# LETTERS FROM WALES

## MEMORIES AND ENCOUNTERS IN LITERATURE AND LIFE

SAM ADAMS

Foreword by Michael Schmidt

Edited with an introduction
by Jonathan Edwards

Parthian, Cardigan SA43 1ED
www.parthianbooks.com
First published in 2023
© Sam Adams 2023
ISBN 978-1-914595-07-3
eISBN 978-1-914595-08-0
Editor: Jonathan Edwards
Cover image: 'Darn o Dîr / A Piece of Land' charcoal, ink and pastel on
handmade Indian Khadi paper by Iwan Bala
Cover design by www.theundercard.co.uk
Typeset by Elaine Sharples
Printed and bound by 4edge Limited, UK
Published with the financial support of the Welsh Books Council
British Library Cataloguing in Publication Data
A cataloguing record for this book is available from the British Library

*To Muriel*

# CONTENTS

# FOREWORD

In the more than quarter century since Sam Adams started writing his 'Letters from Wales' for *PN Review*, we have met a very few times. Yet we have become old friends. He has contributed (as I write this) 158 items to *PN Review*. Fourteen years before the celebrated 'Letters from Wales', from 1982, he had been a reviewer for us and a contributing poet. His first *PNR* poem was 'Kite Flying':

I thought that I

Should never get it right – perhaps
I had made my cross too rigid,
Perhaps my paste and paper were too frail...

But the kite climbed and climbed.

Sam and I first worked together in 1974, when he edited *Ten Anglo-Welsh Poets* for Carcanet. These were writers born between 1904 (Gwyn Williams) and 1941 (John Pook). The introduction says that poets have a special place in the popular culture of Wales, 'Their names and works are the property of the common people, their memory is treasured, they are not the special preserve of an elite, academic or eccentric, and this is because poetry has always received an affective response from the whole community.' I was moved by this, the term 'affective response' stays with me. And I was moved by his ten poets.

In *PN Review*, very early on, Sam wrote of 'the literatures of Wales'. I came to share his natural instinct for plurality – linguistic, generic, stylistic – and admired the confidence with which he could read and read across, within and beyond his own literatures. There was a 1985 review of books by Roland Mathias and translations of Dafydd ap Gwilym, a connection across centuries and languages. We were well on our way to the 'Letters'.

When we started them, neither of us expected they would result in an amazing *cahiers* exceeding 700 pages in this generously presented Parthian volume. I have very little to add to Jonathan Edwards's introduction which takes the measure of Sam's achievement. This is writing in time and over time; the author's horizons widen as he goes, his impressions change. It is a vivid process, reading the scene and the players in different lights and weathers. What is revealed is the generous deep-rootedness of the author's cultures.

But why did I decide to have a regular 'Letter from Wales' in *PNR* and not one from Ireland, Scotland – or, more exotically, from New Zealand, Trinidad, Singapore, New York? We set out to be attentive to all those other Englishes, but Wales fascinated me, among the constituent portions of the United Kingdom, as having a culture different in kind from the others. Within Wales, Welsh and English seem to enjoy a living parity which has been unbalanced by history elsewhere in the kingdom. With the big twentieth-century exceptions of some Thomases, Joneses and others who retained a connection to the two languages, Welsh culture was taken into account in a different spirit. There were ways in which Welsh resisted assimilation, and English writers with Welsh inflections (in earlier periods, Vaughan and Herbert, for example) at some level puzzled English readers.

As literary alliances were forged, the Irish/Scottish axis, the Irish/American access, Wales seemed to be left out. Yet so much had happened and was still happening in Welsh culture: the persistences, the inventions, the harmonies and disharmonies: it was like a loosely controlled experiment and observing it through the informed, wide-open eyes of Sam Adams was instructive. A *multum in parvo*: the more closely it was observed, the more relevant to the larger culture *multum* became.

Reading these letters, one is drawn into a continuum fascinating not only to the Welsh reader but to any Anglophone reader who loves poetry and how it survives in changing histories, how it is itself able to open out areas that seemed to be diminishing or to have been politically diminished, and how it can engage with the big international movements with names like Modernism and Post-Modernism without losing its identities.

As a reader, it seems to me that Welsh poetry even now sometimes suffers exclusion from the main feast. There are the English, busily regarding themselves, and the Scots, and the Irish with their greater cultural and political complications and clout. The other Anglophone literatures are propelled into focus, too, but Wales stands apart, and this is its fascination: it doesn't seem to be part of the international business of poetry. It insists on its own cultural parameters, patterns and connections, resisting integration but also resisting insularity — in a sense *protected* by its competing and collaborating languages. To be reminded of this by Sam in his Letters every two months is a tonic – and a pleasure that, as an editor, I find I cannot do without. It's half a century since we agreed to publish *Ten Anglo-Irish Poets*. The kites are still flying!

Michael Schmidt

# INTRODUCTION

Writing in March 2020 in 'A Letter from Wales', Sam Adams describes the process of cleaning a brass coal miner's lamp. It belonged to his grandfather and he has looked after it as a tangible reminder of his roots and of the wider history of industry in South Wales. Now he tries a new way of cleaning the lamp, and makes a surprising discovery:

> Recently I tried submerging the lamp in a solution of a new kind of cleaner. It was not a complete success as traces of Brasso remain, but the brass looks refreshed and, much to my surprise, when I emptied the bowl I found at its base a layer of the finest coal dust somehow displaced from recesses in the interior of the lamp. There it was; the very same black death that silted the lungs of my grandfather and snatched him away from us so shockingly in middle age, no more than a week after I was born. That is why I bear his name: Samuel.

This image of coal dust in the bottom of the bowl is a resonant one for Sam's *Letters from Wales*. Passionate about history and about a Welsh way of life, the letters offer us a continuous process of discovery and preservation. Sometimes the writing is explicitly historical, exploring memories of childhood or of wider life in Wales. More frequently, it is concerned with the major writers of Wales's present and past, and Sam shows the same tender care in these pieces for the canon of Welsh writing in English, the same desire to look after, burnish and protect, as he shows for the lamp when he cleans it. His writing respects writers, respects the past and, because of this quality, it continuously offers readers something surprising and new.

One of the most significant aspects of the work collected in this volume is its initial audience, the people whom Sam's discoveries were offered *to*. If gaining coverage of Welsh writing in influential English publications has long been a challenge for all sorts of reasons, Sam's 'Letter from Wales' column is an important exception to this situation. Since 1996, the letters have been appearing in *PN Review*, one of the most highly-regarded English literary magazines. Together, they constitute one of the most significant and sustained attempts during this period to present Welsh writing to an audience throughout the UK and beyond. Their collection for the first time in this volume offers a fascinating cross-section of Welsh literary culture during this period.

When I was approached to edit this collection, the publisher's suggestion was that the letters could be arranged thematically, to give a coherent reading experience to the book as a whole. This has not been easy to do: the letters are precisely that – *letters* – and Sam pursues whichever subjects he is most passionate about at the time of writing, in pieces intended for individual publication. One might as well manage to curate a boxful of diamonds, each of which is singular and beautiful.

My solution has been to create three loosely framed categories: 'On Writers', 'On Wales' and 'On the Literary Scene'. Each section moves backwards in time, starting with the most recent letters, and offering a journey into the past. I've also given each letter a title to give some sense of its most prominent subject but, like any good road trip from Cardiff to Caernarfon, these titles only give a sense of where the letter might take you, rather than everything you might see along the way. My hope is that this approach offers a flexible structure that will allow for sustained reading, as well as allowing readers with special enthusiasms to dip in and browse, using these titles as a guide.

The first section of the book offers fascinating coverage of many of the best regarded recent and contemporary Welsh writers, from Gillian Clarke to Roland Mathias, R.S. Thomas to Rhian Edwards. There are also important pieces about writers of Wales's past, from the familiar to the more obscure. We hear of the Book of the Year and readings at Hay, the passing of important writers is honoured and the emergence of new talent is celebrated. A number of the letters constitute important introductory capsule essays to the work of individual writers, and are part of Sam's attempt to bring the literature of Wales to a wider audience.

Among interesting things about Sam's work in this section of the book is the balance he achieves between respect for writers' public achievement and the close understanding which is generated by his personal knowledge of them as people. His September 2018 letter about Meic Stephens, for example, properly honours the writer's achievement, calling him 'probably the most influential figure in the literary life of Wales in the second half of the twentieth century', and exploring the full range of his political activism, journalism, arts and academic work, alongside his writing. But the piece is also able to offer us a fascinating and telling glimpse of the life lived. In the 1960s, Stephens was invited by Harri Webb to move into a house in Merthyr Tydfil, and Sam's description of the life there and the inception of so many things of cultural significance in Wales is fascinating. The house, he writes,

> was conveniently near Ebbw Vale [where Stephens was about to start a teaching job], space was available at the top of the house and, since ownership of the property was uncertain, no one came to collect the rent. These were persuasive arguments: Meic joined the group at Garth Newydd. Soon, Radio Free

Wales, a pirate radio station, was broadcasting from his room to a few neighbouring Merthyr streets, while downstairs Harri was editing *Welsh Nation*, Plaid Cymru's newspaper. Working alongside Harri, Meic learned essential editorial skills and in 1963 he launched his own publishing imprint, Triskel Press. It was under this banner that the first number of *Poetry Wales* appeared in 1965, price three shillings.

As with any letter-writer, Sam has his enthusiasms, and one of the most interesting we encounter in this section of the book is T.J. Llewelyn Prichard, author of *Twm Shôn Catti*, greeted on publication in 1828 as 'the first Welsh novel in English'. Prichard had an enigmatic and fascinating life, including the loss, at some point, of his nose. Sam summarises the life like this: Prichard was 'an actor in the London theatre, lost his nose somewhere, and died in Swansea in 1862 after falling into his own fire'. I hope the reader will enjoy the several visits to Prichard that are made throughout this book: these enjoyable letters are pieces of writing through which, as Sam puts it, 'Prichard capers'.

The second section of this volume, 'On Wales', explores a number of significant aspects of Welsh history, from the Chartist Rising to the history of mining, from the flooding of Tryweryn to the settlement in Patagonia, from St David's Day to St Dwynwen's Day. The writing here has a great deal in common with those great writers of Welsh history, John Davies and Jan Morris, who are celebrated in a number of the letters.

Another feature of this section of the book is the intensely personal, moving exploration of Sam's childhood in Gilfach Goch. Here, the experience of being young in Wales is examined with an intensity and lyricism worthy of 'Fern Hill', by that other great writer this collection admires, Dylan Thomas. In a letter of March 2012, Sam takes his grandchildren on an uphill hike so that they can look down on his childhood home. In doing so, he outlines a motivation – passing on his own sense of history to others – which can be seen as beautifully achieved in the writing he has done in this book:

> I wanted them to view Gilfach as it is and handicapped myself for the stiffish climb with the weight of a couple of books containing photographs of the way it was when I was a boy and three working collieries filled the valley floor. The coal industry has gone, the close community it engendered has gone; neither will ever return. My sense of personal history, of rootedness, has become more demanding as I grow older, and with it my guilt and frustration that I did not ask my parents all the questions about their parents and their younger days that leave me now searching hopelessly for answers. I want our grandchildren to have the chance to avoid my mistake. I feel very strongly that, whatever route they take through life, they should know at least where the Welsh side of their ancestry comes from.

The third section of this volume, 'On the Literary Scene', will be fascinating for anyone who works in or cares about the arts in Wales. Sam loves Welsh writing and praises everything that is good about the institutions that support it. His love is also manifested in a frustration with petty constraints: Sam is an astute and honest critic. Importantly, he is brave enough to put his name in writing to positions on some of the powerful institutions in Welsh writing, which most people might only whisper about in dark corners. The writing shows, then, a generous and selfless commitment for things to be better for everyone. Reading a number of points that Sam raises, one feels at times a sadness that some of the issues mentioned have not been effectively tackled in twenty years.

Overwhelmingly, then, what emerges from this book is Sam's

love for Wales, our writing, our history, our country: his passion sings from every sentence of these pages, and it's been a privilege to be the first reader of a full collection of these letters. One of the last things I did in the organisation of the volume was to move his letter about his grandfather's lamp to the front of the book. I did so because it is among my favourite of the letters and intensely moving, managing to focus love for family and history in a single object. I'll leave you now to enjoy this letter, and those beyond it – for the letters to release the discoveries generated by Sam's care for Wales and the past, just like that resonant and time-travelling coal dust which appears in the bottom of the cleaning bowl. For the letters to do their work on you, reader, as they have done already so much significant work in giving Wales to the world.

Jonathan Edwards

# MY GRANDFATHER'S LAMP

*March 2020*

My grandfather's lamp, suspended by its hook, hung from a
nail driven high into the wall in our outside lavatory. It was so
familiar a sight for me as a child that I ceased to notice it. When
the house in Gilfach Goch was cleared ahead of sale it was one
of the items I bore away. Even then I gave it little attention.
Many years passed before its significance and worth dawned
upon me. I treasure it now as a twofold connection with the
past, one personal, as an object contributing to the story of my
family, the other general, as an artefact recovered from the
history of the south Wales coalfield.

It is an overman's lamp, somewhat smaller than those one
sometimes sees in bric-a-brac shops, and made entirely of brass
rather than the more usual steel and brass. It is intact, even to
the wick, after a hundred years or so, though dented (wounded
if you like). Sometime during its working life a heavy weight
has fallen on it with force enough to fracture the circular boss
at the top and drive it downwards a millimetre or two. The
broken metal has been soldered in the blacksmith's shop (every
colliery had a blacksmith's shop), but this scarred lid and the
ring of perforations immediately below it remain buckled.

At intervals, I have taken a rag and a tin of Brasso and
brought up the shine on it, but over the years an unsightly white
deposit has built up in inaccessible folds and joints. Recently I
tried submerging the lamp in a solution of a new kind of cleaner.
It was not a complete success as traces of Brasso remain, but
the brass looks refreshed and, much to my surprise, when I
emptied the bowl I found at its base a layer of the finest coal

dust somehow displaced from recesses in the interior of the lamp. There it was; the very same black death that silted the lungs of my grandfather and snatched him away from us so shockingly in middle age, no more than a week after I was born. That is why I bear his name: Samuel.

As overman, my grandfather was responsible for the safe and productive effort of colliers underground in a section of the mine. His brass lamp was a symbol of office. He also carried a cleft stick which allowed him to lift the lamp by its hook to examine the roof of a heading where men were at work and test for the presence of firedamp, the flammable gas readily ignited by a naked flame or even a chance spark from a pick striking rock. The damage to the top of the lamp might have been caused by thrusting it against a low roof, or perhaps when a stone fell on it. 'Stone' is a characteristic understatement of the mining industry: a stone might weigh several hundredweight. Mining was never a safe occupation. I was told that in his tours of the coalface my grandfather would sing hymns (he and his wife were staunch Salvationists), so that men on the shift would know of his approach and would be found busily and carefully at work.

My grandfather's grandfather, William, from the old mining area of Newhall, Derbyshire, and his wife Rachel, a Breconshire girl from Llangynidr, settled in Abersychan in the 1820s and, apart from brief forays to try their luck elsewhere in south Wales, remained there until 1851 and beyond. What brought them to that place? The simple answer is the likelihood of a steady living, for there was a concentration of industry nearby. The Afon Llwyd ('grey river', a name replete with significance for anyone familiar with a mining area) rises on Mynydd Coety overlooking Blaenavon and winds some thirteen miles through Abersychan and Pontypool down to its confluence with the Usk at Caerleon, about half a mile from where I sit. It is one of those curious geographical coincidences, the sort that shouldn't be pressed too far, but nevertheless gives me a sense of connection.

The upper reaches of this Monmouthshire valley, and the six miles between Blaenavon and Pontypool, were the setting of some of the earliest manifestations of the Industrial Revolution in Wales – before the great days of Merthyr and the Rhondda. In 1840, works in that stretch produced and transported by canal fifteen thousand tons of iron. Coal was mined alongside ironstone and there was, within a short distance, a choice of location and heavy labour for men and women, and their young children if they were prepared to risk them. In 1842, a government commission into the employment of children found there were 185 children under the age of thirteen employed at the Blaenavon ironworks. The furnace manager said they sometimes got burned 'but not very bad'.

Search the internet for 'Llanerch Colliery, Abersychan' and you will certainly come across a photograph of the pit – engine house, stacks, pithead winding-gear – and, assembled in the middle ground, a crowd of black-suited men. It must have been taken soon after 6 February 1890. Despite warning from an inspector of mines, in the previous December the mine manager had declared it safe to work the pit with naked lights. On that fateful day in February a massive gas explosion killed 176 men and boys. Long before then my immediate Adams kin had moved on, into Glamorganshire. The role of overman and the safety lamp my grandfather carried were intended to prevent such disasters. They didn't, of course (think of Senghenydd, 14 October 1913, where 439 were killed), though the existence of precautionary measures probably meant there were far fewer than would otherwise have been the case.

There are substantial remains of colliery and ironworks and terraced workers' cottages in Abersychan, but a more complete experience of the industrial past has been preserved at

Blaenavon (a World Heritage site, three miles or so further up the valley), first in the ironworks – including furnaces, foundry and cast house, and via an open square of restored workers' cottages. The 'truck shop', among the cottages was the company store for groceries and all other necessities. No alternative existed: workers were paid in tokens that had value only in that shop, which in the 1830s was providing one-tenth of the company's profits. Less than a mile off, 'Big Pit' provides the faintest taste of a working coal mine, which it was indeed until 1980. A friend from the Rhondda Fach tells how, as a teenager, he was taken down the local pit by his father on a Sunday morning when only repair teams were busy underground. It was not a pleasant experience. 'If you don't work in school, this is what you'll get', his father told him. He became a scientist and successful businessman. Late last year we visited Big Pit together. Mining safety regulations still apply: you leave watches and mobile phones behind before descending 300 feet in the cage, wearing a hard hat and safety lamp powered by an eleven-pound battery on a belt around your waist. No dust now, none of the incessant clamour of coal-cutter, shot-firing, picks and shovels, men's voices, journeys of drams. The stables are there but not the horses that hauled the drams, empty to the miner's stalls and full to the cage waiting at the bottom of the pit. There, too, at the end of the shift the weary, coal-grimed men assembled for the haul to the surface and the blessing of fresh air.

*PN Review* 252, Volume 46 Number 4,
March – April 2020.

# 1: ON WRITERS

# HUW MENAI

*November 2020*

The hooters calling colliers to work are silent, the pit wheels that remain, confined to museums, no longer spin, the black dust has long since settled. But for something like one hundred and fifty years the south Wales coalfield was an industrial hub about which it is not an exaggeration to say a substantial part of British enterprise turned. You would think in that stretch of time an indigenous literature would have emerged to represent the place, its people and, overwhelmingly, the occupation of its menfolk. Yet the one title that readers, and film-goers, most readily call to mind as a summation of coal mining here is Richard Llewellyn's *How Green Was My Valley*. I would be the last to deny its power to hold an audience in either form, but it was written by an outsider who knew next to nothing of life and work in 'the Valleys' and, as I have previously explained (*PN Review* 249), was assisted to his triumphant fictional debut by Joseph Griffiths of Gilfach Goch.

There are not many who, having worked for some years underground, found space in their lives to tell us about it. B.L. Coombes's autobiography *These Poor Hands* is a clear and ringingly authentic account of the miner's work, the conditions in which it was undertaken, and for what grudging, meagre returns, in a way that Richard Llewellyn's fiction could never be. The very thought of spending eight hours a day underground engaged in heavy manual labour, often in a cramped space, is enough to make one sweat, but what if you were aware of the instability of the rock above and around you? Here Coombes and his butties are approaching a section of the mine where there has been a fall. 'All alive it is,' one comments:

> Nearer to the coal-workings the sides and roof are not so solid... Soon we begin to feel the heat coming to meet us, then we sense the movement of the newly disturbed ground; the continual creak of weakening timber; a snapping sound as the roof begins to crack above us; and when we are within a hundred yards of the coalface we hear the roar of falling coal and the sharp staccato cracks as the gas loosens more slips of the coal. Here is our working place for this shift. We hang our clothes on a projecting stone out of reach of the rats...

There were poets of the coalfield, too, but they were few and, with a single exception, Idris Davies, are largely forgotten. 'Huw Menai' (Huw Owen Williams, 1886–1961) came from Caernarfon. He was Welsh-speaking, his parents near monoglot, and went shoeless, he said, to a 'ragged school', though that cannot be strictly true as 'ragged schools' were absorbed into the free elementary education system introduced by the 1870 Act. In any case, his schooling ended when he was twelve. At sixteen, he walked the length of Wales to find work in the Glamorgan valleys, early on (1905) at Aberfan, adding his share of slag from the Merthyr Vale colliery to the enormous tip that five years after his death cascaded down the hill to engulf a school and its children. What would he have made of that one wonders, for in his poetry a sensuous response to nature is ever in tension with an overwhelming awareness of incipient tragedy in the human condition. As a young man he was a political activist on the radical far left, writing essays in the *Socialist Review* and the *Social Democrat*, and making speeches on street corners, on at least one occasion, in August 1908, being fined five shillings for causing an obstruction. His prominent opposition to the political status quo irked colliery managers and he found himself unemployable until, oddly, he was taken up by D.A. Thomas, later Lord Rhondda, and given work as a weighman. In that capacity he was the employer's man, weighing drams, each bearing the individual mark of the collier who had filled it, and estimating the amount of slag or 'muck' to be deducted for the calculation of pay. The union's checkweighman, elected by the men, kept a careful eye on proceedings, but the weighman was unlikely to be popular. Huw Menai was again unemployed after 1926 and might have been expected to forget the favour he had been shown, but a decade later, in a letter to the *Western Mail*, 10 September 1936, he wrote of his 'very genuine' regard for Lord Rhondda, despite suffering 'insidious victimisation' as a consequence of being 'befriended' by a capitalist.

I have a remote connection with Huw Menai. I was told that when he first came to Gilfach Goch he was a lodger with my Aunty Sarah (my great-aunt, that is), before renting a house for himself and a growing family in a terrace a third of the way up the mountain overlooking two of the valley's three pits, named (I hope with intended irony) 'Fairview'. From there his output of letters to the *Western Mail* continued, from time to time varied with appeals for work: 'Huw Menai, the Welsh Poet, who has been out of work for seven months, and whose employment benefit has just been stopped, here makes his third appeal for a job before he is reduced to the necessity of applying for Poor-law relief for himself and family...' On 10 December 1927 the paper reported a court case in which his wife was accused of 'making a false statement to the local guardians for the purpose of obtaining relief', for the *Western Mail* had also been the vehicle of a subscription appeal by others which had raised £70-£80 for the poet. That much of this windfall had gone to pay arrears of rent is clear from another report in the paper, 6

March 1928, when the owner of the property obtained a possession order for a further accumulation of arrears. During the war he at last found work at the ordnance factory in Bridgend, but by 1949, when his cause was taken up by the Port Talbot Forum, Sally Roberts Jones tells us he was living on £2.17s a week. The Forum's efforts gained him an annual Civil List pension of £200.

He published four volumes of poetry: *Through the Upcast Shaft* (1920), *Back in the Return* (1933), *The Passing of Guto* (1929) and *The Simple Vision* (1945): for 'upcast shaft' and 'the return' you need to consult mining terminology. All appeared from significant London publishers, Hodder & Stoughton, Heinemann, the Hogarth Press. If not lionised, he was at least recognised as a worthwhile and unusual talent, but that didn't save him from penury or near it for a good part of his life. In view of the brevity of his formal schooling, what is remarkable about his poetry and his writing generally is the range of reference it exhibits in literature, art, philosophy and what we might today call 'popular science', though that figured rarely in public discourse then. A teenage job as a packer at a bookseller's that for a time gave him access to an unusual range of reading material might be part of the story, but he was certainly a formidable autodidact. In the era of T.S. Eliot and Dylan Thomas (whom he declared '90% Bloomsbury'), his poetic manner, style and diction remained stuck in etiolated Romanticism. Glyn Jones, one of the most benign and delightful figures in twentieth-century Welsh writing, yet with a keen eye for the features and foibles of others, is critical of his 'bogus lyricism' and 'debilitated' language. Having had a glimpse of the man in the round, I find them easier to bear, and when his subject is the pit you know experience speaks:

Where shall the eyes a darkness find
That is a menace to the mind
Save in the coal mine, where one's lamp
Is smothered oft by afterdamp?
Down there is found the deepest gloom,
Where night is rotting in her tomb.
…

But when full work is on, the air
Does a more homely garment wear,
When sometimes, floating on the foul,
Comes 'Jesu Lover of my Soul',
Or, coming from more distant stalls,
The rhythmic tap of mandril falls
Upon the ear till one would swear

The pulse of Earth was beating there.

*PN Review* 256, Volume 47 Number 2,
November – December 2020.

# HARRI WEBB

*September 2020*

As an organisation, Yr Academi Gymreig, or 'Academi', the banner under which the Welsh Academy of writers has operated since 1998, appears moribund. I hope this is a misapprehension occasioned by my failure to keep abreast of its activities, and that writers continue to meet socially and to participate together in literary events. The last such occasion in which I had a part to play was in June 2009: a bus tour with talks of places associated with Roland Mathias. Led by John Pikoulis, biographer of Alun Lewis and then Chair of the English-language section of Academi, it was one of a series that also included visits to what one might call Raymond Williams country, around Pandy near Abergavenny, and Alun Lewis's Aberdare. The buses started from Cardiff, picked up paying customers en route and were invariably well filled with people (mostly of mature years, it must be conceded) who were knowledgeable and interested. The Roland Mathias tour took us to the Plough Chapel in Brecon, to the grave of Henry Vaughan in the churchyard at Llansantffraed, and to Talybont-on-Usk, its reservoir lapping at the tumbled stones of the poet's birthplace. It will be a grievous loss if this kind of experience is no longer offered to a public hungry for poems.

I have written before about the Welsh Academy of writers, which had its origins in conversations between two giants of twentieth-century Welsh-language literature, Bobi Jones and Waldo Williams. Their intention was to gather support for a new magazine to serve the distinctive literary culture that they exemplified brilliantly and an organisation that would enrol and represent writers in the first language of Wales. The *Oxford Companion to the Literature of Wales* notes that the choice of the more generally applicable adjective *Cymreig* in the original title, rather than *Cymraeg,* which applies only to the Welsh language, was designed 'to allow the subsequent inclusion of writers in English'. That is, indeed, what happened, when in 1968 the English-language section was formed at the instigation of Meic Stephens, then Literature Director of the Welsh Arts Council.

In the early 1970s, I thought myself peculiarly favoured to be elected to membership of Yr Academi Gymreig, to attend and contribute to readings, lectures and conferences along with other writers, many of them already acquaintances by correspondence, thanks to my role as reviews editor of *Poetry Wales*. An unforeseen and happy consequence of having re-settled in Wales in 1966 within a short distance of Cardiff was to find that, among the writers Meic had in mind when he wrote, in *Poetry Wales* (Winter 1967), of a 'second flowering' of Anglo-Welsh writing, several lived in or near the capital, or within a short, if tortuous, drive up the Valleys. I remember especially Roland Mathias on the outer rim in Brecon, and Glyn Jones, John Ormond and John Tripp, all at the time Cardiffians; then Dannie Abse could be found enjoying a breath of fresh air at his Welsh HQ in Ogmore-by-Sea, Leslie Norris turned up on poetic missions from Sussex, and Harri Webb rolled downhill from Cwmbach. I admired their work and enjoyed their company, which was always stimulating and occasionally, thanks to John Tripp, verbally explosive.

The centenary of Harri Webb's birth falls in September. He came from a Swansea working-class background, and a family with roots in farming on the Gower peninsula, to win a place at Magdalen College, Oxford, where he studied medieval and modern languages, specialising in French and Spanish (and in 1947, 'in three months of hard work [he] learned Welsh'). During the war he served in the navy in the Mediterranean theatre, where he acted as an interpreter with the Free French, and in the North Atlantic. On shore leave in Scotland he encountered the writings of Hugh MacDiarmid, which introduced and quickly committed him to republican nationalist politics. After demob in 1946, early work as a librarian and bookseller took him to genteel Malvern and Cheltenham, but he was already a polemicist for *The Welsh Republican*, a bi-monthly newspaper, and in 1953 became its (unpaid) editor until the collapse of both newspaper and movement in 1957. In 1954 he returned to Wales as a librarian, first in Dowlais, Merthyr and, a decade on, at Mountain Ash where he remained until retirement in 1974.

The Merthyr connection is important. Harri was already a resident at Garth Newydd, a large house in the town, abandoned and apparently ownerless, when in the summer of 1962, on a day out in Cardiff, he first met Meic Stephens enjoying a pint at the Old Arcade, a venerable hostelry. They fell into conversation and soon found they had much in common, linguistically and politically. There and then the budding relationship underwent a baptism of fire. A relic of Cardiff's great Edwardian coal-exporting days, the bar where the two were leaning had a small gas lighter above counter height where wealthy customers would lean to the flame to light their cigars. Engrossed in discussion, Meic was unaware his jacket had come within range of this unusual facility until Harri poured a pint over the smouldering leather patch on his sleeve. Meic, in search of lodgings within easy reach of Ebbw Vale, where he was about to take up a teaching appointment at the local grammar school, was delighted to accept Harri's invitation to join communal life at Garth Newydd. *Poetry Wales* and a great deal more derive from that chance encounter at the 'Old A'. It was Harri Webb who suggested to Yr Academi Gymreig that it should sponsor the compilation and publication of what became the *Oxford Companion to the Literature of Wales*.

He was well known as a polemicist to readers of *The Welsh*

*Republican* and, later, to those of Plaid Cymru's newspaper *Welsh Nation*, which he also edited. His poems began appearing in *Poetry Wales* in 1965, and in 1969 his first book, *The Green Desert*, won a Welsh Arts Council prize. It was followed by *A Crown for Branwen* (1974), *Rampage and Revel* (1977) and *Poems and Points* (1983). The last named was a collection of verses, clever, humorous and scurrilous, many marked by the same trenchant wit that characterised his polemical writing, which had featured in, or been inspired by the opportunity of writing for, the HTV television show 'Poems and Pints'. Some of his squibs incorporating clever use of the demotic have been absorbed into the culture, while his song *'Colli Iaith'* ('Losing Language', with music by Meredydd Evans) has become a regular feature of the National Eisteddfod. His *Collected Poems*, edited by Meic Stephens, which appeared posthumously in 1995, revealed a prolific verse writer and an accomplished prosodist, notably in the sequence 'Sonnets for Mali', two of which not only fulfil the metrical requirements of the form but are also macaronic acrostics, the final letters of lines forming appeals in Welsh, *'Tyrd yn ôl gariad'* ('Come back, darling') and *'Dere lan eto Mali'* ('Come up again Mali'). He died in 1994. In characterising a fellow republican (the wife of a friend) whom he felt he strongly resembled, he offered a moment of self-analysis: 'subjective, romantic, loquacious, artistic, over-personal, with a talent for mimicry, a creative urge, and a too-ready tongue'. His wit was, indeed, sharp and could be merciless. It is said he had his faults (don't we all?), but in my experience he was a man of considerable charm and good humour. In the 1970s and 80s, he was unquestionably the best known and most popular living poet in Wales.

*PN Review* 255, Volume 47 Number 1, September – October 2020.

# RHYS DAVIES, ALICE B. TOKLAS AND LOUISE HAYDEN

*January 2020*

*Rhys Davies – A Writer's Life* (Parthian, 2013) was one of the late major achievements of Meic Stephens's own exceedingly busy career as writer and editor. It won him the 2014 Wales Book of the Year non-fiction prize. Meic brought to the task his vast accumulated knowledge of Welsh writing in English, familiarity with M. Wynn Thomas's pioneering article on his subject with respect to covert homosexuality in a symposium on Davies's work, *Decoding the Hare* (2001), which he edited, access to letters and other archival material, and long friendship with Lewis Davies, who was able and willing to confide a wealth of personal reminiscence about his brother Rhys. Lewis, the last of his family, already deep into his seventies, living comfortably in a flat in Lewes, Sussex, and contemplating mortality, was determined his money would not fall into the hands of HMRC, for him embodied in Mrs Thatcher, whom he execrated. I have previously given an account (*PN Review* 209) of how he and Meic thwarted the PM by setting up a charitable trust in Rhys's name to do worthwhile things for writers and writing in Wales.

As a biography of this elusive figure who ranks among the foremost twentieth century short story writers in English, Meic's book is unlikely to be superseded. That much understood, one may still be intrigued by an occasional by-way. I was struck by the information, gleaned from Lewis, that some of the money donated to the Trust (finally amounting to substantially more than half a million pounds) came from Alice B. Toklas via fellow American Louise H. Taylor. There aren't many unfamiliar with the name Alice B. (for Babette) Toklas, and her partner, as we would say, Gertrude Stein, whose memory and literary reputation she preserved devotedly through the years between Stein's death in 1946 and her own in 1967. Few will not have seen and wondered at the photograph of Gertrude in the large studio of the apartment at *27 rue de Fleurus*, Paris, which she shared with Toklas from the early 1900s, the walls densely hung with rows of paintings, many instantly identifiable, like Picasso's 'Fillette à la Corbeille Fleurie', sold a few months back in the Rockefeller sale for $115,000,000. In her will, Gertrude named Alice her heir, but the collection of paintings was to be for 'her use for life' and thereafter pass to her nephew Allan and his children.

Judging from photographs, Alice was not the most prepossessing of life-companions. In a 1915 passport renewal application she described herself as follows: Age: 37; Stature: 5 feet 2.5 inches; Forehead: Low; Eyes: Hazel; Nose: Aquiline; Hair: Black; Complexion: Dark; Face: Oval. Descriptions of her appearance by others invariably mention her moustache and are often unkind. Those who knew her well were impressed by her quiet charm, her warmth and affectionate nature, and her astute judgement in the arts from painting to dress design and cooking. *Staying on Alone* (1973), a selection of her letters from the period after Gertrude's death, edited by Edward Burns, also reveals a colourful and gossipy correspondent.

The passport application tells us Alice was born in San Francisco on 30 April 1877. She was the daughter of Jewish parents who initially said they had emigrated from Germany, though at the 1920 Census her father, Ferdinand, declared he was a retired dry goods merchant who was Polish and spoke Polish. Presumably, post-World War I, with Poland once more independent, he was proud to reassert his nationality. He had begun his business career in Seattle, then moved to San Francisco and made the family prosperous. In 1890 they moved back to Seattle and Alice continued her education at the Mount Rainier Seminary. There she fell in with girls of similar tastes and interests, among them Louise Hayden. Although Louise was five years her junior, Alice would certainly have known her, because, outside school, as talented pianists they shared the same teacher, Mae Potvin, who had a high reputation in Seattle and put on concerts at which both performed. In December 1892, for example, when Miss Potvin's pupils performed at 'Pettis' Chambre de Musique', Alice Toklas, who was fifteen, played Schubert's Impromptu in A flat and the precocious ten-year-old Louise Hayden the first two movements of a Beethoven Sonata. For a time they kept up their musical studies, Alice having lessons from concert pianist Otto Bendix and graduating in music at Washington University, and Louise acting as assistant to the far better known Isidor Philipp in Paris, before both abandoned all ambition in that direction.

Hayden came from an army family. Her father was Major James Rudolph Hayden, who is described as 'one of the pioneers of Washington'. He was manager of the 'People's Savings Bank' and had a 'handsome' home on Boylstone Street. When he died unexpectedly of pneumonia, in November 1902, the *Portland Morning Oregonian* reported Louise and her brother, Lieutenant John L. Hayden, had returned to Seattle for the funeral. In Paris, in 1918, she married Emmett Addis, of Hartford, Connecticut, who had become a Lieutenant Colonel of Infantry during World War I and later served as Instructor at the Army General Staff College. Marriage took Louise back to the US, but during her time in Paris she had attended the salon at *27 rue de Fleurus*, met Gertrude Stein and renewed her childhood acquaintance with Alice Toklas. They became firm friends, as the affectionate warmth of Alice's letters reveals. Louise visited Paris most years and gifts were exchanged.

Addis, recently retired from the army due to ill-health, died in Boston in 1932. In 1939 Louise re-married, in Taunton, Somerset, again to an army officer, Captain Richard Harold Redvers Taylor, known as 'Red', who was eighteen years younger than his wife. His army career had culminated in 1937 in a posting as Assistant Military Attaché at Addis Ababa, but with the outbreak of war he was recalled to serve in the War Office. There he met Rhys Davies, also doing his bit for king and country. Red had artistic tastes and as it transpired artistic ambitions. After the war he became a painter and sculptor of recognised quality, with exhibitions in London galleries and at Kettle's Yard in Cambridge. Like Gertrude and Alice in Paris, Louise and Red welcomed writers and artists to their London flat in King's Court North. Rhys Davies who never aspired to much more than a humble bedsit, was a regular at this salon and sufficiently trusted to be allowed to use the flat when its owners were away to entertain young guardsmen.

Lewis Davies suggested the relationship between Louise and his brother was particularly close. When she died in 1977 she left half her estate, some £65,000, to Rhys, the other half going to short story writer Bill Naughton. Did this include money left her by Alice Toklas? Louise was executor of Alice's will (some sources say her adopted daughter), but all agree in her declining years she had little personal wealth. Even the precious pictures were taken from her. While seeking relief from crippling arthritis at a spa in Italy, and living there in a convent (she had converted to Catholicism, which, she was assured, allowed a heaven where she would be reunited with Gertrude), the widow of Allan Stein had the entire collection seized and locked away securely at the Chase Manhattan Bank in Paris. But Louise did receive a waistcoat and two brooches that had been worn by Stein. One of the brooches is of lapis lazuli; the other, of coral in a silver setting, which appears in the iconic portrait of Stein by Picasso, was of monumental significance for Alice, harking back to her first meeting with the love of her life. Louise donated the brooches to the Fitzwilliam Museum in Cambridge; the waistcoat she gave to Rhys, who sold it for £100 early in 1978 to the University of Texas. When Rhys died intestate in August 1978, the net value of his estate, £80,000, came to Lewis, the one survivor of his family, and he, by care, frugality and shrewd investment, built up the capital and with extraordinary generosity gave all away to the memory of his brother.

*PN Review* 251, Volume 46 Number 3,
January – February 2020.

# RHYS DAVIES

*November 2019*

We are becoming accustomed to assertions in public life that are less than the whole truth and all too often downright lies. In literature we meet, increasingly it seems, narrative fiction based on skeletal fact, as well as work planned and presented to deceive, like Macpherson's Ossian, Chatterton's Rowley poems and Iolo Morganwg's masterly imitations of Dafydd ap Gwilym, as previously mentioned (*PN Review* 249). While searching for a reference I knew to be found in Rhys Davies's *Print of a Hare's Foot*, I was so charmed, once again, by the stories and their telling that I re-read the whole book. It comes into the category of unreliable memoirs, its primary function to entertain rather than factually inform. Davies termed it 'An Autobiographical Beginning', raising expectations of a forthcoming middle and (near) end. But there was no more, for he was nearing the end of a productive and successful writing career, and what we have is filled out with pieces previously published in Geoffrey Grigson's miscellany *The Mint* and Connolly's *Horizon*.

The book begins with a Proustian moment, not a madeleine dipped in tea, but the finger touch of a 'a roll of vividly striped flannel' of the 'old hairy breed' on a stall at Carmarthen market. It brings back the horror of Sunday's fresh-laundered flannel shirt following the weekly bath, the essential preliminary to morning service at Gosen, the tiny Congregational chapel not far from his parents' grocery shop: 'Seated alone in my mother's rented pew... I scarcely dared move within my hairshirt. To rise for hymn-singing renewed the hot itching of my miserable flesh. [The Minister] Mr Walters's demoniac preaching, mounting into *hwyl* sometimes, brought forgetfulness. A good exponent of this chanting eloquence, he roared, thumped the pulpit-ledge, pointed an accusing finger at nastinesses among us, thundered our guilt. He placed a solid load of this mysterious guilt on my back, and I was suitably shirted to receive it.' And he is transported back to historical characters and events and 'Children's Games'.

I am half-inclined to believe this caricature of the Welsh chapel composed for the amusement of English readers. The chapel, or at least the building that once was Gosen, stands near the corner where Thomas Street joins Jones Street, and Mr Walters was my wife's great-uncle. She has no recollection of him, but as a child she took her turn, after elder sisters' strenuous objections had finally obtained them relief from the duty, as overnight companion to her widowed great-aunt, in case she passed away in her sleep. In the candlelit spare bedroom of the gloomy house, desperate for print, she read the yellowed newspapers that lined the drawers of a haughty chest. But how do you square Davies's description of morning service and a sermon in Welsh with what we certainly know from his brother Lewis's testimony: a family connection with St Thomas's, a church even nearer to 'Royal Stores', was strong enough for him to harbour a youthful ambition to train for the Anglican priesthood.

Before the present atheistical, pagan or merely indifferent era, Wales was traditionally associated with Nonconformism and the communion and *hwyl* of the chapel but, as elsewhere, the church, Catholic and, later, Anglican, came first, and is even more deeply rooted. The sadly abandoned and decaying St Teilo's church at Llandeilo Tal-y-bont, Pontarddulais, near Swansea, was dismantled, numbered stone by stone and transported to St Fagans National Museum of History near Cardiff (Art Fund Museum of the Year 2019), where it has been painstakingly reconstructed in a project extending over two decades. On the basis of evidence revealed under centuries of limewash the interior has been decorated with inscriptions, symbols and wall paintings, among them vivid illustrations of the Passion, God the Father enthroned, St Catherine, the St Christopher narrative, and an imposing post-Reformation Royal Arms, all recreated in their original places using authentic techniques and pigments. It is a glorious example of how a church of the Tudor period (c.1510 – 30) would have appeared to its congregation. In 2007, Rowan Williams, then Archbishop of Canterbury, described it as a 'stunning addition to the treasure trove of Welsh history contained at St Fagans'. To the museum's many thousands of visitors, St Teilo's is a paint-fresh visual delight, and perhaps a colourful signifier of the power wielded by the Church over the medieval mind.

A few weeks ago we navigated, with care, the narrow, winding lanes of the Vale of Glamorgan to the village of Llancarfan. Iolo Morganwg knew it very well and in all likelihood as child and young man regularly attended its thirteenth century church dedicated to St Cadoc. It is far less frequently visited than St Teilo's, eight miles off, but more wonderful because it still serves a parish and its decorated interior is entirely original. During the re-roofing of the south aisle in 2005–06 it was found necessary to replace some of the wall plates damaged by death-watch beetle. This latter work dislodged some coats of limewash revealing a thin red line, subsequently identified as the frame of a wall painting. With enormous care and skill over twenty layers of limewash were removed to expose a large image of St George in full armour and crested helm mounted on a superb war horse plunging his lance into the jaws of the dragon, while a king and his queen look on from their battlemented castle and a princess seated on a grassy tump, with her dog on a lead beside her, raises her right hand in a gesture of surprise.

Nor was this all. As the work continued further pictures grew from the plaster. In a window embrasure below the castle of the king and queen a Death emerged, shrouded, worm-infested, a toad squatting on the ribs, part skeleton, part rot. The skeletal hand is holding a well-fleshed hand, pulling the sleeved arm attached into view. What cunning the medieval artist had to withhold from us, if only momentarily, sight of the youthful figure on the adjacent wall, who is being thus led by Death to the burial ground, there outside the window. The young man, smartly dressed, a sword at his side, doesn't realise how close he is to 'drooping, dying, death's worst, winding sheets, tombs and worms and tumbling to decay', as Hopkins put it with an almost medieval admonitory relish. Scholars of ecclesiastical history tell us this belongs to the category of images known as 'Death and the Gallant', and further that the Gallant embodies the Seven Deadly Sins – and they, too, are depicted in a large panel on the other side of St George. Each representation of sin – lust, pride, anger, avarice, gluttony and, in this case, a double vision of sloth, physical and spiritual, the latter illustrated as suicidal despair – is accompanied by torturing demons and suspended over a hell-mouth. It is both revelatory and moving. Looking at those images, silently, one can feel strangely close to the distant generations that congregated in that place on quiet summer mornings.

*PN Review* 250, Volume 46 Number 2, November – December 2019.

# IOLO MORGANWG

*July 2019*


As I was saying (*PN Review* 247), in 1853 Lady Llanover purchased from his son, Taliesin Williams, the precious collection of ancient manuscripts and eighty-eight volumes of assorted papers of Iolo Morganwg, which now reside at the National Library of Wales, one of the three institutions (the other two being a national university and a national museum) the father had foreseen. Iolo Morganwg was not the baptismal name of this cultural icon of Wales, as you will have gathered, but this is a rare case where the bardic name stands on its own rather than being enclosed in parentheses after that recorded in a parish register. The universal familiarity of 'Iolo Morganwg' means that many would not recognise him as plain Edward Williams.

He was born in March 1747, near Llancarfan in the Vale of Glamorgan, the son of a stonemason, also Edward Williams, and his wife Anne, who, having been brought up by an affluent branch of her family at the Seys manor house in Boverton, near Llantwit Major, profoundly influenced this her favourite son with talk of literature, music and the history of the great families of the Vale. The child's first language was English, but Welsh, at that period dominant in the neighbourhood, became the principal choice of his creative aspirations.

It is as Edward Williams he appears on the title page of his substantial collection of *Poems, Lyric and Pastoral – in Two Volumes* (London: 'Printed for the author, by J. Nichols', 1794), while Iolo Morganwg is granted authorship of a six-line epigraph in Welsh. This duality is well-earned inasmuch as he used Welsh and English with equal facility in all aspects of his life and work, but may carry just a hint of shape-shifting inconstancy. He became a master literary forger, far superior to Chatterton and Macpherson. The rather saucy love poems offered to the editors of *Barddoniaeth Dafydd ap Gwilym* (*The Poetry of Dafydd ap Gwilym*) in 1789 as genuine were not identified as actually composed by Iolo until the twentieth century. Is he a reliable witness when offering an account of his early life in the preface to the book? I choose to think he is.

He claims to have had no schooling on account of ill-health as a child, and that his mother taught him to read from *The Vocal Miscellany: A Collection of above Four Hundred Celebrated Songs...* *etc* (the third edition, 1738, which you can now consult, amazingly it seems to me, online) and to write. He was not merely an apt but an avid pupil. He says he 'worked at [his] father's trade from the age of nine', and 'it is of no importance to anyone to know how many stones I hewed, or how many grave-stones I have inscribed with doggerel', but wherever pursuit of his trade took him, he did not cease from study, collecting and writing.

Edward had three brothers. Stonemasons all, they went where they were sure to find a demand for their skills, to London. Perhaps they discovered the building sites were not paved with gold; perhaps, too, they were exposed there to the allure of fortunes to be made overseas. In any event, while Edward remained in the south-east of England, his brothers emigrated to Jamaica, and all three died there. Reading the lives of other families is bound to throw up curious correspondences with one's own from time to time. So it is in this case with me. Three of the five sons of my three-times-great-grandfather, George Williams (1763–1815), rector of Llantrithyd in the Vale, less than three miles across the fields from the new home in Flemingston of the stonemason's family, also emigrated at different times to the West Indies, where in the same dreadful way all died. Whether it was disease that cut them down, or an excess of rum, is now beyond telling. Although they were not, I think, related, that an acquaintanceship at least existed between the two Williams families can be demonstrated from the subscribers' list to *Poems, Lyric and Pastoral*. There we see '*Richard Aubrey, Esq.*' who signed for six sets. I know now he lived at Ash Hall, Ystradowen, where George Williams officiated at the church, having been nominated by his ailing father. Sarah Jones, also 'of Ash Hall', as the notice in the *Gentleman's Magazine* records, married the impecunious curate and thereby secured his preferment to the rectory, then in the Aubreys' gift. If not a relative, she was probably an esteemed nursemaid of the widowed Richard Aubrey's infant children. Later in the list we find 'Rev. George Williams, Llantrithyd' himself.

Subscribers' lists interest me. They are by no means a reliable guide to the life and thought of the writer, but they can occasionally prove revelatory. For example, notwithstanding the entire absence of formal education on the part of the poet, this one includes a high proportion of Oxbridge academics and clerical gentlemen. However, the presence of certain individual names gives one pause. There are a few French residents, including 'Citoyen J.P. Brissot', leader of the *Girondins*, a deputy to the *Convention nationale*, which sentenced Louis XVI in 1793, who, with the overthrow of his party, also died on the scaffold in 1793 – before Iolo's book (long in gestation, because he could not afford to keep up payments to the printer) was published; and '*Mr Thomas Paine*' a name that resonates to this day, '*John Horne Tooke, Esq.*', another radical politician and stirring advocate of parliamentary reform, and 'HUMANITY'S WILBERFORCE' at the head of the 'W' column. Elsewhere we find 'James Boswell, Esq.', 'Mr Incledon' the famous Covent Garden actor, 'Robert Raikes, Esq., Gloucester', founder of the Sunday School Movement, '*Mrs Barbauld*', poet and essayist, who opposed British participation in the Napoleonic wars; '*Rev. Thomas Belsham*', a notable Unitarian minister; and those whose names everyone will recognise, '*Miss Burney*', '*Mrs Piozzi*', '*Miss Hannah More*', and '*Rev. Dr. Priestly*', man of many accomplishments, supporter of the French Revolution and co-founder of Unitarianism in England. Names such as these (and 'the names of my most distinguished friends [are] in italics') tell us much about the character, faith, travels and political allegiances of Iolo Morganwg.

He made his opinions plain (with a little equivocation) to anyone who reads the preface: 'there is too much *Priestcraft* amongst every sect; too much *Kingcraft* in all, even *Republican*, Governments; yet there are many *good Priests*; and, I believe, a brace of good Kings may be found; at least I will venture on *One*'. A footnote advises the One is God. He was a Unitarian-Republican, not an entirely uncommon combination at the time, but doubly suspicious in the eyes of Government and Church. What of the poems? They are examples of competent eighteenth century versification on themes that become common in the Romantic period, including an ode to laudanum, with a strong emphasis on Nature. From a great distance in the mists of time he conjured the Welsh 'triads', how many of his own composition it is impossible to say. One presents, 'The three primary and indispensable requisites of Poetic Genius [...] an Eye that can see Nature, a Heart that can Feel Nature, and a Resolution that Dares Follow Nature'. Wordsworthian you might think, and there is a good deal of evidence to suggest that the poet of Cumbria, the ancient Welsh heartland of Rheged, home of Taliesin, was at one with Iolo in seeing the origins of poetry in the druidic past.

*PN Review* 248, Volume 45 Number 6,
July – August 2019.

# MEIC STEPHENS, BOBI JONES AND CHRISTINE JAMES
*March 2019*


My previous 'letter' was accompanied by a photograph of three important figures in the cultural life of Wales in the twentieth century, the artist Kyffin Williams and two writers, R.S. Thomas and Emyr Humphreys, for both of whom Welsh was a second language largely learned in adulthood. Welsh became their preferred medium of oral communication and both wrote and published work in Welsh, but the creative writing that made and sustains their reputations is in English. A good many contemporary Welsh writers in English have taken a similar journey towards bilingualism as adults, inspired by their late realisation of the long history in these islands and cultural value of Welsh.

There are again those few, who, like Gwyneth Lewis, are thoroughly and creatively bilingual from the outset, and also the unusual cases of writers who, having learned Welsh, choose to engage with the language at the more intense and demanding level of creative expression. It is not a decision to be taken lightly. Conrad thought it demanded 'a fearful effort'. Meic Stephens, who learned Welsh after taking a degree in French at UCW Aberystwyth, was the ideal obituarist when Robert Maynard Jones died in November 2017, for Bobi Jones, the name by which he became known as a writer, had also learned Welsh, beginning at grammar school in Cardiff where the usual curricular limitations meant pupils studied either French or Welsh. He would say later that he didn't choose the subject, it chose him. An outstanding student career at UC Cardiff and in

Dublin in due course took him to the chair of Welsh language and literature at UCW Aberystwyth, a post he held from 1980 until retirement. His enormous contribution to Welsh culture includes co-founding Yr Academi Gymreig in 1957 (with his friend Waldo Williams) and, inspired by his own experience as a Welsh learner, Cymdeithas y Dysgwyr (the Welsh Learners Society). Alongside academic work ranging widely from the middle ages to contemporary literature, he kept up an extraordinary output of poetry, novels, short stories and critical studies – in all, over a hundred books in Welsh. His belief in Christianity was as profound and vivid as his commitment to poetry: in 1958 he wrote, '*Angau, 'rwyt ti'n fy ofni i/Am fy mod yn fardd*' ('Death you fear me/for I am a poet').

In 2012, Meic Stephens published his *Hunangofiant* (autobiography) in Welsh (though there is an English version, *My Shoulder to the Wheel*, also from Y Lolfa, 2015). He regularly competed for the Crown at the National Eisteddfod with long poem sequences, often in Gwenhwyseg, the south-east Wales dialect of Welsh, missing the prize by a whisker on several occasions. For many, his crowning achievement was the *Oxford Companion to the Literature of Wales* (1986), but it may not be as widely recognised that in parallel with the OUP production he also edited *Cydymaith i Lenyddiaeth Cymru*, the Welsh language version, which was published by the University of Wales Press in the same year. His assistant on the latter was Christine James, from Tonypandy, who learned Welsh at a Rhondda grammar school, graduated in Welsh at Aberystwyth and was awarded a doctorate for work on the laws of Hywel Dda. Recently retired as professor of Welsh at Swansea University, she is also a poet of distinction. She won the Crown at the National Eisteddfod in 2005 and the Wales Book of the Year prize for poetry in Welsh in 2014 with *Rhwng y Llinellau* ('Between the Lines'). She became the first woman Archdruid of Wales, presiding over National Eisteddfod ceremonies from 2013 to 2016, and currently she is the first woman to serve as *Cofiadur* (Recorder) of the Eisteddfod's Gorsedd of Bards.

A lecture at the National Museum in Cardiff gave a taste of Professor James's current interests. She is researching popular images of the Welsh as revealed in broadside ballads now preserved in collections at the University of California (the EBBA website) and the Bodleian Library. The best known, as familiar as nursery rhyme, 'Taffy was a Welshman, Taffy was a thief', has an ignominiously long history. As late as the 1890s it was a convenient paradigm for opponents of disestablishment of the Anglican church:

Taffy scoffs at English, and prefers his native bards,
Who splutter Cambrian gibberish at Eisteddfods by yards;
They twingle-twangle creaky harps, they munch their leeks
and cheese,
Hymning to hillside goats their bosom friends the Cymric
fleas.

This late and venomously hostile piece aimed at the Welsh in general includes markers familiar to students of the genre. 'Splutter' is taken from a 'Welsh' oath that appears repeatedly in ballads from the seventeenth century and probably earlier, 'od splutter hur nails', which originally was meant to stand for a Welsh mangling of 'God's blood and nails', though this is not recognised by some commentators. It is an expression used by the Welsh giant even in recent re-tellings of the tale of 'Jack the Giant Killer'. The 'hur', which occurs whenever a Welshman speaks in a ballad, could be put down to an English failure to hear clearly, or listen attentively, but Professor James points out that the Welsh personal pronoun '*hi*', meaning both 'she' and 'her', and pronounced 'he' is a potential source of confusion that may colour aural perception, especially since it is also used to form the possessive. Whatever the source of this curiosity, it had strong powers of adhesion. 'The Welshman's Praise of Wales' from 1700 ends thus:

> Hur has not been in England long,
> And canno speak the Englis Tongue;
> Put hur is hur Friend, and so hur will prove,
> Pray send hur word, if hur can love.

At the nub of it all is the unyielding problem of a different language, 'Cambrian gibberish', deemed impenetrable and, sadly, for most not worth the trouble of trying to understand.

As ubiquitous as 'hur' is the association of the Welsh in balladry with leeks, cheese and goats. 'The Welch Wedding betwixt Ap-Shinkin and Shinny' (1671–1704) is illustrated with a woodcut, in this case representing the bridegroom presumably, though it seems to have been re-used countless times in different contexts. He is a soldier, a pikeman with weapon over his shoulder and sheathed long dagger at his waist. A leek, his badge, is secured by the band of his tall-crowned hat and as shield he bears before him on the end of his knife a round of roast cheese on toast. In the background is a tumbling stream and, beyond, mountains where goats are grazing. Another, cruder, version has Shinkin marching off, pike on shoulder, sword at his side. There is something almost affectionate about these depictions that seems to date from an earlier time, the time perhaps when Shakespeare could create in Fluellen a character eccentric, odd in speech, but worthy, honourable and brave. The goats and the cheese and leeks of the ballads became markers of Welsh peasant poverty and ignorance at a time when the great majority of the English were peasants, equally impoverished and ignorant, though of course there was always the language problem. A brief 'Song to the Old Britons, on St Taffy's Day' (to be sung to the tune 'Of Noble Race Was Shinkin') of about 1715, suggests another reason for the implied gloating superiority of ballad writers:

How are the Mighty fallen!
Is this the Brave, the Haughty!
Highflown Taff, that us'd to quaff
And bear his Head so lofty!
Fa, la, la, lara, &c

The Tudor period had brought the Welsh to prominence in England. Are we seeing in broadsheet ballads an expression of deep-seated English resentment of the Welsh that didn't fade with the passage of time but, encouraged by the popular form (they were all meant to be sung), continued, becoming scoffing or vitriolic as occasion demanded?

*PN Review* 246, Volume 45 Number 4,
March – April 2019.

# R.S. THOMAS, KYFFIN WILLIAMS AND EMYR HUMPHRIES

*January 2019*

A few months ago I received through the post a remarkable photograph, which I believe has not been widely published, as it certainly deserves to be. It is a fine black and white print of three iconic figures in the cultural life of Wales, R.S. Thomas, Kyffin Williams and Emyr Humphreys, and was taken at least eighteen years ago, for RS died in September 2000. The photographer was fortunate, or had planned with exceptional care, to get them together, etched with great clarity against a pale, plain background. All three are formally attired and peer seriously, or questioningly, at the lens; the occasion might have required a sober response to the photographer's request. RS came originally from Cardiff, but in later years settled in north Wales; the other two were born there. Their conversation would have been in Welsh. They belong to an earlier generation, one which witnessed in their own lifetimes enormous changes in the working life, customs and beliefs of the people of Wales. R.S. was born in 1913; Kyffin Williams, who died in 2006, in 1918. Emyr Humphreys, born 1919, will be one hundred years old in April next year. All three dedicated their creative lives to Wales. Roland Mathias – who died in 2007, just short of his ninety-second birthday, lived through the same often devastating transformations and was equally imbued with devotion to the same cause – would have been a wonderful addition to the group.

*Emyr Humphreys* by M. Wynn Thomas, a new addition to the 'Writers of Wales' series, has just been published by the

University of Wales Press to celebrate the writer's centenary. The series was originally intended to provide no more than an introduction to the selected writers and the vast majority are rather brief and do not have the apparatus of notes and index that characterises scholarly productions. In recent years the editorial approach to the series has changed in this respect, and entirely for the better. Wynn Thomas's latest addition to it provides, succinctly, a fuller, more perceptive account of the writer's life than any previously available, and as thorough and detailed a survey and analysis of Humphreys' prose and poetry as one could hope to see. He describes his subject as the 'last great survivor of the heroic age of twentieth century Welsh culture... [that] cohort of writers who dedicated their conspicuous talents to infusing political as well as cultural energy into Welsh life sufficient to arouse their country out of the long torpor of its meekly subservient position within a profoundly anglo-centric "British" polity.' The book is distinguished by the sinew and strength of Wynn Thomas's writing and his unerring selection of example and witness illustrating the nature and scale of this rearguard action to preserve some vestige of the individuality represented by 'Wales' and 'Welsh'.

Emyr Humphreys comes from Trelawnyd, a village in the far north-eastern corner of Wales, close to the border with England, where his father was headmaster of the local C of E elementary school. The nearest towns, several miles away, are the anglicised coastal resorts of Rhyl and Prestatyn. His 'spirited and independent' mother, who came from a farming background, is identified by Thomas as the model of the resolute and mettlesome women that are prominent in his novels and have contributed substantially to his deserved reputation as a creator of female characters. His 'quiet and mild' father, originally from Ffestiniog, of Welsh-speaking, slate-quarrying stock, suffered for the rest of his life from the effects of gassing in the First World War. A Nonconformist by up-bringing, he had converted to the Anglican Church and was withal contentedly anglicised. That, in his youth, the novelist flirted briefly with the notion of becoming an Anglican cleric is perhaps a salute to paternal influence. Certainly, in his case, it signals a serious commitment to Christian belief. When he married, he joined his wife among the *Annibynwyr*, the Welsh Congregationalists.

As a sixth former at Rhyl County School, already sympathetic to the Nationalist cause, he began to learn Welsh, which as his command of the language increased, 'enabled him to read a geographical and cultural landscape that had previously been illegible'. By his late teens he was attending Plaid Cymru meetings, at one of which he met Saunders Lewis, whom he admired both as writer and as one of the trio imprisoned for setting fire to the hutments of the bombing school at Penyberth on Llŷn. Lewis remained a touchstone for the art and attitude of the developing writer.

In 1937 he entered UCW Aberystwyth, where his studies were interrupted by the war. Like Roland Mathias and notable others, he became a conscientious objector on religious grounds. He accepted direction to work on the land and then, in 1943, following training, served with Save the Children Fund in Egypt and, in the wake of the Allied advance, through Italy. The end of the war found him helping to run a large refugee camp in Florence, where he became fluent in Italian, and a confirmed Italophile and Welsh European. Thomas shows that Humphreys' Nationalism never implied turning inwards. Rather it was a creative commitment to Wales in a European context. He believed, in his own words, 'to be more European, we need first to be more Welsh'.

Returned from Italy, he married and, after teacher training

at Bangor, joined the staff of a technical college in Wimbledon. In London he formed important friendships with, among others, Anthony Powell, Huw Weldon, Patrick Heron and Graham Greene, then editor of *The Spectator*, whose advice and encouragement were important factors in his continuing development. His teaching career continued at a grammar school in Pwllheli, but having won the Somerset Maugham Award with his fourth novel, *Hear and Forgive*, in 1955 he left education to join BBC Wales as a producer of radio, and later TV, drama. In this capacity, it was entirely consistent with his European outlook that he put on plays by Dürrenmatt and Brecht and commissioned a Welsh translation of *Waiting for Godot* from Saunders Lewis. His experience in the role also drew him into contact with many of the most significant personalities in the cultural life of Wales at that time, and contributed to an evolution in the style and narrative structure of subsequent novels. In 1965, he left the BBC to establish a drama department at UCNW Bangor. There he exploited his knowledge of the media to the benefit of his students, but finding he was less productive personally, he resigned in 1971 to devote his energies to writing.

Humphreys' first novel, *The Little Kingdom*, though published in 1946, was written while he was in Egypt. His output in fiction has since extended to a further twenty-one novels (including a seven-volume novel sequence 'Land of the Living') and four collections of short stories. There have been, besides, an important book on Welsh cultural history, *The Taliesin Tradition* (1983), and numerous essays and shorter pieces. He began as a poet and has continued to produce poetry as it were in the margins of his long life as a writer: *Ancestor Worship* (1970) and *Collected Poems* (1999) will be followed later this year by another big collection, *Shards of Light*.

His home ground, Wales, is the permanent setting for his

creative expression, but his theme is humanity and its implications are universal. All his writing is strikingly characterised by intellectual and moral consistency. If I were to pluck a single example, *Outside the House of Baal* (1965) is unquestionably a novel of European significance.

*PN Review* 245, Volume 45 Number 3, January – February 2019.

# MEIC STEPHENS

*September 2018*

Meic Stephens has died at his home in Whitchurch, Cardiff, a few weeks short of his eightieth birthday. He was probably the most influential figure in the literary life of Wales in the second half of the twentieth century. A prodigious worker, he was constantly bringing forth fresh projects and restlessly digging at them until they were done, even into his last year. He was a *stakhanovite*, a term (learned in visits to Russia) he enjoyed using, though not in self-regard.

When I returned to south Wales in 1966 to take up a lectureship at what was then Caerleon College of Education, a fellow member of staff, Gwilym Rees Hughes, Welsh editor of the infant *Poetry Wales*, encouraged me to contribute to the magazine and soon after introduced me to Meic. Our friendship began at once and lasted. He and I were contemporaries at UCW Aberystwyth, though I was a few years ahead of him and did not get to know him there. Like many another hopeful English scholar, Meic was felled by Professor Gwyn Jones's Anglo-Saxon axe and pursued honours French instead. He had the better deal, for French was a gateway to a lasting interest in other cultures and languages. More immediately, as a newly qualified teacher, in 1962 it brought him a job at Ebbw Vale Grammar School. He was still wondering how he would get to Ebbw Vale daily, when an extraordinary, serendipitous event occurred. While enjoying a pint at the Old Arcade, a venerable hostelry in Cardiff, which still at that time had little flaring gas jets near counter height where wealthier customers could light their cigars, he fell to talking with a stranger. They found they had much in common: Meic's French matched his Romance Languages at Oxford, and both were poets and staunchly Welsh Nationalist. So wrapped up were they in conversation they did not notice a gas jet burning a hole in Meic's coat sleeve. When the alarm was raised, the new acquaintance doused the minor conflagration with his pint of Guinness. It was one of those curious turning-points at which the direction of a life changes.

The fellow drinker, Harri Webb, was inviting others of similar cultural tastes and political leanings to join him in a large house at Merthyr Tydfil once owned by an ironmaster. It was conveniently near Ebbw Vale, space was available at the top of the house and, since ownership of the property was uncertain, no one came to collect the rent. These were persuasive arguments: Meic joined the group at Garth Newydd. Soon, Radio Free Wales, a pirate radio station, was broadcasting from his room to a few neighbouring Merthyr streets, while downstairs Harri was editing *Welsh Nation*, Plaid Cymru's newspaper. Working alongside Harri, Meic learned essential editorial skills and in 1963 he launched his own publishing imprint, Triskel Press. It was under this banner that the first number of *Poetry Wales* appeared in 1965, price three shillings. The print run of five hundred copies cost forty seven pounds and the editor doubled as salesman: it was a sell-out.

A survey of the contents pages of early numbers of the magazine reveals the vital part it played in what Meic was to term 'the second flowering' of Anglo-Welsh writing (as it was then known), the first flowering having occurred in the 1930s. At once we meet Roland Mathias, Harri Webb, Sally Roberts, John Tripp, Anthony Conran, Leslie Norris, Dannie Abse, Raymond Garlick, John Ormond, Vernon Watkins, R.S. Thomas and more, all poets who would make their mark in the decades that followed, in the 1970s, alongside the emerging new generation, including Gillian Clarke and Robert Minhinnick. Among other features of the magazine that had a lasting impact was the appearance of Welsh-language poets in the same lists, an early expression of Meic's bridge-building between the two language traditions, and the space and prominence given to articles and reviews of poetry publications.

Throughout this time he was also a political activist on behalf of Plaid. To him, mixing literature and politics was not problematic, though he would not have earned himself any credit in the Labour heartlands of south-east Wales, especially after being caught 'white-handed', as he says in his autobiography, *My Shoulder to the Wheel* (2015), daubing the words 'Lift the TV ban on Plaid Cymru' on the wall of Cyfarthfa Castle, and fined twelve pounds by the Merthyr magistrates. He participated in the early campaigns of Cymdeithas yr Iaith (the Welsh Language Society), and was justly proud to have been photographed in February 1963 among the crowd of young people who blocked traffic on Trefechan Bridge, the main road into Aberystwyth from the south. About the same time he added the graffito 'Cofiwch Tryweryn' to a wall near Llanrhystud, which, having been refreshed by others over the years, has become a patriotic rallying cry. Involvement first as agent for the Plaid candidate for Merthyr at the 1964 General Election, then as candidate himself in the 1966 election, brought nothing but lost deposits. It put him off a career in politics, for which the Muse is grateful, but there was an unexpected bonus. He met his future wife, Ruth Meredith, a co-worker, in 1964. Their marriage in August 1965 drew him into a large circle of men and women prominent in contemporary Welsh life. He had begun learning Welsh during teacher training at UCNW Bangor and Welsh became and remained the language of their home, which in August 1966 was in Rhiwbina, a

Cardiff suburb. It was there I think I met him and quite soon after joined him on *Poetry Wales* as reviews editor.

Meic had left teaching to become a reporter with the *Western Mail*. A year later, in September 1967, he was appointed to what was soon after redesignated the Welsh Arts Council and his post within it Literature Director. In addition to an unusually wide familiarity with contemporary writers and writing in Wales, the appointing panel must have seen in him the fire in the belly, the enormous appetite for work and the will to get things done. It was no wonder he could be impatient with those who were less alert and energetic, and that he made enemies during his twenty-three years in the role. Aspiring writers whose applications for grant aid were turned down by the Literature Committee tended to blame him as the figurehead. They were far outnumbered by friends and admirers who appreciated his efforts to promote the culture of the English-speaking Welsh and to build bridges between Welsh- and English-language writers. Much of the achievement in raising the ambitions and standards of writers and critics in Wales, and the quality of book production, can be traced back to him and his productive relationships with a succession of committee chairmen, notably Glyn Tegai Hughes, Roland Mathias, Walford Davies and M. Wynn Thomas. So evident was the worth of several literary initiatives pioneered in Wales that they were adopted by the other UK arts councils.

One might have thought he had enough on his plate, but he also contrived to maintain a high level of activity as writer and editor. As an undergraduate he had seen himself as a poet rooted in industrial south Wales, and was influential as such, but he was not prolific and published little in the English language after *Exiles All* (1973). In later years, however, on several occasions he came close to winning the Crown at the National Eisteddfod for poem sequences in Welsh, his third language. *Linguistic Minorities in Western Europe* (1976) revealed the depth of his interest in the rich diversity of languages and cultures, and again in later years he published translations from Welsh and French. He was an inveterate and orderly collector of quotations and information on literary topics and, above all perhaps, he will be remembered for his scholarship and his remarkable gifts as compiler and editor. These were demonstrated in numerous publications, most notably in his joint editorship (with Dorothy Eagle) of the *Oxford Illustrated Literary Guide to Great Britain and Ireland* (1992), and his crowning achievement, the *Oxford Companion to the Literature of Wales* (1986), which was also published in Welsh and subsequently in enlarged and updated editions.

He left WAC to freelance but soon found himself Professor of Welsh Writing in English at the University of Glamorgan. When, in 2006, he retired from that position, if leisure beckoned he dismissed it with a sharp kick. More important big books followed, among them: *Poetry 1900–2000* (2007), *Rhys Davies: A Writer's Life* (2014), which won Wales Book of the Year, and (jointly edited with Gwyn Griffiths) *The Old Red Tongue* (2017), a monumental anthology of Welsh literature. I was very fortunate to have known Meic as a friend for approaching fifty years. We sent drafts of work in progress to one another for comment, we recommended and exchanged books, we worked together on the Rhys Davies Trust, which Meic founded in 1990. We spoke often and at length on the telephone, rarely without laughter at the vagaries of the world.

*PN Review* 243, Volume 45 Number 1, September – October 2018.

# THOMAS PRICHARD, EDWARD PUGH
# AND KYFFIN WILLIAMS
*July 2018*


T.J. Llewelyn Prichard gave a decade of his life to researching and writing *The Heroines of Welsh History* (1854), convinced that history was the highest expression of the human intellect. Meant to establish his credentials as a serious writer and provide a pension to cushion his declining years, it did neither. But there *Heroines* lies – a small, stout slab of a book, duodecimo, five hundred and eighty-six pages – allegedly published in London by W. & F.G. Cash, a reputable firm specialising in liberal causes such as famine relief in Ireland and slavery in the West Indies, though it is absent from their publication lists. Why *Heroines* you might ponder? For a brand-new feminist slant on narratives hitherto dominated by warring males? To refresh and expand his reading public? To ingratiate himself with his sometime patron, that formidable dragon of Welsh culture, Lady Augusta Hall, who had given him access to her library at Llanover? Probably the last, but things fell apart between them, too late for him to recast the plan of his book. He had the last word, firing satirical blanks at her in a dedication to 'The Virtuous Votaries of True Womanhood [...] as contra-distinguished from The Fantastic Fooleries and Artificial Characteristics of Fine Ladyism'.

I set about reading *Heroines* to see what sort of fist he had made of it, noting, among other things, his sources (where they are acknowledged). That is how I discovered Edward Pugh's *Cambria Depicta*. Looking it up as one does these days on screen, I came across a copy advertised by a bookshop in

California with samples from the seventy-one illustrations that accompany the text, striking hand-coloured views of north Wales at the very beginning of the nineteenth century. I will make sacrifices, I thought, and bought it. I don't regret the purchase. The book is a handsome quarto, the aquatint engravings, from Pugh's grisaille watercolours (originals at NatLib), are fascinating for what they reveal of a varied landscape, with its goodly share of the rugged and sublime, but the real surprise is the natural charm of the artist's account of his travels.

In the late 1820s, Prichard, baffled by a public that could speak and read only Welsh, beat a hasty retreat from north Wales, where he had ventured in the hope of selling his literary wares. But Pugh, born 1763, the son of a barber, was at home there, a Welsh-speaking native of Ruthin in Denbighshire. Although there is no extant confirmatory record, it seems likely he attended the established Ruthin Grammar School, but that was the end of his education, apart from what he taught himself. Of art apprenticeship and practice there is again no sign. All that is known is that he emerged as a painter of portrait miniatures at the Royal Academy exhibition in 1793, and of landscapes with the publication of a collection of engravings, *Six Views in Denbighshire*, in 1794. It seems he took himself to London as a young man and settled there, though changing address quite frequently. In the year of his first RA success he began spending summer seasons in Chester, where he advertised his presence in the local press as 'Professor of Miniature Painting' taking sitters at six guineas a time. He supplied twenty of the twenty-two illustrations of populous London scenes for Richard Phillips's *Modern London* (1804).

In his preface to *Cambria Depicta*, Pugh emphasises the fundamental difference between his account of north Wales and those of the 'tourists' whose publications had preceded his.

With all due modesty he points to 'my knowledge of the ancient British language, *my intimacy with* my native country and its inhabitants, their economy, customs, and character, and [...] the moderate talent as an artist, which I possess'. His own tour was exhaustive and spread over several years. In John Barrell's *Edward Pugh of Ruthin* (UWP, 2013), I learned he spent at least one night in sixty different locations, from Chester westwards to Pwllheli and Nefyn on the Llŷn peninsula, north to Amlwch on Anglesey, south as far as Llanidloes and east again to Shrewsbury. By his own account he travelled 'as a pedestrian between two and three thousand miles, over one of the roughest districts in Great Britain'.

He is referring to the terrain of course and not to the 'unpolished and ignorant people' that many previous tourists assert they encountered in Wales. '[I]f at all ignorant,' he says, 'it must be ignorance of those fashionable dissipations, the never failing promoters of diseases, incident only to the *great* and fashionably *wise,* who take so much pains to secure them; so far as the Welsh are ignorant of such *finished,* such *elegant* refinement of manners, may they ever remain so!' Elsewhere he describes an evening spent at Holyhead in the company of a family and their friends at which 'the cheerful glass went round to every loyal and national toast [but there] was no compulsion to inordinate drinking, nothing was done or said which could offend the eye, or hurt the feelings [...] on the contrary, the mirthful joke, the ready wit, and the harmless song, created an hilarity that pervaded the whole company [...] heedless of the absurd fashion of the times, which prescribes a listless continuance of the table of epicurism, after the just appetites of nature are satisfied'.

Edward Pugh had seen enough of London's binge drinking and loutish behaviour. He continued exhibiting at the Royal Academy until 1807, after which he returned to live with his widowed mother in Ruthin. There he completed the account of his north Wales travels, signing off the preface in May 1813; he died in June the same year. *Cambria Depicta*, his big, beautiful book, was published in London by E. Williams in 1816.

We have just passed the centenary of the birth of another artist who lived for many years in London and made it his life's work to record the character of the scenery and people of north Wales. Kyffin Williams, born 9 May 1918 in Llangefni, Anglesey, is celebrated with sensitivity and style in *Kyffin Williams: the Light and the Dark*, by Rian Evans (with photography by Nicholas Sinclair), whose father, the poet and BBC TV documentary maker, John Ormond, created a memorable film about the artist in 1966. Kyffin was the second son of a bank manager and his wife, both of whom were descended from a long line of respected clergymen. He was educated at Shrewsbury School. While at a cadet summer camp in 1934 he caught meningitis, which may have triggered the epilepsy from which he suffered all his life. At sixteen he was articled to a firm of land agents and began exploring and storing up images of the north Wales coast and mountainous hinterland. In 1937 he joined a territorial battalion of the Royal Welsh Fusiliers, but with the onset of epilepsy he was found unfit to serve and, despite appeals, invalided out in 1940. He attended the Slade School of Art (then based at the Ashmolean in Oxford) from 1941 to 1944, and immediately on gaining his diploma was appointed art master at Highgate School, where he was valued, not least for the inspiration his commitment to practising his art gave to pupils.

In 1947, he began working impasto with palette knives of varying size to express the 'massive bulk' of mountains, and soon with equal facility in portraits. Having settled to his distinctive style, he worked at speed, usually completing even large canvases in a single day. He left Highgate in 1973 and made his home in a cottage on the Menai Straits. Although he was productive on painting tours abroad, notably to Venice and, in 1968, to Patagonia, the landscape and people of north Wales were his constant preoccupation. The sunset seascape is a reiterated theme of his later paintings, the light subdued to a glow in the darkening sky and a reflected broken path upon the water – a meditation on the dying of the light.

*PN Review* 242, Volume 44 Number 6,
July – August 2018.

# RAYMOND WILLIAMS
*May 2018*

I have written before, a long time ago, about driving south from Hay (Y Gelli) or thereabouts and, as the high-hedged country road dawdles this way and that, crossing and re-crossing the border: here we are in England and *Hurrah*, welcome again to Wales! There are so many Welsh names, of villages and farms, on the map of the Southern March to the east of Offa's Dyke – Pen-y-lan, Cayo, Cwmcoched, Bryngwyn, Marlas, Bagwyllydiart – extending as far as Hereford itself, that at fanciful moments I like to think the folk of south Herefordshire will one day vote themselves part of 'Greater Wales'. Though they have since moved to Abergavenny, for some years we regularly visited friends living in the village of Ewyas Harold and, thanks to them, became a little familiar with lanes and villages around and about. No one seems to know what 'Ewyas' means, beyond signifying the territory that still bears the name, but Harold is alleged to be the grandson of Æthelred the Unready. Approaching, within a mile of our friends' door we would pass through the hamlet of Llangua ('church of Ciwan', a female saint who lost the final 'n' of her name in the fifteenth century), take our turn at the lights commanding the bridge over the Monnow and enter England.

A few hundred yards farther brought us to Pontrilas ('bridge over the Dulas'), a Welsh name that superseded the English 'Heliston' as late as the eighteenth century, and soon after we turned sharp left into Ewyas Harold. If you traverse the village to follow another curving country lane for about five miles, doubling back westwards though still in England, you reach Clodock, a straggle of farms and cottages overlooked by Hatterrall Hill to the west and, in the topsy-turvy way of things hereabouts, Mynydd Merddin (Merlin's Mount) to the east. The parish is named after Saint Clydawg, a fifth-century martyr, a Celtic Saint. The site of his ancient shrine is now occupied by a remarkably well-preserved seventeenth-century church, which until 1852 was still in the diocese of St David's. The entire amalgam of local geography and history is expressive of border country. Fragments of painted wall are still visible inside the church and among its treasures is a ninth-century tombstone, discovered when the nave was excavated in 1917. The graveyard is full, crowded with hundreds of old headstones, but in an extension field across the road from the lychgate you will find the spot where Raymond Williams is interred. It is marked with a simple stone inscribed with only names and dates commemorating him and his wife, Joyce (known as Joy), also buried there. He would have appreciated the simplicity of marker and setting in this frontier zone, and ultimately his participation in the ineffable sense of continuity held in the green chalice of a rural parish.

So, in January 1988, the renowned social historian, cultural and political analyst, literary critic, novelist, came home, almost. He was born in Pandy, some three miles from Clodock and just over the border, in Wales. Why wasn't the circle neatly closed to bring him back to his beginnings? He and Joy had a cottage another half-dozen miles up the Monnow valley in Craswall, with Clodock and Longtown one of a group of parishes set on the red soil of south Herefordshire, in the lee of the Black Mountains of east Wales, which supplied the sandstone for the construction of their homes and churches. In Pandy, his father, a World War One veteran, was a railway signalman and avid gardener-beekeeper who supplemented his income by selling produce at Hereford market. He was also an active member of the Labour Party. Raymond Williams attended the Henry VIII Grammar School in Abergavenny, and on the strength of Higher School Certificate results obtained a place at Trinity College, Cambridge, where he read English. His undergraduate studies were interrupted by the war, in which he served in an anti-tank regiment through the Normandy campaign to the fall of Germany. That done, he returned to full exposure with Leavisite practical criticism in Cambridge and complete his degree. Thereafter, a formative stint as staff tutor for the Oxford University Extra-Mural Delegacy, mostly in east Sussex, during which much of his thinking consolidated in *Culture and Society* (1958) was formulated, preceded his return to Cambridge as a lecturer (1961) and professor (1974).

In 1997, among the earliest of the finely crafted commemorative slate plaques put up by the Rhys Davies Trust was unveiled at his birthplace, a house named Llwyn Derw ('Oak Grove') just off the A465 Abergavenny–Hereford road. It is not immediately in the public gaze, but worth the trouble of asking directions. After the unveiling and a buffet lunch in a pub across the road, we dispersed well satisfied. The Trust had done its bit to underline that he was Welsh, one of us. But, of course, it isn't as simple as that. In an interview published in the *New Left Review* in 1979, he speaks of his boyhood, when Welsh was in a box, 'poems and songs... learnt by heart for special occasions', of his 'revulsion against what I saw as the extreme narrowness of Welsh Nonconformism', and the profound Anglicising influence of his grammar school education. With his long immersion in England, geographically and culturally, one would think all attachment to Wales would be severed beyond repair, but that was not the case. As he goes on to say, 'The result was a rejection of my Welshness which I did not work through until well into my thirties, when I began to read the history and understand it.'

In his novels, from *Border Country,* published in 1978 but begun many years earlier, to *People of the Black Mountains* (1989), character, setting, historical background, are consistently in borderland, but on the Welsh side. That creatively and imaginatively he remained in Wales is of no concern to the great majority of commentators who, while writing at length about his contribution as social historian, ignore his roots and his own acknowledgment of them. The work of Daniel Williams, *Who Speaks for Wales? Raymond Williams: Nature, Culture, Identity* (2003), and Dai Smith, his authorised biographer, *Raymond Williams: A Warrior's Tale* (2008), has asserted the opposing view, but it will bear reiterating. When the friend of whom I spoke in the opening paragraph visited Raymond Williams at his Craswall home in the 1970s to ask whether he would be interested in becoming a member of Yr Academi Gymreig, the Welsh academy of writers, without a moment's thought he said, 'Yes'.

*PN Review* 241, Volume 44 Number 5,
May – June 2018.

# WILLIAM SALESBURY
*January 2018*

So precipitate was the cavalry charge of the eager to view Stephen Hawking's PhD thesis that the website of Cambridge University crashed. What the majority of those who clicked in good time made of it is anyone's guess. A fortnight earlier, the digitised version of another document, as epoch-making in its own way, was made available by the National Library of Wales: William Salesbury's translation of the New Testament into Welsh. It was launched with a subdued fanfare to celebrate the four hundred and fiftieth anniversary of its publication, on 7 October 1567. Notwithstanding the distance in time, those who can read Welsh have a better chance of understanding the text than most who struggled to cope with Hawking's opus – once they have come to terms with the obscurity of the Black Letter font.

Salesbury was born in Llansannan, Denbighshire, sometime before 1520. Although it is only eight miles south of Abergele on the heavily anglicised north-east Wales coastal strip, his home village is still substantially Welsh-speaking. It is in a precious rural area on the banks of the river Aled, a tributary of the Elwy, which is far better known thanks to Gerard Manley Hopkins. The English origins of the Salesbury family name must have been long forgotten by the sixteenth century, for William, second son of Ffwg and Annes Salesbury, was securely Welsh in language and allegiance. Of his education we know nothing with certainty, except that he studied at Oxford and gained some knowledge of law at one of London's Inns of Chancery.

His own assessment of his knowledge of languages was modest, but at Oxford he was said to be 'the most learned Briton [i.e., Welshman] not only in British, but also in Hebrew, Greek, Latin, English, French, German...' On the death of his elder brother, he moved some ten miles west to settle at Plas Isa, Llanrwst. He married Catrin Llwyd, of whose death, probably in 1572, we know from an elegy composed about that time. The date of his own death – 1580? 1599? – is hazier than that of his birth, but of the significance of his achievement there is no doubt.

Almost certainly it was at Oxford that he witnessed and internalised the immense power of the printing press, especially as a means of promulgating the word of God in the vernacular, a development already occurring in England and elsewhere in Europe. In all likelihood it was also at Oxford he imbibed the first heady draughts of Protestantism. What we know is that in his maturity he rejected the Catholic faith of his upbringing and conceived it as his duty to give his own people access to scriptural truth and Renaissance learning.

The first printed book in Welsh, *Yn Y Lhyvyr Hwnn* (In This Book), containing the Paternoster, the Creed and the Decalogue, was published under the auspices of Sir John Price of Brecon in 1546/7. Salesbury's *A Dictionary in Englyshe and Welshe* followed in 1547 and in the same year his *Oll Synnwyr Pen Kembero Ygyd* (The Whole Sense of a Welshman's Head), a collection of proverbs. *Kynniver Llith A Ban Or Yscrythur Lan* (As Many Readings and Extracts from Holy Scripture...), containing translations of the gospels and epistles largely from the 1549 Anglican Book of Common Prayer, followed in 1551. These were the foundation stones of literate Welsh culture: words and the Word. The time would come when he would translate the opening of St John's gospel: *'Yn y dechrae ydd oed Gair, a'r Gair oed gyd a Duw, a'r Gair oed Duw.'*

All this and more you will find in R. Brinley Jones's

monograph *William Salesbury* in the Writers of Wales series (UWP, 1994). The list of publications following hard one upon the other bespeaks a man driven, as indeed he was, by interrelated aims – to preserve and elevate Welsh, which he feared was in danger of lapsing into an 'everyday vocabulary of buying, selling, eating and drinking...hardly better than the chatter of wild birds' (in Jones's translation), and to develop a language replete and flexible with 'learning, knowledge, wisdom and godliness', fit for the purpose of translating the scriptures. It seems likely he would have proceeded with similar promptitude to tasks greater in scale and importance than those already accomplished, but was thwarted by the accession of Queen Mary to the throne of England in 1553. During the persecution of Protestants that followed, sensibly he lay low in Llanrwst until, with her death in 1558, his work began again. *Lliver Gweddi Gyffredin* (The Book of Common Prayer) was published in 1567, and (as we have seen) on 7 October the same year his *Testament Newydd* (New Testament), 'printed by Henry Denham, at the costes and charges of Humfrey Toy, dwelling in Paules church yarde, at the sign of the Helmet'. The title page tells us the translation was 'drawn, as far as the different idiom allowed, word for word from the Greek and Latin'. The dedication, in English, addressed to 'The most virtuous and noble Prince Elizabeth...', begins by contrasting the recent past when 'vaine Rites crepte into our country of Wales [and] in steade of the lyvyng God men worshipped dead images of wood and stones, belles and bones...' Salesbury acknowledges contributions to the text from Richard Davies, Bishop of St David's, and Thomas Huet, the cathedral's precentor, but the bulk of the translation and the task of editing the text fell to him. The language of the translation is north Wales Welsh, though south Wales forms appear in marginal notes. Critics say it is marred by archaic forms, Latinisms and eccentric orthography, so as not to be easily understood by contemporaries, but it stood one important test.

'The Newe Testament', Salesbury wrote in his address to Queen Elizabeth, has been 'translated into the British language, which is our vulgare tongue... And would to God that your Graces subjectes of Wales might also have the whole booke of Gods woord brought to like passe.' Through zeal and industry, he was responsible for most of the books published in Welsh up until 1588. In that year Bishop William Morgan published his translation of the Holy Bible, *Y Beibl cyssegr-lan*, which has had a linguistic and literary influence on Welsh wholly comparable to that of the King James Bible on English. In large measure, Bishop Morgan was content to incorporate Salesbury's *Testament Newydd* into his great undertaking.

*PN Review* 239, Volume 44 Number 3,
January – February 2018.

# BERIAH GWYNFE EVANS AND ARTHUR MACHEN
*November 2017*


The 2017 National Eisteddfod, held near the village of Bodedern in the north of Anglesey, closed a few days ago. More than 150,000 attended this astonishingly vibrant annual cultural festival, despite sometimes spiteful weather. The Chair, for a poem in the 'strict metres', was won by Osian Rhys Jones. The subject for the competition this year was 'Yr Arwr' (The Hero), the same as was set in 1917. Then, the winner, Ellis Humphrey Evans, everywhere known by his *ffugenw* (nom de plume), 'Hedd Wyn', did not rise from the audience when he was called. On 31 July that year he had been killed at the battle for Pilkem Ridge. The empty Chair was draped in black.

I did not visit the eisteddfod this year, but was on the *maes,* the eisteddfod field on the banks of the Usk at Abergavenny, last year when a friend gave a talk (in Welsh of course, a rule for all scheduled events) about Beriah Gwynfe Evans (1848–1927), dramatist, journalist and notable *eisteddfodwr*. The topic was well chosen, for Evans was born at Nantyglo, barely ten miles from Abergavenny, and was a great-grandfather of the speaker's wife.

I don't think I would have recalled this old news if I had not been sharply reminded of it by an inspirational book, *The Nations of Wales, 1890–1914* (UWP, 2016), by M. Wynn Thomas. Difficult to conceive of now, the Monmouthshire in which Beriah was born and raised was, like much of the rest of Wales, predominantly Welsh-speaking and a stronghold of Nonconformist faith. He became a teacher at Gwynfe in

Carmarthenshire, adding the name of the village to his own, but like his father, Evan Evans, an Independent minister who spent the latter part of his life (1869–86) preaching in America, he was also a writer, and one with journalistic ambitions. In 1881 he founded *Cyfaill yr Aelwyd* (Friend of the Hearth), a monthly journal of the arts, sciences and topical affairs, which he continued to edit until 1894. By that time, having abandoned teaching, he was working as a journalist in Cardiff. In the words of the *Companion to the Literature of Wales*, he was a 'romantic Nationalist', a supporter of *Cymru Fydd* (Future Wales), a Home Rule movement that was gaining traction in the decade or so about the end of the nineteenth century. Lloyd George, elected Liberal MP for Caernarfon Boroughs in 1890, equally vociferous on behalf of Home Rule and Disestablishment of the Anglican Church in Wales, brought Beriah to Caernarfon as managing editor of his Welsh National Press company, where he quickly established a reputation as a formidable political journalist. In 1895, he gave up the editorship (though not journalism) to become secretary of *Cymru Fydd*, and later still he played a prominent role in the National Eisteddfod.

It is not Evans's life and career, however, that attracts Wynn Thomas, but his novel, *Dafydd Dafis: sef Hunangofiant Ymgeisydd Seneddol* (David Davies: the Autobiography of a Parliamentary Candidate), published in 1898. Dafydd is an innocent propelled into politics by his astute, strong-minded English wife, Claudia. As slowly apprehended by him, the Liberal Party's internal strife over major issues of the day – Home Rule (in which the more vigorous, and violent, Irish approach is contrasted with the Welsh) and Disestablishment – are dealt with lightly. Along with its amused ironic view of contemporary politics, the novel features cartoons, farce and, at the climax, drama. From Wynn Thomas's account and commentary, it seems, in some respects, an unexpectedly modernist text, and not least in the delightful play with language that renders the speech of English characters phonetically in terms of Welsh orthography, as for example in the passage Thomas quotes from an episode nearing the end of the novel when Lord Harcourt, Liberal Chancellor of the Exchequer, says to Dafydd, '*Iwar weiff is a remarcabli ffein wman ... in meni respects ei meit se a gloryis wman ... byt ei thanc hevn shi is not Ledi Harcort!*' This is the book my friend talked about last year on the *maes* at Abergavenny. I should have read it then; I must do so now.

The final essay in *The Nations of Wales*, 'Arthur Machen: Border Disputes', brings us to the southern march and, so far as I am concerned, even closer to home, here in Caerleon. I pass Machen's birthplace, coming and going, most days, and often enough it brings to mind 'The Shining Pyramid', which is set hereabouts, and which has haunted me since I first read it when I was very young. It is a story that transmits a strong impression of an uncertain evil lying just below the surface of everyday existence, one that leaves signs and symbols for those who can read them, and is ready to reach out and grasp the unwary. Wynn Thomas's close probing of the text reveals a level of significance beneath the skin of narrative that my absorbed but superficial reading failed to detect: Machen's mistrust of strangers ('hostility' rather), whether they are foreigners or merely ordinary people differing from him only in being daily engaged in the docks and industries a few miles away in Newport, the Castletown of the story. He notes also Machen's 'multiple identities', his 'indeterminate cultural positioning of himself as a borderer'. Dyson, Machen's protagonist if not alter ego, implicitly presents himself as English, and Caerleon as an English village. Nor was this the only occasion when the writer preferred to identify himself as a 'western Englishman'.

Machen looked eastwards from Caerleon into the Gwent

countryside, which rolls on in multitudinous greens, and onwards again, without break: at the level of landscape there is no border. To the north he saw the industrial valleys and to the west the ports of Newport, Cardiff and Barry, all hazed with coal-dust and pullulating with activity day and night. It is quite clear where his sympathies lay, yet he couldn't entirely shed the badge of his baptismal name, Arthur Llewellyn Jones, and paternal Welsh heritage. Wynn Thomas says he usually preferred to think of himself as 'Celtic English' and, as a son of the rectory, felt strongly drawn to the idea of Celtic Christianity: 'the Mystery Religion. Its priests...called to an awful and tremendous hierurgy; its pontiffs...the pathfinders, the bridge-makers between the world of sense and the world of spirit.' Though never formally a convert to Catholicism, emotionally and intellectually that was where he belonged. There are resemblances in the cast of mind and to some extent the creative juices between Machen and his younger contemporary David Jones, who did convert and was as deep-dyed in the history, mythology and spirituality of Romano-Celtic Britain. David Jones's library, now lodged at the National Library of Wales, includes Machen's *The Secret Glory*, where his propinquity to Catholicism has its fullest expression. They would have been thoroughly at home in one another's company. We have one of Jones's simpler inscriptions, which reads '*Mair Fam Duw Dewi Ddyfrwr ac Holl Saint Cymru Gweddia Drosom*' (Mary Mother of God David the Waterman and All Welsh Saints Pray for Us), to which Machen would have at once added 'Amen', for 'The Waterman', or 'Fisher King', and the Grail legend are as potent in his fiction as they are in Jones's poetry and art.

*PN Review* 238, Volume 44 Number 2,
November – December 2017.

# THOMAS PRICHARD AND CATHERINE WARD

*September 2017*

A few weeks ago I applauded, at a distance, the launch of a fresh reprint of the first, and best, 1828 edition of *Twm Shon Catti*. Its author, Thomas Jeffery Llewelyn Prichard, would have been delighted: a new edition with sundry minor blemishes in the original, like the eccentric numbering of chapters, removed, and it didn't cost him a penny. The book is edited by Rita Singer in the Llyfrau Cantre'r Gwaelod series (a branch of Celtic Studies Publications, or CSP) dedicated to returning to print Welsh literary classics of the nineteenth century. I doff my cap to it, while Prichard capers.

He would have been less cheerful to receive a charge of plagiarism, from an anonymous critic, who alleges he helped himself to verses that were composed by another, namely Mrs Catherine George Ward. I will admit I had never previously heard of her, and hastened to make her acquaintance. The *Oxford Dictionary of National Biography* tells us she was born in 1787, somewhere in Scotland, spent her childhood 'partly in the Isle of Wight' and 'had family connections in Norfolk'. She made a handful of appeals to the Royal Literary Fund to tide her over existential crises, sick children and insolvent husbands dying of TB. The disease may have claimed her, too, for nothing is known of her after 1833. Biographically she is as shadowy a figure as Prichard, or probably more so.

Mrs Ward (Mrs Mason by her second marriage) was a prolific novelist, and for much of her career had a well-known publisher, George Virtue, ready to bring out anything she produced. Several of her books were originally issued in parts, a style of publication that first made Virtue's name. You can find a good sample of her doorstop fictions digitised online. Two I read because they relate to the case, a third, chosen at random, to test whether Jane Austen had anything to fear from this younger contemporary. The short answer is no.

Mrs Ward, unlucky in her husbands and likely driven by the constant threat of poverty, was industrious and possessed astonishing facility. Between 1810 and 1833 she seems to have churned out nineteen novels, most easily exceeding 600 pages. In all circumstances, narrative or descriptive, hyperbole is Mrs Ward's default setting. She attempts wit but is seriously lacking in humour. Irony is unknown to her. In the books I have read her main characters are all titled, 'excessively' handsome or beautiful, 'prodigiously' wealthy and gifted, noble, courageous, sensitive, modest, generous and altruistic. The faults a few may have, due to a quick mind and youthful lack of polite inhibition, they lose at the first serious turn. The conflict in young people between love and duty owed to parents and the magnetic attraction of another is a reiterated theme. They easily betray their true feelings for a blush accompanies any and every emotion.

Women and men are much given to 'colouring deeply'. From time to time, especially when acting or about to act nobly, characters refer to themselves in the third person: 'And when Edwin proves himself unworthy, may he that moment cease to live.' They rarely 'say' anything; even mundane expressions in direct speech are accompanied by, 'he cried' or 'she exclaimed' or even 'ejaculated'. Popular appeal was Mrs Ward's goal and to attain it she created cartoon characters and situations. She is an early nineteenth-century Mills and Boon romancer, love and marriage the fulcrum of action. Thwarted love can lead to sickness and even tubercular death, and tears are shed, copiously, on all sides, but finally romantic love triumphs. Babies are born, without stress, and beautiful, of course. The education of children is entrusted to tutors, male and female, who may be harmlessly eccentric but are devoted to their charges and are likely to get paired off in the knot-tying of the resolution.

This is not to say she never made observations on the social life of the period, but they are rare and lack spirit or spite. Publishers affect to despise authors whose second work cannot be obtained at 'so cheap a price as the first'; women in society disparage 'darkly complexioned' children 'allied to some tawny breed', or any seen to make a successful match ahead of their own; other women, who give up their children to a wet nurse, are derided as 'cruel' and 'unnatural'. Along with the 'penurious and shabby prices of booksellers' that starve authors, breast-feeding was an issue Mrs Ward took very seriously.

Where does Prichard come into this? Mrs Ward's first book was a slim volume of poems, sold by subscription, and most of her novels are liberally sprinkled with poetry. Every chapter has an epigraph, and quite often further lines of verse and even complete poems turn up in the text. Among the acknowledged suppliers of epigraphs are Shakespeare, Campbell, Pope, Burns, Phillips, Goldsmith, Rogers, Moore, Byron, Southey, Scott, Gray and Crabbe. Many more are unattributed, including extracts from early plays. As a young woman, Mrs Ward was an actress (the subscribers' list to *Poems*, 1805, suggests a connection with the Theatre Royal, Edinburgh, though no record of her stage career has emerged) but the lines from, for example Dekker's *Old Fortunatus*, are not quoted from memory, nor do they necessarily indicate familiarity with the play. Rather they are gathered from the selections of poetic and dramatic fragments published in magazines, such as Leigh Hunt's *The Indicator*.

The chosen passages are occasionally abbreviated or otherwise modified. Such is the case with the epigraph to chapter VIII of *The Fisher's Daughter, or the Wanderings of Wolf and the Fortunes of Alfred* (1824), where eight lines are assembled from three separate stanzas of Prichard's 'The Star of Liberty', with his name (misspelled Pritchard) attached. Later in the same chapter the complete poem is presented as the work of the 'young inspired poet' Wolf. In chapter XIV, Wolf's 'tribute to the young sister Anne' is actually Prichard's 'A Quaker Beauty's Likeness'. His authorship is given away by the lines: 'Thy sister-maids my heart admires./Like Cambrian girls of farthest shires,/Simplicity and truth are theirs,/My countrywomen.' Both substantial borrowings, 104 and 72 lines respectively, vary in numerous minor ways from the texts printed in his *Mariette Mouline, The Death of Glendower and other poems* (1823), which may indicate Mrs Ward's taste in punctuation was less prone to the exclamation mark and dash than Prichard's, or that she had copied from earlier manuscript versions.

The title alone which Mrs Ward chose for her next novel, *The Mysteries of St. Clair, or Mariette Mouline* (1824) inspired the charge of plagiarism. *Read on!* one might say, for in chapter XXVI 'Mariette Mouline', the title poem of Prichard's book, all 122 lines, is quoted as the poetic account of 'a lonely and unfortunate woman' to Zosinsky, 'the great Tartarian conqueror' who, in his thoughtless youth, had seduced and abandoned her. Inevitably, at the end of the novel they marry. Prichard tells us he borrowed the story from Kotzebue's *Anecdotes, Literary and Philosophical*. As his notes to the poem go on to explain, to avoid confusion with Sterne's 'Maria at Moulines' in *A Sentimental Journey*, he changed the name of the betrayed woman from 'Maria Moulin', as Kotzebue has it, to 'Mariette'. Far from being stolen from Mrs Ward, 'Mariette Mouline' was his invention. The tale is extrinsic to the narrative development of Mrs Ward's book and might have been added to make up the pages of the final 'part' at its initial publication.

That's speculation, of course, but why stop there? Is the description of Wolf in *The Fisher's Daughter*, with his 'fine intelligent dark piercing eyes', his tall stature and 'great propensity for literature' a portrait of Prichard? Is the concern that lines in 'The Star of Liberty' are 'inflammatory', so that 'it were far better he had not expressed' them, Mrs Ward's concern on behalf of her friend at a time when literary attacks on the establishment could lead to arrest and imprisonment? I have no doubt she and Prichard were friends. They had in common experience on stage and ambition to make a living by the pen and she was a ready customer for Prichard's far bigger collection of poems, *Welsh Minstrelsy*. In the subscribers' list of that book we find '*Warde, Mrs Catherine George, London (6 copies)'. The 'Star' preceding the name denotes an especial closeness, '6 copies' the generosity of her support.

*PN Review* 237, Volume 44 Number 1,
September – October 2017.

# DYLAN THOMAS

*July 2017*

At the end of last week John Goodby was at Cheltenham talking about recent important additions to the swollen archive of work on Dylan Thomas, for which he has been largely responsible. I know from previous experience his audience will have caught the air of fresh excitement he has generated in his study of the poet. He has explored aspects of Thomas's work that earlier critics summarily dismissed, played down or else avoided, such as his debt and contribution to surrealism, in 'The Rimbaud of Cwmdonkin Drive: Dylan Thomas as Surrealist', *Dada and its Legacies* (2012); perhaps more controversially, his centrality to the development of poetry in the 1940s and beyond as far as Hughes and Plath, with a reach into European and world literature that often goes unacknowledged; and his part in the revival of interest in Blake. The spread of Thomas's influence was sometimes thought pernicious, or at best a romantic, obscure, sermonising style to escape from. Among probably scores of examples I think of Dannie Abse and John Ormond, close to home, who fell under the spell – but what an effect to grow creatively out of!

In 2013, Goodby published *The Poetry of Dylan Thomas: Under the Spelling Wall*, the first of his two major contributions to the centenary of the poet's birth, which brings modern critical theory to bear on the oeuvre. Close study of Thomas's poetic language at its densest has had mixed results. While he yet lived and for decades after his death in 1953, if a poem was too difficult for critics to cope with, they threw their hands in the air and declared it rubbish, the meaningless rantings of a Welsh windbag. There is no longer any excuse for ignorance, since Goodby has added *The Collected Poems of Dylan Thomas* (2014), with its hundreds of pages of notes, and now *Discovering Dylan: A Companion to the Collected Poems and Notebook Poems* (2017).

The story of the survival against the odds of Dylan's 'Fifth Notebook' is well known, as probably is that of its purchase at auction by the University of Swansea, where John Goodby is professor of English Literature and Creative Writing. Access to the notebook added a new dimension to a work Goodby had already planned in which he would expand on the notes and commentary in *Collected Poems*. The newly discovered notebook follows the sequence of composition, which ended in the Fourth Notebook on 30 April 1934 with, 'If I were tickled by the rub of love'. It contains sixteen poems, six destined for *Eighteen Poems* and ten for *Twenty-five Poems*, the first dated item (number four) being 'Especially when the October wind', which was added on 1 October 1934. No more than a cheap exercise book, it is nevertheless of major importance, offering a number of insights into a crucial stage of Thomas's poetic development. It shows, for example, that when he left Swansea for London in December 1934 the poetic impetus did not flag, as some critics had speculated, despite the magnetism and temptation of the bars and fleshpots of the city. Rather, he took his poetry forward to explore new subjects and more complex forms, culminating in the formidably challenging 'Altarwise by Owl-light'. Goodby's commentary on this 'sequence of ten inverted Petrarchan sonnets' runs to fifteen closely argued pages, including a historical survey of the remarkably varied critical response it has evoked. In the 1960s, Kleinman saw it as a devotional poem, a 'statement of religious perplexity concluding in spiritual certainty', while Holbrook condemned it as 'pretentious nonsense [...] a kind of verbal perversion'. In the 1980s McKay took the entirely different view that the ten poems create 'a sense of illusion and flamboyance, as each item declares itself, like an item in a Mardi Gras parade, momentous and momentary'.

What might have prompted the poet to embark on a sequence (it was always intended to be lengthy) characterised by exuberant use of language and imagery? It took over a year, 1935–36, for Thomas to complete 'Altarwise'. During its composition he referred to it as a 'work in progress', tacit acknowledgment of a debt to Joyce's *Finnegans Wake*, though not really to the entire novel, which was first published in 1939, but rather to *Anna Livia Plurabelle: Fragment of a Work in Progress*, which Thomas would have seen in the Faber & Faber (1930) edition. I have just read Thomas Dilworth's *David Jones: Engraver, Soldier, Painter, Poet*, a splendid biography, the culmination of many years' study and publication. In it we learn that Jones, too, was intellectually smitten by 'Work in Progress'. He said 'it made a great impression on me' and when his friend Harman Grisewood gave him the recording of Joyce reading the final pages he was so enthralled he set about learning the text by heart, reciting it on walks. Dilworth argues that this was Jones's primary model for the poetic use of colloquial language. In broad terms, what both he and Dylan Thomas saw in Joyce was an intense interest and pleasure in exploiting all the resources of language. If *Anna Livia Plurabelle* had a message for them, it was, 'Let linguistic experimentation flourish'. It gave them endorsement of the direction they had already started out upon and licence to develop their creative expression further, towards similar goals: Jones in *In Parenthesis* and *The Anathemata*; Thomas in 'Altarwise'.

Taking his cue from McKay's view of Thomas's overall design as a 'carnivalesque' sequence, Goodby turns to Notebook Five with its trial stanzas, deletions and variant readings to explore the ambiguities and deeper meanings of the text. It may not persuade every reader but, for now at least, is as close to a definitive analysis as we are likely to get. Notes on the poem bear out the assertion in the introduction that Thomas, omnivorous in his reading, hid the sources of allusions in his poetry rather than 'flaunting them on a broken variable verse surface' like Eliot in *The Waste Land* or Pound in *The Cantos*. (In a distant echo of his poetic practice, for reasons difficult to fathom he would also deny all knowledge of a book or movement with which he was actually very familiar.)

The legend of Dylan Thomas as drunken womaniser, *poète maudit*, has taken hold of the public imagination. It contributes to the tourist industry in south-west Wales, but has done little to enhance wider appreciation of his writing, which few know anything about beyond 'Fern Hill' and one or two other poems. Goodby regrets the perpetuation of the 'young dog' portrait. He argues that it is time for a fresh look at the poetry of the 1930s and '40s, which should reveal in Thomas not an apocalyptic dead-end, but a fusing of the formalism of Auden and his followers with Modernist existentialism. He has completed the assembly of necessary materials: with a fair wind, reappraisal should follow.

*PN Review* 236, Volume 43 Number 6,
July – August 2017.

# WILLIAM WILLIAMS
*May 2017*


On the first Saturday in March we took our seats in the usual place at Cardiff Arms Park for the home match against Munster, in the outcome a disappointing affair. At one stage quite early in the game some ragged, badly-pitched singing broke out – like a rash, you might indeed say for the discomfort it brought, and it soon petered out. 'Guide me O Thou Great Jehovah' can rarely have been rendered so badly. It was emblematic of the change that has overtaken the cultural life of Wales in the last half century. There is no holding out now against the forces of mass entertainment, inane celebrity and internet communication, but some vestiges of a distinctive, common culture still existed even among rugby spectators in Wales when we were young. It manifested itself in the impromptu singing of hymns, in choral harmonies, by many thousands of ordinary people enfolded for a couple of hours in the shared experience of a hurly-burly performance on a muddy field. Although we did not recognise it at the time (it didn't cross our minds), this marked the end of the great Nonconformist chapel tradition that had endured since the early decades of the eighteenth century.

One of the founders of that tradition, William Williams, fourth child of John and Dorothy Williams, was born early in 1717, just three hundred years ago. His father, a small farmer, had the good fortune to marry into a somewhat wealthier family, and his bride, in due course, inherited their farm, which was called Pantycelyn – a long, low whitewashed building on the slope of a lane about four miles from Llandovery in Carmarthenshire. Wales was, and probably still is, littered with

William Williamses (forty-four are listed in the *Dictionary of National Biography*) and as is common the farm name was attached to distinguish him. Now, at least by the older generation, he is immediately recognisable as 'Williams Pantycelyn', or simply 'Pantycelyn'. His family attended an Independent chapel at Cefnarthen, a stronghold of Dissent. These Nonconformist inheritors of Puritanism, seeking a return to the simplicity of early Christianity, set up gatherings, initially often in private houses or barns, that were independent and self-governing. They appointed their own ministers and officers, though they did not see themselves as in opposition to the Anglican Church. When the congregation at Cefnarthen split along sectarian lines, the Williams family became part of a new Calvinistic gathering, which met at a farm nearer their home. Eventually, after John Williams' death, his widow and William, her surviving son, gave the land on which a new chapel was built.

As a young man William was set to train as a doctor. This should have involved apprenticeship to an apothecary for several years before qualifying for a licence to practice, but in 1737 or 1738, while he was still in the earlier stages of a formal education at Llwyn Llwyd, near Hay-on-Wye, he chanced to hear Howel Harris preaching in the churchyard at Talgarth. The direction of his life was changed instantly. Ordained deacon of the Established Church in 1740, he served as curate until 1743, while at the same time travelling and preaching elsewhere, perhaps to the neglect of the duties of his cure. In any event, as with Howel Harris, the bishop refused to ordain him priest. Two other names are linked with these: Griffith Jones (1683–1761), rector of Llanddowror, famous even as far as Russia as founder of the Circulating Schools, and Daniel Rowland (1713–1790), also an Anglican priest. Preachers of immense power and authority, all four were accused by the

Established Church of preaching irregularly, but they were the cornerstones of the Methodist Revival in Wales, and did not spare themselves in their determined evangelism.

Determination was essential. Harris was a diarist; a posthumous 'autobiography' created from diary extracts reveals how they could suffer in the cause. In the summer of 1740, he and a fellow preacher came to this place, very close to where I am writing: 'When we came to Caerleon everything seemed calm and quiet whilst Brother [William] Seward [...] prayed and discoursed sweetly by the Market-house, but when I began to discourse after him, then they began to roar most horribly, pelting us with dung and dust, throwing eggs, plum-stones, and other hard substances even in our faces, and hallooed so loudly as to drown my voice entirely. Brother Seward had a furious blow in his right eye, which caused him much anguish; and as it affected his left he was obliged to be led by the hand [...] till at last he became totally blind of it.'

Through their endeavour and sacrifice, all four sowed the seed of Methodist fellowship groups or associations. By the 1750s there were four hundred such *seiadau* throughout Wales. Reviewing his 'glorious work in the world', William Williams calculated he had travelled one hundred and fifty thousand miles on horseback, preaching and tending the fresh shoots. In the midst of what appears to be non-stop evangelism, in 1748 or 1749 he married Mary Francis, daughter of a fairly well-off farming family. They had seven surviving children (a direct descendant farms Pantycelyn today). He had sufficient means to amass a substantial library of books in Welsh and English. Glyn Tegai Hughes, whose Writers of Wales monograph *Williams Pantycelyn* (1983) is an accessible and reliable source, says English writers, notably Milton and Bunyan, were the chief stimulus of his own literary endeavours. His output, overwhelmingly in Welsh, was prodigious. He published

*Pantheologia, neu Hanes Holl Grefyddau'r Byd* (A History of All the Religions of the World) serially between 1762 and 1769, and between 1756 and 1764 published three epic poems, each of about six thousand lines, two in rhyming four-line stanzas and one in blank verse, which he told his readers 'allows the poet to put all his gifts to use, his imaginings, his tropes, his flights of fancy [...] where elsewhere he is so much a slave to having to put together words of the same sound, and that in a language without many words at its disposal'. My Welsh hymnbook includes no fewer than one hundred and fifty-two hymns by Pantycelyn, but that is a fraction only of a total of more than three thousand. The epic poetry is uneven, partly, as Hughes shows, because of the self-acknowledged difficulty he encountered in forcing vigorous expression of his condemnation of sin and love of God into a constricting metrical form, but he nevertheless composed passages 'of great beauty and power'. It is above all the hymns that earned him the title 'y pêr caniedydd' – the sweet singer.

William Williams died in 1791. A brief review of his remarkable life and achievements leaves the impression of a man of Dickensian energies, if not appetites. Did he sleep, and write, in the saddle?

The English words of 'Cwm Rhondda', which we heard murdered last Saturday, are his own. They are not a translation of the original Welsh but another sacred poem, that in this present irreligious age (so the Census takers say), despite constant repetition has all but lost its meaning.

*PN Review 235,* Volume 43 Number 5,
May – June 2017.

# THOMAS PRICHARD
*November 2016*

At the beginning of the 1960s, in the absence of any formal interest on the part of university departments here in what has since become known as 'Welsh writing in English', it was left to Roland Mathias to cultivate an almost entirely neglected field. As editor of that quarterly doorstop *The Anglo-Welsh Review*, he led the way in writing carefully considered reviews of books by Welsh poets and authors and long editorials and critical articles that set the standard for later academic studies. His influence can be seen in the emulative efforts of *Poetry Wales*, founded in 1965 by Meic Stephens and edited by him. Stephens, too, sought to expand reviewing beyond scant notices of recent publications to close scrutiny and assessment, and in those special numbers of the magazine devoted to individual writers (Dylan Thomas, R.S. Thomas, David Jones), to which Mathias usually contributed, gave academic critics, like Jeremy Hooker and Anthony Conran, the opportunity to begin building a conspectus of the subject on scholarly lines. To their lasting shame, neither the then federal University of Wales, nor any of its constituent colleges, awarded Roland Mathias the honour he so richly deserved, but before the end of the century, the seeds he planted, nurtured by gifted scholars of the calibre of M. Wynn Thomas, had established Welsh writing in English as a course of study available to students. The metamorphosis of *Welsh Writing in English: A Yearbook of Critical Essays*, which began appearing in 1995, to the *International Journal of Welsh Writing in English* in 2013, is an indication of the subject's status in Wales and in universities overseas.

It still has a long way to go to make any impression on English studies in England, as on the stone-faced or arrogantly dismissive metropolitan media – which is a pity, because it throws up curiously absorbing Welsh-English interests. Almost forty years ago, Roland Mathias, in the way he had, invited me to interest myself in Thomas Jeffery Llewelyn Prichard, and see if what I found might suit *AWR*. After a stint turning over old books and a surprising hoard of manuscripts at Cardiff Central Library I produced an article that corrected the Prichard entry in the *Dictionary of Welsh Biography*. I have written extensively on this topic before (*PN Review* 192, 2010) and will not repeat myself aside from mentioning that he wrote what was at the time greeted as 'the first Welsh novel in English', *Twm Shôn Catti* (1828), had earlier been an actor in the London theatre, lost his nose somewhere, and died in Swansea in 1862 after falling into his own fire. As an antecedent of the present race of Welsh writers in English, he is now attracting the attention of academic critics, who tend to focus their attention on the novel, which was Prichard's greatest success. Indeed, having made a little money from the initial publication, he expanded it considerably for a second edition (1839), and at the time of his death was working on a yet longer version, which was eventually published in 1873.

Even allowing for this unfinished attempt at the 'triple-decker' of his dreams, to be auctioned among a score of competing publishers, he probably wrote more poetry than prose. I have taken pains to read all I could, but for the best part of the several decades Prichard and I have been acquainted I have chafed at my inability to obtain a copy of one of his books of poems. I knew it existed because he referred to it on the title page of another publication, *Mariette Mouline*, where he declares himself 'Author of "My Lowly Love", "Theatrical Poems", &c.', but as none of the great libraries of the land possessed a copy of T.J. Llewelyn Prichard's 'Theatrical Poems' I gave it up as lost – several times. Knowing how lost stuff sometimes reappears, I recently approached the National Library at Aberystwyth and asked them to try again. On this occasion, my request reached Martin Riley, senior enquiries assistant at the library, and as usual he drew a blank. Then he searched simply for 'Theatrical Poems' and produced an unexpected result. Yes, the library had a copy of 'Theatrical Poems', not by Prichard, but Jeremy Diddler. This had come to the library in the collection of Joseph Joseph (fl. 1855–1890) and his grandson Capt. James Buckley (1869–1924) of Castell Gorfod, St Clears, Carmarthenshire. Joseph had roots in Brecknockshire, Prichard's home county, and had taken the trouble to bind Jeremy Diddler's slim volume with Prichard's *My Lowly Love*. So there we had it: Diddler was Prichard by another name. When he began to publish poems, in a short-lived magazine *The Cambro-Briton*, he used the nom de plume 'Jeffery Llewelyn', which he later incorporated into his own, plain Thomas Prichard. He was not averse to appearing in disguise, and in this case he might have thought it wiser, because most of the poems in the book are satires of contemporary actors and theatre managers and their devious practices. A self-confessed admirer of Charles Churchill (1732–1764), when he compiled the collection, he almost certainly had in mind the latter's *The Rosciad*, originally published anonymously in 1761. The name Jeremy Diddler he borrowed from the chief character in a popular farce of the period, *Raising the Wind*, by James Kenney (1780–1849), first produced at Covent Garden in 1803. 'Jeremy' is a conman, whose aim in life is to marry an heiress. When we are taken in, deceived by a trickster, and say we have been 'diddled', we owe the word to him, or rather to James Kenney who created the character. Prichard had in mind a particular revival more than a decade later when the lead role was played by Richard Jones, to whom *Theatrical Poems* is dedicated.

In the Writers of Wales monograph *Thomas Jeffery Llewelyn Prichard* (UWP, 2000), I proposed that he acted at Covent Garden as 'Mr Jefferies', sharing the stage with celebrated players of the stature of John Philip Kemble and his even more famous sister, Sarah Siddons. In the absence of proof, doubts have been cast on the hypothesis. It was pleasing to find in this late discovery support for my case (in addition to the circumstantial evidence adduced previously). Satire was ever Prichard's strongest suit and anger the inspiration. The most vitriolic attack in *Theatrical Poems,* in a poem entitled 'A Wise Man, A Fool', is aimed at someone he knew well:

Ch— Kl—'s but a sorry actor,
A fop by art, a fool by nature,
A grovelling squab in form and feature: –
That he ne'er play'd a single part
Consistent with dramatic art,
Except, perchance, once in his noon
Whil'st Covent Garden's pantaloon.

It is not exquisite verse making, but it is deeply felt. A little research identifies the target: Charles Klanert, and a collection of Covent Garden playbills reveals a curious, reiterated juxtaposition. At the opening of the 1805/6 season, in the cast of *The Padlock*, a 'musical farce', we see 'Scholars, Mess. Klannert and Jefferies'; in *Hartford Bridge* they are paired as 'Waiters'; in *Othello* Klanert plays Antonio, Jefferies Julio; in *Hamlet* (20 March 1806), Rosencrantz is played by Klanert, Guildenstern by Jefferies. In these and many other examples the size and importance of the roles are very similar. All are minor. It might be objected that Prichard, born 1790, would have been only fifteen in 1805/6. But youth was no impediment to a stage career. Many major actors of the period began as children: in the production of *Hamlet* noted above, the leading role was taken by 'Master Betty', a fourteen-year-old phenomenon.

*PN Review* 232, Volume 43 Number 2, November – December 2016.

# WALES BOOK OF THE YEAR 2016

*September 2016*

Just a week ago, early evening, we set out for Merthyr Tydfil. The A470, that joke of a trunk road running from Cardiff almost two hundred miles to Llandudno, is dualled at least as far as Merthyr and, the crawl of commuter traffic over for the day, we made good progress to the gates of the town. Then things went badly awry. After a while of blundering into cul-de-sacs and halting, baffled, at *No Entries*, we saw a sign to Twynyrodyn. It was the memory of a fine poem, 'Ponies Twynyrodyn', that prompted me to point the car that way. At once we found ourselves on a steep hill, heading north, out of town. We stopped and asked directions. Discussion ensued about a number of options. The simplest appeared to be to keep going until we reached a roundabout at the top and there turn left. After that advice the road continued, if anything more steeply, up. No wonder the ponies in my old friend's poem came down that way in winter: the top is at the very edge of the Brecon Beacons. But our advisers were wise indeed, the left turn brought us steeply down and precisely to our destination – the Red House, Merthyr's old Town Hall, restored, in part with European Development Fund money, and re-opened on 1 March 2014 as a 'creative industries centre'. This was the venue for Wales Book of the Year 2016. In recent years these events have alternated between Cardiff and Caernarfon; bringing it to Merthyr has underlined a sense of inclusivity in the arts in Wales that has long been an aspiration of Literature Wales and the Arts Council.

The evening was remarkable for revealing two triple prize-winners. Caryl Lewis swept the board in the Welsh language: her novel *Y Bwthyn* (The Cottage), published by Y Lolfa, won the People's Choice Award (online voting), the fiction prize, and the overall Book of the Year Prize. And Thomas Morris did the same in English with his collection of short stories *We Don't Know What We're Doing* (Faber).

Philip Gross won the Roland Mathias Prize for poetry with *Love Songs of Carbon* (Bloodaxe), his eighteenth collection. The poems reflect the experience of a Cornishman long resident in Wales. In Cornwall there are strong ties, vibrant still in memory, with loved parents; in coastal south Wales, the living connection of married love. The collection is dominated by Time (as are we all), and persistence is the message echoed from poem to poem. Art can, or must, persist against all odds, as in 'Paul Klee: the late style'. In 'Thirty Feet Under', the hermit crab and sea anemone on the foreshore, exposed by the retreat of the huge Severn estuary tide, convey the same message: love must go on regardless of statistical evidence. 'Coming of Age' sees us propelled willy-nilly through life's stages, and still what matters in the end is love. 'Watermark', that 'line in the sea made of nothing', where gulls gather to feed, and 'Several Shades of Ellipses' are multifaceted images of love continuing to the ultimate full stop. Gross's poetry has acute observation of the natural world and human relations, and phrase-making that often stops the reader in his tracks. It is both profoundly serious and, on occasion, playful, and always alert to the fresh perspectives on life afforded by science and technology. In 'Mattins' it wrestles with the imponderables of faith and the human condition in a way that Roland Mathias, whose name is preserved in the prize he received, would recognise at once as akin to his own precarious knowledge of uncertainty.

The prize in the English-language fiction category was for the first time sponsored by the Rhys Davies Trust. It was peculiarly appropriate that it went to a short story collection, for Rhys Davies was, and is, an acknowledged master of the genre. The setting of Thomas Morris's stories is the town of Caerphilly, dominated by its colossal Norman castle and the mountains beyond. True, one story takes its cast of young men on a stag-do to Dublin, and another takes the town into some future or parallel time, but all are permeated with its unique character and nearly all with recognisable localities.

Although he has studied and lived in Dublin for the last eleven years, Caerphilly remains Morris's home. He can recreate it wherever he happens to be, much as Joyce carried Dublin around with him and drew upon his memory of it constantly. Like Joyce again, his vision is clarified by being away from the inspirational place. Even if not quite to Joyce's capacity to entertain and confound the reader, there is enough variety in Morris's approach to storytelling – first, second and third person narratives, past, continuous present, even future tense – to interest a creative writing class.

The voices Joyce heard in exile were Dublin voices, and the language of Morris's stories is a version of the contemporary south Wales demotic. It lends itself readily to hyperbole and humour. Things rarely go well for the characters, and they are frequently afflicted by the manifold 'issues' of modern life, but humour is never far away from the troubling surface of events. With one exception, 'Strange Traffic', which concerns a pensioner couple, the stories involve men and women in their twenties, often the late twenties. They are people who are lonely, depressed, pinworm-infected, self-harming, drunk, hungover, aimless. That is, people who should 'know what they are doing', but do not. The stresses of life and mental fragility in situations where the old, fundamental certainties and expectations – work and a wage, and secure, lasting relationships – no longer obtain are themes that run through the book. In an interview, Morris has said he is interested in 'the idea of adulthood [...] the lines between being a boy and a man'. He identifies the distinguishing feature of adulthood as being given 'genuine responsibility'. Here he has hit upon one of the important factors influencing the nature of society in post-industrial south Wales, and probably wider afield. In the harsh environment of the pits and steelworks, adulthood came early, as men still in their teens took on daily and lifetime responsibility for themselves and their fellows. Such was the nature of the work. Today, employment, where it is available, is usually physically safe, often highly individualised, and too often temporary. If this does produce men – and women – who grow older without becoming adult, it is a problem for society and we are a long way from a solution.

For all their underlying seriousness, the stories are constantly engrossing and shimmer with memorable images: 'smiling like a bag of chips', 'pale and thin, like semi-skimmed milk', 'street lamps glowing like electric lunch boxes', 'her mother was still percolating after her father's death'. In Dublin, Morris edited *Dubliners 100* (Tramp Press, 2014), an anthology of short stories to celebrate the centenary of the publication of Joyce's *Dubliners*. He is editor of the literary magazine *The Stinging Fly*, which encourages new writers. I'm afraid he was a new writer to me; we shall, I'm sure, hear more of him.

*PN Review* 231, Volume 43 Number 1,
September – October 2016.

# IFOR AP GLYN AND GILLIAN CLARKE
*May 2016*

On 1st March, St David's Day, Literature Wales, the administrative and funding agency for literature this side of the border, announced the appointment of a new National Poet: Ifor ap Glyn. In the words of the press release, he will represent 'the best writing from Wales on the national and international stage'. From its inauguration in 2005, it was intended that a Welsh-language poet should alternate in the role with one whose work was largely, if not entirely, in English. Ifor ap Glyn has twice won the Crown at the National Eisteddfod (in 1999 and 2013) and published five volumes of poetry in Welsh. Unsurprisingly, Welsh is his first language, but he was born and brought up in Pinner, in the London borough of Harrow. Elton John and Michael Rosen were near enough neighbours and contemporaries. Therein lies an important lesson: as long as the family remains proud and firm in the Welsh language, the children will thrive in it, despite the omnipresence of English.

Traditionally, Crowned Bards, and Welsh poets in general, have risen from the ranks of teachers, academics and ministers of religion. Ifor ap Glyn, born in 1961, is from a newer mould. Since graduating from Cardiff University he has had a career in the media. He has a considerable reputation as television scriptwriter, producer and presenter. If you can call to mind a BBC 4 series called 'Pagans and Pilgrims: Britain's Holiest Places', or another programme on the same channel, 'The Toilet: an unspoken history', then you will have had an opportunity to appreciate his skill as writer and producer, and (Praise be!) an easy, undemonstrative style of presentation, which in these days of waving arms and heavy, misplaced emphases, few seem capable of. He is a founder member and creative director of *Cwmni Da* ('Good Company') a television production company based in Caernarfon, and a major creative force in Welsh-language media. He was shortlisted for the Grierson Award in 2008, for 'Frongoch: Birthplace of the IRA' and has won BAFTA Cymru awards for the series *Popeth yn Gymraeg* ('Everything in Welsh') and *Lleisiau'r Rhyfel Mawr* ('Voices of the Great War').

The public dimension of his new role will not disconcert him. At university in his twenties he was the front man of a rock group called *Treiglad Pherffaith* ('Perfect Mutation' – make of it what you will), and in 2008–2009 he was Wales' Children's Laureate. He has twice performed at the Smithsonian Folk Life Festival, Washington DC, where the Welsh language and culture are celebrated in a way London has never yet considered. In short, he is a splendid representative of the bilingual Welsh in the technological world, justifying all that is being done by activists and Welsh Language Acts to secure the continuation of the language, in the face of indifference and even hostility from within Wales and without.

Ifor ap Glyn is our fourth National Poet, having been preceded by Gwyneth Lewis (2005–2006), Gwyn Thomas (2006–2008), and Gillian Clarke (2008–2016). At the outset, it was envisaged that the role would change hands fairly frequently, but it has lodged with Gillian Clarke for the simple reason that her performance of it has been exemplary. She has been an outstanding ambassador for poetry and for Wales, here and overseas.

The beech buds are breaking. I feel so happy.
I snapped the bare twigs in a wood
A month ago. I put them in a wine bottle

Filled with water, not for the twigs, for the light
Blown bubbles to float in the shine of the water.
[...]

The floor of the wood glimmered with white bones;
Little, silver skulls eyed us darkly, and the lambs
Leapt away round the hill. The blood of birth
And life stained the pale bones of the past.
[...]

The child sleeps, and I reflect, as I breathe
His brown hair, and watch the apple they gave him
Held in his hot hands, that a tree must ache
With the sweet weight of the round rosy fruit
[...]

It was very strange to watch him sail
Away from me on the calm water,
The white sail duplicate [...]
When they returned the exhilaration
Of the familiar morning had gone. I felt
As though on the water he had found
New ways of evasion, a sheet
Of icy water to roll out between us.

I remember the excitement I felt when, in the summer of 1970,
Meic Stephens, editor of the magazine, showed me the four
poems a complete newcomer, Gillian Clarke, had submitted to
*Poetry Wales*. There was a marked preponderance of male poets
in the lists of contributors at that time, though Ruth Bidgood,
Sally Roberts Jones and Alison Bielski appeared fairly regularly.
The outlook has changed since. Even now, typing the above
extracts from Gillian's poems, I receive an echo of that sense of

discovery we experienced then. Whatever may have been happening elsewhere, or may have happened since, there was no precedent in the scores of fat envelopes addressed to the editor that prepared us for them. Here was a young woman, mother to three children, writing directly out of life, existentially if you like, about relationships, interests and concerns, including the quotidian and domestic, with acute observation, delicacy and tact, and unstrained phrase-making that excited the ear and mind. In another year she had published enough poems to make an impressive booklet, *Snow on the Mountain*, which I edited in the Triskel Poets series. Since then she has been constantly productive. There are a further fourteen books by my count, ten from Carcanet, including *Collected Poems* (1997). With all that, and more, she has given readings at venues throughout the UK, in Europe and America, and devoted much of her time to encouraging interest in poetry among young people in schools and colleges. She became the second Welsh poet (after R.S. Thomas) to win the Queen's Medal for Poetry in 2010 and was admitted to the Gorsedd of Bards at the National Eisteddfod in 2011.

Although her primary creative medium is English, she has long since 'crossed the bridge' to become a Welsh speaker. She occasionally writes in Welsh and employs her second-language skills in translations of both poetry and prose. In all her travels she is as enthusiastic a champion of Wales and Welsh culture as she is of poetry.

Ifor ap Glyn's first appearance in the role of National Poet will be on 31 May at the Hay Festival, when he and Gillian Clarke will share the platform.

*PN Review* 229, Volume 42 Number 5,
May – June 2016.

# IAIN SINCLAIR
*January 2016*


Iain Sinclair was in Cardiff a few weeks ago to talk about his latest, *Black Apples of Gower*, a hardback just published in the neat, pocket-sized Little Toller MONOGRAPHS series. The last book I read of his was *Ghost Milk*, a sustained polemic in which he condemns 'the age of multi-layered development agencies, the tearing out of gardens, the expulsion of small traders, the removal of travellers', specifically, in this case, to make way for London's 2012 Olympic Park. For Sinclair, what remains as a legacy of the peripatetic Olympics adds salt to the wounds inflicted by developers on the traditional urban environment. This is a theme he explores on the ground in Berlin and on the mouldering site of the Athens 2004 games – 'the symbol of a nation's bankruptcy'. He has his heroes, in *Ghost Milk* Thomas de Quincy, revered as the first psychogeographer, and J. G. Ballard. With Paris in his sights, he might embrace the redoubtable Richard Cobb (a self-styled 'walking historian' and one of my heroes), to whom Haussmannisation and the Périphérique were triple-dyed sins. As a worker in and with film and photography, he probably has Cobb's *The Streets of Paris* (with splendid photographs by Nicholas Breach) among his books.

The walks that inform his writing occasionally take him beyond London, once (to the best of my recollection) even as far as Wales, or at least the southern March, with *Landor's Tower* (1999), which, he seems to think, did him no good in the land of his fathers. In any event, he was soon tugged back to London. Readers may be forgiven for thinking him a

Londoner; after all, he has lived in Hackney for more than forty years. It may surprise them to find him exploring the Gower peninsula, that boot-shaped projection into the Severn Sea to the west of Swansea. What took him there? Well, *hiraeth*, we would say: the event in Cardiff was a homecoming. The evidence has been clear enough in autobiographical asides in Sinclair's substantial output and in interviews from time to time. He was brought up in Maesteg, an old coal-mining town in the Llynfi valley. His father, a Scot, practised as a GP there, but his maternal grandfather was a miner, and Welsh-speaking, as were all his mother's relatives. Like a great many born in the south Wales Valleys in the 1930s and 1940s, he was familiar with two languages and cultures.

He mislaid his Valleys accent at Cheltenham College, where, as a sixth former, with an eye to university entrance, he wrote a paper on Dylan Thomas, for which he did original research, 'tracking down witnesses, walking around potentially significant territory, taking photographs, scribbling notes'. This approach he has replicated since – and expanded, with intellectual embellishments from the Courtauld Institute of Art and the London Film School. It is the foundation of his writing. At Trinity College, Dublin, he tells us, 'I read Charles Olson', and, he might have added, became, first, a poet. Since, he has carried Olson's definition of poetry as a 'high energy construct' into his prose writing, which crackles with vitality. Part of his personal rhetoric derives from the apparent freedom with which he allows the force of the moment, acting upon a great reservoir of eclectic reading, to take him where it will. A friend of mine, viewing a piece of wayward writing which juxtaposed disparate observations, used to say it was like taking his nosy terrier for a walk with constant tugging of the leash in different directions. There is something of that in *Black Apples of Gower*, but it is an illusion of freewheeling thought association. Sinclair knows where he is going and the book may be seen as a running (or walking) commentary which introduces, as imagination prompts and opportunity allows, reference to David Jones, Graves, Yeats, William Blake (a particular favourite), and much else.

As a boy he holidayed with his parents in a caravan set in a farmer's field near the village of Horton on the southwestern coast of the Gower, and he returned there with friends as a teenager, cycling the thirty-five miles or so from Maesteg. It was then that he first walked as far as the extraordinarily beautiful Rhossilli Bay and searched out the sea caves scattered along the rugged coastline. It was at that age, too, industriously alone, that he visited Vernon Watkins at Pennard, to ask about his friendship with Dylan Thomas, and found the poet unwell, but ever courteously obliging, sitting up in bed ready to receive him. Watkins's determination not to advance his lowly career behind the counter of a bank in order to dedicate his life to poetry seems even more eccentric today, when many (most?) writers find a niche in university departments of creative writing, but he maintained as well vigorous outdoor interests. As a sure-footed Gower cliff and foreshore scrambler and indefatigable tennis player (until it stopped him in his tracks), he advised his young interrogator not to give up rugby. Wise words. Sinclair also has a longstanding interest in another sometime Gower resident, and friend of Watkins, the artist Ceri Richards, whose inspired super-doodling in the margins and spaces of a copy of Dylan Thomas's *Collected Poems* created a unique artefact. An image that decked the lower blank portion of the page ending 'I dreamed my genesis', evolved into Richards's enigmatic painting *'Afal du Brogwyr'* ('Black Apple of Gower'), the words his own invention, which gives the book its title. This large-scale work presents what appears to be an enormous black sun, with pips of regeneration at its heart. Much as Watkins's poetry reveals the essence of Gower, says the writer, so does Richards's art.

The incandescent blackness of Richards's sun is paralleled by the black entrance of the Goat's Hole cave in a limestone cliff above blue sea in that part of Gower known as Paviland, where in prehistory the 'Red Lady' was interred. A visit with a like-minded friend in January 1973 failed to find the cave, but at another attempt, in 2014, he entered the cave and looked on the famous burial site. His (because it was a young man, not – as originally thought – a female) red ochre stained bones, thirty-three thousand years old, were excavated by the Reverend William Buckland in 1823, and are now displayed, controversially some would claim, at the University Museum in Oxford, when they should be in Cardiff, or Swansea, or Gower. Another sidestep near the end of the book, one among scores of entertaining 'by-the-way' stories, throws light on Buckland's extraordinary digestive sampling of all creatures great and small, including the long-preserved heart of King Louis XIV.

If, after Trinity College, Sinclair had come back to Wales, instead of going off to London to study art and film and be a Hackney council gardener, and a bookseller and publisher, he would have joined in the second flowering of Welsh writing in English. We here would have gained much from his talent and energy. I am sorry, for example, that he has not had the time to bring to other Welsh poets, notably Roland Mathias, whose work he would find full of landscapes viewed through the prism of time, the powers of perception and analysis he reveals in his commentary on Vernon Watkins in this latest book. But it pains me to admit a nagging suspicion that, deprived of the experiences London brought, he would not have flourished as a writer in the same way, nor found the wide readership and admiration he now enjoys.

*PN Review* 227, Volume 42 Number 3, January – February 2016.

# ALUN LEWIS AND ROLAND MATHIAS

*November 2015*


All day it has rained, and we on the edge of the moors
Have sprawled in our bell-tents, moody and dull as boors,
Groundsheets and blankets spread on the muddy ground
[...]
And we stretched out, unbuttoning our braces,
Smoking a Woodbine, darning dirty socks,
Reading the Sunday papers – I saw a fox
And mentioned it in a note I scribbled home; –
And we talked of girls, and dropping bombs on Rome,
And thought of the quiet dead and the loud celebrities
Exhorting us to slaughter, and the herded refugees ...

Early in my first university year at Aberystwyth I heard someone read the poem of which these are the opening lines and soon after made my way to the upper gallery second-hand section of Galloway's bookshop in Pier Street and found *Raiders' Dawn*, the first of two books of poems by Alun Lewis, the second, *Ha! Ha! Among the Trumpets*, published posthumously. It is easy to understand why 'All day it has rained' caught my attention. In 1952 there were fellow students who had served in the war. One, David Pritchard, later professor of Education at Swansea, who had been promoted major at the crossing of the Rhine, became a good friend and led a quartet of us on an adventure in France and Spain in the summer of 1954. But it wasn't just that the poem was about the war that won my attention, it was the register, somewhere between the familiar nineteenth-century poetics of school English and twentieth-century journalism, and the closeness of the language and ideas to those of my everyday life, and again the mood – ennui, surely, but poised on the edge, as it were, of chaos or epiphany. *Raiders' Dawn* was published in March 1942; eighteen months later, October 1943, it had reached a fourth impression, as the copy I bought in Galloway's shows. It was the same with *The Last Inspection and other stories*, also published in 1942, which had run to a third impression by 1947, for Alun Lewis won a considerable following in his short lifetime. However you look at him, he was a writer of substantial achievement and huge promise. The war may have forced him, impelled creativity with its threat of life foreshortened, filled him with longings and fed him impressions, particularly of India, but it was sheer talent that made him a writer, arguably the finest of the Second World War. Only Keith Douglas and Sidney Keyes come near him.

Lewis was born in Cwmaman, a former mining village near Aberdare, on 1 July 1915, and was educated at Cowbridge Grammar School, UCW Aberystwyth, and Manchester University. His formative years coincided with the prolonged industrial strife and depression of the 1920s-30s and from family and community he imbibed nonconformist, socialist and pacifist convictions. The six weeks he spent in the summer of 1937 at an International Peace Conference in Pontigny, northern France, he described as among the happiest of his life. It needed a particular kind of courage to deny these principles and enlist at the beginning of the war. In 1941 he married Gweno (Ellis), a teacher, and was commissioned second lieutenant in the south Wales Borderers, and by 1942 he was serving in India. There are indications that his was a conflicted personality: a pacifist who enlisted; an officer who disliked the officer class and preferred being with the men of his platoon. His experience of the landscape and peoples of India was shocking and profoundly moving and, though he never lost his sense of loving responsibility for Gweno, he found there another love, one that bowled him over. At their fine house in the Nilgiri Hills, Wallace and Freda Aykroyd hosted army officers on leave. The moment he saw Freda, he was lost. In February 1944, now an intelligence officer with the Borderers, Lewis was posted to the Arakan in Burma. Soon after he died of a revolver shot wound to the head from his own weapon. He was twenty-eight. Although he probably committed suicide, a subsequent inquiry, which concluded his death was the result of an accident, brought an atom of comfort to his widow and family at a time of overwhelming sorrow.

When in 1974, as editor of *Poetry Wales,* I brought out an Alun Lewis special number, it was with the willing cooperation of Gweno, his mother, Gwladys Elizabeth, and his sister, Mair, and included letters, photographs and personal reminiscences previously unpublished. There is far more available now, all from Seren: the *Collected Stories* and *Collected Poems* (both edited by Cary Archard), *Letters to My Wife* (edited by Gweno Lewis), *Morlais,* a novel about the Valleys Lewis wrote as a young man, and *Alun, Gweno and Freda*, by John Pikoulis, which offers a fresh slant on the biography. Not to read, or read again, for instance, 'In Hospital Poona' (1 and 2), 'The Mahratta Ghats', 'The Jungle', and 'Goodbye' among the poems, the stories, 'Ward "O"3(b)' and 'The Orange Grove', and a sample of his letters, is to miss, in this centenary year of his birth, connexion with a writer of extraordinary power and a consciousness at full stretch under the pall of impending doom.

Roland Mathias, too, was a child of 1915, born in September at Ffynnon Fawr, a farmhouse on the hillside above Talybont-on-Usk, Breconshire, only a couple of months after Lewis. They had a good deal in common. They came of families intimately connected with nonconformist religion: Lewis's mother was daughter of a Unitarian minister; Mathias's father was a Congregationalist minister and army chaplain. Highly intelligent and academically successful, both took Firsts in history and went on to do research – in areas both found dry and tedious. Both became teachers, remarkably good teachers. Both were energetic and committed players on the sports field, though for Lewis it was hockey, while Mathias chose rugby. Both felt a strong bond with the common working man, and were by instinct and breeding pacifist. Both were primarily poets, who also wrote short stories.

The clash of military aggression and pacifism resounds more strongly in Mathias's case. At the time of his birth his father was serving in the Dardanelles and, in those circumstances, it took a strong personality to uphold the banner of peace. Yet that is what his mother did, and continued to do, throughout the war – and beyond, because, when it ended, her husband remained with the army. It took extraordinary courage to be pacifist and enlist to fight, as Alun Lewis did, and just as much, for Roland, to resist call-up and all accompanying social (and legal) pressure and persist in his conscientious objection to anything and everything connected to war – apart from the friends who had joined up, and nevertheless remained friends throughout the conflict.

Much time and effort has been expended this year on what might be called a memorial season to remind us of Alun Lewis, mostly on the part of Seren as the publisher of work by and about him. In the absence of a similar impetus to remembrance in the world at large, last week, reading poems and stories I have read many times before with, as always, affection and awe at the achievement, I held my own quiet celebration of the centenary of the birth of Roland Mathias.

*PN Review* 226, Volume 42 Number 2,
November – December 2015.

# WALES BOOK OF THE YEAR 2015

*September 2015*

At the recent 2015 Wales Book of the Year presentations, Tiffany Atkinson was awarded the Roland Mathias Prize for the outstanding book of poems published in 2014. I was not surprised, for she missed the same award in 2012, with *Catulla et al* (Bloodaxe), by a hairsbreadth. Then, in the person of 'Catulla' she took her cue from the Latin poet and added a layer of classical reference to her witty, often acerbic, observations on life and love. This latest, *So Many Moving Parts*, also from Bloodaxe, continues her examination of self, human motives and contemporary mores directly, while allowing us to eavesdrop on aspects of her daily work, travel and relationships, and guess more about her background – parents, siblings, a Catholic education. 'Nightrunning', which begins the book (and a theme passed like a baton to later poems) contains a hint of gratitude for divine grace: 'It's all such a blessing, this body,/this job, this love', and something akin to confession about the animal self within that is 'neither kind nor unkind, just restless'. The problem of the irrepressible ego is revisited later in one of the book's longer poems, 'Mantra': 'The ego's a mistake/with a finely tuned appreciation/of nicotine and Sancerre …//a mistake/that runs on good days twenty/hot miles on its own grease//…that writes into the night/and puts in overtime/and talks if need be to the bloody document/and god deserves promotion'. The flow of meanings, almost always unhampered by end-stopped lines and usually by punctuation, rewards careful reading, occasionally with a sharp jolt, as in these lines from 'Guts': 'Yesterday I ran/three hours on caffeine: at mile ten/I ducked beneath a bridge and squatted/like a dog in dead leaves feeling occult,/hooked up to a secret sphere of minuscule/fauna and landscapes, twenty-five feet/of watery engine churning at the river-/mouth, that dark unloved star.'

The collection includes a pack of holiday postcards and a memoir album of younger days. Whatever the subject, the poetry is intriguing, cerebral, a play of intellect on daily experience. Often, too, the experience is troubled with existential angst or by the universal application of sod's law: 'At three a.m. on the longest night/and no sleep since Monday I park/in thick wind and scoop my career/from the passenger seat in inches of/loose pages. The wind has it in for me./Oh my nightshift oh my annotations –/what a huge magnolia in slow detonation,/what an angel, what a din of unhinged/wings. I stand in my lozenge of dark/as the wind shakes my bones. Oh. Oh'. This flat arrangement of the poem's lines disguises an intuitive sense of form but cannot hide the conversational tone and rhythmic ease of Atkinson's writing. It has a rare quota of refined intellect into the bargain. 'On crying', for example, brings Montaigne to mind and has verbal play on the subject of tears of Metaphysical complexity.

I was misled by the italicised title of 'The Starling Cloud', a melancholy observation on exclusion from the joy of others. It did not refer, even glancingly, to one of the sights of Aberystwyth, the amazing swells and eddies of an immense flock of birds before they settle to roost for the night. The poet would have watched the display often enough, because she taught literature and creative writing at the University. More recently she has been appointed Professor of Creative Writing (poetry) at the University of East Anglia.

*My Family and Other Superheroes*, which brought the Costa Poetry Award to Jonathan Edwards, was shortlisted for the

Roland Mathias Prize. It has a strong following in the literary prize stakes, but juries do not think alike. On this showing at least, his is essentially performance poetry: if you don't grasp its meaning at once, you have not been listening. This is not intended to denigrate. He is a gifted storyteller, with an ease in attaining the right measure of fanciful hyperbole the current crop of stand-up comic entertainers might envy, the occasional vigorous punchline ('Brothers'), and a refined ear for speech and speech rhythms. His standard medium is a literary approximation to the demotic of the south Wales Valleys. As you read, you can hear the voice, the emphases: 'His foot on the accelerator/makes the world go, his right arm at the auction//can't say *No* and when the day is over,/that's him, that's him – he's snoring on the sofa' ('How to Renovate a Morris Minor'); or, 'in his wallet//is a licence from the Queen and what it means/is he can say what the hell he likes and you/can't do nothing.' But then the odd line brings you up short: 'and look, that's him now, twiddling his thumbs/so furiously, it's like he's knitting air./It's only him can hold the air together' ('Bamp'). The same playfulness in affectionate portraiture can segue into moving tribute and mild satire, the latter as in 'Girl': 'In diamanté//scarlet heels, six inch/when she walks everything sparkles, everything//limps.' This is not the antithesis of 'poetic' writing (Tiffany Atkinson makes as telling use of the vernacular when it suits her purpose) but it enjoys its lack of sophistication. 'The Bloke in the Coffee Shop' makes a joke of it: 'How is the weather? Pissing down. Umbrellas//hover over heads like oh-so-faithful,/massive-winged and oh yes, somehow, handled//blackbirds. So much for similes.' Love of place – the Valleys – is expressed with the same affection as that bestowed on people, except that it tends to generalise, to deal in stereotypes. 'The Chartist Mural, John Frost Square, Newport' (a wonderful memorial mosaic destroyed by the local council last year) does not contain the expected political statement, though it does have striking images of fallen chartists 'bleeding from their mouths, their hearts, red tiles', and 'the king's men firing the slowest bullets in the world at those whose screams shatter their faces into pieces'. There is nothing in the book about the 1984 Miners' Strike, but 'Capel Celyn' revisits the drowning of the north Wales village to supply water to Liverpool, and 'Raskolnikov in Ebbw Vale' has the notorious survivor of a Siberian prison drawn to Wales as a 'welcome escape from industrialisation'. This is a very mild comment on the state of things. With its animal poems ('Seal', 'The Hippo', 'Flamingos') and as a whole, the book reminds me of the poetry of John Tripp, but without the anger.

In 2012, Patrick McGuinness walked away with the fiction award and the major Book of the Year prize for *The Last Hundred Days*, a gripping novel about the final days of the Ceauşescu regime in Romania. He had already a formidable reputation as a poet; it was his first novel. In 2015 he made a first appearance in the 'creative non-fiction' list with *Other People's Countries: A Journey into Memory* (Jonathan Cape). I bought it as soon as the early reviews appeared, read it avidly and with delight, and would have been prepared to wager it would be on the short list when the time came. It was, of course, and it went on to win its category award and, once again, to give Patrick McGuinness the overall prize. What can one say? Congratulations hardly seems enough.

*PN Review* 225, Volume 42 Number 1,
September – October 2015.

# DYLAN THOMAS AND JAN MORRIS

*March 2015*

Dylan Thomas was born on 27 October 1914, and centenary celebrations in his name are winding down. It is not long since we celebrated the R.S. Thomas centenary. Predictably, that was a low-key affair compared with the events of Dylan's year, for apart from a tendency to be brusque on occasion, and stiff and ascetic almost always, nothing vaguely controversial attaches to RS. The life of Dylan Thomas on the other hand was full of the scrapes beloved of the media. As well as a truly wonderful poet, he turned out to be a posthumous celebrity. Events organised by Literature Wales included marathon readings of his work, theatre and dance productions, and literary tours – by boat, on horseback and on foot – exploring Dylan Thomas haunts and habitats in Wales and Fitzrovia and New York. The Welsh Government funded creative writing workshops in schools that involved more than 8000 young people. An exhibition at the National Library of Wales brought the poet's notebooks back from the University of Buffalo, NY. Radio and television joined in: it is unlikely the centenary passed you by.

The broad appeal of the programme has won praise, but there have been dissenting voices, prominent among them that of Professor John Goodby of Swansea University, whose new annotated edition of Thomas's *Collected Poems* (Weidenfeld & Nicolson, 2014), is a major contribution to this past year and a fuller appreciation of the poetry. The critics complain that a rerun of the familiar, popular writings, emphasis on the rackety life, and activities that were at best tangential (something entirely different 'inspired' by Dylan Thomas) sold the poet short. John Goodby compares Thomas's output in the winter of 1933–34, 'brilliant lyric after brilliant lyric', to Keats's *annus mirabilis* more than a century ago, and finds in 'I see the boys of summer' and 'If I were tickled by the rub of love', neither a popular favourite, 'poems of Shakespearean richness'. For all the popularity of 'Fern Hill' and *Under Milk Wood*, Thomas has been neglected of late by scholars and critics. These challenging claims argue that he is an important modernist poet, whose early, less accessible poems must not be ignored. Discussion of this kind did not feature prominently in the centenary year, although the notebook containing the 'brilliant' lyrics of 1933–34 was, briefly, at Aberystwyth. Just a week or so ago, a fifth notebook, saved from a bonfire, was sold at auction for £85,000, the purchasers, remarkably enough, Swansea University. And soon after, the Welsh Government, working in conjunction with Literature Wales, announced that henceforth 14 May will be known as Dylan Day. The choice of date, which may seem odd or arbitrary, commemorates the first public reading of *Under Milk Wood* in New York in 1953. It is Wales's hopeful answer to Bloomsday.

Jan Morris lives in Llanystumdwy, north-west Wales, close to her father's old home, a place 'between the mountains and the sea', where even now Welsh can be heard daily in streets and shops. More than most she qualifies as a citizen of the world, but is firmly Welsh by choice and conviction, devoted to the language and culture of Wales. Her son and occasional collaborator, Twm Morys, won the Chair at the National Eisteddfod in 2003. Via journalism with the *Times* and the *Guardian*, she began publishing books in the late 1950s. The long list of publications includes fiction and history (the *Pax Britannica* trilogy) but is mostly the product of travel. She is a superb travel writer, one of the very best, acute in observation and graced with a wit that, to misquote Dickens, is apt to make the best of places, not the worst. Behind the limpid prose is a wealth of research, but she visits without agenda and to follow her meandering footsteps is a privilege and delight. If I am not greatly mistaken, Jan Morris is eighty-eight. Earlier this year she published what may be her last book, though I doubt that: how does one give up the authorial practice of a lifetime when there are places still to go, if increasingly in memory, and pleasures to enjoy in the moment or recall? This latest then, *Ciao Carpaccio* (Pallas Athene, 2014) is a gem. Pocket-sized with a hard cover, it is portable but safe from the depredations paperbacks are prone to, so that when quotidian business yawns ahead, or the scene before you has nothing to light the eyes, you can take it out and dwell for a while on the beauty and complexity of Carpaccio's art and the charming friendliness of Jan Morris's commentary. The text directs your attention to the intricacies of the reproduced paintings (all in colour), and your feet, if you are lucky enough to find yourself in Venice, to the galleries where many of the originals are displayed. Vittore Carpaccio (c.1465–1525), a Venetian precursor of the High Renaissance, produced portraits and large-scale narrative paintings, mostly on religious themes. Often, what fascinates in the latter is not so much the principal subject but what is going on around it: other people, who may appear watchfully interested, or preoccupied with business of their own, and creatures, especially birds – and dogs, some perhaps with an allegorical part to play, while others have wandered in, on the artist's whim, indifferent to the event. I read the book at one sitting, but since then have turned again and again to the pictures. One traditionally entitled *Duck Hunt* has men in punt-like boats actually fishing with bows and arrows. They are accompanied by cormorants (that ought not to be mistaken for ducks), acting as retrievers. In the distance geese are taking off from the reedy marsh and heading in a skein towards mountains on the far horizon. It is a composition of extraordinary beauty but, as Jan Morris shows, that is only part of the story. A blossoming white lily in the left foreground of the fishers' picture is growing from a pot on the balcony in another painting, *Two Venetian Ladies*, for originally they were one, panel-shaped, tall and rather thin. It is these bored women (*Two Courtesans* is an alternative and probably more accurate title in view of the picture's symbolism) who should be the focus of our attention. A pair of doves are perched separately on the balcony and a boy (or a dwarf) seems about to restrain a dowdy peacock, in the sexless autumn of its days, from slipping through the balustrade where one woman leans, indifferent alike to the masculine activity on the lagoon behind her and the parrot approaching the hem of her flowing robe. The second woman plays listlessly with a fierce-looking dog, of which we see the head and forepaws only, teasing it with a thin whip that the beast has seized in its teeth, while her other hand holds the front paws of a second dog, a white lapdog, in begging posture, which looks out at us with bulging eyes, questioningly. What do you make of this? It says, the fishermen, all action, and the idle women, past their prime, waiting.

I admit I had not previously come across Carpaccio, but that is one of the many gaps in my knowledge I shall hasten to repair. I wonder what Jan Morris thinks of Piero di Cosimo, a Florentine and close contemporary, whose work I have long admired for reasons possibly not greatly different from those that initiated her infatuation with Vittore.

*PN Review 222,* Volume 41 Number 4,
March – April 2015.

# DANNIE ABSE AND JOHN HUGHES

*January 2015*

Not much more than a year ago, I met Dannie Abse crossing the car park of the Bull Inn here, on his way to give a reading in one of Caerleon's remarkable Roman remains, the fortress baths. He was as effortlessly charming as ever. 'There's a photograph of you in here,' he said, extracting a copy of *Goodbye, Twentieth Century*, his autobiography (the real, not the fictionalised one), republished in the Library of Wales series, from the bundle under his arm. He flicked the book open to the page. It wasn't easy to recognise myself, dark-haired and darkly bearded, about forty years younger, but there I was indeed, one of a sizeable group, on a sunny day, enjoying the hospitality of Dannie and Joan in the garden of their Welsh home, 'Green Hollows', at Ogmore-by-Sea. John Tripp, cigarette to lips, is turning around to the camera, Herbert Williams leans against the white-painted wall, Aled Vaughan, rich-voiced Welsh-language author and broadcaster, sits next to Gillian Clarke, on my right stands a small dark-haired figure, possibly Sheenagh Pugh, and Glenys, John Ormond's wife, sits in front of me, but I cannot see John – a wonderful poet and documentary film-maker, who was familiar with the poetry of camera angles: perhaps he is taking the photograph. Beside the French doors Meic Stephens towers over Dannie (and just about everyone else) and Joan, nearest to the lens, is smiling broadly.

I have no direct memory of the occasion, but this commitment of time and generous encouragement of Welsh writers and writing was the sort of thing Dannie did.

Encouragement is often little more than a generalised expression of good will; that was not Dannie's style. His was practical. Cary Archard has told how he was behind the founding of Poetry Wales Press (which became Seren), not only inspiring the project by his enthusiasm for Archard's idea, but also providing office space for the fledgling press at that same Ogmore home. Although based in London and ever busy with his daily work as diagnostician at a chest clinic as well as his writing, he preserved a part of his life for Wales. He rounded on a BBC Wales interviewer who asked whether he had a sense of Welsh identity: he was not constantly preoccupied with the idea of being 'a 5 foot 8 1/2 inch Welsh Jew' he said, though it was, after all, pretty close to the mark, except he was very much more than that. He frequently returned to Wales, if he could manage it combining a rendezvous for business or pleasure with active support for Cardiff City FC, through thick and (mostly) thin. He was a good friend of Yr Academi Gymreig/The Welsh Academy of Writers, and President of its English Language Section. In the summer of 1981, he had been booked to lecture at an Academy conference held in Dyffryn House, near St Nicholas in the Vale of Glamorgan. Dyffryn is a grand late-Victorian extravaganza, now, along with its magnificent gardens, restored and in the keeping of the National Trust; then it belonged to the Glamorgan authority and, somewhat dilapidated, was used as a conference centre. Dannie came with his lecture typed and double spaced for ease of reading. As chair of the session I introduced him to the packed room and settled back to enjoy what I knew would be beautifully delivered, thought-provoking, entertaining. About ten minutes in, the audience rapt, he stopped, visibly upset and, though he tried, could not speak another word. He signalled to me to take his place and for a few minutes I carried on reading the text, until he was ready to continue. He had stopped at an Old Testament quotation that flooded his mind with thoughts of his mother, who had recently died, aged ninety. From time to time we will read again some poem by Dannie Abse, or a passage of his prose, and memories will crowd in – of a warm and decent human being who happened to be one of the finest writers of his generation.

Earlier this year, troubles in the Ukraine for a time dominated the headlines, and still they reverberate, waxing and waning according to the political mood of the moment, but ever present. Russia and the West, equally convinced of the rectitude of their case, pursue their ideological goals, while on the ground, in towns and villages, the people suffer. A proportion of the population in eastern Ukraine has Welsh ancestry. This is particularly the case in and around Donetsk, where, even as I write, fierce fighting continues at the airport. Donetsk was not the original name of this city at the centre of a former Soviet industrial heartland. In a map of 1917 it appears as Yuzovka. A commoner transliteration offers a form that more closely echoes its origins: Hughesovka. In 1870, the government of the reforming Tsar, Alexander II, informed the British Foreign Office that it had high expectations of a concession for the exploitation of mineral rights in the Ukraine granted to an 'Englishman of the working classes' named Hughes. But John Hughes was not English. He was born in Merthyr Tydfil about 1815, the son of an engineer in the Cyfarthfa iron works. His own career in industry took him to the Uskside Engineering Works, which was located a few miles from here in a district of Newport known as Pill. There he married a local woman, Elizabeth Lewis: their eight children were all born in Church Street, Pill. At the Uskside works, which specialised in the production of equipment for ships and collieries, Hughes developed an interest in marine engineering that led to the patenting of inventions in armaments and armour plating, and these in turn gained him a directorship of the Millwall Engineering and Shipbuilding Company in London. That company's success in Admiralty trials of armour plating led to an order from Russia and brought John Hughes to the attention of the Russian government. He was taken to the Donbas region, an endless empty grassland, intensely hot in the summer and bitterly cold in winter, where surveys had shown there were vast deposits of coal and iron ore. Hughes took the challenge. He set up the New Russia Company Limited and in 1870 brought there by ship and bullock train essential equipment and about a hundred experienced ironworkers, mostly from south Wales. Starting from scratch and working against a tight schedule set by the Imperial government, they built a blast furnace and, after an initial failure, rebuilt it, so that regular production of rails for the Russian railway system began in 1872. Within a decade open hearth furnaces had been added and steel rails were being produced. John Hughes died in 1889, but his four sons carried on the business and in the 1890s the 'Hughes factory' was the largest in the Russian empire. Following the Bolshevik Revolution of 1917 the great majority of foreign workers left, but the business continued. Hughesovka was renamed Stalino in 1924 and then became Donetsk in 1961. The New Russia Company was finally wound up in 1970. The whole remarkable story is told in *Hughesovka – A Welsh Enterprise in Imperial Russia* by Susan Edwards, published by the Glamorgan Record Office (1992). The extensive and important Hughesovka Research Archive is held by Glamorgan Archives in Cardiff.

*PN Review* 221, Volume 41 Number 3,
January – February 2015.

# RICHARD LLEWELLYN

*November 2014*

John Edmunds, a friend of many years' standing, spent a day with us recently, breaking his journey back to London. Some will remember him as a regular BBC TV newsreader, and he has also been prominent in theatre, as an academic and, more recently, as a translator of Lorca, *Four Major Plays* (for the OUP World's Classics series), and *Four French Plays – Corneille, Molière, Racine* (for Penguin Classics). We hadn't seen him for some time and there was a lot to talk about. One of the tales he told us concerned the novelist Richard Llewellyn (1906–83), author of more than twenty novels, but remembered for only one, *How Green Was My Valley*, his debut in the genre. First published in 1939 and an immediate bestseller, it has never been out of print. It garnered a huge international readership, has been translated into thirty languages and frequently reprinted in several of them: by the 1970s the bulk of the author's income came from translations. Llewellyn had a military bearing, acquired by service as a captain in the Welsh Guards in World War II and six years in the pre-war army, mostly in India, and was a tweedily stylish dresser. Much of his life after the war was spent travelling to collect stories and local colour, but he occasionally returned to Wales, where he had spent part of his boyhood with grandparents living in St David's, Pembrokeshire, and found in the history of the south Wales coalfield and the Griffiths family of Gilfach Goch the theme and setting of an enduringly memorable book. Those of my acquaintance who met him found little to like in him, perhaps because they sensed his habitual dissimulation. He hid his formative years, growing up in London and apprenticeship in the hotel-keeping and catering trade, as he did his real name, Richard David Vivian Llewellyn Lloyd, under a smokescreen of pretension.

In the 1970s, he wrote to Sir Goronwy Daniel, principal of UCW Aberystwyth, to say that he was available to tutor students during the summer term. As 'creative writing' did not exist at the time, John Edmunds, who, not long before, had been appointed professor of the newly created bilingual drama department, was invited to make appropriate arrangements for Llewellyn's extended visit. This was well-nigh impossible, for by the time he arrived teaching was almost over and the students were either revising for exams or sitting them. When the famous author turned up for sessions there were no students; and when a few of them were cajoled into appearing, he didn't arrive. A public lecture was scheduled and advertised and a small audience cornered. Perhaps the latter took Llewellyn by surprise, because he came unprepared and in ten minutes had finished all he had to say. With his customary gruff courtesy the principal thanked the guest speaker, who liked to live in style, but in later life could not be relied upon to pay his way, or indeed, deliver what he promised.

Within the last week I have re-read two courtroom episodes in *How Green Was My Valley*. At least that was my intention, but once the book lay open on the table before me I was drawn to other scenes, and was soon adding to layers of marginalia from previous readings. The grip it has on my imagination has scarcely lessened since I first picked it up many years ago. When I arrived at them, the courtroom scenes were a little disappointing. I thought perhaps they would convey a flavour of the trials of miners during the strike of 1910–11 (mentioned in my previous Letter, *PN Review* 218). They do not, but one is a fictionalised version of the successful case Joseph Griffiths brought against coal owners and management when he was financially penalised for union activity. In the novel, Davy, the narrator's brother and a union firebrand, sues the company for paying him less than the agreed minimum wage. The company argues that his money reflects his incompetence in the workplace but, because he is able to present before the judge years of carefully preserved pay dockets showing he has regularly earned several times the amount of the claim, he wins the case. Davy has already planned to emigrate to New Zealand, knowing there will be no more work for him in the Valley – the actual fate of Joe Griffiths.

While not so melodramatically lit as the action of the novel by Llewellyn's often rhapsodic, biblically inflected prose, newspaper accounts of the trial of miners more than a century ago are in their own way fascinating. So they seem to me at least, and I offer that as explanation for my return to this theme. I have just discovered these primary resources, the raw material of history, which are now generally available at 'Welsh newspapers online', a free treasury of digitised information, courtesy of the National Library of Wales. The *Weekly Mail*, a forerunner of today's *Western Mail*, was one of the papers to cover events in Gilfach Goch on 29 November 1910, where 'violence and intimidation' against William Gould, an assistant manager of the Britannic Colliery, was witnessed by his police escort, and on 24 December in Pontypridd, where some at least of the perpetrators were brought to trial. In Gilfach, Gould had been on his way to the (steam) engine house, where a worker named Rees Jones was feeding the fires to keep the pumps going and prevent the pit from flooding, when he was approached by a large and hostile crowd. A police witness testified: 'Some of them shouted, "Kill the —" and "Chuck him in the river."' Gould himself claimed a number of men attacked him, striking him about the head, forcing him to the ground and kicking him until he promised to leave the valley. 'We will see you don't come back', came from the crowd. The defence lawyer pointed out that, apart from a minor bump on his face, Gould bore no sign of injury, and extracted from the police the admission that there had been 'laughing and chaffing as well as booing' among the crowd, but there was no mitigation: on 20 December, in good time for Christmas, two of Gould's assailants were jailed and several more convicted with fines.

The same newspaper confirms the daily attendance outside the court of several thousand miners, adding that on 14 December over ten thousand had gathered at the Rocking Stone, a famous (and still existing) landmark on the common overlooking Pontypridd. A photograph of the mass meeting showing thousands in the universal miners' uniform of Dai-cap and white muffler accompanies the text. Noah Rees, a respected miners' leader, tried to dissuade them from besieging the court, arguing that aggression would be 'suicidal' in view of the large force of military and police stationed in the town. The reporter estimated about half the assembly heeded his appeal. The rest marched into town as they planned, but there was to be no dramatic rescue of the defendants, who were spirited away from the courtroom by a back door.

All that occurred more than a century ago: how can it matter now? Data published in a recent academic study show that in 2012, the average number of jobs per hundred residents in Great Britain is 67; in the former coalfields as a whole, it is 50; in the south Wales coalfield it stands at 41. Perhaps because the communities of the south Wales Valleys still suffer in the aftermath of what was thoughtlessly, peremptorily removed, that old lump of history still sticks in the throat.

*PN Review* 220, Volume 41 Number 2,
November – December 2014.

# RHYS DAVIES

*September 2014*

Meic Stephens's splendid biography, *Rhys Davies – A Writer's Life* is shortlisted in the creative non-fiction category for Wales Book of the Year 2013, the winner to be declared at a ceremony in Caernarfon in July. The book is the summation of many years' study of Rhys Davies as author and service to the charitable trust set up in his name through the philanthropy of his brother Lewis. Meic brought to the task of biographer unprecedented access to the materials of a life dedicated to writing, lived simply and, to a large extent, secretively. He also brought a knowledge of the history, the character – and the characters – of the south Wales Valleys, the source of much of the best of Rhys Davies's writing. He was, as they say, cut out for the job, and he has done it exceedingly well.

In 1969, Davies published *Print of a Hare's Foot – An Autobiographical Beginning*. It is a typically fluent and entertaining account of his life as he sped, light-footed as a hare, to and fro between Blaenclydach and London (the former to recharge batteries with the stuff of valleys life, and his pockets with the wherewithal to maintain existence in the latter), leaving hardly a sign of his passing, for he travelled light and had no interest in personal space or possessions. The second part of the book describes travels farther afield, notably to the south of France and into the orbit of D.H. Lawrence. He was a staunch friend to Lawrence in his later years when many erstwhile supporters had drifted away and he was vilified by a large section of the British press. If you would like an insight into life with Lawrence and Frieda you could do far worse than consult Rhys Davies. Yet he is not to be entirely trusted, because he brought to autobiography the instincts of the indefatigable writer of fictions (forget fact if you can tweak a good story to make it better), and because he wanted, and needed, to disguise his homosexuality.

The probable tweaking of one particular story has fascinated me for some time. Towards the end of his unreliable autobiography he spends considerable time and trouble over a young man he met on the train returning to London, a twenty-year-old trooper, returning from leave, 'Iberian dark, misleadingly glowering [who] always remained lean and lithe despite his insatiable eating'. He calls him 'Caerphilly Jones', because of his fondness for the cheese toasted. In Davies's account he had worked with horses underground in the pit and had been taken in by the Household Cavalry 'of their charity'. At one point, in a mounted troop of plume-helmeted and breast-plated cavalry returning to barracks, he shouts to the writer, '*Shw mae? Caws Caerffili gartref?*' ('How's things? Any Caerphilly cheese at home?'). Later he is observed losing a boxing match. He gets a girl 'from Leytonstone way' in trouble and is obliged to marry – most fortuitously. Bought out of the army by his father-in-law, who owns a mattress factory, he is employed in the business and seems set fair for life. But as a reservist he is called up in 1939, and dies in the war.

That is not the end of the story, however. The part that long ago caught my attention describes the writer, in search of Caerphilly's family, walking over the mountain to a neighbouring valley: 'one of those small, tucked-away valleys [...] in self-contained privacy outside the Rhondda', where 'a stream of copper mountain water ran through'. There are mining villages in tributary offshoots of the Rhondda and other larger valleys, his own Clydach being one, but very few that fit the phrase 'self-contained privacy'; and what is the significance of the copper-tinged stream? An OS map of the area shows that a mile-and-a-half walk due south over the mountain from the writer's Blaenclydach home would bring him to Gilfach Goch (in English, 'little red nook'), so named because of the stream of reddish water that ran into it. The valley is a cul-de-sac; even today, having looped around the top, you leave Gilfach by the same road that brought you in. And the pedestrian route over the mountain to Clydach and the Rhondda, though never more than a well-worn, grassy track, was once a high road indeed, especially for miners seeking work, or better paid work, in the Rhondda. It was the way my mother's father trod during the 1910–11 Cambrian Combine strike when, with a wife and ten children to feed, he walked in the other direction, from Clydach to Gilfach, looking for work in a pit outside the Combine. Topographically, Gilfach is the only valley that fits Davies's description. Details such as the absence of a railway station, a bus stop near 'the Spout' (code for the Squint, one of Gilfach's collieries) and the 'crossroads at the valley's mouth' confirm the identification.

But what of Caerphilly Jones, the trooper who died in the war? Internet records of military personnel do not tell the whole story. There was only one thing for it: I went up to Gilfach. At the Social Club, a British Legion memorial board reveals thirty-six men from Gilfach gave their lives in the 1939–45 conflict, among them trooper Robert Leonard McDonald of the 10th Royal Hussars. On another visit I traced a much younger brother, who had little direct memory of the soldier, but was able to tell me he had been a wireless operator in a tank, who died fighting in the North Africa campaign, January 1942. But he hadn't worked in the pit; their father, a miner, was dead against it. Rather, an interest in things mechanical took him to what was formerly a cavalry regiment, mechanised before the war. He did know a bit about pugilism, because his father had a reputation as a boxing trainer. He did not marry into a family that owned a mattress factory, but his wife, who came from Tonyrefail, worked in a mattress factory. Where does the cheery greeting from a cuirassier come from? Possibly Davies's imagination, but then he was friendly with a number of guardsmen.

Robert Leonard McDonald's family was well known locally because his grandfather, Michael, was one of thirteen miners from Gilfach Goch tried at Pontypridd in December 1910 for their part in the Cambrian Combine unrest. Ten thousand miners marched to support them but could not prevent sentences of from two to six weeks being handed down. That was not the first bitterly fought strike and many more followed as miners sought a decent wage for their labour from wealthy absentee coal owners. The last, however, began in March 1984, thirty years ago. In 1983, having secured a double victory, in the Falklands and at the ballot box, Margaret Thatcher turned her attention to the miners. She laid the ground carefully: Ian MacGregor, who had pushed through closure of much of the British steel industry, was made chairman of the National Coal Board, coal was stockpiled at power stations and, in 1984, the Trade Union Act, which would deny state benefits to miners and their families, was added to anti-union legislation already in place. Police were trained and equipped for 'riot control'. The hate generated by the rhetoric of the prime minister on the one hand and the miners' leader Arthur Scargill on the other, the intensity of the struggle and, in the end, the futility of it all are well documented. The strike lasted a whole year and, as in 1926, the south Wales miners were among the last to yield. The pit closure programme, which had been gradual since the 1950s, was accelerated without thought of the consequences for communities where little or no alternative employment was to be had. The only industrial activity visible in Gilfach these days is the slow churning of wind turbines desecrating the beautiful mountain landscape.

*PN Review* 219, Volume 41 Number 1, September – October 2014.

# HENRY GREEN AND GORONWY REES

*May 2014*

My interest in Henry Green (see *PN Review* 216), further stimulated by Jeremy Treglown's *Romancing: The Life and Work of Henry Green* (Faber, 2000), has led me in strange directions and furnished unexpected connections. The biography is, all things considered, a gloomy read, because eventually we see in it the self-indulgent unravelling of a rare literary talent. His father, the industrialist Vincent Yorke, owned Pontifex, an engineering works in Birmingham, and was chairman of the board of Compañia Limitada del Ferrocarril Mexicano. Henry did not see eye to eye with Vincent, but neither could he break entirely free of his influence. Between 1926 and 1952 he published ten novels, but after the last, *Doting*, nothing of consequence. Physically undermined and, though he never gave up the desire to write, creatively impaired by alcoholism, he died in 1973.

Green (it is simpler to stick to his deliberately low-key pen-name) was a formidable drinker and womaniser. His 'recreation', declared in *Who's Who*, was 'romancing over the bottle, to a good band'. He had an enormous circle of acquaintance, literary and aristocratic, including Anthony Powell, Maurice Bowra, Robert Byron, Nevill Coghill, the Mitfords, Ottoline Morrell, Koestler, Aly Khan, and, among Americans, Terry Southern and Eudora Welty. To the latter, whom he met in London in 1950, he was 'terribly attractive' and she admitted to being 'captivated' by him and his writing. They did not meet again but continued to correspond and she never lost her high regard for his talent: in 1961 she published a long essay praising Green as 'the most interesting and vital imagination in English fiction in our time'.

Although he remained indissolubly married to 'Dig' (Mary Adelaide Biddulph), the list of Green's lovers is as impressive as that of his acquaintance. Notable among them was Kitty Freud, whose huge eyes stare out of portraits by her husband Lucian, the writers Elizabeth Bowen and Rosamond Lehmann, and Mary Keene, a great beauty, who was also the lover of the artist Matthew Smith. In May 1944, at the height of the flying bomb attacks on London and the south-east, Mary gave birth to a daughter, Alice, who was acknowledged by Green. To escape the ever-present threat of bombing Mary took the child as far west as she could, to the coast of Cardigan Bay, where, perched on the cliffs in the outskirts of New Quay, she found refuge in a bungalow constructed of wood and asbestos named 'Majoda', then occupied by her friends Dylan and Caitlin Thomas.

In this dwelling the poet had been more productive than for some time, writing radio and film scripts and poems, and beginning 'Llareggub', arguably based on New Quay, which would grow, slowly, into *Under Milk Wood*. Nearby lived Vera Killick, a friend of his childhood in Swansea, whose husband was a serving soldier. What followed has become part of the romantic drama of Dylan Thomas. When Captain Killick, who had been fighting behind enemy lines in Greece, turned up on leave, he found his wife had been generously supporting the poet with cash and, he suspected, gifts of another kind. After a drunken altercation in a local pub, Killick launched an assault on Majoda, firing several shots into the flimsy building and, allegedly, threatening to blow it up with a grenade. He was arrested, tried at Lampeter for attempted murder and acquitted. The Thomases fled to safer accommodation and Mary Keene reported to Henry Green that New Quay was 'an open air loony bin' and life there worse than London in the blitz.

One cannot help reflecting that Majoda is fifty miles as the crow, or the seagull, flies from Tan-yr-Allt, the hillside cottage in the armpit of the Llŷn peninsula, where Shelley had (apparently) been the target of a shooting incident in 1813, but that is a connection too far-fetched. The one that really caught my eye in Treglown's book is with Goronwy Rees, who took up his appointment as principal of UCW Aberystwyth in September 1953, the beginning of my second year. He was forty-three, perfectly at ease in his new role, with an exceedingly attractive wife. We took to him at once. One of his early decisions was to have the stone walls of 'Quad', the balconied space where students gathered between lectures, painted. My memory tells me he chose pink gloss. With the giant black plaster statues of founding fathers in full academic fig and oratorical postures at either end, critical observers might have dubbed it 'Nero's bathroom'. But he came along, with his wife, for a formal relaunch, spoke beautifully, charmed everyone. Well, perhaps not everyone. He had powerful detractors on the college council who had opposed his appointment and, still unconvinced, were eager to find any reason to unseat him. He gave his critics what they were waiting for when in early spring 1956 the *People* published a series of anonymous articles about the Cambridge spies and it emerged that Rees, who knew them all and was a particular friend of Burgess, was the author. A committee of enquiry found that in selling the story he had acted against the interests of the college. He left Aberystwyth in April 1957.

Goronwy Rees, born in Aberystwyth in 1909, was the son of a notable Calvinistic Methodist minister. He won a scholarship to New College, Oxford, where he took a First in PPE in 1931, and in the autumn of that year was awarded the first prize fellowship at All Souls. He played rugby for New College in the same team as Richard Crossman, to whom he was 'an extremely brilliant and handsome scholar who took Oxford society by storm'. His ambition was to write and, in 1932, his novel *The Summer Flood* was published by Faber. In the early 1930s, having travelled in Austria, Germany and Russia, and then returned to Berlin in 1934, he had first-hand knowledge of totalitarian states, fascist and communist. He brought his expertise to the *Spectator* as leader writer and, wherever he could, opposed the policy of appeasement towards Germany widespread in the British press. In 1940 he was commissioned in the Royal Welsh Fusiliers, served in military intelligence and finished as a lieutenant-colonel in the Allied Control Commission after the capitulation of Germany. While still in the Territorial Army at the beginning of the war and stationed in Bloomsbury, he had met Henry Green who had joined the Fire Service. They were both novelists, and had friends in common, such as Maurice Bowra and A.J. Ayer, and they were alike in their drinking habits and an attractiveness to women that they were ever ready to exploit. At different times, they were involved with the same lovers – Elizabeth Bowen and Rosamond Lehmann – and Rees had in Diana Trilling, who thought him 'probably the most attractive man I have ever met', an American champion to match Green's Eudora Welty. An informant told Treglown that Green's sister-in-law, known as 'Miss', declared she had 'always loved Henry but Goronwy Rees was the love of her life'.

In 1946, Green invited Rees to join the board of Pontifex, where, admired for his brain, he was well paid, had a variety of roles and was on hand as a drinking companion – when he wasn't engaged in political intelligence work with MI6. In 1951 he picked up another part-time job, as estates bursar of All Souls, but still contrived to live beyond his means. The two remained friends (a decade later, to encourage him to write, Rees's daughter Jenny came regularly to Green's home to take dictation), but in the early 1950s Nemesis stole up unseen on both of them. In 1952 the publication of *Doting* brought the curtain down on Green's literary career and a year later Rees went to Aberystwyth and found notoriety.

*PN Review* 217, Volume 40 Number 5,
May – June 2014.

# DYLAN THOMAS, FORD MADOX FORD, JOHN UPDIKE AND HENRY GREEN

*March 2014*

As I write I am conscious we are sliding, as when young we used to down the mountain on candle-wax-slicked bits of cardboard, helter-skelter towards 2014. Behind us lies 2013, the year we celebrated the centenary of the birth of R.S. Thomas, and before us the year we celebrate that of his namesake Dylan. R.S. served a rather lengthy apprenticeship to the muse during which an accretion of characteristic poetic themes and gestures enveloped him like a horny carapace and a characteristic style emerged. He was thirty-three when he published *The Stones of the Field* and almost forty at the publication of *An Acre of Land*. Dylan, on the other hand, was a boy wonder. He was twenty when *18 Poems* appeared, twenty-two at the publication of *Twenty-five Poems*, twenty-five at that of *The Map of Love*. More remarkably, many of the poems in these books had their substantial genesis in his adolescent years: the Rimbaud of Cwmdonkin Drive, indeed.

It is sixty years since Dylan Thomas's death in 1953. As a representative of the gradually diminishing band of those present at the poetry reading he gave to students at Aberystwyth in the autumn of 1952, I have from time to time rehearsed the occasion in conversation and print and cannot be sure now whether what seems still so clear in my mind is true to the original. I am nevertheless prepared to vouch for the extraordinary impact of the performance on the audience packed into the Exam Hall (the largest venue then available in the Old College building on the seafront). Do not believe denigrators critical of Thomas's 'plummy' voice and reading style: he was a superb reader of verse, his own and, as he demonstrated long ago in Aber, that of other poets he admired. He was above all a poet of the spoken word. The sounds words made combined in his head and, as he habitually chanted them aloud in the process of composing, mattered a very great deal. The perennially popular *Under Milk Wood* could only have been written by someone who had a highly developed sense of the power of the human voice. One of the problems early American commentators had in interpreting Thomas's writing was that their transatlantic accents did not allow them to *hear* accurately what they read on the page.

In 2014 we shall also be remembering the beginning of the First World War. The unspeakable horror of the battlefields and waste of millions of lives will again be brought home to us in image and writing. I have been reading Ford Madox Ford's *War Prose*, a collection of published and unpublished pieces written during and immediately after the war, edited by Max Saunders (Carcanet, 1999). 'Why Ford?' you may ask. The quality of the writing is reason enough; and then there is the Welsh connection. Ford Hermann Hueffer, as he was before changing his name post-war, enlisted in 1915, at the age of forty-two, and was commissioned as a second-lieutenant. After training in Wales, in July 1916 he sailed for France, 'attached', in military parlance, to the 9th Battalion of the Welch Regiment. If we are to believe what he wrote, it proved an attachment altogether stronger than the Army probably reckoned on. *War Prose* tells us that before going to war, he had felt an even-handed sympathy for all those involved, friend and foe alike, but experience altered him. He soon found he hated the Hun and wished them all dead, and cared with an extraordinary depth of feeling for the men of his battalion and those others of the Welch Regiment who served alongside them. 'Pon...ti...pri...

ith', originally written in French for *La Revue des Idées* (translated by Saunders and reprinted in *PNR* 127), exemplifies this heightened comradely feeling. A vessel is carrying a boatload of Welch Regiment troops, 'eight hundred men and two hundred and fifty officers who had all come from south Wales', up the Seine on their way to the Front, where they will arrive at the height of the battle of the Somme. Ford was fluent in German and French, but the language of the Tommies, over forty per cent of whom would probably have been Welsh speakers at that time, is alien to his ears, 'as if you were hearing ravens chatting'. More remarkably, when you think of the importance of communication in the ranks, '[s]everal thousand of them could not make themselves understood in English'. But '[t]hey sing at all times and for all reasons; and they play football – at all times and for all reasons! It was the Welch Regiment that advanced at Etreux in 1914, kicking a football and shouting "Stick it, the Welch"; and singing in chorus.' And a little later, 'They sing like angels and the prophets...and like men who are about to die [...] for in six days, the majority – the majority, alas! – of them would give their lives in Mametz wood'.

In another piece, 'A Day of Battle', which was written 'in the Ypres salient: 15th Sep. 1916', he attempts to explain how a rational human being can keep going in the face of bombardment and terrible destruction, of bodies mangled or 'burst into mere showers of blood and dissolving into muddy ooze', and of his own expectation of imminent death. For him at least, the answer was concentration on the task in hand, especially as it involves 'hypnotic' responsibility for the lives of others. Here again, sympathy is reserved principally for his own battalion. He barely notices as he passes by the straggling bands of wounded from other regiments, but remembers individually 'the wounded of my own Bn. that I have seen. The poor men, they come down from Pontypridd and Nantgarw and Penarth and Dowlais Works and they have queer, odd, guttural accents like the croaking of ravens, and they call every hill a *mountain*… and there is no emotion so terrific and so overwhelming as the feeling that comes over you when your own men are dead [...] the little, dark, raven-voiced, Evanses, and Lewises, and Joneses and Thomases…Our dead!'

The 'Land of Song' trope, tellingly exemplified above, had turned up earlier in 2013. I had been reading two big books of John Updike's shorter prose, *The Early Stories 1953–1975* (2004) and *Higher Gossip – Essays and Criticism* (2011), and his memoirs, *Self-Consciousness* (1989). I am one of those who believe he was among the greatest of twentieth-century writers, and recall with pleasure that I met him once, by chance, in Bristol, where he was signing copies of *Rabbit Redux* in George's bookshop, an opportunity not to be missed: I bought a copy. 'What name?' he asked. I told him. 'Ah, the old rabble rouser,' he said and signed with a smile.

From *Higher Gossip* I learned of Updike's admiration for the novels of Henry Green, an author I had never read; it seemed a good time to start. The Penguin Classics one-volume edition of Green's three novels, *Loving*, *Living* and *Party Going*, with an introduction by Updike (which he terms 'a piece of homage'), was a revelation. I soon found other admirers. Although he is these days far less well-known, Green is esteemed by some, not least among them Frank Kermode, as a modernist writer deserving recognition alongside Joyce and Virginia Woolf. Pondering the background of a novelist capable of descriptions of working-class life so remarkably insightful and empathic as those contained in *Living*, I turned to *Pack My Bag*, an autobiographical work as disarmingly self-deprecating as one could hope to find. The child born 'a mouth breather with a silver spoon' at Forthampton Court, near Tewkesbury in 1905,

the disaffected Eton pupil, the Oxford University drop-out who
at twenty-one published a novel, *Blindness*, he had written
while still at school, had some affection for Wales – as a
wilderness: 'It is [...] distressing to come back to London
Sunday evenings with one's heart still beating by a marsh near
Builth perhaps'.

Down ignominiously, if happily enough, from Oxford, he
began a career in industry on the shop floor of an engineering
works in Birmingham owned by his father (who had taken a
double first at Cambridge). He found satisfaction in a routine
of manual labour that left little time for leisure, and enormous
pleasure in the conversation and laughter that often accompany
it. How people spoke meant a very great deal to Green, to the
extent that his later novels are almost entirely dialogue. *Living*,
the novel that came out of the works experience, has a single
Welsh voice, a voice raised in song:

> Then, one morning in iron foundry, Arthur Jones began singing
> [...] When he began the men looked up from work and at each
> other and stayed quiet [...] He was Welsh and sang in Welsh.
> His voice had a great soft yell in it. It rose and rose and fell
> then rose again and, when the crane was quiet for a moment,
> then his voice came out from behind noise of the crane in
> passionate singing. Soon each one in this factory heard that
> Arthur had begun and, if he had two moments, came by iron
> foundry shop to listen.

It is little wonder that our singing reputation, embedded in
literature, lingers – despite evidence to the contrary. You can
go to international rugby matches in Cardiff these days, with
crowds of more than seventy thousand, the vast majority Welsh,
and hear almost nothing you could describe as tuneful. The
Welsh words, all those majestic hymns everyone once knew,

have gone, and the music has shrivelled away, to a few pathetic choruses of 'Delilah' and 'Hymns and Arias'.

*PN Review* 216, Volume 40 Number 4,
March – April 2014.

# RHIAN EDWARDS AND CLIFF MORGAN

*January 2014*

I met Seamus Heaney (twice, I think) in Cardiff in the 1970s, at a time when it was not unusual for Irish poets to give readings here under the auspices of the Welsh Arts Council, and I spoke with him again in the 1990s at a university ceremony, also in Cardiff, where he was about to receive yet another honorary degree. He had already an assured place among the literary elite at our earlier encounters and by the 1990s was famous indeed, but for all that I felt at once comfortable in his company. He had that gift among many others of making strangers at ease, or better still, no matter where you were, at home with him. The unexpected news of his death brought an acute sense of loss, for, though the time I spent in his company could barely have been counted in hours, it seemed I knew him well. It is the poetry of course that made him, makes him still, the close companion of many years.

I felt even more keenly another death, which occurred on 29 August, the day before Heaney's, that of Cliff Morgan. Readers of this magazine may not be familiar with the name, but he too was widely loved, not least because, like Heaney, he had the ability to be comfortably at ease with friends and strangers and, though the accent was different, a memorably pleasant voice and manner, the kind that engages people. He was an excellent radio presenter and interviewer. But that came later.

Cliff was born in Trebanog, Glamorgan, in 1930. The name of his birthplace means 'high dwelling', an accurate enough description for a small pit village about seven hundred feet up on the haunch of a mountain between Tonyrefail in the valley of the Ely and Cymmer-Porth in the Rhondda. Dauntingly steep hills climb on either side to its cluster of terraces. Muscular development of the lower limbs was a *sine qua non* for inhabitants in those days. Cliff's father, a miner, had a lot of sporting ability, though his choice was the round ball game. Cliff went to Tonyrefail Grammar School, where only rugby was played. It was a two-form-entry mixed grammar school with about 200 girls and hardly more than 120 boys. Not in the front rank academically, it was nevertheless a good place to be. When I entered the school in 1945 Cliff Morgan was a senior and showing remarkable ability at outside-half on the rugby field. He would have been a boyhood hero for that alone, but he was much more. He had just the right degree of cockiness that made him a favourite with fellow pupils and teachers, would address, exhort, entertain the entire school from the platform in the hall with as much aplomb as any member of staff, and rather more than most. Sometime in my first year he was picked to play in the final trial for the Wales Secondary Schools XV at Pontypool Park. On a cold, wet day a bus full of us, mostly juniors, went to Pontypool to support him. I was eleven and it was the furthest I had ever travelled. And there was an occasion after that I shall always treasure. Sometime in my second year I was sitting on the bank just above the school field to put on new rugby boots for a games lesson when Cliff sat beside me. 'New boots?' he said. 'Let's have a look.' He handled them carefully, testing their lightness and flexibility. 'Good boots,' he said, helping me to complete the lacing. While he probably forgot that spontaneous expression of a generous nature immediately, I recall it now with a kind of joy and real gratitude. Within a couple of years he was playing regularly for Cardiff RFC and in 1951 I watched him win the first of twenty-nine Welsh caps against

Ireland at the Arms Park. The following Thursday evening he came back to the school for the usual Urdd ('Welsh League of Youth') meeting and presented his precious red jersey to Ned Gribble, the master in charge of rugby, an act of astonishing generosity. This was long before replica kit made jerseys of all clubs and countries commonplace and we crowded around to see and touch it. In 1955 he was the outstanding player of the British and Irish Lions drawn test series in South Africa, and the heartbeat of the touring party off the field.

If, when his playing days were over, he had quietly subsided from public view, he would still have been remembered for his prowess on the field, but he went on to become a key figure in broadcasting. Starting with radio sports coverage in Wales, he became producer and editor of BBC TV's *Grandstand*, was for two years editor of ITV's current affairs flagship *This Week*, became a face familiar to millions as team captain in the TV quiz show *A Question of Sport*, and from 1976 to 1987 a BBC executive as Head of Television Sports and Outside Broadcasts. He gave away the accumulated memorabilia of his rugby career to charity auctions and, notwithstanding the increasingly onerous demands of broadcasting, still answered requests to speak at rugby club dinners, usually declining the fee. He was a brilliant speaker, known, admired and loved everywhere. His death was not unexpected, because he had been suffering from cancer of the larynx for several years, yet the public expression of grief was on a scale usually reserved for royalty. The first five pages of the *Western Mail* on 30 August were wholly given to tributes and photographs and there were two full pages of reminiscences from sports reporters at the back. More appeared on 31 August and more again followed the funeral a few days later.

It is perhaps puzzling that a rugby player should be so venerated. Is there something peculiar in the Welsh psyche to account for this? Possibly. A nation even now barely awake to its own history must find its heroes somewhere. But in this case there is a simpler answer: Cliff Morgan was a very remarkable man, hugely and variously talented, who had the ability to communicate personally to, and gain the affection of, individuals, even when he spoke to a mass audience. We will forget any number of politicians, generals, rogues and royals, but we will remember Cliff.

Back in high summer, the Welsh College of Music and Drama was the venue of another Wales Book of the Year awards evening, for books published in 2012. The event is well paced and smooth running. Prizes are awarded for poetry (the Roland Mathias Prize), fiction and creative non-fiction, in Welsh and English. The shortlisted books in each category are introduced by brief films, which include an extract from the text, read by an actor, before the panel chairman delivers an adjudication and announces the winner. Finally, overall winners in Welsh and English are declared. There are also 'People's Choice' awards in both languages: online voters' verdict on the books. The event was marked by two achievements unprecedented in the annals of the ceremony. The first had emerged at an earlier stage, when books by Meic Stephens and published by Y Lolfa were nominated for the 'creative non-fiction' shortlists in both Welsh (*Cofnodion*, his autobiography) and English (*Welsh Lives*, a collection of his obituaries of prominent Welsh people first published in the *Independent*). Although he was not among the award winners, that these two books caught the eye of entirely separate panels of judges is testimony to the quality of his writing in both languages, and to his continuing productivity as a writer. The second emerged in the course of the evening and was even more remarkable. Among the English-language books, Rhian Edwards's first collection of poetry, *Clueless Dogs* (Seren), which was earlier shortlisted for the Forward First Collection Prize, gained the People's Choice award, then the Roland Mathias Prize and at the end was judged overall winner.

A chance introduction to an open mic session ten years ago at a Covent Garden pub set Rhian Edwards on the path and she has not looked back. She has a fine reputation as a performance poet on stage and on the radio and won the John Tripp Award for spoken poetry in 2012. Her work has also appeared on the page in metropolitan newspapers and magazines, and her *Parade the Fib* became Poetry Book Society Pamphlet Choice in 2008. She has said her poems 'tend to be very confessional and autobiographical', and clarity and directness of communication are to be expected where poems and songs are written for performance. Human and sexual relations, domestic and local events are the stuff of *Clueless Dogs*. An extract from 'Alison', an office manager perhaps, is illustrative:

Tanya is flapping again,
her daughter keeps nicking her fags
and trampolining the dog till it's sick.
No time for coffee, I scold her for asking.
The phone bleats from my handbag.

Somebody's fucked up somewhere,
I don't know where but I'll find out,
I'll give that girl hell now,
gave me the wrong bloody keys, didn't she.
My head's in the shed again.

But this demotic simplicity is a façade behind which lurks the unflinching eye and sophistication of an LSE law graduate, viewing herself and others with a steady gaze:

Like a crack in the egg,
a lash in the eye,
a smattering of black grass
marring the blanch of the moon,

black hairs spear through the pale
pink wheel of my nipple,
whisker-thick to the pinch,
sprouting sheer as a thorn.

[...]

Eight threads puncture the thin
limpid membrane of the halo.
This breast is gravid
with a hatching of spiders.

The first Rhys Davies Short Story Conference, a new venture of
the Trust dedicated to the writer, was held at Swansea
University in September. It began with the launch of Meic
Stephens's splendid biography *Rhys Davies: A Writer's Life*, the
first full-length treatment of its somewhat enigmatic subject.
Stephens had access to a good deal of new material from Rhys's
brother Lewis, the Trust's generous benefactor; it is very
unlikely his book will be superseded. D.J. Britton's play
*Silverglass*, a two-hander, followed later the same evening.
BAFTA-award winning actors Richard Elfyn and Eiry Thomas
played Rhys Davies and Anna Kavan in a drama still in
development that speculates upon the psychology of the
relationship that bound these unlikeliest of mutually dependent
friends. Nearing the close of the conference, Will Self, who, with
Edna O'Brien, was a key speaker, cast doubts on the
continuation of the short story genre because, he said, stories

no longer sell. That the audience disagreed did not shake his view, but this was before the world learned that Alice Munro had won the Nobel Prize for Literature.

*PN Review* 215, Volume 40 Number 3, January – February 2014.

# TONY CONRAN AND DANNIE ABSE

*November 2013*

So far as I am aware, the only poem to have come out of the Falklands War has as epigraph lines from the sixth-century heroic poem by the bard Aneirin elegising warriors of 'Y Gododdin', a British (that is, Welsh-speaking) tribe of what is now south-east Scotland, who lost their lives fighting the English at Catraeth, or Catterick, in Yorkshire: '*Gŵyr a aeth Gatraeth oedd ffraeth eu llu,/Glasfedd eu hancwyn, a gwenwyn fu*' ('Men went to Catraeth, keen was their company,/They were fed on fresh mead, and it proved poison'). The poem, 'Elegy for the Welsh Dead in the Falkland Islands, 1982' is by Tony Conran. Albeit in another language, it mourns the twentieth-century fallen in imagery, phraseology and rhythms that echo Aneirin's commemoration of those slain in the sixth century. And in the same way it names them:

> Malcolm Wigley of Connah's Quay.
> > Did his helm
> Ride high in the war-line?
> Did he drink enough mead for that journey?
> The desolated shores of Tegeingl,
> Did they pig the steel that destroyed him?

> [...]

> Certainly Tony Jones of Carmarthen was brave.
> What did it matter, steel in the heart?
> Shrapnel is faithful now. His shroud is frost.

Figment of empire, whore's honour, held them.
Forty-three at Catraeth died for our dregs.

So the poem ends, with an entirely contemporary bitterness against the tenacity of the notion of empire, but it is incontestably a warrior elegy in its sinewy expression of pain and regret.

Anthony Conran died in January this year. He was everywhere admired for his skill as writer and critic, and (a far rarer thing) loved for the man he was. I met him in the 1970s at Lampeter, in the company of a mutual friend. Since he would have no truck with euphemism or polite avoidance of the truth, there is little point in disguising the fact that Conran was severely disabled. Cerebral palsy twisted his spine and contorted his limbs; every word he spoke demanded a writhing effort. It was not easy, initially, to understand what he said. But his disability did not inhibit his talk and far less his work. That his tortured body housed a smoothly whirring intellectual machine, if it wasn't known before, became clear when, still a young man, in 1957 he reviewed (for *Dock Leaves*, no. 22) *The Burning Tree*, an extensive collection 'from the first thousand years of Welsh Verse' translated by Gwyn Williams, then the doyen of translators. While acknowledging certain strengths in the book, Conran brilliantly analysed its flaws, including the omission of key poets, failures of poetic sympathy for the original and plain inaccuracy in Williams's versions. It is a courteous and typically robust critique that continues its arguments beyond the covers of the book to the monoglot community it was intended to enlighten:

Now, the Anglo-Welsh are in Wasteland. The only way to get them out is by showing them that poetry is what it is, and not some other thing; that religion, politics, good manners, are what they are, and not something else; that art is delectable only if you treat it seriously as art, and not trivial excitements...The great need is for critical appraisal... One or two poems, adequately translated, and suitably publicised, could do more for Welsh culture than a whole battery of third programme entertainments on Welsh themes.

Having issued the challenge, during the next decade Conran worked on his response, published in 1967 as the *Penguin Book of Welsh Verse*. The introduction sets out the history of Welsh poetry from its beginnings in post-Roman Britain and explains its essential difference from the poetry of other Western European cultures that do not have the 'intense Welsh preoccupation with the *bro*, or district you come from...crucial to their history'. It is an elegant and erudite exposition of Welsh poetics and the practice of individual poets, foremost among them Dafydd ap Gwilym, 'one of the supreme wizards of poetic sleight-of-hand the world has ever seen'. As an exposition of the sadly underestimated (indeed, still mostly ignored) wealth of Welsh-language poetry his book has not been superseded.

I have written previously (*PN Review* 155 and 186) about Conran's interest in drama, his championing of Idris Davies, best known for his poem sequences about the 1926 Strike, and his standing as a modernist poet of great skill and versatility. As in the elegy quoted above, his sense of the intimacy of the *bro* coloured much of his writing, which was often dedicated and addressed to friends and involved the mutuality of the neighbourhood. Most important of all to him was the embrace of family, his wife Lesley and two daughters. It was Lesley who read extracts from his work on his behalf at Brecon when he was shortlisted for the Roland Mathias Prize in 2009. If you have not previously read Conran, that book, *What Brings You Here So Late* (Gwasg Careg Gwalch, 2008), a modernist verse autobiography, is the place to begin.

Caerleon, where we live, has an annual festival. While no rival to Hay, it does have substantial literary content. This year's celebrated Arthur Machen, that remarkable hack writer, actor and author of cult fantasy fiction, born in the heart of the village, a short walk from here, one hundred and fifty years ago. There was plenty to engage Machen enthusiasts, but Dannie Abse was the major attraction among living writers. The youngest child of a wonderfully talented Jewish family, he was born and brought up in Cardiff, like his brothers, Wilfred, who became an eminent psychiatrist in the United States, and Leo, a lawyer and outstanding backbench Labour MP. Although his career took him away from Wales, Dannie remained true to his Welsh roots, preserved a loved foothold on the south Wales coast at Ogmore-by-Sea, and supported Cardiff City FC through all the lean years at last to a place in the top rank. He qualified as a doctor in London and after National Service settled there, working at a clinic where he specialised in the diagnosis of chest complaints. His daily routine at the clinic, he says, rarely stretched him. Indeed, it usually gave him time to fulfil that 'imperative need' he felt to write poems and often supplied the stuff of them, in a way rather reminiscent of R.S. Thomas, who found the Anglican priesthood similarly compatible with his poetic vocation. Again like Thomas, he has been prolific: since 1949, in addition to novels, plays, autobiography, collections of essays and memoirs, and editing work, he has published (by my count) seventeen books of poems. The latest, *Speak Old Parrot* (Hutchinson – as usual – 2013), he brought with him to Caerleon.

He was launched early on the poetry reading circuit in the 1950s, became a regular at poetry and jazz evenings up and down the country in the 1960s and by the 1970s was giving about thirty readings a year. I have listened to him read many times and always with pleasure. Good poets are not necessarily good performers of their poetry, but Dannie Abse is. Whatever natural gifts of that sort he possessed have been carefully honed by practice at home and abroad, before audiences of all sizes and cultural complexions. He has earned in broadsheet review columns and on the road the reputation of being among the finest and most widely appreciated poets of the last century, and this. And with all that he has no side, no pretensions, which in part explains his wide circle of friends, at home and abroad. 'Letter to Stanley Moss in New York' (*PN Review* 162) is characteristic of the wit and humanity of his poetry and expressive of his gift for friendship.

Dannie Abse will be ninety in September. He is a little bent, his face a little bonier, but the social ease, the charm, are not one jot diminished. We met at the Roman baths, the evening's venue. Caerleon, a highly important Roman settlement, home of the Second Augustan Legion, has an amphitheatre and barracks, both remarkably well preserved, a Legionary Museum and, most recently excavated, the baths. A narrow walkway around the walls of the containing structure allows visitors to view from above, to the left, the hypocaust that heated the smaller of the two pools and to the right the much larger cold plunge. A light display simulates the rippling of water, convincingly when viewed between the slats of the walkway, which affords the only seating space. A full house sat around the larger pool, backs against the wall. It was an unpromising arrangement for a reading, but one the poet overcame with ease. He read some old favourites – 'The Uninvited', 'Not Adlestrop', 'Olfactory Pursuits' – all quite beautifully, the voice sure as ever. Meditatively he observed, 'I have it seems two voices in me, one more conversationally pitched, one more lyrical. I think the lyrical is fainter now'. 'Moonlight' and 'Sunbright', first published a couple of years ago in *PN Review* 198, suggest otherwise. The 'old parrot' of his latest book, his inspirational self, is apostrophised in the opening poem, 'Talking to Myself':

In the mildew of age
all pavements slope uphill

slow slow
towards an exit.

[...]

The aspen tree trembles as I do
And there are feathers in the wind.

Quick quick
speak, old parrot,
do I not feed you with my life?

At Caerleon, the evidence of both poems and performance suggested that there has been no falling-off in the old imperative to write, nor in having something worthwhile to say.

*PN Review* 214, Volume 40 Number 2,
November – December 2013.

# R.S. THOMAS
*July 2013*

As we still await the coming of spring, which for him was a matter of the greatest consequence, we begin celebrating the centenary of the birth of R.S. Thomas. He was born in Cardiff on 29 March 1913, the only child of a merchant seaman and his wife, who were English-speaking. When he was five the family moved to north Wales, where his father worked on Irish ferries out of Holyhead. They settled in the town, a predominantly Welsh-speaking environment. The growing child explored with delight a rural landscape at the edge of the sea.

When, later, people came to the poet seeking answers, asking Why this? and What is the meaning of that?, he would slam the door in their faces, sometimes literally. Yet he could be surprisingly open to enquiry in congenial company. *All Things Considered*, a religious affairs programme on BBC Radio Wales (9am each Sunday) is, I am confident, one of the best of its kind. A recent edition marked the centenary by repeating an interview with R.S. Thomas originally broadcast in 1995. The presenter, Roy Jenkins, a Baptist minister and most accomplished of gentle interrogators, described the poet's arrival at the BBC studios in Bangor. Divested of long scarf and heavy overcoat, he said, 'You know I get paid according to the number of poems I read,' and with a relaxation of the characteristic scowl, ' – so I shall read slowly.' In addition to the readings, listeners were given an insight into a system of belief that some will have found worryingly unorthodox and some intensely appealing. To him, he said, God had chosen to reveal Himself through nature. His awareness of the enormous size of the universe, and all that physics and mathematics have shown, do not dismay; we can believe in a Resurrection, he said, on the basis of the annual rebirth of nature. When others point to the violence and suffering at nature's core and ask what place they have in God's love, he replies (as a Buddhist might) that all living creatures have a claim on one's love and we should not despair. The problem, he said, is not the being of God, but the nature of God, and prayer at its best is not talking but listening, waiting upon a revelation of God's nature.

His openness on this occasion should not have surprised, for despite his reputation as a poet resentful of intrusion, he had before been responsive, in the right circumstances. In an earlier broadcast interview (a transcript was published in *Poetry Wales* Vol. 7 No. 4, 1972) he confessed to John Ormond, 'I'm a solitary, I'm a nature mystic; and silence and slowness and bareness have always appealed'; and again, 'I firmly believe this, that eternity is not something over there, not something in the future; it is close to us, it is all around us and at any given moment one can pass into it'.

Another remarkable interview, with Ned Thomas and John Barnie, the magazine's editors, was published in *Planet* No. 80, 1990. On this occasion he spoke of his schoolboy apprenticeship in poetry 'based entirely on my reading of *Palgrave's Golden Treasury*', and his first published poems in the college English-language magazine while he was a student of classics at Bangor. For the latter he adopted the 'astonishing' pseudonym 'Curtis Langdon', an implied rejection of Welshness. As a student his habits were already solitary, and when he spoke it was with a deliberately acquired English accent, which re-emphasised the distance he felt from his Welsh-speaking fellows, and which he never discarded (in this he resembles his namesake and near-coeval, Dylan, whose Swansea accent was modified by elocution lessons). His attitude to Wales and the language changed gradually, and then more dramatically when, in the early 1940s, as rector of the upland parish of Manafon, he applied himself intensively to learning Welsh. Asked how he came to enter the Church, he replied, 'Who can deny the finger of God?':

> It may have been a disaster for other people but it was a blessing for me...It has given me time which is the most necessary of all to a poet...I loved the country, was not ambitious, and thus had no feelings of guilt about remaining there...the Anglican custom of putting such a man in a country cure and leaving him to pursue his studies was congenial to me in my efforts to see things in perspective...

He thus became an inheritor of that long tradition of studious, creative country clergy, extending at least as far back as George Herbert (whom he mentioned in this context) but including those in the eighteenth century whose antiquarian interests did so much to rescue the manuscript history of Wales. He deployed poetry in his battle to preserve the language and his own vision of a pristine Wales unsullied by the hated noise of mechanisation and the tawdry inroads of tourism and immigration from England. He saw this was a fight doomed to fail. No wonder the scowl became habitual.

To save himself, he 'turned to the birds'. 'Instead of being asked into a modernised cottage with the television's St Vitus's dance in the corner, I went out seeking birds,' he says, and 'God worships Himself in mountains, flowers and bird-song'. His answer to the imperious voice of science comes with the same calm certitude:

> The sub-atomic world, like the extra-galactic world, depends to some extent on the imagination. One realises that the greater

the magnification the more territory comes into view at either end of the optic. Because of the concept of infinity, all these spaces are as infinite as they are meaningless to the human observer. So why should not another invisible dimension, infinitely close, be equally valid.

Listening to that slow, quiet, ineradicably English intonation, almost a drawl, is strangely moving. I heard it, in my mind's ear, as I read his latest, posthumous publication. *Uncollected Poems*, edited by Tony Brown and Jason Walford Davies and published for the centenary by Bloodaxe, includes 139 poems from a wide variety of journals. The bibliography reveals that a further 48 poems plus nine translations from the Welsh were excluded by editorial decision; probably to the poet's relief, in his other dimension, the Curtis Langdon poems are absent and unacknowledged. Nevertheless, the chronological arrangement enables the reader to trace the development of Thomas's poetic style from 1939. They also reveal his studious acquisition of knowledge about Welsh history and literature and his regard for contemporaries who wrote in Welsh, like the poet Gwenallt and, with particular emphasis, Saunders Lewis, while at the same time acknowledging his indebtedness to English literature: 'No patriotism dulls/The true and the beautiful/bequeathed to me by Blake,/Shelley and Shakespeare and the ravished Keats'.

All the early poems have rhyme, even 'Welsh Shepherd', which appeared in the *Dublin Magazine* (as did many others) in 1949 and marked the first appearance of 'Poor Iago Prydderch ...A scarecrow of a man, becalmed in the unreal/Tides of light', who in future observations of the hill farmer's life would be exposed to harsher weathers. By the chronology of this book the first unrhymed poem is 'Darlington' (1953), and soon after, from the *TLS* in 1954, 'Somersby Brook', alluding to the young Tennyson in his rural Lincolnshire birthplace. To my mind, this poem is the first to be permeated with the turn of phrase, the metaphoric way of thinking, the authentic cadences of the poet's maturity. R.S. soon reached the stage when he no longer submitted poems hopefully to editors; editors sent begging letters. A few of his contributions recognisably respond to his perception of a magazine's particular bent, but mostly he is off on his own, by turns dramatic in setting and register and, as in 'The Question' (1962), meditatively questioning and self-questioning. An autobiographical thread also runs through this collection, prompting the speculation that the poet omitted these poems from his many books for other than critical considerations of quality. 'Yesterday's Farm' (1964), for example, tells plainly of calling at a farm to ask directions of the women there:

I examine one as she stands close:
There is a roundness of the figure
That is not bad; and the good teeth –
[...]
It is not girls like these
Are the daughters of Prydderch.

That is, she did not fit into his poetic scheme of things. She had only an 'appeal/To the male in me'. It is a confession of physical attraction and unusual on that account. 'Autobiography' (1973) casts light upon his relationship with his parents which, presumably, he did not want to see in a book:

Nothing they have they own;
    the borrowed furnishings of their minds
    fray. I study to become the rat
    that will desert
    the foundering vessel

of their pride; but home
is a long time sinking. All
my life I must swim
out of the suction of its vortex.

Perhaps it was sensitivity to the predicament, theirs and his, that made him decide not to include the poem in a book, though what he describes is hardly unusual. The same could be said for 'The Father Dies' (2002), worth a place in any collection, which concerns the emotional impasse between the poet and his own son. Most of Thomas's later poems are confessional in the broad sense that they are constantly the conduit of sober meditation on the state of Wales and the world, his own soul and eternity.

*Uncollected Poems* is an important contribution to a celebration of R.S. Thomas that will continue throughout 2013.

*PN Review* 212, Volume 39 Number 6,
July – August 2013.

# RHYS DAVIES

*January 2013*

I have written previously (*PN Review* 159) about the Rhys Davies Trust and its principal aim of preserving the memory of an important writer of short stories and novels by supporting Welsh writing and writers in English. The trust was set up in 1990 through the generosity of Rhys Davies's younger brother Lewis, born like him over the shop, a general grocery store at Blaenclydach, barely a mile up a steep hill from Tonypandy, the heart of the Rhondda Fawr, in 1913. Lewis was the last of six children, having two brothers and three sisters to look up to. The eldest of the boys, a youthful flyer in World War I, was killed in action in 1918; the girls grew up strong-minded to the point of domineering, two becoming primary school teachers and the third a hospital matron. Rhys, born in 1901, was determined not to be shackled by home and community. Against his parents' wishes, he left grammar school for employment at the earliest opportunity and soon made his way to London to fulfil his ambition to write. Although he returned to the Rhondda occasionally, usually when short of money, and travelled a little, he lived in or near London, and published there, for the remainder of his life. He was a totally professional, committed writer, and quite prolific, his output including twenty novels and more than a hundred short stories, besides limited forays into non-fiction, biography, drama, autobiography, and numerous articles and reviews for newspapers and journals. Several of his stories were first published in the *New Yorker* and the *Saturday Evening Post*, including 'The Chosen One', which appeared in the former and won the Edgar for the best short story of 1967 from the Mystery Writers of America. His writing was accorded serious appraisal and generally well received by the critics of his day. Half the novels were also published in the United States and several of his books were translated into German, Danish, Swedish, Norwegian, Icelandic and Hungarian. Something about his fiction, a good deal of it set in the mining valleys of south Wales, appealed to Scandinavian taste. Re-reading him now, I wonder how he fell into neglect after his death in 1978.

He was not the kind of writer to be noted for stylistic individuality, but possessed a fine, flexible technique, far more than merely serviceable for the narrative purposes to which it was put:

In those days [he is writing of a visit to France in the autumn of 1928] you could go most of the way from Nice to Monte Carlo by interlinking tramcars on the low coast road, at a cost of a few pence. The florid old casino, all dusty plush, chandeliers and religious hush, was beautiful to me. Very aged cocotte-like creatures, with strange scalp-growths of dyed seaweed for hair, sat calmly beyond locomotion at the afternoon tables, as if they had been born, earned their living, and become mummified before those spinning wheels [...] I left while the going was good, and alighted from a tramcar somewhere near Beaulieu, deciding to walk the rest of the way to Nice in the warm magnolia light of late afternoon. I stretched under a sea-wall and went fast asleep. When I woke, a round bronze shield hung low over the authentically wine-dark sea of Homer [...] I lay drowsing in the same awareness that had come on a cold winter night in Wales, the voice of a brook in my ears. Once more I knew we are always alone, and never bereft of identification with the endless past. Only the future was anonymous. Why should that be hostile? [...] My grimy load of undeserved guilt seemed to have gone from my back. Its substitute of self-expression in writing, some of it impure, might always be weighty, but this was of my own choosing, and it was a full wineskin on my back.

This extract from *Print of a Hare's Foot* (Heinemann, 1969), an 'autobiographical beginning' as he put it, describes a kind of epiphany, or at least a coming to terms with himself and the life he had chosen. He was, to use the word he chose for males of his acquaintance whose sexual orientation he shared, 'queer', in the eyes of the law a transgressor and well advised to disguise his preferences. The habit of discreet subterfuge was ingrained in him; from his writing you would not readily guess he was gay. It is only recently, notably in an essay on Davies's fiction by M. Wynn Thomas ('Never Seek to Tell Thy Love', in *Rhys Davies – Decoding the Hare*, edited by Meic Stephens, UWP, 2001), that the extraordinary care he took to cover his tracks became thoroughly known and understood. Forewarned, by a subtle shift of focus the reader is able to see, for example, that the description of a young woman washing her brother-in-law's coal-grimed back in the story 'A Bed of Feathers' is supercharged with sensuous appreciation of male beauty: 'she began to rub the soap into his flesh, disregarding the rough flannel used for that task. Into the little hollows of his muscular shoulders, down the length of his flawless back, over the fine curves of his sides, she caressingly passed her spread hands'.

When I first read the short stories – all, that is, in the *Collected Stories* published by Heinemann in 1955, which has been royally superseded by the three-volume *Collected Stories* edited by Meic Stephens (Gomer, 1996) – I was struck by Davies's mixing of the mores and topography of the mining valleys, which were familiar to me, with narratives and characters that were often distasteful – 'impure' was the word he used in the extract above – and sometimes violent. His descriptions of the inner turmoil of characters, of changing moods, emotional conflict, flesh and spirit, reminded me of D.H. Lawrence, but the Lawrentian influence, though present, is not that large; he was always his own man. He was, however, a close and valued friend of Lawrence towards the end of the latter's life. The story of their association forms a major part of *Print of a Hare's Foot*.

Having sold the American publication rights of his first novel, *The Withered Root*, Davies determined to go to France for six months to work on his next book. That was where we found him visiting the casino at Monte Carlo and meditating on life and the future on a beach near Beaulieu. Having been informed of the young writer's presence in Nice by a mutual friend, Charles Lahr, who had published Davies's first short story in his magazine *New Coterie*, Lawrence wrote inviting Davies to join him and Frieda at Bandol, about fifty miles west along the coast. There were the usual ups and downs, but from the outset they got on well together. Davies thus became a companion and observer of the exiles and one of the most important witnesses of their relationship in the years of Lawrence's physical decline. Frieda having travelled to Germany for a holiday with relatives, Davies, on his way back to Britain, accompanied Lawrence to Paris, where it was hoped a publisher could be found for a cheap popular edition of *Lady Chatterley's Lover*. Sylvia Beach turned the opportunity down but found Lawrence another Paris-based American publisher, who made a fortune out of the book. It was March, still cold and damp, and Davies, sharing a room with Lawrence, saw how frail and wracked by disease he was. Lawrence's final collection of poems, *Pansies*, had been accumulating during the Bandol weeks and Davies had the task of smuggling the complete manuscript back to England in his luggage, a risky undertaking (copies posted to Lawrence's

London agent had been seized by the postal authorities following a 'random search'), but he got away with it and the text was eventually used for the printing of a 'private' edition. When, a year later, in March 1930, Lawrence died in Venice and his critics, no longer fearful of a whiplash response, rounded on him, Davies, angered by their 'indecent' attacks, stood up for him.

In later life, Rhys Davies, who lived by his pen, frugally, mostly in bedsits, received two substantial legacies. The first he inherited from Anna Kavan, the heroin-addicted writer with whom he had a long-standing friendly relationship and whom he saved from overdoses on more than one occasion. The second came from another close friend, Louise Taylor, the adopted daughter of Alice B. Toklas, who with her husband, the painter Red Taylor, welcomed artists and writers to their house in Chelsea. He had little time to enjoy his wealth: diagnosed with lung cancer, he died in August 1978, leaving everything to his brother, Lewis, who also lived in London, where he was chief librarian of Odhams Press. He, too, was gay and they moved in similar circles, though not often in one another's company. In retirement Lewis Davies moved to Lewes, not far from Brighton, where he bought a flat in a nondescript modern block. He lived alone, comfortably, without extravagance, and the inheritance piled up in banks and investments.

At length, all his family having died, Lewis determined that when his turn came the money would go to a cause of which he could feel proud. In 1990, he inaugurated the trust in his brother's name with an astonishing initial gift and further undertook that, in the fulness of time, virtually his entire estate would follow. The trust's first act was to place a memorial plaque to Rhys on the wall of the dwelling in Blaenclydach that had once been Royal Stores, birthplace of all the Davies children. Lewis, a dapper figure, unveiled the plaque and afterwards we walked a little further up the valley to the site of the Cambrian colliery, now an open green space, while he recalled the good times and the bad in the mining community that had given his brother a rich seam of story. He was a lovely man, gentle and quietly spoken, and maintained a keen interest in the work of the trust. In recent years he had become frail and when he could no longer manage on his own he went into a nursing home where constant support was available. He died in December last year, aged 98, and later that month Meic Stephens and I, co-executors of his will, went to the flat in Lewes, which had been unoccupied for three years. Apart from the dust, it was as he had left it – the pictures, all the books and records and theatre programmes, all the smart clothes (he and Rhys were a little dandified), all the crockery, cutlery and glassware, and the mementos: Rhys's OBE, the caricature statuette of Poe, his Edgar, and a small bronze of a naked youth, in the antique manner, with a full wineskin on his back, in the act of pouring wine into a beaker, his image of the burden of self-expression in writing, joyfully borne.

*PN Review* 209, Volume 39 Number 3,
January – February 2013.

# GWYNETH LEWIS AND PATRICK MCGUINNESS
*November 2012*

About a year ago I received the first box of books from Literature Wales, the literature promotion agency. Its home is the Wales Millennium Centre in Cardiff Bay and its chief executive, successor to Peter Finch, is Lleucu Siencyn. I believe Peter was the lone male in the operation until his retirement last year; now the entire staff is female, a reminder, if one were needed, that gender inequality is not an issue in the province of literature. The book box was the first of several that came with the role of judge of Wales Book of the Year 2011. It was a shared task: my fellow judges on the English-language panel were Trezza Azzopardi, the Cardiff-born novelist whose first novel, *The Hiding Place* (2000), won the Geoffrey Faber Memorial Prize and who now teaches creative writing at the University of East Anglia, and Spencer Jordan, who directs the MA in Humanities at Cardiff Metropolitan University. When the invitation came, having previously served several years on the committee deciding the biennial Roland Mathias Prize, I was not enthused at the prospect: I knew what lay ahead. Reading for pleasure is like a stroll in a landscape where every turn brings fresh sights to delight and amaze, or, depending on your choice of book, shock and appal. Judging is like a forced march. But significant changes in the organisation of Wales Book of the Year were persuasive. As with other major literary awards, prizes are now given to the winners of three categories – poetry, fiction and creative non-fiction – as well as to an overall winner, in both Welsh and English. For me, a more important consideration was the merger of the Roland Mathias Prize with

Wales Book of the Year, with the certainty that, henceforth, the award in the poetry category in English would continue to bear the name of Roland Mathias.

With as much zeal as I could muster, once again I established for myself a routine of reading and note-making. Often enough the books I took out of a box I would have chosen to read anyway, and read with pleasure, but many pages might have been made of lead so heavily did their turning weigh upon me. Among the latter were solemn, and ultimately useless, attempts to apply what passes for academic literary criticism to the work of writers who deserve better. Inadequate proofreading was an irritant to all three of us, but judging presented few problems at the shortlist stage and only one issue, quickly resolved, at the selection of category winners. The awards ceremony was held on a rainy night at the beautifully extended and refurbished Welsh College of Music and Drama in Cardiff. Two of the category winners are well known to readers of this magazine: Gwyneth Lewis took the Roland Mathias Award for poetry with her collection *Sparrow Tree* (Bloodaxe), and Patrick McGuinness the fiction prize for his novel *The Last Hundred Days* (Seren). The best of the creative non-fiction was a memoir, *The Vagabond's Breakfast* (Alcemi) by Richard Gwyn.

Patrick McGuinness was the unanimous choice as overall winner. The action of the novel is worked out against the background of historical events in Romania (and eastern Europe generally), culminating in the execution of the Ceauşescus. It is a first-person narrative reminiscent of *The Third Man*, for the regime has created an environment of dearth, criminal double-dealing and suspicion as grim as post-war Vienna's. The narrator begins his adventure as an innocent abroad but quickly learns the arts of survival under the tutelage of Leo O'Heix, 'Bucharest's biggest black-marketeer', behind whom looms Belanger, a consummately evil trader in human misery, whose influence persists in his absence and who is glimpsed at the end of the book returning to cash in on the new order. Character development is one strength of the book: Professor Ionescu, ruthless party member and 'expert purger' of discredited academics, and Sergiu Trofim, old-style communist and patient strategist, are wonderfully well done. Bucharest, the city itself, in a state of flux as old quarters are systematically destroyed to be replaced by jerry-built modern trash, emerges as a key character. The pungency of dust clouds from bulldozed buildings and the rot of decaying new concrete permeate the novel. While Party propaganda boasts the successes of the system, the constantly spied upon and brutally repressed people live in poverty, surrounded by the insane destruction of everything of cultural value. McGuinness is a gifted phrase- and image-maker and has a convincing command of atmospheric detail. Speaking at the ceremony, he said that *The Last Hundred Days* had its origins in his experience of Romania at this critical period in its history, which left so strong an impression that it brought on recurring nightmares. Readers will understand why. Since writing the book his nightmares have stopped.

I briefly outlined the three books in the shortlist for the poetry prize in *PN Review* 206: *Deep Field* by Philip Gross, Tiffany Atkinson's *Catulla et al*, and Gwyneth Lewis's *Sparrow Tree*. All three are excellent and deciding the winner entailed a great deal of head-scratching by the judges, though in the end there was no disagreement. The award went to Gwyneth Lewis, who graciously acknowledged her debt (a debt that as readers or writers we all share) to Roland Mathias. Although very different, her poetry can be as challenging as Mathias's, so subtle and evocative is her imagery, so deft her conjuring with metaphor and symbolism. There is a vogue for plainness in poetic expression (exemplified in much of Philip Gross's impressively serious and sustained focus on his father's final months), but Gwyneth Lewis's is as brightly plumaged as her birds. The title poem announces that the poet is setting out in a new direction. It is an invitation from the Muse, who, with her creative gift, bears also thorns. In this book dark shadows fall across the loveliest of life's promises: the active brain is prey to migraine, the visual cortex is thwarted by glaucoma, the primal urge to bear children negated by failure to conceive, the anticipated pleasure of a sea voyage turned bitterly to ash by sickness, life itself constantly threatened by time. The poems possess this realm of meaning below the surface, which is itself an elaborate filigree of imagery close knit with rhyme, rhythmic patterning, verbal echoes and cunning line-breaks – the signature of a conscientious prosodist. They are also illuminated by extraordinary wordplay drawn from knitting and quilt-making, the sea and navigation, the cosmos and the microcosms of atoms and cells. And, with all their brilliance, they are carried on a strong current of human love.

Within a month of her success at Wales Book of the Year, Gwyneth Lewis won another major prize, on this occasion for poetry in the Welsh language. She was awarded the Crown at the National Eisteddfod for a sequence of poems on the subject 'Ynys' (Island). The Crown is a competition for a long poem or sequence in the 'free metres', that is any form that does not employ *cynghanedd*, described by the *Companion to Welsh Literature* as 'an ancient and intricate system of sound chiming within a line of verse,' for which the Eisteddfod has a separate 'Chair' competition. On one recent occasion, presumably by oversight, the Crown competition rubric omitted to mention the free metres requirement, and the judges gave the prize to a poet who broke the well-established convention and used *cynghanedd*, much to the annoyance of a number of commentators, and the chagrin of Meic Stephens, who might otherwise have won. There were no such problems this year.

151

Gwyneth's poem is based on the concluding part of the story of Branwen in the *Mabinogion*, where, having been mortally wounded with a poisoned spear, Bran orders the seven survivors of the battle on the Island of the Mighty to cut off his head and carry it to the White Hill in London for burial. On their way they spend eighty years in a great hall on the island of Gwales (Grassholm) off the coast of Pembrokeshire, during which they do not age and the head is as it was while Bran lived, as long as no one opens a door looking over the sea towards Cornwall. Once the door is opened, all remember every grief they have ever suffered, and they know they must go at once and bury the head. I have not seen Gwyneth's poem, but would not be surprised to find the theme of change and a longing for the suspension of change loom large in it. The adjudication spoke of the poet's mastery of her craft and how she had this year raised the standard of the Crown competition. Nor was that all. Later in the week her highly praised Welsh adaptation of Shakespeare's *The Tempest* was performed at the Eisteddfod by Theatr Genedlaethol Cymru.

The Eisteddfod was held this year at Llandow, in the Vale of Glamorgan, on the site of an abandoned airfield near Llanilltud Fawr (Llantwit Major), the small coastal town where, about the end of the fifth century, Saint Illtud founded a monastery and one of the most famous of Christian colleges. The caravan parks for long-distance *eisteddfodwyr* were there, hundreds of tents and stalls representing cultural institutions, providing food and drink, proclaiming this and selling that, and in the midst the great pink pavilion, venue for all the competitions in music and dance and the major ceremonies. Among the stalls on the *maes* was one bearing the banner *'Teyrnged i'r Beaseleys'* ('Tribute to the Beaseleys'). It was empty, symbolising a family home stripped of its furniture by the bailiffs.

In writing about Saunders Lewis recently (*PN Review* 205)

I referred to the lasting impact of his BBC lecture 'Tynged yr Iaith' ('The Fate of the Language'), in which he concluded by saying Welsh could survive, but only by the exercise of willpower, determination, struggle and sacrifice, and he gave the example of Trefor Beaseley, a miner, and his schoolteacher wife Eileen: 'In April 1952 [they] bought a cottage in Llangennech, near Llanelli, in a district where nine out of every ten of the population are Welsh speaking. In the rural council to which Llangennech belongs all the councillors are Welsh speaking. So are the council officials. So, when they received the rate demand from "The Rural District Council of Llanelly", Mrs Beaseley wrote to ask for a Welsh version. She was refused. She in turn refused to pay the rate until one was forthcoming. Both she and Mr Beaseley were summoned before the magistrates court more than a dozen times…Three times the bailiffs collected furniture from their home…This continued for eight years. In 1960 Mr and Mrs Beaseley received a rate demand from "Cyngor Dosbarth Gwledig Llanelli", and the Welsh in it was as good as the English'. The cause and the sacrifice of this couple have not been forgotten. Trefor Beaseley died in 1994, and on 12 August, at the end of the Eisteddfod week, his widow, Eileen, died, aged 91.

*PN Review* 208, Volume 39 Number 2,
November – December 2012.

# POETRY OF 2011

*July 2012*

Yesterday evening was as wet and chilly as the second week of May could ever have been. We drove up to Brecon, to Theatr Brycheiniog, for an event organised by Literature Wales, the newly rechristened literature promotion agency, at which the shortlists for Wales Book of the Year 2011, both Welsh-language and English, were announced. It was a well-attended event, as it should have been, given that, before the announcements, the audience was entertained by a bilingual poetry reading. Gillian Clarke and Carol Ann Duffy, National Laureates both, supplied the English, and Eurig Salisbury and Ceri Wyn Jones, the current Young Person's Laureate in the Welsh language and his immediate predecessor, read, of course, in Welsh. As usual, simultaneous translation facilities were available. I recalled hearing Yevtushenko reading poems in Russian and being excited by the force of rhetoric in a language of which I had not the slightest understanding, and wondered again whether it is better to listen to a poem read clearly in its proper language without its being overlaid by an inevitably prosy version in another.

Brecon was a wise choice as venue. It is not as conveniently central as Llandrindod Wells is deemed to be for people travelling from the four quarters of Wales, but not as remote as Cardiff for those coming from the west and north. Besides, Brecon was the home of the Roland Mathias Prize and, while that formerly independent literary event has been rolled up and joined to Wales Book of the Year, it still retains a separate identity within it. Wales Book of the Year is now organised along the lines of other major literary prizes; that is, books are judged first in categories: poetry, fiction and creative non-fiction. Yesterday's shortlists named three books in each category. In July, at a grander event at the Welsh College of Music and Drama in Cardiff, the winner from each category will be announced, and the overall winner. That the name of Roland Mathias will continue to be associated with the prize delights me.

The shortlist of poetry books contains two familiar names: Gwyneth Lewis, the first National Poet of Wales, whose work is well known to readers of *PN Review*, and Philip Gross, who won Wales Book of the Year in 2009 with *I Spy Pinhole Eye*, and the T.S. Eliot Prize in 2010 with *The Water Table*. The third poet is Tiffany Atkinson, who like Gross teaches creative writing, but at Aberystwyth University, whereas he is professor at the University of Glamorgan. All three have produced books of high quality and choosing a winner is going to be difficult. Atkinson's book, *Catulla et al*, includes a series of twenty-first-century feminine variations on the Latin of Catullus, sharp in observation and satirical wit. In *Sparrow Tree*, Gwyneth Lewis reveals her knowledge of avian taxonomy, quiltmaking and knitting, and seafaring, which are the frequent sources of metaphor and analogy in poems about human pain and mutability, the terror of losing a loved one and the leap of hope. Philip Gross's subject in *Deep Field* is his ageing, dying father, who fled Europe in the aftermath of the Second World War and came to Britain possessed of several languages. The book is a sustained elegy, which focuses particularly on the father's loss of language as a result of deafness and aphasia. It is unflinching in its honesty, acutely observational and deeply melancholy.

Whichever wins the prize, we will hear more of all three shortlisted books. If we consider these alone, 2011 was a very good year for poetry, but several other poets, unrewarded this time, published books that are well worth reading. Among them is Ellie Evans, originally from Carmarthen, who read English at

Oxford, taught English in Hong Kong and London, travelled extensively in other parts, and lives now in Powys. She is a postgraduate student of creative writing at Bath Spa University and came late to poetry. Among her earliest poems are those published in *PN Review* (No. 167, 2006), two of which are drawn from her life in China and a third about experience of the Okefenokee Swamp, from her time in the United States. Her first collection, *The Ivy Hides the Fig-Ripe Duchess*, published by Seren in 2011, includes all three poems, 'Okefenokee' and 'Trip', the longer of the two China poems, somewhat altered. It is interesting to see in the former a few phrases changed, a word and a detail about the size of an alligator 'twelve feet long' added. That the changes are as much concerned with the balance and stresses of the line as they are with lexical matters becomes more obvious with the formerly formless 'Trip', which has undergone radical change into a prose poem set out in five paragraphs. Some of her more recent poems have conventional rhyming forms; in several others rhyme is used occasionally, perhaps opportunistically. She is learning the craft to accompany her gifts for recreating the remembered incident, skilful contrivance and neat cleverness. Ellie Evans is a poet of sights, sounds and sensations, and much of her work is infused with female sensibilities, whether it is about family relationships (often involving furniture and household impedimenta), or derived from exotic travel, in which a travelling companion or lover may be present or implied. What distinguishes her, and may point to her future development, is an edginess that emerges with added force in the final sentence or line of a poem, as in 'Setting the Scene':

How would a *noir* director dress your sitting-room
prior to shooting? He'd change your lighting for a start,
chuck out those ceiling saucers which cast an amber mist

speckled with dead flies...
He'd focus on the cage, the budgie with
my face, a close-up of your nails gripping my arm, leaving
a smear of machine-oil. Your eyes are flakes of slate
concealing whirring fan-blades, clacking like a clapper-board
ready for the take.

Film noir, perhaps, is for her a natural environment, but not the only one in which she is at home.

I first met the poetry of Susan Richardson in *Creatures of the Intertidal Zone* (Cinnamon Press, 2007). I thought it an interesting first collection, not least in her use of rhyme and conventional metrical forms. She is a writer much concerned with environmental issues. Poems about the landscape and creatures and historical explorers of Iceland, Greenland and the eastern seaboard of Canada were particularly striking, including 'Eiriksdottir' – the story of Gudrid, daughter of Eirik the Red, which Richardson might have read about in Gwyn Jones's *Eirik the Red and other Icelandic Sagas* (OUP, 1962), although there are now other sources. Eirik reappears briefly in her latest book *Where the Air is Rarefied*, from Cinnamon Press. This too is a remarkably focused collection taking as its subject the imminence of environmental disaster in far northern latitudes. It draws on various narratives of the region, from folk tale to Icelandic and more recent exploration sagas. Richardson employs a variety of forms from prose poems to experimental unspaced blocks of words, but the rather spindly short line, in which assonance is a key device and rhyme falls as it may, predominates. Read aloud, some poems seem allied to shamanic incantation. Personification, a key device in this book, is surprisingly effective. The frozen north, in the grip of man-made thaw, is a female figure in several poems:

I can no longer staunch
the drips from the tips of my fingers
or the sag of my once firm drifts.
Since my flesh turned to slush,
my musk ox escorts have dumped me,
the tongues of my raunchiest glaciers
are in retreat.

A barely subdued cold rage sparkles with verbal inventiveness, as in 'The White Dark', a poem about the monitory deaths of Arctic explorers:

They died with tongues frozen to beards.
They died of a diet of boot leather and each other ...
They died freeze-dreaming wives
in baleen-stiff underwear.
They died of too much tilt and shipness.

Susan Richardson comes from Monmouthshire and is another well-travelled poet, having spent time in the United States, Canada and Australia. A Churchill Memorial Trust Travel Fellowship took her to the icy north on the trail of Gudrid. She is a committed and energetic teacher in creative writing at workshops and has a following as a regular 'poet-in-residence' for BBC Radio Four's *Saturday Live*.

Ann Cluysenaar belongs to an earlier generation. She is a poet of distinction. Two of her books, *Double Helix* (1982) and *Timeslips: New and Selected Poems* (1997), are from Carcanet, and twice in the 1980s she contributed long autobiographical poems to this magazine (*PN Review* 11, 1980 and 21, 1981). Born in Belgium, but with an Irish passport, she came to Wales relatively late, but transplanted to the lower Usk valley she has flourished in the Usk Valley Vaughan Association and an editorial role with *Scintilla*, the association's splendid magazine. Her latest book, *Migrations* (Cinnamon), displays the technical skill, poetic eye and powerful meditative current that have long characterised her poetry. Many of the poems are about mutability – observations of decay and departure, while the stream of life goes on. 'The Pear-Tree' describes a familiar tone of evening light and distant cows seen through the tree's branches, and concludes: 'I love change all the more. Free of waiting,/expecting, straining, and whether/I see it or not, that light will come.' This quiet insistence on the continuity of life (reminiscent of Vernon Watkins) blends with a heightened sense of geological time and the brevity within it of humanity's span on this planet. The final section of the book is wholly autobiographical and elegiac, as the poet relives loving relationships. The poems are full of the experience of long looking and shared quiet wonder, and meditation upon inevitable partings.

If you look at the Literature Wales website and, in particular, at its 'Writers of Wales' database, you will see that the number of poets who are of some significance has grown remarkably, as has the number of those who are graduates of creative writing courses, or teach on them, or both. I used to meet most of the poets whose work appeared regularly in *Poetry Wales*, and was reasonably well acquainted with many. Although my recollection of those times is fresh still, it was, perhaps, further in the past than I care to think, but the point is this: when I look at the contents lists of magazines published in Wales currently, with a few exceptions, the names of contributors are unfamiliar. I have fallen into the generation gap. The Book of the Year event gives a chance to catch up and, in striving to do so, it is impossible to miss other differences, such as the high proportion of women poets and, to turn to the magazines again, the greatly increased number of writers and editors who are not

Welsh by birth or even upbringing, but have come to Wales in adulthood for employment, frequently in higher education. There is also a surprising amount of writing, from all over the world, in translation. Although the landscape is occasionally invoked, as in the poetry of Ann Cluysenaar, there is not much poetry that touches, however fleetingly, on things Welsh these days. The magazines and books may be published in Wales, but their outlook is international.

*PN Review* 206, Volume 38 Number 6,
July – August 2012.

# SAUNDERS LEWIS

*May 2012*


Saunders Lewis (1893-1985), 'generally regarded as the greatest figure in Welsh literature of the twentieth century', was born in Wallasey, just north of Birkenhead, across the Mersey from Liverpool. His ancestry was impeccably Nonconformist, both his father and maternal grandfather being notable Calvinistic Methodist ministers. He was educated at Liscard High School for Boys and Liverpool University, where he studied English and French. He interrupted his university studies to volunteer for the army in November 1914. A small, spare man, one of that minority of officers no taller than the other ranks they led, he was commissioned in a 'bantam' battalion of the south Wales Borderers. He saw action in France, and is described by a close friend, D.J. Williams (of whom more later), in the trenches at Loos reading a book by his favourite French author, Maurice Barrès. There was little enough time for reading and it was not a place for quiet contemplation. The conditions were often appalling. In January 1917 Lewis wrote to Margaret Gilcriest, a fellow student at Liverpool and his future wife, 'Nothing...of what I have seen before of trench warfare was at all like this. In the line we held we were in shell-holes waist-high in slime, without even the least semblance of a trench: dead men were as common as the living. They had died in all kinds of positions – numbers had merely drowned – until your attitude towards them became one of mingled tenderness and sympathy and humorous acceptance. One joked with them and often joined them.'

In April 1917 he was wounded (the following July his brother Ludwig was killed in action). After convalescence he was posted to the War Office in Athens and remained there until the Armistice in 1918. He returned to Liverpool University, took first-class honours in English and wrote a thesis on the English influences on classical Welsh poetry of the eighteenth century. In 1922 he was appointed to the Welsh department of University College Swansea. A safe and smooth academic career beckoned, but his was never the safe way.

Unlike a good many Welsh writers, Saunders Lewis was not a pacifist at heart, far less one who held a conscientious objection to fighting. D.J. Williams suggested that his love for France and French literature may have prompted his decision to join up and his reading of Barrès would have reinforced his instinctive commitment to patriotic causes. Through Barrès, he told Williams, 'I discovered Wales'. So it came about that, in war-torn France, with a French writer as his guide, he saw how he must dedicate himself to the service of Wales, its culture and traditions. He emerged from battle a convert to Welsh nationalism, and in 1932 a long journey from the faith of his home ended in his conversion to Roman Catholicism.

Experience on the Western Front, conversion to Catholicism, love of Wales – the combination recalls another English-born writer: David Jones (1895-1974). He and Saunders Lewis were almost coevals and, with such significant experiences in common, it is no wonder they became close. In his introduction to *Presenting Saunders Lewis* (edited by Alun R. Jones and Gwyn Thomas, UWP, 1973), Jones writes of Lewis as 'a personal friend…a very remarkable man indeed – the width and range of his abilities is astonishing, his ruthless expression of what he perceives to be true, or what he believes to be true, with regard to any given matter, seems to me one of his exhilarating qualities'. And there was also 'his width of appreciation of the arts of man, especially of Western man...his love of France and Italy, his ability to read Dante' and so on. Here was one, above all others, whom David Jones held in affection and respect. On his deathbed, in some mental turmoil over his last will and testament, it was to Saunders Lewis he turned for advice, which in the event was less than helpful (see *PN Review* 200). They were both influenced by the Catholic philosopher Jacques Maritain and saw their own principal concerns within the overarching tradition and continuity of the European Catholic Church.

Lewis was wonderfully gifted. In addition to English and Welsh, he had a deep knowledge of Latin, French and Italian literature, and was capable as no other of placing the hugely impressive contribution of Welsh writers of the fourteenth and fifteenth centuries in a European context. He was, at the same time, politically active, one of the founding members of Plaid Cymru in August 1925. In 1926 he became its president, a position he held until 1939.

His predecessor, the first president, was Lewis Valentine, a Baptist minister and pacifist, who had spent three years in the army as a non-combatant in the RAMC. D.J. (David John) Williams (1885-1970) was another of the founding members. He had come out of Rhydcymerau, deep in rural Carmarthenshire, to work as a collier in the Rhondda, before returning to education and taking degrees in English at Aberystwyth and Jesus College, Oxford, and becoming a teacher. These were friends who knew Saunders Lewis well and found him 'delightful, charming, loyal...warmly affectionate'. Others, Williams admitted, regarded him as 'a snob, a little aristocrat, stand-offish, hyper-highbrow, who would freeze you stiff with one glance of that pair of large and wonderful blue eyes of his. Naturally,' he went on, 'you cannot expect a man of his type to suffer fools gladly'. Others testified to the same qualities. To Emyr Humphreys, it seemed 'his dignity [was] often taken for aloofness', and short-story writer and dramatist Gareth Miles placed him among 'the most brilliant sons' of the Liverpool bourgeoisie, from which he inherited 'his energy, his fearlessness, his self-confidence, his arrogance, his uncompromising individuality'.

I am thinking of him now because of a nexus of significant anniversaries. In 1936, four hundred years after the first of the Acts of Union, which insisted that English was to be the language of law and administration in Wales and that only those who spoke English could hold public office (that is, about five per cent of the population at that time), Saunders Lewis, with D.J. Williams and Lewis Valentine, set fire to huts and building materials at Penyberth on the Llŷn peninsula, which were destined for the construction of an RAF bombing school. They immediately informed the local police of their action. In court at Caernarfon, Lewis argued on their behalf that Penyberth was a place of great significance in Welsh culture: 'Penyberth farmhouse...was one of the most historic in Llŷn. It was a resting place for the Welsh pilgrims to the Isle of Saints, Ynys Enlli, in the Middle Ages. It had associations with Owen Glyn Dŵr. It belonged to the story of Welsh literature. It was a thing of hallowed and secular majesty. It was taken down and utterly destroyed a week before we burnt in its fields the timbers of the vandals who destroyed it. And I claim that, if the moral law counts for anything, the people who ought to be in this dock are the people responsible for the destruction of Penyberth farmhouse.'

And that was only the beginning. They had acted, he said, because widespread protest against the selection of Penyberth for the bombing school had been ignored. Earlier proposals to site the development at Abbotsbury in Dorsetshire and Holy Island in Northumberland had been withdrawn because of campaigns against them in *The Times* and parliament. Despite interventions from the judge that these arguments were meaningless in law, he continued with an extraordinary outright attack on governments that assert 'they are above the moral law of God'. The jury failed to agree and the three were sent for trial to the Old Bailey, where they were found guilty and sentenced to nine months with hard labour.

Towards the end of 2011, a seminar at Swansea University commemorated an act of which the institution is now ashamed. It was the seventy-fifth anniversary of the sacking of Saunders Lewis from his post in the Welsh department, before the trial had ended. D.J. Williams returned to his school and Lewis Valentine to his ministry; Saunders Lewis alone was doubly punished for a symbolic act that has assumed monumental significance in the history of modern Wales. He found employment where he could, in farm work and teaching, and in journalism, before he returned to university teaching at Cardiff in 1952. As a journalist he was quickly acknowledged the foremost political voice in Welsh-language periodicals. His work was widely admired for its stylistic elegance as well as its trenchancy, and added to a reputation already gathered as dramatist, poet and literary critic.

Although he was not a prolific poet, any collection of the best Welsh poems of the twentieth century will certainly include examples of his work, and his historical and critical studies of Welsh literature, published in Welsh and English, had set standards in scholarship and analysis since the early 1920s. However, it is as a dramatist that he made his most important contribution. French drama from Corneille to Sartre is a major influence and his twenty-two plays include translations into Welsh of Molière's *Le Médecin malgré lui* and Beckett's *En attendant Godot*. His plays explore deeply serious themes in which moral values are tested and often involve characters in situations of conflict between public and private life. Twice in the 1970s he was nominated for the Nobel Prize for Literature. Had he won, which would have been well deserved and would have done wonders for Wales and the Welsh language, his acceptance speech would have been potent and memorable. It is too late now; he died in his ninety-second year in 1985.

There is yet another anniversary to remark. Fifty years ago, in February 1962, Saunders Lewis gave the BBC Wales Annual Lecture. His theme was *'Tynged yr Iaith'* ('The Fate of the Language') and he began by predicting the demise of the Welsh language by the year 2000. He charted the course of its decline from the Act of Union of 1536, focusing in particular on the anti-Welsh attitudes of the Victorian establishment, typified by remarks in the official report on the state of education in Wales (1847): 'Whether in the country or among the furnaces, the Welsh [i.e. Welsh-speaking] element is never found at the top of the scale...Equally in his new as in his old home, his language keeps him under the hatches, being one in which he can neither acquire nor communicate the necessary information. It is a language of old-fashioned agriculture, of theology and of simple rustic life, while all the world about him is English' (the same profound, smug ignorance is still about us today, as revealed by a comment in a recent restaurant review, of all things, in the *Guardian*, by John Lanchester, whom one might have hoped to be a little better informed, but let it pass). Lewis's analysis is conducted with a scalpel and without denunciation of the English, or even the Westminster government. His bitterness is reserved for the Welsh, who allowed themselves to be blinded to the value of what they uniquely held and its infinite capacity, as demonstrated by reinvented Hebrew, to adapt itself for all purposes and innovations.

*'Tynged yr Iaith'* galvanised the youth of Wales, mainly of course Welsh-speaking youth, but many more who, though their

command of the language was imperfect, were vitally concerned for its continued existence. Cymdeithas yr Iaith (the Welsh Language Society) was formed as a direct consequence of the lecture. The movement's fiftieth anniversary will follow in August this year, and it has every right to a grand celebration. Among other things, its campaigns have brought us bilingual road signs (probably the highest profile change to outsiders), bilingual signage of all sorts, everywhere, and bilingual official notices and documents. Welsh-medium schools have been established in every part of Wales and Welsh has a place in the curriculum in all schools. We have broadcasting in Welsh on radio and on television (S4C), and Welsh has official status following the passing of the Welsh Language Act 2010 at the National Assembly in Cardiff.

The devolution of powers to Wales would almost certainly not have occurred when it did, following the 1997 referendum, if at all, without the thrust of Cymdeithas activists over the previous thirty-five years, which brought a consciousness of Wales as a political entity into popular culture. And all is ultimately owed to Saunders Lewis. I count myself fortunate to have seen him on a few occasions (that is, simply to have been in the same room as him), because no other individual has had so great an influence on the shaping of contemporary Wales.

*PN Review* 205, Volume 38 Number 5, May – June 2012.

# GWYNETH LEWIS

*January 2012*

Little more than a week ago, a piece by Gwyneth Lewis appeared in the *Guardian*. Readers of this magazine, knowing her a poet of formidable intellect, who draws on contemporary science and technology thematically and metaphorically in a way that prompts comparison with the Metaphysical poets of that other great age of discoveries, might be surprised at her subject. She wrote about rugby, though distinctively, in a way recognisably her own. What other rugby writer would see in the progress of Wales in the World Cup 'the model of a mind'? 'As Welsh supporters watch the match,' she explains, 'mirror neurons in their brains will be in a high state of arousal. These are the cells that fire both when we perform an action and when we observe it. This may be a physical description of empathy. When the Welsh team plays...with its characteristic combination of close teamwork and flair, these qualities will be rehearsed in the temperament of the nation they represent'. This is a passage that would not be out of place in a book by Oliver Sacks.

Lately we have seen discussion of the relative paucity of novels and stories in which rugby union football plays a significant part. The outstanding exception is Roland Mathias's wonderful short story 'Match', which has it all: an account of a (real) schoolboy game that is as acutely observed as only a dedicated player could make it, poetic description and psychological truth. Apart from episodes in novels such as *Times Like These* by Gwyn Jones, I can think of no other fiction worth mentioning (rugby league has, of course, David Storey's *This Sporting Life*). There are well written memoirs by rugby union players, notably John Daniell's *Confessions of a Rugby Mercenary*, and well written histories of the game, the best of which, by a distance, is *Fields of Praise*, the official history of the Welsh Rugby Union, by Gareth Williams and my old friend Dai Smith, professional historians both, with a fine turn of phrase and a secure consciousness of the social context of the game in Wales. Living in Wales, you will, however, hear an enormous volume of well informed, insightful and frequently amusing talk about games and personalities, anecdotes in profusion, some of them true. Discussion of the finer points of play is, I was going to say, a national pastime, but really the phenomenon is largely confined to the old industrial south of the country, where village teams were an expression of community spirit, a controlled and benign hangover of tribalism from the remote past, as those who, like me, remember with painful nostalgia the Christmas 'local derby' encounters between Gilfach Goch and Tonyrefail will agree.

Part of Gwyneth Lewis's argument is that the 'strong communitarian flavour of Welsh life...found an outlet in our national sport, both on and off the field', and the historians also conclude that, to us, rugby has long been more than a game. It is said that success on the field has been a valve to release the pressure of discontent, and provided 'compensation for economic and social deprivation'. If this is so, politically we have not asked for much. Nevertheless, perhaps she is right to claim that in the decade since the devolution of powers to a National Assembly in Cardiff Bay 'the drive to excellence has been finally decoupled from a lack of self-determination'.

The *Guardian* piece appeared on the day of the World Cup semi-final between Wales and France. We saw the game unfold at breakfast in the comfort of our home, thanks to television. Travelling support coloured the match venue, Eden Park in Auckland, with great patches of red and blue. By 9am well over

60,000 – a crowd larger than that filling Eden Park – had gathered at the Millennium Stadium in Cardiff to watch the match on a giant screen, and many more thousands were packed into clubs and bars all over Wales for the telecast. Having seen the British and Irish Lions well beaten by the All Blacks at Eden Park in 2005, and Wales play Fiji in Nantes at the 2007 World Cup, I know a good deal about hope and anticipation where rugby is concerned, and the despondency that descends upon supporters of the losing side. We saw grown men weep coming from the stadium in Nantes. On that occasion Wales had been expected to win and, thrilling as the match was, the defeat felt catastrophic: as ever, the higher the expectation, the bitterer the blow. So it was on that day a little more than a week ago.

'The biggest game in Welsh rugby's 130-year history': Gwyneth Lewis was at one with sports journalists in that estimate. Those of us who saw Wales beat New Zealand for the third (and last) time in 1953 might debate the point, but only academically. This is the era of the World Cup, global audiences and International Rugby Board rankings. As with the Olympics and Association Football ('that round ball game' as Ned Gribble, rugby master at Tonyrefail GS, disparagingly labelled it), the opportunity to excel comes once every four years, and the intensity of competition increases with each quadrennium. Having beaten Ireland in some style to gain a place in the semi-final, Wales became the focus of media attention as never before, even from the metropolitan press, which usually can barely raise a pen to mention any team other than England. And France, our opponents, appeared peculiarly out of sorts. A New Zealand-Wales final was widely expected.

'The fair breeze blew, the white foam flew,/The furrow followed free': there are times in life when you are sailing along so smoothly you hold your breath waiting for the inevitable something to go wrong. I am sure I was not the only remote spectator to feel a sense of impending doom that Saturday morning. And of course it descended with the sending off of the Welsh captain, Sam Warburton, for what is now termed a 'tip tackle', and the withdrawal through injury of Adam Jones, keystone of the pack. Wales fought on with fourteen players against a French team curiously devoid of ideas beyond resolute defence, and lost by a single point. Being brave in defeat was once considered a virtue; now it is of no account. Winning is all. I fear the poetry has gone.

Gwyneth Lewis, equally and brilliantly creative in Welsh and English, became our first National Poet in 2005, principally as a writer in English. As the post alternates linguistically, she was followed by Gwyn Thomas, a leading poet in the Welsh language. And, since taking over the role in 2009, Gillian Clarke has been a splendid ambassador as, thanks to her indefatigable industry and fervour for the cause, many of us have witnessed. The first Bard Plant Cymru (Children's Poet for Wales), appointed specifically to encourage reading and writing in Welsh, was named twelve years ago, and the latest incumbent, Eurig Salisbury, was announced at the Urdd Eisteddfod last June. Just a few days after the failure of our rugby team to reach the final of the World Cup, I saw Catherine Fisher formally announced as the first Young People's Laureate, at an event held at the Literature Lounge in St David's Centre, Cardiff. We now have a triumvirate of laureates with active roles in promoting reading and writing and literature generally.

St David's is a vast arcade of shops and, in the quarter where the Literature Lounge is situated, restaurants. This is bringing literature into the market place and the media age. Thousands walk by daily, and the Literature Lounge is there with comfortable seating, coffee and a book exchange to tempt people in, and regular events to create a stir. How was it possible to initiate an attractive cultural zone in a highly desirable precinct when those arts organisations that have survived exist on a knife's edge and public libraries are being closed? John Pikoulis, joint chairman of Literature Wales, explained that the centre's management had been persuaded that a busy space (albeit non-retail) is preferable to a vacant shop, and gave it free for a limited period. Wine and soft drinks were available on the evening and canapés came gratis from the Italian restaurant across the arcade. Nor was this all. Copies of Catherine Fisher's books had been donated by Hodder, her publisher, for distribution to young people, who came in large numbers.

It was a highly successful event. Charlotte Church, once 'the voice of an angel' and now singer, TV presenter and media celebrity, was there to say how much reading and creative writing have meant to her, and emphasise how important it is for mothers to read to young children daily, as she does. The 'Writing Squads', organised by Literature Wales in conjunction with local authorities throughout the country, were represented by a teenager from Merthyr who said how much it means to have workshops with 'real' writers, even, on occasion, Gillian Clarke and Robert Minhinnick. The new laureate spoke of books, such as *Alice in Wonderland*, which caught her imagination as a child and began a passionate interest in reading and, later, writing stories. Having first attracted critical attention as a poet with *Immrama* (1988), *The Unexplored Ocean* (1994) and *Altered States* (1999), all published by Seren, Catherine Fisher has established herself as a highly successful writer of fiction for young people. *Incarceron*, the latest of more than twenty fantasy novels, was named *The Times* Children's Book of the Year and entered the *New York Times* bestseller list. Born, brought up and educated in Newport, she is already a star in the local firmament and beyond the mere threshold of an international reputation. There could hardly have been a better choice for the role she has taken on. As I left she was being interviewed by a group of young readers. The Young People's Laureate has a busy time ahead.

*PN Review* 203, Volume 38 Number 3,
January – February 2012.

# DAVID JONES

*June 2011*

H.S. ('Jim') Ede created Kettle's Yard, a lovely home and haven from the busy streets of Cambridge, in his own impeccably aesthetic image. Among its art objects are several important paintings by David Jones. Jones, the author of *In Parenthesis* (see review, *PN Review* 197) was a decidedly untypical modernist artist, while Ede was a curator at the Tate and discriminating art lover. He was one of the network of 'friends in need', on whom Jones came to rely for psychological and financial support. They had much in common. Born in the same year, 1895, both served on the Western Front in the First World War, albeit as officer (Ede) and eternal private (Jones); both were wounded in action, and enrolled at London art schools when demobbed in 1919. Jones, whose father was Welsh, became fixated on Wales; Ede, cosmopolitan in taste, was born there. They became close friends in the early 1920s, about the same time that Ede and his wife Helen became friendly with Ben and Winifred Nicholson and Christopher Wood, who, like Jones, were members of the Seven and Five Society of artists.

Jones had already joined the commune of artists and craftsmen at Ditchling, Sussex, presided over by Eric Gill, a fellow convert to Roman Catholicism and, when the Gill entourage removed to Capel-y-ffin, in the Black Mountains, near Abergavenny, he became friendly with a young Irishman, René Hague, who fell in with the group there. Jones had something in common with Hague, too, for he was engaged (although it didn't last) to Gill's daughter, Petra, while Hague later married another daughter, Joan. We have Hague's testimony, in *Dai*

*Greatcoat: A Self-portrait of David Jones in his Letters* (Faber, 1980), that in 1930-33, 'for a good deal of time' Jones lived with him and Joan in a small cottage at Pigotts, the Gill home near High Wycombe, Buckinghamshire. They knew one another very well, and exchanged letters for more than fifty years. Hague's book contains a selection of these letters along with some from Jones's correspondence with other friends, among them Jim Ede.

In recent months I have accompanied my wife as she gathered material for a project on David Jones as watercolour artist. The quest has taken us to the Jones archives at Kettle's Yard and the National Library of Wales. We have had a remarkable experience. It needs to be understood at the outset that the letters of David Jones were not business-like and brief. Many run to hundreds, even thousands, of words, written on plain foolscap sheets. The text tends to meander more or less diagonally down the page, leaving large irregular spaces on either side, which are often occupied by sentences or paragraphs written parallel to the edge of the page, and sometimes by illustrative sketches. This eccentric epistolary habit is itself beguiling, but the letters have more than charm to offer; they are vehicles for reporting discoveries and sorting out issues arising from work in hand, and of course for exchanging news with understanding friends. Those to René Hague in particular are often delightfully merry with colloquial expressions picked up from the common soldiery, with which Jones identified. There are hundreds of letters, by no means all of them in public collections. At a conservative guess Jones's output in this form exceeds a million words.

No commentary on Jones's life and work can ignore the severe breakdowns he suffered in 1933 and 1946, because they cost him years of creativity as writer and artist. It is hard to avoid speculating upon what might have triggered these devastating events. The obvious cause was shell-shock, delayed perhaps, but still full-blown post-traumatic stress disorder of the sort that, sadly, we hear of increasingly. Yet, in *Dai Greatcoat*, Hague takes pains to deny this: 'It has often been said that David's breakdown in 1933 was caused by his war experiences. For my own part, I believe this to be completely untrue. David enjoyed the war.' And in the introduction to the book, Hague writes that 'his four years in the army, the months in the trenches and the bloody battle of [Mametz] Wood, left him spiritually and psychologically unscarred and even invigorated'. The evidence of army slang and 'bad language' in the very familiar, light-hearted letters he wrote to Hague might be thought to support that view.

But, if the cause did not lie in appalling conditions on the Western Front – then where? There was to begin with the potential for fearful inner conflict in the great and growing contrast between his interior world, stuffed with knowledge (self-acquired) of Catholic liturgy and psalms, classical and Welsh history and Arthurian Romance, and the mechanised 'world of steel' outside the door. Hague suggests his neurosis arose out of 'the difficulties he met in his work', the struggle of 'wedding form to content', and then enlarging the content to include 'every sort of allusion, belief, tradition, hope, love'. This was, indeed, a tall order. Then the note Jones wrote for Dr Stevenson, who treated him during his 1947 breakdown, shows (not unexpectedly) that a previous nerve specialist had explored with him the possibility of an underlying sexual cause – 'my fears etc. with regard to sex' – which he dismissed, while defending his celibacy 'in order to pursue...a greater good' – his artistic vocation.

There were three loves in his life, whom René Hague refers to as his 'cult figures'. The first, and (according to Hague) 'most beautiful' was Petra, second daughter of Eric and Mary Gill. They became engaged in 1924, but by 1927 the engagement was off and Petra later married Denis Tegetmeier, another of Gill's followers. There are not many references to her in *Dai Greatcoat*, but those that are there are still warmly affectionate. At the end of a letter to Hague written in 1934 he adds 'My love to my dear Petra'. In 1929 Jones met Lady Prudence Pelham, daughter of the earl of Chichester, who had commissioned Gill to design a memorial stone for her father and her elder brother, both of whom had died recently. She wrote to Jones and visited him frequently at his various addresses from 1935. Hague says this was 'the most important relationship in David's life', and there is evidence in the letters of the depth of his feelings for her: 'I love her very very much and our friendship has meant everything to me'. When he thought of her it was as 'sweet high bright Prudence'. They shared artistic and literary interests and, like other close friends, she helped with domestic chores. The book she sent as a Christmas gift in 1946 has the dedication: 'Dai, with love from Prudence. Shall I mend your other sleeve or have you done it yourself?' They also shared a common affliction, 'all my kind of neurasthenic stuff' as Jones put it. The death of her husband, Guy Branch, an RAF pilot, in 1940, clearly didn't help and she struggled with this unidentified nervous disorder. Prudence, who subsequently found another loving partner in Robert Buhler, died in 1952 of multiple sclerosis.

Chance or fate, he couldn't determine which, brought a third muse into Jones's life in 1958, when Valerie Price, a young woman from Cwmllynfell in the Swansea Valley, wrote to the correspondence column of *The Times* on the decline of the Welsh language and the failure of government action to arrest it. In the weeks that followed her views were opposed by David Llewellyn, MP for Cardiff North, but a scion of Monmouthshire landed gentry, and Lord Raglan, from the same Welsh borderland, and supported by the Bishop of Bangor, and David Jones. In the first of his letters (11 June 1958), reprinted in *Epoch & Artist* (Faber, 1959), Jones argues that the loss of Welsh would impoverish England, 'for the survival of something which has an unbroken tradition in this island since the sixth century, and which embodies deposits far older still, cannot be regarded as a matter of indifference by any person claiming to care for the things of this island. It is by no means a matter for the Welsh only, but concerns all, because the complex and involved heritage of Britain is a shared inheritance which can, in very devious ways, enrich us all'. On 22 August, he added 'even to understand [the place of Welsh] in history and its mythus, is something. I should have thought that ordinary *pietas* asked that much. Especially considering how very bleak is the prospect of that tradition in face of the civilizational pressures of our present-day technocracy. Miss Valerie Price is to be greatly thanked for the historical awareness and cogency of her letter...'

We went to see Valerie Wynn Williams, the former Miss Price, at her home in north Wales. She told us she had initially gone to London to train as a physiotherapist and had become involved in raising funds for the magazine *Wales*. Keidrych Rhys, its editor, seeing journalistic potential in the *Times* correspondence, invited Lord Raglan to expand his views in the magazine and was no doubt delighted that the resulting piece was controversially anti-Welsh. He also suggested that David Jones might be invited to a Plaid Cymru party Valerie was organising in her flat. Jones declined, instead inviting her to visit him at Northwick Lodge, Harrow. She was a very attractive twenty-four-year-old and, although at that first meeting she was accompanied by her boyfriend, Michael Wynn Williams, whom she later married, it seems likely that Jones fell for her at once. He was sixty-three, but the sight of her leaping up the stairs 'like a gazelle' (with a nod to Yeats perhaps) revived his belief 'in the reality of "Romantic Love"'.

At his invitation she went again and again to take tea with him and talk deep into the evening, when, at last, he would put on the famous greatcoat and escort her to the tube. We gain an insight into the inspiration of her presence and how it affected his ability to work from a letter written to Hague in April 1960, when he felt he had lost it: 'Can't get on at all with my picture [Tristan and Iseult]. Feel quite exhausted with the complications of it. What a long time ago it is when I did the bloody things about 20 times more quickly – but they will never return. Last year when I was seeing Elri (that's the Welsh form of Valerie) I felt quite young again...' For her marriage to Michael in 1959 he had designed the cover of the order of service and he made an exquisite inscription for the couple as a wedding gift, but inwardly he was torn. In a letter (27 June 1959) to his old friend Harman Grisewood, he confessed 'my feelings are...of exceptional confusion' and that he was 'surprised at the *intensity* and *ubiquitousness* of the distress', because he had, as it were, lost her. In the same letter to Grisewood, while admitting that he half expected her to marry 'this bloke' and denying that he ever 'wished for marriage in itself, *very far from it*', he writes, 'I know that an involvement in "Welshness" has an awful lot to do with my intrication with Elri... She's the only Welsh woman I've met really'. She was furthermore a Welsh-speaker (which meant a great deal to Jones) and, as an active member of Plaid Cymru, introduced him to fellow Welsh Nationalists. As one consequence of this, David Jones joined the group that attended the House of Commons to argue for a Welsh TV channel. But his 'involvement in Welshness' began long before the infatuation with 'Elri'. At Kettle's Yard we found autobiographical notes written for Jim Ede in September 1935, in which Jones writes of the influence of his mother, who 'drew extremely well' and of his father, 'singing a Welsh song', with the comment 'and as long as I can remember I have cherished, through him, a sense of belonging to the Welsh people'.

David Jones and Valerie remained close friends. In March 1964, he reported to René Hague (with evident pride) that he had come across a copy of the Welsh edition of the *Radio Times* with a photograph of Valerie, who had appeared in a Welsh-language television play, and a brief note of her career, which he painstakingly translated, retaining the Welsh word order: 'Girl versatile is V.P. who plays the part of Tessa...Nurtured (was) she in Cwmllynfell and among other things has been a physiotherapist, a (school) teacher, a model and champion hurdler of Wales'. She was more than that. One of her programmes as a Welsh-language ITV producer was on David Jones.

At our meeting a few weeks ago, she told us that when David was seriously ill in 1974, she arranged at his request for Ben Jones, a barrister and Nationalist politician, to visit the Calvary Nursing Home in order to help him make a will. He wished to leave all the paintings and manuscripts still in his possession to the National Museum and National Library of Wales, and to make a bequest to Cymdeithas yr Iaith, the Welsh Language Society, then campaigning vigorously for Welsh-language broadcasting services on TV and radio. The barrister suggested that the latter was unwise and Valerie was sent to telephone Saunders Lewis, an old friend of David's, and arguably the greatest figure in Welsh politics and literature in the twentieth century, the instigator of Cymdeithas, to ask his advice. By the time Valerie returned with the reply, 'He must do as he wishes', David was too tired to continue. Making the will was postponed. Within the week, David Jones died, intestate, and Wales lost a gift of inestimable value.

*PN Review* 200, Volume 37 Number 6,
June – July 2011.

# JOHN AUBREY

*February 2011*

I have discovered a connection with John Aubrey, whose *Brief Lives* are a constant delight. I had dipped into the book often enough before, but, newly conscious of a link so faint as to be invisible to all but me, I have just read the whole with some care. Aubrey was careful in matters of lineage so I had better admit at the outset that we have no shared ancestry.

As a convinced astrologer he was also conscientious about the date and time of births, wherever the information was available. His mostly third-person autobiographical notes tell us he was born 'about sunriseing' on his father's estate at Easton Pierse, Wiltshire, 12 March 1626. The date and time were astrologically inauspicious, for he was thus condemned to labour 'under a crowd of ill directions'. We can be easily reconciled to that since, if he had not been so fated, whatever else he might have accomplished as antiquary, proto-archaeologist and 'natural philosopher', we would not have had his potted biographies of characters from the times of the first Elizabeth to the second Charles. An 'ingeniose youth', he became competent in Latin and Greek in his schooldays, and spent his best years at Trinity College, Oxford and Lincoln's Inn, interrupted as they were by Civil War and smallpox, which he caught at Oxford. As the eldest of three sons he inherited his father's encumbered property in 1652 and was immediately involved in lawsuits.

A major source of the family wealth, which was dissipating during his father's lifetime and entirely lost in his, was his great-grandfather, William Aubrey, Doctor of Laws. Born at Cantref,

Breconshire about 1529, he came out of Wales to serve as lawyer and statesman to Queen Elizabeth, who 'loved him and was wont to call him "her little doctor"'. His way to court may have been smoothed by a kinsman, the earl of Pembroke ('the Welsh men are all kinne', Aubrey observes parenthetically), although it is *not* William, the first earl, who may have been active on William Aubrey's behalf, as his biographer confusedly suggests, but Henry, the second earl. William Aubrey hardly needed a push, having already become Fellow of All Souls and Jesus and Principal of New Inn Hall. His involvement, from about 1555 until his death in 1595, in important cases in ecclesiastical, international, constitutional and maritime law, and special commissions at home and abroad, was gained entirely by his own merit. He repurchased his ancestral home in Breconshire, built a 'great house' with views over the river Usk, and increased the family estate to the extent that he 'could ride nine miles together in his owne land'. He was worth '2500 *li.* per annum', but proved less successful as a judge of character than as judge advocate. The man he chose as his chief clerk and executor turned out a fraud, who cheated the legatees, including Aubrey's grandfather, of their inheritance.

The estate was entailed. Although a lowly eighteenth in the entail, disregarding his stars, Aubrey began a lawsuit in Brecon, 'which cost me 1200 *li.*' Marriage to a wealthy woman appeared a promising solution, but it was Aubrey's fate to become engaged to a litigious termagant, who ultimately ruined him. He spent his life thereafter avoiding creditors and arrest, never in employment, a peripatetic guest at the mostly rather grand houses of relatives and friends. He must have been remarkably good company, for they never let him down.

His Welsh kin were among those whose hospitality he enjoyed. From them he acquired some knowledge of the language and antiquities of Wales. A cousin living in Llanelly, Breconshire (not the former industrial town of the same name in south-west Wales), he terms '*Penkenol, i.e.* chiefe of the family', which, for a Wiltshire man, is a reasonable attempt at '*pencenedl*'. Similarly, an account of the ancestry of another branch of the powerful Herbert clan (to which the earls of Pembroke belong) includes a Welsh verse presented in an eccentric 'phonetic' script: '*Ô gway vinney (dhyw) râg wilidh/Vôd vinhad yn velinidh*' and so on. It is clear the lines were not copied from a text, which probably would have read '*O gwae finnau (Dduw) rhag cywilydd/Fod fy nhad yn felinydd.*' Aubrey's translation of these two lines is passable, but more precisely they say 'Woe is me, God, for shame/That my father is a miller.' It is, perhaps, a surprise to conclude that he must have learned the verse aurally. By his own account, as a young man, 'Much of his time [was] spent in journeying to south Wales (entaile) and Herefordshire.' In addition to a continuing interest in his Welsh roots, he could hardly have avoided some familiarity with the everyday language of virtually the whole of Wales in the seventeenth century (as well as anciently Welsh parts of Herefordshire).

At much the same time Aubrey was looking to another Welsh connection to improve his lot – 'I expect preferment through Sir Ll. Jenkins.' That his expectation came to nothing did not leave him embittered, as we see from his portrait of Sir Leoline Jenkins, one of the most generous of the *Lives*, which begins: 'Sir Lleuellin Jenkins, knight, was borne at Llantrithid in the countie of Glamorgan. His father (whom I knew) was a good plaine countrey-man, a copyholder of Sir John Aubrey, knight and baronet (eldest son of Sir Thomas), whose mannour it is.' After an Oxford education Jenkins returned to Llantrithyd as tutor to Sir John Aubrey's son and, for companionship, several other boys from gentry families nearby. His 'vertue and assiduity' in all he undertook were noted and on the restoration of the monarchy, Sir John recommended him to the king, in whose service he rose to the rank of Principal Secretary of State. 'He haz a strong body for study,' Aubrey observes, 'indefatigable, temperate and virtuous. God blesse him.'

Llantrithyd, a modern spelling, is mentioned elsewhere in the *Lives*. Writing of himself again, Aubrey tells us, 'He began to enter into pocket memorandum bookes philosophicall and antiquarian remarques, Anno Domini 1654, at Llantrithid.' He notes that Archbishop Usher of Armagh, celebrated for his dating of Creation in 4004 BC, was also at Llantrithid 'for severall moneths, and divertised himselfe much to talke with the poore people to understand Welsh'.

Sir Thomas Aubrey, second son of the Elizabethan Doctor of Laws, acquired Llantrithyd Place, a Tudor manor house in the Vale of Glamorgan, by marriage in 1586. Thereafter the property passed to Sir Thomas's second son, Sir John, a staunch royalist, created baronet on the Restoration in 1660, whose son, also Sir John Aubrey, second baronet (c.1650-1700) took as his second wife the heiress of William Lewis of the Van, Glamorgan and Boarstall, Buckinghamshire, thus considerably extending the Aubrey estates.

Several other Sir Johns inherited the title, but when Aubrey visited Llantrithyd in the second half of the seventeenth century, house and land were possessed by the royalist second baronet. It was probably the heyday of the property, before the acquisition of the estates in Buckinghamshire divided the attention of subsequent heirs. Eventually Boarstall replaced Llantrithyd as the family seat. Early nineteenth-century sketches suggest the scale and magnificence of the Tudor residence, built around a courtyard open to the west, with deer park, ornamental fishponds and terraced gardens, but it was then already abandoned, in a state of dilapidation. Today it is roofless, a ruined shell.

What has all this to do with me? One of the sketches mentioned above shows to the east of the great house, very close, Llantrithyd church, a benefice in the gift of the Aubreys. I have before me a copy of a document dated 27 March 1790 in which Margaret Aubrey, half-sister of Sir John and Sir Thomas (the fourth and fifth baronets) and by this time principal leaseholder of the 7000 acre Vale estate, presents to the Bishop of Llandaff 'my beloved in Christ George Williams Clerk humbly praying that your Lordship would be graciously pleased to admit and canonically to institute him...to the Rectory and Parish Church of Llantrithyd'. George Williams was my three times great-grandfather, and the stars had been kind to him. On 31 January 1786, his father, also George Williams, Vicar of Penlline, had informed the same Bishop that he had appointed him curate at his church, promising to pay him 'the yearly sum of twenty pounds for his maintenance'.

George Williams was not a university graduate or otherwise particularly well qualified: why, then, was he preferred to the rectory? During the brief four years that he had been a clerk in holy orders he had also served as curate in the church at Ystradowen, a hamlet only a short distance from Llantrithyd, where Margaret Aubrey's nephew, Richard Aubrey, lived at Ash Hall, another grand, elegant house. Here I must speculate a little: Richard, his family and household servants doubtless attended Ystradowen church, and in this way the curate met Sarah Jones, who seems to have been nanny or governess to Richard's daughter. Acquaintance, we assume, led to friendship and tender emotions and so to a proposal of marriage. Sarah was in her late twenties, somewhat older than George, perhaps her last chance, and the Aubreys blessed the relationship. They married in 1789 and soon after moved into the rectory, a fine sixteenth-century building. I am a descendant of their firstborn, a son they named Bloom – but that is another story.

I owe my existence to the Aubrey family of Llantrithyd. Though to be sure he had other influential friends who gave him bed, board and protection, John Aubrey may well have owed them not much less. His affection for Wales gleams here and there through the *Lives*: William Aubrey, Doctor of Laws and his learned kinsman John Dee; the poet Henry Vaughan and his twin, Thomas, also kin (their 'coxcombe' father notwithstanding) and Edmund Gunter, the mathematician, like them of Breconshire; Sir Leoline (or Llewelyn) Jenkins; Walter Rumsey of Llanover, one of his lawyers in lawsuits in Wales; captain Robert Pugh, an 'honoured friend' who died in Newgate; Vavasour Powell, 'allyed to most of the best families in north Wales'; David Jenkins, of Hensol in the Vale, imprisoned eleven years 'for his loyalty...the only man that never complied... always excepted by parliament in the first rank of delinquents'; Owen Glendower, who 'dyed obscurely (I know where)'; William Cecil, Lord Burghley, whose 'true name is *Sitsilt*... an ancient Monmouthshire family...'Tis strange that they should be so vaine to leave off an old British [i.e. Welsh] name for a Romancy one'; Sir Thomas Morgan, the diminutive giant in battle 'of meane parentage in Monmouthshire [who] seek't his fortune (as a soldier) in Saxon Weymar [and] spoke Welch, English, High Dutch, and Lowe Dutch, but never a one well'. Not all of the Welsh portraits are uncritical, but they clearly include some personal heroes.

In his life of the historian William Camden, Aubrey writes, 'Mr Camden much studied the Welsh language, and kept a Welsh servant to improve him in that language, for the better understanding of our antiquities.' '*Our* antiquities' – is he thinking of himself as Welsh? Possibly. There is a bigger question, which would startle Aubrey, who thought inclusively about such matters: when since Camden has an English historian taken such pains? I wonder how Simon Schama or David Starkey would answer.

*PN Review* 198, Volume 37 Number 4, February – March 2011.

# FFRANSIS PAYNE
*January 2011*


Long ago, during my years as HMI, I was for a time district inspector in Powys. Extending along much of the border with England, Powys has the greatest land area of all Welsh counties, and is sparsely populated. Most people live in small towns and scattered villages and hamlets. Newtown, birthplace of Robert Owen (1771–1858), the social reformer, and Geraint Goodwin (1903–41), the novelist and short story writer, and the largest town, has a population of fewer than 13,000.

I had then an enviable job; liaising with the smallest local education authority in Wales and visiting its schools was pleasant enough, but the freedom to travel the county was much more. There were twelve secondary schools and some 115 primary schools, and visiting them invariably involved driving along roads made for contemplative plodding not speed. In the old days, I was told by A.G. Prys-Jones, a retired colleague who was a considerable poet and survived into his nineties, HMI would have travelled by train to a convenient station (decades before Beeching) where a pony and trap would be waiting that would carry them along narrow country lanes between verdant and blossoming banks and hedgerows to small, remote schools. One-horse-power travel meant there was time to look about and appreciate the landscape. Driving, I covered the distances between schools in a fraction of the time, usually with a fraction of the pleasure HMI of the past had enjoyed.

There were occasions when I could not forbear stopping. One winter's day, crossing the Epynt, a mountain the military use as a firing range, I hit a patch of ice and the car spun a complete circle so that I was facing the way I had come. I got out and stood beside the car shakily; and looked over the great expanse of frost-crusted moor under the spell of a most extraordinary silence. Nothing moved; not a breath, the army's red warning flag hung limp, and I got back into the car, turned it warily to face the right direction and drove on, slowly. More often it was spring or summer when for a few minutes I would be distracted from my official duties by experiences almost visionary. I recall once, while driving east from Llandrindod Wells along the A488 via Bleddfa and Whitton towards Presteigne, it was no more than the movement of the wind through tall grass that made me stop: an unfenced quiet road about twelve hundred feet up, wind fretting the grasses, high white clouds and two buzzards circling – all apparently just for me. 'Powys Paradwys Cymru' (Powys the Paradise of Wales) is an ancient descriptor that still holds.

Powys is named after the post-Roman kingdom of Powys, which roughly occupied the same area, plus a wide swathe of what is now the west Midlands of England. The modern county, following Local Government Reorganisation in 1974, merged old Breconshire, Radnorshire and Montgomeryshire. Shortly after I took up the district inspector role, a senior colleague urged me to read *Crwydro Sir Faesyfed* by Ffransis Payne. The title means 'Wandering [in] Radnorshire' and it was a well-intended suggestion. I read Welsh slowly so that it would have taken a little effort and time to tackle the book. I had the excuse then of busyness and, to my shame, postponed the attempt long enough to forget his urgent prompting. He was right of course; no matter how long it took to read, the book would have done me a power of good. Now, however, it is available to all English readers in a translation published as 'Exploring Radnorshire' in *The Transactions of the Radnorshire Society*, volume LXXVIII,

2008. *TRS* is co-edited by Peter J. Conradi, whose *At the Bright Hem of God* (2009 – see *PN Review* 190) might be viewed as continuing the theme of intense, rather melancholy, appraisal of the fragile beauties of Radnorshire begun by Ffransis Payne.

Payne was born in 1900 at Kington, just across the border in Herefordshire, where his father, a Glamorgan man, was farming. He was not brought up Welsh-speaking and only later became aware of his *bro*, his home patch, as an area from which Welsh had receded, though, in his judgement, not as fully or as long ago as English scholarship alleged. One of his themes is the tenacity of the language into the late nineteenth century and its capacity for revival in the twentieth, albeit on a small scale, in isolated spots along the border. Writing in the 1960s, he sees the southern March as part of Wales's history, where 'the overwhelming majority [of inhabitants are] Welsh by blood, although they do not know it, or wish to know it any more'. Travelling in Herefordshire he likens to 'a journey through the most beautiful graveyard of the Welsh nation'. The list of Herefordshire place names that are Welsh tells its own story.

At fifteen, Payne left school in Kington to seek employment in the heavy industries of the south Wales coalfield, and he was briefly an RAF wireless operator in the First World War before returning to his agricultural roots at a time when a good deal of farming practice was still in touch with centuries-old traditions. He learned Welsh and, when he began writing about rural folk culture, it was this lately acquired language that he turned to. In 1941 he became an unusually mature graduate of University College, Cardiff. Several years earlier, via librarianship, he had discovered his métier – the museum service, in which he eventually became head of the Department of Material Culture at what is now known as the National History Museum, at St Fagans, near Cardiff.

The guiding principle of Payne's thought and writing is his

sense of 'the unity of history and literature and locality'. This is very reminiscent of the major impulse underlying so much of Roland Mathias's poetry. Neither can take in a view without a sharp consciousness of the layers of human endeavour on which the present is built. And because the poet was a Breconshire man, it is not surprising that from time to time they write about the same scene and the same people – Sarnesfield church and the tomb of John Abel, Gladestry Court and Sir Gelli Meurig, Castell Maes-llwch and Maesyronnen Chapel. Medieval manors, most in various stages of ruin, which were the homes of the *uchelwyr* (literally 'high men') are another of Payne's special interests, and with these hall-houses, the histories of the families that owned them, and the praise poems of wandering poets who existed by their patronage. His own researches uncovered more than forty poets who had sung their way around Radnorshire between 1400 and 1600 and a number of their poems are included in the book, in the original Welsh, with translations.

He is, as one might expect, a Kilvert enthusiast. 'I must have seen,' he writes, 'as unremarkable middle-aged women, some of the little lively, red-cheeked, black-eyed girls who pierced his heart so much. But I only know them in his diary. Know them, too, as you know rural people in the pictures of old Breughel and his peers, people caught by the unsparing but affectionate eye of an artist.' He is of course expressing his closeness to Kilvert in time; he does not have the diarist's particular predilection for young girls. But he is like Kilvert in his simple love of rural folk and old rural places and pastimes, and in the elegance of his expression of that love. He celebrates the village of Weobley, for example, with its 'beautiful magpie-coloured street', and notes how 'untidy and clumsy' a startled heron appears 'as it hung for a moment above the water flapping like a shirt on a clothes line'. Above all he conveys a sense of the exquisite simplicity that is so easily missed (and as easily destroyed): 'There is little here, and that little is perfect. The green meadow under the hill, the church in it as bare as an anchorite's cell, its old stones and woodwork, and the limewash on it as bright as the river. And the arch of the bridge looking from the river like a young moon.'

Payne has a wealth of stories, many of them historical, like that of Tomas ap Rhosier, who fell at the Battle of Banbury in 1469, and who owned *Llyfr Coch Hergest*, the famous 'Red Book', which contains the manuscript of 'The Mabinogion'. The tale of a ghostly black dog that in later times haunted the rooms of the fortified mansion of Hergest may well have inspired Conan Doyle's hound, as the family name of the Baskervilles, four miles away at Clyro Court, certainly gifted him the rest of the title of his story. Among memorable encounters with people, we have Payne's recollection of Locke, the gipsy fiddler of Weobley, among whose family inheritance of songs was a version of 'Greensleeves' and whose skills and repertoire died with him, and the farmer met in 1937 near Llowes, the parish from which the novelist Anthony Powell's ancestors came. 'Are you Mr Williams?' he asked. 'There was silence for a few seconds, and then the traditional watchful answer, "Well – maybe." Silence again, and then the usual perplexing confession, "And if not, who I wonder?"' Near Old Radnor, to the west of Hergest Ridge, he visits Hindwell, a large farmhouse where Thomas Hutchinson, Wordsworth's brother-in-law, lived. The poet and Dorothy stayed there from time to time, and Wordsworth may well have planted the large pine tree near the pond at the front of the house.

As I well remember, barely a mile of the A44 separates New Radnor and Old Radnor (or Maesyfed and Pencraig, to give these villages their original names). Hereabouts the great landowners were the Lewises of Harpton, who claimed ancestry stretching back to the bard Llywelyn Crug Eryr in the twelfth century and died out in 1911. For hundreds of years the family had been patrons of Welsh culture, but by the nineteenth century their Anglicisation was complete. One of the last of the line, Sir Frankland Lewis, is reported to have declared, 'I never countenance Eisteffods and other contrivances for keeping the use of Welsh. Want of English is the cause that principally keeps down the people of Wales. It excludes them from domestic service, it prevents their employment in English towns, it indisposes them to emigration.' The theme is well known to any who have even a passing acquaintance with the 1847 *Report into the State of Education in Wales*, wherein three English forerunners of HMI utterly condemned the Welsh language. It is easy to understand Ffransis Payne's sorrow and exasperation that the views of men like Sir Frankland, whose Welsh-speaking forebears bequeathed him his comfortable acres, should have prevailed to such pernicious effect on humbler natives of Radnorshire.

*Exploring Radnorshire*, charming, interesting, thought-provoking, is a delightful book. The translation, by Dai Hawkins, is very fine. It has a useful map and index, and a number of beautiful black and white photographs, which with the text might tempt you to your own exploration. The author identifies roads and describes routes, even tracks to hidden caves, in sufficient detail to serve as a guide, but he must have hoped holiday crowds would not hasten to follow in his footsteps.

*PN Review* 197, Volume 37 Number 3,
January – February 2011.

# ARTHUR MACHEN
*July 2010*


When my great-grandfather, Thomas Adams, married Hannah Evans in December 1856, both signed the certificate with an X. He had come from Great Bridge, Staffordshire, initially to labour in iron or tin plate works at Abersychan, near Pontypool, though by the time of his marriage he was a mineworker. Hannah was born in Rhymney, another early industrial town at the head of the valley of the river Rhymney. But could it be my Hannah who in 1851, at the age of fourteen, is living with her parents in Bassaleg, near Newport, and working as a tin plate roller? If so, perhaps she, too, moved on to Abersychan, a far shorter distance for her, in pursuit of employment, and there met her future husband. In any event, meet they did, and marry. One may reasonably ponder where in their lives there had been time for literacy before they put their marks on the heavily creased and coal-dusty fragment of marriage certificate that has survived.

In the 1861 Census Thomas's occupation is given as 'pit sinker'. His job was to 'drive the hard headings', my father told me, which means he and his fellows cut through rock to reach the coal seams. His lungs were silicotic, caked with stone dust, and he died, aged 61, in 1887. He did not see his son, my grandfather and namesake, marry Margaret Williams in January 1891, but widowed Hannah may have been at Sardis (Independents) Chapel, Pontypridd, for the occasion, perhaps accompanied by three younger sons, aged thirteen, sixteen and nineteen, all coal miners. Whether the Adamses and the

Williams family were acquainted some time earlier it is now impossible to tell, but in 1891 the newly married couple lived in Gilfach Goch next door to Margaret's parents, William Williams, a coal miner, and Mary, his wife, with the two youngest of their family of eight, Julia (12) and Amelia (14), and no more than a few hundred yards from Sam's mother. They were part of the Gilfach Goch community of that time, thoroughly Welsh in language and life (the Williamses declared they spoke only Welsh), right at the top of the valley, the mountain rising steeply behind, the pit before them, thumping and clanging beneath a pall of smoke and dust.

That Sam Adams, born in 1869, had worked underground alongside his father from the age of twelve. He would have needed to show competence at reading, writing and arithmetic to gain early release from elementary education, but the standards set were not stringent. Nevertheless, the confident, neat cursive of both signatures on their marriage certificate is an index of progress in the education system. So was the determination that their second child, a boy they named Bloom (highly unusual, but a tradition in his mother's family), should stay in school beyond the elementary stage. He went to the grammar school at Ogmore Vale, in the next valley to the west, which must have meant lodging there during term. Bloom became a mining engineer. My father, another Thomas, three years younger, was not so lucky. Was there not enough money to support both boys through secondary education? Or was he considered unlikely to benefit from it? The 1911 Census tells me he was, at fourteen, a baker's assistant, but that didn't last long. However fervent his mother's pleas, they failed to keep him out of the pit: he became a colliery electrician.

My father was an intensely practical man: electrical and mechanical motors, closed to me, were his open books. He had no formal qualification for what he did in the mine, where he was in sole charge. Several stout volumes with 'Electrical and Mechanical Engineering' in gilt on the spines lay on a shelf in a cupboard. I never saw him open one; they were pristine when we threw them out. The other books we possessed were also in cupboards: a large two-volume Bible with some wonderful copperplates by John Martin, and an almost equally large biography of William Booth (wherever my grandparents began their religious journey, they ended staunch Salvationists). I do not recall anyone settling down to read these either. My father was not bookish, nor was my mother, until I was at university, when she read through the fiction on my honours syllabus with relish. But we had three newspapers delivered daily and a bundle at weekends, though not major London broadsheets.

I read comics of course, but my introduction to the pleasure of books began when I was twelve. Then Aunty Lil, one of my mother's five sisters, and Uncle Percy, an unmistakeably frail and wheezing colliery blacksmith, with no children of their own, would feed me sardines on toast at teatime and lend me items from their lightly loaded bookshelf. The one that made the most immediate and biggest impression was *Welsh Short Stories*, published by Faber in 1937 in series with similar anthologies from Scotland and Ireland.

I could make nothing then of Caradoc Evans's terrifying vision of warped humanity, and little enough of the warped version of English he perfected in his stories: he was surely among the first to invent an idiom as a medium for his storytelling and stick to it. A youthful Dylan Thomas, raving with words, but with not much to say, was also too far off from me. But other stories I took in at once, swallowed whole and licked my lips. There was E. Tegla Davies's 'The Strange Apeman', translated by Llewellyn Wyn Griffith, Glyn Jones's 'Wil Thomas' with its unforgettable portraits: 'Evans was a queer-looking chap, tall and dark, dressed from head to foot in black clothes, having his mouth half-way up his face and filled with big false teeth that were broken in the plate and rattled when he was talking like a pocketful of taws. He had big nostrils too with tufts of black hairs sticking out of them, hooked and black like little bunches of candlewicks.' And Geraint Goodwin's 'Janet Ifans's Donkey', which made me laugh aloud again, many years later when, with a monograph of Goodwin to write, I re-read it. I was gripped by 'The Black Rat', an understated, almost casual tale of omens and death in the First World War by Frank Richards, who served on the Western Front throughout the conflict and knew what he was writing about, but the story that fascinated me was Arthur Machen's 'The Shining Pyramid', which haunts me still. When, in the late 1960s, Roland Mathias and I collaborated on our anthology of short stories by Welsh authors, we approached the tasks of reading and selecting with open minds. Of one choice I was fairly confident from the outset, however, and in the end the book was called *The Shining Pyramid and other stories* (Gomer, 1970).

Machen has a niche in the Hay Festival this year; and I attended a day school devoted to him at the University of Newport last year. It isn't that this venerable author is staging a comeback; he never went away. Here, as I write, I am only a few hundred yards from his birthplace, and when I went to the post this morning I passed the very house, which has a memorial blue plaque.

What we call progress has not yet entirely destroyed the magical view of his home village with which Machen begins *Things Near and Far* (1923), the second of two volumes of autobiography:

The road from Newport to Caerleon-on-Usk winds, as it comes near to the old Roman, fabulous city, with the winding of the tawny river which I have always supposed must be somewhat of the colour of the Tiber...And then there came a certain turn, where suddenly one saw the long, great wall of the mountain in the west, and the high dome of Twyn Barlwm, a prehistoric tumulus; and down below, an island in the green meadows by the river, the little white Caerleon, shining in the sun. There is a grey wall on one side of it, a very old and mouldering wall to look at, and indeed it is old enough, for it is all that remains of the Roman wall of Isca Silurum, headquarters of the Second Augustan Legion.

But there, white in the sun of some summer afternoon of fifty years ago or so, Caerleon still stands for me shining, beautiful, a little white city in a dream.

It is truly beguiling, prose that seems written in a trance and trance inducing.

Machen was born in 1863 (six years before my grandfather) and died in 1947. He was baptised Arthur Llewellyn Jones. 'Machen', his mother's maiden name, was added with a hyphen when he went to Hereford Cathedral School (where he was educated in Latin and Greek, but learned no French: that is significant). Later, in London, he dropped the Jones. His father was an impecunious, eventually bankrupt, cleric, lacking the means to provide for his son the Oxford education he had enjoyed. Denied the opportunity of following his father into the Anglican Church, after a few false starts Machen became a hack writer. In 1884 he published *An Anatomy of Tobacco*, which, he said, he had written in a '10 by 6 cell'. On the strength of this he was commissioned for a pittance to translate *The Heptameron* (1886) from the French, and for not much more *The Memoirs of Jacques Casanova* (1894) in 'twelve sizeable volumes'. His output was prodigious, his remuneration pitiful: 'I have just been running through a list of my books from 1881 to 1922, and reckoning...how much money I have made by them...and my total receipts for these eighteen volumes, for these forty-two years of toil, amount to the sum of six hundred and thirty-five pounds. That is, I have been paid at the rate of fifteen pounds and a few pence per annum.'

In 1901 he became an actor, playing Shakespearean bit-parts in the Frank Benson Company. It is all curiously reminiscent of another old acquaintance, T.J. Llewelyn Prichard, except that Machen did not lose his nose and was a far better writer. He is known today principally as a creator of curious tales of the supernatural: you will usually find his books on shelves labelled 'Fantasy'. By his own account this came about as the result of a stint as bibliographer. The books he was asked to catalogue opened his eyes and mind to occultism in its various forms, ancient and modern, which reinforced the tendency in his own writing towards tales of mystery and evil nameless things. *The Great God Pan* (1894), 'a rare fantasy set in a rarer atmosphere', brought a certain notoriety. He became an associate of the fin de siècle decadents, and like Yeats a member of the Hermetic Order of the Golden Dawn.

The story most frequently associated with him, while still concerning the supernatural, is of a somewhat different cast – 'The Bowmen', written as news of the terrible retreat from Mons began appearing in newspapers and originally published in *The Evening News* in September 1914. It tells how an invocation, 'Adsit Anglis Sanctus Georgius', uttered almost thoughtlessly by a soldier in the heat of battle, summons up 'Saint George [and] his Agincourt Bowmen to help the English'. Within days rumours spread that this was not fantasy but the truth, and despite Machen's careful account of how he came to write the story in his introduction to its first publication in book form, *The Bowmen and other Legends of the War* (1915), there are some still who prefer to believe in the veracity of 'The Angels of Mons'.

Machen may not be to everyone's taste, but he is an old-fashioned stylist, a wonderfully elegant and persuasive writer. If you haven't yet done so, I urge you to dip into *Things Near and Far*, or its companion volume *Far Off Things*, and for the frisson of his supernatural tales, of course, 'The Shining Pyramid.'

*PN Review* 194, Volume 36 Number 6,
July – August 2010.

# THOMAS PRICHARD
*March 2010*

My interest in Prichard began thirty-five years ago, and I am still in pursuit of him. I blame Roland Mathias. He suggested I write something about Prichard for the *Anglo-Welsh Review*, the magazine he edited with such distinction for sixteen years. I had never heard of him, and since there was always a good deal of levity in our conversation, for all I knew the invitation might have been a joke. But no, it was meant seriously. He told me that in 1828, Prichard had made a modest stir in Wales with the publication of a novel, *The Adventures and Vagaries of Twm Shôn Catti*, and for that alone deserved to be better known among Anglo-Welsh antecedents. The enlargement of knowledge about writers and writing from Wales was one of the sacred duties of *AWR*; I was conscious of the responsibility I had been given.

The *Dictionary of Welsh Biography* gave me the name, Thomas Jeffery Llewelyn Prichard, told me he was both writer and actor, that he was born in the parish of Trallong, Breconshire and, on the evidence of one of his letters, 'dated 24 Nov. 1875' quoted in a journal, *Cymru Fu* (1889), that he died in 1875 or 1876. As I discovered, much of this is incorrect, but the greater surprise is that the entry does not mention that Prichard lost his nose. It was perfectly obvious to the few who met him and wrote about the encounter – as plain, you might say, as the nose on your face. Among these was the author of the essay in *Cymru Fu* that *DWB* refers to: Charles Wilkins, at the time clerk in the post office at Merthyr Tydfil, which, without being too inquisitive, might explain why he had one of Prichard's letters. 'He was gaunt and grey,' wrote Wilkins, 'with thin features and lustrous eyes, a false nose – having lost his natural one in a fencing match – and he spoke with an earnest snuffle – I say this kindly – from which most people would quickly have turned away.'

I began my quest thumbing through the card catalogue at Cardiff Central Library, which then housed the capital's principal collections. The library had *Twm Shôn Catti* and several other books by Prichard – *Welsh Minstrelsy*, a volume of poetry, *A Cambrian Wreath*, an anthology of poems on Welsh subjects by several hands including his own, guide books to Aberystwyth and Llandrindod Wells and their mineral springs, and *Heroines of Welsh History*, an episodic view of centuries past focusing upon the role of women (much later I discovered he had published more poetry in four pamphlets, one of which, *Theatrical Poems*, is sadly lost – unless a reader of this piece has chanced upon a copy). *Twm Shôn Catti* was fine, an old-fashioned picaresque tale interspersed with jolly poems and satirical remarks about unscrupulous English landowners of low morals, which might be more highly regarded had it been written in, say, 1758 rather than 1828. In any event, the novel was by far the most successful of Prichard's books. Much of the rest, especially two poems of epic length in *Welsh Minstrelsy* (1824), I found frankly depressing.

Nevertheless, I remained hot on the scent of the man with no nose. I spent fruitless hours with the parish registers in the church at Trallong, a hamlet perched above the Usk and the A40 Brecon to Llandovery road. He certainly lived at Trallong as a child, on a farm, Bryn-du, high on the mountain above Sennybridge, as he tells us in a poem included in *Twm Shôn Catti*. But he was not born there, and, if not there, then where? Having read in his work several references to Builth, I made an expedition to that prominent market town and pored over the registers in the frigid vestry of its parish church. Although several Prichard families of long standing presented themselves in the late eighteenth and early nineteenth centuries, none had sons named Thomas. But an incoming family, which the registers show to have spent only a few years in the town, provided a precious exception: 'Thomas Prichard, lawyer and his wife Anne', of whose three children only one seemed to have survived, a son, also called Thomas, baptised 29 October 1790.

This was not a 'Thomas Jeffery Llewelyn', but then, where (outside the aristocracy) would you find offspring of that period baptised with several forenames? Not in Wales anyway. I had by this time bought a worn copy of *Welsh Minstrelsy* in a second-hand bookshop and had begun working on it from title page (where the notorious radicals 'Messrs. John and H.L. Hunt of Tavistock-Street, Covent Garden' are declared publishers) to the list of subscribers at the end. The latter told me that among those who had signed up in London were a number with theatrical connections, but the great majority were in south Wales and among these was the 'Revd Jeffery Llewelyn' of Llywel, another hamlet just off the A40 a few miles from Trallong. It could hardly have been a coincidence, and it wasn't. A short and pointless enquiry into the historical Twm Shôn Catti (Thomas Jones, *c.*1530-1609, antiquary, genealogist and bard) led me to the hoard of manuscripts and ephemera accumulated by the Revd William Jenkins Rees, Rector of Cascob in Radnorshire, which was bequeathed to Cardiff library and is known there as the Tonn collection. Among the papers I found the prospectus that Prichard had issued for *Welsh Minstrelsy* and another circulated by John Humffreys Parry for a journal, the Cambro-Briton, also published in London. One thing leads to another: in the short-lived *Cambro-Briton* I found Prichard's earliest poems, over the pen-name 'Jeffery Llewelyn'.

He must have liked the name, for he added it to his own, often thereafter signing himself 'T.J. Llewelyn Prichard'.

It was some time before I came across an aside on page 536 of *Heroines of Welsh History* in which the author describes himself as 'a native of Builth'. I was on the right track with regard to his origins; what about his end? *DWB* said he died in poverty in Swansea in 1875 or 1876. I went to Swansea and spent many hours turning the yellowed broadsheet pages of the *Cambrian*, the earliest national newspaper in Wales, which was printed and published in the town. No word of Prichard through the 1870s, though his reputation as an author might have earned him a line or two. When I had almost given up hope, it occurred to me that if he had died there, surely a death certificate was issued. At the local registrar's office they turned it up in a couple of minutes. I have the copy before me: Prichard died of burns 'caused by his clothes taking fire in his bedroom' on 11 January 1862, aged 72.

Poor Prichard – but wonderful news: he was indeed born in 1790, and now I knew precisely where to look in the cumbersome bound volumes of the *Cambrian*. They told me more than I had expected. He had been found in the most abject state towards the end of November 1861, the butt of the malice of young ruffians, who were throwing stones at 'Major Roteley's Cottage', the hovel where he lived. The newspaper got up a fund to help him and appointed a committee to see all was properly done. He was given food, clothing and furniture, and a woman, Esther Bird, was paid to look to his daily needs and tend a fire to warm his old bones. It was she who found him horribly burned on 9 January 1862. At the inquest the coroner wondered whether he had been drunk, but there was no clear evidence of that. Esther Bird testified that his last words were 'Oh! the boys – the boys' – make of it what you will.

I had the beginning of Prichard's story and the end, but what happened in between? I had seen him in the guise of 'Jeffery Llewelyn' place two (heavily edited) poems in the *Cambro-Briton*. Editor's notes in the magazine reveal he failed in several more attempts: he could not have lived by his pen. Charles Wilkins described a man who had once been familiar with the London stage, and the subscribers' list discloses Mr C. Baker of the Theatre Royal, Covent Garden, Mr Hastings and Mr John Haines of the Coburg Theatre, Mr Frederick Mortimer of the Theatre Royal, Brighton and Mr Macready of the Theatre Royal, Bristol, most of them known to theatre history. A certain warmth of acquaintance between poet and subscriber is indicated, since *Welsh Minstrelsy* boasts nothing that might have been of intrinsic interest to actors and theatre managers. In Cardiff library I found passing references in reminiscences and diaries of the 1840s to Prichard performing on stage in Brecon and Aberystwyth. It seemed reasonable to suspect he had also acted in London. I pursued my enquiries at the Theatre Museum, Covent Garden, spooling through microfiche images of hundreds of playbills, but there was no sign anywhere of a Prichard. As with his poetry, might he have adopted a stage name? I began again, looking for a likely contender – and found one: Mr Jefferies.

Although I had no proof, I was already, in optimistic moments, confident that Prichard was related on his mother's side to the Jeffreys, a Breconshire clan, members of which had from time to time since the seventeenth century become extraordinarily wealthy. Their ancestral home was Bailie Cwmdwr, in the parish of Llywel (where the Revd. Jeffery Llewelyn was curate) within reasonable walking distance of Bryn-du farmhouse in the neighbouring parish of Trallong. In Prichard's lifetime, the owner of Bailie Cwmdwr and extensive lands contiguous was 'Rees Jeffreys, Gent', whose will I examined at the National

Library of Wales. When he died in 1811, apart from a few minor legacies to family members, including ten pounds to a niece, Anne, he left all his property to the unrelated Revd Jeffery Llewelyn.

I followed Mr Jefferies' acting career at the Theatre Royal, Covent Garden between 1814 and 1823, in the days when John Philip Kemble was manager and leading player. He had minor roles, among them Benvolio in *Romeo and Juliet*, Bernardo in *Hamlet*, Lennox in *Macbeth*, which he retained whenever the play was performed. Between November and mid-December 1822, however, his parts were given to Mr C. Baker. Where did Mr Jefferies go in those six weeks? I have become convinced he went to Brighton, where Prichard persuaded Mr Mortimer of the Theatre Royal to subscribe to *Welsh Minstrelsy*, and to Worthing, where he employed William Phillips (who already had Shelley's *Necessity of Atheism* to his credit) to print *My Lowly Love*, his first pamphlet of 'petite poems/chiefly on Welsh subjects'. Mr Jefferies resumed his usual roles at the Theatre Royal from 16 December 1822 until 23 June 1823, after which the name disappears from the playbills. It could, of course, be coincidence, but shortly afterwards Prichard began recruiting subscribers across south Wales.

On his way to Wales he may have met, in Hereford, Naomi James, whom he married at Abergavenny in January 1826. She was at the time perhaps only sixteen, certainly no more than eighteen, and already pregnant, as Prichard confessed in a letter to the Revd William Jenkins Rees (who had somehow become a staunch friend), which the good rector squirreled away among his papers. The newlyweds lived for a time in Aberystwyth, where they enjoyed the brief success of *Twm Shôn Catti*, then, until 1839, in Builth, after which Prichard seems to have abandoned wife and family and taken to the road as actor, at least until he lost his nose, and door-to-door salesman of his own books, declining all the while towards that hovel in Swansea and death by fire.

In 2000 I published *Thomas Jeffery Llewelyn Prichard* in the Writers of Wales series, an account of all I had discovered up to that time about a very elusive character. Since then I have found an unpublished Prichard manuscript, forty 'historical' sonnets with accompanying brief essays, in the basement stock room of Swansea Museum and, near enough one might say, his grave at Dan-y-graig Cemetery in Swansea, where he had a pauper's burial in a plot now unidentifiable because the numbered iron markers were recently stolen by scrap metal thieves. In the Writers of Wales book I set down the sparse facts as I had found them and came clean about the web of speculation on which they hung. It is all really unsatisfactory, but I keep looking for clues. Sometimes I feel it is less a case of me pursuing Prichard, than of him snuffling and stumbling after me.

A few years ago, despairing of finding evidence of his childhood at Bryn-du, his connection with the man I supposed his great uncle, Rees Jeffreys, Gent, and the Revd Jeffery Llewelyn of Llywel, I began inventing a life for him. To that I added a youthful journey to London with drovers, an uncle Richard (in 1823 a Richard Prichard of Regents Circus ordered six copies of *Welsh Minstrelsy*!) who took him in and found him employment as an apprentice accountant (when asked about his employment by the census enumerator in 1851, Prichard replied, 'Accountant'), and a career on the stage at Covent Garden in the company of John Philip Kemble. With this imaginary autobiography I fulfilled a promise Prichard himself had made – and not kept – in the preface to another of his pamphlets, *Mariette Mouline* (1823). Hence, for me, his story ends with his return to Wales. Great gaps remain in the rest of his life, not to mention the puzzle of his missing nose. These I decided to leave to two researchers, whose story is now interwoven with that of my fictional Prichard. The resulting novel, *Prichard's Nose*, will be published by Y Lolfa in Spring 2010.


*PN Review* 192, Volume 36 Number 4,
March – April 2010.

# R.S. THOMAS

*November 2009*


R.S. Thomas is a poet of consequence. He wrote prolifically (his *Collected Later Poems 1988-2000*, published by Bloodaxe in 2004, has 183 poems) and there are few troughs in his output. He is reputed a great religious poet, though certainly not of Christian orthodoxies. His power did not diminish with age. Like Thomas Hardy, as an old man he could look back upon a marriage for which austere might be the kindest epithet, and astound with the poignancy of the lyrical impulse. You cannot read 'A Marriage' without recognising that an extraordinary delicacy lies in that spindly assemblage of words:

> We met
>   under a shower
> of bird notes.
>   Fifty years passed,
> love's moment
>   in a world in
> servitude to time.
>   She was young;
> I kissed with my eyes
>   closed and opened
> them on her wrinkles.
>   'Come' said death,
> choosing her as his
>   partner for
> the last dance. And she,
>   who in life

had done everything
    with a bird's grace,
opened her bill now
    for the shedding
of one sigh no
heavier than a feather.

You might think a man of philosophical bent, possessed of such depth of feeling for the natural world, and antipathy to all manifestations of our modern materialist society, would be an interesting correspondent. If *R.S. Thomas: Letters to Raymond Garlick 1951-1999*, newly published in hardback and some style by Gomer Press, is representative of his epistolary manner, you would be mistaken. He began the exchange ('29.vi.51') by writing to congratulate Raymond Garlick on some salient remarks the latter had made in the course of a radio discussion, and volunteering contributions to *Dock Leaves*, which Raymond edited. As an earnest of his intent he enclosed six shillings and sixpence for the next three numbers, adding 'Please let me know if I can help in any way' – a generous offer.

The six and sixpence was no small gesture either from a cleric who, while he despatched his son, Gwydion, to fee-paying independent schools, chose a comfortless existence for himself and his wife, Elsi (the notable artist Mildred Elsie Eldridge). Money is a recurring theme in the letters: 'I never refuse the BBC as I am always in need of cash, although I have felt many times I ought to on the score of integrity'; and, of an invitation to speak to students at Bangor University, 'I wish they would state a fee when they write. The universities have plenty of money. Aberystwyth offered 6 guineas when I spoke there.' I can vouch for the latter, because in 1956 I was chairman of the English Society that invited him to Aber and had the difficult task of formally thanking him for a talk on imagery that added nothing to what we heard in lectures, and in the course of which he did not once mention he had ever written a poem.

There is a certain playfulness in one of the earlier letters: 'If you are having good discussions about "gnawing the carcase" etc. I don't see why I should put a stop to them by explaining what I mean! After all, so much poetry is the result of a mood.' But the usual tone is different, more acerbic and grudging: 'I have done what I can [as reviewer] with Mathias' poems', that is, Roland Mathias's third book *The Roses of Tretower*. Of the broadcast of Raymond Garlick's radio ode, he writes, 'I hope you were pleased with it – the whole thing is a bit questionable as people rarely listen to verse for so long – but there you are – 30 gns are quite useful'; and of his own long poem, 'I was astonished at the BBC's reading of *[The Minister]*, I thought they read it appallingly.' And so on. He has little time for fellow poets. Dylan Thomas, he says, 'wrote some half dozen first class lyrics – the rest is dross', and he dissents from the critical lauding of Seamus Heaney (Geoffrey Hill, however, is very much to his taste). Reviewers are pooh-poohed: 'I see some people are still nit-picking about my so-called lack of form. I wish they'd catch up. John Wain, one of the Movement bunch seems to have begun it, and Donald Davie, another Movement fan, agrees, carrying on about "enjambement" etc., as if that mattered any more.' The eulogistic introduction John Betjeman had written to *Song at the Year's Turning* (1955) he describes as 'almost drivel', and later, with a stiff broom he sweeps away all the critics: 'English criticism is a morass and is made worse by certain dons, who should know better, who delight in saying stupid and impossible things in public'. To Raymond himself (one of the key figures in post-Second World War Anglo-Welsh writing) he offers school-masterly advice: 'As you go on you will, I am sure, eliminate the echoes of other people's voices, discipline your easy rhymes, and refine your alliterative and assonantal obviousness.' What response this elicited we do not know, since only one of Raymond's letters survives. Perhaps that too says something about R.S. as correspondent.

Several postcards are included in the 152 items in the book, and most of the letters might easily have fitted on a postcard without cramping the writer's hand. Over the years I received the odd postcard from him. I was not invited to be on first name terms, a status achieved by Raymond Garlick five years and thirty-two letters into the correspondence, and implemented two years later with letter 43. He was all stiffness and had no small talk – there is the story of him leaping a wall to avoid meeting parishioners – and he had a limited range of interests. He liked walking and was a devoted birdwatcher; at home he read and meditated, and he wrote poems. He did not like the English, or tourists of any stripe, and almost despaired of the 'supine' Welsh, who were complaisant about, if not complicit in, the destruction of their language. Even so, he didn't entirely give up. The letters show how he was involved in protests on behalf of the language, and later active in the appeal to buy Ynys Enlli (Bardsey), reputedly the burial place of twenty thousand saints, off the tip of the Llŷn peninsula, and in the local branch of CND.

The later letters, though usually still brief, have a greater ease of familiarity, not least in expressions of concern about and interest in Raymond's family and career. But R.S. rarely gave anything away, as audiences found at readings up and down the land. How they would have warmed to the occasional less guarded glimpse of the man and poet, such as: 'The first poem I wrote about [Prytherch] – A Peasant – certainly was written in the evening after visiting a 1000[feet]-up farm in Manafon where I saw a labourer docking swedes in the cold, grey air of a November afternoon. I came later to refer to this particular farmer jestingly as Iago Prytherch' (letter dated 15.iii.69).

Notwithstanding the omission of a few passages, for

'personal reasons', the letters exude the authentic aura of this odd, thorny mystic, this strange man. They reveal him more strangely still nearing the end of his life when, a widower, he got married again, to an old acquaintance whose character and temperament were polar opposites to Elsi's, and went happily jaunting around the world with her. The book is patiently and meticulously introduced and edited by Jason Walford Davies.

You learn nothing new from the letters – certainly not if you have read Byron Rogers's consummately readable, finely balanced (and James Tait Black prize-winning) 'life of R.S. Thomas's *The Man Who Went Into The West*. Rogers's recently published joust with autobiography, *Me – the authorised biography* (also from Aurum), has already attracted much media attention. No surprise, since it is highly entertaining. It begins with a teasing foreword, 'A Warning to the Curious', which quotes from Henry James (*not* the James we expected) to justify an approach that is altogether different from the usual chronological narrative and 'terrible fluidity of self-revelation', and presents the past randomly disordered in the way that memory works. Interviewers and commentators thus far have tended to focus upon his time as features writer for the *Daily Telegraph* magazine, which is indeed where the book begins, with two letters and a story guaranteed to hold the normal adult reader as spellbound as was the wedding guest by the ancient mariner's glittering eye. You might prefer to follow his lead and start at the end of the book, where, entering his sixties, he attempts authorship and, *faute de mieux*, salesmanship, retailing his book at the local butchers' with a pound of sausages for each buyer. Reviewers admired the quirky humour (the *New Statesman* thought him 'radically weird'), but found 'the early emphasis on Wales ... a little heavy going', which, he remarks, was not something they 'would have dared say about the Jews. Or the Scots. Or anyone really, apart from the Welsh'.

All his adult life Byron Rogers has lived and worked in England, but he retains a deep and passionate sense of rootedness in Wales. His *bro* is the town of Carmarthen and the countryside around; as a five-year-old he spoke only Welsh and he has not lost the language. If he writes of family, background, schooling, as the autobiographer must, then Wales will get its due measure of emphasis. That it is not 'up front' is perhaps a lesson learned from the reviewers. His tales are by turns whimsical, nimble-witted, pungent, always diverting, for he writes beautifully and is a gifted anecdotalist. Distinctly odd characters flock to him, or he has that knack, the curiosity to find them and then the social ease and intuition to make the most of them. Inevitably, too, looking back makes for an element of nostalgia. For all its humour, the book is an elegy to departed relatives and friends, lost paths and places of childhood and youth and, among other vanishing particles of tradition, derelict pubs where once regulars gathered to drink a pint or two and talk, actually talk.

The life journey of Peter J. Conradi, the biographer of Iris Murdoch, an Englishman with Polish ancestry, has taken him in the opposite direction. He first came to Wales in 1965 and has a house at Cascob, Radnorshire, which having once been a retreat from academic life in London has become over the years his principal place of residence. It is a former school, quietly beautiful, set in a bowl of hills, neighbouring an ancient church in its circular graveyard. From the start he found this part of the Welsh March congenial, and he has increasingly devoted his life to learning about it, on foot, through meeting and talking with locals and extensive reading. He has happily embedded himself there and co-edits the *Transactions of the Radnorshire Society*. Radnorshire is the subject of his latest publication.

Cascob itself is not far from the border with England, and some are happy to see that demarcation blurred, to think, for instance, of Hay, the festival town, as English. But Conradi is in no doubt – this is Wales and many of the sources he has drawn upon for his book are Welsh. Its title, *At the Bright Hem of God* (Seren, 2009), is taken from a line of Welsh poetry, *'Yn ymyl gwisg Duw'*, as translated by R.S. Thomas, one of three poets (the others are Roland Mathias and Ruth Bidgood) whose Radnorshire connections are discussed in some detail. But that is only one facet of a book that is extraordinarily rich in narrative and scope of reference, and often poetic in its evocation of this loneliest of rural places, a landscape of 'golden silences'. Wandering smoothly and beguilingly among topics, personalities and historical periods, startling with little known facts, both celebration and elegy, it is a lovely book. 'You will recognise,' Peter J. Conradi recently wrote to me, 'it is of course a love poem.'

*PN Review* 190, Volume 36 Number 2, November – December 2009.

# RICHARD LLEWELLYN

*August 2009*

At Tonyrefail Grammar School, some time in 1947-8, I first became aware of the source of the core narrative of Richard Llewellyn's *How Green Was My Valley*. I remember the occasion well because it was a revelation that the novel was about a family from Gilfach Goch, my home valley, and I recall it now because 2009 sees the seventieth anniversary of its publication.

It was probably during a wet lunch hour, when, as a relatively senior pupil, I was keeping an eye on a well-behaved first-year class. I wandered among the desks exchanging a few words with individuals and looking at an exercise book here and there. One of the books I picked up, intending no more than a cursory glance, at once caught and held my attention. Among the earliest pieces of writing was an account of how the boy's grandfather had told Richard Llewellyn about the early days of coal mining in Gilfach Goch, and the struggle between miners and coal owners at the end of the nineteenth century and beginning of the twentieth. The boy's name was Teifion Griffiths, and the incident I have described certainly occurred in 1947-8, because (as he has recently told me) before that school year was over, his family left Gilfach for London and he continued his education there.

I have long thought *How Green Was My Valley* easily the best novel to come out of the experience of the south Wales coalfield. Re-reading it in the last week has served to confirm my view. It has many admirers all over the world, but has always been considered controversial and is even now often reviled in Wales.

My heavily annotated paperback copy was published in 1978 – the forty-fourth printing since Michael Joseph, newly in business on his own account after parting from Gollancz, risked all on a first book by an unknown author. In days when initial print runs for novels by established writers rarely exceeded a couple of thousand, Joseph ordered 51,000. It became an immediate bestseller in Britain, and when Macmillan in New York brought it out in 1940, sold 176,280 copies from United States bookstores in the first year (outselling Steinbeck's *The Grapes of Wrath*, published in 1939), before John Ford's cinema adaptation, which won the best film Oscar for 1941, increased its popularity.

What is the secret of the book's appeal? It lies in part at least in the first-person narrative, which might have begun, 'Whether I shall turn out to be the hero of my own life, or whether that station will be held by anybody else, these pages must show', if the words had not already been given to David Copperfield. The story unfolds in the memory of Huw, youngest of the Morgan family, whose understanding of events and the motives of others is imperfect, as, often, is his response to them. He is about to leave the Valley (unnamed but capitalised throughout) at a point in time near the publication date of the novel. His dwelling, the home his parents made, is about to be engulfed by colliery waste; it is a time for looking back fifty years or so to his early childhood and his family as it was then, and charting his own stumbling growth to manhood. Like Dickens's novel, the book ends with a march past of major characters, but more briefly and on a sustained melancholy note. The ungreening of the Valley by the collieries and their waste heaps is the other major theme: Llewellyn's suggestion that 'Slag' should be the title of the novel was rejected by Joseph.

Huw is courageous, but lacks boyish belligerence and has to be taught how to fight; he is intelligent, but determines to join his father down the pit rather than progress to Oxford; he is endlessly selfless, courteous and caring, but in his relationships with women, apart from his mother, he is a fool to himself. His failings count for naught. What matters is the way he expresses his sensuous perception of the world, for which Llewellyn created a resonant style. The dialogue imitates Welsh idiom and word order, and descriptive passages borrow from the sonorous language of the Authorised Version. Paragraphs taken in isolation are not to modern taste. Here, for instance, Huw and an alarmingly sensual Ceinwen make love on the mountain: 'An anthem rages as a storm, with chanting in poetries that never knew a tongue, and strange music, and crackling fires of primal colours burst behind the sight-blind eyes and myriads of blazing moons rise up to spin for ages in a new-born golden universe of frankincense and myrrh.' It is surprising how even this seems less unbearable in context and, with a moment's thought, reminiscent of Dylan Thomas. The book is luscious with verbal imagery of sights and sounds, and often redolent of the savours of an honest, wholesome existence, a kind of demi-paradise. The Valley is not far from 'Fern Hill'.

At the outset we find Gwilym and Beth Morgan and their children in a state as close to prelapsarian content as it is possible for a working-class family to be. The men of the village work hard underground, are paid in shiny sovereigns, and sing together tramping from the pit to their warm homes where wives have steaming suppers waiting. When the mood takes them, they stroll out into the clean air of the mountain, and on Sundays they fill the chapel. The Morgan family are the aristocrats of the Valley, the father and his sons all strong, handsome and talented, the women beautiful and loving. They are highly moral models of integrity, looked up to by all, and spitefully envied by a few.

Within a dozen or so pages the Fall is foreshadowed and the unravelling of family ties begins. Thenceforth, the story and most of the dramatic incidents are driven by failure in the relationships between the sons and the young women they fall in love with, and profound difference in opinion between father and sons over the necessary response in increasingly bitter disputes between miners and mine owners. Gwilym, the father, is seen to represent the voice of reason, speaking against strike action on the grounds that it does more harm to the strikers and their families than it does to the owners (an attitude not far removed from that of the early miners' leader, William Abraham, known as 'Mabon'). His most outspoken opponent is his socialist son Davy, who 'wants a union with everybody in it, all over the world' and carries with him his brothers Gwilym and Owen. Young Huw observes all, at first with imperfect understanding, but eventually as a fellow miner, on his father's side. At the climax of the novel, he is with his father striving to save the pit from flooding when strikers threaten to sabotage the pumps, and it is Huw who is first to reach the body of his dying father, buried in a roof fall underground.

Welsh critics of the novel are uninterested in failed human relationships, but they castigate what they perceive to be distortions of history. They support their views with facts. When mining began in Gilfach Goch in the 1860s, the wage for a 'hewer' was about 25 shillings a week; other colliery workers were paid less. The terraced dwellings the miners called home, some still standing at the top of the valley when I was a boy, were two-up, two-down hutches of local stone, each with a couple of undersized windows. The mountain was close at hand, but to see it you needed to crane your neck over the encroaching slag heaps. How families existed in them is now beyond imagination. Certainly, there was nothing idyllic about the life, especially as owners became increasingly remote from pits, and even from the coalfield, and interested only in profit. Unionism and a succession of strikes were the inevitable response.

The first strikes in the novel are over the imposition of pay cuts as cheaper labour becomes available and to take account of the amount of unsaleable dirt brought up with the coal. Those that follow are fictionalised reflections of the long-running dispute over the 'Sliding Scale', by which wages fluctuated according to the market price of coal, a system (as John Davies points out in *A History of Wales*) 'which encouraged the employers to undersell and overproduce', to the detriment of their employees. The history of these conflicts, which culminated in the 1910-11 strike, has been thoroughly researched: for example, the story of the south Wales Miners' Federation, which was born of them, is fully and vividly told in *The Fed* by Dai Smith and Hywel Francis (UWP, 1980).

But historical accuracy should not be expected of a novel, especially one that is deliberately vague about details such as the names of places and chronology. There is a lesson even in the identity given to the Valley's first mine owner, 'Christmas Evans'. Historically, as Llewellyn well knew, it should have been 'Evan Evans', but that is not nearly as interesting, even for a marginal character. The real Christmas Evans was the son of Evan Evans, who inherited his father's property and sold the Gilfach pits to a major historical figure, D.A. Thomas (later Lord Rhondda). Under Thomas, they became part of the Cambrian Combine, about which you will gather a great deal from *The Fed*, but nothing from *How Green Was My Valley*, except an impression of the bitterness and violence of the struggle between striking miners and the establishment ranged on the side of the owners.

The novel tells of the deployment of police and of soldiers in the Valley by 'Mr Winston Churchill' – as they were historically in Gilfach. Meirion Davies's fine *Glynogwr & Gilfach Goch: A History* (1981) has a photograph of Royal Munster Fusiliers billeted in Gilfach. He also tells how Samuel

Thomas, a 'check-weightman', urged the strikers who were attempting to stop the pumps at the Britannic pit 'to restrain themselves', and how the day after the disturbance fifty Lancashire Fusiliers and twenty mounted Hussars were despatched over the mountain to Gilfach in a show of strength. In the novel Gwilym Morgan is the check-weightman who, we recall, strives to preserve the peace and keep the pumps working at the 'Britannia' colliery.

There is every indication that Llewellyn had been engaged on a novel about the coalfield for some years before he learned about Gilfach. The story of the Griffiths family and what he saw when he visited their home showed him how he could focus on a group of characters and thereby contain and shape within a community a story that threatened to sprawl. Typically, as coal was exploited along the 'glove shaped' valleys of Gwent and Glamorgan, villages and small townships coalesced in one continuous ribbon development (travelling the roads there today, you move imperceptibly from, for instance, Penrhiwfer to Williamstown to Penygraig to Tonypandy to Llwynypia and so on). But Gilfach Goch occupies a valley of its own between Rhondda to the east and Ogmore to the west. It is a cul-de-sac into which the road enters and loops at the top end like a noose. When, late in the novel, the case against Huw at a trial 'over the mountain' is dismissed, he returns home, 'Back to the wide greenness of the Valley', a place unrecognisable in the topography of the Rhondda valleys, but descriptive of the entrance to Gilfach Goch.

The mythic quality of the novel is starkly demonstrated by the contrast between life 'over the mountain' (bad) and in the Valley (good – though increasingly poisoned by contact with the world beyond): paradise on its way to being lost. At the end, with the rest of the Morgans – father, mother, brothers, sisters – all dead or dispersed abroad, we find Huw, their remembrancer, about to be expelled as the slag heap reaches the walls of the family home. Even this finality, however, is not symbolic only, but also an echo of the Gilfach story, where, Llewellyn learned, a farm, a school and a street of houses lay under a tip.

The author's first contact with Gilfach was through Will Griffiths, who, blackballed by pit managers because of his union activities, had left the village to find work as a musician in London. He played the violin in silent cinema and theatre orchestras and subsequently worked in Foyles, becoming head of the bookshop's Welsh department, which issued its own publications under the imprint 'Gwasg Foyle'. 'Will Griff', as he was known, told Richard Llewellyn about his own village, and how he and his three brothers worked in the pit alongside their father, Joseph. All four brothers were talented musicians and the home was cultured and Welsh speaking. With this knowledge and the sense of a story cohering around it, Llewellyn visited Gilfach. He viewed the singular valley, the pits, the enormous slag heaps that almost filled its upper end, and the rounded outlines of the green mountains beyond them. And he met Joseph Griffiths in his book-lined room, from whom he acquired the lore of the early days of mining. He might have spent some little time working on the surface of a colliery; there were three to choose from, including the Britannic, within a stone's throw of one another. With his imagination, and some experience as a film-script writer familiar with the appeal of romance and drama, he had enough to go on.

Will Griff eventually attracted his brothers to London – hence Teifion's departure from Tonyrefail GS. There they joined him in a bookselling business, 'Griff's', in Cecil Court, off Charing Cross Road, which became a Mecca for Welsh writers living in or visiting London. I called in whenever there was time after meetings in London in the 1970s. Richard Llewellyn carried on writing novels, but never with anything like the success he achieved with the first. Those of my acquaintance who met him say he was not likeable. He was born Richard Lloyd, in London in 1906, but was reluctant to disclose the circumstances of his upbringing, which were nothing to be ashamed of. If you would like to know more about him and his book, read the splendid articles by John Harris in *Planet 73*, 1989 and *Welsh Writing in English*, Volume 3, 1997.

The artist Kyffin Williams, hearing I was from Gilfach Goch, told me that during a visit to a remote village in the Patagonian Andes he discovered to his surprise that Richard Llewellyn had been there not long before and, against all precedent, had persuaded the authorities to allow him to build a house in what was designated a National Park. Llewellyn, who had upset the locals by arriving with a female companion not his wife, proceeded to live as handsomely as local provision permitted, while the building went on. Having accumulated large debts on construction and high living, he and his partner did a moonlight flit, though the part-finished house remained. Some years later the artist noticed in a bookshop a new paperback edition of *How Green Was My Valley*, which had as cover illustration a reproduction of one of his paintings, taken without permission. He couldn't blame Llewellyn, who was already dead, for that, but the fact that it was a painting of a village in north Wales did, he thought, add insult to injury.

*PN Review* 188, Volume 35 Number 6,
July – August 2009.

# MEIC STEPHENS, TONY CONRAN, GRAHAM HARTILL AND ROBERT MINHINNICK
*March 2009*

End of year leisure has, as usual, brought opportunities to review recent events and publications. October saw Meic Stephens's seventieth birthday celebrated at St Fagans National History Museum, on the outskirts of Cardiff. I don't believe I have previously mentioned this wonderful branch of the National Museums of Wales, where farm buildings, shops, a chapel, a school, a row of workers' cottages from Merthyr Tydfil and much else, most recently a now gloriously refurbished medieval church, dismantled from sites all over Wales, have been faithfully re-erected on a hundred-acre site, to stand more or less as they were originally. I visit frequently with grandchildren; it is one of the most popular cultural tourist destinations in Wales, in terms of our folk culture, the most richly rewarding.

Meic's event was held in the miners' institute, transported from its original place at Oakdale in the Gwent valleys. Well over a hundred filled the upper room to hear friends and literary associates going back to the 1960s, Arts Council colleagues, a student from his final career destination as professor at the University of Glamorgan, who recalled a sample of the wide range of his achievements, particularly as writer and editor. It was a fitting celebration for one who, in 2008, published an acclaimed first novel, *Yeah, Dai Dando* (Cinnamon); *Necrologies* (Seren), a collection of obituaries, mostly from *The Independent*, which is an essential supplement to any history of modern Wales; and as editor, *The Complete Poems of Leslie Norris*, with a fine introduction by Patrick McGuinness, a handsome production by Seren and the definitive text. Virtually from the moment he founded *Poetry Wales* in 1965 Meic Stephens has been a major literary figure. His output over the years has been prodigious. And there is no sign of letting up.

Despite manifold difficulties, there has been no diminution either in the productivity of Tony Conran, an old friend of Meic's, who was unable to attend at St Fagans. In 2006 he published *The Red Sap of Love*, a big collection of lyrical poems and sequences culled from almost fifty years of writing (1951 – 2000), which reveals his journey as a poet intellectually and stylistically, in these relatively shorter forms, from his late teens (another volume at least as large would be needed to display his parallel development as a social, polemical and dramatic poet). In prefatory paragraphs he remarks how he was bored by and reacted against the 'rarefied up-market journalism' that characterised the poetry of the 1960s and 1970s, and strove to 'recreate paradigms of the recovery of experience, metaphors of rebirth'. A web of metaphor, of classical and biblical allusion, in the earlier work veils a preoccupation with love and desire and, more opaquely, his affliction as a sufferer with cerebral palsy. It is poetry of mind, internal, bookish, playing out obscurely his anguished contemplation of the barrier his disability placed between him and the fulfilment of human relations, friendship and sexual love. Often abstruse and allegorical, but shapely, too, and highly polished, rather than sprawling across the page, without imitating them, his writing leans towards the poetics of Vernon Watkins or Dylan Thomas.

His mature poems have less surface glitter, less intellectual challenge. As he begins to look about himself and trust observation, he learns how lyricism can be simply playful and, more important, how it is possible to write about his disability and relationships straightforwardly. 'Daughters and Family' and

'Personal Talk', which includes the memorable elegy, 'The Great
RS is Dead', are composed in something very like plain style –
the sort of thing he once abjured. After those later poems in
*The Red Sap of Love*, Conran's most recent publication, *What
Brings You Here So Late?* (Carreg Gwalch, 2008), may come as
a surprise. An epigraph, 'from the singing of Frank Quinn, Co.
Tyrone' explains the title: '"What brings you here so late?" said
the knight on the road./"I go to meet my God," said the child
as he stood."' The book is a fragmentary verse autobiography
in twenty chapters, and the style modernist.

This is not so much stylistic reversion as another shake of
the kaleidoscope, for Conran is above all an experimenter with
form, here to combine confessional poetry with layered
allusiveness, a collage of impressions, language and styles
drawn from a variety of sources. It's the kind of writing that
from time to time might have the reader wishing for explanatory
notes – and he will find them at the end of the book. Chapter
12, 'Possessions', for instance, borrows from *Beowulf* and the
Anglo-Saxon alliterative line to describe how, having been set
up in a house in Bangor, he was robbed by an acquaintance.
Chapter 13, 'The Pit' melds classical mythology – 'And at last
we crowd on sail,/Glide under the Euboean coast by Cumae [...
] The Sybil/In the pit of years/Is the mare he must break and
ride' – with the history of the south Wales coalfield, epitomised
in the experience of the poet Idris Davies, whose dramatic poem
sequences, *The Angry Summer* and *Gwalia Deserta*, Conran has
championed. Although it refers to 1979, Chapter 14 could
hardly be more contemporary in its analysis of society and the
threat of rampant capitalism: the poet as prophet! In the last
three chapters the damaged 'poor love' of the opening section,
grown old, is metamorphosed into the platypus, 'Floating on
his back like a dead dog/ On to the mudbanks', in an allegory
of the life-threatening operation he endured in the hope of

preserving a small measure of mobility. As the duck bill oxygen-mask slips,

> A faraway
> Voice like a tin soldier's
> Echoed in his consciousness:

'Well, I'm still dancing,' I said.

Conran is probably still best known outside Wales as the translator of *The Penguin Book of Welsh Verse* (1967). He is much more than that. This late offering, with its wit and complexity, deserves to be widely read.

A more familiar style of modernism, with italicised quotations and unexplained esoterica, is represented in Graham Hartill's latest book, *A Winged Head* (Parthian, 2007). A poem may be conveyed in a series of brief gnomic utterances, or taking its cue from Abiezer Coppe, suddenly explode in ranting denunciation of the war in Iraq: 'Rumsfeld, Wolfowitz, Cheney, Blair:/their throats are open sepulchres ...'. Elsewhere the varying space between lines seems to assume significance, and integrated prose quotation functions as chorus or explanation. Essentially, however, these are poems placed in the communion of friends (to whom several are dedicated), and in the resonating landscape of the southern March – Gwent, Powys, Herefordshire – studded with ancient churches. Hence, for example, the long sequence 'Jesse', inspired by the fifteenth-century carving in St Mary's, Abergavenny; and 'Cwmyoy, July', which takes us to a church that looks as if at any moment it might tumble downhill, where there are memorials by the Brute family of Llanbedr (who appear in an epigraph to another poem, 'Winged Heads'), and a unique image of the crucified Christ upright rather than depending from the nails (or as the poet sees it 'arms stretched straight/as if those starving ribs need *us'*).

It is a territory well walked and deeply considered, into which the present from time to time intrudes with its political and environmental concerns and insistent demotic. If the latter are plain enough, the same cannot be said of all the references to places and features. Perhaps that is why the parenthetical commonplace, 'barbaric/(means spoken with a foreign tongue)...' irritates, though not as much as finding 'span' where the past tense of 'spin' is intended. Hartill is widely admired, deservedly so. Irony is not his strong suit, but he has an excellent eye and ear (his phrase 'a scrawny iron gate' lingers) and at his best commands language sonorous and dramatic, as in 'Brochwell Looks Back On Melangell': 'I felt like a bird that stooped to the hare in me./All my life I'd been told to trample the womanly thing,/our game being power and heavy skill,/but when I fell, my sins/flew off from me like flies from cess'.

Even if a few of the rockets splutter and fall prematurely, Robert Minhinnick's *King Driftwood* (Carcanet, 2008) is a brilliant pyrotechnical display. The serious political and environmental issues that underlie the poems cannot be ignored, but the energy, the sweeping power of expression, the constant effervescence of imagery astonishes. Few contemporary poets can equal his inventiveness as a creator of images, or his linguistic resources, increasingly enriched by the vocabularies of science and geology. In one of the shorter poems, 'The Weighbridge', there is a reminder of the Minhinnick of *Native Ground* (1979), where in his 'Images from Tremorfa' he wrote of '[sliding] off early' from a day's 'clerking in the ferrous trade' – 'Passing East Moors, a blitzed town/Burning and deserted, fire's//Intricate horizon a yellow/Thread woven into the dark'. The strength and profusion of especially visual imagery was there 30 years ago,

but constrained by formalism. That old loyalty was waning in
*Hey Fatman* (1994) and had gone by the time *After the
Hurricane* appeared from Carcanet in 2002. Without resorting
to the commoner manifestations of 'free' verse, he achieves
untrammelled, logical expression and extraordinary music. If
Minhinnick's art now is reminiscent of anything, it is the
accomplished jazz musician improvising with no appearance of
effort. The poetry seems to unwind seamlessly, a kind of
freewheeling, but it has a strong basis of personal experience
and political conviction, for he is, too, a troubadour of the air
age, bringing fresh inspiration from distant countries, Iraq to
Argentina, to delight with exotic visions, and sometimes make
us squirm with guilt. But home, the south Wales seaside resort
of Porthcawl and its environs, is where the book's heart lies –
the beach, the sea's edge, its creatures and detritus, the
fairground, the dunes – 'And sand, of course'. It is difficult to
select from poems that unspool like magnetic tape, but if
pressed I would choose 'The Fairground Scholar', a fantasia on
the theme of language with tidal riffs, 'The arm of the Atlantic
round your waist', and echoes of the world's pain:

Okay
we are doing it
your way: watching
the storm destroy its text,
the tattooist become his own prosody,
ants conspire on the forest floor
in syllables of carbon and hydrogen,
the child emerge from the surf
with all the tide's codes broken in her
head;

[...]

MEIC STEPHENS, TONY CONRAN, GRAHAM HARTILL AND
ROBERT MINHINNICK

Rimbaud's black and green vowels
marching out of Somalia to meet him,
the drowning man arguing semantics
with the sea.

Turn any page, Minhinnick's visionary wordscape is endlessly
beguiling.

*PN Review* 186, Volume 35 Number 4,
March – April 2009.

# ROLAND MATHIAS
*January 2008*


Roland Mathias died on 16 August 2007, a few weeks short of his ninety-second birthday. He had suffered a stroke in May 1986 from which he never fully recovered. With typical fortitude, and with the constant support of his wife, Molly, he slowly regained the use of limbs and learned to speak again. He had from his school days preserved items of interest from newspapers and magazines, not least concerning his own career and achievements. There were already a few old and well-stuffed scrapbooks and during his long recuperation he made several more, carefully adding captions to cuttings and photographs. By the beginning of the 1990s he was corresponding with friends, though more briefly than hitherto, and setting aside hours in the week when he would sit in his study and try to write poems.

He saw himself first and foremost as a poet, but had filled his life so completely with labours, never undertaken lightly, or given short measure, as educationalist, short story writer, historian, editor, reviewer, literary critic, committee chairman, lecturer, preacher, that his poetry blossomed in odd corners of his life. During his days as teacher and headmaster, poems begun during one school holiday might be finished in the next. Now, with time enough and to spare, composition was difficult and very slow. Seven poems were written between December 1991 and 2000, five (including a short sequence after the manner of Edgar Lee Masters) were included in *A Field at Vallorcines* (Gomer, 1996), his last book. They lack the linguistic sinew and muscular energy he had commanded at the height of his powers, but a flavour of that verbal concentration and rhetoric remains in another still later poem, 'Peter Has Been Digging', which he wrote in 2000 and which, unmistakably his, stands at the end of the *Collected Poems* (UWP, 2002):

> Peter has been digging the beds, swaying
> Under forget-me-nots, as he always
> Does, but there is no honour nor contentment
> Since Molly has gone. Each of these days
> Has its parley on, its heredity buried in
> The summer. The Buff Beauty roses are perking
> Now, defining the beds. But this is a conceit, a gipsy
> Wandering, to make magical these petering last
> Ragged days, looking for appetite to answer
> Those blackbirds singing like incendiaries.
> This is what summer does, stops and tries
> Out old habits, girds the visitor with crumbs.
> No, this is not what Isidore of Seville may say
> In the old world, nor the notary at the gate,
> This is Molly's garden, schooling for the arrival of
> The right and quiet assertion that it formerly was.

Reviewers, who from the later 1980s had begun to find his wavelength, greeted *A Field at Vallorcines* with warm approbation, but the contents had been largely written, and in many cases published in magazines, in the 1970s. The appearance of the book after a decade of silence was a painful reminder, if one were needed, of the incalculable loss to the literary culture of Wales wrought by his illness. The extent of the personal loss to this most articulate of men is beyond imagining. It could have surprised no one had he been afflicted by frustration and bitterness. Nothing of the sort. Nor was he changed by the sudden terrible loss of his wife in 1996. His

Christian faith remained steadfast, his warmth and generosity to others did not waver, his cheerful enjoyment of company and conversation was the same as ever. If a word or distant memory would not come when bidden, he would smile, 'Can't do it.' The guessing game that followed could be hilarious, and sometimes triumphantly produced the right result.

We had been friends since 1969, when I'd had the (relatively) youthful audacity to write to him out of the blue and ask his collaboration in editing a book of short stories by Welsh writers, particularly for use in schools and colleges. The project appealed to him. He was committed to the cause of Welsh writing in English at a time when it was dismissed or wilfully ignored by reviewers and literary critics, and even by the University of Wales, who refused to see anything in it worth their attention. Roland was not alone in arguing for critical reading and evaluation, but his were the most persistent voice and cogent arguments. In the editorial pages of *The Anglo-Welsh Review* and his own painstaking analysis of texts in reviews and essays he laid the foundations of a new discipline in English studies that has its roots in Wales. By 1986, when he was struck down, the developments he had sought and worked for were beginning to reveal themselves in higher education institutions, but *The Shining Pyramid and other stories by Welsh Authors* (Gomer, 1970), which we had co-edited, was long forgotten.

We collaborated again, on *The Collected Stories of Geraint Goodwin* (Five Arches Press, 1976), and continued regularly in contact, particularly while he remained editor of *AWR*. Some time in 1973, in his editorial capacity, he suggested I should interest myself in Thomas Jeffery Llewelyn Prichard (1790 – 1862), an actor who lost his nose, allegedly in a fencing match, and author of *Twm Sion Catti,* 'the first Welsh novel in English'. Prichard was, I soon discovered, a hopeless case, but nonetheless fascinating for that, and I have been digging and conjecturing ever since. In our last conversation, a few days before he died, Roland asked again, as he always did, how Prichard was getting on, as though he was a mutual acquaintance.

Our relationship was always warm and easy, because, with all his intellectual gifts, he was a wonderfully amiable man, often jolly, sometimes mischievous, though not hurtfully so. It deepened when, in 1993, I was invited to write the Writers of Wales monograph on Roland Mathias. We met frequently at his Brecon home, where I was given access to those scrapbooks I have mentioned, everything else I asked for and much beside that I didn't know I would need. With the help of Roland and Molly I began to understand more fully his achievement and the principled motivation that underpinned it.

He was a committed Nonconformist Christian, a Congregationalist, as his parents had been. His father, Revd Evan Mathias, newly married, had just been called to a chapel in Pontypool when the First World War began. He volunteered immediately to serve as a Chaplain, and when the war was over stayed with the army. He preached in both Welsh and English and was, I suspect, a man who enjoyed company and conversation: he was a notable *eisteddfodwr*. All I have read and was told about her suggests that Roland's mother was a pillar in the home, but indifferent to society. She did not like army life and was an ardent pacifist. Her puritanical faith, her pacifism and her strength of character were major formative influences on the poet. His determination to yield to nothing in doing what he judged morally right is illustrated by his appearance before the Lancashire and Cheshire Tribunal for Conscientious Objectors in 1940. He refused military service and direction to what were termed 'non-combatant duties'. A local newspaper reported that he told the tribunal, 'The war is indefensible. He did not carry a gas mask. He would not take cover if a bomb fell.' Nor did he. While the authorities considered what to do with him, he continued teaching, but, at his request, without pay. Such are the strictures of a moral conscience. At a subsequent trial he was found guilty of refusing to attend a medical examination under the Armed Forces Act and sentenced to three months imprisonment with hard labour. Walton, he told me, gave intimations of Hell, but did not weaken his resolve.

With Roland's faith came a work ethic that demanded he used his gifts and filled each day with endeavour. He had, furthermore, extraordinary energy, so that it was not sufficient to be headmaster and writer, he must also serve the chapel and society at large, take part in amateur dramatics (he was a fine actor) and, in the aftermath of the war, support international youth organisations. Wherever his career in education took him – Pembroke Dock, Belper in Derbyshire, Birmingham – he made a strong impression on pupils, staff and community. The same ethic required self-assessment. In poems like 'A Stare from the Mountain' and the allegorical 'Burning Brambles' he revealed how far short he felt himself to be of the high standards he set:

… in the back ditch the tins are so many
Rust-flakes that part in the fingers, dusting on black
    bottles rainy

Yet stoppered, a heap of old sins without consequence, save
Deep in the land's heart where the sods of the field wall gave

Them summons for turbulence.
[…]
        The clog of leaves and sticks must be left
Momentarily on the ground. It is enough to unpile and shift

The endless loops of this waste, hearing the crackle behind
And knowing the smell of a life ill lived as it passes down
 wind.

When, in 'They Have Not Survived', he compares his life and its rewards with those of his peasant forebears, there is no satisfaction in the greater affluence and comfort he has attained. 'Why am I unlike/Them', he asks himself, 'alive and jack in office,/Shrewd among the plunderers?' Furthermore, their simple belief, preserved in the face of hardship, stands as a reproof to one who constantly interrogates his own belief and deplores his shortcomings.

In 'Brechfa Chapel', a poem of the early 1970s, black-back gulls gathered at a moorland pond afford the poet an image of contemporary society that is far from reassuring, and reminiscent of the conclusion of the Hitchcock film –

 ... shifting
Like pillagers from weed to shore, settling
And starting raucously, hundreds of testy
Black-backs utter their true society, bankrupt
Hatred of strangers and bully unrest whichever
Marge they think themselves forced to.
It is a militant brabble, staked out by wind
To the cropped down pasture.

Uproar and mindless violence formerly had their answer in the chapel that stands beside the pond:

 A light from this
Tiny cell brisked in far corners once, the hand held
Steady. But now the black half-world comes at it,
Bleaks by its very doors. Is the old witness done?

The question strikes to the heart. What can preserve us now from the 'hellish noise...harrying the conversation/Of faith'? Do we surrender belief? Roland's answer is clear:

> Each on his own must stand and conjure
> The strong remembered words, the unanswerable
> Texts against chaos.

For the attentive, he has another message, or rather a moral, in the poem 'Grasshoppers', drawn from observation of the creatures on the Rhinerhorn in September 1982. He saw that they did what they had to do, 'Knowing there's no survival/Except in the eggs that instinct/Buried in the entablature at the/Inevitable season'. For us, he concludes,

>                ... it is right
> To climb as we can, to the limit
> Of will. To do less,
> Is unworthy of such sun, such far
> Blue purpose as the distance is,
> Folded back and back, fainter
> And fainter always, surpassing
> Peak with peak, till the day
> Is what we can never be and scarcely
> comprehend.

Roland Mathias will surely survive as a writer of great seriousness and consequence, the most significant poet of Nonconformist Christian belief of his time.

*PN Review* 179, Volume 34 Number 3,
January – February 2008.

# RUSSELL T. DAVIES AND JOHN HAYNES

*March 2007*

The revived *Doctor Who* has survived two series with no diminution of critical and popular acclaim. It continues to attract large, 'family' audiences, win media awards and make household names of individual actors. To the surprise, possibly chagrin, of other BBC regions, it is produced in Wales, which hitherto has enjoyed little success as a maker of networked products. As we are tuned to BBC Wales and S4C (the Welsh language channel), from time to time we wonder about this. A fair amount of dross is broadcast from Cardiff, as elsewhere, but there are good things too, superior in our estimation to certain programmes from London and the other regions. Anyway, *Doctor Who* has overturned the barriers, and has been followed by *Torchwood* (for the uninitiated, an anagram of 'Doctor Who'), another sci-fi adventure series, but aimed at a post-watershed adult audience – and well-aimed at that.

The lead writer and executive producer of both series is Russell T. Davies, who now lives in Manchester but was born in Swansea in 1963 and educated at a large comprehensive school there and at Oxford, where he studied English. An apprenticeship in theatre, a director's course at BBC TV and early employment as a producer, mostly of children's programmes, preceded discovery of his true metier, writing television drama. Since the late 1990s, *Queer as Folk, The Second Coming* and *Casanova* have in turn stirred some controversy and raised his profile. He has earned a reputation for television writing that is daring, exciting – and often plain fun.

The special effects essential to science fiction fantasies are made in Wales by artists and a production team that, to judge by the names listed in the credits, are largely home grown, and locations in schools, public houses, coffee shops, London, Scotland and alien planets are, remarkably, also Welsh. Gelligaer Common, near the old mining village of Fochriw, where once I had a prized umbrella whipped out of my hand and destroyed by the gale, does duty as a Scottish moor, while the Scottish baron's turreted, gloomy mansion is represented by Craig-y-nos Castle, in the upper Swansea Valley, an early Victorian country house, to which Dame Adelina Patti added her own private theatre and the wonders of electric lighting. In another episode, Dyffryn House and gardens in the Vale of Glamorgan and Tredegar House in Newport looked splendid as simulacra of aristocratic eighteenth-century France. And how many viewers identified the Thames-side setting of one scene as a prospect of the River Usk at Newport from the city's new Riverfront Theatre? The camera lies! Much of the location shooting for *Torchwood* takes place in instantly recognisable parts of Cardiff Bay, where the underground headquarters of the eponymous small anti-alien task force, close to a monstrously menacing 'rift in Time', are adjacent to the Wales Millennium Centre. It all *looks* good, and the overhead night scenes in particular have a rare beauty. For the moment at least Wales has its own spectacular niche in popular culture, and whatever body is responsible for tourism these days should be rubbing its collective hands and thinking how best to exploit the opportunity.

WMC, which incorporates gallery space, has recently been the venue of an unusual exhibition of paintings by the artist and illustrator Lorraine Bewsey, the outcome of a year-long project to portray contemporary poets. Among the twenty subjects are a number who contribute to *PN Review:* Gwyneth Lewis, Patrick McGuinness, Robert Minhinnick, Dannie Abse, Tim Liardet among them, and others hardly less well known, such as Owen Sheers, Zoë Skoulding, and Pascale Petit. Most are on Seren's list. The artist works in pastels on paper and the portraits, all of head, shoulders and chest against a plain black background, are as remarkably like life as spouse or parent could wish. The exhibition was launched with readings by some of the portrayed poets, who were clearly pleased to pose again for the occasion. There will be further launches and readings as the exhibition tours other parts of Wales including Bodelwyddan Castle in the north and galleries in St Clears, Brecon, Swansea and Aberdare.

Last summer *(PN Review* 169) I wrote about the development of Seren/Poetry Wales Press Ltd over the past twenty-five or so years from early days in Cary Archard's (and then Dannie Abse's) front room to a publishing house with a fair sprinkling of successes in terms of Poetry Book Society recommendations and nominations for the shortlists of UK literary prizes. I remarked also that it had a quite delicate balancing act to perform in continuing to serve writing from Wales, while embracing with understandable enthusiasm work of quality submitted by writers from other countries attracted by its growing reputation. Seren has just achieved its biggest coup to date with the Costa Poetry Award going to *Letter to Patience* by John Haynes in the face of stiff competition. Without a notion of the book's planned (or even then achieved) scope, I had picked out his extract (XXVI) from *Letter to Patience* in *Poetry Wales* a couple of years ago, perhaps more for its unusual form (terza rima is not an everyday offering in magazines) than anything else: I keep a look out for rhyme and metre. Having heard nothing of him since, I had almost forgotten the name. With the sudden focus of media attention, I wondered about his Welshness. By his own account his paternal grandmother came from Llangynidr in Powys, which would have satisfied the Welsh Rugby Union in more desperate times. 'Where does he come from?' we invariably ask in Wales (and then, more colloquially, 'Who is he belonging to?'). Similar curiosity may well have manifested itself elsewhere as readers awoke to the success of a long-odds outsider. After all, everyone knows about Seamus Heaney. Haynes was born at Newquay, Cornwall to parents who were musical and had careers 'in showbiz'. He was an unhappy boarder at prep school and left public school at sixteen. Three years in the RAF and a brief flirtation with the theatre in a rep company preceded training for primary school teaching, after which he did a degree at Southampton University. The 'lack of imaginative freedom' in primary teaching disappointed him and he returned to Southampton to do research on 'criticism and metaphors from the sciences' under the supervision of F. T. Prince. He lectured for a while in teacher training and then found a post – and contentment – at Ahmadu Bello University, Zaria, Nigeria, where he stayed for eighteen years through the 1970s and 80s, and became deeply involved in African concerns and African literature. His parallel intellectual journey has taken in Marx and Wittgenstein, Pound as imagist, Hughes and Plath, Arthur Waley, Yeats and Lowell, Nadine Gordimer and Edgar Rice Burroughs among others. Doctoral research in applied linguistics on free verse had the contrary effect of turning him on to metre and rhyme. *Letter to Patience* was begun in 1992 – 3, following his return to England with his African wife.

Although elections to the National Assembly and the Scottish Parliament are four months off, there are already signs of anxiety in the higher echelons of New Labour over the possibility of nationalist gains, and faintly in the distance (perhaps indeed only a ghastly mirage) a vision of independence for Wales. For Scotland, this very day marking the 300th anniversary of the Act of Union with 'England and Wales' on 16 January 1707, the prospect may be a little more realistic. A BBC/ORB opinion poll informs us that 32% of Scottish residents support the notion, compared with 19% of those living in Wales. Nevertheless, Peter Hain, Welsh (and Northern Ireland) Secretary, has raised the bogy of the break-up of the United Kingdom and the terrible financial consequences of this for Wales. He writes dismissively of the fantasies of separatists 'like creating a Welsh foreign secretary and costly embassies worldwide, while simultaneously disbanding the armed forces'. Those of us who hadn't thought of that might consider it a good idea. Do embassies have to be costly? And are armed forces necessary to an essentially pacific nation? Viewed even from a distance, of far greater concern to Mr Hain are the devastating consequences at Westminster for a Labour party, new or old, deprived of its traditional Welsh and Scottish seats.

It may be recalled that about a year ago, Alun Pugh, Minister with responsibility for the arts in Wales, caused consternation by proposing major changes to the remit of the Arts Council of Wales. Henceforth, he declared, the major arts organisations, including Academi, the literature promotion agency, and Welsh National Opera, would be directly funded by Wales Assembly Government. The furore that followed, which focused on the dangers of political interference in the arts, might have surprised him but did not change his mind. Defeat in the crucial vote at the National Assembly obliged him to postpone his plan until a committee set up to consider the issue had reported – which it did in November. The report's major recommendation was that responsibility for funding should remain with the Arts Council but, with a nod to the Assembly, that the minister should join a committee of major figures from the arts who would outline strategy for ACW. The saga ended in December when Alun Pugh formally accepted the recommendations. Perhaps the 'bonfire of the quangos', that crippled element of Wales government policy, will now limp away.

I have been visiting parts of Breconshire that are associated with poems by Roland Mathias. More than ever convinced that he is a poet of high significance, and most mysteriously neglected, I have attempted to experience for myself the locations, all rural, some rather remote and wild, where the first impulse to write occurred, or which 'recollected in tranquillity' were an inspiration. Frail now, at 92, he looks back on the days when he was a great walker and can still describe the routes he took. And he advised, if I were to follow in his footsteps, I should go alone, as he did almost always. He is a poet of harsh conditions, preferring intellectual and moral rigour, and autumn and winter to spring and summer. So, having driven up the steep lane and across the rattling cattle grid at the top, I found myself recently on Llandefalle Hill, moor as bleak as he could wish, in dreadful weather. The wind was rising to a gale bearing with it rain in waves that broke over the car one after the other and swirled away to the east. Before me scattered clumps of gorse and rushy patches started up from the rough grass and there was a line of stunted trees, an old hedge perhaps, in the middle distance. Beyond that there were only irregular masses in various shades of grey; the darkest, furthest off to the west and disappearing fast, were the Beacons. To venture outside would have been foolhardy. Unlike Roland, wary of my fallible memory, I make notes on the spot. So it was, with a useless, barely visible map spread over the passenger seat and notebook and pen in hand, while the wind shook the car, I was concentrating on recording a few observations. I cannot be sure what made me look up, but when I did there was a horseman on a tall dark horse pacing silently by the car. I felt my nape hair rise. If that was an epiphany, I can do without them.

*PN Review* 174, Volume 33 Number 4,
March – April 2007.

# RAYMOND GARLICK

*January 2007*


A couple of issues ago I mentioned the launch at the Hay Festival of the hundredth publication in the Writers of Wales series, Tony Brown's *R.S. Thomas*. The first monograph in the series was *An Introduction to Anglo-Welsh Literature* by Raymond Garlick. I remember my interest, indeed excitement, at its appearance in 1970. I was lecturing at what was then Caerleon College of Education and Garlick was similarly employed at Trinity College, Carmarthen. There he had pioneered teaching about the English-language literature of Wales, a topic outlawed in the University of Wales, where English departments held fast to syllabuses and set books that might have been handed down by Oxbridge with the same injunction to eternal observance as the Ten Commandments.

Anglo-Welsh literature was deemed academically unacceptable in part because it was seen to lack a history. In an influential public lecture in 1956, Professor Gwyn Jones had declared that the tradition in which, as a distinguished novelist and short story writer, he practised, began only in 1915, with the publication of Caradoc Evans's *My People,* a perverse and caustic vision, by turns horrifying and hilarious, of the manners and morals of rural west Wales. The school of writing that Caradoc led, the professor argued, could not exist until the more radical anglicisation of Wales in the nineteenth and twentieth centuries, and the institutions that accompanied it, produced a population of educated English speakers – whose minds were opened only to mainstream English literature. In 1956, many of the writers who might figure in a course on Anglo-Welsh writing were, therefore, still alive, or anyway, like Caradoc, not long dead, and while it was vaguely hoped students would read their work, it had not been through the several stomachs of academia to arrive at a suitably digested form for university study.

As a young teacher in the early 1950s, Raymond Garlick started to gather evidence to demonstrate that Welsh writing in English had a history, extending as far back as the first Welshman to write a line creatively in the tongue of the coloniser (about 1470 so far as he could discover) and continuing, albeit in a dotted line, down the centuries to a burgeoning of talent in the 1920s and 1930s that Gwyn Jones pointed to and that we think of as 'the first flowering'. I recall Garlick lecturing on this topic in September 1969 at the 'Taliesin Congress' on literature in Celtic countries, a remarkable event, which, in addition to speakers from Wales, brought Derek S. Thomson and Alexander Scott from Scotland, Per Denez from Brittany, and Máirtín O Cadhain and Austin Clarke from Ireland. The force of Garlick's argument and the lustre of the occasion – and the subsequent publication of his Writers of Wales monograph – did much to confirm the academic respectability of his subject. I was deeply indebted to him then and later for the ideas and materials he gladly shared with fellow teachers who were seeking to bring into college courses writing that was more relevant to students (the great majority of them Welsh) in terms of time and place, than conventional syllabuses allowed, with no loss of literary quality.

Much later, when he was close to retirement, I had the privilege of observing him at Trinity College presenting the introductory session of a day course on 'Dylan Thomas Country' to a large group of sixth formers. Carmarthen was a convenient starting point for an expedition taking in Laugharne, Fern Hill, the Taf/Tywi estuary so brilliantly evoked in the 'Prologue' to

*Collected Poems,* and so on, and it would not have been possible then, or now, to find a better speaker to send them on their way. As a teacher in schools and college, he was one of the rare sort who held a class not by exuberance and party tricks (and certainly not by lowering his own high intellectual standards to some perceived level of their understanding), but by stillness, by calm, quiet, beautifully modulated speech, and of course by the depth of knowledge and love of his subject.

Raymond Garlick is an unlikely but passionate Welsh patriot. Born in London in 1926 and of English ancestry, he found his own way into the heart of Wales and its bilingual culture, at first through holidays in north Wales with English relatives who had retired there, and later, during the war years, through school in Llandudno and then university in Bangor, where he read English. As a student, he was already a pacifist, and influential friendships confirmed him in this conviction. They also gave a European dimension to his thinking and persuaded him that, having read poetry avidly from early childhood, he could also write it. Among Garlick's friends were the writer and artist Brenda Chamberlain (collaborator with John Petts and Alun Lewis on the Caseg Broadsheets) and her Dutch partner, who then lived in a cottage, Ty'r Mynydd ('the Mountain House') at the end of a steep path high above Llanllechid in Snowdonia. When Chamberlain moved, he rented her former studio at the cottage for £13 per year and lived there until 1949, when he became the first member of staff to be appointed by the new headmaster of the grammar school at Pembroke Dock – Roland Mathias.

So began (as I have mentioned before), one of the longest lasting and most productive literary friendships in twentieth-century Wales, without which we would not have had the magazine *Dock Leaves/The Anglo-Welsh Review,* which Garlick edited from its inception in 1949 until 1961, when Mathias took over, and the major anthology *Anglo-Welsh Poetry 1480-1990,* which Garlick and Mathias co-edited. As editor of the magazine he made lasting friendships with a number of important writers. That with R.S. Thomas gave rise to a life-long exchange of letters, which was highly valued by the poet's biographer, Byron Rogers. There was similar extensive correspondence with Idris Davies, David Jones, George Ewart Evans, T.H. Jones and Henry Treece. In keeping with Garlick's aim to bridge the gap that then existed between the two cultures of Wales, the range of contacts included also some of the most revered Welsh-language writers: Saunders Lewis, Waldo Williams and D.J. Williams. In 1955, a chance encounter on a rainy day in Blaenau Ffestiniog, where he had moved to take up a new teaching post, led to a close friendship with John Cowper Powys which lasted until the latter's death in 1963.

The number and depth of these friendships speak volumes for the man, but they are only part of the story. Raymond Garlick is from first to last that rarest of birds, a formal, rhyming poet of real substance. His craft in intricate verse-making is both servant to his convictions as staunch Nationalist and European, pacifist, non-violent protestor against the more asinine elements of British justice and the establishment at large, and medium for the celebration of Wales, its languages and people. His *Collected Poems 1946-86* (Gomer, 1987) is essential reading for anyone with an interest in Welsh writing in English.

At the end of September, I participated in an eightieth birthday tribute to him in Carmarthen. It was a fine occasion, which ended fittingly with words from the poet. He has been disabled since childhood as the result of a crippling illness, but incapacity has only strengthened his resolve to see things through. He described how in fairly recent years, in the course of a long-anticipated journey to the lands of classical antiquity, he visited Delphi. Not content to rest on the lower slopes of Mount Parnassus, with what difficulty it is hard to imagine, he climbed the steep path to the remains of the temple of Apollo. It was a story imbued with allegorical significance. Nonetheless, travel, he concludes (in 'Here'), seems best designed to sharpen appreciation of returning, for thus Garlick's sense of belonging to a particular Welsh locality, or *bro,* essential to his poetic persona, is expressed:

> Sometimes I think that coming home
> Is really why I go away:
> That moment when the diesel swings
> Round the curve from Carmarthen Bay
> Into the Tywi's wide embrace
> Is the one that crowns my day.

There have been celebrations of one kind and another elsewhere. The Arts Council of Wales, having been saved from summary execution at the hands of Welsh Assembly Government by the loss of Labour's knife edge majority (though it still awaits the outcome of an enquiry that will decide its future role, or indeed whether it has a role of any significance), has just achieved its sixtieth birthday. It has not always been popular with the institutions and individuals it represents, but when it was being dragged to the block, they stood up for it and the 'arm's length' principle in arts funding that it represents. Over the years, Council officers, members and committees (when they existed) have not lacked ideas or endeavour; funding has been another matter, particularly for literature. But there has been improvement in this respect also. The Council's budget for 2006 is £37 million – £26 million from the Assembly and £11 million from the National Lottery. The Lottery has made a difference: £200 million has been invested in arts projects in Wales from this source since 1996-7. While some may turn out duds, surely the law of averages will bring a quota of success.

There is a new National Poet for Wales. Gwyneth Lewis has been succeeded in the role by Gwyn Thomas, formerly Professor of Welsh at University of Wales, Bangor, one of the very finest of contemporary Welsh-language poets. He spent his young life in Blaenau Ffestiniog and – now I come to think of it – might well have been a pupil of Raymond Garlick at the grammar school there. He certainly grew up steeped in the bardic tradition endemic to that part of the Welsh heartland, but has consistently sought to interpret what might be considered an esoteric system to modern readers. He has published sixteen volumes of poetry. The addition of modern colloquial expressions, and an unexpected levity, to the matrix of traditional allusion in his later books has broadened his already wide appeal. He writes effectively about and for children (his translations, with Kevin Crossley-Holland, of tales from *The Mabinogion* are among the finest available). He is an enthusiastic proponent of film and television as cultural media. Not to put too fine a point on it, he has been a populariser of Welsh-language literature and culture, and there are never too many of those.

The historian Peter Stead, another gifted populariser, perfectly at ease before a microphone, seems to have been the moving force behind the Dylan Thomas Prize, which was inaugurated, fittingly, on the poet's birthday, 27 October, at a gala dinner in his home town, Swansea. It is a big award, even by modern standards: £60,000 for a book by a writer under 30. Among the fifty submitted were five volumes of poetry, none of which impressed the judges, who shortlisted six works of fiction by authors from as far afield as Northern Ireland and the USA. It was reported that the panel, chaired by Andrew

Davies (famed for his adaptation for the screen of *Bleak House* and so much more), argued long and hard before declaring their winner – a collection of short stories by Rachel Tresize, who comes from Treorci in the Rhondda Valley. I have read the book, *Fresh Apples,* and notwithstanding Andrew Davies's bold assertion that it is comparable to Joyce's *Dubliners,* will only say it would not have been my choice. My disappointment at the outcome may be exceeded by that of the organisers in respect of the feeble media coverage of the event, which is a sign, perhaps, that (winners excepted) we have had a surfeit of literary prizes.

*PN Review* 173, Volume 33 Number 3,
January – February 2007.

# R.S. THOMAS
*November 2006*

I thought in my last letter, with its closing critique of our prying cult of celebrity, I had written as much as I would wish to write for a while about R.S. Thomas. But I had not then read the recent biography of the poet by Byron Rogers, *The Man Who Went Into The West* (Aurum, 2006). At a time when literary biographies are typically heavyweight, almost day-by-day accounts of their subjects, this manages to reveal R.S. in all his complexity without wearying the reader with exhaustive detail. There is not an ounce of solemnity in the book and, though I can envisage a reaction in some quarters against what might be perceived as undue levity in the unfolding of the story, I prefer to think of it as lightness of touch that will commend it to the general as much as to serious students of the man and his work. If you have previously seen R.S. as 'the ogre of Wales', you will find here evidence of eccentric asceticism, extraordinary solitariness within marriage (to Elsi, who, as Mildred Elsie Eldridge, had been one of the brightest young artists of the late 1930s), failure to connect with others, including his own son, and antipathy to contemporary life amply to support your opinion. If you were previously an admirer of his subtle intellect and straight-speaking honesty, his granite principle and, above all, his poetry, here too you will find vindication of your views.

He was an unusual vicar: he disliked *all* hymns and had no small talk for parishioners, preferring to hide behind hedges to avoid meeting them and even to vault the churchyard wall rather than condole with the bereaved. But then again he performed his pastoral duties religiously, sat with the sick and

dying, wrote in parish magazines, urged backsliders to attend
services, preached hundreds of sermons. John Ormond, himself
a poet of real stature (who has had nothing like the recognition
he merits), and an outstanding BBC film-maker, interviewed him
in 1972 for *R.S. Thomas, Priest and Poet.* I remember it well as
I was given the job of approaching Ormond to ask if a transcript
of the broadcast could be made available for publication in
*Poetry Wales,* and having obtained it, of writing an introduction
that appeared with it in an R.S. Thomas special number (Vol.
7, No. 4, Spring 1972). I read it then, as I do now, with
astonishment at the interviewee's readiness to speak about his
first encounters with hill farmers, the physical paradigms of
Iago Prytherch, and with a frankness that, at the time, probably
gave his bishop qualms about the unorthodox nature of his
belief, when I knew him to be the most obdurately taciturn of
men. Ormond told me it had been far from easy but he had
managed it by joining R.S. watching seabirds from a cliff top
near Aberdaron. For a long time they sat together in silence
before he risked a question: did the poet-priest seek out lonely
spots to think? The seabirds wheeled, the wind blew, the tide
began to turn and, at last, R.S. admitted that in such places he
did indeed think. Ormond tried again: what was it that he
thought about? A pause ensued during which the tide receded
a fair way down the shore, then, 'Oh, this and that.'

However slow and halting the initial exchange, Ormond won
his trust and with marvellous tact obtained from him a more
complete statement of his poetic and religious philosophy than
he had ever confessed before, and worth repeating now:

I'm a solitary, I'm a nature mystic; and silence and slowness
and bareness have always appealed...God, reality, whatever it
is, is not going to be forced, it's not going to be put to the
question, it works in its own time...The message of the New

Testament is poetry. Christ was a poet, the New Testament is a metaphor, the Resurrection is a metaphor...My work as a poet has to deal with the presentation of imaginative truth. Christianity also seems to me to be a presentation of imaginative truth...Of course, I'm using the word imagination in the Coleridgean sense, which is the highest means known to the human psyche of getting into contact with the ultimate reality... one has been blessed with these sudden glimpses of eternity... glimpses of this eternal ultimate reality which one gets in Wales when the sun suddenly strikes through a gap in the clouds and falls on some small field and the trees around. There's a kind of timeless quality about this, one feels. Well this is eternity, if only one could lay hold on it...I firmly believe this, that eternity is not something over there, not something in the future; it is close to us, it is all around us and at any given moment one can pass into it; but there is something about our mortality... that makes it somehow difficult if not impossible to dwell, whilst we are in the flesh, to dwell permanently...in what I would call the Kingdom of Heaven. But that it is close and that...we get these glimpses of it, is certainly my most deeply held conviction.

He didn't shirk the duties that earned him a meagre living from the Anglican Church, which in return allowed him the time to practise his true vocation. Towards the end of his life, in his last parish at Aberdaron and especially in retirement in a cottage named 'Sarn' overlooking Porth Neigwl or 'Hell's Mouth' at the tip of the Llyn peninsula (leased to him for life by friends), he was at last socially at ease in a remote Welsh-speaking community. Even then there was a curious epilogue. After the death of his wife of almost fifty-one years, in 1996 he remarried. Betty Vernon, like him an octogenarian, had three previous husbands to her credit, smoked and swore and drank. They travelled widely and were happy together. And he continued to write prolifically to the end. The exuberant Betty told Rogers that she had burned three bags of poems after he died, claiming, 'We had a very close understanding, and I can judge poems. He just churned them out.' There were plenty left for Wynn Thomas to bring out the posthumous *Residues* (Bloodaxe, 2002), and they continue to turn up unexpectedly in odd corners and between the pages of secondhand books.

In the second half of the twentieth century Wales had in R.S. Thomas the foremost religious poet of the Anglican persuasion (a denomination surely supple enough now to accommodate a nature mystic without demur), and the foremost Nonconformist poet in Roland Mathias. They were very close contemporaries (Thomas was born in 1913 and Mathias, happily still with us, in 1915) and had much in common. Both played rugby, Mathias a good deal more successfully, both were great walkers, at home on mountain and moor, both were pacifists, Mathias coming to that determination earlier and sticking to it despite prison, while R.S. later became active in CND. They knew one another, of course, and had (have) a lifelong mutual friend in Raymond Garlick, first editor of *Dock Leaves/The Anglo-Welsh Review*, whose correspondence from Thomas is extensively quoted by Rogers.

Garlick persuaded Thomas to review Mathias's third book of poems, *The Roses of Tretower*. He might have taken on the job with gritted teeth, for as a rule he didn't write reviews or commit time to literary criticism. In any event, the review (in *Dock Leaves* No. 8) begins inauspiciously – 'Mr. Mathias is one of the younger members of the, by this time, rather tatterdemalion school of Anglo-Welsh writers' – and goes on to censure the 'younger' poet (by two years) for being stylistically 'Protean', for having fallen under the influence of Dylan Thomas, and for 'rather contorted' lines that raise the 'vexed question of intelligibility'. He has praise for language used 'in a taut and robust way' and those poems that have a connection with Wales, but there is no acknowledgement of the many poems in the book that have Christian themes or allusions – a curious omission for a practising poet and Anglican cleric. Mathias, one of the finest critics of his time, regularly reviewed Thomas's books and wrote an important article about his poetry. While admiring the other's great strengths as a poet, he cannot disguise his disappointment at the absence of clear religious and moral guidance in what is, after all, the work of a priest. That R.S. appeared unsympathetic to Nonconformist faith did not help. Both visited, at different times, and wrote poems on 'Maesyronnen', a sadly dilapidated 300-year-old chapel in Radnorshire. While Mathias is inspired by the evangelical spirit that spread forth from one of the historic homes of Puritanism and confirmed in his faith, Thomas sniffs 'the stale piety mouldering within' and is more interested in birds singing among the rafters. Mathias's religious conviction was not easily won, nor is it held without rigorous self-interrogation (one of the main-springs of his finest poetry), but in the end it is always there. He is at one with the founding fathers of his faith, though doubting his capacity to live up to their exacting standards. No wonder he has found it difficult to come to terms with R.S.'s failure clearly to profess his religion. 'I should have liked,' he wrote in a review of Thomas's *H'm,* 'to feel that that through the struggle of a poet who is also a priest (and who wasn't quite so glib about equating the two functions) I was being shown something that might be my struggle too.'

The argument could never be concluded, but we must regret that, because of the stroke he suffered in 1986, Mathias did not have the opportunity to discuss Thomas's later writings, such as his prose contribution to *Britain: A World by Itself* (Aurum, 1984), which is quoted by Rogers. Entitled 'A Thicket in Lleyn', it is, I think, more moving than the poem of the same name, which, I admit, I had forgotten. The narrative is the same: the poet enters a spinney where the trees are October bare, but just then leaved with tiny birds, goldcrests on their migration route. He enters so quietly that they perceive and accept him as no more than another tree and for a moment, before they fly on, the 'other realities' of his human existence are somehow suspended and he is elsewhere, 'part of the infinite I AM'. I don't know whether Mathias read this, but if he did, I am sure he must have been spellbound by its description of mystical experience, as I was last week.

*PN Review* 172, Volume 33 Number 2,
November – December 2006.

# TRANSLATION

*July 2005*

Two recent literary events have prompted me to revisit a time in the late 1960s and 1970s when, at some point in the proceedings, every gathering of writers in Wales was sure to debate the health and status of Welsh-language writing vis-à-vis English, the validity and usefulness of translating Welsh literature for the monoglot audience, and the suitability of the term 'Anglo-Welsh' as a label for those Welsh by birth or allegiance who wrote in English.

The Poetry Society's Translation Reading Series brought Michael Schmidt, Patrick McGuinness and Robert Minhinnick to an upstairs bar in the Wales Millennium Centre, where they discussed the 'Ethos of Translation'. They had plenty to say: Carcanet's impressive record as a publisher of literature in translation is well known to readers of *PN Review,* and Patrick McGuinness now offers advice on the subject to Seren, while, as editor of *Poetry Wales,* Robert Minhinnick has laboured to transform an introspective magazine into an international journal by introducing scores of poets from overseas, usually in translation. And, besides, all three are highly skilled translators. For stimulating talk the occasion lacked nothing but the size of audience it deserved. Minhinnick was particularly quick on his feet. Perhaps he anticipated challenges to his editorial policy, which has alienated some regular readers of *Poetry Wales* who would prefer to see the magazine continue as of old, focused principally, if not exclusively, upon the home-grown product, and to the swashbuckling approach to translation manifested in *The Adulterer's Tongue,* his anthology of six Welsh-language poets, typically published by Carcanet. In the event, none came. However, whether you can or should attempt to translate poetry, and whether, having decided to do so, a more or less literal, prose translation is better than one that aims at being poetic at the expense of being less accurate, continue as live and contentious issues. And, of course, they have been with us for centuries.

As will appear, I have been re-reading Keidrych Rhys's *Wales* recently, or rather skimming and reading intensively here and there, where something caught the eye. I would not claim this as an experience to rank with thumbing through its contemporary, *Horizon,* but *Wales* caught the mood of its various times and, if not momentous, had its moments. Reviews were often plainer speaking than they are today. In one (from *Wales* No 46, November 1959), Harri Webb takes to task Gwyn Williams, a translator whom he describes, without irony, as 'a scrupulous and deeply informed scholar with a genuine poetic sensibility', for the failings of *Presenting Welsh Poetry* (Faber, 1959). Webb argues that Williams is less successful in treating the poetry of the medieval period than previous translators, who captured the spirit of the original better in prose, and that he is 'irritatingly' at fault in rendering the work of several very different poets in a voice recognisably his own.

From the translator's point of view, the problem with early Welsh poetry is that its prosody is utterly alien to English. Gwyn Williams gave further offence to Harri Webb by his 'comparison of Welsh alliterative speed [sic] with cockney rhyming slang' and quoting 'a line of *cynghanedd* salvaged from Shakespeare'. Yes, *cynghanedd* can be found embedded, by accident or design, in English poems (Hopkins usually provides the example), but it is never structurally integrated into an entire poem, as it must be to satisfy the metrical rules of traditional Welsh poetry. Translating it is 'largely impossible', writes Minhinnick in his introduction to *The Adulterer's Tongue*. But it is necessary to give due acknowledgement to the current renaissance of this tradition, and he goes on to describe how he dealt with the work of 'a modern master' of it, Emyr Lewis: 'Working on poems such as ['M4'], I wished to somehow continue the poem where the Welsh left off. For me, studiously translating [such poetry] is hard graft. Why do it? Some poems don't want to be translated. But attempting to restyle 'M4' in another language is fantastic fun.' You can bet, however, that it will not please the purists.

Whereas bards of the ancient past have no say in the matter of translation, contemporary practitioners in the 'strict metres' do, and a few bluntly refuse to submit their poems to the process. Twm Morys, who has emerged as spokesman for this group, recalls the immense history of his craft, 'three-quarters as old as Christ', which constitutes 'another language yet again within the language'. In a note to *Poetry Wales* (Volume 38, No 3, 2003), he argues that poems in *cynghanedd* 'lose so much in translation as to make the effort almost worthless' and takes a hard line: 'When I have occasionally wanted to reach an audience that doesn't speak Welsh, I've written in English. Otherwise I write in Welsh because I'm speaking with Welsh-speaking people. If others would like to join in, well they can bloody well learn the language!'

Grahame Davies, the Welsh-language poet who joined Jeremy Hooker and Sheenagh Pugh to give the poetry reading that preceded the Roland Mathias Prize award ceremony (the second of the two events mentioned at the outset), stands somewhere close to the other end of the spectrum of views on translation. *Finiau/Borders* (Gomer, 2002), the book he brought out with Elin ap Hywel, is (like *The Adulterer's Tongue)* a facing-text anthology. It contains poems in Welsh by both writers, accompanied by translations that are the result of a joint approach to the project. 'Sometimes,' they say in an introductory note, 'we have translated our own work, sometimes each other's. Sometimes the translation is a fusion of the best elements of two versions.' And they proceed to identify the impetus that drove them: 'the constant attempt to find that Holy Grail of translation, the *mot juste,* and also the awareness that these are poems to be heard, either in the individual reader's head or in front of an audience. In the process we [...] came to understand anew that the poem's energy, either in the original language or in translation, lies in the hearing.' It is fascinating to see on the page in parallel Welsh and English, and hear, Grahame Davies working in another traditional form, the villanelle. His is a far from solitary voice proclaiming the value of translation to contemporary literature in Wales, as well as to the development of his own art. There are also the outstanding examples of Menna Elfyn and Gwyneth Lewis, who demonstrate convincingly that possessing two languages and the entry they give to two distinct cultures is far better than being restricted to one. And if the creative impulse is confined to one, why should it always be English?

Brecon was *en fête* for the inauguration of the Roland Mathias Prize, or at least the venues for both the reading and the ceremony that followed were crowded and the occasion generated a great deal of local enthusiasm. The shortlist included *A Glorious Work in the World* (UWP) by David Ceri Jones, a history of the Methodist Revival, in which Howel Harris, from nearby Talgarth, was a prominent figure; *The Canals of Mars* (Carcanet), Patrick McGuinness's stylish and highly praised first volume of poetry; and the eventual winner, Christine Evans's *Selected Poems* (Seren), which evokes rural life, particularly that of Bardsey, the island steeped in history off the tip of the Llŷn Peninsula, with persuasive clarity and sympathy. Since the prize-giving, unquestionably a successful occasion, there has been barely a whisper about it. Public relations is a tarnished trade but, goodness knows, we have need of some modest flag waving to celebrate the occasional literary success.

In his talk at WMC, Patrick McGuinness used 'Anglo-Welsh' in preference to the currently approved 'Welsh writing in English'. The former, he says, is a term that has a substantial weight of tradition behind it, has the merit of brevity, and is well understood (if you pause to analyse it, especially where translation enters the frame of reference, 'Welsh writing in English' can have a different meaning from that usually intended). But this has long been a contentious issue. I banged my head against it in the early 1970s, when I was editing the anthology *Ten Anglo-Welsh Poets* for Carcanet. I wanted to include Emyr Humphreys, the distinguished novelist and also a very fine poet, among the ten, but he courteously declined, saying that, as a matter of principle, he would not allow his work to appear in any book bearing the term 'Anglo-Welsh' in the title. He was, he insisted (and, now in his eighty-sixth year, thankfully still is), a Welsh writer. In a lecture as far back as 1938, Saunders Lewis, by common consent the greatest figure in Welsh literature in the twentieth century, asked 'Is there an Anglo-Welsh literature?' and concluded that there was not, because there are no Anglo-Welsh people. Nor, he argued, is there an Anglo-Welsh dialect, with its own idioms and rhythms and folk poetry, like that in Ireland, which gave writers such as 'Yeats and Synge and Lady Gregory a basis for song and drama'. There are dialects in Welsh in rural Wales, he went on, as there are in English in the English countryside, which afford similar scope for literary development, but 'the extension of English [in Wales] has everywhere accompanied the decay of [Welsh] culture, the loss of social traditions and of social unity and the debasement of spiritual values. It has produced no richness of idiom, no folksong, but has battened on the spread of journalese and the mechanised slang of the talkies'. In Saunders Lewis's eyes, 'Mr Dylan Thomas is obviously an equipped writer, but there is nothing hyphenated about him. He belongs to the English.'

Wyn Griffith, eminent in his day as novelist, poet and translator, contributed 'A Note on Anglo-Welsh' to the first number of the revived *Wales,* July 1943, which begins: 'No man born ever wrote poetry in two languages' – a view he would now be obliged to change, on at least two counts. Getting to the point, he echoes Saunders Lewis: 'In Wales I can find nothing 'Anglo-Welsh' [...] the description 'Anglo-Welsh' is never claimed by any except by Welshmen who cannot speak Welsh, and then only when they are writers', and there, too, time has proved him wrong. But the debate went on, fuelled as frequently as he could manage it by Keidrych Rhys, in the pages of his journal. 'Do you consider yourself an Anglo-Welsh writer?' was the first question in the *Wales* questionnaire, to which there were eleven respondents between No 8/9, August 1939, and No 23, Autumn 1946. George Ewart Evans, probably best known now for his work as oral historian in East Anglia, did not like the category: 'It suggests an artificial... fusion of cultures'. 'I would indeed like to be an Anglo-Welsh writer,' wrote John Cowper Powys, 'and I hope in time when I have succeeded in at least learning to read and write Welsh that I may be in a position to take a part in Welsh life worthy of my ancestors.' David Jones did not 'feel very happy about this kind of classification, but if by 'Anglo-Welsh' a person of mixed English and Welsh blood and affinities is meant, then I suppose I could be so described.' Predictably, R.S. Thomas exclaimed, 'No! A Welsh writer [...] the question of a writer's language is a mere matter of historical accident and will be seen to have little ultimate significance.' Vernon Watkins agreed, 'No. I am a Welshman, and an English poet' and then added, intriguingly,

'I would be Anglo-Welsh only if I could write also in Welsh.' B.L. Coombes replied 'I do, very definitely.' But he had lived on a farm in Herefordshire until he was eighteen, then sought work in the south Wales coalfield, settled here, learned Welsh and wrote 'the autobiography of a miner', *These Poor Hands,* which earned critical accolades from Cyril Connolly and J.B. Priestley. Glyn Jones's reply was a simple 'Yes', but when he came to dedicate his splendid *The Dragon Has Two Tongues* to Keidrych Rhys in 1968, he began 'I address this introduction to you because in a way it was you who started it all. By 'it' I mean this particular book and the general enquiry into the Anglo-Welsh, a term, by the way, I know you dislike as much as I do.' It has taken a little time, but a strong consensus has grown in favour of 'Welsh writing in English', due in part to the recently achieved respectability of academic studies in the field. The important Universities of Wales Association for the Study of Welsh Writing in English has adopted the formula and applies it as a brand to all its publications.

More than half a century ago, in a talk to the Dunedin Association *(Wales* No 30, November 1948), R.S. Thomas said: 'It is one of the dearest achievements of a certain mentality in Britain to convince others that they will never produce any literature of worth until they write in the English language.' In general, attitudes over the border may have altered very little, but there has been evolution here. Fundamentally, what is at stake is national consciousness. Among writers, the change began in 1968, when Yr Academi Gymreig, until then a Welsh-language academy of letters, after lengthy debate, acceded to the request of a deputation of Anglo-Welsh writers to admit an English-language section. Mutual suspicion lingered, but the readiness of the membership of the new section to support Welsh-language causes was an important factor in strengthening the bridge that had been built. Over the years it has become the norm rather than an exception for writers in English, if not already Welsh-speaking, to learn the language. Translation of contemporary Welsh poetry into English, once rather rare, has become almost commonplace: both *The Bloodaxe Book of Modern Welsh Poetry* and Robert Minhinnick's splendid *Adulterer's Tongue* were published in 2003. And, as previously noted, we now have fine poets such as Gwyneth Lewis, Menna Elfyn and Grahame Davies, who, flying in the face of orthodox opinion, are creatively at home in either language.

Since 1968, more widespread influences have come into play, notably the increase in education through the medium of Welsh and later the inclusion of Welsh as a second language in the National Curriculum for pupils in all primary and secondary schools, the implementation of a Welsh Language Act and, after one missed opportunity, the establishment of a National Assembly in Cardiff. In the street, too, and the pub and the newspaper, attitudes have changed. A few become apoplectic over bilingual official forms and road signs and would be happy to see *Cymraeg* slide to oblivion, and one or two powerful voices are raised on behalf of the monoglot English-speaking majority, who, they say, are short-changed when it comes to cultural support and development, but on the whole there has been a healthy increase in recognition of the different identity the Welsh language confers on Wales, and in pride in being Welsh – never more obvious (and perhaps this betrays an underlying fragility in the national psyche) than in a year when Wales wins rugby union's Grand Slam title.

*PN Review* 164, Volume 31 Number 6, July – August 2005.

# DYLAN THOMAS AND T.H. JONES

*May 2004*

To adapt his namesake RS, there was, as predicted, a deal of 'picking the carcase' of an old poet before midnight bells brought 2003 and celebration of the fiftieth anniversary of Dylan Thomas's death to a suitably sodden end. One might have expected it to be the occasion of sober revaluation of Thomas's art and assessment of his place in twentieth century literature. Nothing of the sort came to my attention. The tawdriness transfiguring almost everything touched by the press these days is epitomised by a crop of newspaper headlines that caught my eye in October and November. The *Western Mail* gave its readers 'Dylan Thomas tricks BBC from the grave' – about the careless inclusion in a BBC Wales radio tribute of a poem, 'His Requiem', that Thomas filched from the *Boys' Own* and passed off as his in the same *Western Mail* in 1927; 'How Dylan's life and wealth were hijacked', allegedly by unscrupulous, unsympathetic and even criminal trustees of the Thomas estate, and the response the following day from Thomas's biographer Paul Ferris, 'Why Dylan trustees don't deserve to be labelled villains'. The *Guardian* did its bit for literature with 'Dylan Thomas's granddad was a model of lust' and 'The cut-price Dionysiac'. The latter headed one of Hywel Williams's viciously acerbic essays that did have a few words to spare for the poetry, although one could hardly consider them balanced: 'His poems, in all their babbling weariness, try to recover a baby's view of the world. Which is why reading him is like stumbling into a one-infant workshop in automatic writing'.

Williams is paid to offend our sensibilities on the grounds that controversial lambasting of a public figure sells newspapers. He is too intelligent to let the opportunity pass without offering some observation that pulls us up short. In this case it is a critique of *Under Milk Wood* as 'the single most important anglophone text in providing the English with an essentially treacherous view of Wales'. The writer is suggesting that *UMW*, a 'literary exercise[s] of the colonial mind', demeans the Welsh. Similar accusations have been levelled at another bestseller, Richard Llewellyn's enduring, and immensely appealing, myth of the south Wales coalfield, *How Green Was My Valley*. Are the English incapable of distinguishing fiction from fact? Does anyone think that Thomas's cartoon characterisation of a Wales that never existed is anything like the real Wales? Hywel Williams does, for the sake of his essay at least, and he has a brickbat to spare for the 'generations of Welsh actors [who] have colluded in this sorry little tale by a man who was the literary agent of the colonial condition'.

My first instinct is to disagree profoundly with the *Guardian* writer, but then I ask myself what alternative visions of Welsh life are available to the wider world in our literature. We can do anti-English pretty well, as the poems of R.S. Thomas, Nigel Jenkins, Harri Webb and John Tripp, among others, amply demonstrate, but where can one find writing that expresses something of the essence of Welshness? The work of Emyr Humphreys (especially *Outside the House of Baal*) comes at once to mind, but after that not much. Perhaps we are doomed to be thought either sub-human chapel-going hypocrites (by readers of Caradoc Evans's short stories), or, in Hywel Williams's words 'irresponsible charmers...[with] a national talent for genial submissiveness', like Dylan Thomas's creations. If one has to choose, the latter is more appealing. Anyway, what has literature got to do with it? For all the multitudinous views of the national character that might be gathered from the books of English writers, it is a very much simplified – and unflattering – caricature of the English that persists in the minds of the citizens of other countries, including Wales.

Among the books that caught the fiftieth anniversary tide is *Dylan Remembered, Volume One 1914-1934* (Seren, 2003). This is a transcript, edited by David N. Thomas, of part of the collection of about 150 interviews conducted between 1958 and the mid-1970s by Colin Edwards, a Welshman then domiciled in California, among relatives and friends of the poet. It is the source of the *Guardian* story of the poet's lustful grandfather and could be a mine of trivia for future biographers. It also offers a few facts about Thomas that are generally under-emphasised, such as his interest in theatre and practical experience of the stage long before he became a celebrity as a performer and wrote the best known of all radio plays.

One of the earliest book length studies of Thomas's poetry, *Dylan Thomas* in the *Writers and Critics* series (Oliver & Boyd, 1963) was written by T.H. Jones, another Welsh poet, whose life was almost as colourful as Thomas's and whose death was equally tragic. A recent biography, *T.H. Jones, Poet of Exile* by P. Bernard Jones and Don Dale-Jones (UWP, 2001), which benefits from interviews or correspondence with many relatives and friends and the cooperation of his widow, Madeleine, tells the whole rather gloomy story. Thomas Henry Jones, known as Harri, was born in December 1921 on a small farm high in the mountains above Builth, Powys, and brought up in circumstances of conspicuous rural deprivation. Recollections of him as a boy and young man mention his scrawniness and pallor and threadbare clothing. The disadvantages he suffered did not dim his intelligence. He gained a scholarship to the county grammar school at Builth and went up to UCW Aberystwyth in 1939.

At Aber he soon became known as a character. He was a left-wing political activist, a drinker and an ambitious writer. His work appeared in the college magazine, *The Dragon*, under the name T.H. Jones, following the example of Yeats, Eliot and Auden, all of whom had some influence on his early poetry, though the seductive rhetoric of Dylan Thomas had by far the greatest effect. The local recognition he won at this time was as an essayist and short story writer, but he always saw himself as a poet. How far this was a fate laid upon him by his paternal grandfather, a shepherd and chapel deacon, who was literate in Welsh and English, is not easily determined, but the old man became a key figure in Jones's nostalgic myth-making of his rural childhood.

In 1942, at the end of his second year at UCW, he joined the navy – not the predictable choice of a young man from the hills of Powys. Nevertheless, his fascination with the sea, begun with the books he read as a child, continued throughout his life, though he never learned to swim. As is usually the case, the war exposed him alternately to mindless *ennui* and appalling stress. He served as a telegrapher on a minesweeper escort attached to Malta convoys and had spells of riotous shore leave in North African ports that left a bitter aftertaste of guilt. In the later poems sex is the original sin.

He met his future wife while shore-based after the war, was demobbed and returned to Aber in 1946 to do honours English. He was awarded a First and did research on the imagery of the metaphysical poets. His studies gave him more than an MA in 1949: they added lasting elements of seventeenth-century poetic style to his own voice.

During these years the ex-serviceman student created a self-image that left an indelible impression on all who knew him. He was a hard-drinking, charismatic character, and devoted to poetry. Women were drawn to him. He had married Madeleine in 1946, but at this time, while she pursued a course in ceramics in London, they lived apart. Alone in Aber, he continued to have relationships with others, notably the young Rachel Roberts, a fellow student, destined to become a very fine film actress – and wife of Rex Harrison – before alcoholism destroyed her talent and she took her own life.

Jones tried desperately hard to obtain a post in a university English department but without success, until he was recruited by the fledgling university college at Newcastle, New South Wales. In 1959, full of hope, he set out for Australia with his wife and three small children. His first book of poems, *The Enemy in the Heart*, published by Rupert Hart-Davis in 1957, had attracted favourable reviews in the metropolitan press. He seemed on the threshold of limitless promise and quickly gained a reputation on the campus as a wonderful reader of poetry, in the tradition if not the manner of Dylan Thomas. Robert Lowell was a favourite in his performances, an indication of his enthusiasm for American literature, which developed strongly in Australia. The confessional mode was absorbed into his writing.

Encouraged by the cheapness of drink and permissive attitudes among college staff, Jones hit the bottle harder than ever. He had long been convinced that drink and women were essential to maintaining his contact with the poetic muse and in his new role he had access to a surfeit of both. Within a few years he had declined into alcoholism and, though he never ceased protesting his love for her, become the despair of his wife. When on the afternoon of 29 January 1965 colleagues brought him home drunk, Madeleine and the children went off to the library and left him. He was missing when they returned and a few hours later was found dead in a swimming pool cut into the rock of the nearby shore. The inquest found that he had died accidentally, but the confessional poetry of his final months suggests it might have been otherwise.

We are within a year of the fortieth anniversary of the death of T.H. Jones. He has been so long neglected I doubt the media will make much of it: little enough attention has been paid to the biography that, late in the day, has prompted these remarks. But is he worth remembering? Yes, very much so. After the promise and achievement of the first book, his second, *Songs of a Mad Prince* (Hart-Davis, 1960), was simply more of the same and a disappointment, but he wrote prolifically in Australia and in *The Beast at the Door and other poems* (Hart-Davis, 1963) reveals unexpected strengths that have developed out of the more complete assimilation of those influences – Dylan Thomas, Auden, Eliot and metaphysical poetry – that had manifested themselves separately and more obviously in his earlier poems, combined with a lacerating self-analysis that he learned from his study of contemporary American poets. In 'Llanafan Unrevisited' (the title a denial of *hiraeth* or nostalgia for home), he mingles ideas of exile and human love. It begins: 'I took for emblem the upland moors and the rocky/Slopes above them, bitter parishes', and ends:

And now I live in the good meadows, and I have
No emblem except your body, and I am
Still a member of a narrow chapel, and a boy
From a hungry parish, a spoiled preacher,
Greedily taking the surplus of your sunshine,
And still afraid of hell because I've been there.

He was a gifted poet of both the physical and the psychological aspects of sexual relations, and as honest about them as he was about the sickness that was destroying him. He concludes 'Lines on the Death of an Alcoholic' with extraordinary prescience:

269

Lapped now by deeper waves he lies,
An ague stilled, untwitching bones,
Taut tongue unswollen and relaxed,
And silent all hysteric moans.
Only the stink around his grave
Says, Here was one we could not save.

Another book entitled *The Colour of Cockcrowing* came out in 1966, again from Hart-Davis. It was assembled by his widow, with the assistance of colleagues in the English department at Newcastle, from the 'Black Book' in which, from 1949 until his death, Jones had copied some four hundred poems as they were composed. The posthumous volume is, if anything, even surer in its display of the complex of poetic skills he had refined in the years of his physical decline. Scores of poems still remain unpublished. A new 'collected poems', edited by the same team that brought out the biography, is on the stocks. It will be worth waiting for: a proper first evaluation of T.H. Jones is long overdue.

*PN Review* 157, Volume 30 Number 5, May – June 2004.

# TONY CONRAN AND IDRIS DAVIES

*January 2004*

In 1995, the Welsh Union of Writers marked the UK Year of Literature by publishing *Thirteen Ways of Looking at Tony Conran,* a book celebrating the writer's life and work. I have mentioned Yr Academi Gymreig, (which, as 'Academi', is now the established agency for literature promotion in Wales) in previous letters, but not, I think, the union. It was set up in 1982 to represent writers vis-à-vis publishers, broadcasters and public institutions and is open to any prepared to pay the modest annual subscription. A parallel body, Undeb Awduron Cymru ('Union of Writers of Wales'), founded almost a decade earlier, in 1973, functions in much the same way for Welsh-language writers. Contributors to the celebratory volume include members of the Undeb. Anthony Conran may well be one himself: as an outstanding translator of Welsh verse he is ideally qualified to have a foot in both camps.

Conran's *Penguin Book of Welsh Verse* (1967) did more to inform readers about the essential nature and quality of Welsh poetry from the sixth century to the twentieth than any other book before – or since. To some, it was a revelation. Nor was its impact confined to those like myself, then freshly returned to Wales from occupational exile in England and striving to gain a fingerhold on the great monolith of the Welsh language. Thanks to the publisher's cachet and distribution network, it reached into minds open to the experience throughout the world. *Thirteen Ways of Looking* reprints a review written for *Planet* 66 (December/January 1987-8, on the occasion of the publication of Seren's revised edition) by Les Murray, in which he expresses his 'amazed delight in Conran's pioneering Penguin book' and acknowledges 'its importance in the development of [his] own writing'. Part of Murray's delight was in his discovery of 'a whole ancient and in the full sense classical tradition', which is still extant, one might add. But it is his lavish tribute to the intoxicating power of Conran's rendering in English of *cynghanedd* that most surprises: 'What echoed continually and fascinatingly for me out of Conran's translations was an all-over patterning of cross reference and cross resonance, a kind of ever-growing crystal lattice of sound and sense at once. I was amazed by the continual fine shifts of key, of vowel colour, by how a sequence of consonants would appear with dark vowels between them, then immediately recur with an infilling of light vowels, like shadow and sunlight chasing each other across a rippling current. It was a powerful, ever-recurring mantra against randomness and chaos.' Murray saw it as a necessary antidote to *vers libre* on the one hand and 'the stiffer march of English rhyme, with its ever-successive finalities' on the other. He was glad to acknowledge that in the flexibility of the kind of fleeting, resonating rhyme he saw in Welsh poetry he found a resource of substantial importance to the development of his own writing.

In his autobiographical essay in *Artists in Wales 2* (edited by Meic Stephens: Gomer, 1973), Tony Conran states baldly, 'I was born a spastic' and it was for health reasons that he was brought up by grandparents, first in Liverpool and then Colwyn Bay on the north Wales coast, rather than his birthplace, Kharghpur, in Bengal, where his father was a railway engineer. He describes himself as a young man having a life of the mind and the imagination and being passionately excited about 'real or imaginary knowledge'. That might be thought to predicate an adult intellect effete and unworldly. Nothing could be further from the truth. His intellectual power, energy and determination earned him a First in English and Philosophy and a post in the English department at University of Wales, Bangor, from which he retired in 1982.

He has strong views about the function of poetry. It is not merely for self-expression and self-gratification, but to render coherent the values of the community for which the poet writes. This view, influenced by his profound study of the Welsh poetic tradition, finds expression in his own poems, many of which were written for friends and specific occasions – 'Elegy for the Welsh Dead in the Falkland Islands, 1982' is probably the best known. As we approach the fiftieth anniversary of the death of Dylan Thomas, it is worth recalling that Conran first became involved in the 'Anglo-Welsh' literary scene as the winner of a competition organised in 1953 by *Dock Leaves* (later, *The Anglo-Welsh Review*) to write a memorial tribute to Thomas. The competition was judged by Louis MacNeice, who (in No. 13) took exception to the 'emotional clichés' and the 'many tags from Thomas's own poetry' that disfigured the majority of entries, as well as their lack of 'real shape which is something which Thomas himself insisted upon'. These are judgements that could have applied with equal force to many poets and would-be poets of the time. Conran's entry, for which he had chosen the Burns stanza, stood out as something entirely different:

Poor poetry is gone to seed;
Damp footnotes in dull verse must plead
The rigour of her proper creed
    In their excuse,
While prosemen with her direst need
    Play fast and loose.

And he has remained different, very much his own man, with strong, often controversial views, not least as a literary critic. He thrives on the clash of opinion. Although I admired Gwyn Jones enormously, I could not forbear a sly chuckle at the vigorous shoeing his *Oxford Book of Welsh Verse in English* received from Conran (in *Planet* 45/46, November 1978). He is not one to mince matters, especially when it comes to the selection and translation of early Welsh language poets, although he saves his sharpest censure for the editor's choice of Anglo-Welsh poets, several of whom, like Edward Thomas and Wilfred Owen, have doubtful claims to Welshness and none of whom is under fifty-five. And then there is the question of the poetic standing of Idris Davies as implied by the three poems Gwyn Jones allows him – 'a selection that belittles him,' Conran fumes, 'makes him a local bard, a half-way house to McGonagall'.

By the time we get to 9 November this year, few people with even a superficial interest in literature will have managed to escape a reminder that Dylan Thomas died fifty years ago. Few beyond our borders, or even within Wales, will have any notion that it was the fiftieth anniversary of the death of Idris Davies on 6 April. If Davies is not entirely forgotten here, it is in some measure due to the critical influence of Tony Conran. In the same *Planet* review he writes: 'There's a range of attitudes and techniques in Idris Davies that make him one of the most sophisticated poets the Anglo-Welsh have had. His ruthless demand for clarity of expression sometimes topples over into the trite or the embarrassing; but it is a small price to pay for his dramatic masterpiece, *The Angry Summer*, a piece that ought to be as common in our theatres as *Under Milk Wood*.' It was Glyn Jones, reviewing Davies's *Selected Poems* in *Dock Leaves* (No. 11) who first urged consideration of *Gwalia Deserta* and *The Angry Summer* not as books of individual poems, but integrated sequences on the themes of industrial depression in south Wales and the 1926 general strike respectively. Tony Conran, who brought out a scholarly edition of *The Angry Summer* (UWP) in 1993, and is himself an experimental dramatist of considerable note, has established recognition of them as unified dramatic works.

Idris Davies was born in 1905. His birthplace, Rhymney, at the top of one of those ribbon-like south Wales industrial valleys, has the Brecon Beacons at its back. Although founded on iron working, by the beginning of the twentieth century its whole economy and *raison d'être* was coal mining. Davies left elementary school at fourteen to go down the pit. He spent seven years as a collier before a combination of circumstances, first the loss of a finger while working underground, then the seven-month miners' strike of 1926, and finally the closure of the pit where he worked and consequent unemployment from 1927 to 1929, forced him into another way of life. He had been a young man, not friendless, but happy in his own company, content to while away leisure hours in the reading room and library of the local Workmen's Institute, or roaming the mountains. Briefly, he took WEA classes, matriculated and completed his education and training as a teacher at Loughborough and Nottingham University, qualifying in 1932.

While still in the pit, a friend and fellow collier had introduced him to the poetry of Shelley. It is not easy to imagine now slogging at the coalface and coming up at the end of the day shift with the pit grime still on you, looking at the mountains, and thinking, 'What shall I do with what remains of the day?' This is what Davies recorded in his diary: 'As soon as I had dinner today I bathed and went up the field with a book in my pocket. There was nobody I knew about, so I went to read some of Shelley's poems as I lounged on the grass. I read the 'Skylark' over again. It is amazing stuff. Then I read

'Men of England'. The best poem about the workers ever written. And Shelley was a rich man's son! What if he had been a coalminer? Shelley was a real extremist, if ever there was one. He's a dazzler!' Young people today, granted far easier lives, rarely react to Shelley at all, far less with that kind of simple enthusiasm.

Davies had tried his hand at writing before he began his teaching career in London, but there, in that curious Welsh *salon* at Griff's bookshop in Cecil Court, off Charing Cross Road, he found like-minded exiles, including Dylan Thomas, who afforded him friendship and encouragement. He began to be published in magazines such as *Poetry Review*, *Adelphi* and Keidrych Rhys's *Wales*, and in 1938 his first volume of poetry, *Gwalia Deserta*, came out from Dent. Davies was politically alert and astute, a socialist of course, and his mind and senses were attuned to poetry (he had a prodigious quantity of English verse by heart). Furthermore, he had lived through the worst times in the industrial history of south Wales. It was natural that he should find his subject in that turbulent period. *Gwalia Deserta* was indifferently received by reviewers who failed to appreciate both its cumulative effect and Davies's self-confessed 'unpayable debt to the mighty Wordsworth' in his choice of 'incidents and situations from common life' and 'selection of language really used by men'. Some who will say they have never heard of the book will, however, remember Pete Seeger's plangent 'Oh what can you give me?/ Say the sad bells of Rhymney', which is number XV in the sequence.

The fifty lyrical and passionate poems that comprise *The Angry Summer* were written in June and July 1941, while Davies was teaching his evacuee pupils in the village of Anstey, Hertfordshire. It was accepted by T.S. Eliot and published by Faber in 1943. Subtitled 'A poem of 1926', it is more concentrated in theme and effect than *Gwalia Deserta*. The pits have long gone, and even in Davies's lifetime the sense of community in the valleys that had been engendered by shared toil, hardship and aspiration had begun to ebb away, but it still has a powerful impact.

Idris Davies returned to the Rhymney Valley in 1947 to teach at a local junior school. He found: 'the social and cultural life of the region to be very impoverished in comparison with what he remembered from his youth', says Dafydd Johnston in his introduction to the *Complete Poems* (UWP, 1994), and was doubtless disillusioned. It did not help either that the marriage he so earnestly desired was put off because his fiancée, also a teacher, was caring for her invalid mother, and, after *Tonypandy and other poems* (Faber, 1945), he could find no one to publish his work. Eventually, in March 1953, Faber brought out his *Selected Poems*. A month later Davies died of cancer. For all the well-rehearsed wonders of *Under Milk Wood*, I think I should prefer to hear a radio performance of *The Angry Summer* before we stumble to the end of 2003.

*PN Review* 155, Volume 30 Number 3,
January – February 2004.

# ROLAND MATHIAS AND WILLIAM JENKINS REES
*September 2003*

We passed through Y Gelli Gandryll (Hay-on-Wye) recently, on our way to a pub meal just across the border. It was a blustery, showery day and the book town was quiet, few cars in the car park and bibliophiles thin on the ground. In a week's time it will be very different. The programme of the Hay Festival has that starry look that should attract punters from afar. A scattering of Welsh items might bring in local supporters, or so I hope. I have a small part to play in the celebration of Roland Mathias, the man and his poetry, along with Professor Wynn Thomas, Robert Minhinnick, Gilllian Clarke, Anne Cluysenaar and Peter Finch. All of us count Roland as a friend of many years standing and are delighted to participate in an event honouring him.

I cannot be sure now, but I think the first Mathias poem I read was 'Cascob', which appeared in *Dragon,* the magazine of UCW Aberystwyth, in 1958 (that year, a farsighted editor had the good sense to invite contributors from outside the student body). 'Cascob' is a strange poem and I continued uncertain about it, even after lengthy discussion with the poet, whose recollection of places and events, once perfect, has become unreliable since he suffered a stroke.

> Just here's the middle of a silence that
> Has already sung the centuries like a gnat:
> The valley's middle too, by the hill sound
> Topping the trees. Perhaps the full circle, for the bound
> Of the churchyard circles, and the black yews
> Are markers.

A comprehensibly descriptive opening, but a few lines further in we begin to wonder what is going on:

Blank wall facing west, belfry of weather-board
Raised on a druids' mound, none of it
Reassuring. Within, a brass of familiars, habit
Of clergy, *pater pater pater noster noster noster*
Three times for Saturn, *O save our sister*
*Elizabeth Lloyd from spirits, amen.*
[...]

Sister, sister, night follows day
Out of these bounds, loping beyond the yews, away
Giddily over wall and number and ken.
Quiet these centuries. Who is it going now? Amen, amen.

Cascob, not far to the north of Hay if you take the crow's road, is close to the border – as Mathias's poem seems to be, though its borderland lies in a twilight zone between pagan and Christian, good and evil, heaven and hell. The notion of relating poem and place had long fascinated me and I had, too, a second motive for going there in the knowledge that Revd William Jenkins Rees (1772-1855), staunch friend of T.J. Llewelyn Prichard, one of my other literary projects, had been Rector of Cascob. We allowed ourselves a rainy detour.

For most of its length, the winding lane that leads into this remote valley is wide enough for one vehicle only. A prayer is the fee at each blind corner, but I would not discourage travellers who have time to spare. After a few miles of hazardous meandering you come upon the church and ease the car on to the weed-covered bank by the red telephone kiosk with the kitchen chair inside. To the left of the churchyard gate is a stone house that looks vaguely ecclesiastical: the rectory you think. Across the narrow road is another far smaller house where a dog barks. This is it. You have arrived.

As though in preparation for our visit, a few sheep had been turned loose in the circular churchyard to trim the grass but, while leaving ample droppings, had hardly got to grips with the task. We slithered among the gravestones in a dank and flowery meadow until my brown shoes were black and my socks wet. No sign of Rees's last resting place and no one to turn to for advice. The church, a strangely stunted building, ineffably medieval, was locked. I completed the circuit of the yard, noting the elms, the mound on which, or into which, the church tower is set, the weather-boarded belfry, the absence of windows to the west – all just as Mathias had observed them almost fifty years ago. The incrustation of lichen on gravestones has increased and their lettering advanced further towards obliteration, but I doubt there has been a change worth noting in the building or the landscape of multitudinous greens that encloses it since the thirteenth century. It is a diminutive and plain coeval of Notre Dame.

I was keen to see as much as I could of the rectory, where I knew Prichard had been holed up during the long and vicious winter of 1847, availing himself of Revd Rees's excellent library, but could hardly advance uninvited to the door. Then, as luck would have it, we came upon an electoral roll pinned up in the low porch of the church that supplied the name and telephone number of the current occupant. I phoned from the kiosk, explained my interest and received an immediate, unqualified welcome. I sat on the chair for a moment or two to gather myself then walked the dozen yards to the front door of the house alongside the churchyard gate.

The man who opened the door was clearly surprised. I felt obliged to identify myself as the person who had just phoned asking to see the rectory. 'Ah,' he replied, 'you're in the wrong place.' He was kind enough to direct me to the much altered eighteenth century dwelling, now a farm, a half-mile away, where I was expected. So it was I viewed the rectory, upstairs and down, and learned that the house by the church, formerly the school (though where its pupils came from, goodness knows), is the home of Peter Conradi, the biographer of Iris Murdoch. This was the rural retreat in Wales where she and John Bayley would stay.

I lacked the courage to go back and introduce myself, but we did go to the house across the road, where the key of the church is kept. Inside the thick walls it is bare, simple, primitive even, and gloomy on a showery late afternoon with dark clouds scudding. But there is a commemorative tablet to Revd William Jenkins Rees, 'Priest, Author, Antiquary, Litterateur', and something far stranger – the Abracadabra Spell, a quaint and curious form of exorcism, mingling Christian prayer and astrological conjuring to preserve 'Elizabeth Loyd from all witchcraft and from all evil...the witches compassed her abought [sic] but in the name of the Lord I will destroy them Amen ***** pater pater pater Noster Noster Noster...' There lay the source of that eerie departure from normality in the second part of Mathias's poem. Alas, you will not find this explanation in my notes to his *Collected Poems*.

Travellers in the southern March find themselves constantly welcomed to Wales and, a few miles further on, to England, as the road winds this way and that across the national boundary. This produces occasional aberrations – like the bilingual signs indicating that men are working '400 yards/llath' ahead, but which on the English side have 'llath' blacked out with tape. Did the censor think a word of Welsh would disorientate or enrage the unwary monoglot? It is far too late to expunge such impurities, for the Welsh language is anciently well established in Herefordshire. A glance at a map of the March reveals how the Welsh tide receded to the west, leaving in its wake scattered salt pools on an otherwise unseasoned shore. Llanerch-y-coed, Penhenllan, Mynyddbrydd, Cae Mawr, Coed Poeth, Maes Coed, Gilfach, Maerdy, Caradog, Cwmdulas, Dyffryn, Bagwyllidiart are all to the east of Offa's Dyke. On the other hand, there are Welsh places to the west of the Dyke, like Hay, whose names have been Englished almost out of existence, but not for much longer, perhaps. Cymuned, the organisation that lobbies for the Welsh language and Welsh-speaking communities, has begun a campaign to reverse this trend with efforts to re-establish the Welsh names Yr Wyddfa and Eryri, for Snowdon and Snowdonia. Will book lovers turn up as readily for the 'Y Gelli Festival' and, while there, go on jaunts as far as Llanandras (Presteigne) and Tref-y-Clawdd (Knighton)?

Though you would not suspect it now, there is ample evidence that Welsh-speaking enclaves persisted throughout this region in the tenth century and later. David Powel's *Historic of Cambria* (1584) tells us that 'the Welsh toong is commonlie used and spoken Englandward...a great waie, as in Herefordshire, Gloucestershire, and a great part of Shropshire'. In the early 1720s, Daniel Defoe noted that the 'whole county of Hereford was, if we may believe antiquity, a part of Wales, and was so esteemed for many ages'. Now, there's a goal for the ambitious Welsh nationalist: why stop at independence within the existing border, reconstruction of the Dyke, when a claim can be made for the old territories and reestablishment of Greater Wales?

Independence is a live issue, at least for Plaid Cymru, the Party of Wales, for it is strongly suggested that a failure of faith or courage that caused party leaders to play down nationalism, which is its *raison d'être,* led to the losses it suffered at the National Assembly election early in May. The electoral system combines elements of 'first past the post' (for forty constituency seats) and proportional representation (for twenty regional seats, four in each of five regions). Voters make their mark twice, once for a named constituency candidate and once for a party, to decide the regional representation. At the first election in 1999, Plaid did far better than expected: as well as holding its own in the Welsh-speaking areas, it won seats in the traditional Labour constituencies of Rhondda, Llanelli and Islwyn and finished with seventeen AMs. It became the largest party in opposition, larger indeed than the combined forces of Conservatives and LibDems. In order to become the party of government, Labour was forced into a coalition with the latter. In 2003, however, it has regained Rhondda, Llanelli and Islwyn and now with thirty seats, precisely half the total, has decided it can rule alone. The LibDems, still with six seats, seem content to be marching on the spot and the Conservatives with eleven (two more than in 1999) are hugely pleased with themselves. For twenty-four hours after the election, Plaid Cymru, down five seats to twelve, was in a state of shock. Then the recriminations began. Much of the blame was laid at the door of its president and party leader, Ieuan Wyn Jones, a man of principle who may simply have got his tactics wrong. Within the week he resigned and threw the party into turmoil.

Although it was not always so, Plaid is now clearly left of centre, which may help to explain its appeal to communities in the old industrial south in 1999. But to retain its hold on these new supporters, the leadership sought to cast off its old garments of nationalism and greater self-government and oppose Labour on social issues alone. Blairite Labour's shift to the right should have benefited Plaid – if the party in Wales followed Westminster's line. But it does not. Rhodri Morgan, who retains the role of First Minister in the new administration, is Old Labour and has contrived to put 'clear red water' (his phrase) between the Assembly's policies and those of Downing Street, effectively pulling Plaid's plank from under its feet.

A major problem facing all parties is voter apathy. Only 38

per cent of the electorate turned up at the polling booths. One cannot, then, look to politics or politicians to stimulate interest in the culture and identity of Wales. Would poets fare any better? Sales of the new *Bloodaxe Book of Modern Welsh Poetry* (edited by Menna Elfyn and John Rowlands) might give an indication. Although there is a measure of overlap, it will serve as a companion volume to Anthony Conran's justly celebrated *Penguin Book of Welsh Verse* (1967), now available revised and expanded from Seren under the title *Welsh Verse*. They offer together an overview of Welsh poetry from the sixth century to the twenty-first. The Bloodaxe book, a Poetry Book Society Translation Recommendation, will put paid to the common notion the other side of Offa's Dyke that hardly anyone speaks, far less writes, in Welsh these days. The team of translators includes poets whose names will be familiar to readers of *PN Review,* such as R.S. Thomas, Gillian Clarke, Rowan Williams, the new Archbishop of Canterbury, and Robert Minhinnick. Notwithstanding the usual caveats, some of their work is striking, such as this of Ceri Wyn Jones's 'Honour – to the first child born after the IRA ceasefire' by Minhinnick:

This mild child's not turned her face
to the spyhole of our race;
so cannot see she will inherit
the certain shaming of the spirit.
She's not been bothered about blood
or the nagging tooth of nationhood.
She's not scrawled slogans of the schism
or learned her Semtex catechism
or glimpsed us as we grind the bones
of children on sectarian stones.
Still, pretty soon she must discover
that life is one side or the other.

It is a splendid anthology. I would hazard a guess that the modernity, and occasionally the unrestrained contemporaneity of themes and language will be the biggest surprise to readers unfamiliar with writing in Wales.

*PN Review* 153, Volume 30 Number 1, September – October 2003.

# PETER FINCH, JOHN DAVIES AND SHEENAGH PUGH
*March 2003*

Peter Finch was among the first writers to have a website. He has always been at the forefront of developments at the confluence of literature and technology. Back in the 1970s, I found neither reason nor euphony in the distortion of words and odd sounds he and Bob Cobbing vented in public performance with the aid of microphone and tape-recorder. But then, I am (to be kind to myself) a sad reactionary in most matters artistic. I have, too, learned to appreciate the intelligence, wry humanity, variety and abundance of Finch's creativity. Some time ago, given a half-hour on Radio Wales, he produced a gem of a programme that might have taught the broadcasters a thing or two about the use of the medium. And he is constantly adding to his technical bag of tricks: his most recent productions are accessible only on mobile phones with WAP facility.

The design of the website (www.peterfinch.co.uk), which greeted me as visitor number 29792, is exemplary. I went in after *Real Cardiff* but was soon browsing the history and bibliography of *Second Aeon*, the magazine Finch founded as a nineteen-year-old in 1966. From the mimeographed issue 2, it set out an inclusive worldview of contemporary poetry and attracted an extraordinary array of contributors, including Allen Ginsberg, Gary Snyder, Charles Bukowski, William Burroughs, Theodore Enslin and Theodore Weiss, among others, from the United States. There is nothing to compare with *Second Aeon's* resonating roll call in any other magazine from Wales and, I suspect, few from England.

Later numbers, conventionally printed and bound, achieved a circulation of 2500, but the magazine could not survive without the subsidy it received from the Welsh Arts Council and a generous private benefactor. In 1975, when Finch was appointed manager of Oriel, the WAC gallery and bookshop, he ceased publication because, as an employee of the Council, he was no longer eligible to receive its grant aid. It was not a question of running out of editorial steam, though that would have been understandable, since he had sustained the magazine and its spin-off, Second Aeon Publications, as a one-man show for nine years. Nor was that all. He had made himself a key figure in the UK small press scene and was an indefatigable organiser of readings in pubs around Cardiff.

This conveniently brings us back to the book, *Real Cardiff*, which has recently appeared from Seren. Finch advises dipping into it and, since water is a recurring theme, the metaphor is peculiarly apt. He traces the histories of the multitudinous watercourses that predated the town and needed to be re-routed, covered, lost if possible, before construction on the silt and mud of the flood plain could begin. Even then you could not rely on the stuff staying put, what with a fifty-foot tidal fall ('second largest in the world') and the reliability of heavy rainfall on the moorland and valleys only a dozen miles or so to the north. The book is not a whitewash job: readers will learn as much or more about the mud of the hinterland, the littering of streets and the culture of drunkenness among the young as they will about the undoubted beauties of the city, the concentrated convenience of its commercial centre and the promise of the Bay. The travel section of the *Observer* highlights Wales (along with China and Libya) as a 'place to visit' in 2003. If you are persuaded, and would like a genuine flavour of the capital in advance, read Peter Finch, who has studied the city in historical depth and quartered it on foot and will entertain you all the way.

As chief executive of Academi, the literature promotion agency, Finch continues to have oversight of poetry readings, now anywhere in Wales. One series of Academi-sponsored readings attracted good audiences to an upstairs bar of Chapter Arts Centre in Cardiff on the first Thursday in each month through the autumn. At the November session, Robert Minhinnick was teamed with John Davies. The former, like a migratory bird, constantly in flight between exotic places, told us of the limo due at the end of his set to whisk him off to darkest Islington and read with the assurance of long practice. Since he became a Carcanet author, his poetry has changed gear. Its wealth of precise imagery remains, more lapidary still if anything, but the formal straitjacket it once wore with more than a touch of elegance has loosened. The change gives free rein to invention, and often motive force to rhyme. Ideas seem to skip along the lines but the message is global and serious. Man has an appetite for destruction that scientific knowledge and technical skill are serving chiefly to increase.

John Davies may be less well known to readers of *PN Review*, but he has been a significant figure here for a considerable time. I brought out his first pamphlet, *Strangers*, in the Triskel Poets series, in 1974, when he was already a regular contributor to *Poetry Wales* and the *Anglo-Welsh Review*. A major theme in the pamphlet poems was the separateness of people and the increasing distance that grows between members of ostensibly the same community as they get older. Ambivalence about Welsh, the first language of his wife and his daughter, also registered early and was perhaps a factor of distancing that, as a monoglot English-speaker, affected him personally. Davies subjects both country and culture to serious scrutiny and harbours no illusions about either. He has a keen appraising eye, can spot a phoney from afar and stoops like a hawk on glib naïvety and cliché. He struck a chord with 'How to Write Anglo-Welsh Poetry', one of the few pieces from his first book, *At the Edge of Town* (1981), preserved in *North by South*, his 'new and selected poems' just out from Seren:

First apologise for not being able
to speak Welsh. Go on: apologise.
Being Anglo-*any*thing is really tough;
any gaps you can fill with sighs.

And get some roots, juggle names like
Taliesin and ap Gwilym, weave
a Cymric web. It doesn't matter what
they wrote. Look, let's not be naïve.

Now you can go on about the past
being more real than the present –
you've read your early R.S. Thomas,
you know where Welsh Wales went.

And so on in the same vein. If you are impelled to write about Wales, you do a proper job. More than twenty years ago, he was honing his metrical skills on versions (in sonnet form) of Welsh language poems that he studied in translation, along with all their historical ramifications. In the 1990s, he found new themes and, rather like Minhinnick, a freer poetic in the United States, where he has travelled often and had a few long stays, in Michigan and Utah. The sonnet still fascinates but he is less obsessed by metre these days. He spread his wings, so to speak, with *Flight Patterns* (1991), his fourth book, in which roughly half the poems are in one way or another about Wales, while the rest reflect his experience of the USA. Whatever the landscape or people, there is a philosophic toughness at the core of his writing that reminds us of his other craft, wood carving, especially, if not exclusively, the carving of birds. The analogy occasionally finds expression in poems like 'Power Carving' – 'With a chisel, once you'd peel back/leaves from a bird and not ransack the wood...It's tricky,/advancing without losing your way or voice', and 'Decoys', which offers a metaphor for the constant effort and dissatisfaction of artistic creation:

> Beyond wood: an airy something
> from nothing wood's a pretext for.
> Alone at last with the whole mind's scope,
> you drift. Almost a familiar shore.
> Stirrings, gleams are stalked, and springing
> this time they are yours, you hope.

Five years have passed since Davies's previous book, *Dirt Roads*, and the eight new poems he has selected for *North by South* suggest a diminishing interest in poetry, which, if that is so, is a pity, for there has been no diminution in the quality of the writing.

Sheenagh Pugh's poetry shows no sign of declining output. Rather to the contrary. And, since she moved to Wales in 1971, her prize winning has been almost as prolific as her writing. She won the Babel prize for translation in 1984, the British Comparative Literature Association's first prize for translation in 1986, the Welsh Arts Council's 'Poem for Today' competition in 1987, the Cardiff International Poetry Prize in 1988 and 1994, and the Welsh Arts Council's 'Book of the Year' prize, for *Stonelight*, a collection of poems, in 2000. Now with her tenth book, *The Beautiful Lie*, published by Seren last April, she has found herself short-listed for the Whitbread Poetry Award. Even as one accustomed to climbing the victor's rostrum, she was surprised, but not so surprised that she did not pause to wonder why. Why this book, which is certainly good but not better than some she published previously, *Stonelight*, or *Sing for the Taxman* (1993), for instance, or *Id's Hospit* (1997)? Interviewed in a recent number of *The Big Issue (Cymru)*, she gave her answer to this puzzle. 'The first thing I did was look up who the judges were and I thought, Ah, I know what's happened here.' For the panel included Wendy Cope, who had been one of the judges of the Cardiff International Poetry Prize a couple of years ago when Pugh came second with a poem 'about the guys who built the Millennium Stadium, and how much I fancied them.' Wendy Cope had liked the poem enough to include it in an anthology she later edited.

As I found with Peter Finch, familiarity with a writer's work is an important basis of an understanding and appreciation of it. We are again reminded of the controversy, aired in *PN Review* and elsewhere, about the tendency for the awarding of poetry prizes to degenerate into mutual backslapping involving a small number of close acquaintances. It is perhaps more understandable when you consider the unenviable role of the judges, seeking to relate to individual books among the dozens or scores in competition, many by poets they have never heard of, let alone read, and working to a deadline that does not allow to them anything like mature consideration. We would be wise to forget about literary prizes, apart from the Eisteddfod chair and crown. They are, after all, simply media events, akin to those ghastly charades *I'm a Celebrity – Get Me Out of Here!* and *Popstars* – though even to be short-listed must be rather fun.

*PN Review* 150, Volume 29 Number 4, March – April 2003.

# ROWAN WILLIAMS, EMYR HUMPHREYS AND GORONWY REES

*November 2002*


The Tawe rises in the Black Mountain, west of the Brecon Beacons, and flows southwestwards to the sea at Abertawe (or Swansea, if you prefer the Viking version, though who Sveinn was no one seems to know). The river passes Craig-y-nos, an early Victorian castle where the prima donna, Adelina Patti, unwound after triumphant tours of the world's opera stages, before entering Cwmtawe, the Swansea Valley. A twisting chain of villages and small towns follows the river from Abercraf, where the mountains rise steeply behind to the cliffs and scree slopes of Cribarth, down to Pontardawe, now virtually on the outskirts of Swansea at the valley's southern end. This is an old industrial zone, its communities owing their existence to coal mining and work with iron and tinplate. For a couple of centuries until the destruction of our heavy industry, it was predominantly Welsh in its language, its socialist politics, its Nonconformist belief, its culture of chapel, choirs and workmen's halls and institutes.

This was what the eminent artist, Joseph Herman (1911-2000), found when he arrived in Ystradgynlais, at the upper end of the valley, in the mid-1940s. He had left Warsaw in 1938, as disaster threatened, with his mother's tearful valediction ringing in his ears, 'Don't come back'. They were wise words: the Nazis killed the entire family. As a refugee, he had tried and failed to discover in London and Glasgow a place of healing and inspiration, but his first sight of Ystradgynlais miners trudging home from the pit in the ruddy glow of a setting sun told him he had found what he sought. He spent a decade there. Looking back, he considered the experience crucial to his artistic development. The community took him in and gave him an equal share of all it had to offer. He established a studio in the neglected bowling alley of a local pub and the figures of miners and their families, monumental whatever the scale or medium, became iconic in his art. He was still working in Ystradgynlais when, in 1950, Rowan Williams was born there.

The newly appointed Primate of All England is interviewed in the latest issue of *Planet* (No.154, August-September 2002): the editor, John Barnie, was evidently prescient or quick off the mark. Archbishop Williams, who is far cleverer, and immeasurably more modest, than those Fleet Street hacks that are currently eager to denigrate him, foresaw that Canterbury would mean, among other things, offering himself as a target for the media's petty snipers. But even he must have been bemused by the libel that he is dabbling in paganism by accepting an invitation to join the Gorsedd of Bards at the National Eisteddfod, continuing as I write, at St David's, Pembrokeshire. It is, to say the least, a disappointing display of ignorance by the newspapers concerned.

The Archbishop, who speaks Welsh (and several other languages), was perfectly at home on the *Maes* at St David's, having attended his first National Eisteddfod as a three-year-old, when it was held at Ystradgynlais in 1954. Furthermore, he has published two volumes of poetry: *After Silent Centuries* (1994) and *Remembering Jerusalem* (2001). The first includes versions of two deeply religious Welsh-language poets, the hymnist, Ann Griffiths (1776-1805), and Waldo Williams (1904-71), patriot, pacifist (he was twice imprisoned for withholding income tax that would contribute to the military at the time of the Korean war) and probably the most admired

Welsh poet of the twentieth century. In the *Planet* interview, Rowan Williams pays tribute to the Chapel culture of his birthplace and, his family having moved to the Mumbles, the 'actively bilingual' environment of Swansea at the time of his secondary schooling there in the 1960s. Following studies at Cambridge and Oxford, he embarked on a career in higher education, though his jobs have almost always granted him 'double citizenship – Church and academic work'. During his first three years as a lecturer at Cambridge University, he held a part-time curacy on the council estate where he made his home. He is no ivory tower theologian and all who have met him speak of the ease they feel in his company.

If you would like to know what Rowan Williams thinks about the current state of education, the ordination of women and homosexuals, Christianity and Islam, Islamic schools, Palestine and Israel, the aftermath of 11 September, you could do worse than read *Planet*. This timely interview confirms that the magazine has maintained the high standards set by its founder, Ned Thomas, in providing a thoughtful and often trenchant commentary on political, social, cultural and environmental issues principally affecting Wales but embracing other cultures and continents. It is also a showcase for contemporary writers. The same number has impressive contributions from five poets and a wonderfully downbeat offering on Jubilee Year by Jan Morris that the *Daily Mail* commissioned but lacked the courage to print.

The many column feet of discussion of Dr Williams's impending move from Newport to Canterbury include occasional references to the meeting of St Augustine, his ancient predecessor as Primate, with bishops of the Celtic church in AD 603. The story derives from Bede's *History of the English Church and People*, the principal purpose of which was to demonstrate that the English were God's chosen people. In

Augustine, emissary of Pope Gregory and Bede's hero, they had a formidable leader, far more sophisticated and ecclesiastically street-wise than the Cambro-Britons. The fact that most of the English still clung to their pagan gods, and that the Celtic church had long been a great engine-house of Christian learning and evangelism, was neither here nor there.

The story is retold in *Emyr Humphreys: Conversations and Reflections* (University of Wales Press, 2002), an outstanding collection of essays and lectures interspersed with conversations about the issues they raise with the book's editor, M. Wynn Thomas. Humphreys, whose *Collected Poems* was published by UWP in 1999, is one of that increasingly rare breed, a writer who holds that literature should have a moral purpose. Wynn Thomas sees him as 'an intellectual in the Continental tradition – one who believes it is a writer's duty to bring intelligence to bear on any issue that concerns the preservation of a civilized social order'. In an article he published in *The Listener* in 1953 Humphreys wrote, '[the writer's] attitude to life...must be grounded on a faith which his reason, his conscience and his experience can accept and serve'. He is an admirer of Graham Greene (with whom he was personally acquainted) for this reason. His own faith is Protestant and he writes of it as guide and inspiration: 'Personal responsibility is a Protestant principle – one of the few Protestant principles that still retains its pristine force and power... Often, in the recent past, the artist has shied away from the crude strength of the Protestant conscience – that constant, hoarse, dynamic whisper. But it possesses an exciting paradoxical combination of simplicity and complexity; an awareness of the great mystery, the infinite unconditional nature of God, and the egocentric solitude and sin of man in the trap of time... The New Testament founded the idea of Christian progression, faith, hope and love; and these are the weapons the aspiring novelist needs not only to save his art but also to work out his own salvation.' This is a long way from the cheap tricks of contemporary bestsellerdom and may explain why a writer of Humphreys's stature (he won the Somerset Maugham award for *Hear and Forgive* in 1954 and the Hawthornden Prize for *A Toy Epic* in 1959) has not in more recent times received the attention he deserves outside Wales. But he has never moved from his position of principle, nor has he deviated from his aim to write 'the Protestant novel', perhaps most fully exemplified in *Outside the House of Baal*, first published in 1963 and reprinted in paperback by Seren in 1996. It is by any measure one of the finest novels of its era.

Emyr Humphreys was the one Anglo-Welsh writer to whom Goronwy Rees (in a *Spectator* review of *Outside the House of Baal*) gave unmixed critical blessing. Rees's own story, which reads like an extraordinary fiction, is told in one of the finest examples of the long-running Writers of Wales series: *Goronwy Rees* by John Harris (UWP 2001). Harris is blessed in his subject and has made a splendid job of it. Rees, a son of the manse, is taken from childhood in Aberystwyth via grammar school in Cardiff and an open scholarship in modern history at New College, Oxford, to a Fellowship of All Souls in September 1931, a couple of months short of his twenty-second birthday. A comfortable academic life lay ahead one might have thought, and one would have been wrong. He beat Quintin Hogg (the Lord Chancellor's son, scholar of Eton and Christ Church) for first prize in the Fellowship, was well acquainted with notable contemporaries, Richard Crosman, Douglas Jay, John Sparrow and Freddie Ayer, and regularly contributed poems and reviews to *Oxford Outlook*, then edited by Isaiah Berlin, who became a lifelong friend. As an undergraduate, he was (I am tempted to say, of course) writing a novel – *The Summer Flood*, published by Faber in 1932 – and with his handsome looks and sparkling intellect attracted many admirers, of both sexes, and the envy of a more than a few. Of all the career doors that were ready to open for him, he chose journalism.

He was, by inclination and rigorous analysis, a social democrat and, in 1934, during a second extended visit to Germany (having quit his post as leader writer for the *Manchester Guardian* to make the trip) he wrote anti-Nazi copy for Social Democratic broadsheets. His travels also took him to Russia, Austria and Czechoslovakia, accumulating information about the forces deployed in the political turmoil of the 1930s. He wielded this first-hand knowledge effectively in a long series of lead articles for the *Spectator*, which he joined as assistant editor in 1936.

Commissioned in the Royal Welch Fusiliers in 1940, he was soon active in military intelligence and during the final stages of the war served as liaison officer under Montgomery before finishing as a lieutenant colonel with the British Element of the Control Commission. When demobbed, he was recruited to MI6, serving in political intelligence at the Russian and German desks, a job he had no difficulty in combining with that of co-director of Henry Pontifex Ltd, which had come at the invitation of the manager, Henry Yorke (the novelist Henry Green), who was a close friend. In 1951 he took on the additional role of estates bursar of All Souls, renewing acquaintance with two more old friends, Maurice Bowra and John Sparrow. It was they who backed his nomination for his next appointment, as Principal of the University College of Wales, Aberystwyth. I was at the beginning of my second year at Aber when he came in 1953. Like most other students, I knew nothing of his career but was struck by the glamour and ease of his appearance with his wife in Quad, a dim and dingy gathering place between lectures, which he caused to be transformed with a lick of paint soon after his arrival.

If this homecoming was a kind of pinnacle (though he had

no illusions about academic and social life in Wales), it was one on which he was not destined to perch for long. Indeed, he fell headlong from it when it became known that the story of Guy Burgess, serialized anonymously in the *People* in March/April 1956, had in fact been written by Rees. John Harris's account of Rees's involvement with the Cambridge spy ring and the way his opponents in Aberystwyth seized the opportunity given them by the *People* serialisation to oust him makes interesting reading, even after this lapse of time. He left 'the college by the sea' in April 1957 and, not without difficulty, returned to writing via reviewing and journalism. This was the period of his acclaimed autobiographical books *A Bundle of Sensations* (1960) and *A Chapter of Accidents* (1972), which, edited by John Harris, were reprinted together in 2001 as *Goronwy Rees: Sketches in Autobiography* (UWP).

What, one wonders, would Rees have made of Devolution? He was philosophically opposed to the priorities then set out by nationalists, an important factor in his removal from Aberystwyth, but had huge sympathy for the working class of every country in all its travails. He was intensely moved by the conditions he observed in Merthyr in 1931: what would he have thought of Ebbw Vale in the wake of the final closure of the steelworks there? How would he have responded to 'post-industrial' Ystradgynlais or Tonypandy, when for so many young people that term is synonymous with 'post-employment'? We could do with his acute and well-informed intelligence as we try to make sense of the economic, social and cultural issues that face the Assembly and affect the lives of all of us.

*PN Review* 148, Volume 29 Number 2,
November – December 2002.

# GWYN JONES AND THE RED POETS
*May 2000*


In a recent editorial (*PN Review* 131), Michael Schmidt paid tribute to Penguin Classics as a storehouse of ancient literature and learning in translation and asked pertinent questions about the exceedingly precarious position of Latin and Greek in our schools and universities. He remarked too upon that small number of poets in this new century and the last who have consistently exploited a knowledge of the classics in their writing, and the unexpected success of translations or versions of Homer and Ovid in the last few years. He might have mentioned the rather different case of the popularity of Herodotus occasioned by *The English Patient*. All are reminders of the undiminished, if latent, power of ancient texts to enthrall a modern readership once attention has been drawn to them. Now we have the fresh example of the Whitbread Book of the Year, Seamus Heaney's translation of *Beowulf*. Suddenly everyone is acknowledging not only the translator's skill but the extraordinary craft of the eighth century poet.

As a teacher at a Bristol comprehensive school in the early 1960s I enjoyed introducing pupils of all ages and abilities to the stories of *Beowulf*, *The Battle of Maldon*, *Sir Gawain and the Green Knight*. It was always an additional pleasure to observe the surprise of the class when I wrote a few lines from the original text of whichever story I had been telling on the blackboard (a feat I was capable of then) and told them it was English. My own introduction to Anglo-Saxon and Middle English occurred at Aberystwyth, where, as in most university

English departments at that time, they were unavoidable. I was not alone in finding the weekly doses of Anglo-Saxon grammar in the first year hard to swallow, and the examination in that part of the course correspondingly difficult. Success in it was however a condition of progress into the honours class. Only those who carried a sufficiently heavy load of Anglo-Saxon avoided slipping through the sieve into outer darkness. At the beginning of the second year the queue of aspirant honours students would trail across the quad and wind up two flights of spiral staircase to the door of Professor Gwyn Jones's circular room in one of the towers of that extraordinary nineteenth century gothic building on the seafront. The vast majority would emerge crestfallen. There were six in the honours class in my year. If I had not been possessed by some uncharacteristically argumentative demon after Gwyn had glanced at his mark sheet and delivered the standard negative, 'No, I don't think so,' there would have been five.

Reading and translating *Beowulf* with Gwyn Jones in that same circular room, book-lined from floor to ceiling except where windows looked across to a substantial remnant of Georgian Aberystwyth (including the former Assembly Rooms, then the students' union), demanded assiduous preparation and a quality of concentration that I have rarely been able to summon up since. In two years we covered all 3182 lines of *MS Cotton Vitellius A15*, in the edition of Wyatt/Chambers, and every session had its quota of illustrations and anecdotes delivered with the flawless syntax and the smile in the voice that were Gwyn's trademarks. He was an inspirational teacher – and a formidable presence: the breadth of the shoulders and the noble head, for which, it seemed to me the Sutton Hoo helmet was designed, have left an unfading impression. Perhaps a decade ago he appeared on television, to talk about the 'first flowering' of Anglo-Welsh literature in the 1930s. He was never a hat man, but one sequence showed him strolling the promenade in Aberystwyth, wearing what appeared to be a forage cap of uncertain provenance. It reminded me of apparently contradictory aspects of his character. He could be the most formal of men, yet often chose to appear casually dressed; he was solidly working class in his origins, democratic and anti-establishment in his views, and at the same time elitist and autocratic. There was no doubting who was in charge of English at Aber in his time, and he viewed with undisguised distaste the contemporary notion that headship of a university department can be an elective office and can rotate among staff.

In Thomas Jones, Professor of Welsh at Aberystwyth, Gwyn had the perfect partner for one of his most ambitious undertakings, translation of *The Mabinogion*. Once embarked on the project with the blessing of Christopher Sandford, whose Golden Cockerel was the only private press in operation in the immediate post-war period, they enlisted the support of the finest that Welsh scholarship had to offer, to ensure that it was the most accurate translation of the best possible text. Gwyn's concern was to wed this accuracy to a style that would sound in English 'the same kind of great literature as the original sounds in Welsh' – a tall order. In his essay on the whole experience in *Background to Dylan Thomas and Other Explorations* (OUP, 1992), he shows how nearly they succeeded. Michael Schmidt's observation that leadership in teaching Latin and Greek has passed to the United States does not surprise me. It is, however, a shock to discover that the Penguin Classics edition of *The Mabinogion* is translated by Jeffrey Ganz, a product of Harvard University's school of Celtic Languages and Literature. Ganz's aim 'to present an accurate, readable rendering into modern English', which nevertheless does not attempt 'to be absolutely literal' largely comes off, but it lacks the nobility of the great Golden Cockerel translation, which was published in 1948 (and, supplanting Charlotte Guest's version, as an Everyman book in 1949).

Gwyn Jones served his apprenticeship as a translator tackling *Four Icelandic Sagas* (1935), significantly, in view of the American source of Heaney's commission, for the American-Scandinavian Foundation. His outstanding contribution over almost thirty years to international appreciation of Nordic literature and history was recognised in 1963 by the award of the highest honour Iceland had to offer, and some of his finest work in that field was still to come: *The Norse Atlantic Saga* (1964) and *A History of the Vikings* (1968). Closer to home, he was also the translator of *Sir Gawain and the Green Knight* (1952) for the Golden Cockerel Press, a typically elegant and eloquent piece of work, which is well-matched by the quality of the book production. I have written about Gwyn Jones before (*PN Review* 118). This fresh spate of reminiscence and information is inspired by news of his death, in December last, aged 92.

I was recently at Blackwood, where Gwyn Jones was brought up (though not, as I had thought, his birthplace, that honour going to New Tredegar, a few miles away in a neighbouring valley), for a gathering of the Red Poets Society to launch the latest issue of its annual *RPS* magazine, number six. The society 'was set up in 1993 as a loose collective of mainly performance poets'. Since 1999, it has been a 'joining organisation' – a change of policy which has brought in thirty new poets, without changing its political stance, as Mike Jenkins, prime mover in the society and joint-editor of the magazine, points out in his introduction: 'I don't believe there's an Establishment and anti-Establishment in terms of writing in Wales. We include both Robert Minhinnick and Peter Finch in this issue, both of whom hold important posts in the literary world yet are happy to contribute to a mag that has never hidden its commitment to politics which envisage revolutionary changes in our society.' Membership is not expensive (your five pounds a year includes a free copy of the magazine), nor is it exclusive, though it is a decidedly uncomfortable zone for Tories and 'New Socialists'.

The reading was well attended, which is more than could be said of that evening at the same venue (*PN Review* 127) when three of the leading lights in contemporary English-language poetry in Wales – Tony Curtis, Duncan Bush and Nigel Jenkins – shared the stage. Furthermore, it offered plenty of variety and a fair measure of entertainment. Complexity, profundity and craft were in short supply, but there was plentiful evidence of what can be achieved by grabbing contemporary themes by the throat and shaking them for all they are worth. Political cliché, delivered with the kind of self-satisfaction that politicians commonly develop, if they were not born with it, was mercifully rare. The audience responded best to performance that was somewhere between rap and rant, and to a memorably sustained poetic howl about the ills that afflict the have-nots in what remains of our welfare state. In the authentic voice of the underprivileged anger is spiced with bitter humour. Frankly bleak and depressing subjects are galvanized by high-octane nervous energy and wit – and occasionally rounded off with blues harmonica. Much of this works far better on the stage than on the page, but *RPS* 6 is worth the small outlay, if only for Robert Minhinnick's 'For Nazar Jassim Noori – on the bombing of Baghdad, December 1998'.

Not many weeks previous to my January visit to the Blackwood Miners' Institute I attended a reading at a venue which, in Welsh terms, is its polar opposite: the vast hotel complex that commands the eastern approaches to Newport. Here, in a bar that resembled nothing so much as a rejected set for *Citizen Kane*, the poets assembled. That they included some of the most talented currently available – Sheenagh Pugh, Peter

Finch, Catherine Fisher, Paul Groves and the Welsh-language poet Grahame Davies – made not the slightest dent on the aesthetic awareness of the braying golfers gathering between the vast pillars that gradually diminished with perspective down an endless hall. The cowed writers soon gave up the notion of bringing poetry to a wider audience and addressed themselves, still with some difficulty, to the small group of promoters and friends who accompanied them. They would have been better off performing in the underground car park. So much for National Poetry Day. Mike Jenkins, echoing Shelley, says poetry plays a vital role in his vision of revolutionary change in our society. His method of tapping the energies of active cells of proletarian writers may be more successful than Shelley's distribution of his pamphlet, *An Address to the Irish People* (the style 'adapted to the lowest comprehension that can be read') by throwing them through the open windows of passing carriages or from his balcony to likely looking pedestrians below, but the increasingly materialist mass of the population will take some shifting in the direction of visionary ideals, and receptiveness to poetry.

*PN Review* 133, Volume 26 Number 5,
May – June 2000.

# RICHARD LLEWELLYN AND THOMAS PRICHARD
*March 2000*


Last year (1999) saw the sixtieth anniversary of the publication
of Richard Llewellyn's *How Green Was My Valley*, which gained
a huge and immediate popular readership in spite of the war
and remains in print after goodness knows how many editions
and in a babel of languages. In the past few weeks I have
become accustomed to seeing in the press Llewellyn pictured,
thin-lipped, bushy-browed and wearing a perky hat that looks
a mite small, against a background that I recognise as home:
Gilfach Goch. There is the stream, the Ogwr Fach, its course
somewhat altered by the landscaping of the centre of the valley,
but undefiled now. And there, in line with the brim of the
writer's hat, Glenavon Terrace, which once overlooked the
railway track that carried coal, only coal. Mistier, behind
Glenavon Terrace, in a faint crenellation, are the chimneys and
the backs of the houses of High Street, stretching up the valley
and merging imperceptibly with the blurred mass of the hillside.
It is no longer the place I grew up in where, though they were
separated by only a few hundred yards, one side of the valley
was hidden from the other by black mountains of pit-waste.

Topographically, my old home is unlike the Rhondda, whose
twin ribbons of development (the westerly fingers of
Glamorgan's 'glove-shaped valleys' which, Auden imagined,
'hid a life/Grim as a tidal rock-pool's'), came to represent 'The
Valleys' in the minds of most outsiders. Gilfach Goch, a little
to the west of the Rhondda Fawr, is a cul-de-sac; a single road
like a lasso leads you into the village, loops around the valley

sides and takes you out again. But it shared with the Rhondda its *raison d'être* – coal-mining. In my boyhood its entire life was dominated by three working pits. Their noise and filth were constants and touched everyone, but the employment they provided for every able-bodied male during the war years, and for a time afterwards, was a blessing, which, if not unmixed, was real and, as things have turned out, irreplaceable. The pit where my father worked was the first to close, in September 1949, and he was a member of the small team left to dismantle machinery after the closure of the last in 1960. It is a painful irony that nationalisation, which improved the miners' lot, also precipitated the first wave of mine closures.

It may have been chance that brought the young Richard Llewellyn to Griff's bookshop in Cecil Court, off Charing Cross Road, sometime in the late 1920s. Or possibly he was attracted there by the welcome the Griffiths brothers, who kept the shop, gave to anyone, and especially writers, with a claim to Welshness. The brothers told him their story and, more importantly, the story of their father, Joseph Griffiths, who had experienced the early days of mining in Gilfach Goch. This gave Llewellyn the raw material for his novel, and explains why, some time in the 1970s, he came to Gilfach to have his photograph taken and found all evidence of the recent industrial past had been removed and the valley was green again.

While everywhere else in the English-speaking world readers were bowled over by *How Green Was My Valley*, in Wales it was met by a barrage of criticism. Some, confusing fiction with the textbooks that were their usual diet, pointed to its historical and topographical inaccuracies; others could not tolerate the novel's remarkable success. John Ford's film of the book added insult to injury on both counts. Even today there are hacks and historians before whom it is unwise to mention its name. In truth, they cannot touch it: *How Green Was My Valley* has outlived the coal industry and will survive its critics, though they have experienced a glow of vindication with the discovery that Richard Llewellyn was born in Willesden, north London and christened Richard Herbert Vivian Lloyd and that, though his parents were certainly Welsh (his father, William Llewellyn Lloyd, came from Tongwynlais, near Cardiff, and his mother's family from St David's, Pembrokeshire), a number of the connections he claimed with Wales were as fictional as his novel. The novelist's assumption of a name partly borrowed from his father, and his fabrication of a few inconsequential links with Wales, have been gleefully seized upon by journalists as a fresh proof of the duplicitous nature of the Welsh. Or was Llewellyn English anyway, as an *Observer* headline asserts? He behaved like an English toff, living in Claridges on the proceeds of his book until army service took him to North Africa and Italy, and soon after the war he became a tax exile; but they can't have it both ways.

It is not difficult to see why *How Green Was My Valley* has an enduring appeal, when more historically accurate novels of the south Wales coalfield, like Lewis Jones's *Cwmardy* and *We Live* are forgotten, except by a few academics. Worthy the latter may be, but they are also, for the most part, numbingly dull. When it came to writing fiction, Llewellyn had the advantage of a mind uncluttered by communist manifestos and miners' lodge meetings. Given the simple framework of Joe Griffiths's story, he could concentrate on character, relationships, dramatic incident and language. With the passionate intensity of an exile, he imagined a time when the miners and their families existed as a cohesive, Welsh-speaking, chapel-going society, moral, hard-working, unselfish, with close-knit family and community ties, and then he plotted the breakup of this working-class paradise under the influence of malign external forces. It is the stuff of myth, against which deconstruction is a pointless exercise. The theme of the novel is also that of 'Fern Hill' and, as the child's eye dominates the poem, so in the novel events unfold through the heightened perceptions of an intelligent boy, who doesn't fully understand them. In terms of diction too they have a good deal in common. The resonant style Llewellyn created for the novel slips easily into biblical language and imagery and liturgical rhythms. In the twenty-odd competent novels that came after he never repeated the success of his first, but that is hardly grounds for criticism.

Though some journalists appear surprised by such a turn of events, Richard Herbert Vivian Lloyd was by no means the first writer to employ a *nom-de-plume*. Probably the earliest example among Welsh writers in English was born at Builth, Powys, in 1790 and baptised plain Thomas Prichard. He is best remembered now as the author of 'the first Welsh novel in English', a primitively expanded version of popular folk-tales based on the life of one Thomas Jones of Tregaron (c. 1530-1609), entitled *Twm Sion Catti* (1828). He was also a poet, of some quality when satire was his object, but his attempts at long narrative poems are generally woeful. The hard facts of Prichard's life are frustratingly elusive. It appears that, having spent his boyhood in Wales, he lived as a young man in London, where he began a career on the stage and occasionally published poems in magazines like John Humffreys Parry's short-lived *Cambro-Briton*. He returned to Wales to sell his first substantial book of poems, *Welsh Minstrelsy* (1824), largely by banging on doors. In 1826 he married; at some point he lost his nose, he claimed in a fencing accident; he was battered by the vicissitudes of life and, at last, rescued from dereliction by some good citizens of Swansea. A few weeks later, in January 1862, he died as a result of falling into his own fire, perhaps drunkenly. There is circumstantial evidence to support the conjecture that he acted at the Theatre Royal, Covent Garden as 'Mr Jefferies'. We know he published his first poems as 'Jeffery Llewelyn' – a name he borrowed from the curate of the Breconshire parish of Llywel, near his boyhood home. Whether this was to flatter the Reverend Jeffery Llewelyn who was well-off, and possibly a distant kinsman, or as a calculated insult to him we cannot tell. He reserved his hottest strictures for men of substance who bequeath their estates to individuals outside the immediate family, and this was how the curate had acquired his wealth. Later, he incorporated the *nom-de-plume* into his own name, becoming Thomas Jeffery Llewelyn Prichard or, more usually, 'T.J. Llewelyn Prichard'.

Prichard is an interesting case not least because we see in his writing a change from ardent advocacy of the Welsh language to outright opposition to efforts to preserve it. This was not the result of prolonged inner debate. He was an embittered man, one who bore grudges, and having suffered a real or imagined injury at the hands of Lady Llanover, determined thereafter to oppose everything she held dear. Lady Llanover, wife of Benjamin Hall, whose memory we celebrate whenever 'Big Ben' is mentioned, was the most powerful supporter of the Welsh language in the first half of the nineteenth century. She orchestrated and funded protest against 'The Treachery of the Blue Books' (*PN Review* 131). The barbs in the dedication to Prichard's last book, *Heroines of Welsh History* (1854) – 'To the Virtuous Votaries of True Womanhood...As Contra-Distinguished From The Fantastic Fooleries And Artificial Characteristics of Fine Ladyism In The Middle Walks of Life' – are directed at her. In the preface he quotes with approval the 'eminent critic, William Taylor, of Norwich' who urges that the inhabitants of 'inconsiderable districts, such as Holland, Denmark, Piedmont, and Wales, should not endeavour to immortalize their respective phraseology, but contentedly slide into the speech of the larger contiguous nations'. As for political independence, 'the final conquests of Wales and Scotland, and the union of all Britain under one Sovereign' Prichard considers 'the greatest of blessings', and he castigates 'the most rude and ignorant worshippers of the past, who perversely turn their backs upon the sun of civilization and the onward velocity of the train of progress – wilfully blind to the inexpressible blessings of fraternal and national unity'.

Almost 150 years on, views like these continue to be echoed by a proportion of the people of Wales, often in very similar terms. They have appeared in the correspondence columns of the *Western Mail* almost daily since the inauguration of the Assembly. We might hope it is a declining proportion, but they represent a substantial challenge to that part of the population committed to the economic and cultural progress of Wales. For all the recent, colourful manifestations of new confidence, there are still those who have little or none. We ignore them at our peril.

*PN Review* 132, Volume 26 Number 4,
March – April 2000.

# DYLAN THOMAS
*March 1999*


The Dylan Thomas industry, fuelled from abroad, shows no sign of recession. The 'highly selective list' of commentaries on Thomas's life and work in John Harris's excellent *Bibliographical Guide to Twenty-five Modern Anglo-Welsh Writers* (University of Wales Press) swells his entry to fifty-six pages. Only David Jones and R.S. Thomas among the other poets represented have more than twenty; Raymond Williams with thirty-one reaches the foothills of his peak. The mantle of the Dylan Thomas School, run successfully for several years at the University College of Wales, Aberystwyth by Walford Davies (still, for my money, the best critical interpreter of the poet) seems to have passed to Swansea. As Thomas's birthplace, the 'ugly, lovely town' ought to have been first in the field, but let that pass. In August, the Dylan Thomas Centre, a fairly recent metamorphosis of the 1995 Year of Literature Tŷ Llên, housed a Dylan Thomas Festival, which aimed at attracting the wider public as well as the usual academic interests, though the latter were catered for in a four-day conference hosted by the University of Swansea's Department of English. The festival closed with a performance of jazz pianist Stan Tracey's *Under Milk Wood Suite*, which accompanied readings from the play by Philip Madoc. However translated and transformed, the play can still attract an audience. A reprise of the festival is planned for next year.

I was present when, in the autumn of 1952, almost exactly a year before he died in New York, Dylan Thomas gave a reading at UCW, Aberystwyth. The venue was the largest space available in the strange gothic revival building on the sea-front that then housed most of the academic departments of the college – the Examination Hall. It seated about four hundred, and was packed. One might suppose this was a sign that the spirit of poetry was abroad in Aber in those days, but one would be mistaken. It was not unusual for students to turn out in large numbers, since they were, for the most part, gregarious, and the town offered few distractions to compete with events organised by their own clubs and societies. This did not mean they were docile. Audiences could be, and frequently were, rough – as a middleweight Tory politician of the day, Sir David Maxwell-Fyfe (known to the mob, with little affection, as 'Dai Bananas') once famously found to his cost.

The Dylan Thomas evening began inauspiciously with the kind of unnecessary formality that could raise student hackles. The poet was processed into the hall between two begowned and impeccably tailored professors, Gwyn Jones, the formidable Professor of English leading. The *pièce de resistance* of this academic sandwich was a small, fat, remarkably dishevelled figure. His suit had never known a crease, and his shirt resembled a washed-out flannel pyjama jacket, perhaps its true identity. From their fit, they might well have belonged to someone else; much later we learned this was indeed a possibility. Above the furled collar was the round face, blob nose and nimbus of curly hair that have become iconic. The contrast with his supporters was grotesque. Gwyn Jones's introduction, eloquent as ever, rose above this Marx Brothers production, and Dylan Thomas began to speak. Having heard recordings of the poet's broadcasts and public readings in the USA, I know now how he managed his word-perfect introduction without notes or pause for thought. That does not make it any the less remarkable. It was a patiently assembled and well-rehearsed tumble of verbal fireworks, the touch paper of which seemed to us just lit for the occasion. It was probably in Aber that, for the first time in public, he described the USA-bound hordes: '...there they go, every spring, from New York to Los Angeles, exhibitionists, polemicists, histrionic publicists, theological rhetoricians, historical hoddy-doddies, balletomanes, ulterior decorators, windbags, and bigwigs and humbugs, men in love with stamps, men in love with steaks, men after millionaires' widows, men with elephantiasis of the reputation (huge trunks and teeny minds), authorities on gas, bishops, best sellers, editors looking for writers, writers looking for publishers, publishers looking for dollars, existentialists, serious physicists with nuclear missions, men from the BBC who speak as though they had the Elgin Marbles in their mouths, potboiling philosophers, professional Irishmen (very lepricorny), and I am afraid, fat poets with slim volumes.' He read his own work beginning with 'some early poems, some fairly hurly-burly poems', and a selection of other poets that included Hardy, Hopkins and Henry Read. I had not before, nor have I since, been so completely bowled over by a poet. It later became fashionable to be critically supercilious about Thomas's 'booming' delivery, but those were attitudes born of ignorance. They did not take account of his ability to modulate a wonderful voice; he was, after all, a highly skilled radio actor. It is no wonder that Americans flocked to hear him. If his fame was clinched by a stupid, wasteful death, it was substantially founded on a handful of miraculous poems, the brilliant posthumous broadcast of *Under Milk Wood*, and the magical appeal of his public performance.

Also in August, George Abbey, son of a woman from Laugharne and, since 1996, head of the Johnson Space Centre in Houston, came to the Boat House with the astronaut Dafydd Rhys Williams to return a signed photograph of Thomas that the latter had taken, with sundry other Welsh items, on his flight in the space shuttle. Now we hear that Mick Jagger's film company is planning a biopic of the tempestuous life of Dylan and Caitlin: this will run and run. Meanwhile one of the more interesting footnotes to Dylan Thomas studies appears in the latest number of the *New Welsh Review*, where Ralph Maud and Robert Williams show that the line 'How time has ticked a heaven round the stars' in 'The force that through the green fuse...' derives from Thomas's (slight) knowledge of Welsh and use of a Welsh-English dictionary. It was no more than a way of multiplying the possibilities of words, akin to his use of Roget, and perhaps one he never resorted to again, but it is a scruple to place in the balance against that famously dismissive quip attributed to him. 'Land of my Fathers. My fathers can keep it.'

Like so many others, the young Dannie Abse fell under the spell of Dylan Thomas, but briefly – and a long time ago. Readers of his autobiography, *A Poet in the Family*, will remember that on his first reading tour in the States, Abse did not take kindly to being constantly likened to Thomas, then ten years dead. When yet another stranger came up to him to say '...you resemble Dylan Thomas's, exasperated, he replied, 'You mean I look like an unmade bed.' The autobiography also tells how Hutchinson accepted his first book of poems in June 1946, and finally published it in February 1949, without realising that some weeks earlier the poet had surreptitiously visited the printers and changed about a third of the contents. That seems to have been the only ripple in a relationship with the publisher that has extended almost fifty years to his latest book, *Arcadia, One Mile*. Early in October, Academi, the new literature agency that has grown out of Yr Academi Gymreig, held a literary dinner at the Park Hotel in Cardiff to celebrate Dannie Abse's seventy-fifth birthday. Apart from the food, it was a pleasingly memorable occasion. The guest of honour remembered old friends – John Tripp, John Ormond, Aled Vaughan – now gone, put in a word on behalf of Cardiff City, and read from his new book as beautifully as ever. It was a performance as unlike Dylan Thomas's as he could wish, other than in the polished certainty of it.

Dannie Abse's latest and many another book notwithstanding, the major Anglo-Welsh publishing event of the autumn has been Meic Stephens's *New Companion to the Literature of Wales* (a revised, updated and greatly extended new edition of his *Oxford Companion*), published by the University of Wales Press. It is, and will remain for a long time, the essential reference book for all who have an interest in literature and things Welsh.

*PN Review* 126, Volume 25 Number 4,
March – April 1999.

# MIKE JENKINS, NIGEL JENKINS AND DUNCAN BUSH
*September 1998*

I have been re-reading Gwyn Alf Williams's *The Merthyr Rising*. The book is a monument to the man, whose voice I hear in every line, and should be compulsory reading in all sixth forms and colleges in Wales. It tells of a working-class rebellion in the wake of the first Reform Bill of 1831, which had its heroes, miners and ironworkers, the common people; its villains, the Masters and the soldiery, eventually eight hundred strong, who bloodily suppressed them; and its martyr, one Richard Lewis, who has gone down in folk history as Dic Penderyn, an innocent, betrayed by false testimony, hanged as a scapegoat. The scene of these dramatic events, far greater in scale and violence than those more readily remembered as the Peterloo Massacre, was Merthyr Tydfil. By 1801 this place had become the most densely populated parish in Wales and in good years in the 1820s it was making almost a quarter of the total British production of iron. The town was overwhelmingly Welsh-speaking, remarkably cultured (eisteddfodau were held in a score of pubs and the chapels resounded with music and poetry as well as hellfire preaching against the manifold and manifest sins of the day), and politicised, 'the heartland of Chartism and the home of the Welsh Chartist Press in both languages'. When the workforce was fully employed, some thirteen to fourteen thousand men were engaged in the ironstone mines, the collieries and ironworks. All this seems distant from us, yet the events of 1831 were within the (admittedly long) lifetimes of the grandparents of Glyn Jones, the late and greatly lamented poet, novelist and short story writer.

Harking back to *The Merthyr Rising* was prompted by two recent news items. I read in the financial pages of the *Guardian* (not my usual spot for breakfast browsing, but the headline caught my eye) that the Bank of England's unexpected increase in interest rates and its urging of restraint in private sector earnings, a decision based on the peculiar myopia afflicting its officials that does not permit them to see beyond London and the abundant south-east, is likely to have a devastating effect in Merthyr. There, workers will be told they must accept low pay deals or face unemployment. The article asserts that Merthyr is too far from the M4 corridor to flourish in today's competitive climate; that, to attract investors, efforts have been made to reclaim land blitzed by the old heavy industries; that unemployment has come down, but 'there is a massive problem of disguised unemployment – the people who are classified as economically inactive because of long-term sickness or disability'. Then come the staggering statistics: 'In Merthyr, just under two thousand people are unemployed claimants, about ten thousand are inactive.'

Within a day or so of reading this, I learned from the *Western Mail* that the Arts Council's Book of the Year award for an English-language publication had gone to Mike Jenkins for his collection of short stories, *Wanting to Belong*. The writer, a former editor of *Poetry Wales*, has taught in a comprehensive school in Merthyr for many years. The town and its people, particularly its young people, are his themes, in prose and verse. A great many of the unemployed and inactive in Merthyr live on a vast local authority housing estate, very like the Penôl (literally 'back-head' = arse) estate, in Cwmtaff, the home of the teenage characters and their mostly appalling parents in *Wanting to Belong*. The stories are not greatly to my taste, which is no surprise since they were intended for teenagers, but they offer shudderingly convincing portraits of young people struggling to make sense of, and find a little pleasure in, a world bereft of purpose and, for the most part, of values. Dialogue in the stories is almost entirely in the aitchless street patois of Cwmtaff. Readers of *Trainspotting* or viewers of Rab C. Nesbitt (have you tried the subtitles supplied by 888?) should have no difficulty. Mike Jenkins has used the same phonetic transliteration for some time, notably in *Graffiti Narratives* (Seren, 1994), his fifth book of poems, many of which are wildly funny, but with a bitter satiric edge:

I come from-a ewgest 'state in town,
second ewgest maze in Ewrop, they say,
coz planners potched it up, the clowns;
I'd give em a proper lampin
on'y they've all gone away...

He is capable of sensitivity and, occasionally, sentimentality, as were John Tripp and Harri Webb. He is like them too in his overt commitment to cultural and political nationalism. Above all, it is his sympathy, and his anger, stirred by the deprivation and mundane cruelties that afflict hopeless families in blighted post-industrial communities that account for his appeal. A volume of selected poems is promised next year from Seren and, meanwhile, he is contemplating a novel. It would not surprise me to see him bring it off: there is a lot more material yet to mine in Cwmtaff.

In 1974, the Welsh Arts Council's Young Poets Competition prize was shared by Duncan Bush, Tony Curtis and Nigel Jenkins. No one would dispute that, on this occasion at least, the adjudicators got it right. All three have since won further awards and established themselves as key figures in the contemporary Anglo-Welsh scene. Nigel Jenkins (unrelated to Mike) won the Book of the Year prize in 1996 with *Gwalia in*

*Khasia*, of which I have written in an earlier Letter (*PN Review* 113), and had his moment of metropolitan fame when his poem 'An Execrably Tasteless Farewell to Viscount No', alias the revered late Speaker, George Thomas, appeared on the front page of the *Guardian*. So far, my intuition that the *Guardian* would be less inclined to review his latest volume of poetry from Gomer, has proved sound. *Ambush* has tributes to Roland Mathias and Tony Conran, and ballads in the manner of Harri Webb. As in his earlier books, politics and love are major themes. Love, though still agreeably physical, is crossed by mortality, but political anger is still there – in the scathing lines on George Thomas, a satire on the blight of second home ownership in Wales, and protest (though somewhat tardy) at the drowning of the Welsh village of Tryweryn by Liverpool City Council, with the complaisance, if not connivance, of Welsh Labour MPs. If he is less exasperated with his countrymen than he was, perhaps it is because he is closer now to the culture of the senior language of Wales, as translations by and from Menna Elfyn in this collection suggest. In the opening poem, one of several on the mysteries of the cosmos, he invites us to sign up to a self-portrait as a particle of matter, 'like an atom...all but void' but, until the time comes to 'crumble to a fine invisible dust', if we take a leaf from his book, we will live passionately.

Duncan Bush is, if you wish for such, an antidote to the nationalism of the Jenkinses. Cosmopolitan man, without a pang of *hiraeth*, that longing for the homeland, he spends half his working life in Europe. That does not mean he is indifferent to pain or injustice suffered in Wales, or elsewhere. He is one of the few who have written anything worthwhile about the ruinous miners' strike of 1984. He too is a former winner of the Book of the Year award, in 1995, with his third major volume of poetry, *Masks* (Seren). The masks of the title are those the poet himself adopts, having decided, as he told

Richard Poole in a *Poetry Wales* interview, that to 'promulgate the personality or personal circumstances of the poet...seems to me excessive'. He has written poems of personal reminiscence – the Cardiff of his schooldays revisited – but in the poem sequences that are at the heart of the book, we hear the voices of men and women at the limits of endurance, most remarkably in 'Are There Still Wolves In Pennsylvania' as a Vietnam veteran and his wife move through their dreamscapes towards an undefined, but, inevitably violent denouement. His latest, *The Hook*, just out from Seren, brings together and back into print nearly all the poems that were gathered in two earlier volumes, *Aquarium* (1983) and *Salt* (1985), and the miners' strike pamphlet *Black Faces, Red Mouths*. As he explains in his introduction (with suitable self-admonition about the dangers of tampering with the products of youthful enthusiasm), the poems have undergone some revision. In the main, this is confined to the adjustment of a line break, the substitution of a word here and there, or a change in word order, but a few have been more radically altered. The title poem was first published in 1974, in *3 Young Anglo-Welsh Poets*, the book that presented the winners of the Young Poets Competition, and a fine poem it is. I admire 'Drainlayer', which shares that provenance, a lyrical treatment of manual labour, its full rhymes, muted by enjambements, glimmering like pale stone in freshly turned dark soil:

> ...The blade
> cuts clean, and brightens;
> glazes earth
> the downthrust frees, the spade
>
> flings. But I bury my own
> work dark. Nothing stands

but me.
I lay veins, straight bone

in earth for earth my daughter.
My hollow son is
earth too,
exoskeleton of water.

Notwithstanding the successes of the intervening years, notably with *Masks* and *The Genre of Silence* (1988), an extraordinary fiction purporting to be the literary remains of a Russian writer, Victor Bal, who disappeared in a Stalinist purge, Duncan Bush has had nothing like the wider recognition that his writing has consistently merited. Perhaps the chance to read again these earlier poems will persuade critics and reviewers outside Wales of his exceptional talent.

*PN Review* 123, Volume 25 Number 1,
September – October 1998.

# PETER FINCH, SHEENAGH PUGH AND NIGEL JENKINS

*January 1998*

With some of the biggest players in Welsh business lining up alongside renegade socialists to work for a 'No' vote, the referendum on a Welsh assembly was always going to be a close-run thing. The capacity of the Welsh for self-abasement is not limitless but, God knows, quite close to it. On the credit side, I know of not a single writer in Wales who was in the No camp, but there were a great many ardent, public and vociferous supporters of the Yes campaign. What influence this had on the vote, and in what direction, is a matter for conjecture. As it turned out, 1997 was not a repeat of 1979, *'blwyddyn y pla'* (the year of the plague) as Gwyn Williams explosively cursed it. This time there was cause for celebration, albeit muted compared to that relished by the Scots.

Earlier in the summer, Seren launched Peter Finch's latest volume of poetry, *Useful,* at Waterstone's in Cardiff. In Wales at least, book launches are often low-key affairs: small beer for the writer and publisher and indescribable wine for the handful of enthusiasts. This was one of the other kind. A substantial throng swilled cheerfully around the ground-floor book stacks and mint copies sold briskly. Peter Finch has a following – and he has earned it. Rather more than thirty years ago, while still in his teens (and employed as a local government officer), he founded a little magazine. Initially, it was to print the work of a group of writers who met in pubs in Cardiff and advertised their saloon bar readings with typically abstruse wit as 'No Walls'. The magazine was a one-man operation. Peter Finch was its editor and publisher; he typed the pages and cranked the cyclostyle machine; he sold it. The magazine's title, *Second Aeon,* was an encapsulation of its manifesto. In a zone where the covers of literary periodicals are characterised by sobriety and sameness *(Wales, The Welsh Review, The Anglo-Welsh Review, Poetry Wales)*, it carried a powerful transatlantic, fantastic, free-for-all charge. Within a remarkably short time it was a substantial journal, earning support from the Welsh Arts Council and attracting the contributions of writers of some distinction, notably from the USA. Sales too were healthy when in 1974, on his appointment as manager of Oriel, the Welsh Arts Council's pioneering bookshop in Cardiff, Peter Finch wound up the magazine. Nothing has arisen since to fill the gap it left.

Peter Finch has continued to be the outstanding, if not the only, representative of the avant-garde in literature in Wales. (Who has England to offer, apart from Bob Cobbing, his long-time friend and associate in poetic shock tactics?) The energy and inventiveness he brought to *Second Aeon* have not declined with the years and these qualities, along with verbal facility and wit, have constantly characterised his poetry. *Selected Poems* (1987) has an introduction explaining the origins and methodology of his experimental work, which owe far more to modern art and music than they do to literature, and *Useful,* his twenty-first collection of poems, has notes quoting sources and describing processes. There may appear to be a hint of self-justification in this, and perhaps it is warranted. Over the years, reviewers have been less than understanding about work so obviously and so far out of the traditional mould:

> rydw i am fod blydi I am
> rydyn ni rydw i rody i
> rodney rodney I am
> rydyn am fod I am I am I am
> rydw i yn Pantycelyn Rhydcymerau
> Pwllheli yes

I am bicupping mainly cym sticker
   ardvark
the dictionary cymro hirsuit weirdo
on fire arrested finger-pointed rydych
   chi
imperialist long-nosed pinky
   cottagers...

rudin wedi dysgu hen ddigon ol'
   mouldering
Welsh Saunders Mabinignog crap
nasty blydi bppks we're a video neishyn
smot superbod sam tan brilliant exampl
('Partisan')

This is transparent to anyone who has been a Welsh learner and knows a little pre-referendum history. It is also hilarious, especially when performed by Peter Finch. What would one make of:

Eeeee e eeeeeee eeee ee e eeeeee's eee?
Eeee eee eeee eeeeee eee eeee eeeeeeooo:
Ooooo ooooo oo ooooo ooo ooooooo
   oooo oo Ooo...

even given the title 'Sonnet No. 18', if the notes did not point out that this is 'Shakespeare's most famous sonnet (reduced) to its component letters restructured to mirror the form of the original work'? Perhaps a third of the poetry is thus concrete or abstract. That which is not invariably has a sharp, satiric edge. In previous volumes this has been directed outwards at society; in *Useful* the target is more often failure in human relations between husbands and wives, parents and children, old age and the relatively young. The satire is tinged with melancholy bitterness, and the kind of humour that hurts. Peter Finch is protean and prolific: a new collection, *Antibodies, is* due out before the end of 1997.

About the same time as *Useful* appeared, Sheenagh Pugh published (again with Seren) her eighth volume of poetry. Its title, *ID'S HOSPIT,* might well have been mistaken for one of Peter Finch's verbal transformations, but it was 'found' rather than coined. It is a borrowing of the remaining letters of a sign over the entrance to St David's Hospital in Cardiff, now closed. Phonology and graphology are as fascinating for their own sake to Sheenagh Pugh as they are to Peter Finch. In addition to lecturing in creative writing at the University of Glamorgan, she is a formidable linguist, and an accomplished translator of poetry, notably from the German, though the present volume also includes a version from the Greek of Kallimachos. She won the Babel Prize for translation in 1984 and first prize in the British Comparative Literature Association's translation competition in 1986; the German poet Hans-Ulrich Treichel is a regular client.

The title poem is not typical of the collection. It is a sad commentary on the new hardness in society that accepts unemployment as normal, 'pubs (that) have dress codes and names like Traders', the homeless existing in boxes and on handouts of soup, and 'the healing word/...flaking off the wall letter by letter'. Only 'Jeopardy', which adds irony and mordant humour to the social comment has a similar theme. An encounter with a 'South Efrican' who sells cigarettes to third world countries and betrays the same ardent desire for the young snooker player in the match they are watching, provides an opportunity for the display of the sharp wit which is a permanent strength of her writing:

I saw my neighbour,

White-knuckled, hungry eyes aching,
fixed on the remote
beautiful face, and nearly said:
'Hey, you too, mate?'

The same wit, playfully employed, in technically polished lines
– she favours stanzaic forms with regular half-rhyme –
distinguishes poems like 'The Embarkation of the Pigs (On
hearing that British publishers no longer welcome pig characters
in children's books)', and 'Booklifting': 'I slipped a Jean Genet
inside my shirt/(he'd have approved, surely?)'.

Sheenagh Pugh has enthusiasms. Snooker and beautiful
young men, together or separately, music from Mozart to rock
but with particular affection for the 'folk' end of the spectrum,
history and the north, often combined, have woven colourful
strands through her writing almost from the start. The Norse
sagas, Iceland, islands, shores and seascapes generally are the
stuff of poetry for her. Several poems in *ID'S HOSPIT* are based
on a visit to the Shetland Islands. The sequence 'Voices on
Mousa Broch', beginning in 1994 ('No-one lives on this island
any more,/but all summer, all day when the ferry runs,/the
tower is filled with languages...'), recreates episodes from the
island's populated past, back to a distant, unfigured time, when
the tower which now draws the tourists was built. There is a
physical and intellectual questing in poems like this that excites
me and I am sure I am not alone in responding to the romance
of the north in Sheenagh Pugh's poetry. 'Sailing to Islands', with
its descriptive echoes of *To the Lighthouse,* reminds all but the
most blasé voyager that such journeys still faintly replicate
those of ancient man and can be a metaphor for life itself:

There is always a time, sailing to
   islands,
when you notice they have turned
   green,
and they weren't when you set out.
   They began blue,
a blur of deeper blue at the sky's edge,

hardly a smudge, an ache on the
   straining eye,
but they are hardening now into solid
   ground,
a green presence, and the sea goes on
beyond them; they are not the end after
   all.

There are signs in this volume that the incongruities of age, or rather ageing, no more yet than a fine thread in the work, may become a thicker strand. I await developments with interest.

Just as I come to the end of my letter, I find that, for the first time since Dylan Thomas died, a Welsh poet has made it to the front page of a national daily – and one of the broadsheets at that. This is good going since Elizabeth Barrett Browning et al, for all the air time lavished on 'The nation's favourite love poem' recently, were granted only a few column inches somewhere inside. Contempt and derision clearly sell more newspapers and this no doubt explains why Nigel Jenkins's satire (in the *New Welsh Review*) on the late George Thomas, created 'The Viscount No' in the poem for his outspoken opposition to an assembly for Wales, caught the eye of the metropolitan press. It could start a fashion for vitriolic verse aimed at deserving public figures. But what did the *Guardian* mean by allocating more space to this on its front page than to the Chancellor and EMU? Only mischief. Will it give as much attention tomorrow or next week to the poet's splendid account of his recent tour of the United States with Menna Elfyn and Iwan Llwyd in the latest number of *Poetry Wales*? Will it review his new collection of poems, *Ambush,* from Gomer, due out early next year? As the saying goes these days, 'Don't hold your breath.'

*PN Review* 119, Volume 24 Number 3, January – February 1998.

# GILLIAN CLARKE AND TONY CURTIS

*November 1997*

Early summer is the season of the Hay Festival and a clutch of literary awards. The town of Hay, more properly *The* Hay, has a musical Welsh name, as David Jones reminds us in *The Sleeping Lord*, '...which place is in the tongue of the men of the land, Y Gelli Gandryll, or, for short, Y Gelli'. Be that as it may, visitors usually need luck and a magnifying glass to detect a Welsh presence at the Festival. Menna Elfyn and Robert Minhinnick were among the few writers from Wales involved this year. They were both at the reception held by the Gregynog Press, where, unnaturally, not a book was to be seen. Instead prints from a selection of its publications were displayed – and very fine many of them were.

At Sotheby's New York sale 'The Book as Art' in June 1995, a copy of *Aesop's Fables* fetched $2530, almost three times the estimate. The book was made in 1931, during the first Gregynog era, when the Press was truly private, the exotic hobby of the Davies sisters, Margaret and Gwendoline. These were ladies of decorum and impeccable taste, granddaughters of the industrialist David Davies, Llandinam. I first saw Gregynog House, a magnificent mock-Tudor pile, almost incredibly built of concrete about the turn of the century, in the 1950s. It is set in glorious parkland near Newtown, Powys, and at the time of that initial visit the surviving sister, Margaret, was still in residence, surrounded by exquisite things, including a collection of French Impressionist paintings that left the viewer pop-eyed and speechless. The paintings were bequeathed to the National

Museum of Wales, where they are the envy of galleries throughout the world and, despite the Arms Park and the Bay development, still the best single reason for visiting Cardiff. Gregynog itself, left to the University of Wales, serves as a conference centre of unusual elegance, with bedrooms the size of dancehalls for special guests. Along with the mansion, the University inherited the stables, which housed the press and all the paraphernalia of types, hand-made papers and fine, imported skins for leather bindings, left over from the 1930s. Largely at the instigation of Dr Glyn Tegai Hughes, the first warden appointed by the University, and Meic Stephens, then Literature Director of the Welsh Arts Council, the Gregynog Press was revived in the 1970s. Since then, it has produced some splendid books, not least among them *Cathedral Builders*, a selection of poems by John Ormond, illustrated with the poet's own drawings, which is beautiful as an object and a delight to read.

Many of those who attended the Gregynog reception at Hay were unaware that the rug of Arts Council of Wales funding had been pulled from under the Press and precipitated its collapse: the highly skilled staff had resigned or been laid off. There is a half-baked notion that it might be resuscitated by the University for special projects, but to all intents and purposes, for a second time, the Gregynog Press is dead. It will be mourned by few – those who could afford, if only occasionally, the high prices that must be charged for strictly limited editions, printed, illustrated and bound to the highest standards by traditional methods. Many more do not realise what they have lost. Something rather rare and beautiful has disappeared from Wales and we are all the poorer for that. Such was the flow of champagne, however, that the Gregynog prints exhibition was outright winner in the cheerfullest wake category at the festival.

Celebratory toasts were in order at other events. The Arts Council's prize for the Welsh Book of the Year in English went to Siân James for a collection of short stories, *Not Singing Exactly*. Gwyneth Lewis, runner-up in the English language prize list last year for *Parables and Faxes*, occupied the same position this year for a collection of poems in Welsh, *Cyfrif Un ac Un yn Dri*, which seems to me more extraordinary than that the top award should go to the short story genre. Within a few days of that announcement, news came of the Cholmondeley Awards to Gillian Clarke and Tony Curtis. The former's work is well known to *PN Review* readers. She has been a Carcanet poet since 1982 and her *Collected Poems* is among the new books promised in the Autumn list. I was fortunate to be among the first to see her poetry, for when, early in 1970, she initially thought of submitting poems for publication, it was to *Poetry Wales* she sent them. At that time, they caught the eye and mind immediately because of the way in which they presented domestic, familial and rural themes from a distinctively feminine viewpoint. Notwithstanding the everyday subjects, there was a shapeliness about the poems, a precision of diction and imagery, and a capacity for artistic objectivity, that placed them far above the commonplace. Those 1970 poems gave notice of a talent with staying power – and so it has turned out. With the development of her craft has come both self-confidence and a well-honed self-critical faculty. It will be interesting to see what of her early work survives her rigorous scrutiny to find a place among the *Collected*.

Tony Curtis, who won the National Poetry Competition in 1984 and was runner-up in the *Observer*/Arvon competition in 1985, must be one of the best known of contemporary Anglo-Welsh poets. American confessional poetry was an early enthusiasm, especially that of Robert Lowell, though he acknowledges also the influence on his own work of Heaney, Walcott and Douglas Dunn. His poems have strong narrative structures, whether they are about his Pembrokeshire roots, home and family, or derive from assiduously cultivated interests in art and artists, and the histories of wars and revolutions in the twentieth century. Death is a recurring theme, and the human capacity to survive through art, books and individual memory. Often too, the story is told in the first person: it is another's confession. As with that of the nurse in 'The Last Candles', leaving the chaos of revolutionary Russia and seeing from the deck of the ship the bodies of Tsarist officers, their feet weighted with stones, floating upright in the port at Odessa:

> Swaying, grey shapes
> I glimpsed from the rail, as if bowing to me.
> The last candles of my Russia
> guttering and going out under the black sea.

The elegiac strand which stands out strongly in Tony Curtis's writing is typified by 'Reg Webb', another poem from his last book *War Voices* (Seren, 1995). It is about a seaman who, after a war spent dodging U-boats and a long peace piloting tankers into Milford Haven, is at last in his final berth:

> Reg becalmed in the straits of morphine
> captaining his bed, full-sheeted, trim,
> away from the port of his front room and tv,
> the photo at the Palace for his OBE,
> floundering and sick of being ill
> sank angrily, far out in the cottage hospital.
> He's lost now, with fire in the hold, and a hard stoke
> for one last evasive action, making smoke.

The poet's interest in art is linked at several points to his study of the two World Wars (research into the war artist William Orpen was the starting point of the prize-winning 'The Death of Richard Beattie-Seaman in the Belgian Grand Prix, 1939') but extends far beyond that. Some of his most recently published poems, in *Poetry Wales*, were from a series written in a collaboration with the New York artist John Digby, and this Autumn will see the publication of a book of conversations with artists in Wales that could open our eyes to talents that have been as little appreciated as those of many Anglo-Welsh poets and, like the poets, deserve closer scrutiny.

Another recent cause for celebration was the ninetieth birthday of Gwyn Jones on 24 May. Although you will find his poem 'The Blue Day Journey' in *The Oxford Book of Welsh Verse in English*, which he also edited, he is far better known as a writer of short stories and novels and a world authority on the Vikings and the Icelandic sagas. If you detect a hint of awe in anything I write about him, I can only plead extenuating circumstances. I fell under the spell of his intellect and remarkable presence as an impressionable seventeen-year-old at the University College of Wales, Aberystwyth, where he was Professor of English. At that time I did not know a fraction of his accomplishments, so that, rather than decreasing with acquaintance, my regard for him steadily grew. At first encounter, he was clearly not a man to be trifled with. His massive head and shoulders powerfully suggested a late incarnation of the hero Beowulf, whose epic tale he taught so brilliantly. He seemed to us as at home in Anglo-Saxon as he was in English and, by whatever standard you choose to mention, he still ranks as easily the most fluently gifted speaker of English I have ever heard – every phrase measured, every sentence perfect, never a pause or stumble. In his seventies, he amazed a TV producer and film crew by speaking to camera, unprepared, in polished paragraphs and a single take. In the quality of his own writing (the evocation of Augustan England in his novel *Richard Savage* (1935) is unsurpassed), in the inspired collaboration with his Aberystwyth colleague Professor Thomas Jones on the translation of *The Mabinogion*, and in the editorial skills he deployed in *The Welsh Review*, which he founded in 1939, he set standards to which the ambitious may aspire, but with scant hope of emulation. For his scholarship he received the Commander's Cross of the Order of the Falcon from the President of Iceland. And Gwyn Jones is, after all, one of us, the son of a miner and the local midwife, born in the Gwent valleys community of Blackwood, ninety years ago.

*PN Review* 118, Volume 24 Number 2,
November – December 1997.

# JOSEPH CLANCY AND MENNA ELFYN
*July 1997*

*PN Review* and Carcanet Press have done more than most to popularise translation as an art form and to increase the currency of writers in other languages among anglophone readers. The current Carcanet list includes translations from French, Catalan, Russian, German, Swedish and Portuguese as well as the collected translations of Edwin Morgan and C.H. Sisson. That there is nothing from the language of England's nearest neighbour doesn't surprise; Welsh writers have ever been poor advertisers abroad of their own talent and have found few to speak up on their behalf. It has become fairly common to hear among the *cognoscenti* acknowledgement of the marvellous medieval lyrical poetry of Dafydd ap Gwilym, but few of these same enthusiasts could name a single contemporary Welsh poet. For the most part, the latter have been content to write for the people in their own backyard. They have competed in eisteddfodau great and small; they have kept up complex, traditional forms of versifying that are exceedingly difficult to render acceptably in another language; they have performed impromptu among friends and neighbours in pubs and parish halls; they have published books for a small, linguistically-defined readership. As in the case of Waldo Williams's single volume, *Dail Pren* (Leaves of the Tree), however, the writing of one or two has had a profound influence on the consciousness of a generation.

That Welsh poetry has flourished in the twentieth century and that there are a number of very fine contemporary poets in the language is not well-known in English-speaking Wales, far less in England. One of Meic Stephens's aims in founding *Poetry Wales* in 1965 was to bridge the ignorance gap between the two linguistic cultures. Actually, the need to improve communication existed on one side only. Welsh speakers tend to buy and read poetry in English as well as books and journals from the Welsh-language presses, but it doesn't work the other way round with their monoglot compatriots. Stephens was determined that *Poetry Wales*, which from the first carried beneath its banner the words *'cylchgrawn cenedlaethol o farddoniaeth newydd'* (a national magazine of new poetry), should include, alongside the Anglo-Welsh contributions, poems in Welsh with translations. This practice continued while he remained editor and for some time after, but has long since disappeared as a regular feature.

Apart from those published in *Poetry Wales*, translations of contemporary poetry have been rare. Books such as Gwyn Jones's *Oxford Book of Welsh Verse in English* (1977), Anthony Conran's *Penguin Book of Welsh Verse* (1967, re-issued by Seren as *Welsh Verse* in 1992), and Gwyn Williams's *To Look for a Word* (Gomer, 1976), excellent as they are in representing the range of Welsh poetry down the ages, contain little that belongs to the twentieth century. Only Joseph Clancy with his *Twentieth Century Welsh Poems* (Gomer, 1982) could claim to represent the modern era adequately.

Clancy is a remarkable case. A New Yorker, formerly Professor of English at the Marymount Manhattan College there, he was first drawn, in the 1960s, to the wealth of medieval Welsh poetry and has dedicated a great deal of his life to researching and translating verse from the sixth century down to the present. Like Anthony Conran and Gwyn Williams (who died in 1990), he is also a poet; his latest collection *Here and There* (Headland), came out in 1994. Now permanently resident in Wales, he is highly esteemed among both Welsh and Anglo-Welsh writers – and rightly so. To my taste, he is currently the most accomplished translator of Welsh poetry. This is not now a judgement that one can reach without some thought, because a number of new poet-translators have suddenly emerged, thanks to the inspiration and will to communicate with a wider audience of two outstanding talents: Gwyneth Lewis, some of whose Welsh poems *PN Review* readers will have seen recently in versions by Richard Poole, and Menna Elfyn, whose most recent books *Eucalyptus* (Gomer, 1995) and *Cell Angel* (Bloodaxe, 1996), have been published bilingually, that is with facing-page translations.

Menna Elfyn (please remember the 'f' in Welsh is pronounced 'v') had published five volumes of poetry in her first language before *Eucalyptus*, a selection of her work from 1978-1994. She dedicated the book 'to the new Welsh speakers', an earnest of her commitment to the concept of a bilingual Wales. Unlike Gwyneth Lewis, her creative output is entirely Welsh, though she is a much-practised and highly-skilled bilingual performer of her poetry, as I witnessed at a pub poetry reading in Newport in January. To produce the English versions, she relies upon and works with her chosen translators, who have included, with Clancy and Conran, Gillian Clarke, R.S. Thomas, Nigel Jenkins, John Barnie and Elin ap Hywel. Those involved in *Cell Angel* provide prefatory remarks. Clancy comments, 'Translating poems is always and never the same. Each time one confronts the impossibility of achieving the Welsh emphasis within the quite different English syntax, the desperate searching for English words that will capture at least some of the associations of the Welsh.' He finds the task of translating Menna Elfyn particularly challenging because she is constantly pushing against the bounds of language to find expression for the nuances of experience she seeks to communicate. The symbolic development of many of the poems adds further problems: some are not easily accessible in either language. Rather to his surprise, the translator finds that the poet is less concerned with the fidelity of the translation 'than with seeing achieved in English an effective poem that conveys the general sense and feeling' of the original. Nevertheless, a large proportion are remarkably close to the Welsh in all but the patterning of sound.

The strength of Menna Elfyn's commitment to causes which do not readily command popular support, and which have often in the past brought her and her family into conflict with the British establishment, is patent in both books. Her social, political, pacifist and feminist convictions are the inspiration and subject matter of a very great deal of her poetry, often combined in a way that is complex and thought-provoking. 'Misglwyf – Mis-y-clwy' ('Bleedings' in Conran's translation), is part celebration of the female cycle, part protest against militaristic blood-letting. Prolonged grief at a miscarriage becomes in a sequence of poems a meditation on relationships, art and life. Poems of feminist protest have an elegiac tone. In 'After the court case', pathetic fallacy and gentle humour are exploited to allay the bitterness of her enforced separation from her husband, a well-known language activist, by legal process. Her own nationalism and commitment to Welsh, tinged more often with sorrow and bitterness than anger, produce poems that are rather like those of R.S. Thomas and, not surprisingly, particularly when he is the translator:

As people we had the death wish
in us, life's zest coming
to us as a nation
at second-hand.

And if we were
to die voluntarily
I daresay it would be
the last sweetener of an item
on 'News at Ten',
an announcer's jovial remark
before the Close Down.

She has herself suffered imprisonment, for contempt of court (she shouted at the judge in a language trial): 'Cell Angel', the title poem of her latest book, is one of several born of this experience. They do not rail against the law; they are not self-pitying, merely determined – 'I could buy my way out of here,/three hours and I'd be home... I'm here for a cause/but found new causes'. They have a strong religious element, for she is the daughter of a Congregationalist minister and is interested in eastern religions. They tell of fellow prisoners who judge her 'not brave, but stupid', of the endless song of the woman in the next cell 'droning on about her sycamore leaves falling my side of the fence', of the spy-hole in the cell door, 'Gaia's eye, sometimes/winking mischief at me', of the manless loneliness of these women –

We are anchorites. After supper
we turn to contemplation. We make
    fleshless
bundles. Like it or not we're spiritual...

Sex – married love – has a stronger presence in these books than readers might anticipate. This too is an expression of Menna Elfyn's integrity as a writer. She celebrates fleshly delights as honestly as she confronts the manifold sins and suffering of mankind, and with a reassuring lightness of touch. As with

Gwyneth Lewis (and even through the distorting mirror of translation) we see in her work a playfulness. It illuminates even elegy, as in the sequence of poems to the memory of the historian Gwyn Williams, and in the unusual blend of lyricism and irony in another sequence, about women's hair, which introduces God as 'Trinydd Gwallt' ('Hairdresser'), fastidiously fashioning Eve's curls, to the envy of Adam, 'the first fool/who brought down snake-spit on his head'.

*PN Review* and Bloodaxe have assisted in lifting a corner of the screen of language and prejudice behind which contemporary Welsh poets communicate with their own small community. While one wouldn't expect to see as a result the kind of international recognition that in the pop and rock world has fallen upon the Manic Street Preachers, there is certainly more poetic talent to be revealed, if the whole curtain can be drawn aside.

*PN Review* 116, Volume 23 Number 6,
July – August 1997.

# ROLAND MATHIAS AND ROBERT MINHINNICK
*May 1997*


The London *Evening Standard* does not reach these parts, but I have occasionally bought a copy at Paddington to while away the journey back to Wales. If my luck was in, I would find some item so infuriating that I would spend most of the time composing in my mind a letter to the Editor, which of course I would not send – arguing with journalists is pointless. Brian Sewell, with his far-back, know-it-all arrogance, could on occasion stimulate that surge of adrenalin. It was enormously satisfying to hear him on television confuse Simon de Montfort, Earl of Leicester (c. 1208-65), with his father, also Simon de Montfort (c. 1150-1218), a petty lord from the Ile de France who led a vicious crusade against the Albigensian heretics until struck down by a mangonel stone (reputedly fired by women and girls) at the second siege of Toulouse. Evidently, we all make mistakes.

I gather from the *Guardian* that A.N. Wilson has resigned as literary editor of the *Evening Standard*. He has not gone quietly: his Parthian shot was aimed at bringing down Seamus Heaney – another mistake. Heaney needs no defence from me, but the terms of Wilson's dismissal of genius made me sit bolt upright. Apparently, in his view, if Heaney had been Welsh, his poetry 'would have been lucky to have made it to the pages of the parish magazine'. It is hard to know whether to be annoyed or pleased about this. In the end, I decided it was a backhanded compliment to poets from Wales and an accurate, if unintended, criticism of the typical metropolitan reviewer's patronising and prejudiced view of contemporary literature as that stuff published within the sound of Bow Bells.

Despite the seven-day wonder of the UK's favourite poems, or what have you, publishers' figures for sales of poetry make depressing reading. I suspect that holds as true proportionally for England as it does for Wales. As the population of the former is some seventeen times greater than that of the latter, so no doubt are the actual numbers of books sold. A fair chance to catch the eye of that larger readership is what Roland Mathias long campaigned for in the editorial pages of the *Anglo-Welsh Review*, but unsuccessfully. Remarkably few London editors and reviewers subscribed to *AWR*.

Now in his eighties, Mathias has recently brought out a new book, *A Field at Vallorcines* (Gomer), his first, not counting a volume of Selected Poems, since *Snipe's Castle*, also published by Gomer in 1979. In between he suffered a stroke which seemed to have brought to an end an extraordinarily busy career as critic, editor, scholar, historian, preacher and lecturer, as well as short-story writer and poet, but in 1992 poems began to appear in journals here again. Jeremy Hooker took some time to come to terms with Mathias's poetic method and moral certainty, but was won over by that splendid book *Absalom in the Tree* (1971), although he felt it 'discomforting to be implicated in another's remorseless self-examination'. Several of the poems he thought 'easily among the finest I have read by a contemporary for some time', and the book as a whole 'as good as it is honest and disquieting'. Within the last year, M. Wynn Thomas, the most respected of Anglo-Welsh critics, has added the weight of his opinion that Mathias 'bears comparison with Geoffrey Hill, whom he resembles in his flinchingly exact use of words, his highly mannered discourse, his pointed use of archaisms...and the acerbic self-distaste that permeates his poetry and in which his resort to language is so ambiguously implicated'. Again, some of the poems, Thomas says, 'are among the most powerful of the last half-century'. I have quoted others because my own regard for Mathias's writing, both prose and poetry, is perhaps already known and my judgement considered partial. Let me say, however, that I think *A Field at Vallorcines* deserves the wide audience that Mathias long argued was the due of fellow writers from Wales. His voice rings true in every poem in the book: the texture of the language (a rough tweed that conveys the physicality of sense impressions and the knotted complexities of a scrupulous concern for truth), the actorly command of dramatic utterance, the numinous landscapes, the self-questioning, the sudden tenderness – are all essentially his. A few lines from the title poem, which at first reading may appear simply descriptive, but reveals itself at last an allegory, a long view back at a shared life, must serve to illustrate the unexpected renewal of mastery represented by the book.

> ... It is calm here. On the old
> Hindmost rushes water gulps
> Out jewels and the seep of the field
> Is audible. To the right the fenced way
>     pushes
>
> Past garden palings and partly tilled
> Vegetable plots to the railway line
> Beyond. But the station building, the
>     immediate goal
>
> Has a kind of grace, a fluted, fine
> Semblance of gothic tricked into metal.
> The run down the gorge to the frontier,
>     the silent place

We peered at this morning with so little
In mind, will be full of jerks and
   slowings
Like the blind climb up. But the station
   has grace. It has borne

The faces of doubt, the comings and
   goings
Of millions. We shall stand there solid
   in
The goodly counsel with which a world
   back we set out.

Robert Minhinnick's new book, *Badlands* (Seren), a collection of travel essays with a strong environmental message, racy and perceptive, is as good a read of its kind as the discriminating reader is likely to find. Minhinnick could, if he wished, turn his hand to most things, from restaurant reviews to TV commercials, or even fiction, and make a killing. But he is a poet and, he told me recently, the poems are 'all true'. He is a latter-day Romantic, writing out of personal experience in a way that has been forsaken by many of his contemporaries. They, when the confessional lode has been exhausted, find *personae* to tell their own or someone else's tale. Minhinnick mines more deeply in himself. After a revolution in style in his fifth book of poems, *The Looters* (1989), in which he employed a symbolist technique to convey sobering messages about human relationships in decline, insanity and the destruction of the environment, he returned in *Hey Fatman* (1994), his sixth and latest, to earlier concerns with family history, memories of childhood evoked by return journeys, domestic activities, bars, macabre events – and writing that is more immediately accessible. For me the gem of the book is again the title poem.

'Hey Fatman' is set in a squalid, beach-side bar in Rio, where the poet observes the 'imperceptible protocols' of the barman boss, four whores and their clients, and local insect life – a huge moth that immolates itself against a neon sign, while over the walls 'the baby roaches ran/Warning of fire, waving their brown arms'. 'Hey Fatman' is the whores' perhaps unspoken invitation to dalliance:

> And they'd suck their drinks and
>    circulate,
> Trailing a perfume through the room
> Of their own sweat, like a herb crushed
>    underfoot.
> *Hey fatman*, it said to the night,
> To the brass propellors of the fan
> That uttered ceaselessly its quiet
>    scream

This Americanisation of Minhinnick's writing, for so I take it to be, highly-coloured, yet relaxed, colloquial and still elegant, is a new departure – more like his essays in tone. Interviewed in *Poetry Wales* in 1989, he revealed himself a poet of and for Wales – 'it's where I've lived and worked, it's also where I've published. It's inevitable'. A.N. Wilson will not have heard of him, but if I were to bet on writers in our small parish who, given the chance, could give the famed Irish a run for their money, Robert Minhinnick would be one.

*PN Review* 115, Volume 23 Number 5,
May – June 1997.

# RAYMOND GARLICK
*March 1997*


On 21 September, the Welsh Academy celebrated the seventieth birthday of Raymond Garlick. The venue was Trinity College, Carmarthen, where for many congenial years Raymond taught, first within the English Department and later as lecturer in charge of Welsh Studies, a course of his own devising, which, uniquely at the time, offered students in higher education a substantial experience of Anglo-Welsh literature. The celebration was a modest affair, but full of warmth and affection. It fitted the man, whose courtesy, gentleness, soft-spoken eloquence and love of literature inspired generations of students. I once sat mesmerised by a talk he gave to a group of sixth formers who were setting out from the college to explore locations in the neighbourhood – notably Fern Hill and Laugharne – associated with Dylan Thomas. He had a similar effect year after year on the trainee teachers and students from Iowa participating in the college's American Programme who were his regular audience. His gentleness is not of the namby-pamby sort. Raymond Garlick is acutely discriminating and tenacious in argument. As one who, virtually throughout his life, has struggled to overcome physical disability and set the highest standards for himself, he has little time for those who lack industry and grit. Like his good friend Tony Conran, he is a pacifist of the kind that does not back away from confrontation but strenuously opposes colonialism and bullying, large-scale or small.

There is every reason for celebrating the life of a gifted teacher (it doesn't happen often enough), but of course Raymond Garlick is much more than that. The University of

Wales Press chose the same birthday occasion to launch formally Don Dale-Jones's monograph on Raymond in its Writers of Wales series. Since 1970 more than a hundred volumes have appeared in the series, and the first was *An Introduction to Anglo-Welsh Literature* by Raymond Garlick. In this essay he proposed an alternative to the view that Anglo-Welsh literature is a twentieth-century phenomenon, a by-product of the English-medium and powerfully anglicising county grammar schools, which were introduced in Wales (before they came to England) by the 1889 Intermediate Education Act. Raymond holds that Anglo-Welsh literature has a long history, extending back at least as far as c. 1470, when Ieuan ap Hywel Swrdwal, a student in Oxford, wrote a 'Hymn to the Virgin' in the English language in which he employed the prosodic devices of Welsh cynghanedd, a feat he challenged his contemporaries to emulate. To be sure, a line can be drawn down the centuries, and it links some notable figures, like Henry Vaughan, George Herbert, Christopher Smart and George Dyer, but it is a dotted line and the gaps in it are often wide.

Raymond also deserves with Roland Mathias a large share of the credit for reviving and sustaining Anglo-Welsh literature after the war. The meeting of these two remarkable intellects came about strangely. Early in 1949, as almost his first significant act as Head of Pembroke Dock Grammar School, Roland appointed the recently-graduated Raymond Garlick to his English department. The scene was thus set for the founding of *Dock Leaves/Anglo-Welsh Review*, which was for some years the only magazine catering for Welsh writing in English. Beyond these historically significant developments, there is also Raymond Garlick's contribution as a poet. Since 1946 he has published twelve books; *Collected Poems 1946-86* appeared from Gomer Press in 1987 and his latest volume *Travel Notes (New Poems)*, also from Gomer, in 1992. A meticulous technician and gifted exploiter of the power of rhyme to make utterance memorable, he has set himself some formidable metrical problems over the years, not least among them pattern poems, like George Herbert's 'Easter Wings' or Dylan Thomas's 'Vision and Prayer'. He has been a stirring polemicist too, in a series of poems protesting against the injustices perpetrated by the English legal establishment against Welsh Language Society activists in the early 1970s. He remains a committed supporter of Wales and Welsh literature in both its languages – a curious commitment, one might think, for one of entirely English background who was born and, until the war years, brought up in the London suburbs. In his account of the writer's life and work and particularly his well-balanced assessment of the poetry, Don Dale-Jones provides a valuable introduction to this important figure in the cultural life of Wales since 1945.

Raymond Garlick and Roland Mathias, who as successive editors of the *Anglo-Welsh Review* welcomed writers from England (and overseas – though rooted in Wales both have strongly European views), will appreciate the degree of openness which emerges from analysis of the contents list of Seren's *Burning the Bracken*, published earlier this year. It claims to be a definitive sampler of poetry in English from Wales, but it is not quite that. Rather it is a collection compiled from the work of that extensive list of poets who have brought out at least one book with Seren in the past fifteen years. Seven of the poets were also included in *The Lilting House* (1969), that landmark anthology of Anglo-Welsh poetry edited by Meic Stephens and John Stuart Williams, and some interesting comparisons can be drawn between the two books. Of the 43 poets in *The Lilting House*, Raymond Garlick was one of only seven who were not Welsh by birth, while almost half the 46 poets in *Burning the Bracken* were born in England. Most of the latter currently live or have spent a considerable amount of time in education or employment in Wales. Even so, this is a considerable shift. Four women were among the poets in *The Lilting House*, compared with seventeen in *Burning the Bracken*. This too is a striking, if not unexpected, change and, like the development remarked above, it is accelerating: of the seventeen younger poets in Seren's anthology, that is those born in the 1950s and 1960s, eight are women. Among these are two of the most accomplished poets in the volume – Sheenagh Pugh and Hilary Llewellyn-Williams. It is the work of Christine Evans, however, one of those born in the 1940s, that I re-read most readily. She has been offering us her quiet observations from her home on the Llŷn Peninsula for some time and conveys with tactile clarity what it is like to live on and off the land. Her poems penetrate beyond descriptive exactness to a sense of the precarious business of survival for individuals and a unique society in her rural, sea-bounded corner of Wales.

Although there are notable exceptions (Tony Curtis, Duncan Bush, Peter Finch, Robert Minhinnick, Mike Jenkins, whose poetic worlds can be urban, industrial, cosmopolitan, routinely squalid, violent), post-Hughes, post-Heaney nature poetry is far commoner in this collection. This is not to denigrate poems that are often replete with acute perceptions and precise images, even if they do not *say* a great deal. In all but a few cases, rural Wales is not distinguishable from rural England, and Mike Jenkins's 'Gurnos Shops', that depressingly accurate vision of a down-at-heel council estate, would serve its purpose as a critique of political neglect almost anywhere. Perhaps it was ever thus and we were wrong to suppose there is anything distinctive about Welsh writing in English; and now Welsh themes are less prominent, because there is less to distinguish society in Wales from that in England. In his introduction to *The Lilting House*, Raymond Garlick identified some poems in the anthology as 'Welsh in the fullest sense', in that 'not only are they written by Welsh men or about Wales – they are written for Wales'. There were not a host of such poems in that book and far fewer can be found in *Burning the Bracken*. Re-workings of Welsh myth or history are rare, and recognisably Welsh, especially Welsh-nationalist opinions are equally thin on the ground, if you set aside the contribution of John Tripp, that remarkable old war-horse, dead these ten years. The poem that leaps out, for its intrinsic quality as well as for its Welshness in Raymond Garlick's terms, is Tony Conran's 'Elegy for the Welsh Dead in the Falkland Islands, 1982' which echoes the great sixth century Welsh poem about a disastrous raid, 'Y Gododdin', and is compounded of anger and praise. I do not think our reserves of that fuel of anger and praise are running low, but they seem now to be spent on social and environmental concerns less particularly Welsh than when Idris Davis wrote 'The Angry Summer'.

*PN Review* 114, Volume 23 Number 4,
March – April 1997.

# GWYNETH LEWIS

*January 1997*


The Rhys Davies Trust was set up in 1990. It owes its existence to the extraordinary generosity of Lewis Davies, the writer's brother. No conditions were attached to the gift and, though the Trustees are much concerned to keep green the name and literary reputation of Rhys Davies, their broad aims to stimulate activity and interest in Welsh writing in English can be satisfied by a variety of outcomes. The Trust enjoys an annual income from investments that, in its first five years or so, has funded an annual lecture, grants for students attending writing courses, predictably (in view of Rhys Davies's contribution to the genre) short story competitions, and in 1993 a pair of European travel bursaries, one of which was won by Gwyneth Lewis. So it was I met her, on the occasion of the formal presentation of the bursaries at Waterstones in Cardiff. That was a low-key event, but since then, and particularly with the publication of *Parables and Faxes*, she has emerged as the most exciting 'new' poet this side of the border.

Gwyneth Lewis was born in Cardiff and educated at Cambridge, at Harvard and Columbia University in the USA, and at Oxford where she did research on literary forgeries. She worked as a journalist in the United States and on the Philippine Islands before returning to Wales; she is now a television producer. While at Columbia, she attended a seminar on translations at which she met a Hungarian translator, Árpád Göncz, who had been sentenced to life imprisonment for his part in the 1956 Uprising. Göncz introduced her to 'A Walesi

Bardok', a dramatic ballad which, he said, was known by everyone in Hungary and recited at the slightest provocation, or none. This work by the revered poet János Arany dates from the middle of the nineteenth century. It was inspired by the spirit of dissent against the occupying Austrian power and retells the apocryphal tale of the Welsh bards who, instead of eulogising Edward I as they were expected to do, heaped poetic curses on him for his bloody conquest of Wales and paid for their honesty with their lives. Gwyneth Lewis's account of her visit, published in the magazine *Planet* (No. 105, June/July 1994), contains some fascinating insights into a country little known to most of us, as it emerges from communism: Árpád Göncz is now its President. 'Old Statues' Park in Budapest', which formed part of her report to the Trust, appears as Parable XXIII in *Parables and Faxes*. But she is not a new poet – at least not to readers of Welsh. Her earliest publications were of prize-winning entries in the Urdd National Eisteddfod in the 1970s and her first volume of poems, published by Gwasg Gomer in 1990, was *Sonedau Redsa*. The title means 'Sonnets for Redsa', her godchild in the Philippines, uniquely named after the initial letters of one of the main streets in Manila down which the crowds surged to secure the overthrow of the Marcos régime.

The ease with which she moves poetically between Welsh and English calls to my mind Euros Bowen, who died in 1988. He was, like R.S. Thomas, an Anglican cleric, and a poet of no less distinction, though far less widely known and acknowledged because he wrote in Welsh. He was also an accomplished translator, having to his credit translations into Welsh from Greek and Latin (Sophocles and Virgil) and, of particular interest in this context, a selection from the work of the French Symbolist poets. He too was a Symbolist, though he preferred to think of himself as a 'sacramentalist'. His imagery, especially of the natural world, was as precise as it was evocative, but many readers considered him obscure. In 1974 he brought out *Poems* (Gwasg Gomer) a selection from the half dozen books he had published up to that point with his own English translations. In his brief preface to this splendid sample of his art he mentions one of the peculiar difficulties that attend the translating of Welsh poetry: rendering into English the distinctive music of *cynghanedd*, 'a system of versification that combines consonantal equivalence and internal rhyme'. He goes on to explain that though he makes use of *cynghanedd*, it is not within the strict metres of classical Welsh prosody, rather 'the movement of the images which convey the meaning... is one of rhythm only'.

All this is germane to recurring themes and the techniques employed by Gwyneth Lewis in *Parables and Faxes* as much as in those Welsh poems elegantly translated by Richard Poole in *PN Review* 110, which naturally owe a great deal to the thought processes of the bilingual writer for whom language itself and the varying forms of its presentation in speech and on the page is an absorbing preoccupation: 'I am the fruit of God's expressiveness to man. I grow on libraries...' What are parables and faxes, in her terms, but modes of symbolist and imagist expression? Euros Bowen would have appreciated the conceit. If language is one theme, transformation is another ('We are all transformers: we change what we see'), and word-play is a constant feature. The whimsical, fantastical elaboration of images occasionally suggests automatic writing, though of a forgivably witty and graceful kind. It is the fate of the would-be critic to see in the work of one writer echoes of others. Here it is Plath and Empson, but that does not mean that I think either was an influence consciously or unconsciously absorbed. What the reader observes is a similar cast of mind perhaps and verbal inventiveness. The Plath-like piling up of images might as readily be seen as an element of Gwyneth Lewis's Welsh poetic heritage to which the term *'dyfalu'* is given. She makes use of ideas and vocabulary drawn from science and technology – a metaphysical habit – that catch the spirit of this age while she explores aspects of the human condition common to all ages. In short, her first English-language collection is both thought-provoking and in its pervading ludic freshness highly entertaining.

*Parables and Faxes* was one of two collections of poetry shortlisted for the Arts Council of Wales Book of the Year Prize; the other was R.S. Thomas's *No Truce with the Furies*. Neither won. To the surprise of many, that accolade went to a travel book, *Gwalia in Khasia* (Gwasg Gomer) by Nigel Jenkins, the Swansea born and based poet and journalist. It tells of the Welsh Calvinist Methodist Mission to the Khasi Jaintia Hills in north-east India which extended from 1841 until 1969 when the missionaries left because of a government edict which insisted that as a condition of remaining they must take Indian citizenship. The Catholic missionaries did so and stayed. Nigel Jenkins travelled to Khasia to find out what the Welsh had achieved over the years and what of their influence remained. Certainly they had brought Christianity and persuaded the warlike Khasis to fire their arrows at targets instead of one another; and they introduced literacy, for there had been no written language before the missionaries came. At the same time they robbed the hill people of many of their tribal practices and a great deal of the natural colour of their lives. Colonialism, even of the non-exploitative sort, finds local distinctions hard to bear. The book is a good read, for Nigel Jenkins knows his subject well and has a keen poet's eye for human foibles and frailties and a light touch. There was a minor furore when the prize winner was announced, somewhat fuelled by the knowledge that one of the three jurors, Belinda Humfrey, dissented from the views of the other two, the historian, Peter

Stead, and Hilary Llewellyn-Williams, a poet. As is the way with such events, controversy soon died down, until it was revived in Robin Reeves's editorial in the latest *New Welsh Review* (No. 33). He calls the affair a 'debacle' and blames the Arts Council for selecting jurors who are not *bona fide* literary critics. The other, richer prizes, Booker and the like, are in his view similarly mishandled. At the heart of his argument is the common conflict of interests between critical appreciation and marketing. However, few care a fig for the former if book sales increase. Gwasg Gomer are satisfied that demand for *Gwalia in Khasia* went up following announcement of the prize and on the strength of that will shortly be bringing out a new edition in paperback. Reviewers have praised the book and it deserves to be a popular success. As for the final literary judgement between it, *No Truce with the Furies* and, indeed, *Parables and Faxes*, we can afford to wait.

*PN Review* 113, Volume 23 Number 3,
January – February 1997.

# LESLIE NORRIS

*July 1996*

In 1995 it was Swansea's turn to host the UK Year of Literature. Why Cardiff decided not to be in the running for the festival remains a mystery, but Swansea bid for it and, with the backing and know-how of the administration team of Yr Academi Gymreig, the Welsh Academy of writers, was successful. It is a matter for speculation whether anyone outside Wales, apart from participating writers and ex-President Jimmy Carter, who was invited to open the Dylan Thomas exhibition, knew much about it. In Wales we wondered what lasting good might come of it: that is still hazy, but there is more promise of useful continuity than at first appeared.

The start was inauspicious. In a small-scale rehearsal of the Cardiff Bay Opera House fiasco, the local council vetoed Will Alsop's winning entry for the competition to design a new library and Tŷ Llên (house of literature) which was to be the major venue for the festival and a permanent landmark. Alsop's colourful, imaginative, flexible design, which might have put Wales on the map architecturally, was altogether too much for the City Fathers, who know what they like and take their cue from Prince Charles. One Year of Literature director came, and went. The next stayed but had less time to prepare. Early events were under-advertised, audiences were disappointing and dire predictions were made. But then the programme got into its stride, writers attracted a good turnout, of mostly local enthusiasts, and finally a success was proclaimed. Many feared that once the festival had closed, the space given to Tŷ Llên in the refurbished former Guildhall would be reclaimed by the council as office accommodation. That has not happened. The programme of events continues into 1996 and by good judgement and, I suspect, good fortune, one of the foremost critics in Wales, Professor M. Wynn Thomas, is associated with a number of them. The past month or so has seen novelists Margaret Drabble and Mordecai Richler at Tŷ Llên, and poets Nigel Wells, Roger Garfitt and, an undoubted coup, Les Murray. At this rate Tŷ Llên could indeed become what its advertisements claim, the National Literature Centre for Wales.

Leslie Norris is probably more highly regarded, better known even, in the United States than he is in the UK. He has been the best survivor of the Welsh poetic exports to the USA. Dylan Thomas, as we all know, died young and debauched in New York. His friend and fellow Swansea Jack, Vernon Watkins, whose orderly life style was as far removed from Thomas's as it is possible to imagine, died a fit man, one might say, on a tennis court in Seattle. Leslie Norris edited the book of tributes, *Vernon Watkins 1906-1967* (Faber) and in 1973 found himself seated behind the same desk Vernon had used, with the immense view of Puget Sound to distract him, in the same role as Visiting Professor of Poetry at the University of Washington. I recall sharing a settee with him at John Ormond's home in Cardiff soon after his return from that stint, listening to his description of the beauties of the Washington landscape, the extraordinary popularity and dramatic death of another poet-teacher at the University of Washington, Theodore Roethke (whose name I found I had long pronounced incorrectly), and his discovery in the drawer of that desk of poems left there by his predecessors. Should he add his contribution to those of Marianne Moore, Watkins and the equally famous others? He had time to consider because he was invited back to Seattle. For many years now, however, he has been resident in the United States as Christiansen Professor of Poetry at Brigham

Young University, Utah. There he is recognised as a first-rate teacher, as one might expect of a former primary school headmaster, and much admired as a writer.

Leslie Norris will soon be 75 and he and his wife, Kitty, are to return to this country. Seren will mark this double cause for celebration with the publication of his *Collected Poems* and his *Collected Stories*, both scheduled for Spring 1996. To have all the poems in one book will be a delight, but it will also disguise a remarkable feature of his career as poet. His first two books, *The Tongue of Beauty* and *Poems*, were published in 1942, the next, *The Loud Winter*, was a pamphlet produced by Meic Stephens's Triskel Press in 1967. Between there was war service, teaching and lecturing and 'years of near silence'. Once he had got his second wind he wrote with a will. *Finding Gold* appeared from Chatto & Windus, also in 1967, and *Ransoms* and *Mountains, Polecats, Pheasants* from the same publisher in 1970 and 1974. The stimulus of friendship with Ted Walker and Andrew Young and the keenness of journals like *Poetry Wales* and the *Anglo-Welsh Review* to display his writing were factors in the creative surge of the 1960s and 1970s. Throughout this time he lived near Chichester, but for his themes he often returned to memories of childhood in Merthyr Tydfil, a birthplace he shared with his lifelong friend, Glyn Jones. It is not the industrial town that preoccupies either of them but often characters, in Glyn's words, 'The legendary/Walkers and actors of it', and the surrounding rural landscape. In a monograph on Glyn Jones that he published in 1973, Leslie Norris did not find it strange 'that a poet bred and born in Merthyr Tydfil should...celebrate so instinctively the peace of small communities and the natural beauty in which they exist'. Glyn Jones, he goes on to say, 'is very properly the poet of such places and of the areas where town and country meet'. He could have been writing about himself. With a precise touch he celebrates the virtue and beauty of simple, often unregarded things and mourns their passing. Poems like 'Early Frost', 'Water' and the much anthologiscd 'Ballad of Billy Rose' have become Anglo-Welsh elegiac archetypes but are distinctively his own. One of the characteristics of his poetic voice is the deft counterpoise of monosyllables, as in 'Early Frost':

> We were warned about the frost, yet all
>    day the summer
> Has wavered its heat above the empty
>    stubble. Late
> Bees hung their blunt weight,
> Plump drops between those simplest
>    wings, their leisure
> An ignorance of frost.

It begs to be read aloud. A very great deal of Leslie Norris's poetry has that appeal to the ear and he is no mean performer of it. Since 1974 most of his work has been first published in the USA. It will be good to have him back.

The Leslie Norris books are the most important items in Seren's list for the coming months, but several others deserve attention. Among the prose is a novel by Rhys Davies, *Ram With Red Horns*, probably the last he wrote before his death in 1978 and now to be published for the first time, and a reprint of Emyr Humphreys's finest novel, *Outside The House Of Baal*. The poetry includes new books by John Powell Ward, whose undemonstrative picking over of the minutiae of life and personal relationships has won many admirers since his Triskel pamphlet *The Line Of Knowledge* (1972), and among the newer writers, Paul Henry, Don Rodgers and Desmond Graham.

It should have come as no surprise to see R.S. Thomas's

name among the ranks of authors supplying samples of their wares in miniature books from Phoenix, but the title *Love Poems* was a little unexpected. They are just that, though of an austere kind, and if Auden's estate can benefit substantially from the opportunistic, and expensive, marketing of ten love poems when everyone wanted only one of them, why shouldn't RST gain some reward from this fairly inspired choice of no fewer than 38 of the *Collected Poems*? It is as good a 60p's worth as you are likely to find.

*PN Review* 110, Volume 22 Number 6,
July – August 1996.

# HARRI WEBB, GWYN A. WILLIAMS, GLYN JONES AND LYNETTE ROBERTS

*May 1996*

It is not too late, as I write, to look back for a moment on the year just ended. Things began badly you might say. We awoke on the first day of 1995 to learn that Harri Webb, poet and patriot had, with a touch of irony, died on New Year's Eve. Harri had been ailing for a long time and, latterly, had acquired the ascetic, bearded mien of an Old Testament prophet, but he was essentially a convivial character (though with an acerbic edge) who loved a pint and a joke. Then Glyn Jones, poet, short story writer, novelist, who had been for many years a touchstone and talisman for all involved in Anglo-Welsh writing, died in April. Lynette Roberts, like Glyn a survivor of the 'first flowering' in the 1930s, died in September and Gwyn A. Williams, that prodigious communicator in every respect but physical stature, in November.

No apology is needed for including Gwyn Alf, as he was known, partly to distinguish him from other Gwyn Williamses, in the list. Although he was a professional historian, he was a member of the Welsh Academy of writers and had a rare way with words. No one who heard him speak is likely to forget how his stammer became not an impediment but another device in the formidable armoury of his rhetoric. His brilliance as a student was such that many believed 'Alf' was a soubriquet, an abbreviation for alpha, the grade he invariably received for essays, and he went on striking sparks from all subjects in the arts, history and politics where his passions led him. Brought up in a strongly socialist chapel-going family in the worst years of the depression, he was not the sort to turn his back on his origins. He was early a communist by conviction and never changed, though his brand of communism was far closer to Tito than to Stalin. He viewed Marxist theory through the lens of Gramsci, of whom he wrote and spoke with persuasive eloquence.

I knew him first at the University College of Wales, Aberystwyth in the 1950s, where he and the late Richard Cobb were colleagues for a time in what must have bid fair to be the liveliest history department in the UK, and saw him last at the packed seventieth birthday celebration in his honour at Chapter Arts Centre in Cardiff. He was even then very ill and, responding to a trio of eulogies, began by saying there was little he could offer in return except thanks. But he drew energy from the crowd and spoke with all the old fire and wit for over an hour. The famous stammer detonated climaxes as sharply as ever, and he sang the *Internationale* in its first language, French, with a firm voice and irrepressible fervour.

His writing was scholarly but never dull. If readers can be persuaded to dip into the preface of *The Merthyr Rising*, probably his finest book, I do not think they will leave the rest unread. In that preface, Gwyn remarks that the grandparents of Glyn Jones, 'a fellow Merthyr citizen,' actually lived through the tumultuous 1830s and the workers' insurrection, bloodily put down, that is the subject of his book. Glyn was 90 when he died last year. He did not wear his political beliefs on his sleeve but, as another who had lived in south Wales through the decades that preceded World War II, he was, almost inevitably, a socialist. More important, he was a devout Christian, and a pacifist: he lost his teaching job during the war because he was a conscientious objector. He was equally unswerving in his commitment to writing – though his ambition as a young man was to be an artist. He transmuted his delight

in form and colour to a lust for words and the texturing of
language that was undiminished into his eighties. An inventive
writer of fictions, short and long, as well as a poet, he brought
to composition an uncompromising determination to follow
Keats's dictum and 'load every rift... with ore.' It was not
enough that a sentence should move a story forward, it had to
have some image, some verbal felicity that would justify its
place on the page. All his adult life he kept notebooks, actually
pocket diaries, in which he jotted observations, ideas, snatches
of conversation, that he later mined to illuminate stories and
poems. Remarkable though his earlier poetry is, notably the
autobiographical poem 'Merthyr', his later writing has a high
seriousness and a limpid beauty that outshines it. He was one
of those poets who continued to improve throughout a long life.
His complete poems are currently being edited for the
University of Wales Press by Meic Stephens, his close friend
and literary executor. Meic has assembled from manuscripts and
published fragments of a long poem in which, he says, another,
unexpected side of the poet is revealed in the persona of Shader,
the artist he had first set out to be. Its belated appearance in
print could prove one of the literary events of 1996.

Like Glyn Jones, Lynette Roberts (born 1909) was a friend
of Dylan Thomas. The Anglo-Welsh writers of the 1930s were
all fairly familiar with one another. Some were close friends who
met often to compare notes, as did the three Joneses, Glyn,
Gwyn and Jack. The London-based members of the group often
gathered above Griff's Bookshop in Cecil Court. Many
corresponded and, in due course, met because they contributed
to the same magazines. First in that field was *Wales*, founded
(in 1937) and edited by Keidrych Rhys. It is to Keidrych that
Glyn Jones addresses the introductory letter that prefaces his
'admirable and humane' collection of essays *The Dragon has
Two Tongues*. Poetry and prose by Lynette Roberts appeared in

the early numbers of *Wales* and she married Keidrych Rhys in 1940. She published two volumes of poetry, *Poems* (1944) and *Gods with Stainless Ears* (1951), both with Faber and Faber. Then she fell silent. In the obituary that appears in the latest number of *Poetry Wales*, Tony Conran sees signs of a revival of interest in her work, and supports it with the weight of his considerable authority. This bears comparison with the renewed regard for the writing of David Gascoyne, another experimental poet of the 1930s and 1940s, who is happily still with us, but has published little since 1956.

In *The Dragon Has Two Tongues*, Glyn Jones tells how, in his grammar school days, Palgrave's *Golden Treasury* was his favourite book, and later Lawrence and Hopkins became his literary heroes. Although his family roots lay deep in Welsh culture, the language of his intellectual awakening was English and so it became the language of his poetry and fiction. Nevertheless, he wrote '...while using cheerfully enough the English language, I have never written in it a word about any country other than Wales, or any people other than Welsh people.'

In his best radical, public bar manner, Harri Webb turned the same sentiment into a piece of 'Advice to a Young Poet': 'Sing for Wales or shut your trap – All the rest's a load of crap.' Harri Webb's *Collected Poems* have just appeared from Gomer Press. Here are all the political squibs and rumbustious crowd-pleasers that made him the 'People's Poet'. He was more complex and subtle than many of his mass audience perceived. Almost a third of the 350 poems in the book have not previously seen the light of day. Among these is a substantial body of work that reveals the poet as an ambitious prosodist, a romantic, an unrequited lover. Meic Stephens, who is editor of this collection also, has done his usual painstaking job in rescuing these poems from the disordered Harri Webb archive

and placing them with the published work in chronological
order. The official launch coincides with the award of the first
Harri Webb prize, to be given annually for poems in the radical
tradition.

Roland Mathias, whose eightieth birthday we celebrated in
October, is the only surviving Nonconformist poet of distinction
(R.S. Thomas is Anglican). There are still politically aware poets
of the radical socialist persuasion but, apart perhaps from Nigel
Jenkins and Mike Jenkins, they do not publish regularly in the
major Anglo-Welsh literary magazines, *Poetry Wales* and *The
New Welsh Review*. Few of the poets represented in the pages
of those journals, most of whom came to print, if not
prominence, in the 1970s and 1980s, have taken Harri Webb's
advice. The finest of them, like Robert Minhinnick, Duncan
Bush, Sheenagh Pugh and John Davies, are more likely to be
writing about the USA or Iceland. The change was inevitable.
In the 1960s we occasionally debated whether there were
features that distinguished Anglo-Welsh writers, not only in
their themes but in the way they used language. It was fanciful
then and is quite pointless today.

Anglo-Welsh writing, or even 'Welsh writing in English', the
politically correct formula, has no distinguishing characteristics
now. A more accurate term would be 'writing from Wales'
(writing in Welsh has always defined itself). However, it has a
surer status than the 'first flowering' and the second ever
possessed, because it is no longer on the defensive in Wales. It
is now academically respectable to teach and research Anglo-
Welsh writing. The goal that Roland Mathias and Raymond
Garlick fought so long and hard for has been achieved. The
establishment of the University of Wales Association for the
Study of Welsh Writing in English has been a giant step forward.
Above all, it means that academics are routinely subjecting
Anglo-Welsh writing to the kind of serious scrutiny that it only

occasionally received before. I hope that my faith in the power of literary criticism to increase understanding and raise standards is not misplaced and that we shall see a re-evaluation of the work of major Anglo-Welsh writers that will gain for them the recognition they merit in Wales and further afield. It will help, of course, if, in succession to Ireland's Seamus Heaney, the 1996 Nobel Prize for Literature is won by the nominee from Wales, R.S. Thomas.

*PN Review* 109, Volume 22 Number 5,
May – June 1996.

# 2: ON WALES

# THE NATIONAL LIBRARY OF WALES AND THE SENEDD
*May 2021*

I recently received via email 'Latest News from the National Library of Wales'. It is the second such document I have received and seems likely to have been prompted by my request for information about last year's review panel enquiry into the working of the library *(PN Review* 258). The first in the series, 'Newyddion o'r Gen' is its Welsh title, concerns new digital resources, an event to mark LGBTQ+ History Month, and a note about the availability of the Welsh Music archive. The second number, a somewhat longer letter, provides information relating to 'The Story of Welsh Art' a BBC2/BBC4 production, skilfully presented by Huw Stephens, son of my old, much missed friend, Meic. The library contributed several items to the programme from its important collection of Welsh art and has gone further by co-operating with the *Guardian*/ArtUK on the 'Great Britain Art Tour', available on the *Guardian* website, and adding an extensive display of its art holdings to the ArtUK website. These developments are very welcome, whether they come as an initial response to the review panel's recommendation that the library should develop an outreach programme, or as the timely realisation of a long-considered project. Visual representations of the library as treasure house of national heritage have an immediate impact; what is contained between the covers of a book or in a bundle of manuscript may be less readily accessible to the public at large, but the second newsletter tackles the problem by highlighting the library's contribution to Women's History Month and its Gareth Vaughan Jones archive. The latter, a journalist from Barry, reported on the Holodomor, the appalling famine in the Ukraine 1932-33, which cost an estimated 3.9 million lives and, soon after, on the rise of the Nazis in Germany, before being murdered by bandits in Outer Mongolia while reporting on the Japanese occupation of Manchuria in 1935. The newsletter signs off with the library's motto, 'Preserving the Nation's Memory', an apt and relevant profession of purpose, but it cannot live up to that without adequate funding, therefore the appended request to 'Keep in Touch' and, of course, donate to the Collections Fund.

The arts always relied upon patronage and their survival increasingly depends on political will, as the recent commotion over the future of the National Library amply illustrated. Wales goes to the polls on 6th May to elect sixty representatives of what has become a plethora of parties to membership of the Senedd. This is likely to prove the most important election since its foundation in May 1999. In 2016 Labour won 29 seats, Plaid Cymru 12, Conservatives 11, UKIP 7 and Liberal Democrats one. A small number of members have changed their allegiance or label since. The objective observer will wonder what way the permanently disgruntled and former UKIP voters will turn. There is plenty of choice. Among the 'parties' in the lists are: 'Gwlad the Welsh Independence Party', not to mention the Greens and the sturdy old Independents, 'Abolish the Welsh Assembly', 'UKIP Scrap the Welsh Assembly' and (begging the question) 'Reform UK'; also, beyond my understanding, almost beyond belief, 'No More Lockdowns', 'Freedom Alliance No More Lockdowns No Curfews' and something called 'Propel', though what and where is anyone's guess. The system allows each voter two votes, one for a constituency representative, the other for a party on a regional basis. There are 40 constituency seats and 20 regional (four for each of five geographic regions), which is where the fringe parties normally figure. Voter turnout in previous elections has varied between 40 percent and 45 percent approximately. Election forecasting will be more difficult than usual this time because of the introduction of an entirely unknown quantity – the effect of the extension of suffrage to all aged sixteen and over.

The presence of two 'Abolish the Assembly' parties (they reject the official name, 'Senedd') posts an existential threat to devolved government in Wales, especially given the present Westminster Tory leadership's lack of respect for, or even acknowledgement of, government in Cardiff. A similar attitude to Scotland is widely held to jeopardise the continued existence of the United Kingdom and will almost certainly lead to another Scottish independence vote sooner rather than later. What will become of Wales then? Its doom is writ large: a permanent position as an unconsidered appendage of 'global Britain', sans culture, sans language, sans everything, or as R.S. Thomas prophetically remarked, we will be left with:

>...only the past,
>Brittle with relics,
>Wind-bitten towers and castles
>With sham ghosts;
>Mouldering quarries and mines;
>And an impotent people,
>Sick with inbreeding,
>Worrying the carcase of an old song.

Martin Shipton, political editor of the *Western Mail* and currently the best informed and most important commentator on Welsh affairs, reminds us that at the last election in 2016, the Abolish the Welsh Assembly party received 44,286 regional list votes, some 14,000 more than the Green Party. He points to evidence that the former UKIP and Brexit party supporters have decamped to 'Abolish' and, furthermore, that in a YouGov poll conducted in March this year, 59 percent of Conservative Party supporters would vote to abolish the Senedd while only 29 percent would keep it. This is where the regional list votes will have the greatest impact in the forthcoming election. The outcome may be that, at the very least, a substantial number of refractory members of the Senedd could act as gravel cast in the machinery of government.

Westminster has already fatally undermined a number of powers that previously resided with the devolved administrations. Thus, their potential ability to veto trade policies that would lower existing (European Union) environmental, food and animal welfare standards was removed by the UK Internal Market Act, which will also allow Westminster to fund infrastructure projects without reference to those administrations. The former EU regional aid money, hugely beneficial to Wales, is to be replaced by the UK Shared Prosperity Fund, and the destination of such aid as may be available will be left to Westminster departments, which, on present evidence, will be manipulated for political purposes by those in power, and in any case will not be based upon local understanding of the needs of communities.

And the needs are great. A Joseph Rowntree Foundation report published in November 2020 states that, before the onset of the coronavirus pandemic, a quarter of people in Wales (700,000) were 'living precarious and insecure lives', while 3 in 10 children, some 180,000, were living in poverty. A Save the Children report says 90,000 live in 'severe poverty'. The Rowntree Foundation report again says Wales has lower pay in every sector than in the rest of the UK. High unemployment and cuts in public spending are prominent among the causal factors, both of great concern to those who will win seats at the Senedd, but for which the UK government is accountable.

*PN Review* 259, Volume 47 Number 5, May – June 2021.

# THE NATIONAL LIBRARY OF WALES

*March 2021*

When I was there in the early 1950s, Aberystwyth was bookended, west to east, by two grand buildings in contrasting styles. On the seafront was an odd jumble of Victorian Gothic, conceived as a railway hotel, the University College of Wales, and some 500 feet up on Penglais Hill overlooking the town, the 'great white stone building...with an understated...classical design' that is the National Library of Wales, or Nat Lib, as I shall always think of it. It is, and I quote again from the *Carmarthenshire and Ceredigion* volume of *The Buildings of Wales*, 'the most important cultural building in Wales'. Even today, Aberystwyth, more or less at the midpoint of the impressive bight of Cardigan Bay, is still fairly remote from the rest of Wales. Having travelled between Gilfach Goch and Aber as a student, by bus, I am allowed to testify to its remoteness, but I recall bridling at Christopher de Hamel's description of NLW in *Meetings with Remarkable Manuscripts* as 'one of the most magnificently inaccessible outposts of learning in the British Isles' (*PN Review* 234), especially since the British Library and the Bodleian are at least as remote from my point of view. In those Aber years I spent little time at the National Library, even in postgraduate studies. It afforded me no more than I could obtain from or via the college library, which was a convenient short step from digs (I should add, the unpublished Thomas Hood letters at Bristol Central Library levered me profitably out of my comfort zone). In recent years, however, especially in my pursuit of T.J. Llewelyn Prichard, I have come to appreciate both the depth of resources and the inspired helpfulness of staff at the National Library, obtainable by email and the mere click of a mouse – and that, it turns out, is vital.

The National Library now shares Penglais Hill with the university campus. While not obscured by the hotchpotch of buildings above it, the site is certainly not 'lonely fair' as it once was. But the view from the library front on a clear day, out over the town to the great sweep of the bay embraced by the curves of the Llŷn peninsula to the north and the Pembrokeshire coast to the south, is still wonderful. I doubt a like institution anywhere in the world could surpass it. The library received its charter in March 1907. Professor Gwyn Jones was born the same year. This coincidence is worthy of mention because, on his death in 1999, the professor left his own substantial library, notably strong in seventeenth- and eighteenth-century literature and private-press books, to the National Library, where the collection is listed as 'Casgliad Castell Gwyn'. This follows the most worthy of ancient traditions: the philanthropy of bibliophiles. As is well known, great libraries have been built on 'foundation collections', the British Library notably on those of Sir Robert Cotton and Sir Hans Sloane, the Bodleian on those of Sir Thomas Bodley, and all he encouraged to follow suit. Sir John Williams (1840–1926), the *Dictionary of National Biography* tells us, was the principal founder of the National Library of Wales. The son of a Welsh Congregational minister and farmer (not an unusual combination), he was educated at a local school and then at the University of Glasgow and, after apprenticeship to a physician in Swansea, at University College Hospital, London. Having qualified MD, FRCP and begun medical practice in Swansea, he returned to London as a surgeon at University College Hospital. It was in Swansea he began collecting manuscripts, books and prints. He was involved with the 'Welsh Library Committee' at UCW, which set itself the target of creating both a national museum and a national library, the first in Cardiff and the second, at his insistence, in Aberystwyth. In 1898, the *Dictionary of National Biography* tells us, 'he purchased the "reversion" [the right to succeed to a property] of the magnificent Peniarth collection of manuscripts in Welsh, Latin, and other languages' with the intention of presenting it in due course to the National Library, which he was able to do in January 1909. He went on to give or bequeath all his books and manuscripts to the institution and a large sum of money. He became the library's first president, a post to which he was re-elected several times.

A press release of 30 September 2020 announced the publication of the first of a planned series of 'tailored' reviews of institutions sponsored by the Welsh government, based on a methodology suggested by the UK Cabinet Office. The privileged institution was the National Library. It has taken a few months for the implications of the review report to sink in and for the first rumours of, or wild guesses, at the Welsh government's response to slither out. The wildest of the latter suggest that the library will somehow be taken over by the British Library.

The number of visitors to NLW is decreasing, while the number of library *users* via the internet has increased remarkably. All major libraries are the same. Nevertheless, the report wants more visitors. In this respect it has a good deal of common sense to offer as well as some absurd tokenism, such as the Library should strive to become more welcoming to the youthful spirit of the age by providing a facility where visitors could have access to the web while eating, drinking and chatting together, the sort of facility apparently now available at the neighbouring university library, or an internet café. What is beyond question, and clearly seen by the review panel, is that the National Library of Wales has been underfunded for a decade. Its income has reduced from £9.97 million in 2007/8 to £9.6 million in 2018/19. In the same period staff numbers have reduced by more than a fifth, from 290 to 224. The review compares the Library's income with that of the National Library of Scotland, which in 2017/18 received £15.3 million, and the British Library, which in 2020/21 will scrape by on £97 million. Furthermore, NLW is entirely responsible for staff pensions, while the staff of Scotland's library and the British Library receive civil service pensions, to which the libraries contribute 20 percent.

While acknowledging that NLW 'has been at the forefront of developing digital skills and services for archives and libraries, in Wales *and internationally over the past decade, before the effects of austerity disrupted this work*' (my italics), the review recommends an increase in the scope of its activities in this field, in other kinds of 'outreach' programmes, and in links with other cultural institutions. All of the above requires increased staffing and funding at a time when the omens suggest further cuts are in the offing. As a user, I have nothing but admiration for Nat Lib and its staff. I have never been less than satisfied with the service it provides and can call to mind immediately several occasions when I have been, frankly, amazed at the ability of staff to respond to my vaguely framed requests. The solution to issues raised by the 'tailored review' panel lies with the Welsh government, which supplies about 93 percent of the Library's income. To simply kill off or sell off a national library would be an unconscionable act of vandalism that any government would shrink from, but many here believe the present Welsh government is in danger of inflicting 'death by a thousand cuts' on the primary repository of the principal expression of the culture of Wales.

*PN Review* 258, Volume 47 Number 4,
March – April 2021.

*The following note accompanied this letter on publication in PN Review:*

NOTE: *The dire situation of the National Library of Wales outlined in Sam Adams's 'Letter' in this issue has been mitigated by a Welsh Government announcement that fresh funding of £2.25 million will be made available for 2021 and 2022 'to safeguard jobs and deliver new strategic priorities'.*

# WORLD WAR TWO AND MINING

*January 2021*

For a few weeks now I have been taking a walk down the hill from our house and, via Broadwalk and the road along the Common, back up the hill. It is little more than half a mile: enough, I hope, at least to keep me mobile. There is a cluster of shops at the bottom of the hill. The small supermarket usually has a well-spaced queue when I pass by on the other side. If I am lucky, a couple of blackbirds are singing competitively part of the way, but my route is just outside the perimeter of the Roman fortress and there is nothing notable to see, far less look forward to, on my brief passage. It was then a surprise to find last Friday three or four houses in Broadwalk had bunting strung along the railings of their front gardens marking the 75th anniversary of the end of the war in Europe.

I remember the beginning of the war, 3 September 1939. At 11.15 a.m. I was with my friends George and Trefor in their house across the road that Sunday when Chamberlain made the announcement on the wireless, and a couple of months short of my fifth birthday. It was not the Prime Minister's words that imprinted the occasion on my memory, but the reaction of my friends' mother and father – a peculiarly penetrating silence. They also had two sons old enough to bear arms. I recall more clearly, on my way home from afternoon school, Tuesday 8 May 1945, walking down the terraced hill of Coronation Road, Gilfach Goch, seeing women in animated conversation over front garden fences and being told, 'The war's over.' That was the year I passed 'the scholarship', as the 11+ was then known (though I was ten), and was soon to embark on new friendships.

The years between five and ten, when I began to become aware of a world beyond immediate family and the valley, were dominated by the war. To me, and tens of thousands like me, it was normality. We had no remembered experience of peacetime; so far as we were concerned, there had always been talk of battles and terrible losses, always cinema newsreels of fighting, always the blackout, always rationing. When was life before we carried a gas mask in its cardboard box? Had school windows ever been other than criss-crossed with glued strips of brown paper to mitigate shattering from bomb blast? I was three weeks past my seventh birthday when, in December 1941, news broke of the sinking of the capital ships HMS *Repulse* and *Prince of Wales* in the South China Sea and, though it did not mean much to me at the time, I saw the devastating effect it had on my parents and my sister, whose husband, a long-serving naval man, was a gunner on the *Repulse*. In due course the official letter arrived saying he was 'missing believed killed'. He is named in the list of more than forty men from the valley on the recently re-dedicated World War II Memorial in Gilfach's Welfare Park. Other families, too, were sorrowing over lost loved ones or in agonies of uncertainty over the missing.

Not long before, miners had been on the scrapheap labelled Depression, but in September 1939 coal was again a precious commodity, vital to the war effort. It powered the ships and fuelled electricity production and the furnaces making steel for weapons. Mining became a 'reserved occupation' – that is, miners were not permitted to enlist (a few years into the war, a tenth of young men called up for military service were drafted instead to coal mining; they were known as 'Bevin Boys', after Ernest Bevin, Minister of Labour and National Service in the coalition government). All across south Wales, the collieries worked non-stop, three shifts a day. My father, sole electrician in 'the Squint', the colliery where he worked, and formally 'days

regular', could be, and not infrequently was, called out to
breakdown emergencies in the depths of night, by loud
hammering on the front door. He also became a 'special
constable'. I do not recall this entailed wearing a uniform or
even an armband, or regular duties of any kind, our local police,
a sergeant and a constable, both of impressive stature and
demeanour, seemingly having everything under control. I
suppose he was available if ever called upon, but the call never
came. His un-service did provide a rare moment of hilarity in
the grey days after the war when he received a commemorative
medal and found from the inscription on the rim that he had
been a sergeant.

Mining towns and villages were potential targets for enemy
bombers, but only Cwmparc in the Rhondda suffered
substantial damage and loss of life. The sound of the air raid
siren was a part of everyday life, and a brick and concrete air-
raid shelter for the street no more than thirty yards from our
door was finally demolished only years after VE Day. It had
never been used, but there was a bomb. It fell in the early hours
a few days before Christmas 1940, jettisoned by an aircraft, as
I think now, limping back to an airfield somewhere in the north
of France from the terrible blitz on Liverpool in which hundreds
were killed, and hit the lower slope of the mountain just behind
the church, where its high explosive made a crater about twenty
feet deep. Although only a few hundred yards from our house,
its detonation did not disturb my sleep. I heard about it at
breakfast and soon joined a small crowd peering into the
inverted cone of reddish clay from which wisps of smoke were
still rising. Here and there in the excavated mud thrown up by
the blast were shards of bomb-casing, jagged chunks of metal
like lightning crystallised, still hot and heavy in the hand. For
a week or two these could be traded for cigarette cards, marbles
or foreign stamps with boys from the lower end of the valley

who had been late reaching the site, but then interest faded. The windows of the church had all been smashed and the roof, though it still appeared sound, so damaged that the building was unsafe. It was not repaired and re-opened for twenty years. Near the church, the local GP's fine, detached house had also been badly damaged, and the doctor and his wife, still abed, had fallen through to the floor below, though whether that was from some freak of blast or another bomb, so far as I am aware, no one ever determined.

My couple of bits of shrapnel rusted on an outside windowsill and eventually disappeared. By VE Day I had a small collection of war memorabilia, some Allied forces cap badges, a few brass cartridge cases, possibly picked up on the Home Guard firing range the other side of the valley and, the most prized, from a Nazi airman's uniform, yellow on green, a stylised eagle, wings spread, a wreathed swastika in its talons. I remember the VE Day festivities, the buns and sandwiches, jelly and pop on trestle tables set up in the Co-op Hall, where Sunday School classes were held. And I remember the red, white and blue lights my electrician father had arranged in a large V-sign at the front of the house that blinked with such speed and ferocity men freshly emerged from the nearby Con Club after a heavy night of celebration were seen to blink and stagger. The awfulness of the war with Japan continued, but that was one down.

*PN Review* 257, Volume 47 Number 3,
January – February 2021.

# THE BUILDINGS OF CARDIFF

*May 2020*

That wonderfully informative series of chunky books, *The Buildings of Wales*, was founded by Sir Nikolaus Pevsner as an extension of his *Buildings of England*, but he was not their author. The much-praised volume on Glamorgan was written by John Newman (who, while a student at the Courtauld, was for a time Pevsner's driver), and it is he who made the bold assertion that 'in Cathays Park, Cardiff has the finest civic centre in the British Isles...where the coherence and splendour of the whole group (of buildings) adds lustre to each individual element'. Most of us, residents in or frequent visitors to Cardiff, are so accustomed to the neat assemblage of a dozen listed, mostly Edwardian baroque, buildings in pale Portland stone on a roughly rectangular grid, with the fine open space of Alexandra Gardens in the midst, that we rarely pause to take it in. It is a pleasant place to stroll on a fine day. You can walk its perimeter roads in twenty minutes without undue haste, as I often did during lunch hours when I worked in the fortress-like 'New Crown Building', clearly designed like the castles of Edward I to keep down the rebellious Welsh, which, since 1979, has closed off the northern end. That and a few more recent additions apart, Cardiff's civic centre is grand without being overbearing, in keeping with the domestic scale of much of the city, until recent years and the construction 'down town' of a cluster of multi-storey monstrosities that crowd the sky without offering a glimmer of aesthetic interest.

Just across the road from the civic centre, to the west, is Cardiff Castle, which has Roman and Norman origins and at the beginning of the fifteenth century fell to the greatest of Welsh rebels, Owain Glyndŵr. The castle owes its present form to the ambition of successive marquesses of Bute and especially to the productive partnership of John Crichton-Stuart, third marquess, with the Victorian Gothic architect-designer, William Burges. The faux-medieval interior of the castle is one of the wonders of Wales and hardly matched anywhere else, though a runner-up might be Castell Coch, just six miles north, a fairy castle overlooking the Taff gorge that you glimpse as you pass by on the M4, which was rebuilt and decorated in similar style by the same partnership of patron and genius. The third marquess owned 22,000 acres in the old county of Glamorgan alone, with its mineral rights, in the great years of coal. His gross income is reported to have been £300,000 per annum, roughly the equivalent of £37 million today. One of the richest men in the world at the time, if not the richest, he could afford Burges's architectural and decorative flights of fancy.

In 1898 the marquess sold 59 acres of what had been Cardiff Castle's pleasure grounds for £161,000 to the local council and this was the land on which the civic centre gradually developed. Today the site has four Grade I listed buildings: City Hall and the Crown Court, both opened in 1906, what was formerly known as Glamorgan County Hall (1912), and the National Museum of Wales, on which work also began in 1912 but, because of delays occasioned by the First World War, opened in 1922. The eight Grade II listed buildings include Cardiff University's main building, the first stage of which was completed in 1909, and the Temple of Peace, a latecomer to the architectural ensemble and somewhat different in style, which opened in 1938. Strictly 'the Temple of Peace and Health', the latter was the gift of David Davies, 1st Baron Davies (grandson of his namesake, the great nineteenth century Welsh industrialist), who had fought in the First World War. His aim was to provide a memorial to those who had lost their lives in the conflict and a home for an organisation dedicated to the elimination of the scourge of tuberculosis. His sisters, Margaret and Gwendoline, who also went to war and served with the French Red Cross, in moments of release from their duties visited Paris in pursuit of art. Their bequests in 1951 and 1963 gave the National Museum, just a couple of hundred yards away, one of the world's finest collections of Impressionist and Post-Impressionist paintings.

The Temple of Peace, which can now be hired for events, has become the new home of Seren's Cardiff Poetry Festival, held this year across a weekend in mid-February. Festival director Amy Wack assembled a programme tailored to a wide range of interests including workshops and readings and a 'Desert Island Poems' session with singer-songwriter James Dean Bradfield, leader of that most literate and poetically aware group the Manic Street Preachers, interviewed by Meic's far-famed broadcasting son, Huw Stephens. Peter Finch, a prolific writer of psychogeography and poetry, read from his latest collection of poems, *The Machineries of Joy* (2020), his thirteenth book from Seren. He is probably the finest living exponent of 'sound poetry' both on the page and, as it needs to be, crisply vocalised. The large audience was duly appreciative. Peter is consistently and richly inventive – and entertaining, but a sharply critical mind guides the ingenious playfulness with 'words... words', and a dark thread runs through this latest book in poems from a road trip to the states, and about old, dead, poet-friends to hospital experiences, carrying the insistent message of mutability. Friday evening brought the inaugural Meic Stephens Lecture, sponsored by the Rhys Davies Trust, on 'creative correspondences' in the poetry of John Ormond. Kieron Smith's timely reminder of his subject's rare talent as both poet and film-maker, was particularly apt, for *Poetry Wales*, launched by Meic Stephens in 1965, helped give John Ormond a reason to turn to poetry again, after early discouragement from Vernon Watkins. He used to say he wrote 'Cathedral Builders', a poem with which he will always be associated, in 'twenty minutes flat' and sent it off to the new magazine with 'Design for a Tomb', a fascinating mixture of the funereal and the subtly erotic. They appeared together in the summer 1966 number and he was once more in the groove. Re-reading his *Collected Poems* (Seren, 2015), which appeared twenty-five years after his death, edited by his daughter Rian Evans, reminds us of the range of his interests – in art and architecture, archaeology, music, philosophy, science and the natural world. All contributed to the rich veins of imagery that thread his poems. He also drew on the inspiration afforded by his home and his family, and by Tuscany, where he was a frequent visitor in his later years. The primary concerns of birth, love and death run through all his work. He found no answers to the fundamental questions, but as he sought them his poetry continued to develop and move along unexpected avenues of thought and feeling. Smith's lecture, and his book *John Ormond's Organic Mosaic* (UWP 2019), remind us he is a genuinely significant poet.

*PN Review* 253, Volume 46 Number 5,
May – June 2020.

# GILFACH GOCH

*September 2019*

A week ago, on Saturday morning, we returned to Gilfach Goch to assist at the unveiling of a Rhys Davies Trust commemorative plaque on the former home, an end of terrace house in Kenry Street, of the brothers, 'Will, Jos, Jack and Arthur' Griffiths, who had jointly owned 'Griffs', a bookshop in Cecil Court, off Charing Cross Road, in London.

Here I pause to consider 'Kenry', an unusual name for a street in a Welsh mining valley. Nearby parallel terraced rows, all dating from the late decades of the nineteenth century, built to accommodate an influx of colliers and their families for newly opened pits, bear similar outlandish designations. Their naming, too, was an act of commemoration, though I doubt anyone living in Gilfach now has any knowledge of that. Wyndham Street derives from Windham Wyndham-Quinn, 4th Earl of Dunraven and Mount-Earl (1841–1926), an Irish peer who had a remarkably full life. After Christ Church, Oxford, he had a career in the army, was a war correspondent for the *Daily Telegraph*, reported on the siege of Paris 1870–71 and presumably the Commune, formed a committee to recruit mounted 'Sharpshooters' in the Boer War, served as under-secretary of state for the colonies, owned an America's Cup yacht, laid claim to 15,000 acres of Colorado as a private game park (now the Rocky Mountain National Park), and was active, as a moderate, in the Irish Home Rule question, eventually becoming a senator of the Irish Free State (1922–26). Given his roots in the Irish aristocracy, it is more than a surprise to learn that from 1889 to 1892 he was a member of the then newly-established Glamorgan County Council. The explanation of the Welsh connection is predictable, however: he had become an extensive landowner and coal owner in south Wales. Thus, humble Adare Street bears the name of the earl's 39,000-acre estate in Adare, County Limerick, and Kenry Street that of a castle and the barony of Kenry, also in Limerick, which became extinct at the Earl's death.

A friend, Teifion Griffiths (son of 'Arthur' above) put me on the track of the Kenry connection, goodness knows, remote enough from the realities of life in a mining community. The same friend, many years ago, and inadvertently, alerted me to a link, previously explained (*PN Review* 188), between Gilfach Goch and the novelist Richard Llewellyn's bestseller, *How Green Was My Valley*, a significant feature of which is the separation of 'the Valley' from those a good deal larger, characteristically the Rhondda, with their ribbon development. Inevitably, the visit for the plaque unveiling has brought to mind what our small cul-de-sac in the coalfield was like when our grandparents were drawn there by the promise of work – and what work! With a population of about 3,500, there were three working pits going full-pelt through the years of our boyhood. Noise and dust were omnipresent, and the river flowed black. But we had a choice of a church and twelve Nonconformist chapels, and four men's clubs (men only then) and nine pubs. We also had a Workmen's Hall containing cinema, library, reading room and billiard hall, a second cinema, and a Welfare Park, with a field for rugby, soccer and cricket, a bowling green, two hard courts for tennis, and a children's play area. The Workmen's Hall and the park were maintained by pennies deducted from mineworkers' weekly pay packets. There was also a silver band and, of course, a Salvation Army band. My maternal grandfather conducted an orchestra of local musicians at the formal opening of the Workmen's Hall in 1924, and that was the venue in the late

1940s and '50s of an annual week-long drama festival involving competing dramatics societies from several valleys townships, one of which, I recall, brought to a packed audience a production of Eliot's *Murder in the Cathedral*.

Coal was the *raison d'être* of the village, but its many rough edges were not a barrier to the infiltration of culture. Teifion has told me that Arthur, his father, and his uncles, Will, Jos and Jack in Kenry Street, had only elementary school education, and left school at thirteen or fourteen to work in the pit. But in their Welsh-speaking home they all played musical instruments, piano, violins, flutes and recorders, and the music of choice was Beethoven, Haydn and Mozart, as well as a huge repertoire of Welsh songs and hymns. In fine summer weather their playing and singing would often attract an impromptu audience of neighbours sitting on the pavement outside No. 15. Will eventually studied at the Guildhall School of Music and became a professional musician.

It was Will, too, who was later employed by Foyle's as head of its Welsh department. It may come as a surprise now to learn that the famous bookshop at that time had its own Welsh imprint, 'Gwasg Foyle', and that, between 1927 and 1944, it published books in Welsh, including *O Law i Law* (From Hand to Hand, 1943), an outstanding novel by T. Rowland Hughes, and Aneirin Talfan Davies's *Yr Alltud: Rhagarweiniad i Weithiau James Joyce* (The Exile: Introduction to the Works of James Joyce, 1944), a pioneering book in the Welsh language on modernist writing. In the 1930s, Welsh writers in London, gravitating towards Foyle's, tended to meet in pubs in St Martin's Lane and Charing Cross Road. It was in this way that the young Richard Llewellyn became friendly with Will and joined him on visits to Gilfach Goch, where he met and spoke at length with Will's father, Joseph Griffiths, about the history of mining in the valley. Subsequently, Llewellyn brought *How*

*Green Was My Valley* to Foyle's for publication. But it was not a Welsh-language book and Will Griffiths, doubting the ability of the bookshop to adapt to a new venture, took the novel to Michael Joseph – and a bestseller was born.

At the end of the war, Will took a lease on 4 Cecil Court to open a bookshop (just as the Foyle brothers had done initially at No. 16 in 1904) and invited his brothers to join him. By 1946 all four were there. The shop soon became a London-Welsh institution, a regular meeting-place for Welsh writers living in or visiting London, a down-market salon where you might bump into Dylan Thomas, or Richard Burton, Gwyn Jones, T.E. Nicholas, Bob Owen Croesor. An interest in Welsh-language publishing lingered: the watchful bibliophile might still come upon a second-hand copy of Geraint Dynallt Owen's *Dyddiau'r Gofid* ('Days of Sorrow', the sequel to his historical novel *Nest*) published by 'W. Griffiths'. When Will died in 1963, Arthur took over the shop until it closed in 1984.

Rhys Davies, another regular visitor to Griffs, was among the favoured taken downstairs to the cellar, where book-keeping and packaging went on, for a cup of tea. Rhys, who in younger days walked over the mountain from Blaenclydach in the Rhondda to Gilfach, would have been pleased the Trust that bears his name has placed a plaque there in memory of his old friends.

*PN Review* 249, Volume 46 Number 1,
September – October 2019.

# GWENT

*May 2019*

Because we have friends there, and commitments of one kind
and another, we are often on the road that skirts Cwmbran
('valley of the crow' – a local stream) and Pontypŵl ('bridge of
the pool') and rises sharply towards Penperlleni ('hill
orchards'), one of the many entrances to rural Gwent, and
heads northwards still to Abergavenny ('mouth of the river
Fenni' – that is, its confluence with the Usk). As you approach
the old market town, if it is a bright, clear day, though you
have done this a hundred times before, you marvel at its
setting. On three sides it is enclosed by mountains: to your left
the Blorenge (the name of uncertain origin, but one of those
rare rhymes with 'orange') at 559m., to the right the rugged
and broken-backed Ysgyryd Fawr ('great split') at 486m, and
straight ahead, dominating the scene, a symmetrical
simulacrum of an extinct volcano, the 590m Sugar Loaf. They
are not high, compared with the Black Mountains, of which
they are the outliers, still less with the Brecon Beacons a little
further to the north and west (some might think of them as
hills), but as a backdrop to the town they are spectacular. You
have a short while to enjoy the scene before the road bends
and dips into Llanofer ('church of Myfor'), and the mind,
pondering time-wrought transformations in place names as all
else, turns from topographical to historical considerations.

English made early inroads into Gwent, the fate of a
borderland, but it was not a steadily advancing linguistic tide.
When industrialisation brought an influx of Welsh from the west
and the north, the Gwent valleys became for a while a

powerhouse of Welsh-language publishing and Welsh chapels flourished. And then there were individuals who devoted much of their lives to stemming the tide, by propagating Welsh language and cultural aims, some of whom had English family origins. Among the latter was a most remarkable woman – Lady Llanover. Augusta, youngest daughter of Benjamin and Georgina Waddington, was born at Tŷ Uchaf ('upper house'), Llanofer, in 1802. Her family had come from Nottingham in 1792. In 1823 she married Benjamin Hall (1802–67). Her husband was third in a line of Benjamin Halls, a family originating in Pembrokeshire. His grandfather was dean of Llandaff cathedral, his father, a barrister, had the enormous good fortune to marry Charlotte, daughter of Richard Crawshay, the Cyfarthfa (Merthyr Tydfil) iron-master, who had come penniless out of Yorkshire and by luck (again a very advantageous marriage), hard work and an instinct for business, created an empire. In 1803, he was able to make Benjamin père a partner in the Rhymni ironworks, and in 1808 presented him with the 3000-acre Abercarn estate, neighbour to the Waddington's Llanover estate. This second Benjamin Hall, I have read, was known as 'slender Ben' on account of his delicate physique. It was not an indication of good health and, having attained a measure of fame as the first industrialist/politician in Wales, he died at the age of thirty-nine. His son, Augusta's husband, also became an MP, in 1831. He was created baronet in 1838 and in 1855 appointed commissioner for works. In the latter capacity he oversaw the construction of the clock tower at Westminster. He is said to have been a large man, well over six feet, and for this reason (underlining the contrast with his father) known as 'Big Ben'. It sounds to me a tall tale, but is nevertheless held to account for the familiar name of the clock tower and its chimes. In 1859, he became a peer, as baron Llanover of Llanover and Abercarn. His steady ascent to the peerage in turn explains why his wife is sometimes referred to as Lady Hall, though more frequently as Lady Llanover.

The devotion to the cause of the Welsh language and Welsh cultural traditions at Llanover is generally thought to begin and flourish under the influence of the mistress of the house, but in his sphere her husband was her equal. A strong advocate of Anglican church services in Welsh for Welsh-speaking congregations, he was active in the Disestablishment movement, which brought about the Welsh Church Act in 1914 and led in 1920 to the creation of a separate province within the Anglican Communion and the election of an Archbishop of Wales. He is remembered also for his battle in parliament against the iniquities of the 'truck system', by which employees in ironworks and mines were paid in tokens redeemable only in company stores – the cause of much unrest in industrial south Wales.

If the genesis of Lady Llanover's commitment to Wales, its language and traditions, can be pinned to any single event, it would be her attendance at a meeting of *Cymreigyddion y Fenni* (the Abergavenny Welsh Society), which was addressed by Rev. Thomas Price, vicar of Cwmdu in Breconshire. Known by his bardic name *'Carnhuanawc'*, he was a writer, an antiquary and an inspirational speaker. He did much to build relations between Wales and Brittany, not least by assisting the translation of the Bible into Breton, a language he had learned. He founded a Welsh school in his parish and, like Benjamin Hall, advocated services in Welsh and an end to the practice of appointing non-Welsh speakers to livings and bishoprics in Wales. This was a time when intellectuals elsewhere in Europe (though not in England) took a keen interest in Wales, its history and language. One among them, Baron Christian von Bunsen, Prussian envoy to the court of Queen Victoria, married Lady Hall's older sister, Frances, and attended eisteddfodau at Abergavenny. At an eisteddfod in Cardiff in 1834, Lady Hall won a prize for an essay on the Welsh language. 'Gwenynen Gwent' (Bee of Gwent), her *ffugenw* (nom-de-plume) on this occasion stuck, for the good reason that it conveyed the extraordinary busyness of her life on behalf of Wales. She had the will (and the wealth) to promote her interests in the playing of the triple harp, in Welsh music and dance generally, in traditionally patterned Welsh cloth and costume – her servants at Llanover Hall wore the traditional costume of their counties of origin. As patron of the Welsh Manuscripts Society she stimulated the rescue and publication of ancient texts; she purchased the precious collection of Iolo Morganwg now in the National Library of Wales.

It is less widely known that she was instrumental in organising the writing – it is now thought by Jane Williams ('Ysgafell') – and publication of *Artegall*, a thirty-two-page pamphlet named after the knight of Justice in Spencer's *Faerie Queene*, as a response to *Brad y Llyfrau Gleision* (the *Treachery of the Blue Books*). It was printed in Llandovery by William Rees. Early in my research on Prichard, almost fifty years ago, I came across a series of letters to Rees in the Tonn collection at Cardiff Library. They were written from 'Llanover' and signed 'A.H.' – Augusta Hall. In one she says 'if Welsh men do not show a little courage, and self-respect now they deserve what they will otherwise have, the contempt of Europe'. Her anger is almost palpable in the vigour of her hand, and we can be sure that whoever wrote *Artegall*, it was A.H. who saw it through the press and arranged publication in London by Longman & Co. Looking over the pamphlet now (as you can do online) you can judge how effectively this rapier picked apart such argument as there was in the three volumes of the 1847 report of the inquiry into the state of education in Wales.

*PN Review* 247, Volume 45 Number 5, May – June 2019.

# FRANK LLOYD WRIGHT
*November 2018*

I have been providing some marginal assistance to a research project on Frank Lloyd Wright and, as often happens in such cases, have had my curiosity aroused by the subject. 'Lloyd' may be sufficiently common in the anglophone world for its Welsh roots to pass unrecognised, but the word is an adaptation of the Welsh '*llwyd*', meaning 'grey'. The '*ll*' is a single letter in the twenty-eight letter Welsh alphabet and its sound is formally described as a voiceless alveolar lateral fricative. The aspirate in the anglicised spelling of the name of the sixteenth-century physician and antiquary Humphrey Lhuyd is an attempt at an approximation to the Welsh pronunciation. 'Lloyd' is not an unusual companion to 'Jones' in Welsh names. Richard Lloyd Jones, Frank's maternal grandfather, borrowed it from his mother Margaret's ancestry, to distinguish, and add distinction to, plain 'Jones', which is a relic of the patronymic ap John (son of John). Kyffin Williams used to tell a story of meeting on the road old Mrs Jones, a farmer's wife, with a pretty lamb on a lead: '"*Bore da*, Mrs Jones," I said, and (pointing to the lamb) who is this?' "Mary," said Mrs Jones. "Oh, Mary Jones is it?" I said. "No, Mary *Lloyd* Jones," the old lady replied.' Anyway, that 'Lloyd' figures in the name of perhaps the most famous of American architects suggests a Welsh connection. But how Welsh was he?

Richard Lloyd Jones, a small farmer and hat-maker, his wife, Mary, and their children emigrated to America in 1844. They came from south-west Wales, the parishes of Llandysul-Llanwenog, in the south of Ceredigion, close to the border with

Carmarthenshire, even now a green place of small towns and smaller villages, drained by the river Teifi and its tributaries. The wave of transatlantic migration from Wales in the nineteenth century was on nothing like the scale of that from Ireland, where starvation drove people to abandon their homes in tens of thousands. A great many of the Welsh rural poor embarked on internal migration routes from homes in the west and the north of the country to the burgeoning mining valleys and steel works in the south-east, taking their language, traditions and Nonconformist religious beliefs with them. We cannot be sure what motivated Richard Lloyd Jones to risk uprooting his family for an uncertain existence far overseas. The promise of religious and political freedom may well have influenced his decision. There is every likelihood he was Liberal in politics and disadvantaged, if not persecuted, by a Tory landowner, the pattern of the times, and his religion was Unitarian. The concentration of Unitarian chapels in that part of Cardiganshire caused it to be known among detractors in the Anglican and Nonconformist chapel communities as Y Smotyn Du (the Black Spot). As late as October 1876, the local Tory bigwig was so enraged by the radical politics and Unitarian preaching of the Revd William Thomas (Gwilym Marles) that he locked him and his congregation out of Llwynrhydowen Chapel. The Revd Thomas addressed a crowd of three thousand gathered outside the locked chapel. He was Dylan Thomas's great uncle and an example of the intellectual energy of Unitarianism. Others might observe that, while it attracted great minds, like Coleridge and Ralph Waldo Emerson, it was, nonetheless, heretical.

The congregations of Y Smotyn Du were visited by that most remarkable of Welsh Unitarians, Edward Williams (Iolo Morganwg, 1750–1813), whose verses were added to tombstones in their chapel graveyards. Iolo's invention of

*Gorsedd y Beirdd Ynys Prydain* (Throne of the Bards of the Island of Britain), its symbols and mottoes, rehearsed once more a few weeks ago at the National Eisteddfod in Cardiff, were (like his forged 'Dafydd ap Gwilym' poems) readily accepted by the majority Welsh-speaking population as true vestiges of a noble, unified Wales. The Lloyd Jones family carried this lore across the Atlantic, and elements of it feature repeatedly in Frank Lloyd Wright's buildings: *Y gwir yn erbyn y byd* (The truth against the world) and a *nod cyfrin* (mystic sign) and the name 'Taliesin' (shining brow).

Having landed in New York, they headed for Wisconsin, where pioneering siblings from Richard's family had settled a few years before. Despite the presence of relatives, their early experience of farming a land only then beginning to emerge from wilderness may have been excruciating, as accounts by a son, Jenkin Lloyd Jones, the notable Unitarian missionary preacher, testify, but nothing dented their resolve or shrivelled their faith. It took them twelve years of trials and errors, and steady expansion of property before, in March 1856, they moved to Spring Green, and thence to Helena Valley, and a landscape reminiscent of the fields and green hills (which they named Bryn Mawr, Bryn Canol and Bryn Bach – big, middle and small hill) they had left in Wales. In 1852, Margaret, Richard's mother, aged and widowed, had written to another son in London: 'I have 30 to 40 between children and grandchildren in America living all in the same neighbourhood and close to Watertown in Wisconsin. There is a house of worship [...] where I hope they all flock on Sundays. Richard has given half an acre of land for a burial place.' It was a tribe of Welsh Joneses, living, working and worshipping together.

When they arrived in America, Frank Lloyd Wright's grandparents and their children, including Anna his mother, were more at ease in Welsh than in English. Jenkin suggests that, at least initially, his father had some difficulty in understanding English. They never lost their first language, because much of the farming day was spent in the company of those to whom Welsh came first to the mind and tongue. Even if they grew up without it, the next generation would certainly have been familiar with the shape and sounds of Welsh. Jane and Ellen (Nell), the architect's aunts, trained as teachers and, having gained valuable experience, in 1887 founded their own school in the valley where their parents had brought them and their four farming brothers. If we judge by the description of Hillside Home School in *A Goodly Fellowship*, the autobiography of Mary Ellen Chase, herself a distinguished educationalist, who taught there 1909–13, it was an extraordinarily enlightened establishment. English was, of course, the language of the school, but *Y gwir yn erbyn y byd* was engraved over the fireplace and Aunt Jane and Aunt Nell, as they were universally known, 'had a way of bursting into stormy Welsh to each other when some one of us [teachers] had displeased them by laziness or lack of attention to detail'.

Marriage to William Carey Wright, a music teacher, for a time took Anna away from the valley, but she returned when they separated and subsequently divorced. Young Frank, who at this point adopted the familial 'Lloyd', attended Madison High School and the University of Wisconsin-Madison, but seems not to have graduated. His training as an architect began in Chicago with the firm of J.L. Silsbee, where in 1887 he had a hand in designing the first Hillside Home School building, in the 'English' style. In 1888 he joined Adler & Sullivan as an apprentice and made rapid enough progress to accept commissions on his own account, thereby breaking the contract with his employers. In 1893 he set up on his own, and in 1901 he designed the second Hillside Home School for his aunts, in the distinctively 'Prairie' style of which he became the most famous exponent. By 1905–08, for the Unitarian Church, he had created a masterpiece, Chicago's Unity Temple.

F.L.W.'s Welsh roots are exposed for all to see; how conscious he remained of them through his long, often turbulent life is impossible to tell. He was happy to accept an Honorary Doctorate of the University of Wales at Bangor in 1956. Ah, if only the 4th Marquess of Bute had not drawn a line under his architectural ventures in Wales after funding the restoration of Caerphilly Castle, but commissioned a Frank Lloyd Wright house, in Ceredigion perhaps, as a grand gesture to the future.

*PN Review* 244, Volume 45 Number 2,
November – December 2018.

# AUST AND ABERFAN

*January 2017*

It is fifty years since we came back to Wales. Work took us to Bristol for a spell and work brought us back – though not to the mining valleys, which we called and, in unguarded moments still call, home. That's the pull, the powerful undertow, dragging you back to origins, which the Welsh call *hiraeth*. While we lived in Bristol, holidays were spent in Gilfach Goch. In the early days of exile, we even went back at weekends. It was not far by train. If you went to Stapleton Road Station at about five-thirty on a Friday evening during a school term you would find scores of Welsh teachers waiting for the train to take them 'home'. The time came when we had a car and drove across the border. It was a lengthy journey, up the east side of the Severn estuary to Gloucester for the first available bridge over the river and down the west side as far as Chepstow, where you could at last head homewards.

Or you could risk the Aust ferry which, if your luck held, would carry you across the Severn to Chepstow and save you sixty miles by road. This was a deplorable alternative that operated only when the tide was amenable. The Severn is a force of nature and there is little you can do about it; the crew of the ferry on the other hand, long familiar with the vagaries of the crossing, could have been informative about conditions on the estuary, but in our experience were peculiarly uncommunicative. At a push, the ferry's open deck would accommodate seventeen cars. There was no explanatory notice; you learned it by counting them on and off. You also counted the number of cars ahead of you to calculate how many crossings you would have to wait before your turn arrived. You might queue two hours or more and then be turned away without a word of apology or regret.

In our last couple of years in Bristol, whenever we waited at Aust hoping to catch the ferry, we would observe building activity only a short distance upstream and the gradual emergence of the two great towers of a suspension bridge. In August 1966, with our meagre array of goods and chattels going the long way in the lorry, we braved the waters of the Severn for the last time. On 9 September, the Severn Bridge opened to traffic, the M4 rolled onwards into Wales and a new era in road transport began. The ferry became instantly redundant. The Labour Minister of Transport announced compensation of £90,000 would be paid to the ferry owners. Feeling no nostalgia for this vanished institution, I would not have awarded them a penny.

Aust is said to be the location of the second, climactic meeting between Augustine, subsequently first archbishop of Canterbury, and the bishops of the Celtic church. About AD 600, Augustine, a Benedictine monk, was sent to Britain by the Pope (Gregory the Great) to convert the heathen English. He hoped to enlist the help of the Welsh, Christianised three centuries before, in the later stages of the Roman Empire. The meeting at Aust was intended to smooth ruffled feathers and align the practices of the Celtic church and those of Rome, with particular reference to the date of Easter, but also in the matter of tonsure design. Bede tells how the British bishops asked an anchorite living nearby whether they should surrender their ancient traditions at Augustine's request. The holy man answered (in Thomas Stapleton's 1565 translation of Bede's Latin), 'if he be a man of God, follow him. But how shall we prove (sayd they) that he is a man of God? The Anchoret answered: our Lord sayeth, *take ye on yow my yooke, and lerne ye of me. For I am milde, and humble of harte*. Yf therefore this Austin be milde, and humble of harte, it is likely that him selfe beareth the yooke of Christ, and will offer you the same to beare. But if he be curst, and proude, it is certaine, that he is not of God, neither must we esteme his wordes.'

But, the bishops persisted, how will we know he is humble of heart? The anchorite proposed they should ensure Augustine and his entourage entered the meeting-place first – 'And if when ye appproche nere, he ariseth courteously to you, thinke ye that he is the servant of Christe, and so heare ye him obediently. But if he despise yow, nor will vouchesafe to rise at your presence [...] let him likewise be despised of yowe.' A simple enough test, which Augustine failed: he remained seated and the bishops were convinced he held them in contempt. Emollient words did nothing to change their minds, nor did the more pressing argument that, if the English remained unconverted, in their brutal heathen way they would surely fall upon the British, persecute and vanquish them. Thus Bede brought together what he had gathered from Gildas concerning 'the ruin and conquest of Britain' and propaganda on behalf of the English church and the Papacy.

Barely two months after our return to south Wales, the Aberfan disaster brought a sickening reminder of the price of coal. Anyone brought up in the coalfield before, in the aftermath of the tragedy, all the tips were modified or swept away, will have strong personal images of the vast heaps of colliery waste that hung over the valleys. They were too much a part of existence to be considered threatening. As children in Gilfach Goch, we viewed with amused indifference the road we walked to school where fissures would open emitting wisps of smoke and where, on damp days, the air stank of combustion. It had been built over a smouldering tip. Houses and Gilfach's first school were hidden beneath another tip, but their burial had been planned and was slow. What happened at Aberfan, soon after the commencement of morning lessons on 21 October 1966, was catastrophically sudden. A black avalanche of slurry and stony debris smashed into Pantglas Junior School and nearby houses in its path, killing 116 children and 28 adults. The engulfing slide had been anticipated and feared by a few, because they knew tipping had proceeded for decades over a small stream and mountain springs. Their voices had gone unheeded and no action was taken. Individual tragedies and disasters had occurred in the coalfield before, hundreds of them, but confined to the underground workings and surface of countless collieries. This time, a generation of the children of a typical mining village were killed. In the enquiry that followed, the National Coal Board and its chairman, Lord Robens, did their best to exculpate themselves. They did not succeed, but revisiting the disaster on this fiftieth anniversary has reawakened grievances over the way the media, the Charity Commission and government bodies responded in its aftermath.

Earlier this year, I met on separate occasions two men, one in the RAF at the time, the other a collier in another valley, who had helped to dig out victims of the disaster. It haunts them still. A boyhood friend of poet and short-story writer Leslie Norris (born in Merthyr Tydfil, a few miles from Aberfan) was deputy head at the school. He and his entire class were killed. When his body was recovered he was found to have spread his arms protectively over five of his pupils as the black tide struck. In his 'Elegy for David Beynon', helpless to express the magnitude of the calamity, Leslie recalled his friend in terms of utmost simplicity:

I think those children, those who died
under your arms in the crushed school,

would understand that I make this
your elegy. I know the face you had,
have walked with you enough mornings
under the falling leaves. Theirs is

the great anonymous tragedy one word
will summarise. Aberfan, I write it
for them here, knowing we've paid to it
our shabby pence, and now it can be stored

with whatever names there are where
children end their briefest pilgrimage.
I cannot find the words for you, David. These
are too long, too many, and not enough.

*PN Review* 233, Volume 43 Number 3,
January – February 2017.

# SHAKESPEARE AND WALES
*July 2016*

As part of its quatercentenary salute to Shakespeare, the National Museum of Wales in Cardiff invited Michael Bogdanov to speak on 'The Welsh in Shakespeare'. His visit drew a large audience to the museum's Reardon Smith Lecture Theatre, attracted by his fame as a multi-award-winning theatre director and his subject. His list of credits for theatre productions – plays, opera, musicals, and in film and television, is of such staggering length, and in so many venues worldwide, you marvel at his creative energy and how he finds time to sleep. With a lot of experience in various media behind him, mostly in Ireland, where he had graduated from Trinity College, Dublin, he joined the RSC in 1970 as assistant director on a production that transformed the presentation of Shakespeare on stage, Peter Brook's *A Midsummer Night's Dream*. (I saw it on tour at the New Theatre, Cardiff, and it remains the most exciting, most memorable, theatrical experience of my life.) He has been a disciple of Brook, dedicating himself, he says, to making Shakespeare politically relevant to people today, and viewing each directorial challenge as 'like reading a detective story, piecing clues together, never taking anything for granted, ignoring received opinion'.

Throughout his international career Michael Bogdanov has maintained a connection with Wales, including a lengthy commitment, 2003 – 2009, as artistic director of the Wales Theatre Company, which had its home in Swansea. The location was a fitting choice for one born just down the road in Neath, to a Welsh mother and a Jewish father whose own boyhood was spent in pre-Revolutionary Russia. And here he was on another visit, picking up the trail and following the clues to the Welsh in Shakespeare, at a brisk pace that pressed the audience to an eager canter to keep up.

It comes as a surprise to learn that some of our neighbours over the Dyke think the Tudors were English. They were of course Welsh, Henry VII being the grandson of Owain ap Maredudd ap Tudur of Penmynydd, Anglesey, who was the second husband of Catherine de Valois, widow of Henry V. At his majority, Henry VI, Catherine's son by that earlier marriage, ensured that his stepfather and half-brothers, Edmund and Jasper, were afforded rank and protection. Edmund was married to Margaret Beaufort and their son, Henry, took the crown from Richard III. The Welsh who had supported him at Bosworth followed him to London. They found places in the law, at court and in parliament; hence, to be Welsh was not a handicap to the able and ambitious in the reign of Elizabeth I. The queen's greatly-esteemed Secretary of State and Lord Treasurer, William Cecil, Lord Burghley, took pains to establish his Welsh pedigree.

In Act IV of Beaumont and Fletcher's *The Pilgrim*, a 'Welsh Madman' enters calling, 'Give me some ceeze and onions, give me some wash-brew' and is dismissed as 'a mountaineer, a man of goatland'. Knowing of their influence at court, no matter what his feelings towards them were, Shakespeare was politically astute enough not to give offence gratuitously in his portrayal of the Welsh (that the Chamberlain's men were accused of sympathy with the Essex faction, though they escaped censure or worse, demonstrates the hair's-breadth hazards of the time). The evidence of the plays suggests an altogether warmer appreciation of the Welsh. He viewed them, as all men, with amusement perhaps for harmless foibles, but also with respect and even affection. It may have counted that he had a Welsh grandmother, Alys Griffin, but there were also fellow actors who, by their names, were Welsh – Augustine Phillips (a shareholder in the Globe), Robert Goughe and John Rice. Textual evidence supports the thesis. It is rare in Shakespeare that a nation speaks in its own language, but in *Henry IV Part 1*, a sequence of stage directions (frequently overlooked in modern productions) demands actors speak Welsh: 'Glendower speakes to her in Welsh, and she answeres him in the same'; 'The Lady speakes in Welsh'; 'The Lady speakes againe in Welsh'; 'Heere the Lady sings a Welsh song'. They tell us that the company also had a Welsh-speaking boy actor.

At the grammar school in Stratford, Shakespeare probably had a teacher of Latin from Wales, Thomas Jenkins, who may well have been the prototype of Sir (not of the knightly sort) Hugh Evans in *The Merry Wives of Windsor*. A good deal of support is given to the suggestion that Fluellen in *Henry V*, the most expansive and memorable of Shakespeare's Welsh, is modelled on Sir Roger Williams, from Penrhos in Monmouthshire, 'an obstreperous and opinionated' warrior in the Protestant cause and expert in the conduct of warfare. Their tricks of speech, in the pronunciation of English words, or the use of a noun for verb or adjective ('can you affection the 'oman?', as Sir Hugh asks), and stock phrases, such as Fluellen's 'look you' were incorporated into the repertoire of comic stage Welsh and may linger still in vulgar performance. But Shakespeare is not laughing at his characters, to whom he gave humanity and even just a hint of noble virtue along with un-English eccentricity. In Henry V, the king sets his seal on this amalgam in addressing Fluellen: 'For I am Welsh, you know, good countryman.' Glendower's brand of high-flown magic realism, in *Henry IV Part 1,* is pitted against the threatening, plain bluntness of Hotspur, and it is the latter who retracts his truculence.

And then there are the plays set in a British past, *King Lear* and, particularly, *Cymbeline,* in which scenes are set in Wales, and more specifically, the great natural harbour of Milford Haven. Had Shakespeare ever been there? Had he even once visited Wales? It seems unlikely, but he had read his histories and had a circle of Welsh acquaintance ever ready to supply local colour. In any case, it is all one, he might have said, for there is no England in *Cymbeline;* Rome, yes, but no England. The 'Great Britain' project was just beginning. To Shakespeare and his contemporaries Britain and British meant Wales and the Welsh language. All this is pretty well known. A splendid book, referenced by Michael Bogdanov, *Shakespeare and the Welsh* by Frederick J. Harries, first published in 1919, is an exhaustive study of the subject, and though fresh nuances have emerged from close textual study, little that is new has been added to it since.

John Crichton Stuart, third Marquess of Bute, 1847–1900, who in a sixteen-year-long partnership with the architect William Burges continued his family's restoration of Cardiff Castle and created Castell Coch, the Victorian gothic masterpiece overlooking the Taff gorge, gave to the people of Cardiff Bute Park and Sophia Gardens, and Cathays Park, where broad avenues are lined with grand Edwardian civic buildings – including the National Museum. Such munificence! – albeit from a man at the very top of the Victorian 'rich list' with an income said to have been £300,000 a year. It seems churlish to regret on this Shakespearean occasion that he did not also give the city the recently authenticated First Folio from his library at Mount Stuart House on the Isle of Bute.

*PN Review* 230, Volume 42 Number 6,
July – August 2016.

# Y WLADFA AND TRYWERYN

*March 2016*


I seem to be remarking significant anniversaries of writers and events with increasing frequency: no doubt a consequence of growing older. The year 2015 saw two that were highly significant in the annals of Wales. They are instantly recognisable to anyone with a superficial knowledge of modern Welsh history by the identifying names: 'Y Wladfa' and 'Tryweryn'.

Y Wladfa (The Colony) is the name given to the one hundred square miles of Patagonia granted to Welsh settlers by the Argentine government. We have been celebrating the 150th anniversary of their landfall at what is now Puerto Madryn on 28th July 1865. 'A cold coming [they] had of it', the depths of the southern hemisphere winter, and a barren shore. It is even now a remote territory eight thousand miles from home, nine hundred south of Buenos Aires. They found it sparsely populated by Tehuelche hunter-gatherers who, after initial suspicion, decided to be friendly and helped to sustain them in the first terrible years. Certainly, it was nothing like the land promised in the glowing report brought back by Lewis Jones and Capt. T. Love Jones-Parry, sent out to reconnoitre and assess in 1862.

The name of Michael D. Jones (1822-98), a Congregational minister and fervent nationalist, born near Bala, north Wales, is the most prominent connected with the venture. Ordained at the Welsh church in Cincinnati in 1847, he hoped life in America, beyond the influence of England, would allow the many immigrants from Wales to hold firm to their language and customs, but soon saw this could not be. Supported by like-minded individuals and groups scattered across America, he sought other locations where a new Welsh colony might be established, and Argentina, where the government was keen to populate empty land in the south to forestall encroachment from Chile, offered the best prospect.

At public meetings up and down Wales the promise of a hundred acres each of land in the Chubut valley attracted individuals and families. Eventually, 153 (a third of them children) sailed in a small converted tea-clipper, the Mimosa, out of Liverpool, where much of the committee-work behind the venture had taken place. The hopeful emigrants included preachers, a schoolmaster, one builder, two farmers, one 'doctor', miners and quarrymen. Three-fifths were from the industrial valleys of south Wales, accustomed to heavy labour and hardship, though not of the sort they encountered in semi-desert at forty-three degrees south, between the Andes and the sea. Even if they had all been experienced farmers, it was too late to plant for next year's crops. Sheep and cattle herded overland for them were stolen en route, food and water were in short supply: it began to look like Chesapeake 1609. Some left in despair, and there were many deaths, especially among the children, but the colony survived.

Within a couple of years an irrigation project, the first in Argentina, inspired by Rachel Jenkins, a farmer's wife, began the creation of fertile wheat lands either side of the Chubut river, and the remaining immigrants were confident enough to explore farther inland and extend the colony to a fertile valley in the foothills of the Andes. Fresh waves, wavelets rather, of Welsh immigrants, five hundred or so in all, arrived within the next decade. By 1875 the new Wales that Michael D. Jones had dreamed of, where Welsh was the language of everyday life, of law and administration, education and religious observance, and every man and woman over eighteen had the vote, existed indeed. It couldn't last. The government in Buenos Aires, determined to assert its authority, insisted military conscription applied equally to the young men of Y Wladfa. In 1896 it declared that all education was to be through the medium of Spanish. Then the economic success of the colony contributed to its undoing: immigrants from Spain, Chile and Italy poured in, until Welsh became once more a minority language.

About fifty thousand Patagonians can claim Welsh ancestry; estimates of the number of Welsh-speakers in 2015 vary from 1500 to (a very optimistic) 5000. Today, there are regular cultural exchanges between Wales and Y Wladfa. Each year three language development officers from Wales spend from March to December in Patagonia promoting Welsh language learning for children and adults. The number of people pursuing Welsh courses rises year by year (985 in 2013) and a Welsh-medium primary school has been established. As in Wales, through education, a new foundation is being laid that should preserve the language for at least another generation.

About nine miles south of Aberystwyth on the A487, outside the village of Llanrhystyd, you see a prominent graffito, over-painted red now, on what remains of a stone wall: *'Cofiwch Dryweryn'*. As he tells us in his lively autobiography, *My Shoulder to the Wheel* (Y Lolfa, 2015), Meic Stephens originally daubed it in white in 1962/3, when he and a friend 'went out into the night to paint [Nationalist] slogans on public buildings'. He was then a young schoolteacher and it was a risky business, not least because of the interest the police and MI5 took in what was construed as anti-establishment activity of any kind. This simple dictum, *'Cofiwch Dryweryn'* (Remember Tryweryn) has achieved iconic status surpassing any effort by Banksy. It has become part of our national consciousness.

In 1957, an Act of Parliament gave Liverpool Corporation

the right to dam the River Tryweryn in north Wales, and so drown the village of Capel Celyn and surrounding farms and farmland. The area was entirely Welsh-speaking. All but one of the thirty-six Welsh MPs voted against the Bill, but it made no difference. Immediate and widespread public protest was similarly ignored. People of Capel Celyn, men, women and children, parading through Liverpool to attend a meeting of the corporation, were vilified and spat upon. From 1960 to 1965, during the construction of the dam, protest continued and intensified. Two sabotage attacks delayed the work, though not for long, and those responsible were arrested and tried; two were imprisoned. At the official opening of the dam on 21 October 1965, a large crowd drawn from all over Wales was in no mood to celebrate. Protesters who lay in the path of the cavalcade of visiting dignitaries and escorting motorcycle police were dragged away. Alderman Sefton reached the podium to begin a planned forty-five minute ceremony. Pandemonium ensued; microphone wires were cut, stones were thrown, scuffles broke out. The event was abandoned – but the dam was there and the Welsh-speaking community erased.

Tryweryn was a late example of colonial exploitation. Wales as a country was defenceless against the expropriation of its land and resource by a single English authority. The city's argument that its need for drinking water gave it an overwhelming prerogative does not stand examination. In a recent television broadcast Lord Elystan Morgan, who as a young lawyer defended the Welsh saboteurs, said the water Liverpool took (and still takes) without payment was sold on as industrial water to twenty-four other English authorities.

The historian Wyn Thomas argues that 1965 was a turning point for Wales and that successive Welsh Language Acts and the establishment of a National Assembly have flowed from the humiliation of Tryweryn. But the language is still under threat, not least because a minority of the population here have no love for it and, with a few honourable exceptions (J.R.R. Tolkien comes at once to mind), no one in England cares a jot. If this is still a United Kingdom, as is alleged, politicians, television, radio and newspapers should play their part in educating the British public at large about the Welsh language, and inspire all with the desire to preserve it. As things stand, the disdainful indifference of Westminster governments and the metropolitan media to the fate of one of the precious ornaments of European culture, with a literature older than English, remains persistent and damnable.

*PN Review* 228, Volume 42 Number 4,
March – April 2016.

# DE CALAMITATE EXCIDIO, & CONQUESTU BRITANNIE

*July 2015*

For more years than I care to contemplate, when they appeared in the catalogues of antiquarian booksellers, and when I could more or less afford them, I have bought books which make a notable contribution to knowledge of the history of Wales. That they do not turn up often is an indication of their relative rarity, and a blessing of sorts: more would be a temptation to imprudence and financial ruin. Some time ago I acquired *De calamitate excidio, & conquestu Britannie* (*Concerning the calamity of the ruin and conquest of Britain*), the earliest surviving account of Britain in the fifth century, written about the middle of the sixth century by the monk Gildas. The text exists in manuscripts from the eleventh century, and the first printed version was published in April 1525 by Polydore Vergil (c.1470–1555), scholar priest of Urbino, who, despatched to England in 1502 as a collector of Peter's Pence, found there ecclesiastical preferment and a niche at the court of Henry VII. In about 1505 he began writing *Anglica Historia*, probably at the king's commission. The quest for materials to assist this project led him to investigate various manuscript sources, among them the Gildas, which is referred to in his history of England, the first edition of which was published in 1534. Detractors later claimed he destroyed manuscripts after filleting them, but the care he took to edit and publish *De excidio* gives the lie to that accusation. The copy I have once belonged to William Constable, Esq., FRS & FSA (1721–91), of Burton Constable Hall, a magnificent Elizabethan house in East Yorkshire. His bookplate is on the front pastedown. It is a small octavo, only 3½ by 5½ inches, printed in elegant italic types, the forty-four leaves unnumbered. Two hundred years ago I might have bought a copy for fifteen shillings – a sum not to be sniffed at in those days, when a Gutenberg Bible changed hands for £199 10s.

It is, of course, written in Latin, which I pronounce without confidence and, despite my school certificate credit, understand hardly at all. More recently, however, the first published translation, entitled *The Epistle of Gildas, the most ancient British author*, came my way and I have read it cover to cover. It was printed in 1638 by '*T. Cotes*, for *William Cooke* ... to be sold at his shop neere *Furnivalls-Inne* gate in *Holborne*'. The author's name is not given, but his identity is known. It was Thomas Habington (1560–1647), whose father, a man of substance, cofferer to Queen Elizabeth, built Hindlip Hall near Worcester. Young Habington, one of Elizabeth's godsons, was educated at Oxford and on the continent, probably at Rheims, where, at the English College, he would have enjoyed the company of fellow Catholics. When his father died in 1581, he returned to England, completing his education at Gray's Inn. He had benefited from a humanist education much the same as that experienced at the beginning of the century in Urbino by Polydore Vergil, one that predisposed him, among other things, to historical interests and the antiquarian pursuits he later developed.

The family had maintained their religious sympathies beneath a discreet façade, but in 1586, Thomas's elder brother, Edward, heir to Hindlip, was implicated in the Babington Plot to assassinate Elizabeth and free Mary Queen of Scots. He protested his innocence throughout the subsequent trial, but was found guilty of treason and executed. Thomas was arrested at the same time and, although not prosecuted, was listed by the Attorney General as 'a dangerous fellowe... [and] dealer with these seminarye priests'. He was imprisoned in the Tower for six years, but emerged firm in his faith and, like other Catholics, hoped the accession of James I in 1603 would bring a measure of religious toleration. The obduracy of parliament ensured it did not.

Hindlip Hall became one of the great houses in the Midlands that afforded protection to Catholic priests – as was well known to Robert Cecil, who ordered a search in January 1606. In Habington's absence, prolonged investigation of the fabric of the house to uncover the many hiding places that had been built into it led at last to the discovery of Cecil's chief quarry, Henry Garnet, head of the Jesuit mission to England, who was later found guilty of foreknowledge of the Gunpowder Plot and executed 409 years ago to this day, on 3 May 1606. Habington was tried with others at Worcester for aiding a known plotter and found guilty. His co-defendants were executed, but he was pardoned, as he later claimed, at the insistence of his brother-in-law, Lord Monteagle (whose earlier intervention had led to the foiling of the plot). This further close brush with the state's agents and a dreadful fate did not deter Habington. He was convicted of recusancy in 1637, 1640 and 1642, suffered another spell of imprisonment and seizure by the Crown of much of his wealth. This part of the historical narrative, which I first explored through my long association with Roland Mathias, endlessly fascinates, not least because such strength of religious conviction is alien to our culture, though not in much of the Arab world.

This, at last you may say, brings us back to Gildas. Habington's translation was completed during his first, long incarceration in the Tower, yet it was not published until almost the eve of the Civil War, and then anonymously. The book begins with a salutation 'To the inhabitants of the island of Great Britain, unity and felicity' and a lengthy preface, which ends with a clear expression of support for Charles I for abolishing old enmities and having made 'a skilfull mixture of the *English, Scottish,* and *Welch,* laboureth now to severe them all into three distinct orders, of the Nobility, Gentry, and Cominalty, of his entire Realm of great *Britaine,* which being of three sundry people framed into one happy Soveraignetie, I beseech the Almighty Trinity, to bring to a most perfect Unitie'. His view was no doubt typical of the landowning gentry of the time, especially those with Catholic sympathies. He lived to see Charles's armies on the verge of final defeat, though the notion of a unified kingdom survived, at least to the present.

Gildas's 'epistle' was not intended to teach historical facts to his own or later generations. It was to show how falling away from God, impiety and immoral behaviour results in destruction. He is not a historian, but a priest, and *De excidio* a sermon, which, long before the end, becomes a rant incorporating every prophetic warning the Bible affords. He mentions (Claudius) Caesar, Tiberius, Diocletian, and Magnus Maximus, who (c.383–88) raised an army in Britain and almost succeeded in taking the throne in Rome, but knows virtually nothing of the Roman occupation. There are no dates, but he tells he was born in the year of the siege of 'Mount Badon', now untraceable, a key event in the wars with the Saxons, where they were defeated and held off for a time, about the end of the fifth century. The wonderful thing about Gildas, a source for the true historians who followed him, Polydore Vergil, Humfrey Lhuyd, Sir John Price, and the rest, to the present century, is that during his boyhood he would have heard from the lips of old men the stories of the immorality of leaders, the plagues and famines, the vicious pirate raids of the Picts and Scots and the coming of the barbarous Saxons, and how the British were driven to the mountainous and forested western edges of what had been their independent, Christian land.

*PN Review* 224, Volume 41 Number 6,
July – August 2015.

# CHARTISM

*May 2015*

Today, 4 March 2015, is the thirtieth anniversary of the end of the year-long 1984–85 Miners' Strike. It is not celebrated, because the miners were defeated, but it is remembered, bitterly, in the pit villages. How long do folk memories last? When I was young, older generations at least still spoke of the strikes of 1910–11 and 1926, which brought untold suffering to the coalfield and ended with the miners worse off in terms of pay and conditions than they were before. But most of the pits were still there, and most of the miners were allowed back to work. Coal remained vital to industry, even if much of it came as cheap imports from abroad, and more vital than ever during the Second World War, as my boyhood memories of Gilfach Goch's three pits working round the clock remind me. When the 1984–85 strike ended, here and there miners returned to the surviving collieries led by brass bands, holding union banners aloft. It was a last, muted, hurrah: they had lost the battle with government, establishment and media, and knew closures would follow, though they did not guess the scale of the programme, nor the speed with which it would be implemented. In the aftermath, the mining communities of south Wales, summarily stripped of purpose, have been devastated. The response of government has been a shrug of the shoulders: 'Too bad. Stuff happens'. Will the memory of this last defeat endure? Not for long, I suspect, because evidence of mining activity has largely been swept away. There are museum pieces for tourists at Trehafod in the Rhondda and Blaenavon, and memorials at Six Bells and Senghenydd, but without mouldering reminders of an industrial past on the doorstep (the sort of thing I knew well), younger people will have nothing to stir a sense of local industrial history. Besides they have other concerns, not least where to find a decent job, or any job.

There were times during 1984–85 when the picketing of miners was viewed by government and press as incipient revolution, and the official response was violently repressive. We had been there before, in 1910–11, when soldiers were deployed in the Valleys to keep the peace, and just 175 years ago, another notable milestone, during the Chartist rising, which had in its south Wales climax in 1839–40 the bloodiest manifestation of the establishment's determination to keep working folk under the heel.

Chartism did not begin in Wales. It was hatched in the mind of William Lovett, a Cornishman who became a cabinet-maker in London. Convinced that political reform was the only answer to the exploitation and grinding poverty suffered by the mass of ordinary workers, he became a co-founder of the London Working Men's Association in June 1836, and in May 1838 published 'The People's Charter', which demanded universal male suffrage, secret ballots, the ending of property qualifications for MPs, payment of MPs, equal constituencies and annual parliaments. Evangelists of the cause recruited support up and down the land. The movement quickly gathered strength in industrial south-east Wales. Henry Vincent, born in London, a printer by trade, and hugely influential orator, toured the coalfield in 1838 and was so impressed with the response he received that he declared Wales would make 'an admirable republic', because 'Nowhere throughout the Empire is a population more discontented than they'. Although he urged his listeners to keep the peace to deny 'our enemies a pretext for letting loose their bloodhounds on us', on 7 May 1838 he was arrested in London and three days later brought before magistrates in Newport charged with sedition. A protest gathering in the town turned into a fight between his supporters and local authorities. John Frost, a Newport draper and former mayor of the town, leader of the Monmouthshire Chartists, subsequently addressed his followers: 'The scene which Newport yesterday presented to our view must, to every honest man, have been painful in the extreme. Numbers of men of the working classes, with broken heads, and their wounds inflicted by Special Constables, sworn to preserve the peace, many of them drunk and under the command of a Drunken Magistrate. My advice to you [...] be cool, but firm. We seek for nothing but our rights as members of a civil society.' In August Vincent was found guilty at Monmouth assizes. His imprisonment for one year may not in itself have precipitated the ensuing violence, but it was a contributory factor.

In the months that followed, Chartists who argued for the use of physical rather than moral force began to gain the advantage. But the government was intransigent. In July 1839, a petition supporting the Charter bearing 1,280,000 names was rejected out of hand by Parliament. During the autumn of that year, a mass protest was planned at meetings in the upper Gwent areas of the coalfield and on the night of 3/4 November 1839 three columns of working men, mostly miners, began to march down the valleys towards Newport, a journey of about twenty miles, gathering numbers on their way. Many bore hard-edged working tools or rudimentary weapons, pikes and clubs they had made themselves, and a few had firearms. They were led by John Frost, Zephaniah Williams, who had been mineral agent for a coal company and kept the Royal Oak at Blaina, and watchmaker William Jones, who had formed a Working Men's Association at his beer shop in Pontypool. The columns were to meet before it was full light and move together to Newport town centre. The night was cold and very wet and their progress through the darkness was slower than anticipated, but the columns led by Frost and Williams eventually coalesced and tramped down Stow Hill towards the town centre. Jones's Pontypool column was unaccountably delayed and, learning that a catastrophe had occurred, dispersed. Perhaps I was lucky in that turn of events: my great-grandfather, Thomas Adams, ironstone miner and pit-sinker, living at the time at Abersychan, near Pontypool, might just possibly have been among them. Nevertheless, a crowd of marchers estimated at between three and five thousand assembled in the open space outside the Westgate Hotel in Newport's main street demanding that Vincent and other Chartist prisoners be released. What happened next is disputed, but there appears to have been an attempt to storm the doors of the hotel, at which a contingent of thirty soldiers from the 45th Regiment of Foot opened the upper half shutters of the downstairs windows and fired their muskets directly into the crowd. Twenty-two died on the spot, many more were gravely injured. Some of those carried away may have died later, but any such cases were hidden, since to give succour to one of the wounded would have amounted to complicity. Ten of the dead were buried in unmarked graves in the churchyard of St Woolos Cathedral, at the top of Stow Hill. You can view a simple stone there dedicated to their memory.

Of course, that was not the end of what has been described as the most serious outbreak of violence associated with Chartism. The Law would have its day. At the assizes in Monmouth, almost sixty men were tried on a range of charges from treason to sedition, conspiracy and riot. On 16 January 1840, Lord Chief Justice Tindal pronounced sentence on the leaders, Frost, Williams and Jones, all three guilty of High Treason: 'that each of you be there hanged by the neck until you be dead, and that afterwards the head of each of you shall be severed from his body, and the body of each, divided into four quarters, shall be disposed of as Her Majesty shall think fit'. In the event the sentence was commuted to transportation for life to Van Diemen's Land.

If the Chartists had won the day at Newport, urban industrial centres across England might have joined in a general rising against establishment, government and monarchy. That is what was alleged and feared by the movement's opponents. But we are where we are. Among the sources I regularly employ in my quest for historical accuracy is the invaluable Penguin *History of Wales*. Sadly, its author, the distinguished historian John Davies, died last month, aged 76.

*PN Review* 223, Volume 41 Number 5,
May – June 2015.

# JOHN PIPER AND ST MARY'S CHURCH, TOWYN
*July 2014*

We have recently acquired a small painting by John Piper. It is a gouache on paper, dating from about 1950, of a 'Church near Rhyl, North Wales'. The church, which has an unusual gable-roofed bell tower, sits in the middle of the painting, a dark sky behind. In the foreground are other buildings, for the most part sombre, but heightened on one side by touches of red, signifying tiled roofs, and elsewhere by narrow vertical bands of pale yellow and blue. Between two blocks of dwellings in the foreground a vivid green oval lies on its side. At first glance the painting is almost abstract, but closer examination of the church reveals lozenge-shaped hatching on the roofs of tower and nave, clearly a distinctive feature, and a minute square outlined in black on the body of the green oval identifies it as a caravan.

A little research on the subject disclosed that this is St Mary's in the parish of Towyn on the north Wales coast, one of those parts of Wales to have endured almost Noah-scale floods in the past few years; the church itself was badly damaged, but has since been repaired. It is not an ancient structure, like many of Piper's architectural subjects, but was founded through the patronage of a wealthy local, Robert Hesketh of Gwyrch Castle, Abergele, and consecrated in 1873. More significantly, from the artist's viewpoint, the architect was George Edmund Street RA (1824–81), a leading figure in the Gothic Revival. He would have known that Street was, like him, the son of a London solicitor, intended to follow his father's occupation, who had escaped the law to embrace the profession of architect, hardly less precarious than his own chosen path. He said he envied

Street's 'well-ordered, rich, selfish, stately, opinionated creative life', but it would have been inimical to his brisk praxis, his industry and assiduity. Nevertheless, he consistently admired Street's work. A sample of it, the Law Courts in the Strand, is viewed by tens of thousands daily; a great deal more is tucked away in small towns and villages all over Britain, for he designed over a hundred churches. Piper's *oeuvre* includes images of at least another two Street churches – St James the Less, Westminster, and St Mary's, Paddington – and, remarkably, three different versions of St Mary's, Towyn, one of which now resides with us.

I was first attracted to Piper's work by magnificent large oil paintings in the Tate collection, and the archival material I saw displayed at the gallery, which included sketchbooks filled with drawings and notes he made as a teenager when he cycled Surrey lanes around the comfortable family home his father had built at Epsom. Although in the early 1930s he was a notable figure in the avant-garde, a member of the 7 & 5 Society, he is quintessentially English, in the long line of artists whose principal interests lie in landscape and architecture, mostly in Britain, although, in common with earlier practitioners, he travelled and painted in other parts. His unique vision of places and buildings perhaps owes something to his lifelong interest in stained glass, for it often seems that the subject of his painting is struck by coloured light cast by some celestial window. No matter what new movements in art come along, or how popular taste is alleged to have changed, the romantic and antiquarian in his work have a lasting allure, and for us, his special appeal lies in certain Welsh connections, foremost among them, because it became the key to others, his marriage to Myfanwy.

Myfanwy Evans was born and brought up in London and educated at Oxford, but her father was from Pembrokeshire and throughout her childhood and beyond she spent whole summer holidays with relatives in the far southwest of Wales, a region of great coastal and rural beauty. They met in the summer of 1934, when Piper, newly arrived by car for a weekend at a cottage in Sizewell, Suffolk, was asked to pick up another guest who was travelling by train. It turned out to be a young woman whose vivacity and intelligence were immediately engaging. Thus began a conversation that endured with few breaks for the rest of their lives. Piper's marriage to a fellow student at the Royal College of Art was breaking up, due in no small part to his wife's affair with the Welsh artist Ceri Richards, and in Myfanwy he found a complementary artistic intellect. They married in 1937. By describing a circle around a pin stuck in a map and exploring the countryside within it, they came upon an abandoned farm not far from Henley-on-Thames named Fawley Bottom. It was without water and electricity, but they settled there and over a couple of decades civilised it. This was where they brought up their children and entertained their many friends; it was Piper's workplace, the home they returned to from their travels.

The artist's association with Wales extended in various directions: H.S. ('Jim') Ede, yet another solicitor's son, from Penarth, was an early influence, encouraging an interest in abstract art; the Howard Roberts Gallery in Cardiff was one of two exceptions when he made Marlborough Fine Art in London his sole representative; a long friendship with Moelwyn Merchant, then lecturer at Cardiff University, began in 1946, when he contributed an article to Merchant's magazine *Cymru'r Groes*; he received an honorary doctorate from Cardiff in 1980; in 1984 he provided exquisite lithographic illustrations for a sumptuous Gregynog Press edition of Dylan Thomas's *Deaths and Entrances*; he and Myfanwy were close friends of Alun Hoddinott and his wife, and as set designer and librettist respectively collaborated with the composer in the creation of five new operas. But most memorable and artistically important was his direct experience of Wales. Shortly before the war began in 1939 they spent a fortnight in mid-Wales. They explored the moorland, a landscape so remote and empty it verges on abstraction, and, inspired by earlier accounts, made several day visits to Hafod, the house and estate created by Thomas Johnes in the eighteenth century. The dereliction of the property and the picturesque wildness of the neglected demesne chimed with Piper's aesthetic interests: 'Hafod is a dream' he wrote to John Betjeman.

Other Welsh interludes were hugely productive. Inspired by Richard Wilson's north Wales landscapes he took his sketchbook to Cader Idris, and by the late 1940s, having developed an obsession with mountain scenery, he and Myfanwy rented a cottage near Bethesda in the valley of Nant Ffrancon as bereft of amenities as Fawley Bottom and far more remote. Then they took another cottage near Capel Curig and Llyn Ogwen. It was what Piper sought – rugged scenery, craggy rocks, sombre, rain-washed, mist-enfolded – and he worked at his drawings outdoors in all weathers. In the whole body of his work, immense and richly varied as it is, some of the greatest achievements are paintings of north Wales.

The subject of our little painting is quite other: a bit of the coast so flat it is prone to flooding, and a church, with (as perhaps even then the artist realised) a portentous green oval before it. Today, St Mary's, much altered internally since the deluge, stands in the midst of enormous static and mobile caravan parks. This is where families from the great cities of the English Midlands take their summer holidays.

*PN Review* 218, Volume 40 Number 6, July – August 2014.

# MINING

*September 2013*

Both my grandfathers, and their fathers, and their fathers before them, worked all their lives, so far as I can tell, in coalmines. Before that, in the eighteenth century, some or all of them presumably laboured on the land. I know my grandfather and namesake began working underground as a 'helper' with his father, at the age of twelve. That was in Gilfach Goch. John Love, my mother's father, began in the same way at the same age in Wellow, near Radstock, Somerset. After thirty years or so at the coalface, Sam Adams and John Love (who came to south Wales as a young man, married and settled here) were promoted within the pit. The former became an 'overman', with responsibility for oversight of the work and working conditions in a sector of the mine. He carried a distinctive brass safety lamp and a stick cleft at one end that allowed him to lift the lamp to the roof of the underground workings to test for the presence of gas. The brass lamp stands on the hearth in our living room. His son, my father, worked fifty years as an electrician in south Wales collieries.

I think now of our children and, more recently, our grandchildren, at the age of twelve, on the way to school, and how very young they were, even for the trials of that experience. I cannot imagine them trudging off to a seven-and-a-half hour shift underground. And what would they have done during those hours hundreds of feet below the surface? I have recently talked with Vernon Harding, whose coal-grimed face you may possibly have seen. He is in that famous Magnum photo *Three Generations of Miners* taken in 1950 by the eminent American

426

photographer W. Eugene Smith. At fourteen, in 1942, Vernon began working alongside his father at Coedely Colliery. His family lived in Coedely, the village of terraced streets you can also see in the photo, within easy walking distance of the mine. He told me what a child did in a pit where, when he began, coal was still cut and loaded into drams by hand.

Those who have never been underground in a working pit (I include myself) can have not the slightest notion what it was like. We have probably seen films or photographs of colliers at the coalface. They invariably convey the impression of a coal seam as a black wall glinting back the light of lamps. But, of course (as a geologist would instantly point out), the wall-like seam is merely a section through a layer of coal varying in thickness from inches to several feet spread over many square miles between similarly blanket-like layers of other rock laid down as sedimentary deposits millions of years ago. The identical coal seams were reached and pillaged by scores of collieries in different valleys and villages in the heydays of mining, and billions of tons of coal remain untapped now the deep mines have all gone.

Colliers were paid by the weight of coal cut and delivered to the weighbridge in individually marked drams, each designed to hold a ton of coal, but by careful packing (termed 'racing') often containing half a ton more. Vernon's widowed father, determined to make the most of each working day, was invariably in the first 'bond' of men in the cage for the 6.00 am descent: five hundred yards vertically down and then a mile walk cushioned by inches of coal dust along a tunnel cut to accommodate the width and height of a dram. There were no footpaths underground. If you happened to be in this tunnel when drams came clattering through hauled by ponies you crouched in the nearest 'manhole' cut into the side until they had passed. This was the main 'heading', the route to the coalface, off which turns were cut into the coal and, as necessary, the layers of rock above and beneath it.

The No. 3 seam where Vernon and his father worked varied in thickness from eighteen to thirty inches. The first task was to create a space six feet wide and five feet deep where a dram could be placed on rails laid back to the main heading. This entailed boring holes and placing charges to break up the layer of rock beneath the seam, which in that place was less hard than the rock above, and then clearing away the rubble. The roof was supported by timber notched and shaped at the ends with axes to make a jointed structure of pillars and cross-beams. Apart from setting the explosive and blowing the rock, which was done by a 'shotsman' on the night shift, all these preliminaries were the work of the miner, who had to drill the holes, complete the excavation, build the roof support and lay the rails, measuring crucial distances. The tools he used were his own, paid for, and at the end of a shift their handles were threaded onto an iron bar locked with his own padlock.

At the face Vernon's father had a safety lamp; he trimmed the wick and filled it with oil to give the light he worked by. Lying on one shoulder, he used a short-handled pick to hack a slot six to nine inches deep in the rock along the base of the seam over a distance of about eight yards and then a longer-handled mandrel to strike down the loosened coal. The fourteen-year-old's electric lamp with its heavy battery was hung from a post behind him, so that he could see little of what lay in his shadow before him. His job as his father's helper was to scoop the fallen coal with bare hands and forearms into a steel 'curling box', and crawling, his back scraping the low roof, tug or slide this hundredweight container several yards back to the waiting dram. As the face moved forward stony waste was cast into the space behind, the 'gob', where a wall had first to be built to retain it. When the roof supports along the gob were removed, the mountain of rock layers above weighed down and sealed the man-made wound.

During the shift you ate your meagre 'snap' when there was a moment's pause at the stall you were working, as when a loaded dram was hauled away; sometimes there was no pause. You drank water from a quart tinplate jack to lay thirst and the constant dust, which you lived in, breathed and swallowed seven and a half hours each working day. The mine was ventilated by air driven by a fan at the head of one ('downcast') shaft through a system of brattice-covered doors that directed the flow where it was needed and up another ('upcast') shaft, but it was warm and had the fustiness of coal about it. To the warmth of the mine was added the heat of intense physical effort. Men worked stripped to the waist and their bodies were painted with sweat and black dust. The No. 3 seam was dry; many were wet and workable only by constant pumping.

In addition to physical strength, miners needed an array of skills not easily or quickly learned – for example, that of notching timber precisely using an axe with a nine-inch blade, so that no time was wasted dismembering a roof support to adjust a joint. They also needed constant wariness. The experienced miner could detect weakness in the roof above by the sound returned when it was tapped with a mandrel handle, but you could never be certain. I remember my father telling me how a collier where he worked had been killed when 'a stone fell on him'. It was a characteristic understatement: a stone might weigh several tons. Vernon Harding was an apt learner, and his father a patient teacher, but it was five years before he was considered competent to have his own working place.

Coedely Colliery was almost a small town. It employed well over 800 men, had a blacksmith's shop, a sawmill, brickworks, coke ovens and, towering above it on the hillside, its own landmark, visible for miles, an enormous conical slag heap. As Vernon wrote to me, 'The noise was always there – the grating chatter of the steel plates in the screens as they sorted the coal, the clang of buffers as the shunting loco moved trucks along the sidings, the rhythmic thump of the steam engines as the winders raised the cages, and the blast of hooters signalling the beginning and end of shifts.' There was also the omnipresent black dust, carried by the westerlies across the valley to the terraced houses on the other side.

The terraces of Coedely were built because of the colliery, to which the lives of wives and mothers were as dedicated as those of their husbands and sons. It was a village community with a single focus, replete with mutual understanding and sympathy, whose families shared alike occasional blessings and years of adversity. Scores of towns and villages much the same lined the valleys of the south Wales coalfield. The settlements are still there, but the sense of purpose and solidarity that animated them as communities has all but died with the closure of the mines. In George Yates's 1799 map of the county of Glamorgan, Cardiff is an insignificant burg with a quay on the estuary of the Taff and Barry barely exists; some growth and industry is emerging around Swansea, Merthyr is beginning to burgeon, and a little activity is occurring in the Cynon valley. But the Rhondda and other adjacent valleys to west and east are virtually empty. Without coal they would all still be empty. Furthermore, it is likely that, without coal, our populous coastal urban areas, most notably Cardiff-Penarth-Barry, would have only a fraction of their current population and significance. The working of iron and other metal ores was highly significant but Welsh coal was crucial to industrial and mercantile development here and elsewhere in the UK. Coal created modern south Wales. The Assembly government is planning a memorial to mining disasters, some 200 of them, in each of which more than five men were killed. It will be sited at Senghenydd, near Caerphilly, where on the morning of 14 October 1913 an explosion at the Universal Colliery killed 439 men and boys. It is long overdue – and it is not enough. What is needed is a memorial to Vernon Harding and tens of thousands like him who worked in the hundreds of collieries that dotted the coalfield, and to the women who shared their lives: a grand memorial to coal, without which south Wales would be largely an extension of the green desert that is rural mid-Wales.

*PN Review* 213, Volume 40 Number 1,
September – October 2013.

# CHURCHES

*May 2013*

The decline in churchgoing and Christian belief is gathering pace here, perhaps more hectically than elsewhere. The falling off began from a high point about the middle of the nineteenth century, when Wales could boast a higher proportion of adherents than any other European country. Only 72 per cent of the population still described themselves as Christian in 2001; a decade later it is 58 per cent. During the same period, the proportion of those who have no religion has increased from 19 to 32 per cent. In my previous letter (*PN Review* 210) I referred to pockets of economic and cultural deprivation corresponding to post-1995 unitary authorities in the former industrial valleys of south Wales. These include communities that experienced the full force of the great Nonconformist revival inspired by Evan Roberts in 1904-5, when chapel membership attained unprecedented heights. Now Blaenau Gwent, Caerphilly and Rhondda Cynon Taf are, according to the census, among the five least religious parts of England and Wales.

The Anglicanism of my experience in the province of Wales seemed so unexacting that lapsing from it carried no burden of guilt. But I cannot deny regret has increased with the passage of years. At the very least, I subscribe to the view expressed by the unnamed narrator in John Updike's story 'Packed Dirt, Churchgoing, a Dying Cat, a Traded Car', first published in the *New Yorker* in 1961: 'Taken purely as recreation, what could be more delightful, more unexpected than to enter a venerable and lavishly scaled building kept warm and clean for use one or two hours a week and to sit and stand in unison and sing and recite creeds and petitions that are like paths worn smooth in the raw terrain of our hearts.'

Whatever I thought at the time, I count myself fortunate to have been, through my childhood and into my later teens, a regular churchgoer, doubly fortunate to have attended schools at which, in assemblies each morning, prayers were said and hymns sung on alternate days in Welsh and English. As a child, and even much later, my understanding of both prayers and hymns, regardless of the language in which they were said and sung, was shallow. But the words and music have proved adhesive, so that from time to time, unprompted, they surface in my consciousness, and I find myself humming tunes I had thought forgotten and repeating phrases that are now surprisingly luculent.

My paternal grandmother was descended from a family of Anglican clerics. Her great-grandfather had been Rector of Llantrithyd, a not inconsiderable living, and *his* father Vicar of Penlline, another village near Cowbridge in the Vale of Glamorgan. How much their religious heritage meant to her immediate family I cannot say, but that her parents' burial plot is within a few feet of the church porch at Coychurch, yet another Vale village, implies a holding priority. It seems likely that the Sam Adams she married was of a Nonconformist family; at least, his uncle was a Methodist preacher in Risca, on the outskirts of Newport. Led by him, I suppose, they married at an Independents' chapel in Pontypridd, but soon afterwards sank whatever denominational differences they may have had in the embrace of a more active Christianity: they joined the Salvation Army. They sang on street corners with the silver band (my grandmother's voice was said to carry clear across the valley), and gave tithes and a terraced house to be the home of successive Gilfach Goch brigade captains. My namesake died nine days after I was born and Mam, my father's mother, survived only five more years; I was not brought up a Salvationist.

It was my mother's influence that made us Anglican. She believed she was related to the Reverend Richard Lewis, Bishop of Llandaff about the turn of the nineteenth century. This story came from her grandmother, who, before marriage, was Catherine Lewis, born into the family of a Port Talbot metal worker. I have a photograph of Catherine with her daughter, Elizabeth Jane, her granddaughter, Edith, my mother, and her great-granddaughter, my sister Joan, then an infant. Catherine, with her bold gaze at the lens, appears strong in body and mind. If she said she was related to the bishop, I am sure it was not whimsy, but I have so far failed to prove the connection. My mother carried in her purse a large and rather fine silver crucifix, the kind a senior cleric might wear suspended from chain or ribbon on his breast; I never thought to enquire where it had come from. Anyway, it was she who, having found me sitting on the stairs in a mote-filled shaft of sunlight singing 'To be a pilgrim' to myself, decided I was old enough to join the choir of the corrugated-sheeting-clad Mission Church near the entrance to our valley, stone-built St Barnabas' having suffered bomb damage a year or so before.

I visited several places of worship in the footsteps of Roland Mathias. He was, first and last, a Congregationalist, a regular at the chapel distinctively called 'The Plough' in Brecon, which originated at the end of the seventeenth century, a time of persecution, when the faithful in the cause met where they safely could; the Plough was then an inn. The present building dates from the first half of the nineteenth century and was restored and extended in the second. Outside, it is typically undistinguished, but the galleried interior is glorious with polished wood and painted dome ceiling. Roland's memorial plaque is on the wall of the porch. I visited medieval churches at Cascob and Sarnesfield, the diminutive box-shaped chapel at Brechfa, by what must be now, after the year's rains, a substantial lake, high on the moor above Llyswen, and historic Maesyronnen Chapel, the first Congregational meeting house in Wales. All contributed to a better understanding of the man and his poetry. Without having seen St Michael's at Cascob, in its mysterious green valley, and St Mary's at Sarnesfield, and walked their ancient graveyards, I should still be baffled by the poems.

In 2012, we have been to churches at Llanilltud Fawr (Llantwit Major), Llanrhaeadr-yng-Nghinmeirch, near Denbigh, and Abergavenny, to view Jesse Trees, those strangely beautiful medieval representations of the lineage of Christ to illiterate congregations, sermons in wood and stone and stained glass. Illtud, the well-attested sixth-century saint, founded a monastery and ecclesiastical college at the small coastal town in the Vale of Glamorgan that bears his name. Among those who studied there were St Samson and St Pol, founders of Breton monasticism, and St Gildas, Britain's first historian. The thirteenth-century church dedicated to Illtud occupies the place where the monastery formerly stood. It has a Jesse niche carved in stone, modest in size, which might once have held a crucifix. The recumbent figure of Jesse rests on his elbow at its base, a stout stem rising from his groin and sprouting stone vines either side of the niche, whose leafy platters support the heads of Christ's ancestors. It is a time-worn image and we could not distinguish the attributes that might have identified them. No such difficulty at the church of St Dyfrog, Llanrhaeadr, where a resplendent Jesse Tree glows in a magnificent window dated 1533. At the foot, labelled 'Radix Jesse', a red- and green-garbed figure reclines on rugs or a mattress within a battlemented enclosure, the spreading tree growing from his breast. Prominent among the branches is David, depicted as the harpist king, and among the other sixteen figures are Joram and Isaiah, Zachariah and Obadiah, all named on flowing scrolls. At the summit, the Virgin with Christ in her arms is revealed in a sunburst of golden rays. This medieval marvel was preserved during the Civil War by being encased in a chest and buried in woodland surrounding the church. It is not the only wonder of Llanrhaedr. An underground stream emerges among tall trees a few hundred feet above the church and cascades down the hillside. This is the *rhaeadr* after which the village is (partly) named. Early in its breakneck descent the stream is caught in a perfectly clear, brimming pool, about the size of a large door, lined with stone slabs: the holy well of St Dyfrog, said to have done penance chained in the icy water, which has curative properties.

St Mary's, Abergavenny, originally the church of a Benedictine priory, founded in 1087, has the most remarkable late-fifteenth-century wooden figure of Jesse bereft of his tree. The structure was damaged at the time of the Reformation and what remained of branches and figures probably destroyed in the Civil War. The Jesse survived, like other monuments and embellishments, through the efforts of parishioners. Ten feet long, carved from a single trunk of oak, it is of the utmost rarity and one of the finest pieces of medieval sculpture in western Europe. Richly bearded Jesse reclines on a cushion held by an angel and, with an expression of resigned content, grasps the stout limb growing from his breast. The rest must be imagined, for when complete the assemblage of branches, foliage and figures would have reached upwards twenty or thirty feet. And it would have been painted in glowing colours, faint evidences of which remain in the folds of Jesse's voluminous gown.

We have visited a small sample of the Christian heritage of Wales. It has made us reflect, as we see understanding of and sympathy for religion decline apparently inexorably. What will become of such treasures and the ancient edifices that have preserved them for centuries? What will they mean to our grandchildren?

*PN Review* 211, Volume 39 Number 5,
May – June 2013.

# THE COUNTIES OF WALES AND *UNDER MILK WOOD*
*March 2013*

The recent release of data from the 2011 census reveals trends in Wales following those in England, though at some distance. The population has grown from 2.9 to 3.06 million in the decade since 2001, immigration accounting for 90 per cent of the increase, and the proportion of 'white' people has dropped from 98 to 96 per cent. Seventy-five per cent of the present population were born in Wales; of the remainder, twenty per cent were born in England and five per cent were born outside the United Kingdom (compared with three per cent in 2001). One set of data makes grim reading: a quarter of Welsh residents suffer from 'life-limiting' illnesses; the counties/county boroughs (or unitary authorities, as they are formally termed) of Blaenau Gwent, Merthyr Tydfil and Neath-Port Talbot, together a substantial part of the old industrial heart of south Wales, have the highest proportion of chronically sick in England and Wales. With the social needs come economic imperatives (for instance, there are more carers in Wales than in any English region), which continue to be largely ignored by a UK government with its mind on other matters.

While we digest what these sad statistics mean in terms of human pain and the depression of expectation and opportunity, it may be instructive to consider how we have arrived at the present administrative system, with unitary authorities bearing names, such as Blaenau Gwent, which are unlikely to mean much beyond Offa's Dyke, and even here mean little outside their immediate boundaries. The Law of Wales Act of 1535 established the traditional thirteen Welsh counties. Seven of these – Anglesey, Caernarfonshire, Cardiganshire, Carmarthenshire, Glamorgan, Merionethshire, Flintshire and Pembrokeshire – had existed since the thirteenth century or earlier. The remaining six – Denbighshire, Montgomeryshire, Radnorshire, Breconshire and Monmouthshire – were newly created out of the Marcher lordships. This was the pattern I grew up with, and many of the older generation, in England as in Wales I suspect, still have it imprinted on their memories. In 1974, reorganisation reduced the thirteen to eight administrative counties: Clwyd and Gwynedd in the north, Dyfed in the west, Powys a huge (in Welsh terms) tract of the east including much of the border, and Gwent, largely old Monmouthshire, in the south-east, while the populous county of Glamorgan was divided into three – Mid-, South and West Glamorgan. There was a little bickering over the loss of ancient names, notably in what had been Pembrokeshire, and the relative remoteness of new centres of administration, but the system soon settled down and functioned satisfactorily. In the main, the enlarged counties were big enough to deal with economic and social issues on their own patch and, typically, had little to do with their neighbours, whom they regarded as rivals, though for what no one could have said, rather than partners.

A consultative document issued by the Audit Commission in May 1994 prepared the way for another reorganisation fragmenting the eight county councils into twenty-two unitary authorities. This product of John Major's 1992-97 Tory administration was intended to offer 'opportunities to achieve better services at lower cost' and, in pre-Assembly days, was brought in under the vice-regency of John Redwood (as Secretary of State for Wales) and his assistant at the Welsh Office, the egregious bully Rod Richards, both pathologically incapable of listening to advice or heeding any opinion differing from their own. Before he left his post in 1995,

Redwood had become a laughing stock for wagging his head and inaccurately mouthing 'Hen wlad fy nhadau' goldfish-like at a televised occasion, which was revenge of a sort. The consultative document contained the helpful suggestion that the new authorities should 'identify needs for working with... neighbouring councils' and make 'joint arrangements'. Anyone with a modicum of experience of local authorities in Wales, or anywhere, would have been able to tell the Audit Commission, and the politicians pushing the plan, that this would not happen. The unitary authorities would determinedly sink or swim on their own, and the fact that, for instance, the education authority in Birmingham is as big as schools provision for the whole of Wales illustrates the absurdity of it all.

The worst aspects of this dreadful idea were compounded by the way the counties were carved up, which created virtually sealed pockets of deprivation in the old industrial valleys of south Wales, such as Rhondda-Cynon-Taff, and those already mentioned, Blaenau Gwent and Merthyr Tydfil. That is not all; since their creation, the unitary authorities of Anglesey, Denbighshire and Pembrokeshire have been declared 'failing' in one or more aspects of their provision. And, predictably, while in these austerity-impoverished zones the pay of council workers has been frozen for up to three years, directors of services have been given huge salary increases in order to match those paid in other authorities. The reorganisation was implemented on 1st April 1996; never was a date for change more aptly chosen. The folly of the whole undertaking, like Rhodri Morgan's 'bonfire of the quangos' (*PN Review* 170), which did away with an effective Welsh Development Agency for the sake of a smart-sounding phrase, is at last being acknowledged by Assembly members, who are desperately searching for some way to mend a broken system (of which further evidences are published weekly) short of another wholesale reorganisation.

The largest stir attending release of the census data concerned the current state of the Welsh language. In 2011, nineteen per cent of people in Wales said they spoke Welsh, compared with 20.5 per cent in 2001. The Welsh Language Commissioner, Meri Huws, and Cymdeithas yr Iaith Gymraeg, the Welsh Language Society, have declared the decrease a sign of crisis imminent if not already with us, especially as the decline is steeper in parts long considered the precious heartlands of the language, such as Carmarthenshire (from 50.3 per cent of the population Welsh-speaking in 2001 to 43.9 per cent in 2011), and Ceredigion (from 52 per cent to 47.3 per cent). This is largely a consequence of that influx of (mostly older) English speakers mentioned above, in flight from the noise and stress of life in the towns and cities of England and, having sold their expensive urban homes, with money enough and to spare for rural properties up quiet country lanes. The value of the heartlands as constant regenerators of the Welsh language cannot be overestimated, but whether the political will exists to curb in-migration in the face of European directives, accusations of racism and the like must be doubted.

A slight increase in the numbers of Welsh speakers in Cardiff and Monmouthshire, viewed in isolation, is good news, but does nothing to mitigate falls elsewhere. If there is a faint gleam of hope, it is in evidence of the effects of Welsh-medium education and, to a far lesser extent, compulsory Welsh lessons in primary and secondary schools. Analysis by age group reveals that the highest proportion of Welsh speakers (forty per cent) is among 10-14-year-olds; thirty per cent of all Welsh speakers are sixteen or under. Another straw to grasp at: two thirds of the population consider themselves Welsh, which would seem to imply concern for the fate of the language. The strongest sense of Welsh identity exists in the old industrial valleys of the south, where the great majority of people were born in Wales, and where parental pressure for Welsh-medium education continues to grow.

Andrew Sinclair has Scottish ancestry, as he is proud to tell you, but an enduring affection for Wales that began in his admiration for the work of Dylan Thomas. I first learned about him when I read his biography *Dylan Thomas – Poet of his People*, which was published in 1975. A richly illustrated book, it sought to place the poet securely in a Welsh context – an approach rarely adopted by writers outside our borders – and revealed an unexpected familiarity with Thomas's Welsh acquaintance, such as Gwyn and Glyn Jones and John Ackerman, whom I knew well, as well as his close friend Vernon Watkins, whom I never met. Sinclair was already then a writer of some distinction. He was twenty-two when his first novel, *The Breaking of Bumbo*, appeared in 1959 and in the next decade he published five more novels and three substantial non-fiction books, including the Somerset Maugham Prize winner, *The Better Half: The Emancipation of the American Woman*. In the same period he had been a Harkness fellow at Harvard, completed a doctorate at Cambridge and become a founding fellow at Churchill College, taught history at University College London – and become managing director of Lorrimer Publishing Ltd, specialising in books about the cinema, and Timon Films.

He has continued to be a prolific writer of fiction and non-fiction, but it was the connection with cinema and film-making that brought him recently to Chapter Arts Centre in Cardiff and, after earlier correspondence arising from his reading of *PN Review*, gave me the opportunity to meet him. In the early 1960s he had begun writing plays for television and film scripts; at the request of Dylan Thomas's literary executors, in 1967 he made a stage adaptation of *Adventures in the Skin*

*Trade*. At Chapter he told us how he had been lucratively employed by Hollywood as a 'script doctor' and had thus accumulated the means to purchase the film rights of *Under Milk Wood*. Sinclair wrote the screenplay and directed the film. His friendship with Peter O'Toole (who would play Captain Cat) facilitated contact with Richard Burton, 'First Voice' in the original radio production, who was at once anxious to be involved. Elizabeth Taylor came with Burton and, at a time when they could name their price for a film appearance, she agreed to play Rosie Probert for ten thousand pounds. With the exception of her largely horizontal part (in which, despite the director's best efforts, she looks more like Cleopatra than Captain Cat's long-dead whore) shooting was on location at Fishguard, Pembrokeshire. The cast included local people, especially schoolchildren, and a crowd of the best Welsh actors of the period, and at its head were three of the world's most famous film performers. No wonder it attracted serious attention and favourable reviews. Seeing it at Chapter forty years on we understand why. It is a delicious experience, Thomas's words embellished by the apt beauty of place and a camera that moves seamlessly from character to character, scene to scene. Andrew Sinclair brought the film back here for a special reason: he is giving all media rights to Wales to be administered by a trust (Milkwood Trust) that will award funds to cultural projects, while the entire archive of materials associated with the making and showing of the film will go to the National Library of Wales. It is a wholly unexpected and wonderfully generous gift, ahead of the celebration of the centenary of Dylan Thomas's birth in 2014.

*PN Review* 210, Volume 39 Number 4, March – April 2013.

# CERI RICHARDS

*September 2012*


In 1951, Ceri Richards was one of the sixty 'distinguished artists' invited by the Arts Council to contribute to an exhibition for the Festival of Britain, an event affectionately remembered at its fiftieth anniversary last year (I doubt it will be possible to say the same about the excruciating Millennium Dome). As his subject Richards chose Trafalgar Square, a great hub loaded with symbolism that he knew very well, because by that time London had been his home for twenty-five years. He filled a book with sketches and produced not one, but a series of large oil paintings in which he isolated and reassembled the familiar features of the square. The paintings are vibrant with colour and movement, scintillant with light. They are modernist paintings.

How distinguished an artist was he? Richards won a scholarship to the Royal College of Art, where his exceptional ability in drawing from the figure was recognised by Henry Moore, who, in the early 1920s, had just begun teaching there. In due course, he taught at Chelsea College, the Slade and, turning full circle, at the Royal College. He became a Trustee of the Tate Gallery in 1959. The catalogue of a retrospective exhibition at London's Whitechapel Gallery in 1960 praised his 'lyrical invention' and a display of technique 'that has no counterpart in England'. In 1961 he became an honorary fellow of the Royal College. His reputation confirmed, he represented Britain at the Venice Biennale in 1962, where he won the Giulio Einaudi Painting Prize.

As so often, the catalogue note says 'England' when 'Britain' is intended, for Richards was not English. He was born in 1903 and brought up in Dunvant, a former mining village to the west of Swansea, on the edge of the upland interior of the Gower peninsula. His parents were Welsh-speaking and the family were faithful members of a Welsh Congregational chapel. Until her marriage, his mother had been a teacher, and his father, a rollerman in a tin-plate works, was a poet in Welsh and English, an eisteddfodwr (one who regularly attends and competes in eisteddfodau) and a notable musician in the locality. Their three children learned to play the piano, Ceri proving a particularly apt pupil. He attended a local intermediate (grammar) school and when he left became an apprentice electrician. His artistic talent had revealed itself early and, having discovered Swansea School of Arts and Crafts, he joined its evening drawing classes. The failure of the firm to which he was apprenticed provided the unexpected opportunity to change the direction of his life towards a career that now held overwhelming appeal. In 1921, with parental support, he enrolled as a full-time art student at Swansea. From there, in 1924, he won a scholarship to the Royal College, where his work caught the eye of Henry Moore.

While still at Swansea, Richards attended a summer school at Gregynog, the great house near Newtown, Powys, which was the home of the Davies sisters, Margaret and Gwendoline. Their ample fortune had come down from their grandfather, David Davies, the coal owner, who had the vision, financial resources and political will to create Barry Docks for the export of coal mined in his Rhondda pits. With their wealth the sisters indulged their interests in art, music, and the making of fine books. Their magnificent collection of impressionist and post-impressionist paintings, now at the National Museum in Cardiff, once graced the walls of Gregynog, as I saw when I visited with an art class from Aberystwyth in 1955, while Margaret Davies was still in residence. To wander the music room, where great works by Monet, Renoir, Cézanne and van Gogh hung, as it were, casually, left us open-mouthed. In 1955 we were at least familiar with reproductions of the work of these artists. In 1923 their impact on Ceri Richards was profound. 'I was staggered by the sight,' he wrote much later, recalling the experience, '[and] fascinated most of all by Monet. Imagine the effect on someone who'd dreamed of great painting but had seen none at all.' He returned to college confirmed in his ambition and with a fresh sense of direction.

The artist's life, career and achievement are fully discussed by the art critic Mel Gooding in *Ceri Richards* (Cameron & Hollis, 2002), a beautifully illustrated and fascinating book, the source of much of the information above. Two aspects of Richards's work are of special interest because of the way they blur the boundaries between the arts. Baudelaire's 'Correspondances' was, for him, more than usually freighted with meaning –

*Comme de longs échos qui de loin se confondent*
*Dans une ténébreuse et profonde unité,*
*Vaste comme la nuit et comme la clarté,*
*Les parfums, les couleurs et les sons se repondent.*

Richards was an accomplished musician: he played the piano daily and the instrument features frequently in his work, sometimes standing on its own with a rush chair before it – a domestic interior – but more often with a female pianist seated on the same chair, her hands on the keys. He celebrated Beethoven, his hero, in a substantial number of paintings and prints, often invoking the composer's suffering and deafness. Debussy is another powerful inspiration. He turned frequently to compositions from the first book of Préludes, such as *'Ce qu'a vu le vent d'Ouest'* and, especially, *'La Cathédrale engloutie'*, responding to the music in a variety of media from large paintings to constructions, collages and small-scale abstract sketches on paper.

As Richards was open in his artistic expression to the sounds of music, so, too, was he receptive to the influence of poetry. He met Dylan Thomas in October 1953, shortly before the poet left on the fateful last trip to the United States, when a mutual friend, the artist Alfred Janes, another of the extraordinarily talented group that emerged from Swansea in the 1930s, proposed a visit to the boathouse at Laugharne. At the time, Richards was convalescing following an operation at a rented cottage in Pennard, on the Gower coast, near the home of Vernon Watkins, who was another friend of long standing. That he and Thomas had not met previously in London, at gatherings literary or artistic, or of the Welsh, is surprising, but Richards had read Thomas's poetry with great interest and his admiration had increased with the publication of the *Collected Poems*, the first response to which was a profound symbolic painting, *'Afal du bro Gŵyr'* (Black Apple of Gower). It was a happy encounter: poet and artist were soon discussing ways in which they could work together. It was not to be, but for more than a decade after the poet's death Richards produced a stream of visual interpretations of Thomas's poetic imagery, among the most potent of which are those exploring 'The force that through the green fuse drives the flower', culminating in 1965 with a series of 'Twelve Lithographs for Six Poems by Dylan Thomas's, described by Mel Gooding as 'his greatest work in a graphic medium'.

Ceri Richards died in London in 1971. In the summer of 1973 I was one of the crowd who attended the opening of a memorial exhibition of his work at the National Museum in Cardiff. The catalogue of the exhibition is prefaced by a lovely essay, the work of John Ormond, describing Richards's trajectory through life as an artist with the insight and sensibility of a personal friend who was also a poet, gifted with a finely tuned visual aesthetic, and no small measure of skill with a pencil. They had a lot in common, for John Ormond Thomas, his full name, was, like Richards, born and brought up in Dunvant (though twenty years later), where his father was a shoemaker. His ambition to study at an art college was opposed by his parents and he went instead to Swansea University where he read English and philosophy, stealing away when he could to attend drawing classes at the art school. In 1946, almost as soon as he left university, Tom Hopkinson, persuaded by the poems that accompanied his application, hired Ormond as a *Picture Post* journalist. In three years with the magazine, on the road with a cameraman, he learned to appreciate the power of the photograph to deliver ideas with an emotional charge, and honed his writing skills contriving text to complement images. This training proved of inestimable value when, in 1955, he joined the BBC in Cardiff, initially as a 'television news assistant'. Two years later he was put in charge of a new documentary film unit and from there progressed to the features department as a filmmaker, where in more than eighty films, several devoted to Welsh poets and artists, including Ceri Richards, he created poetry with the camera lens.

A selection of Ormond's poems appeared as early as 1943, in company with James Kirkup and John Bayliss, in *Indications*, published in London by Grey Walls Press, and he shared *Penguin Modern Poets 27* with Emyr Humphreys and John Tripp, but produced only two more books, *Requiem and Celebration* (Christopher Davies, 1969) and *Definition of a Waterfall* (OUP, 1973). His *Selected Poems* appeared from Seren in 1987. If we believe his own words (in his Artists in Wales essay, 1973) this self-restraint was at least partly due to Vernon Watkins, then in the RAF, who said 'I ought not to publish any further collection until I was thirty ... [and] by the time I was thirty I was completely dissatisfied with what I had written.' He went on to say that subsequently he wrote less and less and destroyed 'nearly all of it'. It depends what is meant by 'nearly'. A few days ago, the opening of a Ceri Richards exhibition at the Martin Tinney Gallery in Cardiff brought a chance encounter with Rian Evans, the *Guardian* music critic, who is John Ormond's daughter. She told us that Seren is to publish her father's collected poems in 2013, coinciding with the ninetieth anniversary of his birth. She has been trying to ensure that there are no omissions by mischance, gathering poems from manuscript and a variety of sources that have, in the main, not previously been published in book form. Four appeared in *Dragon's Hoard*, an anthology for schools I co-edited in 1976, which had originally been commissioned by Tom Hopkinson, after his *Picture Post* days, when he was literary editor of the *News Chronicle* – little poems to serve as captions accompanying the paper's 'Saturday Picture'. They are a delight for any age; rereading them now gives me a pleasure only marginally less than that I received those Christmases when a card arrived, handmade, with picture and verse, signed 'J.O.'.

It was a huge loss when he died in 1990. Among those who contributed to *Poetry Wales* in the 1960s and 1970s, along with Roland Mathias, John Ormond was the poet whose work I valued most. From my present perspective I see no reason to change my views.

*PN Review* 207, Volume 39 Number 1, September – October 2012.

# GILFACH GOCH AND CHILDHOOD
*March 2012*

Last August, while the grandchildren from Greenwich were with us, a rare spell of dry weather gave the opportunity to visit Gilfach Goch. I volunteered to take them and their Caerleon cousins up the mountain to the highest point, actually a 'trig point' on a beautifully symmetrical hill rising above the moor at the top end of the valley – 416 metres. I wanted them to view Gilfach as it is and handicapped myself for the stiffish climb with the weight of a couple of books containing photographs of the way it was when I was a boy and three working collieries filled the valley floor. The coal industry has gone, the close community it engendered has gone; neither will ever return. My sense of personal history, of rootedness, has become more demanding as I grow older, and with it my guilt and frustration that I did not ask my parents all the questions about their parents and their younger days that leave me now searching hopelessly for answers. I want our grandchildren to have the chance to avoid my mistake. I feel very strongly that, whatever route they take through life, they should know at least where the Welsh side of their ancestry comes from. That is why in recent weeks I have been trying to recall what it was like when I was young.

I was three when I followed children on their way to school. They drew me from our front garden, past the corner and the familiar shops, over the First World War bailey bridge with its many criss-crossing bars, where railway engines hauling coal wagons ran underneath, gushing clouds of white smoky vapour through rusted gaps at the foot of the corrugated sheets that stopped you falling onto the track, up the hill called Coronation Road and another short steeper pitch to the schools, infants' and girls' one side of an unsurfaced road, boys' the other. I came home at dinnertime, with the other children, saying, 'I'm not going there again. They make you lie down like a lot of bloody cows'. I can see now the long, low tables at which the youngest children sat in little tub armchairs, and the pillows that, twice daily, were placed on the tables for us to lay our heads on, close our eyes and pretend to sleep.

My mother and sisters repeated this story from time to time, but no one ever mentioned any concern about my disappearance early one day when I was three. Perhaps they guessed what had happened. Perhaps, when they enquired, neighbours said, 'I saw him going off to school with the other boys.' Children were not taken to school in those days; they went unaccompanied. Communication between school and parents was very rare. If there had been some alarm in the infants' classroom at the unexpected arrival of a new pupil, which seems doubtful, it would not have been easy for teachers to get in touch with my mother, for we had no telephone, even if the school did, and that is unlikely. My adventure seems to have been received coolly on all sides. At home, what was remembered was my determination, with an epithet learned from my cousin Bloom, not to go back to school, though of course I did when I was four.

That would have been in 1939. I began properly to learn about things outside home and near neighbours and shops as the war began. I was across the road in the house of Mr and Mrs Vaughan and their five children, all of them boys, when the announcement of the declaration of war came on the wireless. I know now it was eleven o'clock on Sunday morning, 3rd September. For those broadcast minutes everyone was quiet, and we listened. What it meant I had no idea, but something about the occasion, I suppose the reaction of others, imprinted it on my memory. The two older Vaughan boys, Douglas and Glyn, soon joined the forces, Billy worked in the pit, and the youngest, George and Trevor, already in the boys' school, were my friends. My wider explorations of Gilfach Goch and the mountains that rose about it were made in their company.

About the time I was born, in 1934, south Wales was still in the grip of depression with thousands unemployed. Because he was the lone electrician at the drift mine known locally as the Squint, and vital to its maintenance, my father was not among the workless. By the time I became aware of things beyond our doors, the threat of war had brought increased demand for coal and there was work for every able-bodied man, and soon even for some women who, like my sister Joan, travelled daily by train to a munitions factory in Bridgend. The Gilfach of my boyhood was busy and noisy. You cannot live close to a pit, as most of us did, without being aware of it. After hooters calling the men to work, in early morning darkness came the crunch of steel-shod boots on the road, followed soon after by the percussion of steam engines, the creaking and clatter of moving trucks and drams, the grating roar of tipped slag and countless unaccountable thuds and clanks that continued all through the day and, during the winter, deep into darkness once more. So all-pervading was the noise that we did not notice it. A sudden silence would have been startling.

Across the road, at the bottom of the Vaughans' garden, not fifty yards from our front door, was an unfenced drop of about fifteen feet to the railway lines that carried the long, long trains of black wagons empty up the valley and heaped with coal down. On the far side of the double track was the incline along which 'journeys' of drams were hauled loaded with coal from the pit, and the screens, a structure of corrugated sheets within which a moving belt carried the contents of dramload after dramload. There, surface workers separated the coal, large and small, from slag, which was tipped on the further side of the incline, where it crashed and tumbled down into the black river, the Ogwr Fach. Our house was so close to the colliery that, if he were working on the surface, my father would come home for his snack at eleven o'clock in the morning. The kettle was always singing on the hob to make his black tea, and bread and cheese were ready, just in case. I see him still, hanging up the flat cap he always wore to work and sitting at the table in his pit-clothes, his face smirched with coal dust.

Often in the hazy march between waking and sleeping, I go back to the house. I open the front gate and close it behind, listening for that peculiar clink of the latch, and walk up the curving path through the porch to the big front door with its gleaming brass knocker, which Tim, our black and white tomcat, would reach up to and knock as firmly as any human, and I am home. Or I hover wraith-like by the walls, gazing in at windows. My mother is sitting in the kitchen corner, her poor wasted legs close to the fire, my father, his white hair slicked back from the bath, in an armchair in the back room, feet up, newspaper spread across his chest, eyes closed; while my sister Barbara dusts the mirrored sideboard in the front room with swift, vigorous rubs, setting the ornate drawer handles rattling.

Our house stood on its own, atop a little hill of front lawn, separated from its neighbours by narrow gullies. The gate with its distinctive clink was not as tall and barbarously spiked as others along our street, almost all of which hung at an angle from their hinges and ground grimly on the stone threshold as you struggled them open. The bars of our gate were slim and arched at the top and it swung easily between tall pillars of red brick with solid red pyramidal finials. From the gate, a red brick wall ran the width of the property, gradually diminishing in height to another, shorter pillar similarly capped, so that the wall and the low fence, its bars, arched like the gate, set into it, were horizontal against the gradient of the road beyond.

Most of the village shops were close by – a grand Co-op, which had departments for hardware and footwear, general groceries and meat, and on the other side of the road, men's and women's clothes (made to measure if required), and a dispensing chemist. Nearer, within fifty yards, were the post office, Pegler's grocery, and Joe Bacchetta's Italian corner shop. Opposite Joe's was Mrs Griffiths the draper, whose shop was called 'Bon Marché', and then Tambini's fish and chip shop, and Spearing's, a gloomy little delicatessen, where, most Wednesdays, we bought Palethorpe's pork pies to have warmed for dinner. A little further up the road, next door to my Aunty Sarah's, was a greengrocer, a little further again, Jefferies the newsagent's and, at the end of the terrace, Johnny Rabaiotti's Italian corner shop. Beyond that, a broad and steep dirt track led down to 'the Globe', Dai Griffiths's fleapit cinema, which had threepenny benches at the front underneath the screen.

Before I started school, this section of High Street was the limit of my known world. It was only when I climbed the mountain behind our house with George and Trevor that I began to comprehend the valley. The road that passed our house climbed on up to its top, where, balked by the mountain, it swung around a large colliery, the Trane, and its attendant slag heaps, crossed the river and passed in front of Gilfach's third working pit, the Britannic, and an alpine range of tips, before it started down the other side. At length, turning left down Coronation Road and along the planed top of yet another, older tip, which smoked and stank sulphurously in wet weather, it crossed the bailey bridge and closed the loop at the T-junction with its cluster of shops fifty or so yards above our house. At the foot of the smouldering tip the river ran through a circular brick-built culvert, ochre and orange and green with slime at the water's edge. In the summer, when the stream was low, I watched older boys with longer legs traverse this dank tube by zigzag leaping from side to side. Once started it was impossible to stop before a final longer jump propelled a distant jagged figure, silhouetted momentarily in the circle of daylight, out of sight, onto the slag-strewn bank the other end. I tried it once myself before I left the elementary school, my feet landing nearer and nearer the water as I progressed until I slipped and fell in and slid helplessly into the pool gouged at the exit.

In the second phase of my childhood explorations I learned that, down the hill from our house, the road stretched out beyond the Gilfach Hotel, the pub kept by Aunty Bernice and Uncle Reg, past a redbrick urinal on the left and the railway station on the right. There were no passenger trains, apart from rare summer 'specials' to Porthcawl and, during the war years, the daily service for Bridgend ordnance factory workers. A broad path of ginger-stained boards crossed the lines and beyond the fence on the other side was the Squint office. A steep, rubble-covered path led from the office to the colliery, alongside the river at the bottom of the valley. The uncontrolled railway crossing was a route to work for miners and a convenient all-purpose shortcut that I often used.

For a long time there was little development beyond the station, because the pits and the homes of mine workers were at the top of the valley, but by the early 1920s many more houses had been built near its mouth. This part of Gilfach was known as Garden City, or 'the City'. Its children went to a different school and belonged to a different tribe. The intense rivalry between us reached a climax one Saturday in the summer of 1944, when battle lines were drawn up on the mountain above our house, and Top kids and City kids hurled stones at one another. I watched charge and counter-charge from the patch of grass at the back of the house where I lay on a deck chair with my left leg in a plaster cast, having fallen from a tree and torn an ankle ligament a few days earlier. Here and there, stones thrown in skirmishes on the edge of the battlefield fell close to houses and in the road. Clearly something had to be done. The following Monday every boy in the upper classes of the valley's three elementary schools was caned, including a few who, with justification, pleaded innocence.

It should not have been a surprise that boys from different parts of the valley formed gangs and that gangs occasionally made alliances that transformed random bickering into large-scale fights. We in George Vaughan's gang regularly engaged in what he called 'commando training', running, leaping brooks, clambering up quarries and spending hours throwing stones at targets. It was the war, of course, the real war, that inspired and possessed us. The war was in every wireless news bulletin, every daily paper. The school windows were crisscrossed with tape to hold the arrowing shards that would shred us if a bomb fell nearby. Sirens sounded air raid warnings and all-clears. In the early years we carried gas masks. Lights were dimmed; the blackout was policed. My father had become a special constable in August 1938, as the discharge certificate dated 24 July 1942, which he had carefully preserved, later told me. How often he went on duty, or whether he did so at all, I cannot say. The first I knew of his participation in the war effort was when, several years after the end of hostilities, a George VI medal with a smart red, black and white striped ribbon arrived through the post. It was awarded 'for faithful service in the Special Constabulary'. My father's smile was not so much of satisfaction at this tardy recognition, as of puzzlement, more so when he saw inscribed on the rim 'Sergeant T.S. Adams'. No one had told him he was a sergeant.

The war had carried off the young husband of my beautiful

sister, Barbara, killed on HMS *Repulse* in December 1941. As I write on this Remembrance Sunday, I look back and see how much it changed her life, and all our lives, as were the lives of hundreds of thousands of families changed; yes, changed utterly. When my father received his medal we all laughed with him. Time enough had passed for us to see the funny side of that reminder of the war.

*PN Review* 204, Volume 38 Number 4,
March – April 2012.

# WELSH AND JRR TOLKIEN

*November 2011*

Recently (in *PN Review* 200), I quoted from a letter David Jones wrote to *The Times* in June 1958 concerning the Welsh language. The loss of Welsh, he said, would impoverish England, 'for the survival of something which has an unbroken tradition in this island since the sixth century, and which embodies deposits far older still, cannot be regarded as a matter of indifference by any person claiming to care for the things of this island. It is by no means a matter for the Welsh only, but concerns all, because the complex and involved heritage of Britain is a shared inheritance which can, in very devious ways, enrich us all'. Worthy of repetition as it is, I would not so soon have brought it up again if I had not come across a very similar statement from an unexpected source: 'Welsh is of this soil, this island, the senior language of the men of Britain; and Welsh is beautiful...It is the native language to which in unexplored desire we should still go home.' These are the words not of a Welshman, nor of someone, like David Jones, consciously half-Welsh though born a Londoner. They were spoken at a public lecture in Oxford in 1925 by one who considered himself not simply English, but Mercian (which I have now learned means 'of the March'), or better still, Hwiccian, that is, belonging to a kingdom corresponding roughly to modern Worcestershire, Gloucestershire and part of Warwickshire, which was annexed by Mercia in the eighth century.

That, perhaps, gives the game away. They are the words of J.R.R. Tolkien, whose *Lord of the Rings* I have not read, but whom I felt I knew well as co-editor (with E.V. Gordon) of the

OUP *Sir Gawain and the Green Knight*, first published in the same year as that Oxford lecture. My heavily annotated copy is a sixth edition, 1952. Faced with it as a set book in the honours course at Aberystwyth, I cannot pretend I was initially overjoyed, but I soon learned to savour it and am now immensely pleased and grateful that I once read, from beginning to end, a magical poem in its original fourteenth-century Lancashire English.

Tolkien's devotion to 'beautiful' Welsh, the confession of a philologist, was not idly expressed. As professor at Leeds and, later, Oxford, he introduced a mediaeval Welsh option into the Anglo-Saxon syllabus. He found an academic soulmate in Gwyn Jones, professor at Aberystwyth. They shared a professional interest in Old and Middle English and were both, also, writers of short stories and novels. He introduced Gwyn as a friend at a meeting of the Inklings, where, according to W.H. Lewis, brother of C.S., 'he turned out to be capital value; he read a Welsh tale of his own writing, a bawdy humorous thing told in a rich polished style which impressed me more than any new work I have come across for a long time'. Ah, I can just hear the smile in Gwyn's voice. The friendship led to the publication of Tolkien's long poem 'The Lay of Aotrou and Itroun', a tale of mediaeval Brittany, in Gwyn's magazine *The Welsh Review* in December 1945.

I owe much of the above to Carl Phelpstead's absorbing *Tolkien and Wales: Language, Literature and Identity* (University of Wales Press, 2011). It tells us a great deal about Tolkien as a philologist, and as a writer, and suggests how the fantastical inspirations of the latter grew out of the former. One of the prime motives for his fictions was the desire, or need, to create a race of beings who would speak the languages he invented. The process of invention was not merely lexical, but concerned the fundamentals of language structure, such as syntax and the formation of the plural. It was essential, furthermore, that the language had its own linguistic history and the rich patina of legends that living languages possess, and that manufactured (in Tolkien's terms 'dead') systems, like Esperanto, do not. We learn (via Phelpstead) from Tolkien's letters that the Elvish language Sindarin, in *The Lord of the Rings*, was 'constructed deliberately to resemble Welsh phonologically'. But that was not enough. It also has 'a relation to High-elven [Quenya] similar to that existing between British (properly so called, i.e. the Celtic languages spoken in this island at the time of the Roman invasion) and Latin'.

Few of us appreciate the value of learning another language to facilitate communication abroad, far less as the key to the door of another culture. That 'everyone' speaks English is an excuse for not bothering to learn another language. To Tolkien, however, language acquisition was an aesthetic experience, and he profoundly disagreed with those who would promote English as a world language. That was, he wrote in 1925, 'the most idiotic and suicidal [notion] that a language could entertain. Literature shrivels in a universal language, and an uprooted language rots before it dies'. He asked us 'to realise the magnitude of the loss to humanity that the world-dominance of any one language now spoken would entail: no language has ever possessed but a small fraction of the varied excellences of human speech, and each language presents a different vision of life'. If we this side of the March remember that Welsh is beautiful and do all in our power to treasure and preserve it, will the English on their side do so too?

Tolkien thought the greatest of all surviving works in Old English, the epic poem *Beowulf*, more typically Celtic than most things he had met written in a Celtic language. This took me back to Gwyn Jones's teaching of *Beowulf*. In our two-hour-long sessions, severe concentration on the text was leavened with anecdotes concerning matters Scandinavian or Icelandic. Along one of these byways I first heard that well-preserved bodies of Iron Age people turned up in peat bogs in Denmark. In the early 1970s I read P.V. Glob's *The Bog People* (Faber, 1969) where I learned that, along with men and women, artefacts were sacrificially deposited, most notably the Gundestrup Cauldron, a great silver bowl found by peat-cutters in the Raeve Bog, Himmerland, in 1891. It had been separated into sections before deposition, but re-formed is 42 centimetres high, has a diameter of 69 centimetres at the top and weighs almost nine kilograms. Experts still dispute where and by whom it was made, but it is broadly agreed that its repoussé decoration, inside and out, is characteristically Celtic.

In an exquisitely illustrated scene a line of warriors, on foot, is approaching a cauldron, over which one is suspended head-first by a far larger figure. He is being sacrificed: a dog, signifying death, precedes those waiting their turn. Above the foot soldiers, a line of cavalry moves briskly away. While illustrations of the cauldron and Glob's explanation of them were still fresh in my mind, I happened upon Robert Graves's Penguin *Greek Myths*, where, in the introduction, I read, 'If some myths are baffling at first sight, this is often because the mythographer has accidentally or deliberately misinterpreted a sacred picture or dramatic rite'. I was reminded of the strange tale that begins the second branch of *The Mabinogion*. Matholwch, King of Ireland, visits Bendigeidfran, King of the Island of the Mighty, to receive the host's sister, Branwen, as wife. Efnysien, resentful brother of Bendigeidfran and Branwen, maims Matholwch's horses, and when Bendigeidfran hears of this insult, he gives his guest not only a fresh horse for each one maimed but also a magic cauldron that has the power to return to life men killed in battle, in Welsh called *pairdadeni*, 'cauldron of rebirth'. I was at once convinced that the original

Welsh storyteller had seen the Gundestrup Cauldron, and in his narrative 'misinterpreted' the image described above so that its cauldron represents not sacrificial death but resurrection.

This minor revelation occurred almost forty years ago. I was so enthused that I wrote to A.O.H. Jarman, Professor of Welsh in Cardiff and far-famed Arthurian scholar, and laid the theory before him. With courteous academic coolness he dismissed my brainwave, and I put it aside. It is a little gratifying to find a note in Sioned Davies's excellent translation of *The Mabinogion* (Oxford, 2007) informing readers that 'Parallels have been drawn between this Cauldron of Rebirth and a scene portrayed on the Gundestrup Cauldron'. Without claiming proprietorial rights over those of Denmark, I think we ought to have a copy of that wonderful object in the National Museum at Cardiff.

As I write, the aftermath of the riots in England fills the media. Some commentators have reminded us that summer is the favoured time for rioting; others mentioned the possibility of a role for soldiers in keeping the peace and as quickly dismissed the idea. Untypically, the Tonypandy Riots occurred in November 1910. The unrest had begun in September that year when coal owners locked out the work force, with whom they were in dispute over miners' demands for a pay increase to take account of working in geologically difficult conditions, where much of their labour was unproductive, and therefore unpaid. At the height of the conflict on the streets soldiers were called in, and stayed. The strike continued until October 1911, when imminent starvation forced the men back to work. Everyone knows about the Tonypandy Riots, the last time, I thought, soldiers were deployed in a situation of that kind. I was wrong.

A hundred years ago to the day, 19 August 1911, during one of the hottest summers on record (124 degrees Fahrenheit was recorded in Cardiff in July), railway workers rioted in

Llanelli. A national strike over pay had been called on 17 August and the strikers in Llanelli, their numbers swelled by sympathetic tinplate workers and miners, were intent on stopping rail traffic through the town. The press had vilified the strikers, who were among the poorest paid of British workers, and spread rumours that foreign agents were fomenting trouble. At the instruction of Home Secretary Winston Churchill, soldiers of the Royal Worcestershire Regiment were already in place, and when pickets stopped a train their commanding officer ordered a magistrate to read the Riot Act. This did not disperse the crowd and after a minute's warning the soldiers opened fire. Two bystanders, John John and Leonard Worsell, were killed and two others seriously wounded. This was the last time that British soldiers on mainland Britain fired on civilians. The event was commemorated in July on BBC TV's *The One Show* and within the last week by media in Wales and socialist organisations here and elsewhere. But it has been expunged from the history of the Royal Worcestershire Regiment, and London newspapers and broadcasters, if they ever knew, prefer to ignore it. So far as I am aware, there has been no word from David Starkey – surely an opportunity missed.

*PN Review* 202, Volume 38 Number 2,
November – December 2011.

# POETRY AND EDUCATION
*May 2011*

Our grandchildren submit with reasonably good grace to regular questioning about their schoolwork, although their answers are usually vague. Impressions left by most of the week's lessons seem shallow almost to the point of disappearance. Perhaps this is as it should be. I usually ask what poems they have read, or have had read aloud to them. None. Even when (very infrequently) they are asked to write a poem, they do not read poems as preparation. They are now in the first and third year respectively of comprehensive school, but the answer was the same when they were juniors. Have they perhaps forgotten the poem read or heard on Monday by the following weekend? I have to acknowledge that possibility, but I do not think it the case. And I am confident that when they say they have not looked at poems in an anthology as a class, they are neither forgetful nor fibbing. Is there no time for poetry in the contemporary curriculum, at least until an examination syllabus demands it? Is fear a factor – fear that children do not like poetry? Or are teachers afraid?

Is the experience of our grandchildren untypical, I wonder? Do other schools preserve the weekly poetry lesson, which was the norm throughout my days as pupil and teacher? At Abercerdin Boys' Elementary School in the mid-1940s, the best time of the week was Friday afternoon when Mr Williams read poems to us. They were mostly narrative poems of the sort we believe middle-class Victorian and Edwardian families read to entertain themselves around the fireside on long winter evenings, such as Southey's 'Bishop Hatto', 'After Blenheim' and

'The Inchcape Rock', Thackeray's 'Little Billee', Gibson's 'Flannan Isle', all requested week after week. In the 1990s HMI in England rediscovered 'The Highwayman' by Alfred Noyes and so passionate was their advocacy of it that you would not find a primary school in England or Wales where 'The road was a ribbon of moonlight over the purple moor' was not somewhere to be heard or seen illustrated and mounted in a class display. That was another of our favourites at Abercerdin Boys', but best of all was what I assume now to have been a greatly abridged version of Arnold's 'Sohrab and Rustum', the climax of which brought a lump to the throat:

> ... and Ruksh, the horse,
> With his head bowing to the ground, and mane
> Sweeping the dust, came near, and in mute woe
> First to the one then to the other moved
> His head, as if enquiring what their grief
> Might mean; and from his dark, compassionate eyes,
> The big warm tears rolled down, and caked the sand.

More than the death of a young hero at the ignorant hand of his father, it was the weeping horse that moved us. In that class were bareback riders of Welsh mountain ponies – rough boys. A handful of us would pass the scholarship and go to the grammar school in Tonyrefail; nearly all the rest would leave the elementary school at fourteen and follow their fathers down the pit. Whatever their destination, there was not one who thought listening to poetry beneath him, or simply alien.

It was not a rich or artfully stimulating poetic diet, but it was a great deal better than none. I cannot pretend that poetry continued to be an unalloyed pleasure for those who went to the grammar school, where increasingly it was material to be interrogated. And, curiously, whereas in the elementary school we had learned the poems we enjoyed merely by hearing them often repeated, in the grammar school learning became another chore. But we met there, gathered in anthologies, a good range of poetry, mostly Romantic and Georgian, lyrical and narrative, standard school fare at that time. The book I preferred was Methuen's *An Anthology of Modern Verse*, dedicated to 'Thomas Hardy, O.M. Greatest of the Moderns', first published in a cheap school edition in 1921. I see from the copy I appear to have purloined (it bears the Glamorganshire Education Committee stamp) it had reached its forty-first printing in 1945. A. Methuen, the editor, has this message for teachers: 'Some [of you] may think a few of the pieces unsuitable to the youthful mind, but it is a mistake to give the young only juvenile verse... Boys and girls dislike being written down to, and their taste should be fed and cultivated by the very best.' Amen to that.

Thumbing through it again, I see the Great War drifts over the anthology like a smoky pall, and some of the most affecting poems – Wilfred Owen's, Sassoon's, and the far less well-known 'To a Bull-dog' by J. C. Squire – arise directly out of the horror that had ended only three years before it was published. W. H. Davies, Walter de la Mare, Hardy and Yeats are well represented, but modernism as we know it had hardly begun to manifest itself. Eliot appears as the poet of *'La Figlia Che Piange'*. The book is of its time, and the impression it left on me reflects my age (about thirteen I should think, for I was ten when I entered the grammar school) when I first dipped into it. Although it includes a goodly number of poets whose work I have returned to again and again over the years, the one stanza that, once read, I never forgot is that which opens Francis Thompson's 'The Hound of Heaven':

I fled Him, down the nights and down the days;
I fled Him, down the arches of the years ... etc.

That seems a little peculiar now, yet Thompson's distinctive vision and incantatory manner cling like a burr to the memory. I once learned another of his verses on the Underground between Waterloo and Paddington:

It is little I repair to the matches of the Southron folk,
Though my own red roses there may blow;
It is little I repair to the matches of the Southron folk,
Though the red roses crest the caps, I know.
For the field is full of shades as I near a shadowy coast,
And a ghostly batsman plays to the bowling of a ghost,
And I look through my tears on a soundless-clapping host
As the run stealers flicker to and fro,
To and fro:
O my Hornby and my Barlow long ago!

It is the beginning of 'At Lord's', and a rarity: a poem about sport that deserves to be called a poem. Not long ago I received as a gift *Sport* (Parthian, 2007), a hefty anthology edited by Gareth Williams for the Library of Wales series. It includes a couple of dozen poems, by Dannie Abse, Harri Webb, John Arlott and Sheenagh Pugh among others, none of which is more easily recalled than the prose that occupies by far the greater part of the book – with two exceptions: 'The Ballad of Billy Rose' by Leslie Norris and, head and shoulders above that, Idris Davies's 'Send out your homing pigeons, Dai' from his wonderful sequence about the 1926 Strike *The Angry Summer*. There, strength of feeling borrowed from the political circumstances of the time substitutes for the physical intensity which is the best of sport, for athlete and spectator, just as deep melancholy for the passage of the years, the dread acceptance of mutability, informs Thompson's cricketing lines.

In his foreword to the anthology Rhodri Morgan, then First

Minister at the National Assembly, discusses the Welsh relationship with sport: 'what is special is small country psychology – a special kind of need for heroes that could reassure us of our existence as a country. We might not have the conventional signs of life, or the traditional trappings of nationhood, but boy, could we produce runners and footballers and swimmers and fighters we could all look up to...Our heroes reassured us that we were not going to disappear as a nation, that we could not be discarded into the dustbin of history.' This may be a shrewd analysis of the Welsh psyche. It is without doubt deeply disturbing, even humiliating. After seven centuries during which we have looked to England to make decisions for us, is this all we are? Is this all we are allowed to be? Some would settle for that if only we had beaten England in the recent match at the Millennium Stadium, but it is a poor state of affairs. On 3 March 2011, just three weeks' time as I write, there will be a referendum in Wales on a further stage of devolution. A 'yes' vote will extend to Wales the same primary law-making powers already enjoyed by Scotland and Northern Ireland. That this measure of parity was not an intrinsic element of the original devolution settlement is a constitutional disgrace. It has meant that perfectly sound and timely legislation can be, and invariably is, held up by Westminster for many months. In the case of the smoking ban in public places, which our Assembly was the first to declare, there was a delay of three years. Even now procrastination at Westminster is preventing the introduction of a system of 'presumed consent' with regard to organ donation, rather than opting in by carrying a donor card. Meanwhile for those awaiting transplant surgery suffering continues and lives are lost.

In this year of all-round retrenchment (except in the banks) Wales's Assembly Government has cut the Arts Council of Wales budget by four per cent, and told the Council it must trim its running costs by twelve per cent. As the bitter end of 2010 approached, ACW published its allocations of revenue funding to the organisations it will continue to support. All hope of reprieve vanished for the thirty-two notified in June 2010 that funding would stop. Among these were three theatre-in-education companies, Theatr Powys, Gwent Theatre, and Spectacle Theatre. Unlike the Hay Festival, which shrugged off the blow, the T-i-E groups will be sunk: permanent staff will be declared redundant and the valuable work they did lost. Of the seventy-one organisations that will be funded, five must soldier on with substantially reduced allocations. Hijinx Theatre, which toured its productions to small communities throughout Wales, has had its grant reduced by about a third and must struggle to carry on. As the swing door turns and some disappear into outer darkness, new bodies emerge into the light, including Sinfonia Cymru and Independent Ballet Wales, while the great majority of the retained organisations will enjoy an increase in funding. This is the hardest part of the exercise, when the losers and the lost survey the winners, but the Arts Council has done its homework in a painstaking 'Investment Review' and stands by its decisions.

Academi, the literature promotion agency, continues on the same funding as before. A busy, professional organisation, it stimulates and coordinates literary activity for writers and their audiences. The latest number of its information magazine *A 470 – What's On in Literary Wales* lists twenty-eight English-language events to the end of February, one of the quieter periods of the year. Twenty-two are given by or about poets. Poetry readings are popular, especially when they involve audience participation: thirteen of the twenty-two include an 'open mic' session. The John Tripp Award for Spoken Poetry, which goes from strength to strength, will again this year seek out the best performance poet in Wales. The body poetic appears in good health, but the statistics are misleading. How many of those eager to perform their own work buy poetry books and magazines? How many read poems? Really rather few. I wonder how far the wane of the poetry lesson's shared pleasure is responsible for that.

*PN Review* 199, Volume 37 Number 5,
May – June 2011.

# EBBW VALE

*November 2010*


In 2009 the National Eisteddfod was at Bala, in north Wales, the still beating heart of Welsh-language culture and all that is traditional, rural, Nonconformist. There, at the beginning of the nineteenth century, Thomas Charles, leader of the Welsh Calvinistic Methodists, who instigated the movement that became the British and Foreign Bible Society, was delighted to observe that religious revival had put an end to 'dancing, singing with the harp, and every kind of sinful mirth which used to be so prevalent among young people here', and export sales of woollen stockings, largely to America, reached £18,000 annually. Bala was, predictably, a very successful Eisteddfod, including dance and singing and, I have no doubt, a good measure of mirth among folk of all ages.

In the week just past, the Eisteddfod has been held at Ebbw Vale, Blaenau Gwent, which, two hundred years ago, was a virtually uninhabited upland area, a thousand feet or more above sea-level, where the Ebbw Fawr branch of the River Ebbw quits the moor and begins its descent some twenty miles to the coast at Newport. Exploitation of the geographical coincidence of iron ore, coal and limestone in the vicinity began in 1778 and population growth, at first steady and then explosive, followed. Iron was the magnet drawing in people from the rest of Wales and increasingly from over the border to work in forges, coalmines and quarries. The world's first steel rail was rolled in Ebbw Vale in 1857 and by the 1880s eight hundred tons of rails were being produced weekly for export all over the world. Sydney Harbour Bridge is built of iron and steel from Ebbw Vale. In the 1930s, the Ebbw Vale steelworks were the largest in Europe. Post-war, the decline of heavy industry here as elsewhere in Wales did not occur in all sectors at once or overnight, but it was inexorable: the last coal mine closed in 1989, the last steel-making operation in 2002.

A Thomas Charles might have observed that since then the town has had little enough cause for popular merriment, but the cleared steelworks site offered a location for the enormous, pink Eisteddfod Pavilion and its satellites – more than four hundred tents and stalls representing a vast array of organisations and aspects of contemporary life in Wales. This year the *maes* was not a field but dusty hardstanding damped by passing showers. The pavilion offered its usual week-long programme of musical events, literary ceremonies and evening concerts, while discussions, receptions, exhibitions, performances, chance encounters with old friends, eating, drinking, book browsing, strolling, idle gazing went on all over the place. *Eisteddfodwyr* (those who diligently attend the event wherever it is held) testify to the warmth of the welcome they received at Ebbw Vale. There was no doubting the engagement of the community in the festival, though (as all knew) it could not be as Welsh, linguistically, as the experience at Bala the previous year.

By the middle of the nineteenth century in the Gwent valleys English was overtaking Welsh as the language of home, street and work, and without the national and political will to do so, there was no preventing the Anglicisation of Ebbw Vale along with virtually all industrial south-east Wales. In those decades, embracing the new meant junking the old, for the bilingual possibility seems not to have occurred to our forefathers as the great tide of English speakers swept in. It has now – let us hope, not too late. I recall visiting Welsh-medium infants' and junior schools in these parts in the 1970s, where teachers strove, heroically I thought, to instruct whole classes of pupils in a language none of them heard at home or anywhere outside school. And this was at the insistence of parents, and very often their persistence in the face of opposition from the local education authority. It has not been cheap or convenient to satisfy the demands of parents in this regard, and local difficulties still arise from time to time, but the principle has been conceded. Today, Blaenau Gwent, in common with all other authorities in Wales, has a Welsh Language Scheme; Welsh is taught in all schools, adult learners' classes rapidly fill up and Welsh-medium education is available for those who want it. A new, purpose-built Welsh-medium primary school opens at Nantyglo, near Ebbw Vale, in September. Those who wish to continue learning through the medium of Welsh at secondary level are bussed to Ysgol Gyfun Gwynlliw in the neighbouring authority, Torfaen, which is being expanded to accommodate 1100 pupils.

That the social and media environment is saturated with English cannot be denied, so that those who acquire their command of Welsh through education must take it upon themselves to keep it up. This is where S4C, the Welsh-medium TV broadcaster, eisteddfodau large and small, the workplace (where work is to be found), and all manner of community enterprises have their part to play. That's all very well, you may say, but what about the bottom line? Does all the commitment and expenditure show results? In Blaenau Gwent, at the 1991 Census, of the population aged three or over 1,696 (2.4%) spoke Welsh; by 2001 this figure had risen to 6,241 (9.5%). By 2011 there will certainly be a substantial increase in consequence of enhanced provision during the decade.

Responsibility for education in Wales is devolved to the Assembly in Cardiff, where a Labour-Plaid Cymru coalition has been in government since July 2007. But we are no more protected from the prevailing economic climate than any other part of the UK. Education here will not be immune from cuts, which will surely test the resilience of the still relatively small Welsh-medium sector.

There could hardly have been a less propitious time for publication of the report of the Holtham Commission, 'Fairness and Accountability: A New Funding Settlement for Wales'. Central government funding to Wales (along with Scotland and Northern Ireland) is doled out in line with the 'Barnett Formula', which the then Secretary to the Treasury, Joel Barnett, worked out on the back of an envelope in the late 1970s. It is based on population statistics of that period and has remained the same since then regardless of demographic change or any other factor. This is unfair, says the report, calculating that on grounds of social need, Wales should receive £300 million more in its settlement each year. The Westminster coalition agrees with this assessment, remarkable enough in itself, but will do nothing to make amends, because that would entail reducing the allocation to Scotland just as public sector cuts begin to bite, which they fear would drive the Scots towards independence. Holtham goes on to say the Assembly cannot properly and accountably represent the people of Wales without being able to vary the tax rate. While constitutionally desirable, this seems unlikely to be helpful to those who, early next year, will try to persuade us to vote in a referendum in favour of the transfer of law-making powers to the Assembly. Nevertheless, it is what Carwyn Jones, new leader of the Labour Party in Wales and chief minister in succession to Rhodri Morgan, will argue, as he did in a speech on the *maes* at Ebbw Vale.

On our way home from the National, a slight detour into the valley of the Ebbw Fach, the smaller of the tributaries of the River Ebbw, brought us to Six Bells, a former mining village now tacked on to the town of Abertillery. Six Bells Colliery closed in

1986; every vestige of it has been removed. On 29 June 1960, forty-five men were killed at the colliery 'by an ignition of firedamp'. It could have been a lot worse. Routine maintenance meant that 125 men who would otherwise have been working where the explosion occurred were deployed elsewhere. As it was, this stands as one of the most terrible post-war mining disasters. Fifty years on, a memorial to the men who died has been raised on the hillside: the statue of a helmeted miner, sixty-six feet high, by the sculptor Sebastien Boyesen, overlooks the colliery site. Made of corsten steel, which has the natural colour of dark rust, the figure stands with arms partly raised – in supplication perhaps. Or is it the moment before the arms spread wide in greeting? For it seems again, somehow, just risen to the surface, to gaze across the absent pit to the rows of terraced houses on the populated side of the narrow valley. On the plinth the names of the men who died, the youngest eighteen, the oldest fifty-eight, will be inscribed. It is a fitting memorial to them, enormously impressive. And there is still room for the great memorial to the mining industry in south Wales, to which the estates of the coalfield landowners and mine owners should be the first to contribute.

In 2010, for the first time, none of the shortlisted writers for Wales Book of the Year came from Wales. Nikolai Tolstoy was born in England and lives near Oxford. Terri Wiltshire, born in Alabama, arrived in Wales from the USA in 1988. Philip Gross, Cornish by birth, has lived and worked in Wales, as Professor of Creative Writing at the University of Glamorgan, since 2004. Nikolai Tolstoy's *The Compilation of the Four Branches of the Mabinogi* was deemed eligible because of its 'relevance to Wales and Welsh culture', but you don't have to write about Wales as long as residence is established: Terri Wiltshire's novel *Carry Me Home* is about racism in the 'Deep South' of America. In 2007 Philip Gross came close to winning the Roland Mathias Prize with a collection of poems, *The Egg of Zero*. We hardly knew him then, though, goodness knows, he had form: ten novels for children, six earlier volumes of poetry and a big collection, *Changes of Address: Poems 1980–1998* from Bloodaxe. *The Egg of Zero* brought to my attention a poet both cerebral and effortlessly charming, whose fresh observation of the domestic and commonplace and toying with words are immensely beguiling. He easily trumped the near miss in Brecon with the T.S. Eliot Prize for *The Water Table* in 2009, and it was he who in July carried off the Book of the Year award with *I Spy Pinhole Eye*, a collaboration with the photographer Simon Denison.

*PN Review* 196, Volume 37 Number 2,
November – December 2010.

# ST DAVID'S DAY

*May 2010*

It is 1 March, Saint David's Day. This morning we went to Cardiff to join the seventh National St David's Day Parade. It is an occasion for wearing national emblems, colours and costumes, and hoisting flags, St David's gold cross on a black ground alongside the ancient Dragon. There are enormous horses to lead the procession, pipes and drums, marching bands, dancers, hoary old patriots and a crowd of young people from schools within and outside the city.

Their route is along St Mary Street and into the newly elegant pedestrianised area of The Hayes, where a pavilion is set up alongside the statue of John Batchelor, 1820-83, 'The Friend of Freedom'. Batchelor was a staunch Liberal and 'champion of municipal reform' in the days when to oppose the Tory Bute family, landowners of great swathes of Cardiff, was distinctly unhealthy, as he found to his cost. From the pavilion, speakers in Welsh and English address the throng, the biggest cheer going to the one who vows to fight on for St David's Day to be declared a public holiday in Wales – a plea rejected by Tony Blair when he was PM. On an almost Spring-like sunny day, it seems an excellent idea.

On this occasion in previous years the principal speaker has been Professor Hywel Teifi Edwards, who died in January. The name may not be familiar to readers to the east of Offa's Dyke (though they will almost certainly recognise the television broadcaster Huw Edwards, his son), but he was very well known everywhere in Wales, universally among the Welsh-speaking population. In the 1950s, he was my contemporary at the University College of Wales, Aberystwyth, and one of those who soon emerged from the anonymous ranks of the student body as a character. From the outset a gifted public speaker, with a big gruff voice and unforced wit, he had the knack of reaching all sectors of his audience. He might have made a considerable name in politics, if, careless of allegiance, like so many others he had thought of it as a career. But he was from student days a member of Plaid Cymru, even now not a party that has safe seats into which the ambitious can be parachuted by HQ and the machine. He was Plaid candidate in two elections, at Llanelli in 1983 and Carmarthen in 1987, but sturdily as he fought, the electoral tide was set against him. Denied the opportunity of shining at Westminster, he continued to devote his talents to the culture and history of Wales, becoming the outstanding interpreter of the revival of the National Eisteddfod in the nineteenth century, and the conflict in Welsh nationality between the proponents of English above all and those who, in defiance of this flawed and spurious notion of moving with the times, held fast to Cymraeg (Welsh). In his professional life Hywel Teifi was a highly regarded academic and writer, and his rhetorical gifts ensured he was always in demand as a public speaker and broadcaster. On his feet he was a splendid entertainer, though trenchant and forceful when occasion demanded. And he never lost touch with the society in which he was rooted. He would have been surprised at the many tributes and the depth of feeling news of his death evoked throughout Wales.

Twenty-five years ago this week the 1984-5 Miners' Strike ended. It had engaged not just pit workers, whose jobs were at stake, but whole communities and, although the men marched back to Maerdy, the last pit in the Rhondda, led by a brass band and with union banners waving, they knew it was doomed like all the others. As John Davies points out in *A History of Wales*, with what irony in view of recent events, 'At the end of the 1980s, with more Welshmen working in banks than in pits, one of the most remarkable chapters in the history of the Welsh had closed'. And the mining communities, which had been as one during the strike and for decades before, began to fall apart in earnest.

If I could choose a voice and personality to propose the setting up of a memorial to the mining industry in Wales, they would have been those of Hywel Teifi Edwards, who, though he was born in rural Cardiganshire, had family roots in the Glamorgan valleys. At the beginning of his career in education he taught at a school in a mining township in the Ogmore valley, over the mountain from my home, Gilfach Goch, and in 1994 he published *Arwr Glew Erwau'r Glo* (Brave Hero of the Coal Acres), a study of the miner in Welsh literature between 1850 and 1950. The cause is good, because the passing of the coal industry has not been sufficiently memorialised and needs a passionate orator. Here and there across south Wales there are humbler statues to remind us, but quite soon, like the statue of John Batchelor, they will cease to have meaning to younger generations. There are places you can go, like the Rhondda Heritage Park at Trehafod, near Pontypridd, and Big Pit, Blaenavon, both wonderful in their way, where a visitor can have the slightest, fleeting impression, like the flicker of a butterfly wing, of what it was like to go down a pit and hew coal for a living, but they are not enough. A grand gesture is needed, something large and permanent, sited in a spot where it cannot be missed, to represent the dignity, pride and suffering of generations of miners, men, women and children (the grandfather whose name I bear was working underground at the age of twelve), who were forced to fight for a decent wage, while the great landowners, like the Butes and the Beauforts, grew fat on their thousands of acres. Whether we like it or not, Wales became synonymous with coal mining, notwithstanding its diversity and a history extending further back in these islands than England and anything English.

That is why (apart from his extraordinary fondness of himself) David Dimbleby's TV series *Seven Ages of Britain*, for all its pretty pictures of glowing artefacts, is so infuriating. 'For a thousand years,' the programme summary says, 'the British Isles were defined by invasion, each successive wave bringing something new to the mix. The Romans...the Anglo-Saxons...the Normans... ' It is as though the Romans found an uninhabited land, as though the name 'Britain' was conjured out of the air. And, as we saw, it is as though Christianity did not exist hereabouts until the pagan Anglo-Saxons were converted. Yet there were three bishops from Britain at the Council of Arles in AD 313, and St David, whose death in AD 588 we celebrate today, preceded Augustine's mission to convert the Anglo-Saxons in AD 597, by which time there was already a well-established, evangelising Celtic Church. It is curious, too, that unlike James I and VI, who, we were told, came from Scotland, the Tudors seem to have arrived from space. Some viewers must have wondered where Henry VII (ignored apart from his magnificent tomb), Henry VIII and Elizabeth I found that peculiar name. I could go on picking away at the series, but I realise that the Welsh are not the only ones to be given short shrift by this historical farrago (with which the Open University should be ashamed to be associated). The series would be more honestly entitled *Seven Ages of England* or, in view of the substantial preponderance of artefacts from one city, *Seven Ages of London – and a few other places of less significance*. In short, it is emblematic of the stranglehold the centralising principle has on British politics and life, which, like Empire, has surely had its day.

*PN Review* 193, Volume 36 Number 5, May – June 2010.

# GILFACH GOCH AND MADRESFIELD
*January 2010*

I ended my previous letter (in *PNR* 190) with a few brief reflections on Peter J. Conradi's *At the Bright Hem of God*, an excellent book, which is suffused with a tender melancholy evoked by contemplation of the passing of a traditional way of life. It was in 1965 that Conradi first tasted 'the colossal, timeless, golden silence of the hills'. Again he testifies, 'I did not think on that first visit to Wales that I had ever visited a place of such transcendent magic...Here were sublime views over ancient hills, the shock of silence, and then the surprise of a new feeling compounded of exhilaration, trust, and peace of mind.'

I fully understand the sensations he describes, although the upland moors of my experience are neither as remote nor as extensive as those of Radnorshire, and are, furthermore, hacked into by valleys that, collectively, were one of the cradles of industrialisation. Books, photographs, films of the industrial valleys in their heyday (and I suppose reputation) have given outsiders an impression of unalleviated toil, noise and black dust. But that is a false picture, or at least one not entirely true. I stepped out of our back garden gate onto the mountain, Mynydd y Gilfach. If I chose the direct route, a stiff climb of a few hundred feet brought me to the crest of a steep slope. At the crest I was still within hailing distance of home, with much of the village, its three working pits and all that pertained to them in view. A few yards further, I was on the rolling moor and in a different world. There you could lie back and watch the clouds tumbling overhead, hearing only the sound of the wind in the grass and the marvellous, evocative song of the skylark. Escape from dark and daily concerns was never difficult in Gilfach Goch, while the mountain was free to be roamed.

The moor, rising at the top of the valley by way of an extraordinarily symmetrical hill, like a bell curve, to a height of twelve hundred feet, was otherwise undistinguished. The grass was rough and tussocky. Low tumbled walls of local stone made lines across it here and there, marking the boundaries of something forgotten, or anyway no longer significant, and there were patches of bracken. Sheep tracks were etched into it that had no particular sense of direction: there were always sheep, and sheep droppings. A stranger might well consider it uninteresting – a waste space, and to us then it was simply there, an enormous, slumbering, available plaything. Only now I savour its beauty in recollection.

A few weeks ago, my cousin Jean, now in her mid-eighties, who lives in an old people's complex in Llanelli, gave me an aerial photograph of Gilfach that, long ago, my sister had given her. It is rather fine. It shows the post-industrial valley, predominantly green, and you can pick out the house where I was born and the pub my sister kept for almost thirty years. And on the hill to the south of the pub you can see twenty wind turbines. Among the earliest of their sort in Britain, they were put there in 1992, a boon to the farmer on whose land they were erected. In the past few years, applications have been made by energy companies to plant wind turbines on Mynydd y Gilfach, and to the north and west of the valley, so that, if the plans are approved, the valley will be surrounded on all sides by these hideous excrescences. As though a century of coal mining were not enough, the valley will undergo another period of gross industrial exploitation.

Of course, Gilfach is not alone in falling foul of the combined interests of giant commercial companies and landowners. Mynydd y Gwair on the Gower Peninsula, an area of natural beauty, is also under attack. The landowner in this case is the Duke of Beaufort. You may wonder what the Gower has to do with him. Charles Somerset (1460?-1526), illegitimate son of Henry Beaufort, third duke of Somerset (beheaded by the Yorkists in 1463), gambled on the success of Henry Tudor and prospered when he became Henry VII. In 1492 Charles married Elizabeth, daughter of William Herbert, second earl of Pembroke (who had died the previous year), and in 1504 assumed the title of Baron Herbert of Raglan, Chepstow and Gower, 'iure uxoris'. As the first Somerset earl of Worcester, he was named specifically in the 1536 Act of Union, which confirmed his rights as Lord of the March and controller of Chepstow, Magor, Gower and their surrounding areas. In due course, Henry Somerset (1629-1700) succeeded to titles and land and was created first duke of Beaufort. Raglan Castle, the family seat, was so badly damaged during the Civil War that he decamped to Badminton. Nevertheless, until the end of the nineteenth century nine-tenths of the land owned by dukes of Beaufort was in south Wales. So a duke of Beaufort profited handsomely from leasing the mineral rights of land in the Swansea area during the industrial revolution. Now one of his successors has a second windfall. This might be more acceptable, if the Beaufort family, or trustees of the estate, were to set a good example by having a wind farm at Badminton. The Cotswold Hills, with a highest point over one thousand feet, offer sites as suitable as the Gower or Gilfach.

This despoliation of Wales makes one think of Tryweryn. On 1 August 1957 a parliamentary bill was passed allowing Liverpool Corporation, in the face of heated opposition from all over Wales, to acquire land by compulsory purchase and build the dam that drowned the Welsh-speaking community of Capel Celyn, near Bala, Gwynedd. The lake Liverpool created is called

Llyn Celyn, but is commonly referred to as Tryweryn, after the river valley that was dammed. In 1963, Meic Stephens, then recently graduated from UCW Aberystwyth, painted a slogan *'Cofiwch Tryweryn'* ('Remember Tryweryn') on the roadside wall of a ruined farmhouse in Llanrhystud, not far from Aber. Over the years this graffito has been repainted several times. Early on, 'Tryweryn' was amended to *'Dryweryn'*, as required by the system of mutations in the Welsh language (Meic had been a learner at the time) and it is now somewhat smaller than the original to occupy the space left after a corner of the wall collapsed, but very fresh and bright. The coming of the National Eisteddfod to Bala this year provided an opportunity for commemoration of these events of the 1950s and 1960s. Alun Ffred Jones, the Heritage Secretary of the National Assembly, announced a Welsh Government grant of thirty thousand pounds towards the eighty thousand needed to buy the wall and the land around it and preserve it for the nation. Meic has called it 'my most famous statement, my best-known poem, my most eloquent speech, and my most influential political act'.

Mutations are no longer a problem to Meic. He came second in the competition for the Crown at the National Eisteddfod this year for the third time, and in controversial circumstances. The Crown is awarded for a poem or a sequence in free verse (as against the Chair competition for poetry in the strict metres of Welsh prosody). This year a lacuna in regulations governing entries for the Crown allowed a previous winner of the Chair, Ceri Wyn Jones, to submit work in which *cynghanedd* and traditional measures were used throughout. Although contrary to the spirit of the competition, his sequence was judged worthy of the Crown. In 2010, trusting the regulations will be suitably tightened, Meic will have another chance, when the Eisteddfod will be held at Ebbw Vale, the former industrial town in Blaenau Gwent.

Some weeks ago I viewed the Malvern Hills (another site with wind farm potential?) from the beautiful park of Madresfield Court. We were there, at the invitation of very good old friends, as guests of John de la Cour, Director of the Elmley Foundation, which was endowed by the late Countess Beauchamp of Madresfield to encourage arts, crafts and design in the counties of Herefordshire and Worcestershire. As a small invited group we were to see some of the principal rooms of the house, which is still a family home. At the beginning of his introductory talk, John de la Cour handed out a sheet headed 'The Lygon Family Tree' and I knew at once where we were – as would anyone who has cultivated an interest in Evelyn Waugh. Madresfield and the sons and daughters of William Lygon, seventh earl Beauchamp, are the sources of much that is memorable in *Brideshead Revisited*.

Waugh met the eldest son, William, Lord Elmley, at Oxford, and through him his brother Hugh, the inspiration, in part at least, for the character of Sebastian Flyte. 'Hughie', who drank heavily and had been unwell for a considerable time, died in 1936 (aged 32) during a motoring tour in Germany. Getting out of the car to ask directions, he fell and fractured his skull. The death was an especially terrible blow to his father, Lord Beauchamp, the seventh earl (typically, and irrationally, the name is pronounced 'Beecham'. Waugh has a little joke about this in *Brideshead*, when photographs of Julia, Sebastian's sister, are said to appear 'as regularly in the illustrated papers as the advertisements for Beecham's Pills'.) Beauchamp was living in exile as the result of a campaign against him waged by his wife's brother, the Duke of Westminster. The Duke was perhaps motivated by envy of his brother-in-law's success in public life, but his ostensible reason was to defend his sister against the increasing threat of the exposure of her husband's homosexuality. His righteous indignation on this account knew no bounds: he hunted Beauchamp down at court, through his political connections and with the Attorney General. The threat of arrest made it imperative for Beauchamp to go abroad and never come back. How then attend his favourite son's funeral? It was with extreme difficulty that the authorities were persuaded to allow a temporary waiver of the warrant so that he could return for this occasion. In Waugh's novel, this situation is palely reflected in Lord Marchmain's exile in Venice.

Madresfield Court, a moated manor house, is a beautiful hotch-potch with origins in the twelfth century. It was considerably enlarged in the reign of Elizabeth I, further extended in 1799 and underwent wholesale reconstruction in 1865. It was during this last phase that the chapel was created under the direction of the sixth earl, though the wonderful decoration of chapel and library are owed to the seventh earl. Waugh visited frequently, but the great house described in *Brideshead* is not Madresfield – except for the chapel: 'The whole interior had been gutted, elaborately refurnished and redecorated in the arts and crafts style of the last decade of the nineteenth century. Angels in printed cotton smocks, rambler-roses, flower-spangled meadows, frisking lambs, texts in Celtic script, saints in armour, covered the walls in an intricate pattern of clear bright colours...The sanctuary lamp and all the metal furniture were of bronze, hand-beaten to the patina of a pock-marked skin; the altar steps had a carpet of grass-green, strewn with white and gold daisies.'

Yes, that's it, though the reality is more glowing than Waugh's description, and he doesn't mention that the seven children of the seventh earl are portrayed in the frescoes. Also, it suited the writer's purpose that the family should be Catholic, rather than High Anglican.

Madresfield is an extraordinary experience, even in a visit of a few hours. It is no wonder that Waugh, hospitalised from the army in December 1943, during 'a bleak period of present privation and threatening disaster', should turn his recollection of the place and its inhabitants over in his mind and begin writing 'with a zest that was quite strange to me' so that the book is 'infused with a kind of gluttony, for food and wine, for the splendours of the recent past'.

*PN Review 191*, Volume 36 Number 3, January – February 2010.

# MONMOUTHSHIRE

*September 2008*

Not long since, rugby players from Monmouthshire clubs could opt to represent England. Thus, W.G.D. (Derek) Morgan, born in Maesycwmmer and educated at Lewis School, Pengam, who played for Newbridge, won nine English caps in the 1960s and later became chairman of selectors for the Rugby Football Union. This blurring of boundaries began in the reign of Henry VIII. John Davies's *History of Wales* describes how the so-called 'Act of Union' (1536) designated the lordships that would compose the new counties of Wales, and how the eastern edges of the shires of Monmouth, Brecknock, Radnor, Montgomery, Denbigh and Flint for the first time created a border with England. However, when in 1543 a system of courts of justice was introduced as 'the Great Sessions of Wales', Monmouthshire, 'no less Welsh in language and sentiment than any of the other eastern counties', answered to the courts of Westminster, thus engendering the presumption that the county had been annexed by England. Abolition of the Great Sessions in 1830 removed the anomaly but, as we have seen, didn't quite dissipate the erroneous belief.

Under Local Government Reorganisation in 1974, with minor adjustments of the border, old Monmouthshire became Gwent (from the name of a post-Roman kingdom of south east Wales). Few minded the name change, notwithstanding a characteristic squib by Harri Webb, aping the demotic:

I'm a citizen of Mummersher,
I'm as English as the Queen,

And I 'ates them rotten Welshies
Wot paints the signposts green.

I've always lived in Mummersher,
Now they wants to call it Gwent,
But I can't pronounce that 'ard foreign word,
It do make my teeth all bent.

In the nineteenth century, industrialisation drew in workers
from far and wide. My great-grandfather, Thomas Adams, from
Great Bridge in Staffordshire, came to Pontypool probably to
find employment in the metal industries. He didn't come alone;
a street there was named Staffordshire Row. By the time he had
met and married Hannah Evans, a Welsh speaker, he had turned
collier. Their union is an illustration of the way in which, well
into the century, the indigenous population, swelled also by
incomers from other parts of Wales, maintained the linguistic
balance, particularly in the Gwent valleys, but gradually they
lost their numerical advantage and English became dominant.

There was a rearguard action, however, surprisingly led by a
young woman, Augusta Hall, wife of Benjamin Hall, later Lord
Llanover. She was inspired by a speech given at the second
eisteddfod of the Cambrian Society of Gwent in 1826, which
was unaccountably held in Brecon. The speaker was a great
champion of the Welsh language, the Reverend Thomas Price
(1787-1848), who is known by his bardic name 'Carhuanawc'.
The effect of his oratory was immediate and lasting. The Halls'
household at Llanover was organised on the grand lady's
interpretation of traditional Welsh lines: the servants (all required
to speak Welsh, though her own was weak and wobbly) wore her
versions of the traditional dress of the counties they came from;
the Welsh harp was played and Welsh folk songs were revived;
Welsh books and manuscripts were collected. She and her

husband were among the first to join Cymdeithas Cymreigyddion y Fenni (the Abergavenny Welsh Society) when it was founded in November 1833, and their presence brought in wealthy and influential friends. Although the membership included highly literate Welsh-speaking manual workers, the gentry was well represented, as was the Church, thanks to the proliferation of clerics with eisteddfodic and antiquarian interests, and the aspiring bourgeois, who relished the opportunity of rubbing shoulders with landed celebrities of the age.

In 1834 the first Eisteddfod y Fenni organised by the Society was a notable success. Many competitors were attracted by the monetary prizes donated by wealthy members, whose ostentatious presence at ceremonial and staged events drew gaping crowds. The popular appeal of the eisteddfod increased in subsequent years, when it was often attended by foreign dignitaries. Prominent among the latter was the eminent scholar and philologist Baron von Bunsen, Prussian Ambassador at the Court of St James and friend of Prince Albert, who in 1817 had married Frances Waddington, the older sister of Lady Hall. There were other links with the continent: Carnhuanawc was particularly concerned to establish ties with Brittany, and German scholars won eisteddfod prizes for essays on aspects of Celtic studies. For a decade or more the annual celebration expanded, until it became the whole purpose of the Society, and the original pledges of the membership to do all in their power to foster the Welsh language were largely forgotten.

When, eventually, financial support for the eisteddfod dwindled, the Cymdeithas itself began to fall apart. It was wound up in 1854. Much of its contemporary success had come from what we might term froth and celebrity, but there were a few achievements of historical importance. At the 1836 eisteddfod, Thomas Stephens, a chemist from Merthyr, won the prize of £25 donated by the Prince of Wales for an essay on the early literature of Wales. Enlarged and published as *The Literature of the Kymry* (1849), it is recognised as an outstanding example of the scientific approach to philological and literary criticism. Another notable development occurred in November of the same year when the Cymdeithas heard a proposal to establish as an offshoot the Welsh Manuscripts Society, which, under the chairmanship of Lord Llanover, took as its aim the publication of 'manuscripts relating to Wales and the Marches' that resided in private collections. And the Eisteddfod y Fenni itself was a model (albeit imperfect) for those contemplating an annual festival of this kind on a grander scale; the first National Eisteddfod was held at Aberdare in 1861.

In the second half of the nineteenth century Monmouthshire produced two English-language writers who, against the odds, became famous in their lifetime and are still read: W.H. Davies, 'the tramp poet', and the prose author Arthur Machen. The latter was born just down the road from here, opposite a pub in the centre of old Caerleon. As a young man he turned out vast quantities of saleable hackwork for a pittance, was at various times journalist and actor, and went on to write extraordinary tales of the supernatural – stories like 'The Shining Pyramid', I first read as a boy – which have lost none of their strange, other-worldly power.

Although their subject matter might appear similar, Machen owes nothing to Poe, but another Gwent writer, whom I have come across only recently, fell under the influence of Poe's poetic style. Evan Frederic Morgan (1893-1949), second Viscount Tredegar, might well have thought himself a scion of the house of Usher, for he was the last of his line to live in Tredegar House, the beautiful seventeenth-century mansion just off the M4 at Newport. His ancestor, Sir Charles Morgan of Tredegar, was a friend of Benjamin and Augusta Hall, and became a member of the Abergavenny Cymreigyddion. Evan was educated at Eton and Oxford, served in the First World War, and was for a time active in public life. In the 1920s, as a Roman Catholic convert, he became a Chamberlain to Popes Benedict XV and Pius XI. He seems at the same time to have developed a taste for the baroque and outlandish, and a reputation as an eccentric. He married first an actress, the Honourable Lois Sturt, who numbered Prince George, Duke of Kent among her lovers, and whose papers, archived at the National Library of Wales, include an album of her sexually explicit verses; and after her death in Budapest in 1937, the Russian Princess Olga Dolgorousky, who obtained an annulment in 1943.

In Evan Morgan's day, Tredegar House had a menagerie, including a bear, an anteater, a boxing kangaroo, a baboon, and a macaw, 'Blue Boy', which perched on his shoulder. Odder still, he acquired a formidable reputation as an occultist. He was a friend of the self-styled 'Great Beast', Aleister Crowley, who named Evan his 'adept of adepts'. As a young man he was considered able and talented. His paintings were exhibited at the Paris Salon and he was an art collector, specialising in the Italian Renaissance. And he wrote several volumes of poetry, among them *Fragments* (1916), *At Dawn, poems profane and religious* (1924), and *The Eel and other poems* (1926), all Poe-like, or possibly Swinburnean, in their incantatory indulgence, all now forgotten. Among the famous or notorious who attended his extravagant weekend parties at Tredegar House were (in addition to Crowley) Alfred Douglas, Aldous Huxley, Nancy Cunard, Augustus John, Noel Coward, H.G. Wells, Ivor Novello, Terence Rattigan – and W.H. Davies, whose birthplace was less than a mile (and a world) away in Newport, on the other side of the River Usk. A bust of Davies by Epstein was one of the items of the estate dispersed on the viscount's early death in 1949.

Evan Morgan would have been a strong candidate for *Big Brother* or the Hay Festival (what Peter Florence would give for a cast list like that at Tredegar House in Morgan's heyday). Those who visited the festival site on Bank Holiday Monday could have been forgiven for thinking three witches were stirring a cauldron up on Hay Bluff. The weather was appalling. Fearing tractors would be needed to extricate cars from the bogs adjacent to the site, I tried to park in town. Impossible: Hay was full. Eventually I found a gap across the border in England, on a narrow side road to Cussop Dingle, and set off on foot for the shuttle bus stop, where literary festival veterans in rain gear and wellingtons were queuing. On the road to the festival we glimpsed through the streaming windows a windswept notice inviting the hardiest to take Pimms and champagne in the garden of an inn. A Pimms bar was also a feature of one of the refreshment tents, but there were no takers; a paper cup of coffee to warm the hands was a far better idea, while clusters of spherical paper lampshades swung gaily in the breeze above our heads.

It was 'Welsh day', though you would not have known that from the *Guardian,* the major sponsors, or Sky TV. That *Eagle in the Maze* (Cinnamon), the collection of winning entries to last year's Rhys Davies Trust short story competition was being launched, that Peter Finch was reading from his splendid *Selected Poems* (Seren), that Dai Smith was lecturing on Raymond Williams, the subject of his acclaimed biography *A Warrior's Tale* (Parthian), and the shortlists for the Wales Book of the Year 2008 in Welsh and English were being announced made barely a ripple in the expanding lake. Instead we have had little from the media apart from blanket coverage of the usual line-up of celebrities with autobiographies to sell. The clouds of a dismal day pursued me all the way home.

*PN Review* 183, Volume 35 Number 1,
September – October 2008.

# THE NATIONAL ASSEMBLY

*November 2007*

Since my account of the aftermath of the National Assembly elections in *PN Review* 176, political affairs in Wales have moved on – though not 'apace' as the cliché often has it. They have moved on very slowly, to the disgruntlement of many voters and, of course, media commentators, who prefer outcomes disappointing, if not disastrous. In the absence of real news, much was made of an intervention by Dr Barry Morgan, the Archbishop of Wales, who does not shirk controversy. While greeting the new Government of Wales Act as a 'momentous' event, he criticised the mechanism by which legislation proposed by the Assembly can be vetoed first by the Secretary of State for Wales and then by Parliament. The Archbishop contrasted this situation with that in Scotland and declared the Act 'demeaning' and 'patronising' to Wales. It is, in his view, intended to serve the ends of the Labour Party, not the needs of Wales: a Machiavellian act, then, designed to keep the Welsh under the thumb of Westminster. Will anything ever pass this double scrutiny that is not strictly in line with Government policy? Highly unlikely, certainly so long as Labour remains in power, such is the ill will borne towards the Assembly and devolution generally by the great majority of Welsh Labour MPs.

Almost to a man this body vehemently opposed attempts to weld a Labour-Plaid coalition in Cardiff. Nevertheless, a series of meetings took place with the aim of establishing a basis of mutual understanding and agreed policy. Eventually, in the second week of July, Labour, in the person of First Minister Rhodri Morgan, and Plaid, in that of its leader Ieuan Wyn Jones, shook hands over a joint document, 'One Wales', which contains a number of key elements in Plaid's prospectus, including the promise that there will be, in due course, a referendum on full law-making powers for the Assembly, and a proper examination of the 'Barnett formula', by which Treasury funding to Wales is allocated on the basis of population rather than assessment of need. However, it is commitment to true socialist values of the kind that Plaid MP Adam Price would endorse that catch the eye: in the NHS, the ending of the internal market, Private Finance Initiative Schemes and the use of private hospitals; the introduction of powers to scrap the 'right to buy' council houses where there is a shortage of such housing; the provision of grants to first-time house buyers; the establishment of a Climate Change Commission for Wales; and the improvement of transport links between north and south. Even with a fair wind, changes of this magnitude cannot be brought about speedily. Given the likelihood of opposition at Westminster, if not at the first hurdle with the Secretary of State, all could be lost.

No sooner had the Labour-Plaid partnership been blessed by party conferences and work begun on the formation of a new cabinet, than Rhodri Morgan fell ill. While he underwent a heart operation, Ieuan Wyn Jones, elevated to the role of Deputy First Minister, undertook his duties. These included attending the British-Irish Council in Belfast, where the new Prime Minister, Gordon Brown, met leaders of the devolved administrations, Revd Ian Paisley, Alec Salmond, and Ieuan Wyn Jones, not one of them from Labour ranks. Later the same week the coalition cabinet was unveiled. It has fourteen members – ten ministers and four deputy ministers. Three of the ministerial posts have gone to Plaid Cymru, all of considerable importance: economy and transport; rural affairs; and the heritage portfolio, which includes tourism, sport, the arts and the Welsh language. The single Plaid deputy minister has responsibility for housing. Immediately after the announcement the politicians went on holiday, so we shall wait to see what happens next, but there is a general acceptance that the psyche of Wales has undergone a fundamental change. The bleak and sodden summer has not dispersed an unwonted air of anticipation in Welsh political life. There is greater confidence in our capacity to manage the affairs of Wales, and in the positive impact that will have on our cultural life.

An advertisement in the latest number of *Poetry Wales* (Vol. 43 No. 1) invites applications for the post of editor. The Spring 2008 number will be Robert Minhinnick's last. He began in 1997 with Vol. 33 No. 2; a decade and forty issues later the end is in sight. At the outset, his concerns were only literary, but looking back, he sees political devolution and the focus of interest upon the future of the Welsh language as important and challenging issues he could not ignore. As he grasped their significance he redefined his role to involve participation in 'a determined effort to show that Wales and its different cultures actually exist'. 'At times,' he adds, 'I've felt like a politician. But a truthful politician, I hope.' Perhaps the alliance of poetry and politics is natural to him, as it is to John Barnie, who recently resigned as editor of *Planet* after many years of diligent and largely successful endeavour, often against the odds, because of a long-standing commitment to the cause of the environment. 'For good or bad,' Minhinnick says, 'the environment is where the political and cultural zeitgeist is today.'

Other developments extending far beyond Wales have also impinged upon Minhinnick's editorship, not least electronic global communication, and the growth of university creative writing departments – the subject of a controversial exchange of articles and letters in recent numbers of *PW,* with proponents and opponents lining up to praise their provision of (at least) 'critical friendship and creative reading', or dismiss them more or less out of hand as marketing ploys by cash-strapped universities and for being no good at what, ostensibly, they pretend to offer.

Minhinnick's stint as editor has itself stirred controversy. Some subscribers complained that he shifted the focus too violently from Welsh poetry, mostly in English, to writing from almost anywhere in the world, for the greater part, inevitably, in translation. Despite the criticism he has not budged. His initial standpoint, 'an interest in the world's poetries', was succeeded by realisation that 'in Wales now a literary editor can be a kind of cultural ambassador'. It is still, however, an uncommon vision. Certainly, none of his predecessors ventured abroad to publicise the magazine, to identify and explain Wales ('I've had to stand up and speak to the media and live audiences in Latin and North America, and across Europe'), and to invite an exchange of poetries. Typical of his regime, the current issue will be launched at the second Novi Sad International Literary Festival in Serbia, and showcases five Hebrew poets.

I have previously mentioned my literary obsession with Thomas Jeffery Llewelyn Prichard (1790–1862), an actor who lost his nose, allegedly in a fencing match, a poet of epic ambition but scant talent, author of *Twm Sion Catti* (the 'first Welsh novel in English'), and almost certainly the first Welsh writer in English to present himself consciously as such. Some time ago Stephen Knight, Professor of English at Cardiff University, told me that an American student had somewhere found evidence of a link between Prichard and his close contemporary Thomas Love Peacock (1785–1866). In the last week or so I have been seeking that evidence in what seemed the likeliest place, *The Letters of Thomas Love Peacock*, brilliantly edited by Nicholas A. Joukovsky (Clarendon Press,

Oxford, 2001) – so far without success. But I have learned a little more about Peacock's life than I had previously gathered from Richard Holmes's *Shelley: The Pursuit,* where his association with the poet is well documented. Despite having been withdrawn from school at the age of thirteen, when the death of his father left the family in straitened circumstances, he made himself a classical scholar. Some of his correspondence was conducted in Latin and much of it is liberally sprinkled with Greek. His literary acquaintance was numerous and impressive, including, in addition to Shelley, his wives and hangers on (he proposed marriage, unsuccessfully, to Claire Clairmont), Byron and his friends, particularly John Cam Hobhouse, Keats, and Leigh Hunt and so on. He was a familiar of all their interlocking circles. Shelley supported him financially until 1819, when he obtained a position by examination with the East India Company. At India House he progressed eventually to the post of Examiner at £2,000 a year and made a notable contribution to the development of steam navigation. He was also of course a poet and the author of *Gryll Grange*, *Nightmare Abbey*, *Crotchet Castle* and the like, slight, elegant and ironic tales that satirise contemporary mores and caricature many of his famous friends.

In the context of my quest for Prichard, *The Misfortunes of Elphin* (1829) is the most interesting of Peacock's books because it deals with, among other events, the drowning of the Lowland Hundred, the legendary pastoral lordship that is said to lie beneath the waters of Cardigan Bay. This is also the subject of Prichard's stupefying epic 'The Land Beneath the Sea'. One of Peacock's sources, of epigraphs if nothing else, was a short-lived magazine, *The Cambro-Briton*, to which Prichard contributed and which he too relied upon for historical colour. This, however, is as far as one can go in linking the two.

Peacock was fond of Wales, and later cultivated an interest

in its ancient culture. On the morning of 6 April 1810 he wrote to his friend Thomas Forster (who had also taught himself several languages including Welsh): 'Here I am in the Vale of Festiniog, the paradise of north Wales, a little spot of most luxuriant beauty, totally embosomed in mountain scenery of the most romantic character'. From Maentwrog Lodge, a few miles west of Ffestiniog and six weeks earlier, he had written to his publisher, Edward Thomas Hookham, 'I wish I could find language sufficiently powerful to convey to you an idea of the sublime magnificence of the waterfalls in the frost – when the old over-hanging oaks are spangled with icicles; the rocks sheeted with frozen foam...and the water, that oozes from their sides, congealed into innumerable pillars of crystal.'

These observations with their characteristic markers of Romanticism are all very fine; but he did not like the Welsh. On 28 July 1810, he wrote again to Forster from Merionethshire: 'There are no philosophers in Wales. The natives have a great deal of religion, without a single grain of morality. Their total disregard of truth is horrible, their general stupidity prodigious, and their drunkenness most disgusting. I have found two amiable girls in this principality, but an estimable or intelligent man I have neither seen nor heard of.' Back in January he had sent Hookham a brief sketch of the parson at Maentwrog – 'a little, dumpy, drunken, mountain goat'. This was John Gryffydh *(sic),* Rector of Ffestiniog and Maentwrog from 1787 until his death in 1812. Whether his goatishness appeared in mountaineering or lechery is not made clear. If the latter then Peacock was in no position to disparage. Though a staunch guardian of the privacy of the individual, especially his own, there is evidence enough to show that he was a womaniser, if mostly manqué; an acquaintance recalled that Peacock's mind was 'a terrible thesaurus eroticus'. One of the two 'amiable girls' he mentions in his letter to Forster was Jane Gryffydh, daughter of the parson. It is both ironic, and I suppose romantic, that not having set eyes upon her since 1810, Peacock wrote to Jane on 20 November 1819 proposing marriage – and she accepted. They were married 23 March 1820. It was not a happy union; Jane is said to have become mentally unbalanced following the death of a daughter in 1826 and thereafter they lived largely separate lives. Given his handsome salary and pension from the East India Company, it is difficult to understand how Peacock was hard up in later life. Joukovsky leaves hanging in the air like a faint mustiness the possibility that he cultivated female companionship of another kind, but we shall probably never know.

*PN Review* 178, Volume 34 Number 2,
November – December 2007.

# THE SIX NATIONS: ROME AND PARIS

*July 2007*

Every other year, between January and March, the Welsh rugby supporter's fancy lightly turns to thoughts of Paris and Rome, where, in contrast to our own washed-out seasons, there may indeed be signs of the return of Spring (I should include Edinburgh too, but for me, Murrayfield does not have the same appeal). Thousands followed their team to the continental match venues, and the crowded stadiums, even the vast Stade de France, were liberally blotched with red. On each occasion we came away disappointed. Usually, by the time we have tramped to metro stations or found alternative transport, passably good spirits have returned at the prospect of a good night out in the bar or bistro of choice, but this year in Paris, the ridiculously late 9 p.m. kick-off meant it was nearly midnight by the time we returned from the banlieu of St Denis to the Gare du Nord. Instead of burly men to keep the over-enthusiastic out, bars near the station had posted desperate staff begging us to come in. Only the very thirsty heeded their siren calls.

Rome and Paris (yes, and Edinburgh) have a great deal to offer beyond the few hours of intense drama played out on a Saturday afternoon or evening during the Six Nations tournament. You will find knots of Welsh, readily identifiable by their red favours and their voices, at all the major sites and in the museums, galleries and great churches of the cities. The visit to Rome and the chance of a hotel on the Aventine, conveniently close to the Cimitero Acattolico, better known as 'the Protestant Cemetery', brought us to Keats's tomb. It is located in the 'Parte Antica', the oldest part of an extensive graveyard, where fifty or so monumental stones are widely scattered over an area amounting to perhaps a fifth of the whole. Graves in the other four-fifths are packed so close that stepping between them is an exercise in balance. The Parte Antica is quite beautiful. It lies behind a high stone wall, beyond which rises the steep-sided marble pyramid that is the memorial to the Roman *praetor* Caius Cestius. Outside traffic rushes by, but within the wall it is surprisingly calm (at this time of year there are few people about), huge pines spread their green canopies and the daisies and blue violets Severn promised his friend already stud the well-tended grass. The final words on Keats's stone are too well known to bear repetition, though I had forgotten that the lines above them contributed to the myth of a poet destroyed by 'the Malicious Power of his Enemies'. A bigger surprise was the discovery that Severn, his 'Devoted friend and death-bed companion', is buried alongside him, with all his later honours writ large, 'An Artist eminent for his representations of Italian Life and Nature/British Consul at Rome from 1861 to 1872' and so on. Even more surprising, between the poet and his artist friend, and slightly behind them, is the diminutive memorial to Arthur Severn, the son of Joseph, 'who was born 22 Nov. 1836/And accidentally killed in July 1837', with the further note 'The poet Wordsworth was present at his baptism in Rome'. We thought of the other children, those of Shelley and Byron, who died in Italy, and of parental grief. Aside from his devotion to Keats, I know next to nothing about Severn. His gravestone tells me he was, or became in the course of his 85 years, a little pompous and pleased with himself, and understandably proud of old friendships. There is no sign or mention of Mrs Severn. Curiously, it was not the grave of the Romantic poet nor that of his loyal friend that held and moved us, but that of little Arthur, baptised in Rome in the presence of Wordsworth, and killed 'accidentally' at nine months.

Having paid our respects to Keats, we wandered into the crowded main cemetery to trace the plot hard under the perimeter wall where, after spending some time in a mahogany chest in the wine cellar of the British Consul, the ashes of Shelley were interred. Trelawny, close coeval of Severn and not entirely reliable witness of 'the last days of Shelley and Byron', designed the memorial stone with its central inscription 'Cor Cordium' and the extract from Ariel's song, 'Nothing of him that doth fade/But doth suffer a sea change/Into something rich and strange.' Finally, in imitation of Severn (?), he contrived to have his mortal remains transported from his last home in Monmouthshire (I rely on Richard Holmes's monumental *Shelley: The Pursuit)* to Rome, where they lie alongside Shelley's.

Before leaving the cemetery we sought out the grave of Antonio Gramsci, whom I had first heard of as the hero of an old friend, and great Welsh historian, the late Gwyn Alf Williams. Freshly laid flowers showed that in these days Gramsci is remembered by supporters of the political left. As a leading member of the Italian Communist Party in the 1920s he was persecuted by the fascist regime. Much of his life, from 1926 until his death at the age of 46 in 1937, was spent in prison or in hospital under guard. His political philosophy became more widely known only after 1945, when notebooks and letters from his time in prison began to be published, but he had attracted attention initially as a journalist and critic in Turin during the First World War. There he had also been a regular speaker at workers' study circles on Marx, the French and Italian revolutions and the Paris Commune.

Even if you search quite diligently, as we did at Carnavalet, the museum dedicated to the history of Paris, you will find little information about the Commune. You might draw the conclusion that whereas successive governments have been prepared to look back upon the Great Revolution and the Rise and Fall of Napoleon with equanimity if not pride, they would wish the Commune to be forgotten. Having some time ago been bowled over by Alistair Horne's *The Fall of Paris* (New York, 1965), and realised that the events he unfolds occurred during the lifetime of my grandparents, I cannot do that. The basilica of Sacré-Coeur, that tourist icon, should be a reminder since it is constructed on the spot where the Commune was proclaimed in March 1871, and was intended as a symbol of reconciliation, but few of the many thousands who climb the steps towards it each year know why it is there, or why it is reputed to be disliked by Parisians.

In a somewhat extended stay, after the rugby, we visited a few of the sites associated with the Commune, beginning at Père-Lachaise cemetery, which witnessed some of the dying moments of the insurrection. There, in May 1871, a battle was fought among the grand sepulchres of bourgeois Paris; the last communard sniper was flushed out and shot near the grave of Balzac. Soon after, having discovered the mutilated body of the Archbishop of Paris in a ditch, government soldiers took 147 communard prisoners who had the misfortune to be at hand, lined them up against a wall in the eastern corner of the cemetery and shot them. In that place, now called the 'Mur des Fédérés', flowers and wreaths are tokens of remembrance. It is not far from the great cemetery to Belleville, in 1870 an impoverished working-class zone, the heart of the Commune and the last redoubt. The defenders fought against government forces that were better armed and led, and numerically far superior, from street to street, barricade to barricade. The last barricade to be overcome, on 28 May 1871, was in rue Ramponeau, now (as then perhaps) an undistinguished side street as steep as any in south Wales. No more than fifty yards off is a park, once no doubt a tangle of alleyways and festering slums, but now an open space of grass, trees, concrete, littered running water. Like rue Ramponeau, it rises steeply and at the top a pillared belvedere gives a remarkable view of two-thirds of the city. Those who stood there as darkness fell in May 1871 would have seen Paris in flames. The Tuileries Palace was burned to the ground, along with the Hôtel de Ville, the Cours des Comptes (where the Musée d'Orsay now stands) and much of rue Royale. The Préfecture also went up in flames, to the horror of art lovers, for the Venus de Milo had been taken there for safe keeping. The statue was discovered unharmed in the ruins, saved by a burst water pipe.

What were the famous artists and writers of Paris doing while all this was going on? Horne tells us. Some, like Monet, fled to England before the Prussian investment of Paris, the ghastly prelude to the Commune, was complete. Hugo, rejoicing in the fall of Napoleon III, returned from exile, survived the siege with the support of doting mistresses, and with his own brand of republicanism contributed to the rabble-rousing of the communards. But he had no real political influence and retired once more to Brussels. Edmond, survivor of the Goncourt brothers, whose sympathies were with the government, continued the *Journal* they had kept together through the Franco-Prussian War, the siege and the Commune, providing Horne and other historians with a major source. Deprived of the consolation of the company of his sixteen-year-old wife (who had sought the safety of the parental home), Verlaine, chief of the Commune Press Office, plotted how to seduce her maid. Renoir was conscripted into the cavalry during the Franco-Prussian war, but did not see the front line or the ignominious retreat from Sedan. He returned to Paris under the Commune and carried on painting, on one occasion, perhaps unwisely, a view of the Seine not far from the fort of La Muette, which was even then under artillery bombardment by government forces. He was seized as a spy and about to be shot when the chance arrival of a leading member of the Commune whom he had previously helped and befriended obtained his release. An active revolutionary, Courbet was given the urgent task of reopening the museums of Paris and demanded the destruction of Napoleon I's triumphal column in the Place Vendôme. Subsequently tried for this act of vandalism, sentenced to six months imprisonment and fined 250,000 francs, he fled to Switzerland and stayed there.

Courbet was luckier than most. In May 1871, thousands died in the street fighting. When barricades were overrun the bodies were tipped into the ditches from which material to build the barricade had been dug and covered over. Traffic rolling around the Place de la Concorde is shaking the remains of the hapless defenders; as we walked those familiar streets – rue St Honoré, rue de Rivoli, up to the Madeleine and the Opéra, back and back to what is now Place de la République and so to Belleville – we were walking on the unmarked graves of communards. And after that 'bloody week' in May it was worse, as revenge and sadistic brutality ran out of control. No one knows how many were killed more or less out of hand: the best estimates suggest between twenty and twenty-five thousand.

For all its egalitarian ideals, the Commune was doomed from the start. Riven by internal disputes, the leadership was paralysed, while the government in Versailles gathered its forces. In London, Marx kept careful watch on events, and later Lenin and Stalin showed that they had learned the harsh lesson well. This history, which has fascinated and horrified me, may throw some light on the convulsions that in my own lifetime have gripped Paris, and the customary violent response of the authorities. One of the memories that Welsh rugby supporters brought away from Paris on this occasion was the menacing stand-off at the Gare du Nord between a crowd of young black people eager to get to their suburban metro and the line of dark blue uniformed police, there – for reasons we could not understand – to stop them.

*PN Review* 176, Volume 33 Number 6,
July – August 2007.

# ALLT-YR-YNYS

*March 2006*

An anniversary of the domestic sort took us in October to Allt-yr-ynys in Walterstone, a straggling rural parish on the border of Herefordshire and Monmouthshire. The name may not mean much to readers who dwell at any distance from the southern March, but to me it conjures up, first, a long and treasured friendship; next, a heightened sense of a particular historical period, the knowledge of which I owe to that friendship; and thirdly, a remarkable manor house in a beautiful setting. The house, which dates from about 1550, appears externally much as it did in Shakespeare's day. Inside, altered and refurbished as a country hotel, it is a good deal warmer and more comfortable. The historical dimension is related to the Gunpowder Plot, which has just achieved its four hundredth anniversary, celebrated with the usual bangs and flashes, and several television drama-docs, one of which focused on the earlier (1601) abortive coup, led by Robert Devereux, Earl of Essex, sometime favourite of Elizabeth I, and its terrible consequences for the earl and his followers. Among the latter was Sir Gelly Meyrick, steward of the Essex lands in the March, executed with his master. Viewers now know more than they did, probably more than they wanted, about hanging, drawing and quartering, though rather less about the bloodiness of beheading than special effects departments are now capable of providing. In 1605, the conflict between Protestant and Roman Catholic interests was not confined to London, but expressed itself up and down the land in deviant forms of worship (in the view of the Crown), clandestine priestly visitations, and occasional turmoil among the populace, which was hastily quelled by the combined efforts of civil and religious law. The southern March saw agitation of this kind, involving ordinary folk and a few of the gentry. The story is unfolded in Roland Mathias's *Whitsun Riot – an account of a commotion amongst Catholics in Herefordshire and Monmouthshire in 1605*, a splendid example of historical detection, published in 1963.

Allt-yr-ynys enters the picture because, from the fourteenth century, it had been the seat of the Sitsyllt (Welsh, *Seisyll)* family, one branch of which, several generations on, had modified the name to 'Cecil' and come to prominence at the court of Henry VII. William Cecil, Baron Burghley, Elizabeth I's Secretary of State and Lord Treasurer, was conscious of his Welsh ancestry and cultivated certain Welsh connections. When, in May 1567, one of the latter, Morys Clynnog, a Catholic theologian of Caernarfonshire stock, wrote from voluntary exile in Rome to advise Cecil that the queen was about to be excommunicated, the correspondence was in Welsh. Although Cecil's more famous younger son, Robert, Earl of Salisbury, who succeeded him as Secretary of State under Elizabeth and continued in that role under James I, dismissed an interest in the 'vain toys' of genealogy as simply absurd, his elder son, Thomas, later Earl of Exeter, was as keen as his father to remember his Welsh descent. The upshot of all this is that the Cecils had lands and support in Wales, centred on Allt-yr-ynys, neighbouring those of the Earl of Essex. About 1600, their steward on the spot, Paul Delahay, compiled a list of questions for the interrogation of members of the rival faction then stirring trouble in Monmouthshire and Herefordshire, which Mathias uncovered in his research and later used as the basis of 'Indictment', his rousing poetic evocation of an early seventeenth-century trial:

Did you, John Arnallt,
Sitting at table
In your house at Llanthony,
Say to your mother Walcot
[...]
And Harry Prosser, servant
In livery to the treasoned Earl,
That Her Majesty's kitchen
Was poisonous full of Cooks,
Naming Sir Robert Cicill
A Cook by his mother, my Lord
Bacon a Cook by the same
Error...

Did you, John Arnallt,
Coming out of your cups,
Clap this Prosser, murderer
Of one Stumpe of Walterstone
At Sir Gelly's command,
Cheerily on the shoulder, swearing
There should be no more *cawl*
In Wales till the Earl
Your Master should choke
These Cooks with their own herbs?

The 'treasoned Earl' is, of course, the earl of Essex, and 'my Lord Bacon', the statesman, writer and philosopher Francis Bacon, first Baron Verulam, who was largely responsible for the earl's conviction.

One of the pleasures of editing Mathias's poetry was the absolute necessity of understanding many historical allusions. As one might anticipate, the history in 'Indictment' is impeccable, and I remember well that the poem was a favourite of audiences at Mathias readings. On those occasions, he gave rein to his sonorous voice and carefully honed talents as a performer, for he was also a gifted amateur actor. The latest number of the *New Welsh Review* (No. 70) includes a timely tribute to the poet from Andrew McNeillie, Literature Editor at OUP, which begins, 'You have only to open Roland Mathias's *Collected Poems,* at random, as I've just done, to hear his unmistakeable voice', and gives just praise to his gifts as a poet and the enormous contribution of his enlightened editorship of the *Anglo-Welsh Review.* In September last, Mathias celebrated his ninetieth birthday. It is a total (and unforgivable) mystery that as one of the outstanding men of letters of the second half of the twentieth century, he has not yet been honoured by the University of Wales.

As I write, it is almost the 150th anniversary of the composition of *Hen Wlad fy Nhadau* ('Old land of my fathers'), the singing of which in packed halls and stadiums can still raise the hairs on my nape and bring a lump to my throat. The words were written by Evan James, a weaver and wool-merchant of Pontypridd, in January 1856, to accompany a melody composed by his son, James James, and it was heard for the first time at Tabor Chapel, Maesteg, Glamorgan, later that year. Thereafter, it was sung frequently at eisteddfodau, and performance at the National Eisteddfod held in Bangor in 1874 seems to have confirmed it as the popular choice of a song for Wales. In the words of Meic Stephens's *Companion,* it now has 'official status as the national anthem of Wales by general assent'. John Redwood, then Secretary of State for Wales, famously made a fool of himself on television by trying to mouth the words as it was sung at some function or other, which he probably attended against his better instincts, but many who join in these days sing only an approximation of the Welsh and have little idea what the words mean. Journalists and others frequently confuse the title with the first line, *'Mae hen wlad fy nhadau'*, which means, '[The] old land of my fathers *is'*, *'mae'* being the verb. Only the first verse is sung, as with 'God save the Queen' (though by some perverse freak of memory I know all three verses of that dreary chant), and in common with other anthems it recalls brave warriors, patriots, who shed their blood for freedom, but first and foremost it celebrates Wales as the land of famous poets and singers (*'beirdd a chantorion'*), and one would not wish it otherwise.

Sundry poets, all published at one time or another in *Poetry Wales,* turned up at The Gate, a pleasant new cultural and community centre in Cardiff, to celebrate the magazine's fortieth anniversary. When Meic Stephens founded *PW* in 1965, taking on the triple role of editor, publisher and salesman, he could hardly have foreseen its survival over four decades. Several editors later, it goes on, though under the latest, Robert Minhinnick, it has been transformed from a journal principally concerned with writing from Wales to one with far wider ambitions. Minhinnick, a great traveller, and an extraordinarily gifted travel writer, has taken *PW* all over the world, and brought back with him for our edification poetry (in translation as necessary) from Canada, the USA, Argentina, Germany, Hungary, Sweden, Holland, the West Indies, West Africa, Slovakia – the list continues. Established (not to mention old) and newer poets from Wales are by no means neglected, but now, as I have mentioned in a previous Letter, some long-standing supporters of the magazine complain that the overseas element is tending to submerge local talent. Though it may have lain somewhere in the background, this was not, however, the reason for the noisy dispute that erupted in the midst of the celebrations at The Gate. Meic Stephens, invited by Minhinnick to read a sample of the late Harri Webb's poetry from *Poetry Wales/Forty Years,* published by Seren for the anniversary, protested, with a vehemence that shook the party's host, that he, a poet too, was represented in the anthology only by a passage of prose. His omission is indeed curious, since Minhinnick has said in the past that reading Stephens's poetry, which concentrates on people and places in south Wales, while he was in school, encouraged his own early attempts at composition. Why had he been omitted, Stephens wanted to know. Because he hadn't published any poetry for ages, Minhinnick replied. This made matters worse, since Stephen has quite recently made a considerable name for himself as a Welsh-language poet. So the argy-bargy continued, and the audience sat absorbed, as by a tennis match between big-hitters at Wimbledon. It made for an evening more memorable than most, and Minhinnick, who misses few tricks and doesn't spurn creative controversy, might plan spontaneous disorder at future readings, though he will be lucky to find an actor as physically and intellectually formidable as Meic Stephens to take on the stirring role.

Professor Stephens was one of the principal speakers at a recent Academi event in Merthyr Tydfil to mark the centenary of the birth of Glyn Jones, whose long career as a writer began in the 1930s and continued into the 1990s. Poet, short story writer and novelist, he has a secure place in the pantheon of Welsh writing in English, and merits consideration alongside his friend Dylan Thomas. But he was not a crapulous womaniser, and did not die young in New York. He was certain of his gifts as a writer, but was modest and gentle withal, an excellent companion, loved, almost revered, by a host of friends. The talk by Tony Brown, which brought proceedings at Merthyr to a close, may well have opened a new chapter in Glyn Jones studies that will lead to the revaluation of his curious and powerful rhetoric and extraordinary imagination.

In 1905, Cardiff was granted city status, and in 1955 it was formally recognised as the capital of Wales. This double anniversary has been celebrated civically and, on the bookstalls, by a hugely enjoyable sequel to *Real Cardiff* by Peter Finch, entitled, reasonably enough, *Real Cardiff Two – The Greater City,* the added phrase indicating exploration further into the city's hinterland than the first volume, though it might be interpreted as a defiant gesture in the ancient rivalry between Cardiff and Swansea. Peter Finch also has a hand in an anthology, *The Big Book of Cardiff,* co-edited with Grahame Davies. The subtitle in this case is 'New Writing from Europe's Youngest Capital', which is on the whole a fair description. It reflects, too (unexpectedly perhaps), the quality of contemporary literature in the Welsh language, provided here in translation. Although Cardiff alone is the subject, for an introduction to the strength and variety of current writing in Wales, especially in prose, you need look no further.

All three books mentioned in the previous paragraph are from Seren, which, as Poetry Wales Press, was started by Cary Archard twenty-five years ago. Its silver anniversary has been celebrated with a series of book launches at venues north and south. It is, of course, the publisher of the magazine *Poetry Wales* and, from very modest beginnings, has grown to be the leading publisher of Welsh writing in English – another cause for festivity in a year of celebrations.

*PN Review* 168, Volume 32 Number 4, March – April 2006.

# THE NATIONAL ASSEMBLY

*January 2006*

I don't always agree with the acerbic observations in Hywel Williams's *Guardian* essays. He would be disappointed if I did. I applauded heartily, however, a recent piece on the Prime Minister's cursing of the Welsh at the time of the first assembly elections, when Plaid Cymru won a few hitherto solid Labour seats. It appears that Blair is not only blind to the manifest flaws in the character of George Bush, but ill-bred and petulant into the bargain. My father would not have given him the time of day, far less crossed a street to listen to him. But then my father had standards. So disgusted was he by the nepotism and cronyism among Labour councillors that, working class and socially conscious as he was, he never voted for the party that claimed to represent his interests. His was one of very few Tory votes cast in the old Pontypridd constituency, into which that part of Gilfach Goch where we lived fell. If I haven't mentioned it before, I should put on record that, when I was growing up there, Gilfach was an electoral anomaly; with only a couple of thousand voters, it had a minuscule influence on three parliamentary seats. Since all invariably returned Labour MPs, this was of no concern to candidates or boundary commissioners. My father voted Tory because there was rarely another alternative, and because my mother would have voted Tory had she been able to reach a polling station. Her father, colliery contractor and gifted musician, who came from Radstock in Somerset, was true blue, and political colour often runs in families. My mother might not have fitted the mould of the all-powerful Welsh 'Mam' in every respect, but she was a formidable woman, absolute ruler of the household from a wheelchair. When she died my father changed his allegiance to Plaid Cymru, which by that time was regularly fielding candidates in south Wales. Had he still been among us, he would therefore have felt the puny lash of Blair's coarse tongue.

The Welsh may not be the Prime Minister's favourite people, but they do at least afford the government an opportunity of experimenting with risky policies. If Margaret Thatcher had heeded the warning of the public outcry following the early introduction of the poll tax in Scotland, she might have avoided the political calamity of inflicting it on England and Wales – and, who knows, gone on to enjoy a still longer tenancy in Downing Street. A terrible thought! Rhodri Morgan, obedient to his Westminster masters, brought in revaluation of housing in Wales in advance of England, and we have recently heard the outcome. Thirty per cent of homes here have gone up at least one council tax band and only eight per cent have gone down. In view of the increase in property prices, this was not unexpected, but having observed the anger it has generated, and realised how many votes are at stake, the government, already anxious that Blair's part in the continuing tragedy of Iraq might turn away erstwhile supporters, has changed its mind about revaluation in England, which is now safely postponed, at least until after the next election.

If the Assembly government were independent of Westminster in these matters, Rhodri Morgan might still have decided that, whatever happened in England, the time was right for revaluation in Wales. (He will, in any case, attempt to argue that in justification.) Householders here could then feel that their increased tax burden was at least the consequence of a decision made at the national level, in the national interest. As things are, they see themselves disadvantaged compared with their counterparts over the border. Now could be the time for the opposition parties at the Assembly to make hay, especially since Labour, still the largest party with 29 seats, is now outnumbered by the combined opposition parties, which have 31. But in the event of defeat for Labour, on this or any other issue, its replacement by the unlikely coalition of Plaid Cymru, Lib-Dem and Tory would achieve little, because the incoming government group would be hamstrung by the limits placed on the powers of the Assembly.

The White Paper, 'Better Governance for Wales', a weak and watery Westminster response to the recommendations of the Richard Commission, accepts that the present devolution settlement does not allow the Assembly 'significantly to influence the legislative framework', and that there is a need to 're-balance legislative authority towards the Assembly'. This appears a sound premise for recasting the role of Assembly members to ensure they examine proposed legislation and debate the issues involved. After all, they will soon have use of a splendid new chamber, designed by Richard Rogers, in which to display their debating skills. Alas, the White Paper does not envisage a development of that sort, at once radical and sensible. It proposes instead that, whenever so moved, Assembly government ministers should send suggested pieces of legislation up to Westminster, to be considered first by the Secretary of State for Wales and his cabinet colleagues. That hurdle safely negotiated, they would go before Parliament and, if Parliament agrees, become law in Wales under a procedure known as an Order in Council. It does not require unusual intelligence to perceive that the generality of Assembly members are likely to play no bigger part in shaping legislation under this system than at present: so much for re-balancing legislative authority.

The most important job of the Assembly is to hand out the

money it receives from Westminster and Europe. As in Scotland and Northern Ireland, the amount of the Treasury's annual block grant to Wales is dictated by application of the Barnett Formula, a calculation based upon population rather than assessment of needs. Some argue that it works to our advantage, others are equally certain it does not. Either way, nothing can be done about it, nor can the Assembly raise a little extra on its own account through taxation. With powers thus circumscribed, and likely to remain so for the foreseeable future, it is no wonder that critics of the Assembly complain it is no more than a talking shop.

Economic development is a major priority of the Assembly government. Vast sums are spent in an effort to persuade industrial concerns from overseas to set up in Wales. The venturing of public funds in this way is always a gamble, no matter how well the ground has been researched, and there have been one or two spectacular failures. It is a commoner complaint that modestly sized companies take the grants and premises on offer, recruit a work force, trade for a few years and then pull out, presumably to benefit from grants and premises available elsewhere. Assembly government nevertheless claims its policy and strategies have been successful and points to significant falls in unemployment over the past several years as proof.

For some time now, a consortium led by Lord (Richard) Attenborough has been in negotiation with local authorities and Assembly government for support in the construction of film and television studios, a media centre and a film theme park on the regenerated site of an opencast coal mine at Llanilid, near Bridgend. From the outset, several years ago, there was no lack of enthusiasm 'in principle' locally for what predictably became known as 'Valleywood', but only now are there clear signs of development. European Union Objective One funding, channelled through the Assembly, will bring £2.4 million to the project, and another five million is being sought from the Assembly's regional selective assistance pot. Work on the main studio complex is expected to start this autumn. The location is conveniently close to the M4 and the coalfield valleys, which still come off worst in any statistics of employment and community health and wealth. It is an attractive project for many reasons, the prospect of two thousand jobs foremost among them. The University of Glamorgan is keen to become involved and plans to set up a film academy directly associated with the studios. In July, Lord Attenborough received an honorary doctorate from the university.

Historians and writers have testified to the contribution of the cinema in its heyday to the culture of the Valleys. Once the various chapel denominations were catered for, the miners turned their attention to reading, entertainment and sport. Pennies deducted weekly from their wages paid for the workmen's halls and welfare parks that sprouted in every village and township. There were scores of them all over south Wales, some very grand, each with its library, reading room, billiard saloon and cinema. At the undistinguished Workmen's Hall in Gilfach Goch, the cinema, typically, doubled as a theatre where our local drama society performed and where an annual weeklong drama festival attracted groups from all over south Wales. I recall seeing Eliot's *Murder in the Cathedral* and Anouilh's *Antigone* during one such week in the late 1940s. But cinema was the staple. Whatever Hollywood, Pinewood or Elstree turned out, sooner or (usually much) later found its way to 'the Hall', where we often queued to get in, especially at weekends. There was a children's matinee on Saturday morning, which invariably had a packed and raucous audience that loved Tarzan, cowboys, as long as they didn't sing and had no girl friends, Flash Gordon and the Three Stooges. In those virtually sweetless wartime days, some of my acquaintance improvised by bringing raw swedes into the auditorium, which they hacked with pocket knives to distribute slices along the row – a healthy option, perhaps. Whether the action could be interpreted as a critique of the quality of the swede or of the film then showing is unclear, but on one occasion a large vegetable stump hurled from somewhere in the darkness of the stalls tore the screen and put paid to matinees for a while.

Gilfach, remarkably for so small a village, had a second cinema, the Globe, all access to which was along frequently muddy unmade roads and back lanes. It was cheap, from the shilling hard plush-backed seats in the back to the threepenny wooden benches at the front, but must have ordered from a different distributor, for it showed films that we did not see in the Hall, frequently in an unorthodox and disconcerting way. Dai Griffiths, the owner and projectionist, had unreliable equipment and liked a drink before the evening showing. From time to time we saw dramatic narrative rearranged in a way that might have appealed to B.S. Johnson, because the reels of film were shown in random order. More often, the celluloid snapped in the projector and the action was halted until a repair could be effected. At such hiatuses, which might occur several times in one film, a cacophony of shouting would ensue, along with thunderous stamping on the bare boards of the wooden floor. No matter. There I saw *The Great Dictator*, *King Kong*, Olivier's *Henry V* and Cocteau's *La Belle et la Bête* and *Orphée*, which I look back on as certainly memorable if not formative experiences. Although they gave us a distorted view of peoples and places, films brought romance and adventure into our lives and were a constant stimulus to the imagination. I am sure that going to the cinema also enhanced the strong sense of community prevailing at that time, in a way that visits to the nearest multiplex or sitting before the television cannot do today. But when I see the work of gifted directors, cinematographers and creators of special effects, I envy those involved in the business. As Hywel Williams points out in the *Guardian,* 'per capita, few countries have produced so many actors as Wales'. With luck and a fair wind, developments at Llanilid will enable us to turn out talented screenwriters and filmmakers to match, build on small but significant achievements of recent years, especially in animation, and perhaps eventually justify the soubriquet 'Valleywood' to cinemagoers all over the world.

*PN Review* 167, Volume 32 Number 3, January – February 2006.

# WALES, NEW ZEALAND AND RUGBY
*November 2005*

Welshmen were among the earliest Europeans to visit the coastline of New Zealand, but they did not arrive in any numbers. They lacked the economic and political incentives to abandon Britain that prompted the flight to foreign shores of the Irish and Scots, and perhaps they were more law-abiding than the English, whose convicted felons turned up by the shipload not too far off, in Australia and Tasmania. In the 2001 census, asked to indicate their ethnic affiliation, 3,784 New Zealanders admitted to being Welsh, barely enough to hold a decent eisteddfod, or maintain the traditions of choral singing, *cawl* and Welsh cakes.

In 2005, between mid-June and mid-July, this meagre total was increased three-fold. Of more than twenty thousand supporters of the British and Irish Lions rugby union party then touring the country, a good half were from Wales. Wherever you went, North Island or South, in that month, there were cheerful Welsh voices. If you started singing that fine old hymn 'Calon Lan' on a crowded bus shuttling between bars and hotels, before you could finish the first line the rest of the hitherto unidentifiable passengers would have joined in. You would be mistaken in thinking this an index of the relative affluence of the Welsh (no matter how carefully you budget, a month in the Antipodes does not come cheaply); rather, it shows how far some people are prepared to save, or run into debt, for the sake of a drink and a good time in connection with rugby. This, too, is a tradition in Wales, and never so well sustained as when the Welsh team is successful, as at present. Had they travelled all that way in the expectation of seeing a strong Welsh representation in a victorious Lions team, they returned disappointed on both counts. Mismanagement and coaching ineptitude put paid to that. Little hope survives of Sir Clive Woodward advancing to a peerage. After the calamity of the First Test, played in atrocious weather, which the All Blacks easily mastered, every knowledgeable rugby follower knew the series was a lost cause and settled for the pleasures that, even in winter, New Zealand affords.

On the roads between Queenstown in the south and Bay of Islands in the north, the visitors saw, from the windows of their tour coaches, or of the convoys of camper vans that carried them to rugby venues and tourist centres, a landscape that was sometimes like a virtual memory of their own rural past, park-like, with green rolling hills parcelled out between overgrown hedges, where sheep and cattle grazed, and modest wooden-framed houses standing in garden plots. And sometimes it was strange, not just with the peculiarity of the other side of the world, but other-worldly strange. In many parts, the green hills, wrinkled with age or soil creep, have a character entirely their own, while the rainforest, a myriad greens, flourishing in the depths of winter, with its tree ferns and festoons of mosses, seems the most primitive environment on earth.

New Zealand (*Aotearoa,* 'land of the long white cloud', in the Maori language) lies between 34 and 47 degrees south latitude. Transposed to our hemisphere, one might think of its southern extremity roughly at Nantes, and its northernmost cape some distance south of Algiers. But Australia, its nearest neighbour of any consequence (and popular rival, to be spoken of scornfully, if at all), is almost a thousand miles to the west, over the Tasman Sea. Set sail due east, out into the Pacific, and your next landfall is Chile, about four thousand miles away. It is remote, far beyond our normal understanding of the word, and exposed to the 'Roaring Forties', the persistent, often violent, westerly winds blowing across the sea, which bring mean rainfall figures of over twenty-five feet to the Southern Alps, while the plains in the lee of the mountains have only sixteen inches. A fault line runs up the western side of the Southern Alps, which were thrust up no more than ten million years ago. The forces that created them are still active, for New Zealand is perched on the geological borderland of the Pacific and Australian Plates. Hence its volcanoes, earthquakes, hot springs and geysers. Although visitors know what to expect, Rotorua is still a surprise: a town with a thousand steam laundries going full blast somewhere beneath the streets. The fault continues under the Cook Strait, through Wellington, the capital city, and on up the eastern side of North Island. Dave, our tour bus driver, whose droll commentary enlivened travel days, says the fault is directly beneath the NZ Civil Defence HQ, the frequently flooded cellar of an official building. No one is concerned: civil defence and the military are not high priorities of government.

Of the significant centres of population on our itinerary, Christchurch, Wellington and Auckland, only the last has the feel of a modern, cosmopolitan city, complete with rush-hour traffic jams and a PR machine that makes the most of its yacht-packed harbour ('City of Sails'), and its needle-like 'Sky Tower' with a revolving restaurant at the top, which trumps the similar but somewhat lower structure boasted by Sydney, Australia. Wellington is pretty grand on a modest scale, and Christchurch, with its fine new art gallery, yellow trams and punts on the river in summer, is a delight – except when blue sky is suddenly devoured by black clouds, a big wind gets up and icy rain comes at you horizontally. There are few other urban areas of any size. For the most part, New Zealand is a place of scattered small towns, usually no more than a single main street of low buildings, shops and dwellings, with overhanging fronts and awnings affording shelter from sun and rain, which would look as much at home in Arizona. A few have tourist attractions. Kawakawa ('Not a one horse town,' says Dave, 'because I've seen two horses there') has a public toilet block that is the envy of the Southern Hemisphere. Designed by the Viennese artist, architect and ecologist, Friedensreich Hundertwasser, this diminutive architectural marvel in the middle of a short, decidedly unlovely street is bejewelled with tiles made in local schools and bottle windows, and it makes you laugh outright, not at its oddity, but in sheer joy at its artistic exuberance. Rarely has design genius been employed on so humble an object to such wonderful effect. Hundertwasser had settled in a farm near the town in 1999. There was clearly something in New Zealand, perhaps the great open spaces and dramatic landscapes, perhaps the sound ecological stance of the government and friendliness of the people, which appealed to him. Sadly, there will be no additions to his *oeuvre* in NZ or elsewhere: he died of a heart attack sailing the Pacific on the QEII in 2000. He was returned to Kawakawa and is buried beneath a tulip tree on his own land.

The journey by road to Queenstown, about three-quarters of the way down South Island, reveals, quite close on the right, big, rolling brown hills, like a heavy swell on a muddied sea, and beyond them, for two hundred miles and more, in a great breaker line, the snow-covered Southern Alps. The town, situated among the mountains on the shores of Lake Wakatipu, is a winter sports resort, but you don't need to be a skier, or a white water rafter, to appreciate the beauty of its setting. Milford Sound, about forty miles to the west as the crow flies, but at least twice that by road, is in another dimension of experience. Towering mountains rise precipitously all around the winding inlet, feeding the tea-dark water constantly with torrents that run like quartz veins down the rain-forested slopes. So dense is the growth, and so shallow the soil, that when, from time to time, a tree loses its grip and falls away, it gathers in its descent an avalanche of vegetation and tears a long scar down the cliff. Any time of the year, Milford has rugged grandeur. On a gloomy day in the depths of winter, with squalls coming in off the Tasman Sea, it is distinctly eerie.

John Grono, a sealer by trade, found this extraordinary place by accident. Desperate for any kind of shelter from a violent storm, he headed for what he believed the merest cranny in a coastline that Captain Cook had twice passed along without noting anything of interest, and found he was able to penetrate deeper, and deeper still, until he was in sheltered water, just like that of his home port, Milford Haven, for Grono was a Welshman from Pembrokeshire. He had no difficulty finding a name for his discovery, and when he traced the main river that feeds the fjord, he named that, too, after a river he knew well, the Cleddau. Another Pembrokeshire Welshman, John Lort Stokes, commander of HMS *Acheron,* who had earlier been on the *Beagle* with Charles Darwin, fully investigated the fjord in the course of the first hydrographic survey of New Zealand, 1848-51, and renamed it Milford Sound. One of Stokes's specialist crew, Frederick John Owen Evans (who, with a name like that, must also have had strong Welsh connections, and should be remembered for other reasons) painted a watercolour of the sound, with its mountains rising majestically above the diminutive shape of the *Acheron,* which is now lodged in the National Library of New Zealand.

True, we might have seen a production of *The Duchess of Malfi* while we were there; Montana, a major wine producer, sponsors a poetry festival; and we caught up with a large and fascinating exhibition of paintings by William Hodges, the artist who sailed with Captain Cook on his second Pacific voyage; but there is little point in going all that way to seek evidence of European culture, for European presence there is of recent date. At Kerikeri, an attractive Northland town at the head of a tidal inlet from the Bay of Islands, you can visit New Zealand's oldest building, the weather-boarded Mission House, built by Rev. John Butler in 1822 and, no more than fifty yards away, the country's oldest stone building, constructed in 1836 as part of the mission station. On a glorious site overlooking the Bay of Islands are the Waitangi Treaty House and grounds, where, on 6 February 1840, local Maori chiefs became the first signatories of a treaty granting sovereignty over the whole country to Britain; by September some five hundred more had followed their example. It did not end endemic conflict among Maori tribes and between the tribes and colonisers, who were less than scrupulous in bargaining for land. A Maori rebellion in 1860 might have ended differently had the tribes been unified, but some, harbouring old grievances, joined the Imperial Forces to crush their own people. By 1869, it was all over.

It *is* worth the long journey to see what survives of Maori culture, not least in the wonderful collection at the Auckland War Memorial Museum, but also in Maori meeting houses, old and new, in song and dance, in carving in wood and stone, in the language and the pride of the people. If you take a boat to Kororareka (Russell) in the Bay of Islands, and join the mini-bus tour, you may be lucky enough to have as your guide Delia, who married a Frenchman and lived in France, but was drawn back to this, her tribal home. She will tell you that one of her ancestors was a chief who repeatedly tore down the British flag hoisted on the hill above Kororareka, when it was still the 'Hell Hole of the Pacific', a riotous haven for whalers and sealers, and how the language, long under threat, survives still and is beginning to gain ground once more since it was given official status in 1987. Her French-speaking children are having a

Maori-medium education, though it means a ninety-minute journey at the high school stage. And when their schooling is over, there is little prospect of employment, and still less of buying a home in Kororareka, which, as Russell, has attracted many wealthy second-home buyers. Although the other side of the world, it is all terribly familiar.

Bound for home, should you fly out of Auckland late on a Thursday, after an hour or so in the air, when your watch tells you it's Friday, it isn't. It's Thursday still – or again, all the way to Los Angeles and beyond. This is partly the doing of Frederick John Owen Evans, who, after painting Milford Sound, became an expert on the magnetism of iron ships and its effects on compass readings, and was a British delegate at the conference in Washington in 1885 that fixed the prime meridian and the universal day. All you know is that after crossing the Pacific and the Atlantic you drop down into Heathrow to find it is just after eleven o'clock on Friday morning, and you are tired.

*PN Review* 166, Volume 32 Number 2,
November – December 2005.

# HAY-ON-WYE

*September 2005*

I first visited Hay before its fame as 'the book town' had spread, and more than twenty years before the first, very small literary festival was held there: it was 1965. Richard Booth, who invented second-hand book buying and selling on an industrial scale, was already there and had begun attracting like-minded traders – and the interest of the media. I was teaching in Bristol at the time and collecting books in a modest way (on a teacher's salary extravagance was unthinkable). I had an old-fashioned gentlemanly arrangement with George's bookshop, where there was a fine antiquarian section and, in David Slade, a friendly and excellent bibliographer, which allowed me to purchase books beyond my means and pay for them gradually, sometimes over many months, with never a mention of interest, never a word of admonition for tardiness. All that changed when George's was taken over by Blackwell's. Almost the first I knew of this was when a Seneca folio of about 1490, which I coveted, was snatched away by Sir Basil, even though I had seen it first. Then the accountants got to work and I was informed that my account had to be regularised, and finally, catastrophically, the antiquarian section in Bristol was closed because the experts advised that part of the business should be centralised in Oxford. George's went the way of all those fine shops which took pride in their individuality and in good relations with loyal customers, destroyed in that ghastly push for bland marketing, commercial growth and the maximising of profit. A rump of George's, now Blackwells, remains in Park Street, totally indistinguishable from any big book retailer. Anyway, I had an interest in old books and when I read, or heard on the radio, that an enormous second-hand collection was accumulating in Hay-on-Wye, I wanted to see for myself.

A family outing was planned – a foolhardy undertaking. Our two boys, then four and five, enjoyed a long car journey no more than most children of their age. And it was a long journey, for the first Severn Bridge was under construction (finally opening the following year, just after we returned here to live). Drivers could either take their chance on the Aust ferry, which was as dodgy as roulette, or flog their way up to Gloucester and down the other side of the estuary into Wales. I looked at the map and chose the latter route.

Happily, any recollection of the hours spent on the road has vanished. At last we reached Hay and, since there is not much to the town, soon found our way to an ancient stone building, where a sample of Booth's vast hoard, plundered by the library-load from all over Wales, and doubtless further afield, lay in mounds a few feet high on the dusty floorboards. The books appeared to have been dropped by a dump truck, unsorted. The method for a prospective purchaser was to select a book, and take it to one of the casually dressed 'staff' loafing about, who would there and then conjure up a price. In this way I acquired unremarkable eighteenth-century editions of Swift's *Miscellanies* and Dryden's poems and a miniature New Testament, which, because it was small, had caught the eye of the children, all for a few shillings. Realising that, however accidental the creation of bookhills might appear, someone had already rifled them for any item of value, I turned my attention to volumes ranked on makeshift shelves low down against the walls, mostly long runs of nineteenth-century magazines, neat in quarter-leather bindings, for sale by the yard to interior decorators. I knew about *Blackwood's Magazine,* famous rival of the *Edinburgh*

*Review,* and notoriously critical of the 'Cockney School of Poetry', but had not until then seen a single copy. Here it was, year after year, stretching away into the distance.

A yard of *Blackwood's* was beyond my means but, as luck would have it, there were a few duplicate volumes from a broken set. I carried off four, April 1820 to December 1821, and have them still. The brutality of the literary criticism shocks even now. Take, for example, these lines from 'Remarks on Shelley's Adonais', five pages of tirade and parody:

> The present story is thus: – A *Mr John Keats,* a young man who had left a decent calling for the melancholy trade of Cockney poetry, has lately died of a consumption, after having written two or three little books of verses, much neglected by the public. His vanity was probably wrung not more than his purse; for he had it upon the authority of the Cockney Homers and Virgils, that he might become a light to their region at a future time. But all this is not necessary to help a consumption to the death of a poor sedentary man, with an unhealthy aspect, and a mind harassed by the first troubles of versemaking. The New School, however, will have it that he was slaughtered by a criticism of the Quarterly Review [...] We are not now to defend a publication so well able to defend itself. But the fact is, that the Quarterly finding before it a work at once silly and presumptuous, full of the servile slang that Cockaigne dictates to its servitors, and the vulgar indecorums which that Grub Street Empire rejoiceth to applaud, told the truth of the volume, and recommended a change of manners and of masters to the scribbler. Keats wrote on: but he wrote *indecently,* probably in indulgence of his social propensities.

Understanding that the motivation for the attack was more political than literary does nothing to mitigate its scornful savagery.

The continuing controversy over a review by Dai Smith of Stephen Knight's *A Hundred Years of Fiction* in *New Welsh Review* (No. 66, Winter 2004) also has a conspicuous political dimension. Professor Knight's book, in the 'Writing Wales in English' series, offers a valuable survey of fictional views of Wales by Welsh writers in English from about 1880 to the present, together with an analysis of them in terms of post-colonial theory. Dai Smith applauds the author for the book's 'careful delineation of story lines and its occasionally riveting critiques of particular books' but castigates the post-colonial analysis. His review opens with use of the demotic ('This book done my 'ead in'), a device which some have seen as an attempt to approach a difficult critical issue, and a somewhat embarrassing situation (Stephen Knight is, after all, a highly regarded Professor of English at Cardiff University, while Dai Smith was then Vice-Chancellor at the University of Glamorgan), with characteristic humour. Others have construed it as an insult. I fear I shall oversimplify a highly complex argument, but the book posits a Wales finally conquered by the English at the beginning of the fifteenth century, linguistically subjugated since the Tudor Acts of Union and, in recent times, industrially exploited, while being deprived of dignity by assertions of the English establishment (in the 1847 'Blue Books') that its language is inferior and its culture immoral. Two questions arise relating to the definition of colonisation. Is the highly simplified sketch above an image of a colony, comparable with, say, British India? Or does the term admit of a more insidious colonising – that constant undermining of traditional values and the language in which they are couched, which, in Wales, has left a scar on the psyche of fiction writers demonstrable by careful analysis? For Dai Smith, among the finest of Welsh historians, recently appointed to a research chair at Swansea University, there is a more important third question:

does the image correspond to the known historical facts? He says it does not.

In the next number of *New Welsh Review* (67), Professor Jane Aaron, head of the Centre for Modern and Contemporary Wales at the University of Glamorgan, took up the editor's invitation to respond to Dai Smith, rebutting his arguments by quoting authorities (Raymond Williams, Glanmor Williams) he drew upon, and adding a few of her own, notably Franz Fanon and Norman Davies. Professor Aaron also suggests that the review was a product of political ideology ('Dai Smith's protest against "psycho-colonialism" is the voice of Old Labour refusing to budge without a struggle') and that there is 'in certain quarters' a conspiracy of sorts, 'a desire ...to stamp out the concept of postcolonial Wales before it is given further opportunity to challenge Old Labour fortifications'. So 'old' Labour cannot, or will not, accept that Wales is emerging from colonial status. One might see in this the implication that those of a different political persuasion, Plaid supporters presumably, can and do. While indifferent to the political argument, I am concerned that postcolonial (or any other) theory should be applied willy-nilly to writers, regardless of their perception, if not their intention, or 'proved' by demonstration of its application to carefully selected and outlandish examples.

One would not expect the debate to end there. Indeed, Dai Smith has replied in the latest *New Welsh Review*, and may well be present at the Hay Festival, where under the chairmanship of its editor, Francesca Rhydderch (who is beginning to display a talent for stirring the prevailing calm that Keidrychh Rhys might admire), the magazine is hosting a poetry reading and a discussion of this and other issues, involving Kathryn Gray, Patrick McGuinness and Tom Paulin. We could do with more literary debate, seasoned, as it may be, with a soupçon of acerbity.

The *Guardian,* broadsheet sponsor of the festival, is the major source of information about the programme, or at least about celebrities, Piers Morgan, the Hitchens brothers and so on. *Guardian* readers would never know that Hay is in Wales, and that there are events, throughout the week, concerned with writing and publishing in Wales. It is rather like living in a parallel universe. One item of news deserving a headline was the formal inauguration there of Gwyneth Lewis as National Poet of Wales. She is a writer of very rare talent in both Welsh and English and an outstanding cultural ambassador. The choice could not have been bettered. On the same day, Mererid Hopwood, the first woman to win the Chair at the National Eisteddfod, was appointed Children's Laureate at that great arts festival for the young people of Wales, the Urdd Eisteddfod, held this year at the Wales Millennium Centre, where Gwyneth Lewis's magical words are emblazoned on the broad front of the building. Media reporting of this event was confined to two inches in the *Western Mail,* which does, however, do the job of a 'national newspaper' in covering the eisteddfod with a thoroughness normally reserved for rugby football.

Early in May I was at WMC to watch the Welsh Union of Writers sail into the sunset. The union was set up in 1982 with the aim of representing authors vis-à-vis publishers, the media, arts councils and the like. The dynamism of its first chairman, the writer and broadcaster, John Morgan, secured for it a dashing start, with campaigns on behalf of writers for more media attention and more widespread use of writing by contemporary authors in schools and colleges. An attempt to found a new magazine failed for lack of funding from the Welsh Arts Council. After John Morgan's early death in 1988, successive chairmen had the support of Robin Reeves, a Fleet Street journalist who had returned to edit the *New Welsh Review* with style and brought a fund of ideas to the union, which he preferred to communicate behind the scenes. Sadly, he too died desperately young, and since then WUW has been largely becalmed. Nigel Jenkins, a former chairman, paid tribute to both and spoke of the committee's long, expectant wait for a youthful coup, which never came. In the end, rather than let the union dwindle away, it seemed better to wind it up and hold a wake at WMC and a curry house in Cardiff Bay: not with a whimper, but a bang.

*PN Review* 165, Volume 32 Number 1, September – October 2005.

# GILFACH GOCH AND CHILDHOOD
*January 2005*

Radio reports today prominently feature a Home Office initiative to counter anti-social behaviour. The citizens of Cardiff, Swansea and Newport are among those to be singled out for special attention. The pleas of victims will be heeded and uncouth louts, graffiti artists and bad neighbours will be purged. Or at least ASBOs will be applied. It is a real enough cause: parts of our towns and villages are befouled, dreary and, sometimes, menacing. Any amelioration of the condition of the communities worst affected will be a godsend. Besides, politicians are always desperate to be seen to be doing something vaguely within their grasp, and never more so than when they face intractable problems elsewhere. The majority of chief constables in Wales may disagree with the plans they are to implement, but the politicians are determined, conveniently forgetting that they are responsible for creating the heartless estates where most of the problems occur.

This news has intensified my brooding upon the lost past, my boyhood in Gilfach Goch. Perhaps it is the time of year that induces melancholy reflection upon change and the state of society. How unsophisticated we were, and how enormously fortunate. Because of the way houses were strung in terraces along the valley slopes, a little above the industrial heart and purpose of the village, few were more than a hundred yards or so from the open mountain. For most of us, the mountain began at the back garden gate. That was the domain of childhood. What we did there on the acres of rough grass, in dense patches of bracken, and the disused stone quarries that scarred the slopes, was out of the sight of

536

adults and usually beyond their care. Only the ubiquitous sheep were the slightest interested in our activities.

My young boyhood coincided with the war years, which had a profound influence on our play. We belonged to neighbourhood gangs. I was in a gang led by George Vaughan, whose brothers, Douglas and Glyn, were in the forces. George led us on what he called 'commando training', which involved a great deal of running, creeping towards imaginary enemies, leaping streams, climbing quarries and scrambling up and down slag heaps. It was inventive, physical and not without risks. Health and safety experts would take a poor view of it. We had target practice, throwing stones at tins and bottles from the nearby ash-tip (a household refuse dump), set up on the broken wall of a long-abandoned pit engine house. Sometimes we threw stones at one another. I was once hit on the head and had the bleeding wound licked by Dash, George's dog, which did no harm and cheered me up. There was no vandalism. The mountain was impervious to damage, if you discount firing the grass, which left great black patches that soon disappeared under fresh growth.

I forget: there was the occasion when the brake holding a line of trucks full of coal was released, with spectacular results when they toppled off the track. The culprit, whom we all knew, must have been terrified, but nothing ever came of it. And then there was the battle on the mountain. This was warfare by arrangement, the sort of thing engaged in by primitive tribes on remote Pacific islands. On a fine summer Saturday morning, the gangs of the top of the valley amalgamated to take on the combined force of the gangs of the bottom end in a 'charge', the local term for a stone fight. They clashed in the middle, on the hillside above our house, where, having torn ligaments in my ankle, I hopped about in the garden in a heavy plaster cast, exhorting the combatants. Inevitably some stones flew wildly and landed in the road near the steps of the Con Club, to the consternation of lunchtime drinkers and other passers-by. The following Monday morning, every boy at the three elementary schools in the valley was caned, whether he was involved or not. The vast majority were, so justice of a sort was done and the engagement was never repeated.

The streets were patrolled by two policemen, Hobbs (the sergeant) and Walker, who stoutly embodied the law. They knew every family in the valley and were capable of delivering summary justice to any man drunk or foolish enough to overstep the boundaries of conventional behaviour. If anything went missing, they knew where to look, but such events were exceedingly rare. Neighbours possessed nothing worth the trouble of stealing and there is little thrill in breaking in where doors are commonly unlocked. All this is so far in the past, and so totally irrelevant to present circumstances, that one could weep. Almost any account of a more or less happy young life can have the same effect. The humour of Dylan Thomas's *Portrait of the Artist as a Young Dog* is permeated with nostalgia, and 'Fern Hill', hackneyed perhaps, and distinctly rural, nevertheless retains its widespread appeal as an elegiac evocation of irrecoverable childhood that stands for our own experience of different times and places.

These days I prefer 'Poem in October'. If Thomas were alive today, he might begin his birthday poem, 'It was my ninetieth year to heaven...' for he was born on 27 October 1914. On the same date in 2004, yet another handsome award for writers to aspire to, 'The Dylan Thomas Literary Prize', was announced simultaneously at the Dylan Thomas Centre in Swansea and the Algonquin Hotel, New York, asymmetrical bookends of his own short story. Every other year, the prize will go to the author of 'the best book published in English anywhere in the world by an author aged under 30' (I do not envy the judges). It should have attracted a whirlwind of publicity, because it is worth

£60,000 to the winner and has the enthusiastic support of Catherine Zeta Jones, who will be its 'international ambassador', but so far seems to have come to the notice of BBC Radio Wales and the *Western Mail* only. Peter Stead, historian, man about culture in Wales and formidable *Round Britain Quiz* contestant, is its local spokesperson, and may even have inspired this answer to Cardiff's Artes Mundi Prize, an international award for artists inaugurated earlier in 2004, without notable acclaim. At its first attempt, this must be accounted a failure, regardless of the quality of the work displayed, since all such prizes pander to the cult of celebrity and are more concerned with self-promotion than promotion of art or artist. For the moment at least, 'Booker' and 'Turner' organisers can rest easy, though Mrs Douglas, who is strongly attached to her Swansea roots, has the celebrity to attract substantial media attention. A personal appearance at the Dylan Thomas Centre or the Algonquin on this occasion would have brought journalists and photographers from far and wide, but not the recorded message she sent.

'Academi', the national literature promotion agency, is about to move into the Wales Millennium Centre, which now dominates Cardiff Bay. There it will join the Urdd (the still flourishing and very remarkable Welsh youth movement), Diversions, the contemporary dance company, High Jinks theatre company, the Welsh Music Federation, Touch (an arts and music trust for the disabled), and the Welsh National Opera. The building, which opens on 26 November, has a 1900-seat lyric theatre, a studio theatre seating 250, a dance studio, an orchestra rehearsal hall, a recording studio, and residential accommodation for 150 young people, as well as shops and cafés. From Penarth, across the bay, on a cloudy day, the massive dome of the building has the appearance of another dark hill, matching those that rise behind it, to the north of

Cardiff – until a gleam of sunlight transmutes it to gold. At close quarters, its slate walls, banded in the stone's natural colours, green, purple, blue, grey and black, remind the viewer of sea cliffs and castles. Black pillars inside are etched in the familiar lozenge pattern of coal measures fossil ferns. Slate, coal and steel, mountains, cliffs and castles have a collective resonance that lacks only language to be nationally representative. And that, too, is present. An inscription runs across the broad front, overhanging the main entrance. The letters, eight feet high, incised into the steel, serve as windows to let daylight in and, when lights go on inside the building, spell out their bilingual message to the night: 'In These Stones Horizons Sing/*Creu Gwir Fel Gwydr o Ffwrnais Awen*' ('Make truth like glass from the furnace of inspiration'). If not the longest, this is, surely, the largest poem in print. At the outset, Academi had a part to play in organising a competition inviting submission of poems or sayings to fill the allotted space. There were over two hundred entries, none suitable. In the end the words were written by Gwyneth Lewis, who has described the bold *façade* as 'the biggest and best piece of paper ever'.

In advance of the opening, WMC has received the kind of media attention normally reserved for celebrity, and attracted generally favourable comment from London broadsheet architecture journalists. At home here in Caerleon, we have watched its development very closely from its first appearance as a design sketch, for (and now I must declare an interest) Jonathan Adams, the architect, is our son.

*PN Review* 161, Volume 31 Number 3,
January – February 2005.

# THE NATIONAL EISTEDDFOD
*November 2004*


As many readers will be aware, the National Eisteddfod, which always occurs in the first week of August, is a movable feast. The venues are announced sufficiently in advance to allow preparation and, especially, fund-raising in the chosen locality commensurate with the scale of the undertaking. Make no mistake, the National is big; in rural parts it can dwarf its host. This is one reason why it is always designated to a town or village '*a'r Cylch*', that is, 'and its surrounding area'. The other, and more precious, reason is that, for that one week in many years, perhaps a lifetime, the people of a fairly wide district can, if they have the inclination, take a share of the responsibility for maintaining a great engine of the Welsh language, and enjoying themselves in the process. The culture of the chapel appears in terminal decline, and the efforts of education and administration to fill the void are, at best, hit and miss. The Eisteddfod, spluttering and backfiring as must be expected from time to time, remains a reliable machine dedicated to this purpose. For the rest, there are only activist organisations like Cymdeithas yr Iaith (the Welsh Language Society).

This year the Eisteddfod returned to Casnewydd a'r Cylch, Newport and District. It had previously occupied the site at Tredegar Park, Newport, in 1988. Despite the efforts of its town, and now city, council in the last decade or so to refurbish the centre and add the odd aesthetic touch, no one could claim that Newport, an old port and industrial centre on the tidal estuary of the Usk, is an attractive place. It doesn't even qualify for the 'ugly, lovely' epithet that Dylan Thomas attached to Swansea. However, in Tredegar House it has one of the architectural gems of Wales. I visited it first in 1970, when it housed a Catholic girls' school and its grandeur had become very shabby. Since purchasing the house and estate in 1974, the borough has invested belief and a great deal of money in refurbishment, and they have paid off handsomely. In the *Gwent/Monmouthshire* volume of John Newman's 'Buildings of Wales' series (a continuation of Pevsner), it is described as 'one of the outstanding houses of the Restoration period of the whole of Britain'. Although its origins are older by a century or more, the present house was largely built c.1664-74 at the command of William Morgan, scion of the Morgans of Tredegar, supporters of Henry Tudor and beneficiaries of his largesse as Henry VII. The architects were probably Roger and William Hurlbutt, master carpenters of Warwick, who clearly knew a thing or two about design. 'What makes the exterior of Tredegar House unforgettable,' writes Newman, 'is the Bath stone enrichments, of a luxuriant bravura, quite unlike the normally restrained Restoration style.' You might view it, briefly, from the M4, down an avenue of trees and through 'sumptuous' wrought-iron gates. Its pale red brick (that modern manufacturers seem incapable of replicating) has the glow of cherished antiquity. If you come within striking distance of Newport, and have a little time to spare, do not miss it.

The estate surrounding the house is much diminished, but still afforded space and to spare for setting up the Eisteddfod on one flat site, which is more than many venues can manage. Across the road, a public park accommodated the caravan village of loyal, mobile *eisteddfodwyr* (eisteddfod-goers). There are many such, who follow it from site to site, no matter how much travelling and inconvenience is involved, and attend the full week of activities. It is an annual reunion as well as a celebration of Welsh culture. As you walk the *maes* (the Eisteddfod field), you are sure to meet friends from other parts of Wales. And this year, with the sale of beer permitted on the *maes* for the first time, you could have a pint together. Eateries of various kinds proliferate among the ranks of tents and stalls and pavilions assembled on either side of metal walkways, designed to keep feet mudfree in the wet. Although, happily, the sun shone on the Eisteddfod in 2004; it is not always so. For ten pounds you could lunch handsomely and in comfort. Eisteddfod catering is superior to anything at the Hay Festival.

At a rough count, some two hundred and seventy institutions, organisations, shops and services were represented on the *maes* at Newport. They included the media, education at all levels, the National Library, the Museums and Galleries of Wales, publishers, charities, religious organisations, banking interests, political parties, the National Assembly. To visit a third in a full day would be a major achievement, without penetrating to the cultural heart of the Eisteddfod, the *Pabell Lên* (literature tent), various performance areas, and, of course, the four thousand seat *Pafiliwn,* (pavilion), where the major competitions are adjudicated and prizes awarded. This is where the Crown and the Chair ceremonies take place, for the winning bards in the competitions for the *pryddest* (a poem in the free metres) and the *awdl* (a poem in the strict metres of Welsh prosody) respectively. Although the routine, repeated year after year, is familiar to all, it still possesses colour and excitement enough to enthral, especially as the climax approaches and searchlights sweep the huge audience to pick out the one standing figure, who will be cloaked in purple and led to the ornate chair at the centre of the stage. And this, remember, is to celebrate the achievement of a poet.

Paul Flynn, the highly respected Newport MP, spent a great

deal of time on the *maes*, finally turning up for the *Cymanfa Ganu* (singing festival) that ended the Eisteddfod, just as the weather broke on Sunday evening. He has learned Welsh and is probably the only Labour politician at Westminster sympathetic to the constitutional reforms proposed by the Richard Commission. By the beginning of August, the notion of extending law-making and tax-raising powers to Wales, five or six years hence, had been so mauled by the great majority of his former parliamentary colleagues that Rhodri Morgan, first minister at the National Assembly, decided he dare not risk putting Richard, unadulterated, before the Labour conference in September. Instead, he and Peter Hain MP, who is, among other things, Secretary of State for Wales, hatched a compromise proposal. This will (if adopted and implemented in due course) allow the assembly to vary Westminster legislation in those areas, like health and education, which are already devolved, and, perhaps, enable previous such legislation to be amended retrospectively. Like all compromises it satisfies no one. Rhodri Morgan has not had a good summer. His failure to attend the sixtieth anniversary of the Normandy landings (he went to lunch at a golf club instead) exposed him to a prolonged barrage of criticism from all quarters. And, just as he was emerging from his shelter, his failure to arrive at the Royal Welsh showground in Builth in time to greet the Queen drew down fresh opprobrium. Whether his judgement is at fault, or that of his advisers, is difficult to determine. Perhaps he has simply been unlucky. Tony Blair might claim as much over the unmitigated disaster that is the outcome of his Iraq adventure.

Weeks before the Eisteddfod, Dannie Abse, uncrowned laureate of English language poetry in Wales, visited Caerleon (whether I like it or not, another part of the city of Newport). He came to read at a local infants' school in aid of the organisation 'Women to Women for Peace', which 'questions war as a means of resolving conflict and supports peacemakers'. He read from his *New and Collected Poems* (Hutchinson, 2003), which is a very substantial testimony to the grace and staying power of his muse and the breadth of his appeal. He remains, as ever, modest, retains his casual, unruffled charm, and makes the reading of poetry seem easy – which it is not. Although, for the occasion, the poems he read were about war and conflict, it is their humanity that lingers, long after the reading is over. There was room, too, for humour. He told the familiar story (which will nevertheless bear repetition) of being asked, not long after the war, to write an article about contemporary Hebrew poets. Having no Hebrew he resorted to translations, but was disconcerted to find the few available had been rendered in an impeccably Georgian manner, 'as though they had all been written by John Drinkwater'. He decided to invent his own Hebrew poet, Dov Shamir, and compose an illustrative 'translation' for him. Hence 'Song for Dov Shamir':

Working is another way of praying.
You plant in Israel the soul of a tree.
You plant in the desert the spirit of gardens.

Praying is another way of singing.
You plant in the tree the soul of lemons.
You plant in the gardens the spirit of roses.

Singing is another way of loving.
You plant in the lemons the spirit of your son.
You plant in the roses the soul of your daughter.

Loving is another way of living.
You plant in your daughter the spirit of Israel.
You plant in your son the soul of the desert.

This was early in his writing career and one cannot help admiring the cheek of it. The article was published without a question raised. Soon after he sent a selection of his work to T.S. Eliot, then with Faber. Eliot's reply offered the observation that his best work was the 'translation', and perhaps he had better stick to that.

*PN Review* 160, Volume 31 Number 2,
November – December 2004.

# PLAID CYMRU
*July 2004*

In the wake of last year's Welsh Assembly elections, Plaid Cymru, which suffered a damaging reverse, found itself in disarray. The party's leader and president, Ieuan Wynn Jones, resigned – and then offered himself for re-election as leader in the chamber only. To the surprise of many he won the contest. The winner of the subsequent presidential election was equally unexpected: Dafydd Iwan. The latter is clearly well known among the party membership, and well supported, particularly by the younger element, but I doubt his past fame and current political eminence in Wales have registered beyond Offa's Dyke.

He was born in Brynaman, Carmarthenshire, in 1943. His father, a bookish Independent minister, was related to a famous family of *beirdd gwlad* (country poets), steeped in the essentially amateur Welsh-language tradition of composition and, often competitive, performance in the community and further afield. In his essay in *Artists in Wales 3* (edited by Meic Stephens, 1977), Dafydd Iwan recounts his introduction to public performance in his father's chapel and at Sunday School and chapel eisteddfodau, before progression, via the village eisteddfod and local Urdd eisteddfod to the Urdd National, singing penillion in the under-twelve competition (I have written – in *PN Review* 135 – about the Urdd, the biggest youth movement in Europe, and rejoice that it continues, still very much the same organisation of which I was a member in my schooldays). He is a graduate of the Welsh School of

Architecture but has never practised as an architect, because he made the most of every opportunity college afforded to appear on stage at social events and, having learned a few guitar chords, transformed himself into a songwriter and performer. Since then he has been a director of a recording company and organiser of a housing association, and he has devoted himself to the cause of Welsh Nationalism.

This brought him early to Cymdeithas yr Iaith Gymraeg, the Welsh Language Society, which he served as chairman from 1968 to 1971. He describes his decade of involvement in direct-action campaigns in support of the language as a time of 'Endless marches, demonstrations and rallies, a long succession of court cases and hundreds of imprisonments', including his own. It was far from pleasant, but through it all, he says, he was energised by 'the happy, heady, determined zealousness of Welsh youth fighting desperately against the tide of the world and of time'. For him, this was the good fight and the stuff of song writing.

Although highly regarded as a performer, he has never seen himself primarily as an entertainer, because he uses song as a medium of political expression. The words of his songs are invariably in Welsh and about Wales. Among the 'love songs, satirical songs, funny songs...sad songs [and] religious songs' are a few that are 'deliberately political', such as his jibing *'Carlo'* and *'Croeso Chwedeg Nain'*, which caused a furore in 1969, at the time of the investiture of Charles as Prince of Wales. But for every establishment critic there was a youthful supporter.

Whatever the occasion and the composer's intention, from time to time the combination of words and music reaches beyond the moment and fixes itself in the collective memory. So what we think of as folk songs are born. Dafydd Iwan's *'Yma o Hyd'* ('Still Here') has made that leap. Rather like 'Flower of

Scotland', it harks back to a distant historical event in order to express a contemporary idea of nationhood, and in much the same way it is beginning to be taken up by crowds at rugby matches, at least in Llanelli, many of whom, however, may have little idea what they are singing about, notwithstanding the club's boast that it has the largest Welsh-language constituency of any in Wales. The verse of *'Yma o Hyd'* recalls Magnus Maximus, the Roman Emperor: *'...Pan aeth Magnus Maximus o Gymru/Yn y flwyddyn tri chant wyth tri/A'n gadael yn genedl gyfan/A heddiw – wele ni!'* ('When Magnus Maximus went from Wales/In the year [AD] 383/And left us a complete nation/And today – look at us!'). As usual it is the chorus that has the reverberative magical property: *'Ry'n ni yma o hyd...Er gwaetha pawb a phopeth/Ry'n ni yma o hyd!'* ('We're still here...In spite of everyone and everything/We're still here!').

Almost the first public utterance of the newly installed President of Plaid Cymru was a rousing speech to the party faithful asserting the aim of independence for Wales. This is at odds with the line taken by Ieuan Wyn Jones, whose nationalist ideals are tempered by a political intuition that the electorate will take fright if Plaid were to adopt a bold 'Free Wales' slogan. News of a split in the leadership of the strongest opposition party in the Assembly brought a smile to Labour faces and even seemed to cheer up the press. But Plaid has discovered it can gain wide support for policies that are to the left of Labour, especially among the disenchanted masses whose dislike of Blairite 'New Labour' is approaching that once accorded Thatcher governments and, try as he might, the First Minister, Rhodri Morgan, cannot entirely divest himself of the taint of the Westminster leadership.

The last day of March saw publication of the report of the commission chaired by Lord Richard, former leader of the House of Lords, on 'the powers and electoral arrangements of the

National Assembly for Wales'. Media coverage of the event on 1 April seemed to be asking for trouble, but it was taken seriously enough in Wales. London-based papers, on the other hand, dismissed it in a couple of hundred words hidden away in some remote corner – which is perhaps no more than merited for, even if the commission's proposals were wholly accepted, little would change in the short term. They say that the National Assembly should have primary law-making powers by 2011. That allows for a general election to be called next year, the requisite 'Wales Bill' to be drafted soon thereafter and brought to the Commons in 2007. The legislative process may be expected to wend its way to the Royal Assent within a couple of years. But a fresh boundary review is scheduled for 2008-10, so they might as well get that out of the way before any substantive change is introduced in the way we are governed. Meanwhile, the Assembly is expected to enjoy a bigger say in those areas already devolved to Wales, notably health and education, but it will never be easy to bring in secondary legislation specifically tailored to Welsh needs in the face of opposition from Westminster, even (or perhaps especially) that of a Labour government (assuming the continuation of the Labour hegemony here).

Even looking that far ahead, while the commission is quite sanguine about granting the assembly tax raising powers, it does not recommend this vital condition of primary law making. A Labour majority in London, if it survives, would hardly embrace the notion, and it will almost certainly oppose other key recommendations: a change to the single transferable vote system for Assembly elections and an increase in the number of AMs. The former would ensure far better representation in the National Assembly of the shades of political opinion in Wales, and the latter would ensure there were sufficient politicians to take on the additional burdens of legislation. Both, however, could weaken Labour's hold on power. Typically,

Labour AMs have been urging a change in the electoral system in the other direction, to 'first past the post'.

For the moment at least, Rhodri Morgan and his colleagues at the Assembly appear eager to accept the main thrust of the commission's recommendations, but the report has been condemned out of hand by Labour MPs representing Welsh constituencies at Westminster, who are convinced that the *Encyclopaedia Britannica* had it right: 'For Wales – see England'. It is interesting to speculate upon what will unfold should the present travails of the labour government and the unpopularity of Blair lead to victory for the Tories at the next general election. Would a Tory government dirty its hands picking the Richard Report off the shelf?

The report of the National Assembly's Culture Committee on 'Welsh Writing in English', also published on 31 March, languished somewhat in the long shadow cast by Richard. Yet it is potentially of major importance to those who care about literature. The committee of AMs gathered written and oral evidence from all the organisations concerned with the English-language literature of Wales, including the Welsh Arts Council, the Welsh Books Council, the University of Wales, the University of Glamorgan, the Welsh Curriculum Council and the Welsh Joint Education Committee, Academi, the BBC, magazine editors, publishers and librarians. What emerged was largely a tale of woe, and one for which it is hard to visualise transformation to a happy ending. Publishing in Wales is 'sluggish' and 'over-dependent on subsidy from public sources'. At the heart of the problem are extraordinary difficulties in marketing and distribution compounded of lack of will, flair and finance among Welsh publishers in relation to the major booksellers, and that stubborn metropolitan ignorance of almost anything Welsh, which means that books published in Wales and sent for review to the London broadsheets are routinely dumped unopened.

Having listened, the committee was persuaded that 'there is real concern about the recognition given to Welsh writing in English, the main language of the majority of people in Wales' and that this writing 'is as distinctive a form of literature as that produced by, for example, English, Irish and American writers'. Furthermore, because it is 'more likely to be understood [than Welsh] by readers outside Wales...it is also our interface with other literary cultures world wide'. It made a series of recommendations, including an increase in grant to the Welsh Books Council (which is, among other things, an agency for distributing funds to assist book production) to allow publishers to commission 'books of popular appeal' in English, augment their editorial and marketing staff, and join energetically in a 'joint marketing strategy'. This could be money well spent, if the publishers can recruit staff up to the job.

Also on the committee's wish list is an increase in funding for the 'writers on tour' scheme; a 'Library of Wales', like the Library of America, where the classics of Welsh writing in English can be collected; improved promotion of the Book of the Year award; an extension of the remit of the Curriculum Council to enable it to commission work by Welsh writers in English for the examinations board's syllabuses; and the creation of a network of interlinked higher education research centres engaged in studies in the field. These, too, are positive suggestions. It is also recommended that libraries should do more to promote Welsh writing in English, which is within the bounds of possibility, and that discussions should be held with major booksellers, whose stock control systems are located in distant places where things Welsh are never heard or thought of, and the media, to encourage them to take an informed interest. One hopes such dialogues will be productive, but if my experience in trying to interest the literary editors of London broadsheets in the *Collected Poems of Roland Mathias* is indicative, it will be an uphill struggle.


*PN Review* 158, Volume 30 Number 6,
July – August 2004.

# EDUCATION AND POLITICS

*November 2003*

I might as well pick up the threads of this letter where I left off at the end of the last, with politics in Wales. In the 1970s, long before devolution, responsibility for all aspects of primary and secondary education this side of the Dyke was handed over to the Welsh Office. Its education department and institutions it set up put a Welsh gloss on education policy emanating from Westminster. Thus, when the National Curriculum was introduced, themes and topics for study at the various key stages were 'naturalised' wherever possible and, of course, there was always the special place accorded the Welsh language to emphasise the curricular difference between schools here and in England. The degree of freedom the system in Wales was permitted gradually increased under the regime of the Welsh Office, but since the advent of the Assembly the concept of separate development has been granted unexpectedly free rein. We have seen, for instance, formal Key Stage 1 assessments (almost universally deplored by parents and teachers everywhere) scrapped and, well in advance of similar changes now proposed in England, the introduction of a Welsh 'baccalaureate', which is slowly beginning to spread in the secondary sector.

With the transfer of control over higher education student support from Westminster to the Assembly in July of this year, it appeared that we were about to witness the most significant departure yet from New Labour education policy, for this ceding of responsibility will enable Welsh Labour to fulfil its election manifesto promise not to bring in top-up fees for university students in Wales – at least for the duration of the Assembly's second term, that is, until 2007. This is a guarantee extending only one year beyond the designated start date for top-up fees in England: not much cause for alarm or rejoicing then. Academics and political commentators were nevertheless keen to examine the reasons for and possible consequences of such action. If it were prolonged, it would unquestionably ease the debt burden of students in Wales relative to those in England and, perhaps, mitigate the danger that able young people, especially those from less-affluent backgrounds, will increasingly turn their backs on university education. But what would be the likely side effects? One might foresee students from homes in England finding study in Wales an attractive option, while for the same economic reasons their counterparts in Wales would be discouraged from seeking places at institutions in England for which they might be ideally suited. Furthermore, deprived of the income that top-up fees will generate in England, Welsh institutions would be plunged ever deeper into financial difficulty. One year of exposure to tensions of this kind will be a trial indeed. However, the education minister has declared that the Assembly Government will make up for any loss in student fee income in 2006-7. What happens after that she was in no position to say.

That the manifesto pledge was well intentioned and deserved the sympathetic support of voters cannot be doubted, but the most cursory examination suggests the effects of a different fee regime for students in Wales for only one year will not be entirely satisfactory. The nub of the problem, for whichever party finds itself in government here, is that the Assembly lacks tax-raising powers. And, without finance, policies, no matter how enlightened, cannot be followed through. When the Assembly will be granted powers equivalent to those enjoyed by the Scottish parliament is anyone's guess, and, notwithstanding the measure of separate development that has occurred in the spheres of health and education, until that happens devolution in Wales will have the aspect of charade, and occasionally pantomime.

The ship of state is steered from Westminster; the best the Assembly can do is rearrange the seating on its own part of the deck. A too literal interpretation of the trope brought about probably the most unpleasant week for Rhodri Morgan since he entered politics. Labour's proposal to alter seating arrangements in the Assembly chamber created an unprecedented furore. No longer encumbered by coalition with the Lib-Dems, it wants to have all its AMs seated together, facing the rag-tag opposition. It is the kind of thing that party representatives can sort out quietly behind closed doors (as, indeed, will now happen), but Labour decided to make it the subject of a full-scale debate. That was a silly enough notion, but when, in an attempt to justify the change and the debate, it was given out that Labour AMs feared their papers were being overlooked, if not looked over, by AMs of other parties, there was the beginning of descent into farce. The seating issue so riled the opposition that they tabled more than eight hundred amendments, which the presiding officer, Lord Dafydd Elis-Thomas, to whom the term emollient does not apply, refused to rule out. Rebuked by Labour, he countered with a scathing critique of the entire institution, thereby adding his contribution to bringing the Assembly into disrepute. It was a painful episode made worse by the scorn poured on it by the media. The public pays little attention to politics (as the election turn out revealed) but can be negatively energised by banner headlines critical of politicians – as happened on this occasion. If only the achievements of the Assembly could be publicised as enthusiastically.

The journal *Planet will* no doubt comment on these events

in due course. It may well be critical of the tactics of Welsh Assembly Government, as the Labour administration terms itself, but the discussion will be considered and balanced, as newspapers rarely are these days. I recently met the editor, John Barnie, in Abergavenny, his home town, though he has not lived there for many years. A poet and polemicist, he combined both callings in his last book, a verse novel, *Ice* (Gomer 2001). It is about our world 'after the famines and the Third Resource War', in the grip of another ice age, a dystopian vision of the ultimate effects of global warming. With bottleneck and open tuning, Barnie is also an accomplished blues guitarist and it was in this capacity he was engaged, at The Hen and Chicks, an ancient Abergavenny hostelry, along with Nigel Jenkins, another politically aware poet and essayist *(PN Review* 146), who plays a mean 'blues harp' (harmonica) and, on the keyboard, Jen Wilson, a leading figure in the Swansea jazz scene. The word 'gig' has been appropriated by poets on the circuit; this was an occasion to which it properly applied, and as stimulating a session of live entertainment as you are likely to witness in a decade of poetry readings. Barnie and Jenkins spoke and sang their words to blues accompaniment, and Jen Wilson's solos were feminist songs by jazz icons like Bessie Smith. The audience, packed into an upper room of the pub, would have stayed for more. This is not the sort of performance that can be put together on the night. If you want to emulate it, be prepared to put in a couple of months of rehearsal. Only poets with a second, musicianly, string to their bows need apply.

The launch of Lawrence Normand's book *W.H. Davies* also brought a full house to Newport Library a few days later. This is the twenty-third in Seren's 'Border Lines' series, which includes, among others, critical biographies of Francis Kilvert, Arthur Machen, Henry Vaughan, Bruce Chatwin and Raymond Williams. The series editor is John Powell Ward, a former editor of *Poetry Wales*, whose own thought-provoking, quietly disturbing poetry deserves a wide readership. Born in Suffolk, educated partly in Canada and, after twenty-five years at the University of Wales, Swansea, almost an adopted Welshman, he is familiar with the cross-border concept. He was not present for the launch, but Normand was in good company. Katie Gramich, now a staff tutor with the OU, who has researched extensively among Welsh writers in English, was on hand to contribute some deft analysis of Davies as man and writer, and Professor Wynn Thomas, chairman for the occasion, stirred the audience to ask questions and offer their own views. Davies, brought up by his grandparents in a dockland pub when Newport was a major port, is, understandably, a local hero, especially among readers of a certain age – as were most of those present. Many were surprised to find that the simple nature poet they so much admired was a highly complex character, a bohemian spirit who hobnobbed with literary high society, a regular contributor to the Georgian anthologies who might have turned out another Frank Harris had not the refined sensibilities of his friend Edward Thomas kept him in check. Eyebrows were raised at the accounts of Davies's consorting with prostitutes – a reaction against his strict Baptist upbringing, ventured Wynn Thomas. A gent in the second row disagreed: 'I was brought up in the same part of Newport and as a schoolboy knew all the prostitutes along our street by their first names.' One began to see that a man who, not because he had no alternative, but with deliberation sought out the low life of slums and dosshouses, could be more at home among women of the street than of the salon, while at the same time self-consciously moulding or at least acquiescing in the creation of a literary persona that would maintain him in polite society. In *Young Emma*, the autobiographical novel he wrote in 1923-4, he described how he met and, in 1923, married a young prostitute. The woman, Helen Payne, was twenty when they met; he was fifty-one. Mindful perhaps of the editorial advice Edward Thomas had given him concerning risqué elements in the draft of *Autobiography of a Super-Tramp* and, to judge by letters he wrote to his publishers, sensible also of the hurt it might inflict on his new wife, to whom he was, after all, happily married, Davies had second thoughts about the novel and suppressed it. Cape did not return or destroy the typescript, but as Davies seems to have half intended, kept it safe until his widow died. It was published in 1980.

J.P. Ward's own remarks on W. H. Davies are to be found in 'Borderers and Borderline Cases', an essay in *Welsh Writing in English* edited by Wynn Thomas (University of Wales Press, 2003). Countering the frequently repeated accusation that Davies is a prime example of Georgian naïvety, he suggests that when we read the simple-seeming lyrics we should listen for resonances of 'William Blake and George Herbert, Ben Jonson and Shakespeare's songs and the anonymous traditional ballad'. As series editor, he has a good deal more to say about writers who have already appeared in the Border Lines list, and some, like Geraint Goodwin, who have not, or not yet. Katie Gramich, another contributor to Wynn Thomas's symposium, takes a different line on cross-border issues. Her essay 'Welsh Writers and the British Dimension', has penetrating observations on Welsh writers who have been, she argues, 'ambivalent in their relationship with their homeland', such as the 'chameleon-like' Dannie Abse, and Leslie Norris, ever mindful of his Merthyr origins but long resident in the United States, 'who proves how fruitful exile and distance can be'.

Although it could not be termed a joint book launch, it was good to see Seren and UWP sharing what one hopes was jointly and mutually profitable. Lawrence Normand's study of W.H. Davies affords an opportunity for revaluation of a writer who has been neglected for some time, and anyone with an interest in what we used to call Anglo-Welsh writing (and sometimes still do) will find the most up-to-date survey of the field in *Welsh Writing in English*.

*PN Review* 154, Volume 30 Number 2, November – December 2003.

# RUGBY

*May 2003*

Wales is in crisis. You might expect this bald statement to be the prelude to a catalogue of disasters, political, industrial, linguistic or natural. Goodness knows, there are enough reasons in the decline of manufacturing, the legislative impotence of the Assembly, the seeping away of Welsh in its traditional heartlands and, until the chilly lull of the last few weeks, the bleakness of daily rain, to cast us into depression if not despair. But no, the crisis is of a different character. Welsh rugby has gone to pot. Assiduous readers of the back pages of dailies will tell you this is not news; the crisis has simply plumbed new depths.

Welsh rugby has been ailing since 16 February 1980, the well-remembered day when Paul Ringer, open-side wing-forward for Wales, was (some will say unjustly) sent off the field at Twickenham by a referee held like a rabbit in the spotlight of a concerted and virulent attack on the Welsh team by the London-based media – press, radio and television. In common with other travelling supporters from these parts, I have a clear memory of the intensity of anti-Welsh feeling in the crowd stirred by the same media frenzy. Wales has enjoyed brief periods of modest success on the rugby field since, but the trend has continued downwards and things went from bad to worse in 1995, when the amateur administration of the Welsh Rugby Union remained in place while the game turned professional. Few governing bodies in sport, or any other walk of life, have been criticised more roundly and consistently than the WRU. Even politicians have their better days, though I cannot bring one to mind: the WRU has none. From time to time it sets up investigative panels whose members have much relevant experience and the good of the game at heart, but it pays not the slightest attention to the reports the panels produce. It is not given to making decisions of any kind, least of all the decision that every rugby supporter most earnestly desires – to vote itself out of office.

These may be matters of total indifference to readers of a literary magazine. And yet, for better or worse, there is something of the essence of Wales in rugby union football that cannot be ignored, even if, as a reader, you prefer lit.crit. to match reports. As John Davies's magisterial *A History of Wales* (1993) succinctly puts it, 'rugby was grafted on to Welshness and became a powerful symbol of the nation's identity'. If London tabloids can devote front pages to the shaky progress of the English soccer team, the affairs of its manager and the toe and eyebrow of one of its key players, we should not be surprised to find banner headlines in the *Western Mail*, which, notwithstanding its broadsheet format, has embraced the cult of celebrity and a tabloid mentality, about the traumas afflicting Welsh rugby. Typically, 'It's another Welsh rugby farce' shrieks the self-styled 'National newspaper of Wales' and breakfast tables up and down the land are plunged into gloom. We could have worse things to worry about, like the Bush-Blair axis and the imminence of war in Iraq.

I read the back pages and have a small library of rugby books, many of which were Christmas gifts. They provide light relief from my normal diet, but that does not mean they lack the power to make one occasionally stop and think. For instance, I find the assisted autobiographies of famous players interesting for their portrayal of family backgrounds and their incidental commentary on social history. The broad development of rugby union in Wales mimics social evolution over the 130-odd years since the foundation of the WRU in a way that is not repeated elsewhere in these islands, because the game was played here by working-class men: 'The rugby clubs could draw upon the strong tradition of communal activity which had taken root in the industrial districts of Wales,' writes John Davies. The vast majority of the 239 clubs that are full members of the WRU are located within the old boundaries of the south Wales coalfield – a meaningless concept these days. Into the 1950s, most Welsh national teams included a number of players who were employed in mining or metal-working. And the decline of Welsh rugby has largely coincided with the waning of heavy industry. Is there a connection, or is it merely coincidence, that in times when Assembly government rejoices in the establishment of another (probably short-lived) call centre, interest and involvement in rugby is falling away in the small towns and villages of the old coalfield?

The change was accelerating even as the Welsh national team was achieving the highest levels of success, during the late 1960s and 1970s. The influence of education, that broad road out of manual employment, looms large in the pen-portraits of players of this era, but their roots were still deeply embedded in the communities and mores of the coalfield. I offer three (chosen not entirely, I must admit, at random) by way of illustration: Cliff Morgan, Clive Rowlands and that remarkable physical genius Gareth Edwards. All three were born in small mining villages, Morgan in 1930 at Trebanog, on the top of a long, steep hill running down to Porth in the Rhondda, Rowlands in 1939 at Upper Cwmtwrch in the Swansea Valley, Edwards in 1947 at Gwaun-cae-gurwen, also in the Swansea Valley. They are, all three, the sons and grandsons of Welsh-speaking miners, who were themselves saved from the pit by their secondary education, Morgan at Tonyrefail Grammar School (where I knew and hero-worshipped him as an older fellow-pupil), Rowlands at Maesydderwen Grammar School, and Edwards at Pontardawe Technical College. They were brought up by devoted, chapel-going parents in humble homes where the notion of spare cash was unintelligible. Rowlands, indeed, had by any of the usual measures a hard childhood. He lost a sister to pulmonary TB while he was himself a sufferer in another sanatorium and, when he was ten, his father died of the coal-dust illness, pneumoconiosis. As was the way at the time, the compensation board refused any payment to the family, but the community rallied round. All three acknowledge a special debt to their secondary schooling and to individual teachers who, for the sake of the game, and for the sheer pleasure of seeing talent develop, coached, advised and, so far as it lay within their scope, promoted them.

With his wonderful talent for communication, Cliff Morgan was soon launched on a quite remarkable career in the BBC; Rowlands and Edwards both trained as teachers and went on to other things. In this respect, they were typical of the new breed of young players who came to prominence in the third quarter of the twentieth century, many of whom were graduates. Nevertheless, they and a multitude of others far less gifted were the products of a time when rugby was a bright thread in the socio-cultural fabric of Wales, where it was interwoven with other features that are now, but not for much longer, part of folk memory – notably, the impromptu singing of Welsh hymns that preceded and often accompanied international matches. This was a wonder to visiting teams and supporters, but it came easily to us because we learned the hymns (which are wonderful when anyone bothers to listen) in chapel or at school, where we sang them daily at morning assembly. The unravelling of all this did not take long. As for Welsh hymns or songs, the best you can hope for now, at the Millennium Stadium, is a raucous rendering of 'Delilah'.

Whenever the decline of Welsh rugby is discussed, a hefty share of the blame is put on the change to comprehensive education, which occurred more rapidly and completely in Wales than it did in England. The 11+, or 'scholarship' as it was still known in my time, fed fifteen per cent or more of local youngsters into mostly small, mixed grammar schools, where rugby was the only winter game available to boys. That did not prevent us playing soccer with a bald tennis ball on the schoolyard, or outside the gates at weekends, but it gave a single purpose to organised games that secured for every boy, no matter what his sporting ability, at least a basic training in rugby and for most a life-long interest in the game. There were often no more than forty or fifty boys in the fifth and sixth forms combined and a substantial proportion played for the school first XV in inter-school matches on Saturday mornings. Many carried on playing at one level or another into adulthood.

The idea of comprehensive education seemed socially right for Wales, with its huge preponderance of working-class families, but the creation of larger schools inevitably involved the merger or closure of the many small grammar schools. The opportunity for inter-school competition was curtailed. Furthermore, the curricula of comprehensive schools were designed to afford pupils more choice and the extension of this principle to physical education meant that rugby was no longer the sole winter sport. It was soon apparent that, although they had a couple of hundred boys to choose from, these schools still ran only one XV at senior level, and occasionally not even that. Well-motivated young athletes still progress, via the structures that exist, from schools to clubs, but there is much more wastage of talent. It is not surprising that many of the old coalfield clubs, with long and worthy traditions, are finding it difficult to raise teams.

For years I have thought of rugby as essentially theatrical;

good matches have many of the attributes of high drama in their combination of physicality and psychological subtlety – and poetry too (Louis MacNeice was perfectly at home penning occasional rugby reports for the *Sunday Times*). The most persuasive, and moving, expression of the game as something more than a violent collision of 'muddied oafs' is contained in the career and life of Carwyn James. A close contemporary of Cliff Morgan and, like him, the son of a Welsh-speaking miner, but from Cefneithin on the western edge of the coalfield, he was staunchly Nonconformist, politically aware and committed to the cause of Welsh nationalism. He graduated in Welsh at Aberystwyth, where his tutors included two of the outstanding poets of the twentieth century, Gwenallt and T.H. Parry-Williams, learned Russian on National Service in the Navy and read the classics of Russian literature in the original. He played twice for Wales (and would have gained more caps had it not been for Cliff Morgan), but became famous wherever the game is played as a coach. Not many coaches visualised the structured approach to rugby adopted by Welsh teams in the late 1970s as *cynghanedd* in contrast to the exuberant *vers libre* of the French, and this was not merely fanciful. He made of rugby a disciplined aesthetic that was effective on the field, in the harshest of conditions. In 1971, as coach to the touring Lions of Great Britain and Ireland, he dictated the style of play that, for the first time, defeated the New Zealand All Blacks in a test series. That this shy, soft-spoken lover of literature could achieve such a thing is a wonderful paradox. But, at the core, he had principles like steel: in the wake of the Lions success he refused an OBE. He wished above all to be coach of the Welsh team, but let it be understood that he would accept the role only on his terms, which meant no interference from the committee of the WRU. To their undying shame, the Union rejected him.

So we find ourselves at what might be the fag end of Welsh

rugby, after years of losses to the major rugby nations, losing now to Italy, where Carwyn James had taken his coaching talents when his own country turned him down, but still a relative newcomer to the game. We go on bickering among ourselves and resolving nothing while a colourful part of our heritage is fading away. A pessimist might see in the fiasco a metaphor for the condition of Wales.

*PN Review* 151, Volume 29 Number 5,
May – June 2003.

# THE WELSH LANGUAGE
*July 2002*

I cannot remember what institutions I listed on my university application form. I know only that Aberystwyth was at the top, one of the few deliberate choices of my life. I had fallen under the influence of a dynamic young teacher freshly graduated from the geography department there, and wanted nothing more than to put what brain I possessed at the disposal of Professor E.G. Bowen and his colleagues at the University College of Wales. Professor Bowen was a brilliant geographer and a remarkable man. He did a great deal of public speaking, in Welsh and English, to audiences of all kinds and earned the reputation of being able to hold forth, cogently, on any topic at virtually no notice. In the 1950s, the academic excellence of the geography department at Aber was already well known. It attracted students from all over the UK, in large numbers; in the first year you had to fight for a seat in 'The Barn', the largest lecture space available at the time. Professor Bowen built the department by recruiting to the staff his own star students. Among them was Harold Carter, who eventually became head of department, and who, now retired, caused the editorial columnist of the *Western Mail* a little while ago to wag his head sadly and deprecatingly over a statement the professor made to the National Assembly's Culture Committee about the cultural significance to Wales of the Welsh language.

The journalist's sad disapproval was somewhat marred by a whimsical confusion of Professor Carter with the man who broached the tomb of Tutankhamen. However, readers might well have been surprised that a geographer should take a stand on the language issue very like that long associated with R.S. Thomas, especially when politicians, even of the nationalist persuasion, do not dare to. He is reported to have told the committee that it should declare 'unequivocally that its concern is the culture of Wales and that all incomers should be prepared to accept that they are moving into a culturally-distinct area where the character of that culture is paramount'. He added that general statements of support for the language were not enough; specific action was needed in areas such as planning. Surprisingly, perhaps, Welsh is not the professor's first language. But then, neither was it R.S. Thomas's.

The journalist might have given Professor Carter the credit of knowing more about the decline of the language in the communities of the Welsh-speaking heartlands than anyone else: it has been his sphere of research for some time. But, that said, I should probably have let this brief episode in the politics of Wales pass, had it not been for events that occurred subsequently. At the end of January, in an effort to stem the tide of incomers, the Pembrokeshire Coast National Park announced a proposal to ban the building of new houses, except to meet the needs and suit the pockets of local people. This is not a strategy made in Wales: policies of the same kind already exist in the Exmoor and Lake District National Parks, and the New Forest is to follow suit. In March, the Snowdonia National Park announced its intention to introduce similar restrictions. These developments have been condemned by the press and by Labour politicians, who fear accusations of racial discrimination and would, in any case, prefer to let the market prevail. Economics is more important than culture. Since the bans will not prevent outsiders buying existing properties in the designated areas, it will be interesting to see whether they have more than a marginal effect on the influx of second-home buyers and, in those parts still predominantly Welsh-speaking, any impact on the fateful drift towards Anglicisation.

*'Tynged yr Iaith'* ('The Fate of the Language') was the title of a radio talk given almost exactly forty years ago as I write, in February 1962, by Saunders Lewis (1893-1985), scholar, novelist, dramatist, man-of-Welsh-letters *extraordinaire*, founder member of Plaid Cymru and its first president. In 1936, he and his accomplices, Lewis Valentine and D.J. Williams, set fire to workmen's huts on the site of an RAF bombing school, which, despite vehement protest from all over Wales, the government was determined to build at Penyberth on the Llŷn Peninsula, a place steeped in cultural history. They immediately surrendered themselves to the police and in due course were tried for arson, first at Caernarfon, where the jury failed to agree, and then at the Old Bailey, where they were convicted and gaoled for nine months. Saunders Lewis lost his lectureship at University College, Swansea as a result, a decision of which the institution is not proud. Towards the end of his long life considerable efforts were made to gain him the nomination for the Nobel Prize for Literature: that might have done Wales and Welsh a power of good. As it is, what has been achieved by way of official recognition of the language is substantially due to the effect that *'Tynged yr Iaith'* had on a generation of young Welsh men and women. His was not the first nor only voice raised in this cause but Lewis's radio talk was the immediate stimulus of the foundation of Cymdeithas yr Iaith Gymraeg (the Welsh Language Society) by a group of students at Aberystwyth. To anyone entering Wales by road, bilingual road signs are the most obvious evidence of the success of the movement. This conspicuous acknowledgement of the equal status of Welsh and English was not easily conceded by the Welsh Office and local authorities. Some travellers hereabouts will recall the time in the 1960s when many road signs were obliterated with green

paint. They can at least look back and say they got lost in a good cause.

It has become clear, however, that bilingual signs and forms, broadcasting in Welsh, a Welsh Language Act and the policies on bilingualism that must now be uttered by companies, authorities and utilities large and small, are not going to halt the decline of the language where it matters most – in the rural communities of the heartlands. A gathering conviction on the part of certain activists that this specific concern is the key to the survival of Welsh led to the formation only last year of another group calling itself *Cymuned* (Community). It wants discrimination in favour of preserving the Welsh character of small towns and villages in the north and west, for example by subsidising the purchase of houses by locals. Whereas the style of campaigning adopted by Cymdeithas yr Iaith has always been highly visible, bill-sticking, protest marches, occupation of official premises and the like, *Cymuned* favours behind the scenes lobbying. That the National Assembly is currently reviewing the state of the language owes something to both, perhaps rather more to the latter.

Jennie Randerson, the Assembly's Culture Minister, declared recently that ordinary folk in other countries should be more aware of Wales 'as a bilingual nation'. Here is something to make the economist's heart leap: promoting that one distinctive attribute that no other part of the British Isles can boast, an ancient, still living language, might attract tourists. Tourism in Scotland and Ireland would surely make the most of Gaelic if more than a handful of native speakers could be gathered in one place. Our tourist board, the minister said, was for many years not allowed to advertise Wales abroad (as the *Encyclopaedia Britannica* put it, 'For Wales, see England'). Furthermore, she admitted that the arts in Wales were so under-funded for so long that the development of a national identity recognisable abroad was impossible. Things are changing. If Welsh rugby is going to the dogs, we have a stadium that is the envy of the world; Cardiff has put in a bid to be named European Capital of Culture in 2008; despite gloomy predictions, work has at last begun on the construction of the Wales Millennium Centre, which will provide a home for Welsh National Opera and several other arts organisations; the Arts Council has received a 23% increase in funding and, by decentralising and simply having more money for the arts, is looking forward to regaining the confidence of artists and the public. We shall find out in due course whether these sparks of optimism can start a fire. It is, nevertheless, now demonstrable that the Assembly not only has a role in preserving and advancing the culture of Wales, but, if it wills, the means to do something about it before it's too late and we forget Offa's Dyke was ever more than a footpath for those who enjoy long walks.

The title essay of Nigel Jenkins's *Footsore on the Frontier* (Gomer), a selection of prose contributed to various books and journals since 1985, is about walking the 180-mile dyke, 'an eighth century work to dwarf all others in Europe', unusually, from north to south. The book will tell you more about the route, and about Jenkins, a relaxed, economical and entertaining essayist. Those contemplating a brief term in gaol, on a matter of anti-nuclear principle for example, might prepare themselves by reading 'The diary of prisoner WX 0674', which delivers the experience as it is, without exaggeration or mitigation. Another autobiographical piece, 'And the dregs are mine...' explains the roots both of his family and of his own radical and culturally nationalist stance: he is one of the more overtly political contemporary Welsh writers. Not least because we are currently in Andy Warhol season, 'The scars of the imagination' is particularly interesting. It describes the extraordinary life and career of John Cale, raised Welsh-speaking in Garnant, a mining village in the Amman valley. Having been classically trained, he turned out an avant-garde musician given to shock tactics, rubbed shoulders with Humphrey Searle, Aaron Copeland and John Cage and, in 1965, became part of The Velvet Underground and Warhol's multi-media arts circus.

Jenkins brings to life (and sees off, to the final scattering of ashes) another character capable of outraging more restrained and politer sensibilities: John Tripp. Anniversaries of his death also fall in the month of February; this year's is the sixteenth. He will be remembered (not always for the best reasons) by all who knew him. I have written of him in *PN Review* before, a poet of his time, particularly the 1960s and 1970s, who had a distinctive voice on the page and on the stage. He was a gifted performance poet and it was a particularly apt notion to commemorate him by an annual award for spoken poetry. The final of this year's competition brought together 24 poets from all over Wales, performing their own unpublished work. Tripp's anger and caustic wit were not much in evidence, and his political vehemence was entirely missing. There was some humour, though not in the rumbustious vein, some sociological analysis of the state of the world, and a good deal of cleverness. The best poetry was certainly accomplished, and subtle rather than obvious – not written with performance in mind. Cliff Forshaw walked off with the prize; I think it likely we shall hear his name again.

Although we were not unprepared, it was still a shock to hear of the death of Robin Reeves, editor of *The New Welsh Review* since 1991. He too knew 'The Barn', having studied geology at Aberystwyth in the 1960s. Journalism with the *Financial Times* took him to Brussels, where he became staunchly European and one of the founders of the Bureau of Unrepresented Nations, and then back to Wales as the newspaper's first Welsh correspondent. He quit the *FT* to become assistant editor of the *Western Mail* and gave that up to take on the editorship of *NWR*. He was not alone in wanting Wales to have a separate and distinctive voice in Europe, but he was among the few prepared to work to that end. He learned Welsh and became a Plaid Cymru county councillor for the Vale of Glamorgan (not a notably nationalist zone). Not so long ago, in his editorial to the fiftieth number of *NWR*, he wrote '... instilling the same cultural confidence in Wales as obtains in Scotland and Ireland remains a wholly valid, honourable objective, however hostile the worldwide market may be to small enterprise. Indeed, in today's Wales, the need to assert the vital role of literature as a key component in the Welsh nation's profile has never been more important.' He was personally committed to that enterprise, as he was to political progress. He will be missed.

*PN Review* 146, Volume 28 Number 6,
July – August 2002.

# THE UNIVERSITY OF GLAMORGAN

*March 2002*

The University of Glamorgan received its charter about a decade ago. In previous existences it had been the Polytechnic of Wales and a school of mines. Its home is Trefforest, an industrial village on the River Taff a little to the south of the town of Pontypridd and, to the casual observer, hardly now separable from its larger neighbour. Those who have wondered about the geography of Auden's lines 'Glamorgan hid a life/Grim as a tidal rock-pool's in its glove-shaped valleys' will be glad to know that the Rhondda Fach and the Rhondda Fawr, the thumb and forefinger to the pedantic, join at Porth and flow united to confluence at Pontypridd with the Taff, which has begun north of Merthyr Tydfil and is itself already swollen by the Cynon, the river of Alun Lewis's Aberdare. The Taff is the river that flows by Cardiff's Millennium Stadium and into the barrage-protected bay where the National Assembly is housed in a nondescript office block while politicians get themselves ever deeper in the mire over a dispute with Richard Rogers about his design for a new Assembly building. In pre-barrage days the tidal Taff, topped-up with floodwater from the regularly drenched moorland and valleys, could on occasion seep into the city streets. At Cardiff Arms Park (a name far preferable to 'Millennium Stadium') in December 1960, I watched Wales lose to South Africa in a continuous downpour. The tide was coming in as the match entered its final stages and not long after the crowd had dispersed the pitch was drowned beneath two feet of water. So much for local colour.

The University of Glamorgan, which, as its separate charter implies, is not a constituent institution of the University of Wales, has grown spectacularly in its short existence and already has a number of academic strengths, including creative writing and English. Among the staff in these areas are several familiar to readers of Anglo-Welsh literature. Sheenagh Pugh is there and Christopher Meredith, who has a well-earned reputation as both poet and novelist; Tony Curtis was appointed Professor of Poetry some time back and more recently Jeremy Hooker and Meic Stephens have been awarded chairs. Last year Professor Dai Smith, an outstanding historian of modern Wales, quit a top job with the BBC in Cardiff to become Pro-Vice Chancellor. Here are intellects and talents enough to strike sparks in the Valleys communities with which the university is determined to maintain a lively connection. Early in November, Dr Stephens's inaugural lecture attracted a large audience, a few of whom might have known him since boyhood, for he was born and brought up in Trefforest. And last summer I attended the launch on the campus of *Imagining Wales: a View of Modern Welsh Writing in English*, Jeremy Hooker's first book since his return.

Readers of *PN Review* will know Hooker as a poet and critic of distinction but may be unaware of his commitment to Welsh writing in English. In an 'Afterword' to his book he confesses that when he first arrived in Wales (in 1965) he 'had no idea that there was a living literature in Welsh or a significant English language Welsh literature, since [his] knowledge was confined to a few individual writers, such as Dylan Thomas, R.S. Thomas and Alun Lewis'. What followed he describes as an 'education' and among his teachers he lists David Jones, Edward Thomas, whom he had previously associated only with southern England, and Roland Mathias who, as editor of *The Anglo-Welsh Review*, invited him to review *The Lilting House*

(1969), a major anthology of twentieth-century Anglo-Welsh poetry edited by John Stuart Williams and Meic Stephens. Mathias had early recognised that Welsh writing, in either of its languages, rarely received a decent hearing from metropolitan critics who were accounted the only judges worthy of note. He also believed that criticism had a role in raising literary standards and, if he could not look to London for the considered opinion on Anglo-Welsh writing that he sought, then he would strive to develop home-grown critics for the job in the pages of his magazine. He set an example of painstaking reading, scholarship and fine literary judgement in his own reviewing and was delighted to find the same meticulous attention to the task, and perhaps a similar moral concern, in Hooker's critical writing. Furthermore, Hooker was English and, though resident in Wales, deeply attached to the landscape and history of his Hampshire home and Richard Jefferies's England: whatever his critical opinion, he could not be thought *parti pris*. It must have stirred in Mathias some sense of editorial satisfaction, mingled with concern, to read in that review of *The Lilting House* (*AWR* No. 42) Hooker's identification of 'a discrepancy in quality between the work of the older poets and that of all but a few of the younger generation...[which] reveals a deep malaise – a softness and failure of astringency – in some of the criticism to which the modern Anglo-Welsh poet is subjected, especially in his own country'.

Hooker was soon caught up in the excitement of being a pioneer in the teaching and criticism of Welsh writing in English. His essays reveal how intrigued he was by the lack of egocentricity in Welsh writers compared with their contemporaries in England and America. They were concerned with identity, but not their own; rather they saw themselves in relation to a community. He quotes Alun Lewis's promise: 'When I come back I shall always tackle my writing through

Welsh life and ways of thought', sadly unkept. Lewis was an early and absorbing interest but others soon followed, notably David Jones and, among writers of fiction, John Cowper Powys and Emyr Humphreys. With the benefit of a fresh perspective he was able to expose the self-disgust that motivated R.S. Thomas's bitter denunciation of the monolingual English-speaking Welsh; he observed Gillian Clarke striking out in a new direction with her 'sensuous recreation of a woman's apprehension of the world' and, having seen through the concentrated metaphor and compacted language to the Puritan seriousness at the core, produced the first substantial treatment of Roland Mathias's mature poetry.

When he arrived in Aberystwyth, Hooker says, 'In literary and academic circles in and outside Wales [Anglo-Welsh literature] commonly elicited hostility or disdain.' I well remember that Gwyn Jones, Professor of English there a few years earlier, would not countenance work on Welsh writing in English although he was one of the outstanding figures in the field. Change came slowly but, unquestionably, it has occurred. Today, we have the Universities of Wales Association for the Study of Welsh Writing in English, which has a yearbook of critical essays and an annual conference, and publishes 'collected works' of key writers in conjunction with the University of Wales Press. A number of acute and well-informed minds are regularly bent to the explication and assessment of Anglo-Welsh literature and the products are readily available. Hooker 'can scarcely recognise the subject' that he began to teach in Aber. Among the critics for whom he has particular regard he mentions Tony Conran, John Pikoulis, Jane Aaron, Belinda Humfrey, Walford Davies, Tony Brown and M. Wynn Thomas.

The last named is an all-rounder, writing with equal authority on literature in Welsh and English and having an extensive knowledge of American literature; as a recognised expert on Walt Whitman, he has twice been visiting professor at Harvard. The seven essays in his book, *Corresponding Cultures; the two literatures of Wales*, (UWP, 1999), impressively demonstrate the breadth of his scholarship and the incisiveness of his analysis. Whether the subject is Henry Vaughan, the 'Anglophile neoclassical' who nevertheless chose to declare himself a 'Silurist', or the complex fertilising effect of the twentieth-century American experience on a goodly number of poets from Wales, including T.H. Parry-Williams and Pennar Davies among those in the Welsh language, Leslie Norris, Tony Curtis, Mike Jenkins, John Davies and Robert Minhinnick in English, and Gwyneth Lewis in both, he is freshly informative. He is equally bold and perceptive in discussion of gender issues raised in the poetry of Gillian Clarke and Menna Elfyn and has the rare talent of being able to discuss lucidly socio-political and more broadly cultural matters in the context of a wide range of literary reference. This is clearly an advantage where Wales is concerned. He is right when he says that we, the Welsh, have 'scarcely begun...to examine the ways in which our two cultures can be co-operative – can make history and make literature, at the same time and in the same place', but he has already made a major contribution to mutual understanding and harmony.

Early in November, the University of Glamorgan was the venue for the Rhys Davies Centenary Conference, one session of which brought together Dannie Abse and Les Murray, a stimulating contrast in vocal and poetic style and size. Davies was born in Blaenclydach, a short and steep sideshoot of the Rhondda Fawr. As a boy he walked the three miles or so home from grammar school in Porth to save the tram fare 'for other purposes' (a secretive formulation, it now seems). From Porth it was and is another moderate walk, downhill, to Pontypridd. Davies, then, is a local boy whose mind first caught fire (if you can believe him) when the headmaster, standing in for an absent English teacher, read an extract from *The Odyssey* to the class. He decided that he would write and spent much of his life in bedsits in London doing just that. His autobiographical *Print of a Hare's Foot*, reprinted by Seren in 1998, is an entertaining, if not wholly reliable, account of what he did when he rested his pen.

The conference was also the occasion of the launch of *Rhys Davies: Decoding the Hare* (UWP), a book of critical essays to mark the centenary of the writer's birth, in which M. Wynn Thomas's examination of the coded fiction of the gay writer out of his time is both keynote and last word. Davies has two undistinguished poems in Keidrych Rhys's anthology *Modern Welsh Poetry* (Faber, 1944) but their appearance there might have involved a deal of arm-twisting: he was a novelist and a short-story writer par excellence (his service to the poetic muse was confined to providing the clandestine means by which Lawrence's *Pansies* were sent safely from Nice to his London publisher). The new book, edited and introduced by Meic Stephens, is further proof that literary criticism in Wales has progressed since Jeremy Hooker first arrived among us.

*PN Review* 144, Volume 28 Number 4, March – April 2002.

# THE WELSH LANGUAGE

*January 2002*

More than a year has passed since Joanna Weston who, though an inside appointment, had announced herself as a new broom with a fresh strategy for the arts, resigned from the post of chief executive of the Arts Council for Wales. Before her departure, and since, consultants and advisers to ACW and the Assembly have had a field day surveying the scene, collecting the views of practitioners and the public, writing reports and making recommendations. Not many of the suggestions to emerge have had the appeal even of common sense and some appeared positively pernicious, threatening to increase bureaucracy while undermining the few more or less successful institutions that crossed regional boundaries. Ms Weston's successor, Peter Tyndall, took over in October. What he will do with the reams of conflicting advice is anyone's guess, but he has arrived with a demeanour hopeful rather than resigned: to everyone's surprise, for the time being at least, the Assembly seems inclined to let the Council work out its own salvation rather than impose upon it new structures and methodology.

Tyndall does not come from a background in the arts or arts administration. His previous job was with the Welsh Local Government Organisation, which he served as head of education, training and cultural affairs. It was a role that brought him into contact with the ACW, so he has some knowledge of its personnel and perennial problems. That will help, but possibly not as much as will his familiarity with the factions and rivalries among local government officers and elected members. Development in the arts depends upon local support. According to the *Western Mail*, the new chief executive aims to bring transparency and accountability to the workings of the Council, and reassurance to staff, who have been so concerned about their own future that they have hardly been in a position to worry about that of the arts. In any case, lack of funding has long clenched the Council in the arts' equivalent of planning blight. Tyndall knows this but feels that, under the Assembly, the position has changed and that there will be sufficient funding 'to get back to where we were some years ago' – a move in the right direction, but not very far. Though long resident in Wales, he is said to be a Dubliner; steady supplies of the blarney and the luck of the Irish will not go amiss.

The survival of ACW and in what form has not been the most controversial issue of the summer months. Indeed, it has raised barely a ripple of interest compared with the amount of media and public attention given to the fate of the Welsh language. No matter what your politics, religious, social or sporting affiliation, in the end you must agree that the one thing that distinguishes Wales from other countries of the United Kingdom is the language. It has been under threat for centuries, officially since the enactment of Henry VIII's statute 27, clause 26, commonly referred to as the Act of Union of 1536, Thomas Cromwell's device for securing the same system of government throughout the king's realm. This, among other measures (notably the appointment of justices of the peace, as in England, and the right to representation by twenty-six members of parliament), declared that English was the one and only language of law and administration in Wales. The effect of the statute was more than symbolic in that it tended to separate the gentry, whose eyes were already turned towards London, and those who wielded power in courts and newly created counties, from ordinary folk. Among the latter, however, the everyday use of Welsh continued as before from generation to generation until the nineteenth century when a number of factors inimical to the language coiled up into a tidal wave threatening to sweep in and swamp it.

One such was the great influx of English, or at any rate English-speaking, labourers to the pits, steel and tin-plate works, the Adamses from Staffordshire among them. But that alone did not undermine Welsh, for industrialisation also sucked in tens of thousands from the west and north of Wales. At Abersychan, a village in the Gwent valleys, Tom Adams met and married Mary Isaac, a young woman from Llanwrda in the depths of rural Carmarthenshire, and their son Sam, my grandfather, was Welsh-speaking. Victorian officialdom's long bombardment of the language as an inferior babble and impediment to the educational and economic progress of Wales towards the shining light of English achievement finally loosened the grip of many who would have kept it up, if only around the hearth. In the end, it was the readiness of Welsh-speakers in the populous south-east to surrender their heritage that did the trick. Welsh still hangs on in the heartlands of the west and north, but the forecast is grim, not least because the protective bastions of the language, the chapel and the rural environment, are both crumbling. We celebrate, and rightly, the remarkable progress in Welsh-medium education, which is adding to numbers with a competence in the language, but not at a rate even to keep pace with natural wastage among those whose first language is Welsh.

The decline of native speakers became the issue of the summer. A Plaid Cymru councillor in Gwynedd began the controversy with public criticism of the uncontrolled flow of people from England into north and west Wales and the effect it had on small, rural communities. At the National Eisteddfod, held in Denbigh early in August, he called upon the Assembly to take action to protect the language by devising a housing policy that would restrict in-migration. The Archdruid joined in, speaking of the impossibility of rebuilding heartland communities whose language and soul have been vandalised by lack of employment and rising house prices. He too called for a political response, a housing act that would discriminate in favour of local people. John Elfed Jones, an important figure in Welsh life, at various times chairman of HTV, the Welsh Water Authority and the Welsh Language Board, published an article in the magazine *Barn* ('Opinion') in which he began by describing the crisis in agriculture brought about by the foot-and-mouth epidemic and the way the Assembly had made strenuous efforts to counter its effects. Then he turned to another threat to the rural way of life: immigrants 'setting foot into Welsh communities' and putting property beyond the means of local people. 'And,' he continued, 'from the mouths of immigrants comes a language familiar to everyone in rural areas – a foreign language. Soon, unintentionally, almost without anyone noticing, the language and way of life of our communities will have changed for ever.' Lest his readers had missed the implication, he referred again to the political action taken to combat the disease affecting farm animals while, in contrast, 'it seems there is nothing our politicians can do to stop the ruinous effect of the human foot-and-mouth.' This is the sort of rhetorical faux-pas that has tabloid editors salivating and John Elfed Jones duly fielded more than his fair share of brickbats, for his concern is real and widely shared.

The Labour party in Wales, which is keener to maximise any electoral advantage that might be gained from rubbishing Plaid Cymru than to preserve the language, fell like a hawk on this opportunity to denounce their opponents as racists. And the Plaid leadership, desperate not to lose the hard-won support of monoglot English-speakers, disowned their people, among them a party vice-president who had aligned himself with critics of the current laissez-faire attitude. The fact remains that incomes in Welsh rural areas are far below those in England so that young people have no hope of buying a home in their own communities in competition with outsiders desperate to escape from urban congestion and stress, and quite small numbers of in-coming non-Welsh speakers can tilt a delicate linguistic balance beyond recall in favour of English as the medium of everyday communication. The politicians shrug their shoulders helplessly: what can be done? European law would prevent the introduction of measures that might restrict the rights of individuals to buy and sell on the open market. But as John Elfed Jones points out, such restrictions already exist in the Aland Islands between Finland and Sweden and, much closer to home, in the Lake District and the Channel Islands.

Into September the fate of the language and other concerns of far less significance but still sufficient interest (the decision of the Office of National Statistics to hunt down those who spoiled Census forms over the absence of a Welsh tick-box; the Scots' determination to have their flag on car registration plates which should mean the Welsh will be allowed to do likewise) were keeping the pot of controversy bubbling. Then came the appalling events in the United States and swept all away, leaving us to wonder when we shall be able to be passionate once more about local and mundane affairs.

A culture under threat of extinction, not this year or in 2002 but perhaps in the next half-century, is no trifle. Welsh will never become a language of international trade or diplomacy, no matter how many dozen or score of students from Japan, Germany, America, Canada, Ireland or France enrol at intensive language courses, as they do. It will survive if the institutions and communities in which it has been long embedded survive, and if writers continue to use it as naturally, flexibly and beautifully as they have in the past.

That is one of the reasons why the National Eisteddfod is so important. This year the outcome of the Chair competition produced a surprise. The Chair is still considered the premier event of the Eisteddfod, the award of a chair to the *Pencerdd* ('Chief Poet') dating back at least as far as the days of Hywel Dda, tenth-century king and lawgiver, a contemporary of Alfred the Great. Competitors must submit an *awdl*, a long poem in the traditional strict metres. Throughout the 140-year history of the modern eisteddfod, chairs have been won only by men, but at Denbigh the prize went to a woman, Mererid Hopwood. She is one of those quietly remarkable people that (Praise be!) Wales continues to produce in these days of self-advertisement and media hype. A Germanist who gained an outstanding doctorate at London University, went on to lecture there and at Swansea and was until recently in charge of the Arts Council's west and mid-Wales office, she plays down her eisteddfodic achievement. There are many women in Wales who are far better poets, she says, and the reason the Chair has not been won by a woman before is that they have not practised the strict metres.

Her example will doubtless inspire others; the Chair is no longer a male preserve. In the pages of English-language magazines in Wales, over the last forty years women poets have become more numerous than men. *Oxygen* (edited by Amy Wack and Grahame Davies, Seren, 2000), an anthology of 'new poets' from Wales, contains substantial (and often impressive) samples of the work of sixteen English language poets and fifteen Welsh. Among the Welsh, six are women, including Gwyneth Lewis; among the English, eleven are women, again including Gwyneth Lewis, who bats with equal proficiency on both sides. Oddly, Menna Elfyn, one of the outstanding contemporary poets in the

Welsh language, who is as actively bridging the gap between English and Welsh audiences as Gwyneth Lewis, is omitted. Sheenagh Pugh, not new enough for *Oxygen*, whose poetry has received widespread recognition and deserves more, would hate this paragraph because she abhors the categorisation 'woman poet'. She is right of course. I plead extenuating circumstances and a long memory.

*PN Review* 143, Volume 28 Number 3, January – February 2002.

# LETTERS FROM WALES
*July 2001*


Joan Abse, wife of the poet Dannie Abse, an art historian whose *John Ruskin: the passionate moralist* (1980) was widely and favourably reviewed, is the editor of one of the most fascinating books published in Wales in the year 2000. Its title, *Letters from Wales* (Seren), might confuse readers of *PN Review*, but Michael Schmidt, who chose the headline for the meandering observations I contribute to the magazine, would not consider it an infringement of copyright.

The book is aptly named. Although extracts from diaries and journals are included, it is very largely a compilation of more than two hundred letters written from addresses in Wales between AD 1200 and 1997. That they are predominantly from north Wales is no surprise. In the earlier centuries this was where the balance of political power lay. In the later, tourists (seeking a cheaper experience than the Grand Tour offered, and still very much abroad in Wales) were particularly attracted to the mountains and castles of the north. The chronological arrangement of the contents and an italicised running commentary highlight the historical significance of the observations made by correspondents and diarists. The earliest are translated from Latin, the medium that connected the minds of the princes, politicians and intellectuals of medieval Europe, and a small number were originally in Welsh, but in the main they are letters written in English to addresses in England. Since seeing the sights is the travellers' main motive, scenery and the weather are constant themes. For the same reason, observations are concentrated in the summer months.

The usual tone of the letters dating from the sixteenth century is obsequious and beseeching; this was the only attitude that appealed to the few in authority who could get things done. Among those of the seventeenth century is a remarkable series that brings the reader directly into contact with the conduct of the Civil War in Wales and the puritan fervour of its aftermath, and a sample of four distinctively scientific missives from the 'vast correspondence' of Edward Lhuyd, Keeper of the Ashmolean, founding father of palaeontology and much else. Although there are earlier descriptions of scenery, it is in the eighteenth century that tourism gathers pace and writers take pains to communicate their response to a country that is scenically impressive. There are exceptions. Having tramped from the south as far as Montgomeryshire, Defoe is 'tired with rocks and mountains'. Swift, storm-trapped in Holyhead, has no Christian thought or word for the captain of the packet, fellow passengers or local people. His mind is entirely, though wittily, occupied by the inconvenience of a situation that contrasts miserably with the Deanery at Dublin.

Soon it is the turn of the Romantic poets. Coleridge, as an undergraduate in 1794, is interested in eccentric Welsh characters met at an inn and, at Abergele on the north Wales coast, the unexpected sight of 'a number of fine women bathing promiscuously with men and boys – *perfectly* naked!' His travelling companion Joseph Hucks supplies the scenic embroidery. For Shelley in 1811, mid-Wales is 'excessively grand', but he sees beneath the grandeur the ills of society and the predicament of the ordinary folk. In a letter from Tremadoc to his friend Thomas Jefferson Hogg (3 December 1812) he comments: 'The society in Wales is very stupid. They are all aristocrats and saints; but that, I tell you, I do not mind in the least; the unpleasant part of the business is, that they hunt the people to death.' On the same day he wrote to Thomas

Hookham, warming to his theme: '[Wales] is the last stronghold of the most vulgar and commonplace prejudices of aristocracy. Lawyers of unexampled villainy rule and grind the poor, whilst they cheat the rich. The peasants are mere serfs, and are fed and lodged worse than pigs – The poor are as abject as samoyads, and the rich as tyrannical as bashaws.' Wordsworth, in the course of a dutifully long epistle to Sir George Beaumont (20 September 1824), describes the 'grandeur' of Snowdon, conveys the kind remembrances of the Ladies of Llangollen to his patron, and meditates poetically upon the valley of the Dee.

Those symbols of subjugation, Edward I's castles, are a great attraction, to the poets as to everyone else on the northern route. Nathaniel Hawthorne, American Consul at Liverpool in the 1850s, came, saw and was duly impressed. His appreciation is tempered by a thoroughly modern insight into the impact of tourism: 'Certainly [Conwy] must be the most perfect specimen of a ruinous old castle in the world; it quite fills up one's idea...I think it added to the impressiveness of the old castle, to see the streets and the kitchen gardens and the homely dwellings that had grown up within the precincts of this feudal fortress...This does not destroy the charm; but tourists and idle visitors do impair it. The earnest life of today, however petty and homely as it might be, has a right to its place alongside what is left of the life of other days; and if it be vulgar itself, it does not vulgarise the scene. But tourists do vulgarise it; and I suppose we did so, just like the others.' A little further in his journal (July 1854), he notes a remarkable discovery: 'I had an idea that Welsh was spoken rather as a freak and in fun than as a native language; it was so strange to find another language the people's actual and earnest medium of thought within so short a distance of England.' A hundred and fifty years on, English-speaking visitors to north and west Wales are still as surprised as Hawthorne by this linguistic diversity, and many are not nearly as ready to understand and come to terms with it.

Charles Cavendish Fulke Greville (a name to conjure with), clerk to the Privy Council, a guest of Lord Anglesey at Plas Newydd in 1841, makes a similar observation. But he cannot resist asking himself why this should be so, and thinking how a situation that is so clearly undesirable might be changed: 'I have never travelled in any country which appeared so completely foreign. The road from Beddgelert is perfectly Alpine in character, and the peasantry neither speak nor understand anything but Welsh, so that it is impossible to hold any communication with them – It is really extraordinary that the English language has not made its way more among the mass of the people...The Welsh are generally poor and wages are low; their food consists principally of potatoes and butter-milk; the average wage of labour is about nine shillings a week. The people, however, are industrious, sober, contented, and wellbehaved; they do not like either change or locomotion, and this makes them indifferent about learning English.' His answer to this irritating problem is education – 'The country seems to be very ill-provided with schools, nor is English taught in all those which do exist'. The Welsh would hear more of this.

The rural poor could not be relied upon to remain docile. At this very time, in southwest Wales, gangs of rioters, each led by a man dressed as a woman and calling themselves the children of Rebecca (taking their text from Genesis 24:60 – 'And they blessed Rebekah and said unto her...Let thy seed possess the gate of those which hate them'), were destroying toll gates belonging to road trusts in protest against exorbitant charges for travel and transport. Their action is justified in the powerful rhetoric of a letter delivered secretly to *The Welshman:* 'The people, the masses to a man throughout the three counties of Carmarthen, Cardigan and Pembroke are with me. Oh yes, they are all my children. When I meet the lime-men on the road covered with sweat and dust, I know they are Rebeccaites. When I see the coalmen coming to town clothed in rags, hard worked and hard fed, I know they are mine, these are Rebecca's children. When I see the farmers' wives carrying loaded baskets to market, bending under the weight, I know well these are my daughters. If I turn into a farmer's house and see them eating barley bread and drinking whey, surely, say I, these are members of my family, these are the oppressed sons and daughters of Rebecca.'

If they had the strength, the oppressed and impoverished in the rural counties could at least look about and see some hope of heaven in the beauty of the landscape. Those in the industrial towns had no such prospect. A number of extracts from letters and journals provide a flavour of the running dispute between the Crawshays and Guests, the Iron Masters of Merthyr Tydfil, and the hard-pressed workers ('the enemy') to whom they owed their vast wealth. The picture of Merthyr that emerges may be summed up in a single short word: hell. With its flaming furnaces, smoke and soot, and the filth and squalor that were the normal conditions of life for the great majority of the inhabitants, it was a living and stinking illustration of Dante's *Inferno*. A climax was reached with the Merthyr Rising of June 1831 (see *PN Review* 123), and its tragic aftermath – the execution at Cardiff Gaol of an innocent man, Richard Lewis, known as Dic Penderyn. The making of a working-class martyr meant nothing to the employers. George Smith Kenrick of the Varteg Hill Iron Works (not far from Blaenavon, recently declared a World Heritage Site) wrote to Josiah John Guest, Charlotte's husband, on 30 August 1831: 'I agree with you that the Miners Union has a most mischievous tendency. If the men are suffered to establish their union upon a regular system nothing but confusion & violence can be expected, and it is better that the evil should be crushed in the bud'. Lady Charlotte Guest was herself a witness of the Chartists' March in November 1839 (*PN Review* 139). Sitting comfortably in her castle she wrote in her journal of the 'poor deluded creatures' who left twenty-two dead and scores wounded at the Westgate Hotel, Newport.

There is little evidence of alleviation of these conditions or alteration in the attitudes that created them into the twentieth century. In June 1912, Keir Hardie wrote an open letter to George V about a proposed visit to Dowlais Ironworks, pointing out that the Iron Masters, who were taking profits of £500,000 annually, had given not a penny back. 'There are no public buildings, monuments, public parks or public institutions due to their generosity or civic patriotism...That, of itself would be a serious indictment, but there is a much graver one to follow... Were it possible for you to leave your carriage and walk round the purlieus, the back closes, the slums, the horrible hovels in which hundreds of the workers of Messrs. Guest, Keen and Nettlefolds are herded together, and for which they pay extortionate rents...Your Majesty would be shocked. And these disgraceful conditions are the direct outcome of the low wages reduced still further by broken time paid by the firm.' Among the most moving letters in the book are those written at the time of the Miners' Strike of 1984-5.

The historical narrative that threads its way through this book is not new to us, but the epistolary presentation lends it an unusual immediacy and a lively impression of the mind and the human spirit that lies behind the written word – as in this final example from the seventeenth century. William Wynn of Glyn, Merioneth, writes to his student son urging him to profit from his studies, and to live sparingly: 'Therefore prayse God that thou hast careful parents to place thee in Oxenford, a famous university, the fountayne and wellhead of all learning.

Keep company with honest students who aphore evill courses as drinking and takeing toebacko, to their own loss and discredit of their friends and parents who sent them to University for better purposes – Speak no Welsh to any that can speak English, no not to your bedfellowes, and thereby you may freely speak English tongue perfectly. I had rather that you should keep companie with studious, honest Englishmen than with many of your countrymen who are more prone to be idle and riotous than the English.'

*PN Review* 140, Volume 27 Number 6, July – August 2001.

# LLANWERN

*May 2001*

The week that bridged January and February was a bad one for the people of Wales. The cursed uncertainty and speculation about the steel industry that had disfigured the headlines in local newspapers in previous weeks gave way to confirmation of serious job losses. Saturday's defeat in the Six Nations tournament at the hands and feet of the English thickened the gloom. Sports journalists, and that large proportion of the population for whom rugby football has replaced religion, spoke of the outcome of the test match as 'a disaster'. The true calamity was that visited by the management of Corus, the Anglo-Dutch inheritors of British Steel, on the workers at Llanwern and Ebbw Vale, on their families and all whose livelihoods depend on supplying the industry's needs. The removal of 780 jobs from Ebbw Vale, where unemployment already stands at eleven per cent, will be devastating.

Train passengers approaching Newport by day or night cannot fail to notice Llanwern. If the wind is in the right direction a roar that I imagine is the blast furnace going full pelt can be heard in Caerleon. The plant extends for miles it seems along what was once a marshy zone between the railway track and the Severn shore. When the pits were being closed and the spoil-heaps of the Valleys bulldozed into a semblance of normal topography, a few alert entrepreneurs made fortunes selling thousands of tons of well-roasted coke and shale (many of the old tips smouldered sulphurously for decades) as hard core for its construction site. In its now distant heyday, which was also the heyday of the trades unions that ruled the plant, it had an enormous workforce, a goodly number of whom, if you were to believe what was sometimes said in the pubs, did little for their wages. All that changed in the 1980s and 1990s as steel production and jobs were cut and cut again. What remained was as highly efficient as steel-making can be; Corus had no cause to complain about productivity. The loss of a further 1340 jobs at Llanwern will have a profound effect upon Newport, a town that has worked hard to overcome its reputation for shabbiness. The upmarket boutiques planners envisaged as occupants of the refurbished shell of the Westgate Hotel, where construction work is now nearing completion, may need to trim their retail expectations.

There was always a hint of irony in the Westgate's transformation, because of the events of November 1839. Soldiers then stationed at the hotel killed at least twenty of the 5000 Chartists who had marched on Newport as the first objective in their design to capture the towns on the fringes of the coalfield and create a separate workers' republic between the Wye and the Severn, from which fortress eventually to spread their revolutionary doctrine to the rest of Britain. The support the insurgents expected to receive from the military and Chartists elsewhere did not materialize and the rising, such as it was, subsided in bedraggled confusion: the marchers had tramped to Newport through torrential rain. Eight of them, including their leaders, John Frost, a draper in the town, William Jones, a former actor, from Pontypool and Zephaniah Williams of Nant-y-glo, were subsequently sentenced to death for treason. The sentences were commuted; Frost, Jones and Williams were transported to Van Diemen's Land, the remainder imprisoned. Schoolchildren in Newport learn about the Chartists' March and Frost is commemorated in John Frost Square; a statuary group outside the Westgate Hotel represents the aspirations of the nineteenth century working class. If the Assembly and

Westminster cannot (or will not) do anything to make Corus think again, the cold furnaces of Ebbw Vale and Llanwern will be their own memorial to the passing of an industry and the destruction of hope for a great many ordinary citizens.

The late Gwyn A. Williams, historian *extraordinaire*, whose rhetoric betrays that his sympathies lay with the Chartists, says the response of the 'respectable press' to this episode 'drenched working people in the spittle of truly ferocious class hatred and contempt'. The broadsheet *Western Mail*, which is making a fair fist of its claim to be the 'national newspaper of Wales' takes an entirely different view. It is as supportive of the workers' cause as it has been of the campaign to have a further tick-box added to the 2001 Census that will allow those who think of themselves as Welsh to register their nationality in the same way as the Scots (see *PN Review* 137). The reasonableness of this is unimpeachable, but when did reason ever persuade civil servants (or politicians for that matter) who had already made up their minds? We now have the absurd prospect of far more being spent on an advertising campaign urging the recalcitrant Welsh to complete the Census in the way the Office of National Statistics thoughtlessly determined than would be needed to change the form and end the dispute with smiles all round. As things stand, there is a likelihood that widespread civil disobedience will follow and, given the chronic immovability of government, legal sanctions, fines and imprisonment after that. That would not be good news for Labour in election year; Plaid Cymru, already a major force in the Assembly, will certainly make a meal of it.

One of the problems highlighted by the Census impasse is the assumption in Whitehall that, whatever the issue, it knows best, certainly far better than any individual or group calling itself Welsh. As history reminds us from time to time, this is not necessarily so. Publication of Lord Phillips's report on the BSE crisis towards the end of October last year offered one such reminder. In 1990, Dame Deidre Hine, chief medical officer at the Welsh Office, urged Whitehall colleagues *not* to tell ministers what they wanted to hear, namely, that British beef was completely safe. Dame Deidre's advice was ignored (so that the public was treated to the lamentable image of John Selwyn Gummer feeding his offspring with a hamburger), and when her group pressed its concern about recently discovered evidence of the transmission of BSE from one species to another, they were dismissed as interfering subordinates. The tone of the response from Whitehall to the Welsh Office is revealing. Dr Hilary Pickles, the Department of Health's principal medical officer, wrote: 'I am surprised you feel it necessary to put so much effort into challenging the views of colleagues at DoH who are more senior [and] more experienced in the area.' The Phillips report concludes, 'We think the Welsh Office was well served by the combined talents of its team of medical staff and the advice they gave during the initial stages of the epidemic...it was unfortunate that their voices were not more clearly heard in Whitehall at the time.' In view of the fresh alarms about BSE that come almost daily, 'unfortunate' is hardly the right word, but I don't expect this demonstration of Whitehall's fallibility to carry the slightest weight with the Office of National Statistics.

Earlier in January the life and poetry of R.S. Thomas were celebrated, first at Bangor in the north and the following night at Cardiff. The twin events were organised by Yr Academi Gymreig, of which he was a member. The full house at Bangor included Thomas fans from as far afield as England, and almost two hundred assembled in Cardiff. Several of the contributors spoke at both occasions and the programmes were substantially the same. Extracts from the poet's television appearances underlined his contradictory nature. He took part in broadcasts more frequently than might be expected of one who was often uncommunicative at readings. And so we saw him again, duffel-coated, walking the Welsh hill-country, Iago Prytherch country, near Manafon or Eglwysfach, his first two parishes; then against the background of that extraordinarily Romantic setting of the church on the shore at Aberdaron, and later still at the fireside of his cottage or beside the small upstairs window of the room where he wrote. He became engagingly thoughtful before the camera and, in the end, even affable.

If we set aside for a moment the admiration expressed for the poetry, most eloquently by Jeremy Hooker (now happily returned to Wales), the most memorable feature of the celebration were the testimonies to the poet's friendliness and humour. Among a series of tributes, Raymond Garlick spoke of a correspondence with R.S. that extended over fifty years; Gillian Clarke recalled hosting him in her own home and finding him laughing and joking with her children; Gwyneth Lewis and Sandra Anstey both asked favours expecting a rebuff and received instead a welcome to his home; and M. Wynn Thomas who interviewed him a dozen times or more, in Welsh and English, before audiences up and down Wales, found him always companionable and alert to the humour in their shared predicament. In the poet's will Professor Thomas has been appointed 'special executor' of the unpublished work, which one might guess includes a substantial number of poems. It will be interesting to see what R.S. has to say to us from beyond the grave. Sober stuff, I have no doubt; all the more reason to remember that other side of his nature intimates knew. He embodied, as Jeremy Hooker said, the mass of contraries that make the great lyric poet.

*PN Review* 139, Volume 27 Number 5,
May – June 2001.

# OWAIN GLYNDŴR
*September 2000*

When I took over from Meic Stephens as editor of *Poetry Wales* in 1973, I introduced a new cover design. Apart from the name of the magazine, the issue date and the publisher its only feature was a facsimile, a little larger than actual size, of the great seal of Owain Glyndŵr. On the front he appears mounted; his horse, richly accoutred, is galloping forward, he is armed with sword and shield, his helmet is crowned with a dragon crest. On the back, he is seated on a throne surmounted by a canopy, hunting dogs are at his feet and, behind him, protective angels spread banners figured with *leopards passans* – from the arms of the house of Gwynedd, with which he claimed an important, if distant, connection. Both are powerful images, loaded with meaning for any with a sense of Welsh nationhood.

A reproduction of the same seal, bought many years ago from the shop at the National Museum of Wales, lies on the desk beside me as I write. I have recently seen the real thing, attached to an original document, the letter, in Latin, addressed by Glyndŵr to Charles VI of France, 'Given at Pennal on the thirty-first day of March AD 1406, and in the sixth year of our rule', on loan from the *archives nationales* at Paris. The man who sought by this letter to establish Wales as an independent Christian principality, owing allegiance to the anti-pope, Benedict, at Avignon, was a Welsh squire, Owain ap Gruffudd of Glyndyfrdwy and Sycharth. The Glyndyfrdwy is commonly abbreviated to Glyndŵr, and Englished to Glendowerdy. It is as Glendower we meet him in Shakespeare's *Henry IV Part One*, where he declares he can speak English as well as his exceedingly prickly ally Hotspur, because he was 'trayn'd up in the English Court'. The historical Glyndŵr almost certainly knew Geoffrey Chaucer, soldiered with Richard II's army in Scotland in 1387, and received a legal training at the Inns of Court. At his fine moated mansion at Sycharth, just inside the present-day Welsh border, about six miles south-west of Oswestry (destroyed during his rebellion by the future King Henry V), he afforded traditional hospitality to poets, who repaid his generosity with paeans of praise linking him to past kings of an independent Wales. He gave his daughter, Catrin, in marriage to Edmund Mortimer, brother of Roger Mortimer, rightful heir to Richard's throne, and co-signatory, with himself and Hotspur, of those 'Indentures Tripartite', the three discuss in Act III Scene 1 of Shakespeare's play, that promised a much-enlarged Wales as Glyndŵr's share of the spoils of victory. Here, Shakespeare, who cared a good deal less for historical accuracy than he did for dramatic characterisation, conflated events. Henry Percy, known as Hotspur, was killed at the battle of Shrewsbury in 1403, his personal revolt against Henry IV having gone off at half-cock, leaving his forces exposed to the full might of the king's army before Glyndŵr and Mortimer could come to his aid, while the planned division of Henry's realm involved Hotspur's father, also Henry Percy, Earl of Northumberland, and occurred in Bangor in 1405.

The Pennal Letter (named after the small village near the estuary of the Dovey, little more than three miles west of Machynlleth) tells us that Owain dated his assumption of power, and the title Prince of Wales, from 1400, though his rebellion against Henry IV, who as Henry Bolingbroke had usurped the throne of Richard II, only began in September of that year. The seeds of insurrection had been sown far and wide in Wales, and long before, in the repressive measures successive kings of England had taken against the common folk and their local leaders. When the Glyndŵr rising began, there were many eager to join a man whose family tree had roots in the old ruling dynasties of Wales, north and south. That alone cannot explain the fervour of the response from the people of Wales to Glyndŵr's call to arms. There was something in his character and personality that brought rich and poor, peasants and soldiers, clergy and lay people, and students from Oxford, flocking to his standard. In Shakespeare's portrait we catch a glimpse of that personal magnetism that inspired his followers: it was they who, at the beginning of the rebellion, immediately conferred the princely title on him.

The accretion of magical signs and powers around Glyndŵr's legend, also present in Shakespeare's portrait, probably owes much to the spirit abroad in Europe as a turbulent century drew to a close: just as at the recent dawning of a new millennium, there were those who expected 1400 to usher in a new order, or even the end of the world. It did neither. For a while, the rebellion waxed strong, reaching momentous high points, as in 1404, when Glyndŵr held his first parliament at Machynlleth. But by 1406, when he wrote from Pennal to the king of France, to cement their alliance and outline his plans for establishing a separate church in Wales, and two universities, the peak had passed. The Earl of Northumberland had already been defeated by King Henry, who, spared that distraction, turned his full might on the Welsh insurgents. In the years that followed, Glyndŵr's power base in the great castles of Wales was gradually eroded. By 1408 he was able to mount guerilla attacks only from the woods and mountains and the last heard of him is in connection with the capture, in June 1412, of an old enemy, Dafydd Gam (the loyal 'Davy Gam Esquire' of Shakespeare's *Henry V* who, as the play reminds us, died at Agincourt three years later). As late as 1414, probably influenced by Glyndŵr's chancellor, Gruffudd Young, the

Council of Konstanz declared Wales a separate nation, but the great leader himself had already disappeared. His death and place of burial were unrecorded, probably deliberately, so that, like Arthur, he would live on. He was a living presence in the minds of a good many people when the National Assembly opened for business in Cardiff twelve months ago, within a jot of time, just six centuries after those last parliaments of an independent Wales.

The Pennal letter is the *pièce de résistance* of a 600th anniversary exhibition devoted to Glyndŵr, running at the National Library of Wales, Aberystwyth until September. It is a noble attempt to make bricks with little straw, for artefacts connected with Glyndŵr are in short supply. There are a couple of the stone cannon balls with which, in 1408, Henry's besieging army battered the walls of Aberystwyth castle where Glyndŵr had established his court and chancery, and an exquisite fragment of harness ornament bearing his arms, from his own horse one would like to think, found at Harlech, where he had hastened to rebuild his administration after the fall of Aberystwyth. Harlech surrendered in 1409. For the rest, there are sound loops and a TV film, religious and medical treatises in glowing manuscripts suggestive of the period, and a series of painted panels illustrating key events in Glyndŵr's life accompanied by a poetic commentary in Welsh and English. Not a great deal perhaps, but at least it gives the visitor more to think about than the Dome (I write as one who can vouch for that) – and it's free. If you go to Aberystwyth, do not leave without seeing the splendid companion exhibition of treasures of the National Library, which include the Book of Taliesin, the White Book of Rhydderch (one of the texts of *The Mabinogion*), the Black Book of Carmarthen and a copy of Bishop Morgan's translation of the Bible.

The English versions of the Glyndŵr exhibition poems are

603

by Gillian Clarke, who, along with all her other contributions to literature in Wales, is fast becoming our unofficial laureate. She was also commissioned recently to write a sequence of poems about the restoration of the gardens of Aberglasne (Aberglasney), a ruined mansion in the village of Llangathen, Carmarthenshire, once the home of the poet John Dyer (1699-1757), whose 'Grongar Hill' celebrates the surrounding countryside. Long before Dyer's time, Lewis Glyn Cothi (*fl.* 1447-80), one of the most important Welsh bards of the fifteenth century, wrote a poem in praise of 'the nine green gardens' of his patron, Rhydderch ap Rhys ap Gruffudd, in the same place. Though others have their doubts, it is these medieval gardens that the restoration team claims to have rescued. Be that as it may, Gillian Clarke's poems accompanied the television unveiling of the grand work and are now gathered in an attractive, illustrated booklet published by Gomer Press, which is based at Llandysul, barely fifteen miles north-west of Llangathen.

Llandysul, Llangathen, and many other small towns, smaller villages and outlying farms in rural west Wales, lie within the shrinking heartland of the Welsh language. What can be done to save them from the common fate of quiet, beautiful places in the throes of depopulation, the closure of schools and post offices, the dread grasp of second-home ownership, baffles the united intelligence of the Assembly for Wales. The sure knowledge that once the language generator of the heartland has lost its power, which resides in the daily use of a living tongue for ordinary purposes of life, there can be no restoring it, has so far lent no urgency to the politicians. They cannot find the money to provide support for the rural economy that would sustain neighbourhood institutions and make it worthwhile for young people to think of careers close to home; and they cannot stop the moneyed from moving into rural areas and inflating the price of property beyond the reach of the locals.

Let us give thanks then for Ifan ab Owen Edwards. 'Who he?' I hear you ask. One of the modest giants of twentieth century Wales, he founded *Urdd Gobaith Cymru*, a cultural movement for the young. Its name is conventionally translated into English as the Welsh League of Youth, but the literal translation, 'Guild of the Hope of Wales', is more suggestive of the patriotic inspiration that lay behind it. From its origins in 1922, it has grown to a current membership of more than 50,000 in over 1500 branches, mostly primary and secondary schools, throughout the country. It was the Urdd that, in 1939, opened the first Welsh primary school, at Aberystwyth, setting in train another movement that has led to Welsh-medium education becoming available to all who wish it for their children.

In the same week as the Hay Festival, the Urdd was holding its national eisteddfod, which is advertised (though not enough) as the largest cultural youth festival in Europe. Annually at about this time, children and young people from all over Wales, having successfully negotiated preliminary rounds, come to compete in a wide range of cultural events. This year, at Penrhyn Bay on the north Wales coast (like the National Eisteddfod, that of the Urdd is a movable feast), there were 14,000 competitors. The eisteddfod cost a million pounds to mount, and, over the week attracted 110,000 visitors, who together contributed some two million to the local economy. The Welsh language television channel, S4C, brings coverage of the highlights and the results of competitions daily fill pages in the *Western Mail*. It is a big event, and enormously important to the education system, and to the culture and traditions of Wales in Welsh and English, but particularly the former, because the Urdd has a mission to preserve and spread the language. It also generates a great deal of fun, to which, as a member in my own schooldays, I can testify. Lest you should think the literary, musical, artistic and dramatic performance of the young in such circumstances unlikely to be of significance, it is worth recalling that many leading figures in the arts world here first came to notice at an Urdd eisteddfod. Gwyneth Lewis won the Literature Medal two years in succession, in 1977 and 1978.

Comparison of the Hay Festival, now sufficiently famous to attract the interest of literary entrepreneurs in the USA, with the Urdd Eisteddfod, which, as I have indicated, gets a fair crack of the whip from the Welsh-based press and television, is pointless. Nevertheless, it is legitimate to wish that one small fraction of the wider media attention given to the goings-on at Hay could have been spared for what was happening in Penrhyn Bay, where the ability of teachers to enthuse and of the arts to sustain the young was daily in evidence.

*PN Review* 135, Volume 27 Number 1, September – October 2000.

# THE NATIONAL ASSEMBLY AND WALES IN AMERICA
*July 2000*

The 'First Secretary' affair created a considerable stir in the media. When the Assembly for Wales was set up no one, least of all the Prime Minister, foresaw the possibility of its activity having the slightest impact on United Kingdom politics. He, and we, were mistaken. The failure of Blair's placeman, Alun Michael, to obtain from the Treasury a guarantee of match-funding that would unlock a hoard of Objective One euros for the impoverished rural and post-industrial parts of Wales was entirely predictable. What the other parties (who, together, hold a majority over the Labour administration) would do when the expected was more or less confirmed was the only question. With barely stifled glee they seized upon it as a confidence issue. In the end, Michael fell upon his sword – to the consternation of Lord Elis-Thomas, 'Presiding Officer' (the local term for Speaker), who had been prepared for a resignation *after* the confidence vote, not before. It did energise the media remarkably: overnight, politics in Wales became headline news in London. Not out of interest in Welsh affairs, however. The fall of Alun Michael and rise of Rhodri Morgan were seen to mirror events unfolding in Media-opolis, where New Labour's arcane selection system was backed to ensure a similar opposition between the party's preference as mayoral candidate for London and the popular choice. The discomfiture of the Prime Minister is the main theme. I had one brief opportunity of observing Alun Michael at close quarters while he was still in post. He was composed, well-prepared, astute, but unimpressive personally and in his rhetoric. We shall see whether Rhodri Morgan, who has strengths in the areas of his predecessor's weaknesses, manages the Objective One problem with greater success. How far all the media hoo-haa reflects the concerns of people in Wales, or London for that matter, is a matter for conjecture. It seems unlikely to increase the interest of the public, other than those with a particular grievance, in the business of the National Assembly. We are told that, two days after his party confirmed Morgan as Wales's second First Secretary, a television programme dedicated to Welsh politics attracted fewer than 2500 viewers, officially a nil response. The impression is growing that, in the main, political journalists speak only to other political journalists.

R.S. Thomas is reported to have said he has given up writing, but he has not done with voicing his own brand of disgruntled patriotism. He labels Wales the *ci bach* (lapdog) of the Westminster government. In his view, we acquiesced in an inferior style of devolution, which would have been unacceptable to the more rebellious Scots, because we were 'so pleased to have some recognition'. This echoes Ned Thomas's critique of Assembly members' efforts in debate last year on the 'image of Wales'. 'We know this tone well from the culture,' he writes (in *Planet* No. 139, February/March 2000). 'It says we know we exist when we succeed in the big world. We're passionate (one of the recommended adjectives of the Branding Wales group for projecting Wales), but unfortunately we're more passionate for recognition than anything else.' Can we actually *do* anything within the imposed framework? Can we, for instance, vary the way in which teachers are assessed under the new pay regime – a move that would be universally applauded here, and, I fancy, from the sidelines in England? The answer, however you dress it up, is a categoric no. Recognition, it seems, is the only thing our politicians are allowed to be passionate about.

The *Western Mail* handed the Assembly the chance of instant popular appeal on 1st March. In a front-page banner headline it demanded St David's Day be made a public holiday for the celebration of all things Welsh, as St Patrick's is in Ireland and the United States. The Welsh-American connection invariably crops up on or about St David's Day – another manifestation of the recognition culture. Once more we are reminded that Thomas Jefferson, third President of the United States and author of the Declaration of Independence, was of Welsh descent, and apparently proud of it; ditto John Adams, second President, and of course his son, John Quincy Adams, sixth President, and my namesake, the great rabble-rouser, Samuel Adams, to the best of my knowledge unrelated to the other two as I certainly am to all of them. A fifth (or is it a third? – a lot anyway), of the signatories of the Declaration of Independence were within a generation or so of humble Welsh homes. America, with its promise of freedom and a fair reward for effort, had attracted their forebears, in flight from rural poverty and religious and political repression in Britain. Further back, legend has it, lies a more fundamental claim to a Welsh role in the American saga, also brought out and given a fresh polish annually as St David's Day comes round. 'Did a Welsh Prince discover America?' was this year's eye-catcher in the *Western Mail*.

This story concerns Madoc, Prince of Gwynedd, and among the earliest printed versions is that of David Powel in *The Historie of Cambria, now called Wales* (1584). On the commission of Sir Henry Sidney, Lord President of Wales, father of the more famous Sir Philip, Powel corrected, augmented and edited for the press the text of a manuscript said to have been written in Welsh by one Caradog of Llancarfan (*fl.* 1135) 'above two hundreth yeares past [and] translated into English by H. Lhoyd'. The last named appears more often as Humffrey Llwyd (or Lhuyd), native of Denbigh, physician, antiquarian, geographer and MP, who had become a collaborator and friend of the great Dutch geographer Ortelius. It is possible that some of the information about Madoc had come to him from scholars overseas as well as from seafaring traditions along the coast of north Wales. In the *Historie*, the tale unfolds thus. Despairing of the strife between his brothers in the struggle for succession following the death of their father, Owen Gwynedd, Madoc 'prepared certaine ships with men and munition, and sought adventures by seas, sailing West, & leaving the coast of Ireland so far north, that he came to a land unknown, where he saw many strange things. This land must needs be some part of that countrie of which the Spaniardes affirme themselves to be the first finders – Whereupon it is manifest, that that countrie was long before by Brytaines discovered, afore either Columbus or Americus Vesputius led anie Spaniardes thither.' A marginal gloss and the use of a different typeface in Powel's text confirms Llwyd as the source of the story. It is clearly a piece of Tudor propaganda, reinforcing the imperial claims that had already been made on behalf of Elizabethan Britain by John Dee, scientist and magician, another of Welsh parentage, as proud of his Radnorshire roots as Jefferson was of his connection with Snowdonia. Dee too it seems owed a good deal to a foreign source for his confidence in a twelfth century Welsh colonisation of America, in this case Gerard Mercator. In a letter to Dee of April 1577, Mercator's presentation of 'evidence' that survivors of an Arthurian trans-Atlantic quest had turned up in Bergen as late as 1364 was re-interpreted by Dee as proof of the Madoc expedition. It is fascinating, and salutary in the age of the internet, to be reminded that, notwithstanding religious and political conflict and the difficulties of travel, the great minds of half a millennium ago and more had a common medium, Latin, which they used to exchange knowledge, even if some of it was fanciful.

The appeal of the Madoc story declined with the eclipse of the Tudors. When interest revived towards the end of the eighteenth century, it had a different focus and triggered a new quest: the search for the Welsh Indians. North America was rife with rumours about a tribe of 'white Indians' whose language was understandable to Welsh-speakers, who had some vestiges of Christianity in their religious ceremonies, had lived in hill forts, abandoned but still extant, and took to the water in craft indistinguishable from the coracles you can see in use on the river Teifi to this day. So persuasive and persistent were these tall tales that one of the specific tasks President Jefferson set Majors Lewis and Clark before they set out in 1840 on their epic journey from St Louis to the Pacific Ocean was to find the Welsh Indians. Not long before this, the story had got back to Wales, where it was received with delight by a new wave of Welsh intellectuals desperate for some confirmation of the influence of their small country on the wider world. Foremost among them was Iolo Morganwg, inventor of the *gorsedd* of bards, reviver of the eisteddfod (*PN Review* 124).

Iolo planned a voyage of exploration to make contact with the descendants of Madoc, choosing as his companion an able and impressive young man from Waun-fawr near Caernarfon named John Evans. In August 1792, however, Evans set off alone, on the strength of a loan of £20 and a handful of letters of introduction to Welsh Americans. By October he had reached Baltimore. Ignoring advice about the dangers of encountering savage tribes, not to mention rival Spanish and French forces in competition for land, wealth and influence, he pressed on. At St Louis he was imprisoned by the Spanish governor and seems to have been converted to the Spanish cause, for it was through membership of an expedition of the Spanish Missouri Company that he gained the opportunity to go on alone, exploring and mapping the Missouri, ultimately some two thousand miles above its confluence with the Mississippi. On the upper Missouri in September 1796 he came across the villages of the Mandans, the tribe upon which, by this time, all the hopes of the White Indian seekers centred. He lodged with them through the bitter winter months and must have observed how much their villages resembled Iron Age forts in Wales, how much their boats resembled coracles, but in subsequent reports he made no mention of either. He served his new Spanish masters well, hoisting their royal standard among the Mandans and seeing off rival British, French and Canadian traders. And when, in July 1797, he wrote to Dr Samuel Jones in Philadelphia giving an account of his adventures he stated categorically: 'I am able to inform you that there is no such thing as the Welsh Indians.' Almost a decade later, Evans's maps and the notes of his journey assisted Lewis and Clark, but their maker had already died of disappointment and drink, aged 28, in New Orleans in 1799.

That was by no means the end of the story of Madoc's discovery of America, as the recent headline in the *Western Mail* testifies. Each age adds a twist to the old tale. In 1953, the Daughters of the American Revolution unveiled a plaque at Fort Morgan, Mobile, Alabama commemorating the landing of Madoc and his company 'on the shores of Mobile Bay in 1170'. Now the call is for DNA comparison of the few surviving Mandans (the tribe was virtually wiped out by smallpox in 1837) with any identifiable descendant of Madoc. Some hope! The legend lives on in such gestures and speculation, and more seriously in works of art and scholarship based on it, from George Catlin's remarkable paintings of Mandan village life in the 1830s, to Roland Mathias's long poem for radio 'Madoc', broadcast in 1971 (the immediate cause, rather than the *Western Mail*, of this particular airing of it), and a wonderful piece of historical writing, *Madoc – The Making of a Myth*

(1979), by Gwyn A. Williams, which I guarantee will entertain anyone who troubles to look it up.

*PN Review* 134, Volume 26 Number 6,
July – August 2000.

# THE WELSH LANGUAGE

*January 2000*

The Welsh language is the one feature that, despite the Acts of Union and the toll of centuries, distinguishes Wales from England. Pockets of Englishry, like that in south Pembrokeshire, have existed here for centuries. If, however, on the threshold of AD 2000, we look back, it should be to acknowledge that for more than nine-tenths of the previous millennia Wales was, north and south, a Welsh-speaking country. This did not escape the notice of the early English tourist in search of exotic experiences cheaper than those obtainable on the continent. In his *Historical Tour Through Monmouthshire* (1801), William Coxe wrote 'The inhabitants [of western Monmouthshire] unwillingly hold intercourse with the English, retain their ancient prejudices and still brand them with the name of Saxons'. Benjamin Malkin visiting the 'immense works' at Cyfarthfa, Merthyr Tydfil, noted (in *The Scenery, Antiquity and Biography of South Wales*, 1804) that the language of the 'workmen of all descriptions...is entirely Welsh', and J.G. Wood in his *The Principal Rivers of Wales* (1813) described the preindustrial Rhondda valleys as 'the wildest region of Glamorganshire, where the English language is scarce ever heard'. Even industrial south Wales retained its distinctively Welsh culture deep into the nineteenth century, while the rural west and north, outside the gates of the wealthy, landowning class, who were a miniscule minority, was yet more indelibly Welsh, preparing for its contemporary role as the precious 'heartland' of the language. It is also of considerable significance that, in contrast to the Anglican squirearchy, the people of Wales were, from the seventeenth century, predominantly Nonconformist. So, when Malkin again observed it to be 'very remarkable that great immoralities do not prevail in any part of Wales, not even in places contiguous to large manufactories, especially if the English language happens to be but little spoken', he was complimenting the decency of the people and the morality of the Welsh chapels.

The way in which outsiders' attitudes to Wales have affected the confidence of the Welsh, especially in relation to their own language, is one of the themes that can be picked out from a splendid new 'pocket guide' from the University of Wales Press – *Wales in Quotation*, compiled by Meic Stephens. It serves to remind us that ordinary folk, labourers in field or mine or factory, were no more illiterate, no more nor less culturally active in Wales than they were in England. The difference between them lay in the language of daily life and in this respect the English held the whip hand in terms of numerical superiority, and political power. They were, however, in no position to argue the superiority of their language and literature over those of Wales, because (with a handful of exceptions) they knew nothing about the latter, and cared less. That did not prevent them exercising a crude cultural imperialism in relation to their neighbour. John Humffreys Parry, Mold-born writer and editor, who shares with Marlowe the distinction of having been killed in a tavern brawl in London, commented, with admirable restraint (in *The Cambrian Plutarch*, 1824), 'While the national peculiarities, whether in manners or literature, of Scotland and Ireland, have been industriously explored, and in many instances successfully developed, Wales has been regarded with an indifference not easily to be reconciled with the spirit of enterprise by which the literary public of Great Britain is known to be animated.' 'Spirit of enterprise' indeed! He was, of course, trying to butter-up anglophone readers – a hopeless task, as the ensuing one hundred and seventy-five years have demonstrated. At least, the Welsh could have gone on talking to and writing for one another confidently in their own language, but, as another fine book from UWP, *The Language of the Blue Books* by Gwyneth Tyson Roberts, makes clear, a quiet and refined act of colonial aggression against Wales put a stop to that for the great majority of its inhabitants.

What the exploitation of the wealth of the coalfields could not do, even when the prospect of paid employment, albeit in the grim and hazardous environments of pit and furnace, brought hapless agricultural labourers in their tens of thousands from adjacent English counties – and much further afield – into south Wales in particular, was finally achieved at the instigation of a Welsh-speaking MP. A government commission was set up to enquire into the state of education in Wales. The three commissioners were upper-middle-class English speakers of the Anglican persuasion, and knew nothing of Wales. This did not deter them. With a confidence born of their origins and their calling (all three were lawyers), they based their enquiry into a very largely Welsh-speaking Nonconformist society on evidence gathered almost entirely from English-speaking Anglicans. Among the gems of the 'Blue Books', as the three official volumes, published in 1847, came to be known, are: 'In the works the Welsh workman never finds his way into the office...His language keeps him under the hatches, being one in which he can neither acquire nor communicate the necessary information'; 'The Welsh language is a vast drawback to Wales, and a manifold barrier to the moral progress and commercial prosperity of the people. It is not easy to estimate its evil effects.' Of course, there was a howl of protest from some quarters and the episode became notorious as 'Brad y Llyfrau Gleision' ('The Treachery of the Blue Books'). The damage, however, was done. To say that the stuffing was knocked out of the Welsh is not to overstate the case. This was not enough: at fairly regular intervals metropolitan bovver boys put the boot into the prone body of Welsh self-respect. Editorials in *The Times* in 1866 opined 'The Welsh language is the curse of Wales. Its prevalence and the ignorance of English have excluded, and even now exclude, the Welsh people from the civilization, the improvement, the material prosperity of their English neighbours...Their antiquated and semi-barbarous language, in short, shrouds them in darkness'; and 'Wales, it should be remembered, is a small country, unfavourably situated for commercial purposes, with an indifferent soil, and inhabited by an unenterprising people. It is true it possesses valuable minerals but these have been chiefly developed by English energy and for supply of English wants. A bare existence on the most primitive food of a mountainous race is all that the Welsh could enjoy if left to themselves.'

It is difficult to understand now why the establishment in England was so exercised about Welsh when, since the consensus was that the language would soon become extinct in the march of progress, the easier option would have been to ignore it. Was there a certain pique at the ingratitude of the people of Wales in clinging to this cultural difference when vast territories overseas seemed happy to embrace English? Could it have been that they shared with John Redwood MP the supremely ignorant view (expressed in his *The Global Marketplace: Capitalism and its Future*, 1994) that 'If an Englishman enters a shop in Welsh-speaking parts of Wales, the locals are likely to switch promptly to speaking Welsh. Thus the Englishman cannot be sure whether they are talking about him'? Or was it merely supercilious disdain for a feeble neighbour? As late as 1971, Elizabeth Beasley (in *The Shell Guide to North Wales*) looked down her superior nose and concluded, 'The visitor to north Wales should remember that, in architecture as in other matters, English standards do not apply.'

Not so long ago, whenever the Welsh looked back on the past, they inevitably viewed it through English eyes, because the major sources of information, writers, historians and publishers, were English. In the last half century this has changed. Thanks to the scholarship and the presentational skills of people like Gwyn Alf Williams, Dai Smith, Kenneth O. Morgan and John Davies, there is now a body of historical knowledge to put in the balance against views such as those quoted above and help us to an understanding of our contemporary condition. At an intellectual level, they have contributed a great deal to the creation of a sense of something hopeful stirring here. Gwyn Alf could always be relied upon to add a spoonful of spice. In his speech to the Campaign for a Welsh Assembly at Merthyr Tydfil towards the end of 1988 he said, 'We as a people have been around for two thousand years. Isn't it about time we got the key to our own front door?'

Sadly, he did not live to see the Assembly open in Cardiff last May. It has already begun to raise the profile of Wales abroad. On holiday in Italy this summer, in the course of halting conversations with locals, the naming of the land of our birth was not greeted with the usual blank incomprehension. 'Ah, Wales,' he or she would say, 'you're independent now?' Lacking the heart and the words to explain the nature of our constitutional position, we would nod confirmation. A handful of Italians are perhaps even now spreading this error among the townships of Lago di Garda, awaking expectations among our European neighbours that the thousand-year-old dragon flag will shortly join those flying at Brussels, Strasbourg, and New York. While that is as likely as heatstroke in Blaenau Ffestiniog, it has to be said that never in its millennial history has the flag been flown, paraded, draped, painted, flaunted, *worn* so much as in the few months since the establishment of the Assembly for Wales.

The current increase in confidence this side of Offa's Dyke is also due in part to the emergence within the last decade of talented actors and entertainers. Welsh rock bands – notably Manic Street Preachers, Catatonia, Stereophonics – share a strong, if sometimes ironic, sense of Welsh identity. 'Every day when I wake up I thank the Lord I'm Welsh' sings Cerys of Catatonia to huge applause, and Kelly Jones of the Stereophonics brings the house down with 'As long as we beat the English!' – referring of course to rugby football. That they have enthusiastic followings outside Wales says a great deal for the open-mindedness of young people compared with John Redwood and his like. I wonder what Harri Webb, Welsh socialist republican and poet, would have thought of it. All his efforts in prose and verse to create a nationalist stir barely raised a ripple in comparison with the tide of feeling that seems to be running in the wake of these contemporary musicians.

Then there is RWC99 – Rugby World Cup. Journalistic queasiness in some quarters about the emphasis given in the opening ceremony to Wales, the hosts, rather than to the visiting nations, showed that metropolitan attitudes to the Welsh die hard. Certainly it featured dragons galore, not least incongruously (and unflatteringly) on the ball gown worn by Shirley Bassey, who shared the singing of the World Cup theme tune, 'The World in Union', with Bryn Terfel. Enthusiasm knew no bounds while the Welsh team remained in the competition and, though much diminished since its departure, is still evident in the popular interest generated by matches involving other countries.

The sceptics say anti-climax and apathy will follow the closing ceremony. They remind us constantly that national identity and pride cannot be built upon foundations as feeble as rock bands and rugby teams, whose success is ephemeral and durability doubtful. If we are to judge by the threats of another referendum at the Tory conference, even the Assembly is not assured of existence beyond New Labour's term in office, especially if it continues to demonstrate how ineffectual it is at accomplishing anything unsanctioned by Downing Street. We have been caught up in a constitutional conjuring trick. Here, the stage magician says, is something a bare majority of that half of you who are at all interested in this show seem to want. For a moment there appears to be a desirable prize in the palm of his extended hand, but then with a deft fluttering of his fingers it vanishes.

Yet, just now, looking forward to the year 2000 and beyond, against all the lessons of the past and dystopian visions of the future, I feel an unaccountable optimism. In this mood, I am inclined to believe that, should the new confidence among the Welsh prove more than an attractive but short-lived mirage, it may well express itself in increasing dissatisfaction with the condescending gift of devolution without a vestige of power.

*PN Review* 131, Volume 26 Number 3,
January – February 2000.

# WALES AND POLITICS

*September 1999*

In the early 1960s, I was for a time a member of a Bristol club at which it was customary to end each convivial session with three verses of 'The Queen'. Since memory lets you down almost as often by its retention of what you would prefer to forget as by failing to lug forward what you wish to remember, I find that I still effortlessly recall those loyal lines. One phrase, 'confound their politics', I frequently take out of context and apply to politicians of all shades. Unlike many of my fellows (if the turn-out for the recent election is anything to go by), I am afflicted not by apathy, but a failure to suspend disbelief in the efficacy of political process and the worthiness of those who engage in it. I know I should be delighted that we now have our own National Assembly, but I find myself trying hard to work up a little trust in the new institution. True it lacks the powers that have been handed back to the Scots, but it is, after all, the nearest thing we have had to a parliament in Wales since the days of Owain Glyndŵr. I still look to our elected representatives to set us an example of principle and common sense and so often they don't. I should have become more forgiving of their human failings, and have to some degree, but the tattered remnants of that naive expectation cling. In my sister's view, it comes of having been brought up in the Valleys of south Wales, where, as she graphically puts it, a donkey with a Labour rosette would win hands down. So it had always been until 6 May, when to everyone's surprise, not least the candidates', Plaid Cymru took the Rhondda and Islwyn, formerly impregnable bastions of Labour.

My sister still lives in Gilfach Goch, where I was born. To visit her I travel via the M4 and the A4119, the main road to the Rhondda, reconstructed in the 1980s on a ribbon of land where once the railway carried long lines of black trucks piled with coal down to Cardiff. Transport is the key to development and the road was seen by the hopeful as a lifeline to the valley, its collieries all closed, its people desperate for new employers. Having removed the railway, did our political masters order the construction of a fine dual-carriageway to Tonypandy? No, they built a country lane: Churchill's revenge. This thrombotic artery is, nevertheless, one of the main routes serving the authority of Rhondda-Cynon-Taff, itself a wonderful new creation of the Welsh Office, in the death throes of the last Tory administration. An economic survey published recently by the authority classifies 56% of its heads of household as manual workers, less than 4% as professional. In a zone where public transport is a joke, 39% of households have no car. Over a thousand homes still have no bath or shower; more than two thousand lack an inside WC. Unemployment runs at 10%, but of these 23% have been out of work for more than a year. Nearly 26% of 19-24 year-olds are unemployed. That other parts of Wales and the UK can present a similar array of statistics does not ease my depression as I contemplate, from a comfortable distance, my home patch.

I should perhaps be grateful that I can go back to Gilfach Goch, a small offshoot of a valley, a cul-de-sac, its floor at some 600 feet, inexorably rained upon, which might be so easily dammed and turned into a reservoir. This is what happened to the area of upland farms near Talybont-on-Usk, where Roland Mathias was born, and, notoriously, to Tryweryn and the small Welsh-speaking community of Capel Celyn, near Bala, drowned in 1965 to create a water supply for Liverpool. A fortnight before the Assembly election, the *Western Mail* was energetically re-playing this political fiasco, when, despite opposition from all over Wales, Westminster voted in favour of Liverpool's scheme. The image of the flooded valley has an important place in the poetry and prose of Roland Mathias, and in the work of R.S. Thomas, whose poem 'Reservoirs' has been absorbed into the national psyche:

There are places in Wales I don't go:
Reservoirs that are the subconscious
Of a people, troubled far down
With gravestones, chapels, villages even...

There are moves afoot to erect a memorial beside the dam at Tryweryn, a tall, bird-like bronze designed by sculptor John Meirion Morris. Funds are being raised: Liverpool City Council has been asked to contribute. In hindsight, the events of 1965 are being seen as a turning point in Welsh politics, which has led us, very slowly, and with barely perceptible enthusiasm on the part of the majority, to an Assembly for Wales. That should guarantee no more Tryweryns – for which we shall be grateful.

Finances permitting, a fair proportion of the population of the Rhondda visit the seaside resort of Porthcawl during what passes for summer in these parts. Trecco Bay there has the largest holiday caravan park in Europe and, rain or shine, the fairground is crowded with folk, the air thick with Valleys accents and the combined olfactory assault of frying onions, doughnuts and candy floss. Robert Minhinnick lives there, in a street behind the promenade that curves away to the quieter Rest Bay, where staid visitors gravitate. The thronged fairground and, when the trippers have gone, the deserted coast, have long been and continue potent sources of inspiration for him. I was there recently, at a locally famous old watering-hole, the Esplanade Hotel, for the launch of his *Selected Poems*. 'The Esp', a bit seedy these days, was welcoming enough, and by sunset a large roomful of Minhinnick supporters were seated comfortably with drinks they had bought themselves. It was a good occasion to reflect upon the writer's emergence in *Poetry Wales* in the early 1970s and his development since as poet and essayist. Although he has often enough in the past drawn sustenance from experiences as widely separated as Penyfai, Saskatoon and Rio to reinvent himself poetically, nothing quite compares with the transformation that has occurred since Minhinnick's poems have started appearing in *PN Review*. In the latest, a new playfulness and ironic subtlety has emerged alongside the lapidary image-making that has always been his trademark. When in due course we look back on it, I rather think we shall see the publication of *Selected Poems* was particularly well-timed, because it marked the end of a long process of development and set the scene for a fresh departure.

The evening in Porthcawl had a second pleasure: songs and poems by Paul Henry, whose third book, *The Milk Thief* (Seren), came out last year. As a singer-songwriter, performing to his own guitar accompaniment, he adds variety and freshness to the conventional reading and deserves to be in demand. His poems about wife, parents, relatives, and Aberystwyth, his birthplace, have an oblique sentiment and make a crafty virtue of nostalgia. The imagery is precise and evocative – 'Boats, like fallen windowboxes/sink in mud, bloom with weeds'; 'A leaking tap's blown glass/pulls and slips, rhythmically' – and the observation of human types acute:

He'd rest his rod in the V
while she stayed in the Robin,
knitting something white or pink,
emerging only to empty the flask

or to be led, discreetly,
down an aisle of leaves

at the side of the bridge
then under the biggest arch.

Click-click went the reel, all evening.
Click-click from daylight to dark
as the line stirred, then pulled
then slackened and came back in.

And later still, barely visible,
on opposite sides of the glass,
they'd mime catches that swung,
hers from a needle, his from a hook

before the full spool of their love
unwound on its three wheels...

Travellers westward along the M4 will recognise Newport, Henry's current home, by a vast blockhouse on a hill commanding the approaches to the town. It is not military, but a new hotel, the modest monument of the first Welsh billionaire. Soon afterwards they join the congestion caused by the notorious Brynglas Tunnels, another failure for which I blame politicians more than engineers or mute geology. Whether the Assembly can succeed in supplying common-sense solutions to problems like this, and the north-south route, and the myriad needs of Rhondda-Cynon-Taff – and the money to implement them, is another matter. If its current preoccupation with beef on the bone is anything to go by, probably not.

*PN Review* 129, Volume 26 Number 1,
September – October 1999.

# ST DWYNWEN'S DAY

*July 1999*

It may not be well known that, while the English and our fellow Celts on these islands (and, for all I know, people everywhere fallen under the insidious spell of greetings card manufacturers) have only St Valentine's Day, the Welsh command two opportunities each year to declare their passion, secret or otherwise, for another. We also have as a patron saint of lovers, St Dwynwen. On her feast-day, 25 January, we can do all the silly things that commercial interests expect the smitten to do, like sending chocolates and flowers, and witty messages through the post or the press. For knowledge of her we are indebted to Iolo Morganwg, of whom I have written previously as the inventor of the Gorsedd of Bards and all-round reliable witness. He says Dwynwen, daughter of Brychan, the king alleged to have given his name to Brycheiniog (Breconshire), was too hotly propositioned by her beloved, Maelon. Her prayer to God to save her from what might have been a fifth century case of 'date rape' was duly answered. In a dream, God gave her a drink that quelled her passion and turned the unfortunate Maelon into a block of ice. To confuse the issue, Dwynwen was then granted three wishes. The first she used to revive Maelon, the second to become patron saint of lovers, and the third to remain ever unmarried. This is only slightly dafter than the story associated with St Valentine, though chaste singlehood is preferable to martyrdom at a club-end. For some years now the *Western Mail* and sundry other Welsh journals have been trying to raise the profile of St Dwynwen, and there are those who are delighted to have the chance to spend their money on Welsh-language cards and, with St Valentine following close behind, press their suit twice, or perhaps two suits.

The publishers Seren and the booksellers Oriel (once the flagship of the Welsh Arts Council, now the HMSO bookshop in Cardiff) celebrated St Valentine's with a poetry reading. Tony Curtis read from the popular anthology *Love from Wales*, which he and Siân James co-edited, and Dafydd Johnston from his *Medieval Welsh Erotic Poetry*, a revised edition under Seren's imprint of a book first published in 1991. Curtis and Siân James have frequently combined forces as effectively in public performances from their book as they did in selecting and editing the text. Though alone on this occasion, Curtis's reading had all the polish and nice timing of a well-rehearsed act, much to the taste of the small audience. Dafydd Johnston's contribution, an illustrated lecture rather than a conventional reading, demonstrated how far we have come in our tolerance of the sexually explicit. It also showed (if one needed reminding in these days of White House scandals) how little we have changed over the centuries, other than in the will to, or capacity for, keeping grosser imaginings hidden, much as the manuscripts of these poems have, until recently, been discreetly catalogued and stored out of the public view. In her *Selections from the Dafydd Ap Gwilym Apocrypha*, handsomely produced by Gomer in its 'Welsh Classics' series, Helen Fulton remarks that the great scholar, Thomas Parry, exercised a peculiar editorial judgement in his magisterial *Gwaith Dafydd Ap Gwilym (The Works of Dafydd Ap Gwilym)*. He refused to admit as part of the canon any of the ribald poems ascribed to the poet, 'even though these were clearly part of the bardic repertoire'. In so doing, he was 'motivated as much by reluctance to see them in print...as by his stated linguistic and metrical criteria'. Dafydd Johnston has no such inhibitions. The selections he has made from Dafydd ap Gwilym and other quite reliably named poets from the mid-fourteenth to the mid-sixteenth century, as well as the inevitable 'Anon', range from the mildly bawdy to the aggressively obscene. Even so, it is somehow pleasing to learn that the earliest recorded use of the word *'gwn'* (gun) in Welsh is by Dafydd ap Gwilym as a metaphor for 'penis': *'pestel crwn, gwn ar gynnydd'* (round pestle, expanding gun).

The book contains a number of surprises. The presence of Gwerful Mechain, 'the only female poet of medieval Wales by whom a substantial corpus of poetry has survived', is one. Born into a family of the landowning gentry in Powys, she was writing about 1480; her *cywydd* on Christ's passion is said to be of exceptional quality. In Dafydd Johnston's book she is represented by a satirical poem 'To Jealous Wives' and another on 'The Female Genitals', in both of which the remarkable harmonies of the *cywydd* form, with its chiming assonances and alliteration and pattern of stressed and unstressed end-rhymes, are employed wittily and to far different effect. The following couplet from the former may give an impression, if only visually, of the poem's metrical complexity and the merest hint of its engaging lewdness:

*Byd caled yw bod celyn*
*yn llwyr yn dwyn synnwyr dyn.*

(It's a bad state of affairs that a cock completely deprives a woman of her senses).

Almost as unexpected is the macaronic verse, in which the mutual incomprehension of dialogue between laddish Cymro and English maid is a barrier to a seduction, such as this example by Tudur Penllyn from the mid-fifteenth century:

*'Dydd daed, Saesnes gyffes, gain,*
*yr wyf i'th garu, riain.'*

*'What saist, mon?' ebe honno,*
*For truthe, harde Welshman I tro.'*

'(Good day to you, fine handy Englishwoman,
I really fancy you girl.'

'What do you say, man?' she said,
'for truth, you're a Welshman I think').

An abiding wonder is the flexible use of *cynghanedd*, the classical strict metres of Welsh prosody, for lewd purposes. Like all poems of the period, these were intended to be performed in public, as they were at Oriel, their message delivered to the accompaniment of the fizz and crackle of metrical fireworks.

It is hard to believe that this all-too-human reaction to the pussy-footing of courtly love was confined to the poets of medieval Wales. That I know of no comparable writing in English may be an indication of the narrowness of my studies at Aberystwyth, which offered nothing tastier than an unexpectedly forward lady in *Sir Gawain and the Green Knight*.

The *PN Review* editor's *Lives of the Poets* makes a number of observations on the quantity of poetry in manuscript at one time dispersed among many houses, ecclesiastical and secular, in England, and on Gower's *Confessio Amantis*, comparing Florent's Tale with that of the Wife of Bath (though neither with the Miller's Tale, which, so far as I am aware, is the nearest Chaucer came to lewd vulgarity). Of 'Summer is icumen in' he asks, 'How many poems of this virtue got lost because people didn't value their own language? Welsh, Scots Gaelic, Irish, Cornish and Manx, all the little languages on which English

played the colonial trick had such verse. Some survives...'
Indeed it does – and among the survivors we have to
acknowledge those poems selected and translated by Dafydd
Johnston, to which the word 'virtue' in its usual senses would
hardly apply.

R.S. Thomas studied classics at what was then known as the
University College of North Wales, Bangor, before his theological
training at St Michael's College, Llandaff. He has settled
recently, with his second wife, in a new home at Holyhead, the
town in Anglesey where he spent much of his childhood. His
alma mater has now conferred on him an honorary chair in the
department of Welsh. This may not rank with the Nobel Prize,
for which he was unsuccessfully nominated in 1996, but will
probably be appreciated by a man for whom conventional
honours mean little. Asked in a rare radio interview a few
months ago what he thought of the suggestion that he might
become the next Poet Laureate, he replied, 'It's ridiculous'. Not
one to be shaken-off by a dusty answer, the interviewer pressed
him: what if it wasn't a laureateship but just the title of the best
living poet? 'No,' he said, 'because it would still be part of the
English establishment and I have nothing to do with that.' Or a
Welsh laureate? 'We have the chairing of the bard at the
National Eisteddfod.' In response to further questions, he
declared he was not writing much these days – 'I'm getting on
in years, and we've been moving house.' 'Poetry is a very minor
art by now,' he went on. 'I hope the wheel will turn again. We
hear of OUP closing its poetry list. I hope other publishers don't
follow suit.' What about the National Assembly? 'I was never a
nationalist, always a patriot. I have reservations because of a
topsy-turvy situation in Wales, with two-thirds of the population
in the south and industry concentrated there. But it's up to us
to make it work.' Listeners to Radio Wales, accustomed this
winter to flood warnings, might have detected a characteristic

self-deprecation seeping over the airwaves and gradually inundating abroad swathes of literary endeavour and political wishful thinking.

In a letter in the latest number of Academi's *A470* information journal, Amy Wack of Seren proposes an Irish-style laureateship for Wales which will give the chosen poets a year on something approaching the UK average wage to divide their time among the various constituent colleges of the university, holding creative writing workshops. It sounds like hard work. She also complains, with justification, that whereas the Arts Councils in England, Scotland and Ireland have received 10% increases, their counterpart in Wales is on 'standstill funding, *again*'. In Seren's case, the effect of this Welsh Office decision is an 11% cut in funding over the last five years: nothing to celebrate in that, apart from the fortitude of the publishers in increasingly difficult circumstances. Those who enjoy hoarding anticipation will be pleased to learn that the first 'Encyclopaedia of Wales' should be in bookshops by 2002. Like Meic Stephens's *Companion to the Literature of Wales*, it is being produced under the auspices of Academi and published in Welsh and English versions by the University of Wales Press. The poet Nigel Jenkins will edit the English and Menna Baines, former editor of *Barn*, a Welsh-language periodical, the Welsh. With the first signs of spring we also glimpse 'academi.org', the Academi's bilingual web-site, which will offer not only information on all aspects of literature in Wales but also 'a real-time forum where users will be able to enter into world-wide discussions of literary topics'. Although it will, I fear, mean nothing to me, I welcome it on behalf of cyber browsers everywhere.

*PN Review* 128, Volume 25 Number 6, July – August 1999.

# THE NATIONAL EISTEDDFOD
*November 1998*


The Royal National Eisteddfod of Wales is a peculiar institution, and I do not mean that in the sense that only the Welsh have an annual gathering of competitors in literature, art and music, or relish the opportunity for a chinwag with old friends from distant parts. It is peculiar because of its origins and history, and most of all perhaps for the extraordinary influence that one man had upon the familiar ceremonies of the event as it unfolds today. It was this man, Edward Williams (1747-1826), the son of a stonemason from Llancarfan in the Vale of Glamorgan, with no formal schooling, who linked the revival of druidism to the notion of bardic competition in a form that still survives. He honoured himself with a bardic name, Iolo Morganwg, and membership of a tradition stretching into the distant Celtic past.

His imaginative leap was in the right direction. The druids seem to have been cult priests and the perambulating repositories of the oral history, knowledge and wisdom of their people. Without books or pictures of the past, they relied upon memory for their learning, and to assist memorising they employed the devices of an extraordinarily complex prosody. Although their religious significance waned with the coming of Christianity, the importance of poetry, and of technical proficiency to the poet, did not. Iolo held – and most agree with him – that the druids evolved into a powerful and exclusive, self-regulating guild of bards, who had the functions of tribal remembrancers. They were the genealogists of noble families, and the media of their day: their voices celebrated heroic deeds and mourned defeats and the passing of princes. When the true princes of Wales were no more, they fulfilled a similar role for the landowning gentry.

Bards competed together, not to entertain an audience, but in pride of craft and for the acclaim of brother craftsmen. If skilled enough, they progressed, by the assent of their peers, through the degrees of their calling to the eminence of *pencerdd* (chief poet). In the sixth century, Taliesin was *pencerdd* at the court of Urien ap Cynfarch, king of Rheged, the land around the Solway Firth, and Aneirin at the court of Mynyddog Mwynfawr, whose tribal lands, Manaw Gododdin, extended south from the Firth of Forth. These geographical locations explain why '*Y Gododdin*', Aneirin's great poem about the tribe's disastrous foray to attack the Angles at Catraeth (which we know as Catterick), is sometimes claimed as the first Scottish poem, though it is written in an early form of Welsh. At the right hand of king or chieftain, the poet was an acknowledged legislator, of sufficient influence for Hywel Dda, who died little more than a century before the Norman Conquest, to devote a section of his kingly code of laws to the bardic orders and their functions.

All this and much more was known to Iolo Morganwg. Though English was his first language, the language of his poetic awakening was Welsh. While still in his teens he competed with local 'bards' in tavern eisteddfodau, and became acquainted with the scholars, dictionary-makers and upholders of the sterner, classical traditions of Welsh poetry in the Vale and the hills that overlook it. Having served a bardic apprenticeship, much as young men of promise might have done in the old days, he became by his own efforts an immensely learned antiquary and indefatigable copyist of ancient manuscripts, while, with little success, plying his trade as a mason in various parts of Wales and England. He published poetry in English, but classical Welsh literature was his passion and by the 1780s he

633

was writing poems in the manner of Dafydd ap Gwilym that his contemporaries were unable to distinguish from the real thing. He must be numbered among the most notable poetic forgers, for the task he set himself was sterner than those faced by Chatterton and Macpherson, and was brought off with greater success. His 'imitations' were still deceiving scholars into the twentieth century.

The culmination of years of inventive proselytizing of his curious druidic lore occurred in 1792, not on his home turf, but in London, where he had the support of the Gwyneddigion, a society of Welshmen devoted to the literature and culture of Wales. On Primrose Hill, at the summer solstice, he set up a circle of stones about an altar 'on which a naked sword being placed, all the Bards assisted to sheathe it', and the bardic traditions were recited. This meeting of bards he called a *Gorsedd* and in the years that followed he strove to make it the focus of the cultural life of Wales. The ceremonial of this year's National Eisteddfod, held at Pencoed, not far from Iolo's Vale of Glamorgan home, closely followed the pattern he set, but over the years there has been some decorative accretion around it. The symbolically coloured robes, green for the Order of Ovates (novitiates), blue for the Order of Bards, Musicians.and Literati, white for the Druidic Order, were designed originally for the Llanelli Eisteddfod of 1894 by Hubert Herkomer (1849-1914), a painter and graphic illustrator, who was Bavarian by birth but was brought up in the USA and England, and married a Welsh woman. Elected to the Royal Academy in 1890 (and knighted in 1907), his brief description as 'Wagnerian, ruralist, Welsh Nationalist, teacher, *batissomane*, motorist and film maker' reveals him a fitting eisteddfodic partner for Iolo Morganwg. The Great Sword and its embossed scabbard, yet more thickly encrusted with symbolism, are also Herkomer's. Considered picturesque on their first appearance, the robes are now jokily referred to as nightshirts, but the invitation to wear one is taken seriously enough.

Though fixed to the first week of August each year, the Eisteddfod is a movable feast. It alternates between north and south Wales and the chosen venue has a couple of years to prepare for its coming – which is just as well, as local organisers are often hard pressed to raise their share of the two million pounds needed to put it on. Over 160,000 attended Eisteddfod Bro Ogwr (that is, 'Ogmore District' – each National is named after the district in which it is held) at Pencoed, tramping the thirty-acre *maes* (field) packed with hundreds of tents, stalls and stands representing institutions, agencies and businesses of all kinds from all over Wales. Even the Welsh Tories had a presence, fleetingly visited by Mr Hague, who (we are told) is learning Welsh. In addition to the 4000-seat Pavilion where the main ceremonies, competitions and concerts are held, there were, as usual, a Literature Tent, dance and theatre venues, and exhibitions of arts and crafts and of science and technology. In a suitably remote corner a *Pabell Pen Tost* (literally 'headache tent') provided a home for Welsh rock and pop, currently a world commodity.

The week had its highs and lows. The rain was heavier, the sun, when it arrived, hotter than expected. Traffic jams around the site held up bardic dignitaries and delayed the start of the opening ceremony. Ron Davies, Secretary of State of Wales, another Welsh learner, was inducted into the White Robed Order of Bards and, with the Assembly in the offing, obtained a courteous hearing from members of Cymdeithas yr Iaith Gymraeg (the Welsh Language Society), who in previous years have been known to wreck the Welsh Office stand. Menna Elfyn, a Welsh language activist (not so long ago imprisoned for the cause – see *PN Review* 116), and gifted poet, was one of the three adjudicators of the first major literary prize of the week – the Crown, awarded for a poem or sequence of poems in the free metres, on this occasion on the subject '*Rhyddid*' (Freedom). All entries are submitted under a pen name and the identification of the winner in the packed Pavilion is a perennial eisteddfodic *coup de theatre*. The winning sequence, by Emyr Lewis, a solicitor from Swansea, was declared the best for many years and enthusiastic applause prolonged the general excitement. To make an attempt at the Chair, the other major prize, to which more prestige is attached, the poet must write an *awdl* (ode) of at least two hundred lines using combinations of the twenty-four complex metres demanded by tradition. There was speculation that the Crown winner might bring off an exceptionally rare double, for he is better known as poet in the strict metres and had won the Chair at the 1994 National Eisteddfod. He did not. Indeed, he may not have entered the competition, but in any event, none of the nine who made the effort was deemed worthy of the honour. For the eleventh time since 1900 a dread sense of anti-climax settled on the audience. Instead of a bard, the Great Sword rested on the Chair. This elegant piece of furniture has since been offered to the Assembly, but it was built for show and one cannot imagine either Ron Davies or Rhodri Morgan, his only realistic opponent for the job of leading the Assembly, sitting comfortably in it.

Only the odd critic of the rule that all competitions and public utterances must be in Welsh disturbed the calm of the *maes*, thus prolonging a dispute that has lasted for well over a century. Otherwise little controversy attended the Eisteddfod, unlike in recent years when political speeches in support of the Welsh language, or in support of those prepared to risk their freedom for it, have enraged MPs from the left and the right. Even Archdruids, elected by the Gorsedd Board to take the lead in its ceremonies, have been known to exceed the normal expectations of their role and smite the politicians hip and thigh. As Ron Davies's quiet reception at the hands of Cymdeithas yr Iaith suggested, however, there is just now a widespread acceptance, even among monoglot English-speakers, of the need to preserve the senior language. Not that the majority of the population would *do* anything to assist its survival – though, if Welsh-medium schools continue to produce better examination results than the great majority of English-medium schools, we may find the parents of school-age children increasingly keen to promote the spread of the former and guarantee that the long-threatened extinction of Welsh will be permanently postponed.

*PN Review* 124, Volume 25 Number 2, November – December 1998.

# 3: ON THE LITERARY SCENE

# LITERARY MAGAZINES IN WALES
*March 2018*

I cannot deny I spend a lot of time nostalgically looking back. It is, all things considered, a pleasant infirmity of age. I have thought a great deal recently of Roland Mathias's skill and judgement, and values system, as a reviewer – and of course of the clarity and trenchancy of his prose thus employed. In his time as editor, the quarterly *Anglo-Welsh Review* grew in size and importance as the journal of record for all creative and scholarly work from and about Wales. Roland's ambition in this direction was boundless. He played the magazine like an accordion, expanding it to accommodate all he wanted to stuff in. My first article on Thomas Jeffery Llywelyn Prichard, written at his suggestion, occupied forty pages of *AWR* No. 52, some fifteen thousand words, but didn't appear disproportionate in an issue that ran to two hundred and sixty-six pages.

The reviews section in that same number extended over a hundred pages. Roland took the word 'review' in the magazine's title seriously. Reviews commonly filled almost half of the elastic allocation of pages, and to serve this policy he recruited reviewers far and wide. He was himself, however, by far his most frequent contributor. I once took the trouble to turn the pages in number after number and count the reviews that appeared over his name: one hundred and twenty-four, the majority lengthy, all deeply considered (I did not bother to add the shorter, though never cursory, notes on other magazines, tracts, pamphlets, spoken word recordings). While he was editor, no creative work with a claim to be Anglo-Welsh or, these days, 'Welsh writing in English', passed unnoticed, and very few concerning the history and topography of Wales. In addition to reviews, from time to time he published long articles in the magazine. He was the first critic to give serious in-depth consideration to writers of distinction, including Dylan Thomas, Dannie Abse, Alun Lewis and Emyr Humphreys.

At much the same time as Roland Mathias was constantly adding to his prodigious output of critical studies in one form or another, Meic Stephens was placing a similar emphasis on reviewing in *Poetry Wales*. He was equally convinced that literary criticism was an essential adjunct to the 'second flowering' of Welsh writing in English he sensed emerging during the 1960s. Articles on individual poets became a regular feature of the magazine and, between 1972 and 1974, a series of special numbers appeared, on the poetry of David Jones, R.S. Thomas, Dylan Thomas and Alun Lewis among others.

Were these the good old days of trouble-free magazine publication, when an editor could set a course confident that subscriptions, sales – and Arts Council subsidy – would keep the vessel afloat? Not really. At least once a year Roland's editorials would announce the imminent demise of *AWR,* and Christopher Davies, then publisher of *Poetry Wales*, regularly pleaded with the editor to bring out more 'specials', because they sold far better than ordinary numbers. There were constant concerns, but nothing like today's pressures from falling subscriptions, the politics of austerity and concomitant squeezed arts grant regimes, and the tsunami of digital media. To be online is now obligatory and our current magazines, the *New Welsh Review*, *Planet* and *Poetry Wales*, have a screen presence that, for all I know, may be attracting a readership far greater than they enjoyed in the past. But in their print editions they do not, cannot, given the constraints under which they struggle to hold on, allow reviews and articles the space they formerly received. The reviews I read in current numbers are well-informed and discriminating; there are increasing numbers of able reviewers for editors to call on, but there is not the scope to give due attention to all the books that merit critical assessment. We look enviously over the border at the *London Review of Books* and wonder if something similar in format and ambition could survive here, not as a fortnightly, but if only twice or three times a year, to review the books and the literary and political state of Wales.

Remarkably, something of the sort already exists, serving Welsh-language books and cultural interests. *O'r Pedwar Gwynt* (From the Four Winds), is an entirely Welsh-language magazine of similar format to *LRB* and about forty-four pages, appearing three times a year at £4.95 per issue. An independent journal published in partnership with Bangor University, it invites us to 'see the world through books'. The latest (Christmas 2017) number has pages given to analysis, for example of the Catalonia referendum, and Welsh culture and the social media; an interview with Emyr Humphreys, one of the most important twentieth century English novelists; new writing including a short story and an extract from a novel; and reviews. In the course of a year it reviews all books of literary merit from Welsh-language publishers. Whether this would be a feasible aim in the field of Welsh writing in English we cannot know, unless the attempt is made.

The need for clear-sighted critical assessment of the political state of Wales has never been greater, but where does one find it? The *Western Mail* still claims to be the 'National Newspaper of Wales', but in common with most print media its circulation has shrunk and it is only occasionally readers find in it a distinctive voice speaking on behalf of Wales that rises above news and 'interest' features that you would find in any newspaper. A few such occasions have occurred recently, two on successive days in the middle of November. In the first, Patrick McGuinness, having moved to north Wales in 2000, gave his perception of the supine posture of Wales politically in the context of Brexit. He writes as one whose vision is clear by virtue of having long experience of other countries and concludes, 'If Wales doesn't stand up to be counted the rest of the world will have forgotten Wales ever existed.' The following day the paper carried an account of the Raymond Williams Lecture, given this year at the Red House, Merthyr Tydfil, by the astonishingly gifted actor Michael Sheen, who has declared an interest in political activism to oppose the widespread rise of anti-democratic forces. I missed the occasion but was glad to be able to catch up with it on *YouTube*. It is worth viewing – a presentation to make any politician deeply envious, thoroughly absorbing, thought-provoking, delivered without a single miss-step or cough or sip of water. Sheen developed the lecture from *Who Speaks for Wales?*, a collection of Raymond Williams's writing about Welsh culture, literature, history and politics edited by Daniel Williams (UWP, 2003), a book to turn to again at this time. Shortly after these two items appeared, in his weekly column for the *Western Mail's* weekend magazine, Lefi Gruffudd, publisher at Y Lolfa Cyf., whose books regularly win Wales Book of the Year prizes, introduced his thoughts on Michael Sheen's lecture with the observation, *'Does dim angen edrych yn bell i weld sut wlad gymhleth, ansicr, hunanddinistriol yw'r Gymru bresennol'* ('You don't need to look far to see what sort of confused, uncertain, self-destructive country Wales is at present'). It is chastening and disquieting to see how bright minds are turning at this juncture in our long history.

*PN Review* 240, Volume 44 Number 4,
March – April 2018.

# THE FOLIO SOCIETY
*March 2017*


I became a member of the Folio Society in the late 1950s, when you signed up to purchase a minimum of four volumes from the annual list and received a bonus book into the bargain. Charles Ede, who (with Christopher Sandford and Alan Bott) launched the society in 1947, when the book trade was still in austerity mode, must have had in mind people like me. Inspired by the sumptuous library of Professor Gwyn Jones at Aberystwyth, which I viewed with awe whenever I dared raise my eyes from *Beowulf*, I wanted a shelf of fine-looking spines to call my own. I relished every Folio Society classic I received, and the free gifts, often profusely illustrated essays on historical themes, were equally desirable. On the basis of what had become, after a shaky start, a commercially successful venture, in 1960 Charles Ede started Collectors' Corner as a branch of the Society. You applied, via your membership, to receive catalogues of original prints, drawings and watercolours, antiquities, manuscripts, early maps, rare books and so on. I had no idea that it was possible to buy genuine art and historical objects, many of surpassing interest and beauty, over the counter, or at least by Royal Mail (postage and packing free!). I was a little slow off the mark, but by 1966 was certainly on the mailing list. Many of the catalogues I received have disappeared over the years, but I still have a bundle of them, starting with number xxxix, which I look over from time to time, my interest tinged with regret. With a modest income from teaching, and family commitments, my purchases were from the lower end of the price range, and carefully thought over at that. They include a north Wales landscape by William Payne, an engraving of sheep by Aristide Maillol for Vergil's *Georgics*, and a portfolio of 'Leaves from Famous European Books' (among them, the *Nuremberg Chronicle*, the second Folio Shakespeare, an exquisite specimen of early Roman lettering from an incunable by Sweynheim and Pannartz), for which I was allowed, by Charles Ede himself, to pay in three or four monthly instalments of five pounds. Five pounds seems to have been about the limit I set myself. For those with deeper pockets there were treasures indeed: in May 1970 you might have bought three very desirable signed prints, by Picasso, Vlamink and Van Dongen, for less than a thousand pounds.

Collectors' Corner was later renamed Folio Fine Art, but the catalogues continued as enthralling as ever and to receive my rapt attention. Among the items that fell most frequently within my reach were single leaves from 'western and oriental manuscripts'. I acquired a dozen or more, from the fourteenth and fifteenth centuries in the main. Framed, they deck our walls; their elegant lettering, intricate tracery and gold embellishment draw the eye and fill the mind with a sense of history. I could never afford one that incorporated a miniature but they were to be had. In that same May 1970 catalogue mentioned above there was a leaf on vellum 'from a Book of Hours written and illuminated not after 1350 in Lincolnshire' on which a 'large initial D for the opening of Lauds shows the risen Christ'. Thanks to the internet, I know where that 'East-Anglian miniature' went: to the British Library, its Folio Fine Art provenance duly noted. I learned from the same source that Christopher de Hamel examined another leaf from the same Book of Hours at the Lilly Library, Indiana University, Bloomington, and wrote it up in *Gilding the Lilly* (2010).

De Hamel's *Meetings with Remarkable Manuscripts* (Allen

Lane, 2016) is a delight – such lovingly detailed descriptions of manuscripts, the boxes in which they are stored, and the various repositories of knowledge where they are now held. It is a wonder of scholarly exactitude and clarity. In the chapter headed 'The Hengwrt Chaucer', some readers may be surprised to learn that 'the most precious manuscript in the Middle English language' – the oldest surviving copy of the *Canterbury Tales*, made about 1400 – is held at the National Library of Wales in Aberystwyth. Another Chaucer manuscript, *Boece*, his translation of Boethius's *Consolatio Philosophie*, of very similar date and 'quite extraordinary significance for English literature' also resides at Nat. Lib., as we familiarly refer to it. Both manuscripts came from the same source, identified by their catalogue entries. The *Tales* is MS Peniarth 392D, and *Boece* Peniarth 393D. The former, he says, is 'the most unmemorable reference to any world-class manuscript', though I cannot say Cotton Vitellius A15 springs readily to my mind. From about 1650 both had been part of the collection of the Vaughan family of Hengwrt, near Dolgellau, Gwynedd, which on the death of the last of the line passed to a distant relative, William Watkin Edward Wynne of Peniarth, Merionethshire. When Wynne's heir died in 1909, they were acquired by Sir John Williams (1840– 1926), royal physician, who is described in the *Dictionary of Welsh Biography* as 'the principal founder of the National Library'. When Cardiff was increasingly becoming the magnet of things of cultural significance, Williams fought for the library to be established in Aber, and won. In 1909, he gave his manuscript collection to the new institution.

De Hamel's quest took him from Cambridge to Copenhagen, Munich to New York. Completing a Russian visa application for a visit to St Petersburg was a tedious business; otherwise the only reference to travel is the unconscionable length and duration of the train journey to Aberystwyth. There he finds that 'everyone can speak Welsh (and they do), impenetrable to the English' so that 'it all feels as foreign as Finland'. 'Why do these English treasures languish in this distant hole?' seems to be implied. A less irritable response might perceive from the tone of his description that he found the seaside town and his reception at Nat. Lib. charming and amusing, as though at the station he had opened a portal into the past. Then again, I wonder whether, on reflection, he might think it rather shaming that Welsh is to him as foreign as Finnish. He is an uncommonly gifted man of formidable intellect, who doubtless has command of classical Latin and Greek, yet his education has not afforded him an opportunity to acquire one of the principal living languages of Britain – the British language, indeed. This is not his fault. It is the fault of Westminster governments of all times and kinds that take no pride in the survival of Welsh, and have done as little as possible (with a niggard hand and under duress) to support it.

As for the journey to Aberystwyth, I am reminded of the story of an old farmer from Gwynedd who is constantly nagged that for once in his life he really ought to see London. He finally yields to persuasion and takes a coach trip. On his return, stiff from the journey, family and friends ask what he thought of the great metropolis. 'London is quite interesting,' he says, 'but, you know, it's very remote.' The remoteness of London, with its vast accumulation of *national* treasures, from by far the greater part of the population of Britain is insufficiently considered and least of all by the so-called 'metropolitan elite'. It is a stunning irony that the British Library is more readily accessible from half of Europe than it is from much of Wales.

*PN Review* 234, Volume 43 Number 4,
March – April 2017.

# TŶ NEWYDD AND M. WYNN THOMAS

*September 2011*

One of the elements in the radical shake-up of arts organisations here, which came as a surprise to me if to no one else, was the merger of Academi, the literature promotion agency, and Tŷ Newydd, the National Writers' Centre for Wales. Academi has been mentioned often enough in these 'Letters', but not the National Writers' Centre, which was established in 1990 at a beautiful house, once the home of David Lloyd George, in glorious landscape at Llanystumdwy, near Criccieth, Gwynedd.

The centre's *raison d'être* and methodology are much the same as those of the Arvon Foundation, freely acknowledged as the model of the Welsh venture. Gillian Clarke, who was chair of the Welsh Academy/Yr Academi Gymreig at this time, with a great deal of experience of Arvon tutoring behind her, and Meic Stephens, then Literature Director of the Welsh Arts Council, were the leading figures in bringing to fruition one of the brightest ideas in the development of interest and participation in writing in both Welsh and English. Their involvement didn't stop at raising money, persuading the reluctant and haranguing the nation; they were both there, at Tŷ Newydd, in the small team of enthusiasts, mowing grass, scrubbing floors and painting walls to allow the centre to open on schedule. Sally Baker, executive director of the centre from its inception, who was made an Honorary Member of the Welsh Academy at its recent 50th Anniversary celebration, has seen its standing grow remarkably. It maintains a simple formula – courses last four days and involve sixteen students under the guidance of two tutors – and now attracts writers as course leaders and members from all over the UK and many other parts of the world. 'Most people say it is their favourite writers' house in Britain', claims the President of Tŷ Newydd, which is no more than one would expect of the titular head of an organisation, but in this case suspension of disbelief may be in order: the president is our National Poet, Gillian Clarke, who was awarded the Queen's Medal for Poetry this year, and is an indefatigable campaigner on behalf of literature and Wales.

Gillian Clarke was a speaker at the launch of the newly merged body, on the first Monday of the Hay Festival. The event was held in Richard Booth's original bookshop, though not the rambling warren of books, sketchily organised at best, that visitors became accustomed to over the years, where the spirit of the quest was invoked, for it was a place where you travelled without a map, hopefully, never knowing what dusty treasure might lie on the next cobwebbed shelf, but a splendidly refurbished literary emporium, with shelved bays like the best of libraries and room to move, and encouragement, and seating, to relax. This is the work of Elizabeth Haycox, who has come all the way from the Pacific coast of the United States, and her wealthy English husband, Paul Greatbatch, and it is a delight. Her grandfather, it appears, was a feted writer of Westerns, the author of (among many others) the short story that was adapted for the screen as the John Wayne classic *Stagecoach*. She promises to revivify Hay, so that the town grows in step with the Festival, which grows year by year. Elizabeth Haycox's fine, bookish upper room, with its polished wooden floor, was a far better setting for the launch than a tent, however grand, on the festival site.

Dai Smith, Chairman of the Arts Council of Wales, who was flying to Venice for the Biennale the following morning (such are the burdens of office), spoke about the distinctive national responsibility and importance of certain of the council's revenue funded organisations – the BBC National Orchestra of Wales, the National Dance Company of Wales, the National Theatre of Wales, Welsh National Opera – and the significance of the addition of Literature Wales to this group. He saw this as a further expression of the advance of Wales as a distinctive, devolved country, with cultural institutions of its own. He paid tribute to the staff of Academi and Tŷ Newydd, who had contributed much to this achievement, and looked forward to enhancement of their role in the merged organisation. Appropriate poetic tributes were paid by T. James Jones, the Archdruid (winner of the Chair and, twice, the Crown, at the National Eisteddfod), in the form of *englynion* to Gillian Clarke and, on his very last day before retirement, to Peter Finch.

I first met Peter Finch in the early 1970s when he was the editor, typist, printer (using the makeshift technology of the time), distributor, salesman and everything else, of *Second Aeon*, which, it is commonly agreed, was the outstanding, if not the only, wholeheartedly modernist magazine in Wales, then – and since. From 1974 to 1998, he was the manager of Oriel, that extraordinary venture, the Welsh Arts Council's bookshop in Charles Street, Cardiff, when the city didn't have a decent alternative. And when Oriel folded he began his long stint as chief executive of Academi and, in the last few months, its successor. He has, he said, found administration increasingly demanding on his time and is giving up now to concentrate on writing. Not that he has been silent during his managerial years. He has continued to be the foremost experimental poet in Wales, while consolidating his standing in more conventional satiric and confessional poetry: his *Selected Later Poems* (2007), with well over a hundred items, has been followed by *Zen Cymru* (2009). At readings, there is nothing to match the urgent tongue-twisting declamation that is his trademark, unless it be those sober reflections on domestic arrangements, broken relationships, loss and death, which (as with most of us) have tended to increase with the passage of years. In prose, he has brought his own brand of psychogeography to the home patch with three entertaining volumes of *Real Cardiff* (2002, 2004 and 2009), plus *Real Wales* (2008) – and much else besides. He has the fertile imagination and creative fluency to ensure that all the years of his retirement will be profitably filled.

Whatever the outcomes of judges' deliberations on the 2010-2011 literary awards circuit, one book dealing with Welsh culture, and particularly Welsh writing in English, stands head and shoulders above all others: M. Wynn Thomas's *In the Shadow of the Pulpit* (University of Wales Press, 2010). It is a big book, an important book, constantly fresh and luminous with observations that are as memorable as they are significant. It is timely, too, because before very long, a book like this will be beyond the capacities of literary historians, however diligent. It needed an author with not only a superb grasp of the literature we used to call 'Anglo-Welsh', but also an empathic, though not uncritical, insider's knowledge of Nonconformity in Wales.

A proper understanding of the role of religion as a shaping force in Welsh culture in the nineteenth and twentieth centuries, as English was first gaining and then assuming the upper hand in education and life in the more populous parts of Wales, is fundamental to an appreciation of that culture. Welsh writing in English during this period is permeated with a consciousness of the chapel, whether the individual concerned embraced or rejected it. Without an awareness of that, a proper appreciation of the writing of, for example, Glyn Jones, Roland Mathias and Emyr Humphreys on the one hand, and Caradoc Evans on the other, is impossible.

The immediate impulse prompting the book, and revealed in

the introduction, is what seems now in hindsight a final incandescent burst of faith before accelerating secularisation in the twentieth century began extinguishing the flame: the Evan Roberts Revival of 1904-1905, 'the Ghost dance of Welsh Nonconformity'. Wynn Thomas's *mamgu*, his grandmother, was one of a group of five young women from Brynteg Congregational Chapel, Gorseinon, on the outskirts of Swansea, who, inspired by Roberts, in November 1904 accompanied him on his mission to the industrial anthills of the Cynon and Rhondda valleys. The great fanfare of faith and wave of conversions that followed was magnified by the newspapers of the day with the voyeuristic zeal today's press bestows on the carnal misdemeanours of soccer players. Wynn's *mamgu* observed at first hand the momentous months of the Revival, watched it become a hysterical media event, and opted out, with her faith intact.

Apart from frank analysis of the events of the Revival and the personalities involved, not least Roberts himself, what distinguishes this wonderful essay, and the entire book, is the clarity and idiomatic forcefulness of the language. It stands as a persuasive argument for rejection of the formulaic impersonal manner of so much stodgy, opaque academic literary criticism. Thomas knows as much as anyone about the apparatus of modern criticism, post-colonialism and the like, but employs them judiciously and with no detectable enthusiasm. After all, they have limited application, and are of interest only to other academics.

The early chapters provide a brief history of Nonconformity in Europe and America before focusing on developments in Wales, where, as a by-product of its spiritual purpose, the chapel elevated the society it served. But preachers and worshippers, being only human, had flaws that undermined the project and opened it to criticism. Writers were among the advance guard of critics. In the first half of the nineteenth century, T.J. Llewelyn Prichard, long the companion of my lamp-lit study, had sharpened his pen at the expense of Methodism. Others stepped up eagerly in his wake before Caradoc Evans appeared, swinging his axe, determined upon extirpation of the culture in which he was reared. Those who followed him, such as Gwyn Thomas, Idris Davies, T.H. Jones, all in their different ways condemned the chapel, while ineluctably bound to its modes of thought and behaviour that were on their minds and under their skins. Magisterial treatment of key texts of these and other writers lies at the heart of the book, along with an examination of Dylan Marlais Thomas's debt to the Unitarian beliefs of his great uncle, Gwilym Marles, whose name he bore. It is characteristic of the breadth of scholarship, including American sources and connections, which informs this book, that the discussion involves Frank Lloyd Wright and one of Dylan's heroes, Walt Whitman, who also figures in the broad sweep of Wynn Thomas's scholarly expertise.

The scale and scope of this work is, in the author's own words, 'indicative of the richness and importance' of Welsh writing in English, too often overlooked. *In the Shadow of the Pulpit* is easily the most significant contribution to studies in this field since Roland Mathias, in the absence of a corpus of critical opinion on the subject, took it upon himself to begin building one.

*PN Review* 201, Volume 38 Number 1,
September – October 2011.

# THE HAY FESTIVAL AND THE TONYPANDY RIOTS
*September 2010*

The Hay Festival enjoyed its best weather for years. There was but one damp day, when the long grass in the car park field soaked feet in open-toed sandals and wet trouser bottoms, and most people wore or carried raincoats. That was the day we chose to visit. Notwithstanding the grey skies, festival-goers seemed to be having a good time. Even those disposed to be churlish will admit the event is well organised, the extensive site skilfully signposted, the variety of provision impressive. The principal bookshop is thronged at those intervals in the day's programme planned to allow readers to buy more books and, for a moment or two, actually get close to writers. Purchasers forego a morning coffee queuing to have the book signed. This is good for business. The tent next door displaying books from Welsh publishers had only a few visitors, but that may have had something to do with the time of the day, for there were more events about writing from Wales this year than in any previous in my recollection. The choice of readings, lectures, discussions is vast and eclectic. We saw the art historian Martin Kemp on the role of science in the highly complex and still risky business of artistic attribution; the eminent Welsh historian and broadcaster John Davies entertaining a large, packed auditorium with a survey of *The Making of Wales*, first published in 1993 and now revised and updated as part of the 25th Anniversary celebrations of CADW, the organisation that looks after historical sites here; and Rick Gekoski, an amiable and unconventional dealer in rare books, delivering anecdotal highlights from his 'bibliomemoir' *Outside of a Dog* ('a book is a man's best friend. Inside of a dog it's too dark to read' – Groucho Marx).

Gekoski is one of those ornaments of contemporary literary culture, like Bill Bryson and our editor, Michael Schmidt, who, though long resident in Britain, come from America. I met him in 1993. At that time I attended meetings in London fairly frequently and, if business ended conveniently early, I would hasten to shop or gallery to make the most of my day in town before catching an early evening train back to Wales. I had seen advertisements of a David Jones exhibition at Gekoski's and with perhaps two hours to spare made that my target. His premises in a far corner of Pied Bull Yard, barely a hundred yards from the British Museum, were as confoundedly difficult for a stranger to find as the trove at the heart of a labyrinth, but it was worth the effort. This was perhaps at the high point of my continuing enthusiasm for David Jones's art and writing, and Gekoski had gathered a fascinating collection of material, I think in the main (if not entirely) from the family of René Hague. In the early 1920s, Hague became a close friend of Jones in the artistic commune set up by Eric Gill at Capel-y-ffin, between Hay and Abergavenny. Years of close association and correspondence followed: *In Parenthesis*, Jones's greatest achievement as a writer, was published by Pigotts Press, co-founded by Hague and Gill, in 1937. David Jones celebrated high days and Holy Days by sending friends commemorative inscriptions. They must have been made quickly for the occasion, and are certainly less formal and 'finished' than the great inscriptions, but they are not slapdash. They have Jones's characteristic signature: a finely balanced, if eccentric, even wonky, lettering in a mix of colours and languages. I was entranced by those displayed in Pied Bull Yard and said so, but the prices were beyond me. It must have been near closing; I was the only customer, and the engaging Mr Gekoski was content to accept staggered payments. We shook hands: I was his friend forever. I reminded him of this encounter when I brought *Outside of a Dog* for him to sign. 'Oh, yes,' he said, 'I remember those David Jones inscriptions. Very fine. Nice to see you again here at Hay.'

A book collector in a modest way for many years, I greatly enjoyed *Tolkien's Gown*, Gekoski's earlier book about 'great authors and rare books', as I have all the author's Radio 4 broadcasts. *Outside of a Dog*, while it has the same urbanely persuasive, often amused, tone of voice, is different. It tells the story of two extraordinary archives of books and papers, those of Graham Greene and Kim Philby, one acquired easily and at huge profit, and the other tantalisingly within his (or the British Library's) grasp and lost, but this is merely to add anecdotal gloss to what is essentially the personal memoir of a reader. 'Reading is what matters,' he says at the outset, 'and has always mattered to me. I can't not do it, any more than I can stop eating or breathing.' The habit is acquired at home (Dr Seuss) and developed through school, university (Pennsylvania and Oxford), university teaching (Warwick) and the rare book trade. The elements readily combine. At Hay he conducted an impromptu seminar on *The Waste Land*, and told how he had once owned a copy of Eliot's *Poems 1920* which he prized above all things. It was inscribed by the poet to Virginia Woolf, who subsequently set and published the first edition of *The Waste Land*. A book-collecting friend came to the shop, saw the Eliot and asked how much. It was not for sale. The friend persisted: 'Name your price'. An absurdly extravagant sum would surely put him off – but it didn't. So the book was sold and a house was bought with the proceeds.

Next year the Hay Festival will receive no funding from the Arts Council of Wales. It is one of thirty-two losers in the round of cuts just announced; seventy-one arts organisations will continue to be funded. Having exceeded last year's box office sales by thirty-five thousand tickets, Peter Florence, the festival director, was unperturbed. He may well remain sanguine, provided the standard of publicity from press and television is maintained – and the sun shines. Is it gratuitously pessimistic to suggest if anything is to suffer at Hay, it will probably be those parts of the programme given to writing from Wales? Among the others to lose their funding will be the Llangollen International Music Festival, ongoing as I write, which draws performers from all over the world, Theatr Powys, an important artistic hub in a large rural county, and Safle, the body concerned with public arts projects throughout Wales. The total savings will be £3.6 million, about 15% of the £24 million currently distributed by ACW. Professor Dai Smith, chairman of ACW, explained this is not a reflex response to the Coalition Government's harsh new economic regime, but the outcome of a consultation and review process that began in the summer of 2009, aimed at identifying those bodies that will give culture in Wales the best returns for investment. Allocations to the seventy-one selected will be decided next December, when ACW receives its share of public finance from Wales's Assembly Government. There may be yet darker days ahead.

Dai Smith makes up for lack of inches by ebullience and power of intellect. You might look over him, but you could not possibly overlook him. He is one of our foremost experts on the history of Wales, with particular reference to the working-class communities of the industrial southeast. We have been friends for many years and I would never miss a chance of hearing him address an audience. Earlier this week we went up to the Rhondda Heritage Park, on the site of a former colliery at Trehafod, for his lecture inaugurating a programme of activities to commemorate the Tonypandy Riots of 1910. The rioting, two days of misrule (as Dai put it), 9–10 November 1910, arose out of a miners' strike and lockout in a group of collieries in the Rhondda Valley and Gilfach Goch known as the Cambrian Combine. The owner was D. A. Thomas, later Lord Rhondda, at the time one of the richest men in the world. The dispute arose over an inequitable and iniquitous pay system that took no account of varying geological conditions underground. Colliers, who were paid by the ton for the coal they cut, argued that where a seam contained a lot of stone, they were unable to earn a living wage if the allowance for unproductive work was not increased. The vast majority supported the strike, so that, as the climax approached in November 1910, 12,000 men were idle. This was the notorious occasion when Winston Churchill, then Liberal Home Secretary, sent first the Metropolitan Police and then soldiers to restore order. It was an absurd over-reaction and has never been forgotten in the valleys.

After years of research ransacking contemporary accounts, Dai Smith knows more about this episode than anyone else, and is concerned that the facts of the case should be known. It is commonly asserted that the riot occurred because a large body of strikers were held off by a force of 120 police defending Llwynypia Colliery, where a number of strike-breakers, 'blacklegs', were being protected in the power house. Police drove the strikers back in the direction of Tonypandy Square, about a quarter of a mile away, where, rebuffed, they vented their anger on shops and a few other premises.

Shop windows were broken and goods looted: that much is true, says Professor Smith, but the trigger of the riot must have been different. Some eight thousand miners marched, most of them strong young men, familiar with the ground, knowing well the many means of access to collieries. There was a noisy demonstration, and stones were thrown at the power house in

Llwynypia; the police made baton charges and there was fierce fighting where they came into contact with strikers. The various forays made by the police were not successful. The crowd filled the road between Tonypandy and Llwynypia and absorbed attacks. A local magistrate observing events sent a telegram to the Home Office saying police could not cope with the rioters and asking for troops to be sent immediately. Nor were the damage to premises and looting violently unrestrained reactions but targeted. For instance, although several chemists' shops suffered (having profited from the high rates of sickness and infant mortality in the community) that belonging to Willie Llewellyn from nearby Clydach Vale, who had played in the victorious Welsh XV against New Zealand in 1905, was not touched.

The press in London and Wales was entirely unsympathetic to the strikers, and strident in denunciation of the hot-headed ideologues who were alleged to have fomented the trouble and the wild disorder of the mob. It was much the same in 1984. At the Rhondda Heritage Park the audience applauded Dai Smith's verbal fireworks and came away satisfied that the record had been put a little straighter.

*PN Review* 195, Volume 37 Number 1,
September – October 2010.

# BOOKSHOPS AND BOOK THEFT
*May 2009*

The advent of the media age has ensured we are constantly reminded of the worst of mankind, almost to the point of becoming unshockable. We have become used to coverage of events that leaves us angry or depressed about the state of the world, though never for long. It is not often that a newspaper story, especially one about books, casts a shadow that lingers for more than a day. This, nevertheless, was what occurred at the beginning of February, when I read a report in the *Guardian* headed 'Book world's silence helps tome raiders'.

It began with a rehash of old news about a Cambridge graduate, who used disguise and several aliases to gain admittance to major libraries, in order to steal rare books – a million pounds' worth from the British Library alone. The item also mentioned the recent case of an Iranian academic who had previously stolen books from the Royal Asiatic Society Library and caused damage amounting to several hundred thousand pounds at the Bodleian and the British Library by removing maps and illustrations from rare, old books with a scalpel. The reluctance of libraries to admit they have been plundered has encouraged the thieves, but this peculiar conspiracy of silence has now been broken, and they are being caught and punished. In a flash of anger when I first read about their activities, I declared gaol too good for them. In addition, they should at the very least serve a week in the stocks at the Hay Festival being pelted with remaindered volumes.

Halfway through the report, however, I was stunned by the

revelation that David Slade had pleaded guilty to stealing books from the library of the financier Sir Evelyn de Rothschild. I used to know David Slade when he compiled the catalogues of 'fine and rare' books issued a couple of times a year by George's of Bristol. I admired his bibliographical expertise and thought him amiable, quick, charming – an altogether delightful young man (as he was then, thirty years or more ago).

I have written before of my association with George's, that venerable and much lamented Bristol bookshop. It began in the early 1960s when I spotted a copy of Hood's *Comic Annual* for 1829, in its original binding, on a packed shelf in the second-hand department. I had done postgraduate research on Hood, using the 1864 *Works* 'with all the original illustrations' edited by his son and daughter, and presuming the annuals ephemeral, never expected to see one. But there at least was 1829, a stout little book with characteristic punning illustrations on the covers. Staff at the shop thought they could probably turn up others for me – as over the next few months they did, until I had the whole set, remarkably cheaply, even for an impecunious teacher.

My first significant purchase from the antiquarian section occurred a few years later, when I found that my share of the cash my father had saved out of the minuscule weekly compensation he received for loss of the use of his right hand in a colliery accident was just enough to buy the Golden Cockerel *Mabinogion*, translated by Gwyn Jones, Professor of English at Aberystwyth, and his colleague in the Welsh department, Professor Thomas Jones. It is a beautiful book and I treasure it as a memorial to my father and for its own sake. The discovery at this time that I could buy books from George's and pay for them over weeks or months started me as a collector, always and still in a small way. Gwyn Jones was an influence here too, for his circular room, high in a tower in the

Old College building at Aber, was lined with shelves carrying a fine collection of seventeenth- and eighteenth-century books, which he eventually bequeathed to the National Library of Wales.

For several years after we had left Bristol, I returned regularly to visit George's antiquarian section, look at the books and make occasional modest purchases. During one of these visits I met David Slade. We got on immediately, and before long he would invite me into a back room to view the books he was then listing for the next catalogue. It was there in 1982 that, knowing my ambition to possess an incunabulum, he placed in my hands a copy of Suetonius's *Vitae XII Caesarum*, pointing to the colophon with its simple woodcut device 'Venetiis per Baptistam de tortis, Mcccc.lxxxx.die.xv.Februarii'. It was irresistible, and in the fullness of time wholly mine.

The earliest George's catalogue I have (I didn't keep them all) is the 1970 'Winter Miscellany', number 593 in a series that began in 1848. The latest is number 718, of 1992. I think that might have been near the end of the line. The shop had been part of Blackwell's empire since the early 1970s, and by 1992 or thereabouts, head office in one of those deplorable spasms of 'rationalisation' had decided to centralise all its antiquarian book business at Fyfield Manor, near Oxford. I remember David Slade telling me that he had been offered a transfer there, but would not take it because he wanted to stay in the Bristol area. Since travelling to Oxford to gaze at bookshelves was out of the question, I felt the loss personally; goodness knows how it affected him. I became aware from odd references that he was still active in the trade, but we no longer met, and I was surprised to learn from the *Guardian* that he had been at one time in the intervening years President of the UK Antiquarian Booksellers' Association.

I receive catalogues from other booksellers these days. About a year ago one listed Sir Thomas Herbert's *Some Yeares Travels into Divers Parts of Asia and Afrique*, 1638, the second, considerably enlarged, edition of one of the most popular travel books of the period. I pay particular attention to books of Welsh interest, and the Herbert name immediately caught my eye. A note to the effect that, the title notwithstanding, the book included 'a dissertation to prove that America was discovered three hundred years before Columbus by one Madoc ap Owen' was totally persuasive.

It was some time later that I decided to look up Sir Thomas Herbert (1606-82) and found to my surprise that he is described as a Yorkshireman: his birthplace in York has been handsomely restored by the York Conservation Trust. Information supplied by the Trust says he travelled to Persia on a mission to the Shah (1626-9) in company with the Earl of Pembroke, which would seem to ally him with the Herberts of Wales. But the *Dictionary of National Biography* has a different story. It says he went to Persia in 1628 with Sir Dodmore Cotton and Sir Robert Shirley. The Trust, again, thinks that, having been a supporter of Parliament (the *DNB* says he was a commissioner with Fairfax's army in 1644, and for the surrender of Oxford in 1646), he turned Royalist. Aubrey's *Brief Lives* elucidates what may seem conflicting evidence in that respect by telling us how Herbert 'the traveller' was 'by order of Parliament made one of his Majestie's Bedchamber'. Duty to Parliament did not preclude the growth of mutual regard between Herbert and his royal charge. All agree that he accompanied Charles on the scaffold and received gifts from the king – a silver watch, the cloak from the condemned man's shoulders and a second folio of Shakespeare's plays that is now at Windsor. He was created baronet in 1660, after the Restoration.

I have nothing more at my disposal to confirm a connection

between Sir Thomas Herbert of York and Wales. Yet there is a strong link. Part of the problem for historians and genealogists may be the vast scale and complexity of the Herbert family tree, which occasional carelessness with the legitimacy of progeny in some of the branches does not help to clarify. What is certain is that it was a very important and powerful clan, having its origins in Montgomery in the reign of Henry VIII. Within a century or so its influence extended to almost every part of Wales and, in due course, Herberts counted lords, barons and knights without number, and earls of Pembroke, Worcester and Powys among their kin, not to mention one of the most remarkable of seventeenth-century poets.

One Earl of Pembroke, William Herbert (*c*.1501-70), said by the *Dictionary of Welsh Biography* to have been more at home in Welsh than in English, was a patron of Welsh letters. His son, Henry (*c*.1534-1601), the second earl, earned the soubriquet '*llygad holl Cymru*' (the eye of all Wales) for his knowledge of Welsh society and regard for the language. William Herbert (1580-1630), the third earl, was a patron of Shakespeare. As a young man, Philip (1584-1650), fourth earl, had Welsh chaplains, tutors and servants; in England he was said, jokingly perhaps, to need an interpreter.

The latter two were contemporaries of Thomas Herbert, the traveller, and his claim of kinship with them and enthusiasm for the Welsh project is manifest in his book. The elaborate woodcut title page includes the Herbert arms with, unusually, a Welsh motto: '*Pawb yn Arver*' (which might mean 'Each according to his custom'), and the dedication of the second edition, addressed to 'The Right Honourable Philip Earl of Pembroke and Montgomery: Baron Herbert of Caerdiff and Sherland' is couched in terms of light-hearted familiarity: 'MY LORD, Having past the pikes, I take new courage to come on again. One blow more and I have done. Ten to one it lights on my own pate ...'. On page 2 of the text he describes his vessel 'coasting close by the Ile of Wight (call'd so from Gwydh a British word signifying, seene at distance ... )'. By '*British* word', of course he means Welsh. And when, nearing the end of the book, he interpolates his account of the discovery of America by 'Madoc ap Owen Gwyneth' to vindicate 'the honour of our Country...[and]...that the truth may prevaile. and the memory of our Heroick Countryman revive' it is Wales that he has in mind.

This is one of the earliest sources in English of the Madoc myth (if myth it is, for there are still staunch believers). While giving Columbus full credit for his voyage, Herbert insists Madoc reached America in 1170, three hundred years before him. As proofs he cites artefacts, beliefs and Welsh words embedded in the language of native Americans: 'bara, bread: Mam, Mother: Tate, Father: dowr, water: pryd, time: Bu or Buch, a Cow: Llynog, a Fox: wy, an egg: Trwyn, a nose: Nef, heaven: and others, Welsh words, and of the same signification'.

Herbert's book has proved useful recently. The Iranian academic mentioned above who, to augment his own collection and for personal gain vandalised rare books, was found out because he was traced by the British Library as a reader of a particular volume from which maps and illustrations had been removed: *A Relation of Some Yeares Travaille, Begunne Anno 1626* by Thomas Herbert – the precious first edition of the curious book that now entertains me.

*PN Review* 187, Volume 35 Number 5, May – June 2009.

# THE NATIONAL EISTEDDFOD AND LITERARY MAGAZINES IN WALES

*November 2008*

After three decades and thirty different venues alternating between north Wales and south, this year the National Eisteddfod returned to Cardiff. It is always held in the first week of August, and experienced *eisteddfodwyr* come with wellingtons and umbrellas prepared for the rain and mud that seem with increasing certainty to characterise our summer. This is just one difference between the Eisteddfod and the Hay Festival, where visitors are encouraged to believe the occasion will resemble a southern counties idyll with picnic baskets on the grass, Pimm's and champagne, thin, crustless cucumber sandwiches and the like, only to be sadly disabused.

You cannot do anything about the weather, except learn to live with it. As it transpired, there was only one day of rain, when the site was awash, but the Eisteddfod can cater for most eventualities. It has an enormous pink pavilion where all the major events are held, six other performance areas, five restaurants, an art gallery, a games field, substantial structures representing every organisation of any account in Wales, and over three hundred stalls, many occupied by smaller agencies, craftspeople, publishers and denominations, many more selling everything from harps to hotdogs, ice cream to antiquarian books. The business of the Eisteddfod is conducted in Welsh, but translation facilities are available and no one who asks for a coffee in English is turned away. Remarkably, given the scale of the operation, it preserves a sense of community; people gather in families and groups and there is constant hailing of

667

old friends. In these commonly churlish days, it has a pervasive friendliness that, if they knew about it, festivals elsewhere would envy.

Few outside Wales have the faintest notion, however. When a *Guardian* leader, for instance, deigns to notice, it is to damn with faint praise, and ask an absurd question, 'Why are four times as many people planning to attend a Welsh festival in France [at Lorient – the annual pan-Celtic music jamboree] than a Welsh festival in Wales?' Displays of ignorance about Wales and its culture are commonplace. I refer again to the *Guardian* and its sport pages, which I read from habit and in the hope that another Frank Keating will come along, or (if only!) another Neville Cardus. There I found recently one Michael Henderson displaying a feeble knowledge of English literature and compounding his errors with a flatulent remark about Welsh writing: 'If we think long enough we might even come up with some [writers'] names of significance from west of Offa's Dyke'. I can hear the defence, a familiar one, 'He's only being playfully provocative'. It is, nonetheless, tiresome.

There was a great deal to celebrate at the Cardiff National, but it might be especially remembered as a landmark in women's writing in the Welsh language. Firstly, Mererid Hopwood won the Prose Medal, awarded this year for a work (of not more than 40,000 words) in an urban setting, and so became only the third Eisteddfod competitor to take all three major literary awards, having on previous occasions won the Crown for a poem sequence in free metres, and the Chair for poetry in the strict metres of Welsh prosody. At the end of the week the Chair was awarded to Hilma Lloyd Edwards for a poem on the subject 'New Land', who thus became the second woman in history to win the Chair.

And for the first time, a woman, Zoë Skoulding, has succeeded to the editorial chair of *Poetry Wales*. All three major

magazines representing Welsh writing in English are now edited
by women – Francesca Rhydderch is at *New Welsh Review,* and
Helle Michelsen at *Planet.* In her editorial in the Summer 2008
number of *New Welsh Review,* Francesca Rhydderch notes how,
in order to create a literary tradition in English, critics here have
seen it as their duty to 'uncover and record history' to pass on
to succeeding generations. She goes on to remark 'the powerful
influence that feminist literary criticism has had upon this
ongoing process', which has come about because the newness
of Welsh writing in English as a subject of literary criticism,
with its origins and early development largely in the second half
of the twentieth century, has made it 'extraordinarily open to
input from feminist critics'. The timing may have been
propitious, but the emergence of critics like Jane Aaron, Katie
Gramich and Kirsti Bohata has a great deal to do with the
outstanding quality of their 'gender inflected interpretations of
Welsh literary culture'.

Zoë Skoulding's academic interest is also focused on feminist
poetics. Born in Bradford, she grew up in Suffolk, worked in
Belgium and India and has lived in north Wales since 1991.
She will combine her editorial role with teaching creative
writing and contemporary literature at Bangor University.
Though they lack the flux of imagination and verbal fireworks
we had come to expect from her predecessor, her opening
remarks suggest continuation of the internationally flavoured
eclecticism that distinguished the magazine during Robert
Minhinnick's tenure, with perhaps a greater emphasis on
'linguistically innovative' poetry, which is given a good airing
in her first number (Summer, 2008). Matthew Jarvis delivers a
keynote essay on '"Alternative" poetry since the Second
Flowering', which mentions, among others, John James, the
subject of an article by Wendy Mulford, who is included in *The
Shearsman Anthology of Innovative Women Poets,* edited by

669

Carrie Etter, who contributes a poem. Mulford, born and again domiciled in England, though claiming strong attachment to Wales, may have been omitted from Meic Stephens's *Poetry 1900-2000* on grounds of eligibility; but there is no place either in that compendious anthology for James, a son of Cardiff, and Gerard Casey, born in Maesteg, whose *South Wales Echo* (Enitharmon, 1973) is praised by Jarvis.

Has 'Alternative' poetry been wilfully neglected in Wales? I would not have thought so. Other practitioners identified by Jarvis – Chris Torrance, a Scot but long resident in Pontneddfechan, Alison Bielski and, of course, Peter Finch (all in the anthology) – have never found it difficult to publish their work in magazines and have had their share of critical attention. I was publishing Torrance in my short stint as editor of *Poetry Wales* in the early 1970s, when he was fresh from Scotland, and Bielski too. James and Casey did not appear in *PW* while Meic Stephens was editor, nor during my term. Looking at their writing now, aside from the (self-acknowledged) derivativeness in Casey's, I am content to endorse Jarvis's high opinion of it. I strongly suspect neither submitted work for consideration, but B.S. Johnson did, and the poems are there.

At about the same time in the 1970s it appears I acquired a reputation as a scourge of what passed for the avant-garde, and it has stuck – to the extent that my strictures are still referred to as intolerant or unwise. Have I changed my mind since? No. I read poetry that is demanding and work with it and through it to understanding and appreciation of the poet's intention. There is nothing in John James or Gerard Casey to match the complexity of some of Roland Mathias's poems, or the genuine modernism of Lynette Roberts. But I have little patience with the tired trick of writing that is unpunctuated or misleadingly punctuated, or with words arbitrarily divided or poems in columns or composed of letters scattered about a page. And an hour or more of performance in which unremitting noise is presented as poetry (no matter how carefully rehearsed and enthusiastically delivered) would be no more enjoyable or interesting now than it was then.

*PN Review* 184, Volume 35 Number 2,
November – December 2008.

# THE CREATIVE WALES AWARD, WORLD BOOK DAY AND THE NATIONAL POET FOR WALES

*July 2008*

The diversion of National Lottery money to fund London's Olympic Games will affect arts provision in Wales as much as that in England. St Donat's Arts Centre, for example, will lose its revenue grant from the Arts Council of Wales. ACW itself boasted of the centre as a unique venue 'in the grounds of a mediaeval castle over-looking the sea'. The castle was bought and renovated by the American newspaper magnate William Randolph Hearst in the 1920s. As a diminutive trans-Atlantic outreach of San Simeon it served the same purpose of providing an elaborately antique setting for entertaining guests. Here Hearst and Marion Davies held court, safe from the prying eyes of rival newspapers. During Hearst's lordship, it was frequented by more or less local cultural icons, such as George Bernard Shaw (though none, so far as I am aware, actually from Wales) and Hollywood stars on European jaunts. Since 1960 it has accommodated Atlantic College, the world's first international sixth form college, where, in addition to their conventional studies, students learn life-saving skills at sea. In 1976, a converted fourteenth-century tithe barn on the site became the centrepiece of theatre and arts provision for the Vale of Glamorgan and soon began attracting visitors from a wider area. Rather more than thirty years ago I recall talking with an almost youthful Andrew Motion on a bus taking a party of us from Cardiff to St Donat's, where he was to give a reading. And on another occasion soon after it opened, we had an Academi trip there to hear R.S. Thomas and the Canadian Al Purdey – as ill-

assorted a pair of poets as you could hope to see. These and
many other memorable occasions will count for nothing, unless
some rich benefactors step in to make up the inevitable
shortfall. The centre is likely to close in July, when its annual
programme of some 180 events will be lost, and the 53,000 or
so who formerly attended them will have to look elsewhere for
their injection of culture.

In the last financial year, however, ACW again allocated the
cash for a set of 'Creative Wales Awards' to enable artists based
in Wales to undertake specified projects. This continues a
programme that began in 2003 to encourage successful
practitioners – the reverse of an anti-elitist policy in arts funding
that had failed not long before. Awards are made in a variety of
fields, from pottery to poetry one might say, considering those
recently announced, and are quite substantial – from twenty to
twenty-five thousand pounds. They are not in the gift of this or
that individual or committee, but are advertised and applied
for. Applicants submit an outline project, recruit referees and,
if short-listed, must appear before the Council and argue the
merits of their case. Gwyneth Lewis received an award in
2006/7, and among the nine winners announced in March
were the Welsh-language poet Menna Elfyn, and Robert
Minhinnick. The latter's political and environmental concerns
will be further elaborated in a series of essays about the
migration of peoples and individuals. What will come out of it?
As in the 2006 Book of the Year winning collection *To Babel
and Back* (Seren, 2005), we might anticipate a view of the
movement of people across our planet from a variety of
perspectives melding reportage and fiction, illuminated by the
transformative power of a poet's eye and language. Minhinnick
is a key figure in contemporary Welsh writing in English,
arguably indeed the outstanding one, energetic, prolific in verse
and prose, with a keen critical intelligence. The Creative Wales

Award is not his only current success. Already this year his fine first novel *Sea Holly* (Seren, 2007) has been short-listed for the Royal Society of Literature Ondaatje Prize; his next volume of poetry, *King Driftwood,* is due from Carcanet in August; and in May, *La Rossa Amica,* a collection of his poems translated into Italian, will be published in Italy, where he will tour schools, colleges and bookshops. His imminent release from editorial bondage to *Poetry Wales* will bring greater freedom to develop his writing in all the genres, though it could hardly be said to have inhibited his output or progress in the decade or so he has been in charge of the magazine.

World Book Day was celebrated at many centres and many levels. Writing squads descended on venues from Gwynedd to Blaenau Gwent; eight new short stories were launched, four in Welsh, four in English, for use with adults beginning to develop their reading skills; poets and fiction authors held sessions at a selection of ancient monuments, including Tintern Abbey and Caerwent, where the remains of the Roman town Venta Silurum are substantial enough to startle visitors unfamiliar with the site; and there were many contacts between writers and schools around Wales.

At the Millennium Centre in Cardiff Bay, the World Book Day lecture was given by the novelist Stevie Davies, whose latest book *The Eyrie* (Weidenfeld & Nicolson, 2007) has been highly praised. She is director of the creative writing course at Swansea University and her academic specialisms range from the Brontës (her selection of poems by Anne, Charlotte and Emily was published by Carcanet in 1986) to Henry Vaughan and seventeenth-century literature generally. Though a writer of prose fiction, she is possessed by poetry. In her essay 'Writing The Eyrie: Living in the House of Memory', dedicated to the memory of her late husband, Frank Regan, she recalls as a student being 'electrified' by lines from 'The Battle of Maldon'

– *'Hige sceal şe heardra, heorte şe cerire,/mod sceal şe mare, şe
ure mægem lytlağ'* – and confesses that poetry 'bubbles around
in [her] head ceaselessly'. Her lecture revealed how a Swansea
working-class family background and deracinating, peripatetic
experience as a child in a Forces family have influenced her
writing, though not in any strictly autobiographical way. Rather
they have supplied her with a variety of social contexts and local
colour, and, perhaps most valuably, the dual perspective on life
and critical distance from human affairs of one who, having
returned to roots, has the sensibilities of both insider and
outsider, that feeling of being on the peripheries of things, that
often distinguishes writers.

Andrew Motion's laureateship is for life, or at least as long
as he chooses to have it. In Wales, the role of National Poet is
a revolving door: we are already on our third in three years.
The role is sponsored by ACW and Academi takes on the PR
and organisation of events: our National Poets are not allowed
to sit back and wait for inspiration. The first was Gwyneth
Lewis (2005), the second Gwyn Thomas (2006), and the third,
just announced, is Gillian Clarke. Although her work had only
begun to appear in *Poetry Wales* in the summer of 1970, when,
as editor of the Triskel Poets Series, I introduced her first small
collection, *Snow on the Mountain* (1971), it was already
possible to delineate basic concerns and poetic preoccupations,
a number of which were linked to a rediscovery of self at Blaen
Cwrt, a cottage and smallholding in Cardiganshire. 'Many of
her poems,' I wrote, 'are about this quieter world much more
involved with the rhythms of the seasons. Here she observes
the constantly changing patterns of nature, the integration of
rural landscape, bird and beast. All this she records with superb
delicacy and tact, finding in her experience of motherhood
analogies for the fertility of the natural world and the pangs of
birth and separation. She takes as her main themes areas of life

infrequently explored in poetry and very rarely indeed illuminated with such honesty and insight...' The last sentence may not be as true now of Welsh poetry in English as it was then (or even then of poetry elsewhere), and of course there has been huge development in Gillian Clarke's art in the thirty-seven years since *Snow on the Mountain,* as successive Carcanet collections have shown, but what I saw in those early poems still holds true. Gillian Clarke is a wonderful public interpreter of her own writing and an inspirational ambassador for poetry with people of all ages, anywhere. She will be an outstanding National Poet.

Apart from a few private drift mines employing small numbers of men, and opencast sites, which invariably provoke passionate objections at planning stage and continuing protest over dust, the constant traffic of heavy vehicles and widespread damage to the environment, coal extraction has ceased in Wales. Two hundred years of Welsh industrial history ended with the closure of Tower Colliery in Hirwaun on Friday 25 January 2008. The village of Hirwaun is at the head of the Cynon valley, which goes down via Aberdare, Mountain Ash and Abercynon to Pontypridd. It has the Brecon Beacons at its back and is at the confluence of roads from Merthyr Tydfil to the east, the Rhondda Fawr to the south and the Vale of Neath to the west. It might have been chosen as a symbolic centre of the coalfield. Tower Colliery opened there in 1864 and was condemned to closure by British Coal in 1994, in the wake of the 1984-5 miners' strike, on the grounds that it was too expensive to run. The miners were offered £8,000 redundancy money and advised to find other jobs. Instead of touching their forelocks and getting on their bikes, as the Conservative government of the day expected, led by Tyrone O'Sullivan, long-serving National Union of Mineworkers branch secretary at the pit, 239 men sank their payout in a venture to buy the mine, and with two million pounds more borrowed from Barclays succeeded in doing so. Eight months later, in January 1995, it reopened. In thirteen years since, seven million tonnes of coal, valued at £300 million, have been extracted. The men were finally defeated by geology: the coal has run out. It has been a triumph of workers' ownership – the Chartists and the Paris Commune could not have dreamed of more – and it deserves a permanent memorial. But then we still await a monument to the end of an era, and to remind future generations of the sacrifice, hardship and pride of the many thousands of miners of the south Wales coalfield.

*PN Review* 182, Volume 34 Number 6,
July – August 2008.

# THE LIBRARY OF WALES AND SPORTING HEROES
*March 2008*


The Library of Wales, a project of Welsh Assembly Government, proves that politicians sometimes get things right. The idea grew from an enquiry of the Assembly's culture committee, where it had been carefully planted by a group of writers and academics called as witnesses. It envisaged re-publication of a series of books representing the best of the English-language literature of Wales, for sale to the public, but placed free in schools and libraries. Since 2005 fifteen books have appeared. The series editor is Dai Smith, who now occupies the Raymond Williams Chair in the Cultural History of Wales at Swansea. He sees it as 'a key component in creating and disseminating an ongoing sense of modern Welsh culture and history for the future Wales which is now emerging from contemporary society'. The series will embrace a variety of prose genres – essays, journalism, memoirs, drama – as well as fiction, though the latter has so far predominated. You can now buy smart new paperback editions (published by Parthian) of, for instance, Raymond Williams's *Border Country,* Gwyn Thomas's *The Dark Philosophers,* Rhys Davies's *The Withered Root,* and *In the Green Tree* by Alun Lewis, all of which had been out of print for many years.

Anthologies also are allowed within the scheme. The first two, one concerned with sport, the other with poetry, launched with some ado early in November at the Wales Millennium Centre, might appear to belong to disparate and mutually exclusive cultures. That, however, is to lose sight of the traditional role of sport as relief and restorative among the working-class communities of industrial south Wales that produced many of the English-language poets of the twentieth century, and of Dai Smith as a historian whose writing can be illuminated by passages of poetic intensity and who is co-author of *Fields of Praise,* the standard history of Welsh rugby.

The task of editing the anthology of poetry happily fell to Meic Stephens. *Poetry 1900-2000* contains representative selections from the work of one hundred poets. Towards the end of his editorial note, Dr Stephens remarks, 'I have been personally acquainted with almost all the contributors – the exceptions are fewer than a dozen.' That is an amazing indication of his centrality in Welsh writing in English in the twentieth century. His knowledge of the field is unequalled and in all probability unrepeatable. He laid the solid groundwork as founding editor of *Poetry Wales* in the 1960s, built the edifice during his long career as Literature Director of the Welsh Arts Council and editor of the *Companion to the Literature of Wales,* and topped it off as Professor of Welsh Writing in English at the University of Glamorgan. He is himself a poet, in English and in Welsh, his third language.

The editor chose 1975 as cut-off point. This makes Owen Sheers, born in 1974, the last poet in the book. Even so, it is a doorstop. Of the chosen hundred, five were born before 1900, another eight before 1910, and eight more before 1920. At this point the influence of state secondary education in the form of the county grammar schools kicks in: fifteen were born before 1930, a further eighteen before 1940, and twenty-three between 1940 and 1950. Finally, fourteen have birth dates before 1960 and nine between 1960 and 1974. Each decade has its stars. David Jones stands out in the first; Idris Davies, Glyn Jones, Lynette Roberts and Vernon Watkins in the second; R.S. Thomas, Dylan Thomas, Alun Lewis, Roland Mathias and Harri Webb make a golden era of the third; Leslie Norris, John

Ormond, Dannie Abse and Raymond Garlick belong to the fourth. These would be on everyone's list and they command about a quarter of the book. Of writers born after 1930, only Tony Conran, Gillian Clarke, Duncan Bush, Paul Groves, Nigel Jenkins, Sheenagh Pugh, Robert Minhinnick, Gwyneth Lewis and Paul Henry are given similar prominence.

Readers interested in trends will note the gradual increase in the number of women poets decade by decade. Ten of the fifty-four selected poets born between 1871 and 1940 are women, compared with fourteen of the forty-six born during the next thirty-five years. However, almost half the poets listed post-1950 are women; and in the period 1960-1975 alone, women outnumber men.

Selecting the poets for an anthology, although it becomes progressively more difficult from, say, the 1960s onwards, is one thing; selecting the poems another. Sifting a century of poetry involved a vast amount of reading, even if the editor's familiarity with the field gave him a good stock of favourites in advance. The aim of including a reasonable sample of the work of each poet did not make the task easier. Meic Stephens has brought it off with accuracy and assurance. And he provides a useful introduction to each poet. While for some, especially those who have made a mark more recently, this is no more than a résumé of career and publications, the selection for each of the major figures is accompanied by an exemplary brief essay that offers more detailed biographical information and a discussion of prominent themes and stylistic features.

In sum, this is the book that anyone with an interest in Welsh writing in English needs as reference text and source of material and pleasure. Poets born before 1940 provide many personal favourites, including items longer than one usually finds in an anthology, such as the extract from David Jones's *In Parenthesis,* Glyn Jones's 'Merthyr', and John Ormond's wonderful 'Tuscan Cypresses', but it is interesting also to reflect upon the strength demonstrated by writers of whom one might confidently expect to hear more. Among the latter are Robert Minhinnick, Christopher Meredith, Oliver Reynolds and Gwyneth Lewis, all securely established, and Catherine Fisher, Paul Henry and Stephen Knight, who may at this stage be less well known. Towards the end of the book, the strength of poets like Pascale Petit, Samantha Wynne-Rhydderch, Deryn Rees-Jones, Frances Williams and Kathryn Gray, who all bring heightened physicality, even a visceral quality, to their descriptions of sensations and reflections upon existence, along with every appearance of effortless facility (always difficult to attain), suggests a fresh direction in Welsh writing in English in the twenty-first century.

'Let us now praise famous men.' The familiar words from Ecclesiasticus have been much in my mind in the last few months. I have written at length about Roland Mathias, whom I admired greatly as writer and friend. His life and contribution to literature in Wales have also been celebrated by others in newspapers and journals here, and the Roland Mathias Prize, which he endowed, will help keep his memory green. Two more local heroes to whom I felt an attachment have died in the same short period. I never met either – but let me explain. We regularly attend matches at Cardiff Arms Park, one of the most famous venues in rugby union football. Quite often we have seen, in the committee box, a diminutive, silver-haired figure, soberly dressed, the least ostentatious of men. This was the President of the Welsh Rugby Union, Sir Tasker Watkins. His death early in September brought many expressions of grief for a great servant of rugby, his leadership and integrity an example to all. Obituaries disclosed much more. He was born into a Welsh-speaking home at Nelson, near Pontypridd, at the end of the First World War and fought in the Second. And how he fought. On 16 August 1944, as a lieutenant in the Welch Regiment, and the only officer left in his company, he successfully led charges against enemy machine gun posts and beat off a counter-attack by a larger force, finally with a bayonet charge. On their way back to the battalion, they found their way barred by another enemy post. He told his men to scatter and single-handedly charged the post with a bren gun, silencing it. He was awarded the VC. After the war he was called to the bar and made an outstanding career in the law, becoming a High Court Judge in 1971, and a Privy Councillor in 1980. In 1983 he was appointed Senior Presiding Judge for England and Wales and Deputy Chief Justice. The Archbishop of Wales, Dr Barry Morgan, summed up a remarkable life: 'Sir Tasker Watkins was a brave soldier, a brilliant lawyer and a humble man.'

The combination of courage and humility characterises the true hero. That is why perhaps we witnessed here an astonishing outpouring of grief at the death of Ray Gravell at the age of 56 on the last day of October. He was a rugby player – a fine centre-three-quarter who played for Llanelli, Wales (twenty-three times, during the golden era of the 1970s), and the British and Irish Lions in four test matches against South Africa in 1980. He was brought up in the mining community of Mynydd-y-Garreg near Llanelli and, wherever his career took him, remained rooted there. The street where he lived is named after him. A big man, powerful on the burst and uncompromisingly hard in the tackle, he played rugby rumbustiously, and without a trace of arrogance. In 1982, still in his playing days, he shared in the first Welsh-language commentary on a televised rugby match and, when he retired from the game, he became a popular broadcaster in English and Welsh. He brought to the media an unaffected, genial sincerity, whether on the touchline at rugby matches or presenting record programmes from the studio. And, to his surprise, he became an actor on the small and large screen:

Louis Malle sought him out to play the chauffeur to Jeremy Irons in his 1992 film *Damage*. He was, too, a member of the Gorsedd of the Bards and Bearer of the Grand Sword on its ceremonial occasions. Those who saw him on the field remember a bearded swashbuckler, who wore his patriotic heart on his sleeve, and to the end he expressed a notion of chivalry rare these days.

Rugby and poetry: of course there are people not much enamoured of either, but there is a thread, bright gold I think, composed of these two still discernible in the fabric of Welsh life.

*PN Review* 180, Volume 34 Number 4,
March – April 2008.

# THE ROLAND MATHIAS PRIZE AND POLITICS
*September 2007*

The Roland Mathias Prize, worth £2000 to the winner, was awarded for the second time at the end of April. It went to Dannie Abse for *Running Late,* a further revelation of the poet's deft ease, whatever the subject. In this predominantly elegiac book the familiar lightness of touch persists. The contents are leavened with a fair measure of wit and humour, and the weightier themes are greeted with a sad smile and shake of the head. What can one do, after all, faced with the accumulating evidence of entropy, and the loss of friends and loved ones? Yes, weep for the moment, treasure the memories, and treasure, too, what the seasons bring to our gardens and what remains of the familiar bric-a-brac of a lifetime. One of Abse's enviable gifts is storytelling, the communication of message or moral in simple narrative without a wasted word; another is his ability to express human love – not the whirlwind of passion but abiding love – in a way unsentimental, yet deeply affecting.

The poet didn't come to Brecon to receive his prize. Just in case, he sent an old friend and editor from Hutchinson with a letter of apology and gratitude instead. His reluctance to travel down from London was understood by all (he is now 84), yet it was a pity. Roland Mathias, whose generosity created the prize, was almost certainly the first critic to give lengthy, well-considered attention to Abse's poetry, a two-part article for the *Anglo-Welsh Review* (numbers 36 and 38) in 1966-7. Forty years ago, Mathias thought *Tenants of the House* the 'high plateau' of his subject's achievement, and that Abse had already established himself as 'one of the few successful contemporary poets of the extended symbolic concept', a point, he continued, 'as far from his beginnings in a natural, discursive eloquence as he could well reach'. The quality he most admired in the other's writing was that 'fundamental belief in man's spiritual potential and a willingness to look at a happy relationship or a pleasant possibility at least as carefully as others explore the counter-balancing glooms'. The reference to spirituality is perhaps wide of the mark in respect of a poet for whom 'Religion is beyond belief!' But, committed Christian as he is, this would not have dismayed Mathias. At the time, and interestingly in view of his own inventive employment of metre, he was more exercised about a dwindling away of that 'common humanity' that had been a characteristic of the earlier work as Abse began to develop more formal approaches. He need not have worried: the loss, if there was a loss, was temporary. It is the 'common humanity' permeating *Running Late* that holds and moves the reader.

The successful formula of the award ceremony requires the authors of the short-listed books to read a sample of their work. In Dannie Abse's absence, Tony Curtis, another old friend of the poet, performed in his place. An appreciative audience was equally warmly disposed to the selection from Tony Conran's *The Red Sap of Love,* a big book of collected lyrics from fifty years of writing, read by the poet's wife. Conran, who was present but prevented from reading in person by the increasing handicap of cerebral palsy, is revered by many as a brilliant translator of poetry in Welsh, for his own stylish and dramatic utterance, and for his poetic loyalty to the community for which he writes. I have referred to him previously *(PN Review* 155, 2004) and would only reiterate that he has had less than his due of formal acknowledgement for a sustained and remarkable contribution to literature in Wales.

The other two writers whose books made the shortlist read

for themselves. Tony Brown gave an extract from his monograph on *R.S. Thomas* in the Writers of Wales series, an excellent short study of the poet that shirks no issue. It casts more light than any previous critique on the major influence that Patrick Kavanagh's *The Great Hunger* had on Thomas's poetry, identifies inspiration and sources (Keidrych Rhys's magazine *Wales* significant among them), discusses the complex relationship between the poet and his wife, drawing on the remarkable sequence of poems written after her death, and simplifies what had seemed to be the thorny tangles of his unorthodox belief. Finally in the running order, Cornish born, Sussex University educated Philip Gross, who came to Wales as Professor of Creative Writing at the University of Glamorgan in 2004, read from *The Egg of Zero* (Bloodaxe), his first book of poems since arriving here. It was a striking performance from a book that is packed with fascinating ideas and images and, even while dealing with the commonplaces of life, family relations, shopping, the fear of burglars, dry rot beneath the floorboards (!), is often simply electrifying.

The shortlist for the prize bore out an earlier impression that, along with the inevitable dross, some splendid work has been published in the past two years: any one of the four books presented would have been a worthy winner. The Roland Mathias Prize itself is proving a winner, too – not least because it is so well supported by the locality. It has a good start in being organised under the auspices of the Brecknock Society and Museum Friends and sponsored by BBC Wales. Another considerable advantage is that the award ceremony takes place in the historic Guildhall in Brecon, where among the paintings displayed is a grand full-length portrait of Sarah Siddons. (The great actress was born in Brecon, at the Shoulder of Mutton Inn, where her parents, Roger Kemble and Sarah [Ward], were lodging during a provincial tour. That was not their daughter's only connection with the town. Brecon witnessed her first stage appearance and, while still a young woman, she precipitated a family crisis there by expressing her determination to marry William Siddons, another member of Kemble's company, when her parents had planned a more secure match to one of the minor landed gentry.)

As on the first occasion two years ago, the ceremony was preceded by a reading, which began with poems from Christine Evans, the inaugural prize winner, followed by novelist and poet Chris Meredith, who read a new short story, then more poems from Gillian Clarke and Peter Finch, both consummate literary professionals before an audience, as in other respects, who have been doing this sort of thing for thirty years or more. The formula of preliminaries, which entertain and whet the appetite of the audience, before the main event, is a feature that other literary prizes might envy and perhaps seek to emulate.

*Agenda* is the thrice-yearly magazine of the Institute of Welsh Affairs, an independent think-tank and research institute with its main base in Cardiff. Its Spring 2003 number included a short article by Adam Price, the Plaid Cymru MP, who famously, but in the end unsuccessfully, led a campaign to impeach Tony Blair for his part in the tragedy of Iraq. He was writing before the 2003 Welsh Assembly elections and speculating on the choice of coalition partner that might be forced on the First Minister, Rhodri Morgan, if Labour were to lose its overall majority. Since a link with the Tories is unthinkable; the choice would lie between the Liberal Democrats and Plaid; he argues the latter would be sounder politics. Price does not mention in his article that very many Labour politicians and supporters would consider Plaid equally unacceptable. Indeed, it may surprise voters to the east of Offa's Dyke that here Labour's most virulent attacks on the opposition are directed not at the Conservatives but at Plaid Cymru. In part this is due to the fervent belief among the Labour faithful that Westminster is the alpha and omega of political life, while Plaid insists Wales comes first. In November 2002, however, Rhodri Morgan had delivered what has become known as his 'Clear red water' speech, affirming a determination to adhere to fundamental socialist principles that were essentially different from those of Tony Blair. Having taken this at face value, Adam Price showed that Plaid, which by its Constitution is committed to the establishment of 'a democratic Welsh state based on socialist principles', was closely aligned to Welsh Labour (and a better coalition partner than the Lib Dems) – if the latter had the courage of its leader's convictions. In the event, speculation about a new alignment in Cardiff Bay came to nothing. Labour emerged from the 2003 election with the narrowest of majorities (which it eventually lost) and soldiered on alone.

The outcome of the 2007 election has proved another matter. 'All is changed, changed...' – well, not 'utterly', but there has been a dramatic shift in the balance of political forces here as in Scotland (though if you rely upon London newspapers you might never suspect it). No party emerged able to govern without the support of another: Labour has 26 seats, Plaid Cymru fifteen, the Conservatives twelve and the Liberal Democrats six. It was the worst election outcome for Labour in Wales since 1918. In the immediate aftermath Rhodri Morgan courted the Lib Dems, with whom he had formed a coalition government prior to 2003, and was rejected. At the same time representatives of Plaid, Lib Dems and Tories were working on a set of policies and principles that all three could agree with a view to taking power with Ieuan Wyn Jones, leader of Plaid Cymru, as First Minister. The 'rainbow coalition', as it became known in the media, needed only endorsement by party members, but there it fell. Just when it was beginning to look all over for Labour in Wales for the foreseeable future, differences within rather than between the opposition parties gave the initiative away.

The Assembly constitution demands that if a First Minister is not in place within 28 days of an election, a new election must be called. This critical period had almost expired when Rhodri Morgan declared he would form a minority government, trusting that the other parties would work with him in the best interests of Wales, and resumed his place. As might be expected, that did not end the political to and fro – far from it. In further meetings and conferences the opposition parties ironed out internal differences. If only more than 28 days were allowed for the detailed discussions that must attend efforts to form political partnerships (as is the case in other European countries where forms of proportional representation almost invariably lead to election results without a clear majority for any party), the 'rainbow coalition' would by now have its First Minister and cabinet.

Unquestionably, we are at a critical juncture in the political history of Wales. Now for the first time Labour's grip on the electorate has loosened; and now, also for the first time, Assembly members are able to think of themselves as law-makers in their own right, though what they propose must be scrutinised and agreed by the Secretary of State for Wales and Parliament in Westminster before it reaches the statute book. This is not the way things have been done in devolved Scotland from the outset, nor for that matter does it apply to restored government in Northern Ireland. Where the SNP will lead the Scots and what effect that will have on politics here are matters for conjecture and a probably distant future, but as I write, despite the old, deep-seated animosities, further discussions are taking place within and between Labour and Plaid Cymru on the subject of partnership in government. Perhaps Adam Price's message on the eve of the 2003 election, 'what unites us [that is, true socialist values] is for the moment far more important than anything that divides us', will guide negotiators on both sides to the 'historic compromise' that he envisaged as the political way ahead.

*PN Review* 177, Volume 34 Number 1,
September – October 2007.

# THE HAY FESTIVAL
*September 2006*


We learn from the media that the Hay Literary Festival was a huge success. Record numbers of visitors braved an unreliable train service and some notoriously narrow, winding roads to reach the new festival site, in a field about twenty minutes on foot from the centre of Hay. The move from the former primary school site has brought gains and losses. The festival is no longer constrained in terms of space, so that it does not need several supplementary venues around the town, and can, if it wishes, shed the shackles of summer half-term holiday (though the latter accounts for the presence of increasing numbers of parents with children as greater emphasis is given to children's literature). But, notwithstanding a shuttlebus service, slipping into town between literary items for the multitude of shops selling second-hand books and prints, not to mention restaurants and bars, is no longer a simple matter. Once on the new site, only the daring and determined are prepared to quit it for the possibility of more interesting fare elsewhere. Being stuck in a field is not so bad if the weather is fine and there is ample provision of places to rest, relax, have a drink, enjoy a meal, but this is not yet the case. Newspaper coverage of events later in the festival made much of the glorious sunny days, which allowed those so inclined to be photographed lying on the grass reading or eating ice-cream. I wish Peter Florence had arranged for the sun to shine from the beginning.

The first Monday was dreadful – and there was little hope of escape from the cold wind and showers, because any tent offering hot food and drinks, for which there was a great need, was either out of commission or already overcrowded with customers who had no intention of soon leaving their hard-won seats and tables to brave the winter outside. Regulars at the National Eisteddfod, which is always in the first week of August, are quite accustomed to harsh weather and turn up in full survival kit, just in case. The Eisteddfod, a far bigger festival, caters for all interests and needs on its out-of-town sites, though it has to be admitted that conditions at Hay were nowhere near as bad underfoot as they were for *eisteddfodwyr* at Bangor last year, when softly treading on sections of plastic walkway over the swamp would unpredictably squirt knee-high fountains of liquid mud over shoes and clothing. Nevertheless, the spirit of literary festivals is somewhat crushed when large numbers of people moving between events are confined to narrow covered routes between billowing tents. Therein lies another problem: whereas the Eisteddfod has a vast flatpack pavilion, in which all the main events are held, and which is annually dismantled and re-erected at the next venue, Hay is now, or for the moment, entirely tented. The cinema, a popular feature, especially in the conditions that prevailed at the beginning of the week, suffered from both the flimsiness of the structure and the vagaries of re-scheduling.

The first Monday featured a number of items of local interest. The short list for Welsh Book of the Year was announced, revealing, alongside Kitty Sewell's *Ice Trap* (Honno) and Ifor Thomas's *Body Beautiful* (Parthian), another nomination for Robert Minhinnick, with *To Babel and Back* (Seren). This is Minhinnick in prose, though you might be excused for thinking the intense visualisation of places and events, and the profusion of metaphor, more characteristic of poetry. He offers readers a peculiarly rich and luminous concoction, actuality lit by arc-lit perception, and a parallel world of dream or nightmare bathed in a radioactive glare. He has won the prize before, in 1993, with *Watching the Fire-Eater,* his first collection of essays, and could well repeat that success in 2006.

Festival-goers with faith and foresight enough to book in advance, or who rose and joined the queue at the ticket office early, had the pleasure of hearing Dai Smith and Elaine Morgan discuss *The Dark Philosophers* by Gwyn Thomas (1913–81), who had a prodigious talent and, some would argue, became a prodigal abuser of it. In novels, novellas and short stories he mediated his concern for suffering humanity through a uniquely humorous portrayal of noble idealists caught in farcical situations. Richly endowed with hyperbolic wit, he was a gift to the media and is probably best remembered now for his appearances on radio and television, but it is high time his work was re-evaluated. Elaine Morgan, who wrote the introduction to this reprint of *The Dark Philosophers* (three grimly humorous novellas) for the Library of Wales series, is one of the better reasons for continuing to read the *Western Mail,* for which she writes a weekly column. Like Gwyn Thomas, she went from the Valleys to Oxford University during a period of working-class strife, and became a writer for television. Three times a BAFTA award winner, she was highly regarded in the media as one of the most accomplished authors of television adaptations *(Testament of Youth, Anne Frank)* before the present era of Andrew Davies, another Welsh writer. She is best known, however, here and overseas, for *The Descent of Woman* (1972), which presents evolutionary theory from a feminist viewpoint in stripped-down language accessible to all. Although not trained as a scientist – she read English at Oxford – a Google search for Elaine Morgan soon reveals how important a figure she is in this field. In an interview for the *New Welsh Review* in 1989 she said she would like 'to live long enough to see the Aquatic Ape Theory accepted as a tenable working hypothesis'.

Now in her eighty-sixth year, with this ambition substantially achieved (she was recently invited to participate in a university conference on the subject in California), she might justifiably consider resting on hard-won laurels. Happily, there is not the slightest evidence of any such inclination.

Later in the day, the weather unremittingly bleak, we joined the crowd at the discussion to launch the hundredth monograph in the Writers of Wales series, which began in 1970 and continues under the joint editorship of Meic Stephens and R. Brinley Jones, and is published by the University of Wales Press. The vast majority are devoted to significant individual writers in Welsh or English, though the medium of publication is English. In all its variety, the series has made a monumental contribution to our better knowledge and understanding of the literature of Wales. The trick is to match essayist to writer subject and just how effective this can be is demonstrated by number 100: *R.S. Thomas* by Tony Brown, Reader in English and co-director of the R.S. Thomas Study Centre at the University of Wales, Bangor, whose earlier work on the short stories of Glyn Jones was critically applauded. His monograph on Thomas breaks with series tradition in having photographic and other illustrations, notes and index, and is, of course, the better for that. It is also splendidly informative and insightful about a poet and a personality who, no matter how often or from which direction we approach, remains enigmatic. Brown sees the poet at the outset as a self-conscious outsider, belonging neither to the people among whom he finds himself, nor to the culture of Wales. He is not spiritually at home in the faith he confesses and, as a pacifist, is at odds with the Anglican Church, which (even now) can countenance young men going off to war. Life frequently falls short of his imagined ideal. Much of the poetry is born out of anxious soul-searching over tensions such as these.

Tony Brown was accompanied on the platform by Gwydion Thomas, the poet's son, whose support in the writing of the monograph is warmly acknowledged. He is unlike his father in being entirely at ease before an audience, and he did not flinch from talking of family relations, though the circumstances of his upbringing precluded conventional family closeness. While under the same roof there was a distance between them ('He was busy'), and the boy was sent away to an English public school – perhaps in his parents' view the best education available, but more or less guaranteed to alienate him from home and community. Again, although an Anglican clergyman, the poet did not expect, far less insist, that his son should attend church regularly. It was no surprise in the circumstances that he had the impression his father did not care much for writing and giving sermons, though some members of the audience protested otherwise. And it was interesting to learn that having taken the far from easy road of learning Welsh as an adult in order to gain entry to the cultural heart of Wales, RS made no effort to ensure his son enjoyed similar access by learning the language in childhood.

Tony Brown quotes Gwyn Jones who, in a radio broadcast in 1983, on the occasion of Thomas's seventieth birthday, acknowledged that he was 'a very fine poet', but went on to accuse him of lacking 'human love': 'the expression of the natural, kind, warm emotions of humanity are too frequently missing. Even the warmth and kindliness and love of the Christian religion seem to me to be very much underdone.' It is an unexpected indictment, and Thomas's response to it is equally surprising: 'I think he's quite right to say so'. This was not, as it were, granting Gwyn Jones the right to his own views. Indeed, in a *Daily Telegraph* interview in 1999 he identified the same failing in himself and attempted to explain it: 'I don't think I'm a very loving person. [...] I wasn't brought up in a loving home – my mother was afraid of emotion – and you tend to carry on in the same way don't you? [...] I'm always ready to confess the things that are lacking in me [...] and particularly this lack of love for human beings.' It is an extraordinary statement, both for its honesty and its content. We are left with the question how far, if at all, the poet's limited capacity for 'human love' diminishes the poetry, as Gwyn Jones suggested. In my view not one whit. Fascinating as it was, the discussion at Hay Literary Festival had little to do with literature. It merely confirmed that we have become horribly and, I suspect, incurably nosey about the lives of writers.

*PN Review* 171, Volume 33 Number 1,
September – October 2006.

# THE ARTS COUNCIL OF WALES
*July 2006*


There has been uproar in the arts in Wales. Loud and angry protests have been heard in the past, from arts organisations and arty individuals with grievances, usually about the share of public subsidy they received. The current furore is due to meddling politicians and, for once, arts practitioners and the Arts Council of Wales are united in opposing them. Politicians talk in clichés and slogans and listen only to what they want to hear. They have a desperate need to be seen to be doing something (and hate being informed of fact or argument that reveals flaws in their one-dimensional thought processes), which is why they do not understand 'leave well alone' and 'if it ain't broke, don't fix it'. Whatever else Rhodri Morgan and his Labour ministers in the Welsh Assembly Government may say, it is for this reason they have chosen to persist with a 1997 election manifesto promise to do away with quangos. Once the snappy phrase, 'bonfire of the quangos', was coined by some political adviser, the die was cast.

This very day, the Welsh Development Agency, which has overseen economic and industrial development here for the past thirty years, will be brought into the Welsh Office. And if Alun Pugh, Minister for Culture, Language and Sport, had had his way, it would have been preceded by the Arts Council of Wales. So confident was Mr Pugh that all would come to pass according to his will, that he told Geraint Talfan Davies, the highly-esteemed chairman of ACW, several months ago that he would not be re-appointed when his term of office expired at the beginning of April.

Mr Pugh claimed that his intention to integrate the policy and strategy functions of ACW with the Assembly was born of the Council's failure to extend access to the arts to all sectors of the community. It is a pretty poor excuse, not because arts sustained by the taxpayer have no such obligation, but rather because there is clear evidence that ACW was mindful of its role in this respect and not only active but successful in pursuit of it. No one asked Mr Pugh what precisely Assembly civil servants would do that ACW was not already doing. Or, if anyone did, he declined to answer, despite many opportunities to do so over several months of controversy. His only response, frequently repeated, was to contrast access opportunities in Cardiff with those available in the old industrial valleys of south Wales. No contest! Cardiff wins, hands down. You might as well contrast London with Lydney, or anywhere else in England for that matter. Mr Pugh, who comes from the Rhondda, might consider how interest in the arts was developed in those parts during the last century. It was partly by the voluntary efforts of schoolteachers, who, out of concern for the proper education of children and pride in their profession, communicated their own artistic interests to their pupils (these days, of course, all politicians meddle in education and teachers are beleaguered in their own classrooms). In far larger measure it was achieved by the communities themselves, in scores of 'welfare halls', built without subsidy, where cinemas doubled as theatres, libraries and reading rooms neighboured snooker halls, a choral tradition was proudly nurtured, and 'The Band Club' had a silver band as well as a bar. Nearly all these active community centres were lost when the pits were closed, and not one politician, national or local (and all invariably Labour) said we must put public money into these cultural engines now, because to rebuild them fifty years hence will be beyond even a National Assembly in Wales, if any such thing (which God forbid!) should ever come along.

In the short term, Mr Pugh proposed that the six major arts organisations – Academi (the literature promotion agency), Welsh National Opera, The BBC National Orchestra of Wales, Diversions Dance Company, Clwyd Theatr Cymru, and the Welsh-language Theatr Genedlaethol Cymru – should be funded directly by the Assembly, thus terminating the 'arm's length' principle, which has sensibly prevailed in government subsidy of the arts until now. Although the proposal carried with it the likelihood of enhanced funding for the six, they were united in deploring the possibility, no matter how faint, of grant aid being tied to political conformity, or political interference of any kind. All the other arts organisations and many individual artists and writers were equally scathing in their condemnation of Mr Pugh's plans for them. Despite the strength and cogency of protest, he was determined to persist. In the end, however, he was scotched by loss of a crucial vote in the Assembly. The plans were put on the shelf pending another review of the arts to be completed by November 2006.

Meanwhile, ACW remained as before, but without a chairman. Would Mr Pugh swallow his pride and ask Geraint Talfan Davies to continue in post till November, especially since there was insufficient time to go through the usual process of advertisement and appointment? No. Instead, virtually on the eve of Mr Davies's departure, he announced that Professor Dai Smith, already a council member, had accepted his invitation to take over. Critics lament the lack of due process in this interim appointment and point to Professor Smith's political compatibility with Mr Pugh. Those who know him, however, acknowledge his immense relevant experience as a top manager with BBC Wales and academic administrator, and his brilliance as a communicator. He will make a splendid job of it.

Professor Smith already oversees the Library of Wales, which at its January launch Mr Pugh was pleased to claim as one of his better ideas. It was not of his devising of course; he found it among recommendations of an Assembly committee investigating Welsh writing in English, which had in turn snapped it up from evidence presented by Professor M. Wynn Thomas. The plan is to reissue in well-produced paperback format a number of long out-of-print classics. The first tranche includes Raymond Williams's *Border Country*, Gwyn Thomas's *The Dark Philosophers* and *So Long, Hector Bebb* by Ron Berry, three novels of true distinction that deserve to find new readerships. A major concern of the project is to make these books known in Wales and to that end all secondary school, college and university libraries will receive a copy of every book published in the continuing series. Parallel launches in London and New York, distributors in Europe and the USA and online information from *www.libraryofwales.org* should secure more than the usual level of attention for Welsh books in English in other countries. It is a good idea.

I first met Leslie Norris in the late 1960s. That initial encounter was a delight, as was each of the infrequent opportunities to be in his company which followed after. From 1973, when he became Visiting Professor of Poetry at the University of Seattle, he lived very largely in the USA, for the last twenty-two years or so in Utah, as Professor of Poetry and later Professor of Creative Writing at Brigham Young University. He was a great storyteller (few who heard his descriptions of Seattle or his account of the extraordinary life and death of Theodore Roethke – 'Teddy Retkey', he told us – will ever forget them), and a patient and thoughtful correspondent. Before the days of email, his letters, penned in a bold and elegant script, were worth preserving for their appearance alone, and they were often intensely interesting. One of the earliest I received from him included an unselfconscious analysis of one of his best known poems, 'The Ballad of Billy Rose', demonstrating how at the dramatic climax, as 'the brave/Blind' boxer leaves the ring, patterns of internal rhyme and alliteration knit and sustain the narrative. He was as careful with his students and with audiences everywhere. Very few could match him as a reader of his own poetry: I can hear his voice now, and the precise enunciation of lines such as 'Late/Bees hung their blunt weight,/Plump drops between those simplest wings, their leisure/An ignorance of frost.' It was wonderful to see how he worked an audience with well-rehearsed anecdotes, quiet humour and gentle, eloquent gestures. I have a copy of *Water Voices* (1980) signed for me by the poet in his unmistakable hand 'with love'. The phrase is not empty. He had a great capacity for love. Indeed, few poets have had and expressed this gift with such constancy and it is no surprise that he was well loved in return. His sympathies (sometimes tinged with elegiac melancholy and nostalgia) permeated his perception of fellow beings and the natural world. Here is his 'Beautiful Young Devon Shorthorn Bull':

> In warm meadows this bull
> Ripens gently. He is a pod
> Of milky seed, not ready yet.
> Not liking to be alone, he
> Drifts on neat feet to be near
> His herd, is sad at gates
> When one is taken from him. There's
> No red in his eye, he does not
> Know he's strong, but mildly
> Pushes down hedges, can carry
> A fence unnoticed on his broad
> Skull. His flat back measures
> The horizon. Get a ladder, look
> Over him. Dream that one by one,
> The far fields fill with his children, his soft daughters.

Such descriptions of creatures avoid the accusation of sentimentality, perhaps by a hair's breadth, but I would not want to do without one of them. From time to time in recent years he contacted us from his home in Oren, saying he and his wife Kitty were coming home to Wales and asking help in finding a suitable place to live. At his request, I sent details of houses for sale in Caerleon and Usk. Other friends, given the same mission, bothered estate agents in Cardiff, Swansea and Hay-on-Wye, but never to his entire satisfaction. After more than twenty years he was thoroughly acclimatised and transplanted in the foothills of the Rockies, and it was there, in his eighty-fifth year, he died, on 6 April 2006.

*PN Review* 170, Volume 32 Number 6,
July – August 2006.

# SEREN AT 25

*May 2006*

I recently visited Cary Archard at his home in the Vale of Glamorgan. The cottage is centuries old and has massive walls. In the huge fireplace, now occupied by a diminutive but efficient stove, bread for the village was once baked. It was a particularly fine late autumn day and the view from the windows over broad fields rolling gently down to the hidden sea was deliciously rural. This landscape was not Archard property, I was assured, carved out of the Vale on the profits of publishing, but what might be termed the Agatha Christie domain, acquired by her surviving relative, the beneficiary of her literary estate.

Although we have met from time to time over the years, at book launches and literary events, I had not spoken at any length to Cary since inviting him to become reviews editor of *Poetry Wales* following an initial encounter at an Academi conference in Harlech, as he told Robert Minhinnick in the interview published in *Poetry Wales* in 2004 (Vol. 40, No. 2). That was probably in the spring of 1974, for I see his name heading the reviews section for the first time in the summer number of that year (10.1), a special devoted to Sir T.H. Parry-Williams. Sticklers for facts will wish to note that he persuaded John Holloway, Professor of Modern English at Cambridge, to consider *Ten Anglo-Welsh Poets* in the *second* number for which he commissioned reviews (10.2), not the first as he said in the interview.

In those far-off days the magazine's publisher was

Christopher Davies Ltd (*'Llyfrau'r Dryw'*) of Swansea, who, in the person of co-proprietor, (Sir) Alun Talfan Davies, a notable figure in public and cultural life, from time to time expressed a view about the direction of editorial policy. When in 1974 I was obliged by my new employers to surrender the editorial chair I had inherited from Meic Stephens, I presume it was they who (perhaps acting on advice from the Welsh Arts Council) invited John Powell Ward, then teaching at the university in Swansea, to take over the editorship with the summer 1975 number (11.1), while Cary remained reviews editor. And thus things continued until the spring number 1980 (15.4), the last to be tied to Christopher Davies Ltd. Summer 1980 (16.1) was co-edited by Ward and Archard. In their editorial they announced with pride and, in view of escalating printing costs, some anxiety, 'the magazine is owned, once again, by private individuals'. With that issue, the magazine was published by 'Poetry Wales' from Cary Archard's address in Bridgend. John Ward appeared at this point to be gradually easing himself out of a role he had fulfilled with energy and flair, but it turned out to be only a slightly delayed goodbye: the next number reveals Cary Archard as sole editor, assisted by Sandra Anstey and, as Welsh language editor, Gwyneth Lewis.

In his note *'Poetry Wales:* The Twenty-First Year' in *PW* in 1985 (21.1) Ward recalls, 'When Cary Archard took over the magazine in 1980, he muttered that he might "print a few pamphlets". I thought he was mad.' He (Ward) had in mind the essential quotidian labour of magazine editing in what little spare time existed from the rigours of teaching. On top of that, Archard was proposing to publish pamphlets! Major progress towards the founding of a new publishing house occurred during the following year. The title page of the autumn 1981 number of *PW* (17.2) names the publisher as 'Poetry Wales Press' for the first time, but the imprint had already featured on the first three books from the press, collections of poems by Nigel Jenkins and Mike Jenkins, and *Miscellany One,* a selection of work by Dannie Abse.

By 1981, then, Poetry Wales Press is already launched, and the initial sample of the output of the press declares the intention of the publisher – that is, firstly, to encourage English-language poets from Wales, especially young and new poets, and secondly, to increase textual resources for the teaching of Welsh writing in English by returning to print selections from writers with established reputations. Work of this kind was not common in schools (rather to the contrary), but even those keen to develop it were frustrated by the absence of useful books. Cary Archard had an answer to the problem: if you cannot find the texts to serve your purpose in bookshops, commission and publish them yourself.

This, then, was the genesis of Poetry Wales Press. Cary Archard founded and developed it and, although he is quick to pay tribute to the encouragement and generosity of Dannie Abse, who gave the fledgling press office space in his home at Ogmore-by-Sea, for several years it remained essentially a one-man operation. If PWP was at the outset a cottage industry, it was at least one fired by intellect and a love of literature. Other publishers in Wales at the time were little more than jobbing printers with some experience of book production in the Welsh language. They were keen enough to take Welsh Arts Council grants to keep the presses busy by printing books in English, but the potential therein of a far larger book-buying public than they were accustomed to meant little to them. They were not ambitious to achieve commercial growth (nor was PWP at the time), or at least they were not ambitious enough to invest energy and cash in commissioning work, grooming writers for success and promoting books. Skills in these directions still are as rare as the enterprise to exploit them.

At the outset, Archard (like the Welsh printer-publishers) applied for Arts Council production grants on a book-by-book basis. A fundamental and far-reaching change occurred in 1982, when PWP became the first publisher in Wales to receive a block grant. This gave the press a measure of freedom and encouraged the planning of an annual programme of publications. The effect was immediate. The autumn 1981 number of *PW* previously mentioned also advertises a further nine books soon to appear, including poetry collections by Richard Poole, John Davies and Sheenagh Pugh, two additions to the 'Miscellany' series, devoted to Emyr Humphreys and Alun Lewis, and two volumes of literary criticism – *Critical Writings on R. S. Thomas,* edited by Sandra Anstey, and *The Art of Seamus Heaney*, edited by Tony Curtis. The titles tell us that Archard's aims in setting up the press still held.

Within a couple of years, the new funding régime allowed an office to be established in Bridgend and the appointment of Mick Felton, who had previous experience in bookselling, to oversee the day-to-day business of the press. Archard, still a full-time teacher, was doubly relieved: there was someone constantly on hand to deal with the minutiae of the business and with Arts Council bureaucracy. Furthermore, as he told Minhinnick, he regained his own front room. Another stage in the evolution of the press occurred in 1989, when it extended use of the Seren imprint (adopted since 1985 for prose only) to all its publications. Certainly the new label was more streamlined than the old (a matter of some presentational significance in book production and marketing), and it confirmed separation of the publishing house from the magazine that begat it, a distancing that began with Cary Archard relinquishing the editorship of *Poetry Wales* in 1986 (21.4). Since then, successive editors have steered *PW* whither they willed without intervention from the press, though none more controversially than the present incumbent, whose international outlook in poetry and eco-politics has left an indelible mark. The divergence is underlined by separate funding arrangements (with the Welsh Books Council these days rather than the Arts Council), the publisher undergoing annual evaluation for its grant, while the magazine, also in receipt of a block grant, is formally assessed every three years.

The proper launch of Seren in 1989 coincided with the appointment of Dannie Abse as a director of Poetry Wales Press Ltd, still the name of the publisher as listed at Companies House. As the output and the business of the press grew in the 1990s, further appointments were made to the board and more staff recruited. Professor M. Wynn Thomas (1993-2003) was probably the most significant of the former, but the register of directors reveals the effort made to maintain a balance between literary and business expertise. As currently constituted, the board, chaired by Cary Archard, has seven members possessing together extensive experience in the book trade and in business generally, and literary expertise, especially in the field of translation, from Welsh and other languages.

By virtue of more than twenty years as manager of PWP/Seren, Mick Felton is well qualified for the post of company secretary, which he holds in addition to a directorship. Even superficial consideration of these three roles suggests he bears a heavy burden of responsibility for production and financial affairs, strategic decision-making and communications within the company, especially since Archard, having delegated these duties some time ago, quite properly stands aside from the daily traffic, other than in exceptional circumstances, such as substituting for the recently departed fiction editor.

In addition to Mick Felton there are two more full-time posts and three part-time, including Seren's poetry editor Amy Wack and one whose role is marketing, an aspect of the business that might be expected to command continuous attention. Although there are strong stable elements, there is some volatility among the staff, which is not necessarily a bad thing when it is energised by ambition. Nevertheless, it would not be surprising if, from time to time, one or other of the jobs that fall to the manager received less attention than it deserved.

As noted above, in order to qualify for renewal of its block grant, about ninety thousand pounds currently, Seren submits to annual evaluation of its operation, a reasonable expectation where public money is at stake. That it has passed this test more than twenty times might be considered adequate endorsement of the business, but it is not, on its own, a satisfactory measure of Seren's achievement. For that we need to look at the other books, those published. Cary Archard says PWP/Seren has produced 'about five hundred' books. Although a twenty-fifth anniversary might be thought the appropriate time to place on record precisely how many in the various literary genres, nothing better than an estimate is available.

The selected stocklist appended to the celebratory autumn 2005 catalogue of forthcoming titles musters 337 books (eliminating duplicated titles), arranged in thirteen categories. The smallest classes, with ten books or fewer, include children's literature, sport, current affairs, photography, and drama. This is not to dismiss them as of little interest; Seren's contribution to drama and current affairs in Wales is already notable. Three categories have between ten and twenty books: art, translations and 'general'. This is the zone containing some of my favourite Seren titles, Joan Abse's *Letters from Wales*, Minhinnick's wonderful collections of essays, *Badlands, Watching the Fireeater* and, just out, *To Babel and Back,* and Tony Curtis's two volumes of conversations with Welsh artists. Cary Archard expects the number of translations to increase, perhaps dramatically, a forecast not unrelated to the expertise in this field now concentrated on the board. Similar growth is expected of art books, an area to which, rather surprisingly, the press is clearly committed; Peter Lord's books for UWP notwithstanding, Seren is now the premier producer of art books in Wales.

There is a degree of overlap between books listed under 'biography and memoirs', which include those in the splendid, and by no means uncritical, Borderlines series, and 'criticism', where you can find both Roland Mathias's magisterial *A Ride Through the Wood* and two volumes of biographical reminiscences of Dylan Thomas. Together the two categories supply almost a fifth of the books published by the press. Despite 'Borderlines' and a few other books, the press's contribution to commentary on Welsh writing in English and lit. crit. in general is at best modest, although the standard of discourse needed is exemplified in M. Wynn Thomas's superb observations on *Outside the House of Baal,* in the Seren edition. Not so long ago it might have been argued that there were not many writers and academics capable of contributing cogently to the debate on Welsh writing in English, but that is no longer the case; the output of Professor Thomas's department at the University of Swansea alone has greatly increased the number of literary critics with the requisite specialist knowledge and skills. What is needed is a visionary commissioning editor.

Emyr Humphreys's masterpiece (with a further six of his novels) is, understandably, in the fiction list. Another fifth of the output of the press falls into this category, ranging from classics by Kate Roberts and Saunders Lewis (in translation), Caradoc Evans, Rhys Davies and Gwyn Thomas, to the freshest of fictions such as Lloyd Jones's *Mr Vogel,* Richard Collins's *The Land as Viewed from the Sea,* Dai Vaughan's *Totes Meer,* and *Love on the Borders* by Martin Bax, which have had a greater impact on the literary reviews than poetry books. At the close of 2005,

*The Shop,* Emyr Humphreys's latest novel, commanded a dozen column inches in the *Guardian* and there is more than an outside chance that a bestseller far exceeding Seren's usual standard of 3000 copies will soon emerge from the fiction list.

About a third of the books in the stocklist are collections of poems by forty-five individual writers, by far the largest of the thirteen categories. This underlines Archard's initial and continuing commitment to poetry above other genres. He is an avid reader of poetry, has long been a key member of the Eric Gregory Awards panel and has a vast library of poetry books. Early in the history of the press he corralled some of the most memorable voices of the 1960s and 1970s, John Ormond, Leslie Norris and John Tripp, with Glyn Jones, whose creative life spanned the first and the second 'flowering' of Welsh writing in English, and later, posthumously, one of the finest poets of the Second World War, Alun Lewis. He attracted two of the three joint winners of the 1974 Welsh Arts Council's 'Young Anglo-Welsh Poets' competition, Duncan Bush and Tony Curtis, drew Peter Finch from his own Second Aeon press, retrieved Ruth Bidgood from Gomer and took Jean Earle from Carcanet. He inherited John Powell Ward, John Davies and Robert Minhinnick from Christopher Davies, and kept them twenty years and more – until he lost Minhinnick to Carcanet. Christine Evans has brought out four collections with Seren, and Sheenagh Pugh eight. This is a fine, and by no means exhaustive, list of poets with established credentials, all Welsh by birth, residence or affinity. Equally impressive is the roster of those more recently recruited, such as Kathryn Gray, Pascale Petit, Fiona Sampson and Owen Sheers, who are earning or have already won dazzling reputations.

A great deal has been achieved in twenty-five years. Wales has been peculiarly fortunate that Cary Archard set out upon his publishing venture, for without him it is hard to see how else Welsh writing in English could have been encouraged and sustained. Certainly it would not be where it is today. There are aspects of the business that were not right at the start and are still unsatisfactory, notably poor discipline with paperwork extending to writers' contracts and the payment of royalties, and (in common with other publishers) the irksome but essential matter of copy-editing. He can, however, look back on a stream of mostly good-looking books (and not many literary duds) with considerable pleasure, and is rightly proud of those that won Welsh Arts Council prizes, have been short-listed for other UK prizes, or received recommendations from the Poetry Book Society. He deserves our gratitude and congratulations.

PWP/Seren was conceived as a publishing house for Welsh writing in English with a particular mission to find new poets; it still is principally, but it is no longer exclusively so. For more than half its life the press was content with modest ambitions, but natural growth and greater diversity in book production in the 1990s seem to have stimulated the notion that it could become commercially successful. Currently the block grant funds about twenty titles and a further half dozen are published out of sales income, but this could change. The press is at a critical juncture: should it go for growth (Carcanet, for example, which began about the same time, and with a similar outlook, has over 700 titles and a host of major writers in its selected stocklist)? Seren has already shown itself more effective in crossing borders than any other Welsh publisher and in consequence attracts submissions from all over the English-speaking world. The bigger the catchment, the better the chances are that writers of outstanding quality will direct their work to Bridgend. With decent marketing, sales income should increase, but the competition from other countries will make it tougher for new writers from Wales to get published. These are among the interesting issues facing

Cary Archard and his board as they contemplate the next twenty-five years.

*PN Review* 169, Volume 32 Number 5, May – June 2006.

# THE ARTS COUNCIL OF WALES AND KEIDRYCH RHYS'S WALES

*May 2005*

Thirty-odd years ago, I was for a time a member of the Literature Committee of the Welsh Arts Council. The committee lacked neither ideas nor energy, and Meic Stephens, the Literature Director, invariably had an initiative or two up his sleeve if we showed signs of flagging. Everything was done tidily and economically, or on the cheap, for there was never enough money to meet the realistic needs of writers, editors and publishers, far less fund anything outrageous. The proportion of the WAC grant allocated to literature was minuscule. There were always critics of the committee and its works, not least among them writers who felt they deserved recognition and hand-outs, and became furious when neither came their way. Nevertheless, it survived pretty well until the nineties, and then succumbed to cuts and wild anti-élitist notions, before the functions of the Arts Council were transformed by new responsibilities in relation to the national lottery.

Labour's manifesto for the 2003 National Assembly election promised to sweep away the quangos that, for good or ill, have had a good deal of influence on health, education and culture in Wales. In the tawdry media world of the political adviser and the soundbite this pledge became known as 'the bonfire of the quangos', though what may be the implications of echoing the title of a novel by Tom Wolfe is anyone's guess. The First Minister, Rhodri Morgan, let it be known that high on the list of bodies destined for the flames was the subtly renamed Arts Council of Wales. Arts organisations, including some that had complained bitterly about WAC/ACW policies over the years, leapt to its defence. Their most urgent concern was the abandonment of the 'arm's length' principle. If the work of ACW were brought within the National Assembly, one argued, what possible chance would there be of financial support for a play like David Hare's powerful, anti-Bush/Blair *Stuff Happens*? In the event, and late in the day, the First Minister discovered that the Assembly did not have the power to do away with ACW. He settled instead for reducing its remit and setting up a Culture Board that will devise a 'national culture strategy' and take over the funding of Welsh National Opera, the BBC National Orchestra of Wales, the dance company 'Diversions', Theatr Clwyd, the nearest thing we have to an English-language national company, Theatr Genedlaethol Cymru, the Welsh-language equivalent, and Academi, the literature promotion agency, which inherited much of the work formerly undertaken by the Literature Committee. In a statement to the *Western Mail,* Alun Pugh, the Minister for 'Culture, Sport and Languages of Wales', said he would have no more influence over grants to individual artists and performers than previously. It may turn out like that, but the record suggests otherwise. Labour politicians, perhaps all politicians, resent criticism, no matter how well founded, just as they are incapable of acknowledging error and apologising, and find meddling irresistible.

Politicians in Wales, and members of the establishment in general, are constantly looking over their shoulder for the reaction of the English. There is, indeed, a tendency among the Welsh (for which some blame that calumny we term 'The Blue Books'), once they have gained a little local responsibility, while they are usually bombastic at home, to fall victim to an atavistic urge to kowtow before supposed authority figures abroad, usually to our disadvantage. Most Welsh politicians, whatever independence of thought they manifest beforehand, once translated to Westminster desire nothing more than to be abject cogs in the party machine, and cannot imagine how Wales could survive deprived of the pernicious influence of Blair and his like. The Welsh Assembly Government, fearing that an entirely sensible scheme to restrict new housing in the Snowdonia and Pembrokeshire Coast National Parks to locals would be declared racist by thwarted incomers and the London media, have told the respective authorities that their 'unitary development plans', which contain these policies and are due to be implemented, must be replaced by 'local development plans'. While Exmoor, the Lake District and the Yorkshire Dales have already introduced precisely similar restrictions, Snowdonia and Pembrokeshire must begin the whole tortuous planning business again. The WAG minister responsible for this fiasco is reported to have said that if the authorities start now, they might complete the process in as little as two years. Even if they had not considered it before, wealthy would-be second-home owners, *faute de mieux,* will now target Wales. The 'clear red water' between Westminster and Cardiff Bay is illusory. Rhodri Morgan does what he is told and is desperate not to upset the New Labour bandwagon as it rolls on to the election.

Happily, a few eccentrics dispute the superiority accorded to all things English, even suggesting that the language fares better as spoken and written by people from other parts. One such was William Ronald Rees Jones, born on Boxing Day 1915, the son of a tenant farmer who did his best with a hundred acres or so in the foothills of the Black Mountain, near Llanddeusant, Carmarthenshire. Stretching a point or two, he later liked to claim that his birthplace was the nearby village of Bethlehem and his arrival on this earth almost a Second Coming. The family spoke Welsh, as did all the natives of those parts at that time, and he acquired English largely through his education. After leaving the grammar school at Llandovery he seems to have been a bank employee. At least, there is a rumour that he lost a job in a bank because of an incident involving a shotgun. At the age of twenty, he decided he would be a journalist and took himself off to London, where he soon became thoroughly at home hobnobbing with writers and artists in the public houses and drinking clubs of Fitzrovia.

A year later he turned up on the doorstep of Glyn Jones's home in Cardiff, smartly attired in tweeds and speaking Welsh with a public school accent. He had also acquired a new name: henceforth he would be known as Keidrych Rhys. Glyn Jones and Dylan Thomas had already discussed the notion of founding a magazine to serve the talented writers then emerging from Wales. The same idea had occurred to Keidrych and he was keen to involve them and press ahead with it. And that is what happened: the first number of *Wales* came out in the summer of 1937. Among the contributors were Glyn Jones (who also read proofs) and Dylan Thomas, and its modernist agenda was apparent from page one where, in 'Prologue to an Adventure', Thomas lifts the veil on a drunken night out in London to disclose a surrealist nightmare. Identification of the editor, delivered in parentheses, '(Keidrych Rhys)', is delayed to the last page, where he invites subscriptions with an extraordinary rant: 'British culture is a fact, but the English contribution to it is very small. McDiarmid told the Scots that they could gain nothing by joining forces with the English and aping their mannerisms...The greatest present-day poets are Kelts. We publish this journal in English so that it may spread far beyond the frontiers of Wales, and because we realise the beauty of the English language better than the English themselves, who have so shamelessly misused it.'

If the belligerent invitation, which was not repeated in subsequent numbers, gave offence, Keidrych would have been the better pleased, for he liked nothing more than a quarrel. In the event, *Wales* was well received, and not only by the Welsh. A review of the second number in Eliot's *Criterion* described it as 'pulsating with good young, red blood' and 'distinguished by poems and criticism that could stand on their own two legs anywhere'. The magazine had arrived just in time to harvest the 'first flowering' of Welsh writing in English and, while Dylan Thomas was the star, the names of several other regular contributors still resonate: Glyn Jones, Caradoc Evans, Emyr Humphreys, Idris Davies, Vernon Watkins, Rhys Davies, George Ewart Evans, and Lynette Roberts (a highly talented modernist poet from Argentina, who became Keidrych's first wife). Although a critical success, it is likely that *Wales* was in financial difficulties throughout its initial run of eleven numbers, 1937-9. The war finished it off. Nevertheless, it has remained a significant feature in the landscape of Welsh writing in English.

Keidrych joined the army and stayed in uniform long enough to edit two volumes of *Poems from the Forces,* before obtaining an early discharge. More or less free again, in 1943 he began the second series of *Wales,* which recruited fresh talents, including Alun Lewis, John Cowper Powys, R.S. Thomas, Robert Graves and Roland Mathias, but folded in 1947. Another series, published in London by his own Druid Press, began in 1958. It boasted, among others, David Jones, the young Harri Webb, Leslie Norris, Raymond Garlick and Alun Richards, and the even younger Meic Stephens. The editorial of the September 1958 number begins, 'We start *Wales* without a subsidy. No private patron or funds from a transatlantic foundation are behind us.' It was, as ever, run on a shoestring and went down for the third and last time in 1960.

Keidrych fancied himself a poet, a point on which he and Dylan Thomas disagreed, and had a pamphlet entitled *The Van Pool and Other Poems* published by Routledge in 1942. In

1945, in the same Druid Press notice that advertised R.S. Thomas's first book, *The Stones of the Field,* he announced that 25 new poems of his own were to appear in a collection called *Storm and Landscape.* No one has ever seen it. The National Library of Wales has a reference to a third title under his name, but declares that too 'a ghost book'. Perhaps he tired of the ambition and resigned himself to being a competent journalist. In this guise he was for some time the combative Welsh correspondent of the *Sunday People.*

Keidrych Rhys revelled in controversy, was a gossip and a stirrer. In later life, he became a seller of 'rare and antiquarian' books in Hampstead. A Johnsonian figure, to the end he affected sartorial elegance and a manner to go with it ('Dear boy' was his usual mode of address to Meic Stephens). And you cannot help admiring the man for his patriotism and his persistence: in that interrupted sequence extending over 23 years, always against the odds, he held to his editorial principles and provided a showcase and sallyport for Welsh writing talent.

Happily, a number of contributors to *Wales* survive, notably Emyr Humphreys, Roland Mathias and Leslie Norris, who are in their eighties, Raymond Garlick, who is almost there, and Meic Stephens, now Professor Emeritus at the University of Glamorgan, who still waves the banner of (relative) youth. Ruth Bidgood, another poet past the eightieth year, is not a member of this club. Preoccupied with service in the WRNS during the war, and then work for *Chambers Encyclopaedia,* she only began writing when she returned to Wales in the 1960s and settled at Abergwesyn, deep in the green heart of south Powys. She established herself almost at once as a poet of the raw material of rural life, which, as a formidable and meticulous local historian, she perceives with all its ballast of recorded and remembered tradition. Evidence of the past in documents and, strikingly, in the ruins of ancient dwellings, frequently finds its way into her poems, along with the constant awareness the country dweller in that part of Wales must have of forest and moor. Her poems are not technically ambitious, but have a characteristic quiet, cultured voice well matched to thoughtful observation of nature and man or the evidence of man's former presence. Change and mortality are the inevitable concomitants of her studious and engrossed sense of history. Ruth Bidgood's first book of poems, *The Given Time,* was published in 1972; her ninth, *New & Selected Poems* (Seren, 2004), is testimony to her poetic productivity and the consistent quality of her writing. Some of her most recent work is, indeed, as profound and moving as any previous, as for example, 'Yard in Winter', and, especially, 'Thirteenth Gate', which begins with country lore: 'There were thirteen gates here once/in five miles; only the last is left./"Why is thirteen unlucky?" – "It's not./Thirteen is twelve, and one to make the meaning."' And ends:

How to sum a journey, how value it,
till it ends? Something
is completed here, defined,
at the end of the gated road.
                    Ahead
A small wind flicks the hill grass, the way
opens towards far summits.
Twelve gates are passed. Now one,
one will make the meaning

*PN Review* 163, Volume 31 Number 5,
May – June 2005.

# THE RHYS DAVIES TRUST, RON BERRY AND ALUN RICHARDS

*September 2004*

The Rhys Davies Trust, which I have mentioned previously, was set up in 1990. It owes its existence to an extraordinarily generous donation from Lewis Davies, the writer's brother. Lewis, a former librarian and now of advanced years, is a delightful man. In making his gift he sought no celebrity for himself, only that the memory of Rhys should be kept green. Thanks to the work of the trust, that aim is being achieved. At least, anyone with an interest in Welsh literature in English is constantly reminded of Rhys Davies and knows him as a successful novelist and short story writer, particularly of the 1930s and 1940s, who, unusually among our contemporaries, lived by his pen. His publications, listed in John Harris's invaluable *Bibliographical Guide to Twenty-Four Modern Anglo-Welsh Writers* (UWP, 1994) runs to eight pages. Almost from the outset, and commencing with Rhys Davies himself, the trust has instigated and substantially funded the raising of elegantly lettered slate plaques to commemorate the life and work of a number of writers. John Tripp's plaque is located inside the library at Whitchurch, Cardiff, which he frequented to write and research, but most find a place on the façade of the birthplace (if it still exists) or former home of the writer.

Unveiling the plaque is attended by some modest ceremony. One such occasion took me recently to a street in Blaencwm, at the top of the Rhondda Fawr. Such was the fame of the Rhondda as a coal-producing region that far beyond our borders people still know the name. Even my spell-checker, which takes exception to almost everything Welsh, recognises it. Most, however (like the spell-checker), do not know there are two valleys, the Rhondda Fach and the Rhondda Fawr, the Little Rhondda and the Big, which run almost parallel until they join at the township of Porth. In both valleys, road and railway are crammed in the bottom of the trench following the river back to its source. There, also, is where the mines once were, but not any more. No acrid smoke, no pall of coal dust now to smirch washing hanging hopefully on lines in the terraces, rank upon rank, a heavy horizontal shading all along the lower slopes of the valley. Beyond the house line the mountain rises steeply to a crest, which can appear claustrophobically close to those accustomed to broader horizons.

If you travel, as I did, via the A4119, you pass imperceptibly along a chain of former mining towns or villages, the litany of Rhondda – Williamstown, Penygraig, Tonypandy, Llwynypia, Gelli, Ton Pentre, Pentre, Treorci, Ynyswen, Pen-yr-englyn and Treherbert, where you branch left. Blaencwm, a tiny community barely a mile off the main road, has a few short terraced streets that rise quite gradually and terminate abruptly at the mountain. It is a dead end like my old home, Gilfach Goch. Buses come there, turn with some difficulty at the top of the road and go back again. If you retrace your steps to Treherbert and follow the main road, such as it is, another thirty miles will bring you to Brecon.

The mountains are much as they always were, but down in the valley changes have occurred. Without the pits and the slag heaps, it's certainly much greener and, though goodness knows there are black spots still, most of the homes look – tidy. Readers unfamiliar with the English of the Valleys should realise that 'tidy' carries a burden of meaning somewhat weightier than it does in England, and possibly elsewhere in Wales. Of course, as with all colloquialisms, much depends on inflexion and the presence or absence of irony, but basically it is an example of ubiquitous meiosis. Thus, while a well-polished front room can be 'tidy' in the usual sense of the word, so can a pretty woman, a respected, well-liked individual or family, a pint of beer, a vigorous game of rugby, or almost anything that meets with the speaker's approval. Anyway, many of the old terraced homes in the Rhondda have had bathrooms fitted and a lick of paint to window frames and front doors and deserve the all-purpose epithet. The streets of Blaencwm are no exception.

The unveiling was at 4 Michael's Road, where Ron Berry (1920-97), the novelist and short story writer, kicked off his literary career. He had several other callings. The son of a miner, at fourteen he went from school to the pit and slogged underground until the war intervened. After undistinguished military service in both the army and the merchant navy, he was a pro soccer player with Swansea Town for a time, and then a boxer, a carpenter, a farm labourer, a steel worker. He worked on building sites in London and was assistant manager at the swimming baths in Treherbert. He was frequently unemployed and short of money. Few if any could match his credentials as a working class writer. When he started writing in the early 1950s his subject was the decline of the mining communities of the Rhondda and his style an edgy, raw demotic. Neither changed in the years that followed. Five of his six novels found London publishers – Hutchinson, W.H. Allen, Macmillan – but failed to attract critical attention. When he found he could no longer place his novels, he turned to short stories, journalism and scripts for radio and television. He bore a grudge against the generality of critics and academics, who, he thought, viewed him and his writing askance, from the safe distance of comfortable lives. This is rather hard on Professor Dai Smith, eminent Welsh historian and now Vice-Chancellor at the University of Glamorgan, a notably staunch supporter, and John Pikoulis, whose article on

Ron Berry in the *New Welsh Review* (No. 34, 1996) is a model of perception and balance.

The size and character of the audience for the unveiling of plaques naturally varies. That commemorating Raymond Williams, author of *Culture and Society*, the splendid novel *Border Country* and so much else, at his birthplace in rural Pandy, near Abergavenny, attracted a small, if select, gathering. On 8 May, a chilly day with rain threatening, the whole of Blaencwm turned out to see Ron Berry's plaque for the first time and there was a fair sprinkling of visitors. The street was packed. Afterwards, there was a cheerful scrum at the community centre, where the buffet and drinks were free. It was tidy. You felt Ron would have enjoyed it.

The speakers at the ceremony were Dai Smith, who has an enviable talent for finding the right, forceful words for any occasion, and Alun Richards. The latter, novelist, short story and TV script writer (much of the once famed 'Onedin Line' was scripted by him), whose work also displays an instinct for the nuances of Valleys life in the post-industrial era, but is far more blessed with humour, spoke of the contradictions in Ron Berry's character. He was 'fun, good company...kept youthful by an alert mind', but again 'awkward', 'an earthy realist with contempt for received ideas' and afflicted by 'a deep-seated pessimism'. It was a bold summing up in the heart of the man's community, and not a soul demurred.

And now, within a month of that chilly, blustery morning at the top of the Rhondda, we learn that Alun Richards has died suddenly at his home in Swansea. He was seventy-three. Alun Richards was a tall, burly man, but it was not his size that made him stand out in a crowd. He was that bit larger than life. The most cheerful of companions, he laughed readily and was a wonderfully humorous raconteur. His story of the Polish pilot invited to address the sixth form at Pontypridd Grammar School during the war years, who graphically described how he had been attacked by 'a fokker' and rejected the headmaster's hurried explanation that the German aircraft bore its manufacturer's name, Focke, by saying, 'No. This fokker was a Messerschmitt', was almost certainly apocryphal, but had the desired effect. This is not to say he took life lightly. He grew up with a strong sense of identity with the proletariat, which meant, for a Pontypridd boy, the English-speaking working class of industrial south Wales, and few who spend two years of their young manhood in a remote TB sanatorium emerge unclear about the value of existence. The view of contemporary society in Wales that you find in his short stories particularly is always acutely informed and untainted by sentiment.

After training to be a teacher, he spent three years in the Royal Navy (during the period of National Service) and then became a probation officer in London, before TB struck. Fit again, he taught in schools in Cardiff for a decade while beginning to make his mark in literature. In 1967 he quit teaching to become a full-time writer. While the BBC and ITV and the Arts Council in England commissioned him, published his books and produced his plays, he continued to live in Wales. There is a good deal more to the Alun Richards story, not least his friendship with Carwyn James, the possessor of that most incisive and lyrical rugby mind, but if you would like to sample the experience of being in Alun Richards' company for a while, you could do worse than read the series of freewheeling autobiographical yarns he published recently in *Planet* (Nos. 162, 163, 164), which describe bizarre encounters with Kenneth Tynan, Peter O'Toole, Katherine Ross and sundry Hollywood moguls.

The Rhys Davies Trust is not the only independent body supporting Welsh writing in English. There is an annual Harri Webb Prize competition, usually for satiric verse but on this six-hundredth anniversary of the establishment of the first and (*pace* the Assembly), only Welsh parliament, in Machynlleth, for a poem on Owain Glyndŵr; and the John Tripp Prize for spoken verse. Another has just been added. Roland Mathias, now in his eighty-eighth year, has generously donated a sum of money that will fund a biennial award for a published work in one or other of the areas in which he achieved distinction as a writer: poetry, the short story, literary criticism, history. The award, to be known as the Roland Mathias Prize, is open to works written in English and relevant to Wales and Welsh culture, by authors who are Welsh born or currently resident in Wales. The £2000 inaugural prize, for a book published in the calendar year 2004, will be awarded in March 2005. Publishers are invited to submit volumes for consideration as soon as possible, but no later than 21 December 2004. It will be interesting to see what advertisement of the prize draws in, and whether it will attract writers and publishers based outside Wales.

*PN Review* 159, Volume 31 Number 1,
September – October 2004.

# REVIEWING

*January 2003*

Not so long ago (*PN Review* 144), in welcoming the return of Jeremy Hooker to Wales, I mentioned how, in the 1960s, he had taken local literary critics to task for failing to supply the 'astringency' writers needed to see their own work clearly. Roland Mathias, then editor of the *Anglo-Welsh Review*, was another convinced of the importance of reviewing to raising standards in literature. In his contribution to a *Poetry Wales* forum on 'Criticism in Wales' in 1979, he set out basic requirements: 'A reviewer has to begin somewhere of course, but he ought not to do so until he is a relatively experienced reader in the Anglo-Welsh field. And having begun, he should apply himself. Read every book, every word. Compare it, if that's possible, with what the poet has written before.' If this appeared to hard-pressed reviewers a doctrine of perfection, they could at least satisfy themselves that Mathias practised what he preached. He is not only acutely intelligent and perceptive, but has always been enormously painstaking in his assessment of the writing of others.

Another, related, concern that Mathias often expressed in the editorial pages of the *Anglo-Welsh Review*, and still does in conversation, is the unaccountable resistance of London-based newspapers and journals to anything published in Wales. The strange case of his third book of poems, *The Roses of Tretower* (1952), is a demonstration of this peculiar blindness on the part of literary editors and consequent loss to the reading public. As published by Dock Leaves Press in Pembroke Dock, where Mathias was headmaster of the local grammar school, it was virtually ignored outside Wales – the standard response. In 1960, by which time his career in education had taken him to Derbyshire, he brought out *The Flooded Valley,* with the London publishers Putnam. As though to prove the point, this was widely, and favourably, reviewed by the metropolitan press. Putnam, who thought it his first book, probably failed to appreciate the irony that twenty-three of the thirty-one poems had appeared in *The Roses of Tretower*. In a letter he wrote to *Poetry Wales* in 1974, during the period of my editorship, Mathias provided another kind of proof of the acceptability of books written and published in Wales once their presence had been registered in a London broadsheet: 'When Maurice Wiggin gave James Williams's *Give Me Yesterday* a fourteen-inch column review in *The Sunday Times* in 1972 – a piece of accidental good fortune not to be repeated – it was a shock of some magnitude, and one that immediately sold 12,000 copies for a Welsh publisher. Now if *Give Me Yesterday* had been a book of distinction...one might have accepted the natural hierarchy involved and whispered to oneself that only the best books published in Wales could possibly hope to "make it" in London. But it was not distinguished: its place in the Welsh league table would not have been much above half way.'

All this was a long time ago, why bring it up again now? Surely attitudes have changed. Everyone agrees that writers too should enjoy the level playing field that our hardy sportsmen claim as their right. Alas, not so. In his editorial in *PN Review* 147, Michael Schmidt considered the closed shop that operates in the awarding of poetry prizes, and appeared rather more understanding of it than 'Bookworm' in *Private Eye*. But from the Welsh perspective, whatever power exists in the making of readerships continues to exclude us. In a conversation recently on the same topic, M. Wynn Thomas was especially critical of the *Times Literary Supplement*, which rarely stirs itself even to notice books from Wales. Some time ago the Welsh publishers clubbed together to send a representative to London to take sundry literary editors to lunch. Those invited were happy to accept the lunch but obdurate in their resistance to things Welsh. One, perhaps having consumed more hospitality than was prudent, cheerfully admitted that review copies bearing a Welsh postmark are consigned unopened to the bin. Meic Stephens told me that it used to be claimed that the London papers do not review books from Wales because Welsh publishers do not advertise in London papers. Welsh publishers, of course, say it's the other way around: if the books were reviewed, they would advertise. Here may be a mission worthy of the Arts Council of Wales: let it foot the advertising bill for a few months, test the theory and, who knows, break this cycle of negativity.

Whether ACW is any longer capable of action of this kind off its own bat is now open to doubt. It has survived the scrutiny of the National Assembly and, according to its chief executive, Peter Tyndall, has made substantial progress in recovering public confidence. A twenty-three per cent increase in the grant it receives from the Assembly and the greater generosity it therefore extends to clients largely accounts for that. But as part of the package it has also accepted restructuring, the most significant aspect of which is decentralisation or, if you prefer, devolution. A consultation paper on the funding of literature proposes that the Academi, the national writers' organisation and promotional agency (which runs literary courses, conferences, events and 'Writers on Tour') will assume responsibility for all writers' services and schemes, while the Welsh Books Council (which, as well as operating a book distribution centre, offers editing, design and marketing services to publishers) will take on all the grant aid responsibilities of the Arts Council in relation to the publication of books and magazines. What remains for ACW? A small share in the work of Tŷ Newydd, a writers' residential centre, the Hay Festival (though what it is to do there is unclear) and 'Welsh literature abroad in partnership with Wales Arts International': nothing of significance. Perhaps it is to be more actively involved in the other arts. Failing that, one wonders what the rump of staff at Museum Place in Cardiff is going to do with its long days. The answer may well be accountancy.

Accountants and their professional practices arouse more suspicion these days than they were wont to do. In the distant past, I briefly employed an accountant. It seemed to me that I did all the work towards the resolution of my miniscule tax problem, while he merely signed his name and took my cheque. Within a couple of years his small company had been swallowed up by a somewhat larger one, at which point the fees rocketed and we parted company. Soon after, the new group merged with another, and then another and so on, until it was recognisable worldwide by its initials. One such alphabetical conglomerate has been appointed receivers following the collapse of the Cardiff manufacturer Allied Steel and Wire, with the loss of eight hundred jobs. A sizeable proportion of the ASW workforce had served the company and contributed to its pension scheme for many years. They now find themselves unemployed and, thanks to the quirks of financial law and accountancy, robbed of their pensions. When affairs are wound up, the people who sweat at the furnaces and can least afford another knock are last in the list of creditors. The accountants, who will be handsomely paid, are hoping to sell the works to another manufacturer, but time is running out. It ran out in Ebbw Vale on Friday 5 July, when the last shift left the Corus works, bringing to an end a history of iron, steel and tinplate making that began in the eighteenth century. The borough of Blaenau Gwent, where Ebbw Vale is situated, has the highest unemployment rate in Wales.

729

We should, I suppose, be grateful that a use has been found for the other abandoned Corus plant, the vast Llanwern complex near Newport. Its water storage tanks will provide a perfect environment for the preservation of medieval ship timbers recovered from the ooze of the Usk estuary in the course of a building project. There is nothing to offset the forthcoming factory closures in west Wales. In 1998, Dewhirst, the clothing manufacturers who supply Marks and Spencer, had five factories here, all of them in rural or former industrial areas where jobs are hard to find. The last two, at Cardigan and Fishguard, will close before the end of November leaving behind only a sense of hopelessness. Dewhirst had no quarrel with its Welsh employees or the quality of the goods they produced; it is moving its operation to Morocco, where at one factory already open in Tangiers workers earn the equivalent of fifty pence an hour.

An observer capable of viewing these events without feeling or prejudice would still remark upon the speed of change. Wales, where the Industrial Revolution hit its stride, that once supplied iron, steel, tinplate and coal to the world, lost the remnants of its heavy industry and a hefty slice of its manufacturing within a decade. That is some kind of record.

Where does one look for light relief? Perhaps to the Office for National Statistics and the aftermath of the 2001 Census. Readers might recall the storm that raged over the absence of a tick box on the Census form wherein those so minded could indicate that they were Welsh. The ONS, which should have got it right in the first place and had ample opportunity to amend the form subsequently but did not, swore it would prosecute protestors who defaced or failed to complete the form. We now know the outcome of their analysis of returns. Sixty thousand people in Wales rejected the form and there will be two prosecutions (I quote the *Western Mail*): an elderly spinster from

North Cornelly, Bridgend, 'who claimed the bar code on the form was the mark of the Antichrist', and a man from Cardiff 'who was sick of bureaucracy and who sent his form back in four pieces and told statistics officials they could rot in hell'.

The media were preoccupied with the Welsh tick-box campaign and imminent steel closures at about the time those of us with literary inclinations were flocking to memorial celebrations of the life and work of R.S. Thomas. It was then we learned that Professor M. Wynn Thomas had been appointed the poet's literary executor with responsibility for the unpublished work. In the course of that conversation with him I mentioned above, he gave some indication of the large quantity of papers, widely scattered among the poet's effects, which remain to be sifted. In *Residues* (Bloodaxe) we have an initial selection of those poems 'perfectly sound in quality' that the poet enjoined him to present for publication. It is a mixture much as before (I am reminded of that self-deprecatory observation the poet himself made at a reading as he searched through a sheaf of poems for his next offering: 'I don't know – they're all the same'). Some raise echoes of that characteristic meditative voice that goes on and on, rising and falling in gentle cadence, the rhythm unvarying, the tone barely changing, as he reflects on man caught in the trap of time and God seemingly powerless to amend the imperfections of his creation, 'the failed garden/poisoned with an excess/of selfwill'. These are the thoughts of an old man, who is seeking to reconcile his pain with faith in a God who sees all but can do nothing about human suffering except acknowledge it with a 'wince'. There is even a weary despair in his art: 'Is age good for nothing/but with its arthritic breath/to dry up the dew/on the poem's petals' – although the poems often contradict him. The book also returns briefly to earlier preoccupations, the unravelling of Wales, and a vision of harsh lives and twisted bodies that is

Thomas's own brand of rural gothic – cold comfort unrelieved by humour. When they first appeared, poems of this kind invited parody and, from time to time, got it. There is a good deal more to wonder at and speculate upon – Thomas's unfailingly vivid response to the natural world, his writing about poetry and, most memorably, the tributes to his wife, the painter Mildred E. Eldridge. Strangely, perhaps, what lingers above all from a first reading of *Residues* is the poet's capacity for love.

*PN Review* 149, Volume 29 Number 3, January – February 2003.

# POETRY WALES
*September 2001*

The first week of April brings precious little sunshine. Yet more rain puddles the saturated lawn where moss and weeds, which seem not to mind it, have all but replaced the grass. Birds are gargling their morning songs and, so pervasive is the gloom, we breakfast still by lamplight. The news media are equally depressing. Once in a while the post lifts the spirits, as it did only yesterday with the arrival of the latest number of *Poetry Wales*.

The magazine has just started its thirty-sixth year. When Meic Stephens launched it in 1965, he declared (in the third number – the first to include an editorial): 'Our business is to publish the best available poems by young men and women who are writing now, in and about Wales.' Reviewers could be let loose on books by Theodore Roethke, James Turner, and George Mackay Brown and, later, the work of major writers from other countries in translation, such as Fernando Pessoa and George Seferis, but in that issue and consistently thereafter the poets were nearly all Welsh by birth or upbringing. Number 3 had only two exceptions: Robert Nye, an English writer who wrote about Welsh rural life from an address in mid-Wales, and Raymond Garlick who, although born in London, had long since declared his allegiance to Wales and had edited that other vitally important showcase of Welsh writing in English, *The Anglo-Welsh Review*, for eleven years.

As it got into its stride, *Poetry Wales* would begin with a lengthy, commissioned article, usually on an individual poet, the quarter's crop of poems would follow and then a fairly hefty section of reviews. The only variation from the norm, the 'special number' on an individual writer or theme, was also Meic Stephens's idea. The first, devoted to R.S. Thomas (spring 1972), sold well enough to impress the magazine's publisher. Soon after beginning my brief tenure of the editorial hot seat, I was invited (with Gwilym Rees Hughes, the Welsh-language editor) to sup at the grand Penarth home of the late (Sir) Alun Talfan Davies QC, who was the power behind Christopher Davies Ltd, at that time the most energetic publishing house in Wales – which, it has to be admitted, is not saying a great deal. The food and wine were persuasively excellent and it soon became clear that our host's generosity was not unrelated to his enthusiasm for special numbers. Why not two a year, or three? We argued the primary purpose of the magazine was to publish poems. Although a Dylan Thomas number and an Alun Lewis number appeared in the next two years, we were not invited again.

Later editors have tacitly endorsed the *raison d'être* of the magazine as expressed in 1966 and done little to change its essential shape and programme, until the recent arrival of Robert Minhinnick. He has overturned the old policy and opened *Poetry Wales* to the world in a way previously unthought of. The cover of the current issue bears the slogan 'young Welsh poets' but it is not a 'special', even in the manner of that 1973 'New Poets' number in which Minhinnick's own work first appeared. Alongside seventeen Welsh or Welsh-based poets are five from other countries: the USA, Scotland and England. Last summer, Volume 36 number 2 displayed sixteen poets from Canada alongside five Welsh. And, since the Canadians' writing tends to ease its shoulders and stretch its legs as it were in reflection of the vastness of their landscape, there was little room for the local product. Three 'Poets from the Netherlands'

734

were highlighted in the number before the Canadian issue, which also included five each from England and the USA and one from Scotland who, together, again outweighed the Welsh contribution. Volume 35, number 3 had contributors from Romania, Holland, Canada, Cuba, England and the USA.

These changes in the poetry content of the magazine have been accompanied by a new direction in the prose contributions. Editorials are often concerned with people and places overseas, usually in connection with the 'launch' of *Poetry Wales* in other countries. As his essays and, in recent years, his poetry have shown, Minhinnick is a great traveller and his travel writing of high quality. He still conjures up the sights and sounds of his home patch, Porthcawl and the south Wales coast, better than anyone, but his gift for the striking image and the shrewd, witty insight is increasingly employed in places overseas. Furthermore, we have witnessed in poems he has contributed to *PN Review* and other magazines a transformation of the controlled style that characterised his output at least as far as 1994 and *Hey Fatman* (though the title poem of that volume, exotically located in Rio, was perhaps a turning point), into looser forms and arrangements of images that occasionally appear freely associative.

Minhinnick abroad is a delight to the stay-at-home mind but something more is going on. Welsh readers of the magazine are not merely being introduced to other cultures, they are being taught to accept a new poetic. More controversially, they are being encouraged to reject the older one associated with the 'second flowering', that burgeoning of poetic talent in the 1960s when poets like John Tripp and Harri Webb appeared regularly in *Poetry Wales*. The editorial in the latest issue hasn't a good word to say for either, on the grounds that their poetry was 'too frequently...a reaction to perceived cultural slights and economic indignities'. The argument continues: 'Our poets

strove to show they were in touch with 'communities'. The price
they paid was imaginative block, the absence of the unexpected
in their work. And they were lesser writers because of it.' I don't
believe that either Tripp or Webb had a sociological cell in their
skulls. To say that Tripp, after a drink or two, was notoriously
anti-social I know is not quite the same thing but nevertheless
true. They carried their own inner wounds and prejudices into
their writing, could not have changed their polemical stance if
they tried and could not be blamed for enjoying the popularity
that falls to those whose writing catches the mood of the times.
A good deal of their output was of indifferent quality (few poets
could escape similar censure) but their lapses had little to do
with nationalism or a sense of grievance at social injustice. They
were failures of poetic art and language; as Minhinnick himself
concedes later in the same piece: 'it is not what [poets] say but
their mastery of saying it that counts.'

The 'second flowering' had more to offer than Webb and
Tripp. It saw the re-emergence of poets like John Ormond and
Leslie Norris, confirmation of the talents of Roland Mathias,
Dannie Abse, Vernon Watkins, Raymond Garlick and Anthony
Conran, the best of Bryn Griffiths, Robert Morgan and Alun
Rees, all of whom were represented in the first four numbers of
*PW*. The new project does not need to ignore the weaknesses of
this heritage, or deny its strengths, in order to justify its fresh
outlook. In any event, the battle has long been won. Forty years
of accelerating change have seen off the dinosaurs, for good and
all in many cases, though eruptions of nationalist spleen and
social conscience shake the scenery from time to time, the usual
suspects being Nigel Jenkins and his (unrelated) namesake Mike.

Minhinnick's liking for outlandish flavours is reflected in the
magazine's prose as well as its poetry. Among his regular
contributors are Landeg White, a Welshman who lives in
Portugal, and Pascale Petit who grew up in France and Wales

and is poetry editor of *Poetry London*. He has also recruited a literary essayist. Lyndon Davies initially appeared as a correspondent congratulating the editor on his novel stance:

I think you're dead right – we need a poetry of risk, to counter the lumbering politics of identity we're burdened with in Wales...As a marginal nation we've tended to cling to those symbols which appear to give us individual, as opposed to merely marginal, substantiality, and, in the language of our literary products, to the old subject/object relationship inherent in the demands of social struggle. This is all very well, but surely there has to be room too for the exploration of different kinds of grammar, for looking beyond the object obsessed notions of a Heaney or a Wilbur, for the creation of a genuine literature of the imagination, where everything is up for grabs and the old spiritual clamps are tossed aside.

I can't claim to understand all that but clearly it represents a literary philosophy close to Minhinnick's.

If tossing aside 'the old spiritual clamps' is equivalent to 'letting it all hang out', albeit only imaginatively, then I am unsympathetic, being temperamentally inclined to impatience with writing that is sprawling, mystical or fantastical, and suspicious of most things mythical and anything astrological. Nothing of that sort has so far found its way into the magazine, though there has been an increase in poetical risk-taking. Meanwhile, readers are being treated to a rousing knock-about debate in which Alun Rees, the poet-journalist, has done a good deal of the knocking – and we are all probably the better for it. In any event, be assured *PW* is now open house: subscribe and join the widening band of readers and contributors across the continents.

To the surprise of many, the refurbished Victorian guildhall in Swansea continues to function as Ty Llên, the 'House of

Literature'. A little while ago the Academi held one of its regular members' lunches there, in the tall-windowed, echoing dining room. The final course was, as usual, literary entertainment. Stan Barstow drew comparisons between lifestyles in the Yorkshire mining village where he was born and Pontardawe, the small township in the Swansea Valley where he now lives, and Gwyneth Lewis read from her own translation of *Y Llofrudd Iaith* ('The Language Murderer'), a poetic sequence or, arguably, an episodic novel in verse published by Barddas in 1999. As we are coming to expect of Gwyneth Lewis, the latter is remarkable both as a concept (a narrative of the death of the Welsh language told in the form of a detective story) and as a display of imagery and linguistic invention. The subject evokes strong feelings: one of the book's spectacular achievements is that its constantly surprising verbal ingenuity does not compromise the emotional content. It has received widespread critical acclaim.

Judging from the extracts we heard in Swansea, the English version of *Y Llofrudd Iaith* is well advanced. Perhaps it will be completed some place where the sun is shining, for this poet, too, is a traveller. She has given up her job at the BBC and (with the aid of a £75,000 grant from the National Endowment for Science, Technology and the Arts) is shortly to set out with her husband on a five-year voyage round the world in a thirty-five foot yacht. I recall the splendid return for the £500 invested in her Hungary project by the Rhys Davies Trust some years ago and know it will be money well spent. She will be posting progress on the internet: if there is one thing that will encourage me to become familiar with the new technology, this is it.

*PN Review* 141, Volume 28 Number 1,
September – October 2001.

# ACADEMI AND THE ARTS COUNCIL OF WALES

*January 2001*

You might just possibly have wondered what has become of Yr Academi Gymreig, the Welsh academy of writers, in its new role as literature promotion agency for the whole of Wales (*PN Review* 120 and 122). It is getting along quite nicely. The Welsh and English language sections co-operate well, a great many events have been promoted in partnership with local bodies in all parts of Wales (over 2500 in the two years or so since the agency was set up, with an aggregate attendance of almost a quarter of a million), and Academi members have had unprecedented opportunities to meet convivially (at their own expense of course) at dinners in places like Cardiff Bay and Portmeirion. This perception of something resembling progress in the right direction was confirmed by a complimentary first evaluation of the agency from the Arts Council of Wales. It declared the administration effective and praised various aspects of the work, including *A470,* the bi-monthly magazine that advertises literary events, the continued success of the Writers on Tour scheme, and technological advances: the database of writers and performers and the Academi website.

The ACW has recently undergone its own evaluation. The outcome has been far less cheerful. It was only two years ago (also in *PN Review* 122) that I remarked the appointment of Joanna Weston as chief executive of the Arts Council of Wales in succession to Emyr Jenkins, famed father of exceptional daughters, one of whom, Ffion, may succeed Cherie Blair as hostess at 10 Downing Street sometime next spring. If a week is a long time in politics, two years must seem an eternity, but few could have anticipated that Ffion's star would so soon be observed in the ascendant. Since arts administration is not usually susceptible to waves of popular protest, fewer still would have expected Joanna Weston's to twinkle only briefly before burning out. Such, however, is the case. After a week of hesitation, during which certain critics wondered whether she would show the limpet-like adhesion to her post in the face of mounting criticism that we have grown to expect from Ministers, she resigned last Friday (22 September).

In that earlier 'Letter from Wales' 1 mentioned her particular pride in being instrumental in securing resources to support community and amateur arts organisations. It seemed reasonable to assume that this glow from Ms Weston's experience as director of the ACW's lottery division would colour her policy as chief executive, and it did. In August this year, fighting what was already a rearguard action, she reiterated the principles that underlay her management of the ACW. The arts, she said, had a role in regenerating deprived communities, the development of life-long learning and the shaping of new technologies. She went on to describe how the Arts Council in Wales had long been saddled with a 'narrow definition of the arts' by the ACGB, and how its new concept 'recognised the value not only of professional arts, but also of community arts, voluntary arts and arts in education, and aimed at equality of esteem in all spheres'. No explanation of 'equality of esteem' was offered, but as a policy statement it clearly implied that the funds the Council distributed, which had never adequately served the arts under the former narrow definition, were to be spread more widely under the new dispensation, or else hard choices made. Since the ACW did not receive the recent cash boost enjoyed by arts councils elsewhere in the UK, this was a recipe for widespread unhappiness. Within hours of her departure, subscribers to the old-fashioned elitist view in the debate about arts funding were imputing her downfall to the relative neglect under her regime of practising artists, musicians and writers, but while this may have been a contributory factor, it was not the main cause.

Ms Weston's goose was cooked by a decision to cease funding certain theatre-in-education (TIE) groups in order to create new companies better suited to the ACW's purposes. It did not take account of the local appeal of the long-established groups, which, for decades, have been recruiting supporters and honing their arguments against the threat of summary winding-up by hard-pressed local authorities, their main providers. The ACW, intent upon implementing its plans, did its best to ignore protests from all over Wales, but the voices did not die away and were soon augmented by Assembly members glad to have the opportunity to be seen actually doing something. In the end the Council was forced into an ignominious reversal of policy; the new TIE companies were stood down and the old, still complaining because they had lost preparation time, cranked-up again.

Just as this affair was sorting itself out, another crisis came to the boil. Looking back, the official opening of the Centre for Visual Arts in Cardiff by the now deposed First Secretary, Alun Michael, was not a good omen. The CVA is for the moment still housed in a rather grand and expensively remodelled building that had formerly served as Cardiff's central library. It has one splendid feature, an interactive gallery designed to educate school children in using their senses and the business of making, both central to the visual arts, and entertain them at the same time. It did not help, however, that the opening exhibition in the main galleries was of 'installations' and 'conceptual art' – the sort of stuff that may attract the sophisticated, or gullible, to the Royal Academy but is generally dismissed as rubbish by hoi polloi here. What was on show may not have been to the taste of prospective customers, but admission charges were too high even to allow them the satisfaction of going inside to criticise. Although there have been better things on display since, the CVA achieved nothing like the number of anticipated visitors and within months needed additional funding to keep its doors open. It was the Dome all over again, but without the safety nets that Tony Blair and the Millennium Commission were prepared to drag into place. Closure is scheduled for November and the blame has been placed squarely on the Arts Council for failing to secure its continued existence.

These and other aspects of management (including presumably the strategy in the distribution of Lottery funds that saw more 'channelled to grassroots projects...everything from carnivals to mobile animation units to youth theatre performance'), were subjected to the scrutiny of Richard Wallace, a former senior civil servant at the Welsh Office, commissioned to assess the ACW on behalf of the Assembly. His report, published at the beginning of September, was described as 'damning' by the *Western Mail*. The response of Assembly Members was predictably furious and, despite promises from the ACW that an 'action plan' would be produced in keeping with the report's recommendations, there was no turning aside of their wrath. Joanna Weston would have to go, and in the end she did. The Wallace Report recommends the establishment of four regional committees, each with its own funds, to replace central administration and funding of the arts from Cardiff. What effect this might have on all Wales bodies, such as the Academi agency, has not been considered. It could be catastrophic.

Reporting on the Arts Council's difficulties has been matched in terms of column inches by the controversy over a question in the form we shall all be required to complete for the 2001 National Census. As it stands, this will allow the Scottish to declare their national identity by ticking a box, but similar provision is not made for those who think of themselves as Welsh. The Office for National Statistics, responsible for devising the form, has said that anyone who feels that strongly about the issue can write 'Welsh' in the box labelled 'Other'. This is the kind of discrimination that comes as naturally as breathing to civil servants trained within the sound of Big Ben. Unfortunately, once they have committed themselves and Ministers (in this case the Home Office) to a course of action, no matter how plainly absurd it is, they cannot be seen to change their mind and apologise. Loss of face is a more serious matter to civil servants than it has ever been to the Japanese. Protest, from local authorities in Wales, political parties, institutions and public bodies, petitions (ten thousand signed up at this year's National Eisteddfod), and letters and emails from hundreds of individuals, have so far failed to move the mandarins. A plea for a distinctive Welsh identification to be added to the European symbol on the registration plates of vehicles from Wales has been turned down for the same empty reason.

It is all a question of attitudes. Why should people in Wales take offence at these vagaries of Anglo-centric government and officialdom? They are after all small matters compared with some of the errors that politicians, their advisers and highly paid consultants are capable of – such as the Dome. Why should I feel intense irritation at Jeremy Paxman's continuing inability to pronounce 'Dafydd', or Robert Robinson amusing himself on radio by pretending that he cannot say 'Gwladys', and even more at his patronising attempt to deflect Welsh listeners from reaching for their pens by dismissing it as a joke? Would either of them have any difficulty with Lech Walesa, for example? Why should I be surprised that the death of R.S. Thomas, announced virtually as I write, was not considered an item worth including in any of the broadcast media from London? (Though it has to be said that the serious newspapers and certain broadcasters made up for the oversight within the next few days.)

It is well known that RS had not a good word to say for the English. He had none for the great majority of the Welsh either, but he thought the English had raped the land of Wales, destroyed its most precious heritage, the language, and rotted the souls of its people. He wrote his poetry in English because, he said, he was more or less forced to: it was his mother tongue. He would have much preferred to write in Welsh, a language he learned in his thirties. He spoke and wrote prose in Welsh fluently, not to say elegantly, but it is difficult to imagine all those hundreds of poems, their contemplation of man and nature and God, their earnest questionings, their distinctive cadences, in any language other than English. Harder still to believe that, had they been written in Welsh, even with the benefit of inspired translation, he would have had the measure of fame that came his way as an English-language poet. For him, that would have been the least consideration; he would not have been the slightest perturbed if his audience had been confined to that stone church wet with the spray of waves breaking on the shore at Aberdaron. The number of listeners or readers would not have affected his sense of calling (for he maintained that poets are born not made), or reduced his prolific output of poems, or improved his famously off-hand manner in public. He was shy, often awkward, curmudgeonly even, and probably most of the time simply preoccupied with his own thoughts and the words he needed to express them. In spite of himself, he became an iconic figure. With the deepening of the lines that etched his face, the seamed brow, the long downward curves of his mouth, came the steady accumulation of great drifts of poems. 'I don't know,' he once said, 'they're all the same.' But they were not, other than in their spare and sinewy power, and their capacity to make us think. His loss is keenly felt all over Wales and, I dare say, far more widely.

*PN Review* 137, Volume 27 Number 3,
January – February 2001.

# THE ARTS COUNCIL OF WALES

*May 1999*

A recent report published jointly by the Arts Council for Wales, the Welsh Development Agency and S4C (the Welsh-language television channel), claims that 28,600 people are employed in the various branches of the arts here, 16,000 of them full-time. The annual turnover from arts activities is said to be £1.1 billion. Served up plain, this takes some swallowing. Using the conventional formula, it should mean something like 486,000 work in the arts in England, producing a turnover approaching £18 billion. How close to the mark is that, I wonder? It helps to define what is meant by 'the arts' in this context. The report says the media in Wales contribute the largest part of the impressive total with a gross turnover of over £346 million; the visual arts and design come in at £213 million, and the performing arts at about £101 million. The contribution of literature, or at least of writers and writing as distinct from publishing and related business, and from journalism, if it registers in cash terms at all, will surely be expressed as a negative number. Only a handful of writers in Wales live by the pen, and far from lavishly. The rest subsidise their art out of their workaday wages. The Arts Council, ever stingy in its handouts to literature, nevertheless underwrites book production on a large scale. In a recent *Western Mail* article, Meic Stephens (who knows more of both arts and bureaucracy and making a living from writing than anyone else I can call to mind) suggests that without the investment of public funds there would be virtually no publishing industry in Wales and, therefore, hardly any new books in Welsh. Book production in English would be little, if at all, better. Stephens lays a large part of the blame on the publishers, who, between them, bring out several hundred titles a year (many of them admittedly insubstantial texts) in Welsh and in English. They have been so long feather-bedded, he says, that they are incapable of rousing themselves to sell even those books for which a market demonstrably exists.

The example Stephens provides of a marketable book, the *Collected Poems of Harri Webb*, which he edited, has sold fewer than five hundred copies, despite the appeal generated by the poet's association with a television series, 'Poems and Pints'. Poetry readings used to be quite the thing. Twenty or so years ago, Harri Webb was not alone in having a considerable following at such events. Now, if my sampling was not hopelessly skewed, they seem at best but indifferently supported. This does not reflect the effort that is being put into reviving them. Since taking over the editorship, Robert Minhinnick has been actively promoting *Poetry Wales*, by organising a 'launch' in the USA, and by readings to raise the profile of the magazine's new writers. I missed New York but made Cardiff for the latter, an occasion on which the performers and their close supporters clearly outnumbered the general. One could churlishly wish that the poets and their audience had turned up for the scheduled start, and that the organisation had included attention to details such as the oiling of door hinges, but as a showcase for the rising stars of the magazine, the evening served its purpose well enough and may have sold the odd subscription. The much-travelled Kerry-Lee Powell, in an accent still a good way west of mid-Atlantic despite a decade in Cefn Cribwr, induced a stillness among those assembled with poems of Plath-like intensity, the most striking of which borrowed its diction from the combat fiction she has been engaged in editing. Samantha Wynne-Rhydderch, better known to *Poetry Wales* readers, read quite elaborately textured poems that demanded more in the way of preliminary explanation and cerebral response. One lingering impression of the evening is the preponderance of women among the new poets; another, the increasing part played by creative writing courses in producing, or refining the talents of, new writers. The world has turned since Gwyn Jones, who included five women among the ninety-four poets in his *Oxford Book of Welsh Verse in English* (1977), told me, 'You don't have to study English to be a writer.' This when I asked if I could join his honours class at Aberystwyth and offered my aspiration to become a writer as explanation of the importunity. He was, as usual, right, but creative writing courses were unheard of in the fifties and English was the next best thing. I suspect he would give a similarly dusty response to would-be writers today – and he would still be right. Nevertheless, graduates of the creative writing course run by Norman Schwenk (no mean practitioner himself) at University of Wales, Cardiff were prominent among Robert Minhinnick's new poets, and among the winners of this year's Rhys Davies Trust/Academi short story competition.

With Peter Finch at the wheel and supplying a good deal of the motive power, Yr Academi Gymreig, or the Academi, is getting under way. The first number has appeared of a bi-monthly information magazine, *A470 – What's On in Literary Wales*. Those familiar with Welsh road maps will recognise in 'A470' the route more or less up the spine of the country from Cardiff to the north Wales coast. Given the most favourable traffic and weather conditions, expect a drive of four-and-a-half hours; in other circumstances you might be better advised to stay at home. As a metaphor for joining north and south (and points between), the interests of two languages and cultures, writers and their audience, it is serviceable, especially if you perceive in it that element of difficulty the journey certainly involves. Among the events listed in the magazine was the second poetry reading I attended – 'Young Again' an evening with Duncan Bush, Tony Curtis and Nigel Jenkins, joint winners of the 1973-4 'Young Anglo-Welsh Poets Competition' twenty-five years on. I have written about them fairly recently (in *PN Review* 123), but cannot resisting adding a postscript.

The reading was held at the miners' institute in Blackwood, a Gwent valleys town, which (for me) is distinguishable from neighbouring townships only by being the birthplace of Gwyn Jones. Others might think it remarkable for its close proximity to Oakdale, where, at the local comprehensive school, the Manic Street Preachers got to know one another. On an evening early in December, the place held little evidence of residual culture of any kind. Robert Minhinnick, again in charge and liberally dosing himself with green fluid carrying warnings against overuse, croaked the story of the competition and the subsequent successes of the poets. All fifteen in the audience knew it well. Minhinnick has written explosively of the philistinism of south Wales, but it was not an occasion to speak of that, not to people who, after all, *were* present. And the poets were good value, each reading a little from their early, competition-winning entry before concentrating on recent work.

Tony Curtis included extracts from his latest book *The Arches*, a remarkable joint enterprise with the collage artist John Digby, who has for some time lived in New York. A significant proportion of Curtis's output over the years has drawn inspiration from the work of artists and photographers, and the results have always been conventionally coherent. Digby is a surrealist and, in this case, the poet's response is similarly surrealistic. Paired with collages, if one is disposed to accept the dislocation of sense inherent in surrealism, many of the poems work, but they do not stand on their own, as for instance do earlier poems based on paintings by Andrew Wyeth. In its more expensive format the book is accompanied by an interactive cd-rom and music by jazz musician Tim Whitehead to encourage readers/users to create their own texts. Although computer programs designed to stimulate a creative response in words and images have long been available, the entire Curtis-Digby package is a pioneering venture and one wonders what will come of it.

In addition to recent poems about journeys in the USA and with American students around Wales, Nigel Jenkins illustrated his new role as 'municipal graffitist'. This has come about as a result of commissions from a local authority and a hospital. A number of these aphoristic meditations are now set in stone in Swansea and stained-glass windows in Bridgend. He is genial and concerned, can wield rapier or bludgeon with equal dexterity and makes poems full of humanity. When I last wrote about Duncan Bush, I emphasised, as he had himself, the denial of the personal in his writing. His latest book, *Midway*, from which he read at Blackwood, has a contrary agenda. In it he takes stock of his fifty years, family, childhood, youth, gathering maturity. Although it contains other subjects and personalities, the predominant mood is confessional, in verse and prose. The book contains an autobiographical essay much concerned to demonstrate how the influence of America, mediated via the cinema and comic books, was far stronger than any tribal sense of belonging to Wales or to Britain. His working life these days is largely spent in Luxembourg, but it is in America that his 'elective allegiance' lies. It can be seen in his poetry and in his fine novel *Glass Shot*, which the essay prompted me to re-read. 'Looking back now,' he concludes, 'it seems inevitable that (I) would try to be an actor or a writer: one of those auto-fantasists who become compulsive fabricators of other selves.' *Midway*, with its *film noir* cover, is a distinctive, varied and unfailingly interesting sample of the wide range of Duncan Bush's talents.

The disappointing turn-out at Cardiff and the dismal failure to stir a response in Blackwood illustrate the difficulty that will be faced by the Academi in implementing the community-oriented policy of the Arts Council of Wales. Given skilful *animateurs*, it will work well for community-based music, drama, dance, film – the common currency of arts experience for cinemagoers and television viewers. To broaden the appeal of literature it will be necessary to educate an audience, and that will take time.

Time, however, may be in plentiful supply in Wales. As we reach the turn of the year news breaks of a three-week lay-off at the Llanwern and Port Talbot steel works, and worse could follow. The fate of the vast LG semi-conductor plant on the outskirts of Newport, which should have brought thousands of jobs to south Wales, hangs in the balance as South Korea strives to rescue its economy. Far from being impressed with the numbers currently employed in the arts, we should be pressing for a great many more, to improve the quality of life for everyone, and to provide a living for those who are likely to have no other prospects.

*PN Review* 127, Volume 25 Number 5,
May – June 1999.

# ACADEMI
*July 1998*


Not a year goes by without a dispute about a public building. You would think the Welsh the most architecturally alert people in Western Europe. The folk museum at St Fagans (certainly 'worth the visit' as the guidebooks say) preserves, among many other vestiges of folk-life in Wales, examples of vernacular architecture – farmhouses, terraced dwellings from the industrial valleys, even a pigsty, reassembled, brick by brick, stone by stone, from their original sites. They are for the most part humble – and strangely humbling, if you look upon them with a half-sympathetic eye. There should be a gallery at St Fagans where the jerry-building of schools in the 1960s is suitably commemorated, along with the half-baked ideas of developers and anti-social notions of council estate designers. An annexe would feature grand projects come to nought: Will Alsop's library and 'House of Literature' in Swansea; Zaha Hadid's opera house in Cardiff Bay. And alongside these now would be some suitable display to symbolise the dreadful bungle over the selection of a building to house the forthcoming National Assembly. This should have been a perfectly straightforward affair, but the Secretary of State for Wales, Ron Davies, and a man called Goodway, 'leader' (as local politicians will have it these days) of Cardiff Council managed between them to make a pig's ear of it. The collapse of the anticipated Labour old pals' act prompted other localities to press their claims to house the Assembly. The correspondence column of the *Western Mail* was awash with special pleading on behalf of

751

that town or this, and proposals of outlandish compromises – a greenfield site on the slopes of Cader Idris, or a portable building, like the Eisteddfod's pavilion, that could be set up wherever there was need to boost the local economy. It soon became clear that the choice was unlikely to fall outside Cardiff or Swansea. Ron Davies's even-handedness, or dithering, depending on your viewpoint, had ardent supporters of Swansea's expensively refurbished Guildhall (the city's alternative to Will Alsop's brilliant design) panting with anticipation and laying out substantial sums on a campaign. Residents in Gwent received an appeal for support from Swansea airport, whose owners must know a thing or two about politicians' preference for flying rather than risking their precious time on coned and jammed motorways, or the execrable rail service from Paddington. In the end, to much wailing from the west, Cardiff won – though, for the time being at least, Ron (who now sees himself as the first 'prime minister' of Wales) continues to spurn the Edwardian elegance of Cardiff City Hall, the original bone of contention, in favour of a glass box down the Bay. This is making certain entrepreneur developers very happy.

The whole saga was strangely echoed by the east-west rivalry that emerged in the competition for the new literature agency (mentioned in my last letter, *PN Review* 120), for the front runners turned out to be Swansea's Tŷ Llên; 'Canto', another west Wales group, that included R.S. Thomas, Jan Morris and Anthony Conran among its supporters, was led by writers with considerable popular appeal to both English and Welsh language readerships, Nigel Jenkins and Menna Elfyn, and had links with the publishers Gwasg Gomer; and, to everyone's surprise, Yr Academi Gymreig, which the Arts Council of Wales had seemed intent on killing off. It was, then, a shock to most watchers of the literary scene in Wales when, on 26 March, ACW announced that the Academi had won. The spokesman for Canto expressed his disappointment bitterly, in terms that drew a comparison with the treatment meted out to Swansea over its National Assembly bid, and seemed disinclined to accept the decision without a fight. But there will be no going back: the 'Academi Agency' it is, at least for the three-year duration of the franchise.

Perhaps unusually for Welsh affairs, where, in the past, who you know has often been more important than what, the quality of the bid tipped the balance. It says a great deal for the chairman of the Academi's franchise committee, Professor M. Wynn Thomas, and the energy of its members. They found an important partner in Tŷ Newydd, a writers' centre set up in a fine house (the last home of Liberal Prime Minister, Lloyd George), near Criccieth in north Wales. The committee's undoubted coup, however, was to enlist as chief executive of the new agency Peter Finch. He has earned enormous respect as manager of the Arts Council's bookshop, Oriel, and is an inspired and original thinker about ways in which literature can be brought to a wider public. As I tried to show in *PN Review* 119, he is also a fine poet, and the only experimental poet in Wales who can cut the mustard. It is not a surprise to learn that his support for the Academi's bid, and his contribution to its formulation, were crucial factors. The wonder is that all this was achieved in a very short time – and withstood unprecedented grilling by the Arts Council over fine points of detail.

The Academi Agency will replace the Arts Council itself as administrator of the 'Writers on Tour' scheme and writers' residencies, and its intentions are all good. It will place fieldworkers in key locations throughout Wales, so that no part feels neglected; it will increase the number and spread of workshops and new writers' groups; it will organise more literary tours, events and festivals; it will exploit the Internet. As Wynn Thomas put it in a press notice, the Agency 'will make literature in all its forms accessible to everyone, from the housebound to the hyperactive, from the young to the old, from Holyhead to Chepstow...Expect fiction on the motorway and poetry in the crags. Harri Webb's *Green Desert* will be filled with bards.' What more could one ask? Privately, he recognises that the Academi will need a new constitution, and a tighter, more transparent and accountable organisation than formerly.

The finessing of all this will be left to existing members, whose first task will be to elect a permanent Council of six, three from the English section, three from the Welsh, to replace the committee Wynn Thomas chaired. The Council will meet annually to cast a monitorial eye over the operations of the management board, chaired by Peter Finch, which will be responsible for the day-to-day business of the Agency. Wynn Thomas himself will not stand for election to the Council. He has, he says, had enough – an understandable, if regrettable, decision, for he was instrumental in persuading the membership of both sections (or those, at least, who turned up at the EGMs in December) that the Academi must make a bid for the franchise or go under. He argued that this writers' organisation is too important to the conservation and recycling of Welsh culture into the future to be cast aside, and that it is capable of somehow satisfying both elitists and populists among the users of literature. The critical issue of whether the Academi can remain essentially a society of authors in these new circumstances remains unresolved. That too, in the short term anyway, is up to the membership.

What the critical Dr Kim Howells MP will think of all this is a matter for conjecture. Not much, I suspect. He may well be pleased, if only for the most old-fashioned of political motives, that Emyr Jenkins (who is likely to be remembered best not for his substantial achievements in arts administration but as the father-in-law of William Hague), has retired as chief executive of the Arts Council of Wales. He has been succeeded by Joanna Weston, born in Ebbw Vale, who accumulated a wealth of experience as an arts administrator, including some in theatre management in the West End, before joining ACW as director of its newly created Lottery Division in 1994, when the council pioneered awarding grants from the lottery capital and Arts for All schemes. She is said to be particularly proud of the part she played in that role in supporting community and amateur organisations. Those who consider themselves professionals in the arts in Wales will already have taken note.

*PN Review* 122, Volume 24 Number 6,
July – August 1998.

# THE ARTS COUNCIL OF WALES AND YR ACADEMI GYMREIG

*March 1998*

The controversy over Nigel Jenkins's poem 'Farewell to Viscount No', savaging the late George Thomas, subsided slowly. In the correspondence column of the *Western Mail* supporters of the former Speaker, beside themselves with fury, lashed out at the poet and the magazine, *New Welsh Review*, that published him. How could a journal, dependent upon public money via Arts Council of Wales funding for its very existence, print such a scurrilous libel on a sainted politician of the socialist persuasion? Someone should put a stop to it. At this not unexpected twist, others joined the argument crying 'censorship'. Since at least one of the former group has a senior position with Labour in south Wales, there are grounds for some concern that, if the defenders of George could have their way, writing here would toe the party line – or else. The self-regard and eagerness to look after their own, regardless of the consequences, which characterised old Labour, appear set to continue in Wales under the Blairite reformation of the party. That should give pause even to supporters of what must be a Labour-dominated assembly for Wales.

It does not require an advanced qualification in conspiracy theory to see the possibility of a connection between the development of the 'Viscount No' affair and another saga that unfolded in the *Western Mail* about eighteen months ago, involving the MP Dr Kim Howells. Writing about this in *PN Review* 111, I questioned the motives for his intervention in one of the regular eruptions of internecine strife between

756

defenders of the status quo – the happy recipients of Arts Council of Wales funding – and the pretenders, who complain of the others' élitism and the lack of support for their community-based (and specifically socialist) vision of literature beyond the Millennium. Anyone with a grain of political nous would see that these are not mutually exclusive aims, but merely mutually frustrating, because there is insufficient funding for both. Indeed, there never has been enough money to fund adequately all that needs to be done to encourage writing at all levels, and a readership for it. New Labour, complaisantly manacled to old Tory fiscal policy, seems disinclined to help the legions of the poor, so what prospects for literature?

However, the balance, which has so long been weighted in favour of the 'literary establishment' (such as it is) in Wales, now seems set to tilt the other way, as a result of policy change at ACW. It has decided to establish a new agency to take on the great majority of the jobs that, up till now, have been stimulated and coordinated by its own Literature Department or by Yr Academi Gymreig/The Welsh Academy. Restructuring within the Council has already done away with the post of Literature Director, the incumbent, Tony Bianchi, having accepted demotion, and the Literature Committee with its specialist panels has been dismantled. It was further decided that to set up the new agency there will be a staged transfer of funds from Yr Academi. The inevitable consequence of this is the collapse of Yr Academi as it is presently constituted.

If only for the historical record, this is a suitable juncture to consider the origin, development and role of Yr Academi Gymreig. It was founded in 1959, initially as a kind of club without premises or programme for Welsh language writers and, after a deal of special pleading, expanded in 1968 to embrace those who publish in English. During these years and for a while

757

after the joint body emerged, it had few ambitions beyond an AGM and the maintenance of communications among the more gregarious of the membership. In these low-key activities it was devotedly and voluntarily served by 'secretaries' (Alison Bielski and Sally Roberts Jones on the English-language side), who were also members. The Welsh section had its magazine, *Taliesin*, which first appeared in 1961 and continues to play an important part in contemporary literature in Welsh. In 1978, largely as a result of the influence of Meic Stephens, then Literature Director of the Arts Council, and annual draughts of grant aid, this literary equivalent of a cottage industry became professionalised, opened offices in Cardiff, recruited salaried staff and substantially increased its activities. It organised readings, writers' workshops, literary competitions and the like; it commissioned translations, reprints of classic texts, the *Oxford Companion to the Literature of Wales* and its Welsh equivalent, *Cydymaith i Lenyddiaeth Cymru*, and a monumental English-Welsh dictionary – all very useful. The English language section was the mainspring behind the Cardiff Literature Festival – lost, alas, in the backwash of the latest tide of local government reorganisation. Yr Academi had its detractors, among them a few eminent writers who resisted all invitations to join, and others because they were not invited. The criteria for membership were never sufficiently clear, or perhaps of late, in view of the length of the English section's list of members, stringent enough. A few academicians of long standing have been heard to murmur, Groucho-like, that there is more distinction in *not* being a member of this club. At the same time, there was no close season on sniping at the so-called élite, which (as we have seen) along with certain journals and publishers, were the targets of the Kim Howells faction.

The mechanics of levering out Yr Academi from its position as a principal client of the Arts Council and ostensibly chief promoter of literary events in Wales, was formal appraisal by an ACW panel. The report of the second such appraisal in three years, published in October, was severely critical of Yr Academi's perceived underperformance. An objective observer will agree that there was some justice in this assessment, but it is at least arguable that there was no lack of ideas and energy among Yr Academi's committee members and officers; what was always in short supply was cash. Tacit recognition of this is contained in the specification for the new agency, which is expected to raise about a hundred thousand pounds annually from the private sector to supplement its Arts Council income. There are those who doubt that much loose change is to be found in Wales. Be that as it may, at indifferently attended 'extraordinary general meetings' of both sections members decided that Yr Academi would draw a line under its past and bid for the new franchise. It will do so under the leadership of Professor M. Wynn Thomas and Ned Thomas (Director of the University of Wales Press) as chairman and vice-chairman respectively, both very well-known and highly respected. Little has emerged thus far about the opposition, except that among five (or seven?) bidders are Ty Llên, which survives yet in Swansea, and Peter Florence of the Hay-on-Wye Literature Festival. The outcome of the competition will be known in March 1998.

What that far-famed rebel and reprobate John Tripp would have thought of all this would probably be unprintable, even in these free-and-easy days. I would still have enjoyed witnessing his wrath – from a safe distance. He had a low flash-point and talk of money would propel him into paroxysms – because, as one who lived by his pen, he had little of the stuff. His rage would erupt in a prolonged series of detonations in the course of which 'the bourgeoisie' always caught it in the neck. It was wise to be wary, because almost anything and anyone might be deemed 'bourgeois' on such occasions. Yet there was great sadness when he died, suddenly and uncharacteristically peacefully just ten years ago, and no one has appeared to fill the gap he left. He will be remembered by those who knew him, a considerable contingent of whom assembled for that purpose in the upstairs room of a Cardiff pub (John's natural habitat) one evening in October. He had a gruff but profound love for Wales, nostalgia for its irredeemably lost past, painful melancholy for its increasingly materialist present, and sufficient ironic self-knowledge to render both, for much of the time, palatable. For all its occasional lapses into hyperbole and commonplaces, his poetry will survive. He had a distinctive voice when he spoke as when he wrote. We listened to those rich, remarkable vocal tones again, on tape provided by the BBC, and a selection of Tripp favourites read by writers, a number of whom, like Robert Minhinnick (who organised the celebration), Peter Finch and Dannie Abse, had shared a platform with him at various times in the past. That reading poems aloud is more difficult than most of those who attempt it suspect was underlined by sundry actors in an 8.45 am slot on Radio 4 recently. Dannie Abse does it superbly – as his reading of 'Connection in Bridgend' demonstrated:

In the bus café, drinking tea, I watch
nothing happening in Bridgend.
I mean, there is rain, some shoppers
under canopies, tyres sloshing them
from the gutters. Otherwise not
much...

In the café a young mother is being
    given
stick by her two boys. They want Coke

and her baby cries for no reason
unless he's seen enough of Bridgend.
I feel an odd kinship with him.

At last my bacon sandwich is done;
it was something to look forward to,
slicing a minute's delight into the murk.
Balancing the plate, I hold the sad babe
while his mother fetches the Coke.

Then a one-armed paperseller comes in
with a strip of frayed ribbons on his
    coat.
He wants to tell me his story,
so I listen while the baby sobs
and his brothers suck straws.

An hour ago, I was alone; now
there are six. Even the café-owner
squeezes out a smile. We are in it
together, until the last buses go out.
One by one they leave the bays.

Not his last poem, and somewhat untypical, but a fitting
valedictory. It is permeated with sympathy and affection for the
unconsidered mass of ordinary folk, and lit with a gentle,
whimsical, self-deprecating humour; its simplicity is deceptive.
It reminds us of John Tripp's considerable accomplishment as a
poet, and of a complex, infuriating, lovely man.

*PN Review* 120, Volume 24 Number 4,
March – April 1998.

# THE ARTS COUNCIL OF WALES
September 1996

For several months readers of the correspondence column of the *Western Mail* have been entertained by a dogfight over the subsidies that the Arts Council of Wales provides to support literature. This is a familiar battlefield, and the protagonists' standards carry the same devices even if the flagbearers have changed over the years. One side complains that public money is poured into the hands of an élite for the production of books and magazines which don't sell, while the claims of its own broad-based appeal to the artistically-inclined man in the street are ignored or fobbed off with a pittance. The other, of course, argues that it represents high standards in writing and publishing and that, in any case, its products have a readership as large as similarly subsidised books and journals in England. The dispute has got no one anywhere in the past and is likely to have the same outcome this time round – and the next. A difference on this occasion is that it has somehow involved Dr Kim Howells, the Pontypridd MP who rose to prominence during the ill-fated miners' strike. He has emerged from behind the portcullis to fire salvoes of withering scorn on the beneficiaries of ACW largesse. 'Self-obsessed' he calls them, and manufacturers of 'boring rubbish'. People in glass houses, or even the Palace of Westminster...

There is then a political dimension to the affair. The Honourable Gentleman, who finds the concept of even New Labour's emasculated Welsh Assembly difficult to swallow, is seeking to represent the views not simply of Valleys constituents but of writers with a declared radical socialist manifesto. Theirs is a perfectly respectable stance which has a long tradition in Wales. It numbers Lewis Jones, Idris Davies, Gwyn Alf Williams, John Tripp and Harri Webb among its dead heroes, and in Nigel Jenkins, Mike Jenkins (unrelated) and Alun Rees has perhaps its best known living practitioners. In the latest *Poetry Wales*, Mike Jenkins, who edits the *Red Poets Magazine*, writes of his amazement at the number of poets in Wales 'willing to call themselves left wing and contribute'. 'It just wouldn't happen in England,' he opines, where 'elliptical wordplay' which is 'so common' does not fit the concern with people and places which is the stock-in-trade of the socialist republican writer. That may be so; English readers will no doubt advise. Anyway, Mike and Nigel Jenkins contribute regularly to the magazines that are in receipt of ACW grants and the recent tongue-lashing from Westminster.

That an MP chose to speak up on behalf of people who are perfectly able to press their own views would not be of the slightest concern if it were not for the steadily growing possibility that he could have a role in the cultural affairs of Wales by about this time next year. His intervention seems to impute a political motive to those in ACW who make decisions about subsidy; it certainly calls into question literary standards and editorial autonomy. We do not know how much of the heat generated by this controversy comes of writers whose work has failed to find a welcome at *Poetry Wales* and the *New Welsh Review*. Disgruntlement has been the source of literary feuds often enough in the past, and the Arts Council has taken a share of the blame for abetting the miscarriage of poetic justice. During his time as Literature Director of the Welsh Arts Council (as it was then termed) Meic Stephens occasionally received hate mail and once a parcel of putrid fish from disappointed poets. Patient explanations that the decisions of his Committee or distant editors were nothing to do with him did not serve to turn aside wrath.

In the business of writers and writing are grounds for disagreement as fertile as those from which the many schisms in Nonconformity were bred, especially in Wales. A faint whiff of the sometimes acrimonious factionalism that produced Baptists, Congregationalists, Wesleyan and Calvinistic Methodists can be detected in the splits occurring in writers' organisations. First came Yr Academi Gymreig, with its Welsh and English language sections, to which new members are elected, therefore deemed elitist. Next arose the Welsh Union of Writers, which welcomes any who will pay the subscription. WUW has a radical tinge, but is no longer radical enough for some. Most recently the Valleys Literature Committee has given birth to 'a new real union' – the Federation of Welsh Writers, a banner which, doubtless intentionally, brings to mind 'The Fed', the South Wales Miners' Federation, the political hub of the coalfield from the 1890s to the end of World War II.

Tony Bianchi, Meic Stephens's successor at the Arts Council, a Welsh-speaking Geordie, has sent Kim Howells a detailed response to his criticisms and the row has settled into rumbles and aftershocks. The simple fact is literature has never had more than a niggardly share of the funding available and as long as that situation prevails there will be squabbles between the haves and have nots. Whether a larger slice of the cake would produce more writing that is worth reading is open to question, but it would be pleasant if, for once, the ACW were able to give encouragement to deserving new clients without prejudicing its support to the equally deserving old. Perhaps Kim Howells could bear that in mind.

Seren, the most constructively ambitious of Welsh publishers, has its detractors, not a few of them inspired by a perception that it enjoys 'favoured client' status with the ACW. No one could argue, however, that it does not deliver the goods for its block grant. In the HMSO Oriel bookshop in Cardiff, and later in a reprise at the Hay-on-Wye festival, Seren will celebrate 15 years of poetry publication with the launch of an anthology, *Burning the Bracken*, compiled from the work of the 46 poets in its list. They include Robert Minhinnick, Mike Jenkins and Hilary Llewellyn Williams (who are to read at the event in Hay), and an array of others from R.S. Thomas and Peter Finch to Tony Curtis and Sheenagh Pugh. Advance publicity claims the anthology is 'a defining text for a pivotal era in British poetry'. That will take a while to digest. What is certain is that it will offer the public and the metropolitan critics with a rare opportunity to assess the state of writing in English from Wales. At a time when, if we are to believe the London press, anything with the taint of Welshness can be dismissed out of hand, the question is, will they take it?

There is nothing in the traditions of publishing or the custom and practice of writing to oblige poets to divulge the influences upon and preoccupations of their art, the meaning of their poems, the story of their life. Many are loath to go into such things, some like to be coaxed, a few preserve a clam-like reticence. R.S. Thomas comes into the last category. In the past it was far from easy to persuade him to take part in poetry readings or make public appearances of any kind other than before his congregation on Sundays. Since his retirement from the Church he has been readier to read to an audience and attend conferences, but it is still extraordinarily difficult to draw him into discussion.

I recall inviting R.S. Thomas to speak to the English Society of the University College of Wales, Aberystwyth in 1956. He had already gained widespread critical acclaim for *Song at the Year's Turning* and was even then considered by some 'one of the best half-dozen poets writing in English'. The English Society had offered him no brief but assumed he would read and discuss his own poetry, and perhaps the works of poets he admired – as Dylan Thomas had done in the same venue a few years before. He did neither. We heard a lecture on poetic imagery which was impeccably, not to say drily, academic in character, and contained not the merest whiff of a reference to his own writing. Some twenty years after that occasion I recall attending a reading at which he was incongruously paired with the Canadian poet Al Purdey. By this time, the splendid books of the 1960s, *Tares, The Bread of Truth, Pieta, Not that He Brought Flowers*, were behind him; he was a major poet. Purdey proved to be a naturally exuberant performer and RS, who had a sheaf of poems two inches thick, had no will to respond. When his turn came, he stood scanning and rejecting page after page in silence before selecting a poem, reading it plain, without preamble or comment, and then settling once more to turning pages until another caught his eye. In the end, with the quiet observation, 'I don't know...they're all the same,' he gave up.

John Ormond, one of the finest of Anglo-Welsh poets and a gifted TV producer, specialising in arts programmes, once filmed a long conversation with RS in which the then Vicar of Aberdaron on the Llŷn peninsula was more open than he had ever been previously, and perhaps than he has been since. The transcript of the broadcast, which went out in April 1972, was published in an R.S. Thomas special number of *Poetry Wales* that same Spring. Setting up the broadcast had called for some tact. John Ormond used to tell how he manoeuvered a chance encounter with Thomas while he was engaged in his habitual pastime of birdwatching on a headland near Aberdaron. A prolonged silence followed the initial exchange of greetings. Why did the poet seek out such a lonely spot, asked the man from the BBC. The sound of wind and waves filled a long pause, then, 'To think'. 'And what do you think about?' And after an interval during which the tide seemed to reach high water and ebb again, 'Oh, this and that'. In fact, John Ormond's success in winning RS's confidence was due in large measure to his personal qualities as a man and a poet, and also to his skill in turning the discussion to metaphysical matters: the blurred boundaries of poetic imagination and religious belief.

All this is to restate what must be as well known in England as it is in Wales: RS is full of contradictions. To mention only two, he is a Priest who constantly questions Belief, and an outspoken polemicist who is remarkably shy. What is probably less well known is that in 1985 he published a volume of autobiography. It is written in Welsh. The enigmatic title, *Neb*, can mean 'no one', 'someone' or 'anyone', and, curiously it may seem, the book is written in the third person. This is not a pompous device, not grandiloquence, but characteristically self-effacing. How else could he respond to a request to write about himself (as a contribution to the Gwasg Gwynedd series 'Cyfres y Cewri')? At the beginning of the book he refers to 'a nervous boy,' 'a sensitive boy', and later to 'the vicar' and later still to 'RS'. It is not a big book and evidently not the whole story. He suggests that the failures of memory are partly to blame, but the important memories remain. 'How does memory work? It holds on to some things while letting others fall to oblivion. One thing stays. One day on the beach at Hoylake his father pointed at a range of mountains far away across the sea to the west. "There's Wales," he said in English.' This is a significant moment from the sketch of a peculiarly peripatetic early life, for his father was on sea in World War I and his mother followed her husband from port to port. His education, his subsequent career and the evolution of his thinking are also outlined in *Neb* in as much detail as the poet permitted himself.

Since 1985, RS has resisted all attempts of would-be biographers. He has said that he would countenance only a biography written in Welsh. In the coming Autumn, however, Harper Collins will publish a full-length biography of the poet, under the title *Furious Interiors*, by an Englishman, Justin Wintle, who now lives in Milford Haven. RS has not cooperated in the project, but nor has he strenuously opposed it, and, in retrospect, Wintle has been glad of the freedom that the poet's non-cooperation has given him. The book draws on *Neb* for biographical detail and also contains information gathered from interviews with parishioners and others who know him.

While writing for publication, RS has always deliberately distanced himself from his readers. He is, by temperament, a solitary being. This paradoxical position was established in boyhood. He says in *Neb*, 'Despite his mother's nervous and anxious nature, he was free to wander the island (Anglesey) from early morn till sunset...There was unmixed, endless pleasure to be had from being alone. Was he preparing himself to be a poet? How does anyone become a poet?...In the school he would write a poem and pass it to his neighbour in the next desk, and he, after reading it, would pass it back, whispering, "Poet Laureate". Was the other being sarcastic? The budding poet accepted the praise as though worthy of it.' RS has always been one for letting his poems speak for themselves, but they do not come out of the air. They have their origins in his experience and his thinking, on both of which, apart from *Neb* and the John Ormond broadcast, he has been largely silent. If Justin Wintle's book helps us to understand better the personal and philosophical context from which the poet writes, it will indeed be enlightening.

*PN Review* 111, Volume 23 Number 1,
September – October 1996.

**Iwan Bala** is an established artist, writer and lecturer based in Wales. Born in north Wales, he spent many years in Cardiff but now resides in the Gwendraeth valley. He has held solo exhibitions annually since 1990, participated in many group exhibitions in Wales and abroad and is represented in public and private collections. His work was exhibited in four Chinese cities in 2009. He has published books and essays on contemporary art in Wales.

**Jonathan Edwards**'s first collection, *My Family and Other Superheroes* (Seren, 2014), received the Costa Poetry Award and the Wales Book of the Year People's Choice Award, and was shortlisted for the Fenton Aldeburgh First Collection Prize. His second collection, *Gen*, also received the Wales Book of the Year People's Choice Award. His poem about Newport Bridge was shortlisted for the Forward Prize for Best Single Poem 2019, and he has received prizes in the Ledbury Festival International Poetry Competition, the Oxford Brookes International Poetry Competition and the Cardiff International Poetry Competition. He lives in Crosskeys, south Wales.

**Michael Schmidt**, founder-editor of *PN Review*, is also managing director of Carcanet Press, Professor of Poetry at the University of Manchester, and a literary historian, author of *Lives of the Poets*, *The First Poets*, *The Novel: a biography*, and *Gilgamesh: the life of a poem*.

# Modern Wales by Parthian Books

The Modern Wales Series, edited by Dai Smith and supported by the Rhys Davies Trust, was launched in 2017. The Series offers an extensive list of biography, memoir, history and politics which reflect and analyse the development of Wales as a modernised society into contemporary times. It engages widely across places and people, encompasses imagery and the construction of iconography, dissects historiography and recounts plain stories, all in order to elucidate the kaleidoscopic pattern which has shaped and changed the complex culture and society of Wales and the Welsh.

The inaugural titles in the Series were *To Hear the Skylark's Song*, a haunting memoir of growing up in Aberfan by Huw Lewis, and Joe England's panoramic *Merthyr: The Crucible of Modern Wales*. The impressive list has continued with Angela John's *Rocking the Boat*, essays on Welsh women who pioneered the universal fight for equality and Daryl Leeworthy's landmark overview *Labour Country*, on the struggle through radical action and social democratic politics to ground Wales in the civics of common ownership. Myths and misapprehension, whether naïve or calculated, have been ruthlessly filleted in Martin Johnes' startling *Wales: England's Colony?* and a clutch of biographical studies will reintroduce us to the once seminal, now neglected, figures of Cyril Lakin, Minnie Pallister and Gwyn Thomas, whilst Meic Stehens' *Rhys Davies: A Writer's Life* and Dai *Smith's Raymond Williams: A Warrior's Tale* form part of an associated back catalogue from Parthian.

# PARTHIAN

## WALES: ENGLAND'S COLONY?
Martin Johnes

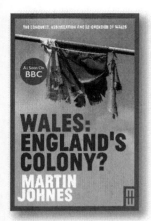

From the very beginnings of Wales, its people have defined themselves against their large neighbour. This book tells the fascinating story of an uneasy and unequal relationship between two nations living side-by-side.

PB / £8.99
978-1-912681-41-9

## RHYS DAVIES: A WRITER'S LIFE
Meic Stephens

Rhys Davies (1901-78) was among the most dedicated, prolific and accomplished of Welsh prose writers. This is his first full biography.

*'This is a delightful book, which is itself a social history in its own right, and funny.'*
– The Spectator

PB / £11.99
978-1-912109-96-8

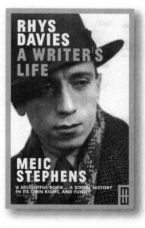

## MERTHYR, THE CRUCIBLE OF MODERN WALES
Joe England

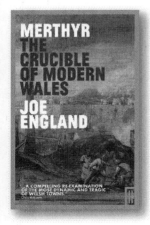

Merthyr Tydfil was the town where the future of a country was forged: a thriving, struggling surge of people, industry, democracy and ideas. This book assesses an epic history of Merthyr from 1760 to 1912 through the focus of a fresh and thoroughly convincing perspective.

PB / £18.99
978-1-913640-05-7

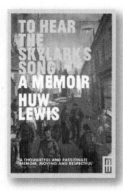

# TO HEAR THE SKYLARK'S SONG
Huw Lewis

*To Hear the Skylark's Song* is a memoir about how Aberfan survived and eventually thrived after the terrible disaster of the 21st of October 1966.

*'A thoughtful and passionate memoir, moving and respectful.'*
– Tessa Hadley

PB / £8.99
978-1-912109-72-2

# ROCKING THE BOAT
Angela V. John

This insightful and revealing collection of essays focuses on seven Welsh women who, in a range of imaginative ways, resisted the status quo in Wales, England and beyond during the nineteenth and twentieth centuries.

PB / £11.99
978-1-912681-44-0

# TURNING THE TIDE
Angela V. John

This rich biography tells the remarkable tale of Margaret Haig Thomas (1883-1958) who became the second Viscountess Rhondda. She was a Welsh suffragette, held important posts during the First World War and survived the sinking of the *Lusitania*.

PB / £17.99
978-1-909844-72-8

# BRENDA CHAMBERLAIN, ARTIST & WRITER
Jill Piercy

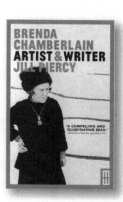

The first full-length biography of Brenda Chamberlain chronicles the life of an artist and writer whose work was strongly affected by the places she lived, most famously Bardsey Island and the Greek island of Hydra.

PB / £11.99
978-1-912681-06-8